The IDG Books Bible Advantage

The *Microsoft Office for Windows 95 Bible, Standard Edition,* is part of the Bible series brought to you by IDG Books Worldwide. We designed Bibles to meet your growing need for quick access to the most complete and accurate computer information available.

Bibles work the way you do: They focus on accomplishing specific tasks — not learning random functions. These books are not long-winded manuals or dry reference tomes. In Bibles, expert authors tell you exactly what you can do with your software and how to do it. Easy to follow, step-by-step sections; comprehensive coverage; and convenient access in language and design — it's all here.

The authors of Bibles are uniquely qualified to give you expert advice as well as insightful tips and techniques not found anywhere else. Our authors maintain close contact with end users through feedback from articles, training sessions, e-mail exchanges, user group participation, and consulting work. Because our authors know the realities of daily computer use and are directly tied to the reader, our Bibles have a strategic advantage.

Bible authors have the experience to approach a topic in the most efficient manner, and we know that you, the reader, will benefit from a "one-on-one" relationship with the author. Our research shows that readers make computer book purchases because they want expert advice on a product. Readers want to benefit from the author's experience, so the author's voice is always present in a Bible series book.

In addition, the author is free to include or recommend useful software in a Bible. The software that accompanies a Bible is not intended to be casual filler but is linked to the content, theme, or procedures of the book. We know that you will benefit from the included software.

You will find what you need in this book whether you read it from cover to cover, section by section, or simply one topic at a time. As a computer user, you deserve a comprehensive resource of answers. We at IDG Books Worldwide are proud to deliver that resource with the *Microsoft Office for Windows 95 Bible, Standard Edition.*

Karen A. Bluestein
Publisher
Internet: kbluestein@idgbooks.com

Microsoft® Office™ for Windows® 95 Bible

Standard Edition

Microsoft® Office™ for Windows® 95 Bible
Standard Edition

by Ed Jones and Derek Sutton

IDG Books Worldwide, Inc.
An International Data Group Company

Foster City, CA ✦ Chicago, IL ✦ Indianapolis, IN ✦ Braintree, MA ✦ Dallas, TX

Microsoft® Office™ for Windows® 95 Bible, Standard Edition

Published by
IDG Books Worldwide, Inc.
An International Data Group Company
919 E. Hillsdale Blvd.
Suite 400
Foster City, CA 94404

Text, art, and software compilations copyright © 1995 by IDG Books Worldwide, Inc. All rights reserved. No part of this book, including interior design, cover design, and icons, may be reproduced or transmitted in any form, by any means (electronic, photocopying, recording, or otherwise) without the prior written permission of the publisher.

Library of Congress Catalog Card No.: 95-79912

ISBN: 1-56884-490-5

Printed in the United States of America

10 9 8 7 6 5 4 3 2 1

1B/SS/QZ/ZV

Distributed in the United States by IDG Books Worldwide, Inc.

Distributed by Macmillan Canada for Canada; by Computer and Technical Books for the Caribbean Basin; by Contemporanea de Ediciones for Venezuela; by Distribuidora Cuspide for Argentina; by CITEC for Brazil; by Ediciones ZETA S.C.R. Ltda. for Peru; by Editorial Limusa SA for Mexico; by Transworld Publishers Limited in the United Kingdom and Europe; by Al-Maiman Publishers & Distributors for Saudi Arabia; by Simron Pty. Ltd. for South Africa; by IDG Communications (HK) Ltd. for Hong Kong; by Toppan Company Ltd. for Japan; by Addison Wesley Publishing Company for Korea; by Longman Singapore Publishers Ltd. for Singapore, Malaysia, Thailand, and Indonesia; by Unalis Corporation for Taiwan; by WS Computer Publishing Company, Inc. for the Philippines; by WoodsLane Pty. Ltd. for Australia; by WoodsLane Enterprises Ltd. for New Zealand.

For general information on IDG Books Worldwide's books in the U.S., please call our Consumer Customer Service department at 800-762-2974. For reseller information, including discounts and premium sales, please call our Reseller Customer Service department at 800-434-3422.

For information on where to purchase IDG Books Worldwide's books outside the U.S., contact IDG Books Worldwide at 415-655-3021 or fax 415-655-3295.

For information on translations, contact Marc Jeffrey Mikulich, Director, Foreign & Subsidiary Rights, at IDG Books Worldwide, 415-655-3018 or fax 415-655-3295.

For sales inquiries and special prices for bulk quantities, write to the address above or call IDG Books Worldwide at 415-655-3200.

For information on using IDG Books Worldwide's books in the classroom, or ordering examination copies, contact Jim Kelly at 800-434-2086.

For authorization to photocopy items for corporate, personal, or educational use, please contact Copyright Clearance Center, 222 Rosewood Drive, Danvers, MA 01923, or fax 508-750-4470.

Limit of Liability/Disclaimer of Warranty: The author and publisher of this book have used their best efforts in preparing this book. IDG Books Worldwide, Inc., and the author make no representation or warranties with respect to the accuracy or completeness of the contents of this book, and specifically disclaim any implied warranties of merchantability or fitness for any particular purpose, and shall in no event be liable for any loss of profit or any other commercial damage, including but not limited to special, incidental, consequential, or other damages.

Trademarks: All brand names and product names used in this book are trademarks, registered trademarks, or trade names of their respective holders. IDG Books Worldwide is not associated with any product or vendor mentioned in this book.

 is a registered trademark under exclusive license to IDG Books Worldwide, Inc., from International Data Group, Inc.

About the Authors

Edward Jones is a leading author of computer books. He has written more than 30 titles, many about database, spreadsheet, and word processing programs. He has also served as a technical editor of many computer books, and has written several magazine articles. Mr. Jones has performed consulting services for major Washington, D.C. based law firms and government agencies, and at the time of this writing is on assignment in the Caribbean. Mr. Jones provides consulting services through his company, Jones Information Services. Raleigh, North Carolina, is his home.

Derek Sutton II is a college computer science student who minors in journalism. As a coauthor with Mr. Jones, Mr. Sutton has published titles about Windows databases and Windows 95. Mr. Sutton also provides training and consulting services in Windows and Windows applications through his company, Derek Sutton and Associates.

ABOUT IDG BOOKS WORLDWIDE

Welcome to the world of IDG Books Worldwide.

IDG Books Worldwide, Inc., is a subsidiary of International Data Group, the world's largest publisher of computer-related information and the leading global provider of information services on information technology. IDG was founded more than 25 years ago and now employs more than 7,500 people worldwide. IDG publishes more than 235 computer publications in 67 countries (see listing below). More than 60 million people read one or more IDG publications each month.

Launched in 1990, IDG Books Worldwide is today the #1 publisher of best-selling computer books in the United States. We are proud to have received 8 awards from the Computer Press Association in recognition of editorial excellence, and our best-selling ...For Dummies™ series has more than 17 million copies in print with translations in 25 languages. IDG Books Worldwide, through a recent joint venture with IDG's Hi-Tech Beijing, became the first U.S. publisher to publish a computer book in the People's Republic of China. In record time, IDG Books Worldwide has become the first choice for millions of readers around the world who want to learn how to better manage their businesses.

Our mission is simple: Every one of our books is designed to bring extra value and skill-building instructions to the reader. Our books are written by experts who understand and care about our readers. The knowledge base of our editorial staff comes from years of experience in publishing, education, and journalism — experience which we use to produce books for the '90s. In short, we care about books, so we attract the best people. We devote special attention to details such as audience, interior design, use of icons, and illustrations. And because we use an efficient process of authoring, editing, and desktop publishing our books electronically, we can spend more time ensuring superior content and spend less time on the technicalities of making books.

You can count on our commitment to deliver high-quality books at competitive prices on topics consumers want to read about. At IDG Books Worldwide, we value quality, and we have been delivering quality for more than 25 years. You'll find no better book on a subject than an IDG book.

John Kilcullen
President and CEO
IDG Books Worldwide, Inc.

IDG Books Worldwide, Inc., is a subsidiary of International Data Group, the world's largest publisher of computer-related information and the leading global provider of information services on information technology. International Data Group publishes over 235 computer publications in 67 countries. More than sixty million people read one or more International Data Group publications each month. The officers are Patrick J. McGovern, Founder and Board Chairman; Kelly Conlin, President; Jim Casella, Chief Operating Officer. International Data Group's publications include: **ARGENTINA'S** Computerworld Argentina, Infoworld Argentina; **AUSTRALIA'S** Computerworld Australia, Computer Living, Australian PC World, Australian Macworld, Network World, Mobile Business Australia, Publish!, Reseller, IDG Sources; **AUSTRIA'S** Computerwelt Oesterreich, PC Test; **BELGIUM'S** Data News (CW); **BOLIVIA'S** Computerworld; **BRAZIL'S** Computerworld, Connections, Game Power, Mundo Unix, PC World, Publish, Super Game; **BULGARIA'S** Computerworld Bulgaria, PC & Mac World Bulgaria, Network World Bulgaria; **CANADA'S** CIO Canada, Computerworld Canada, InfoCanada, Network World Canada, Reseller; **CHILE'S** Computerworld Chile, Informatica; **COLOMBIA'S** Computerworld Colombia, PC World; **COSTA RICA'S** PC World; **CZECH REPUBLIC'S** Computerworld, Elektronika, PC World; **DENMARK'S** Communications World, Computerworld Denmark, Computerworld Focus, Macintosh Produktkatalog, Macworld Danmark, PC World Danmark, PC Produktguide, Tech World, Windows World; **ECUADOR'S** PC World Ecuador; **EGYPT'S** Computerworld (CW) Middle East, PC World Middle East; **FINLAND'S** MikroPC, Tietoviikko, Tietoverkko; **FRANCE'S** Distributique, GOLDEN MAC, InfoPC, Le Guide du Monde Informatique, Le Monde Informatique, Telecoms & Reseaux; **GERMANY'S** Computerwoche, Computerwoche Focus, Computerwoche Extra, Electronic Entertainment, Gamepro, Information Management, Macwelt, Netzwelt, PC Welt, Publish, Publish; **GREECE'S** Publish & Macworld; **HONG KONG'S** Computerworld Hong Kong, PC World Hong Kong; **HUNGARY'S** Computerworld SZT, PC World; **INDIA'S** Computers & Communications; **INDONESIA'S** Info Komputer; **IRELAND'S** ComputerScope; **ISRAEL'S** Beyond Windows, Computerworld Israel, Multimedia, PC World Israel; **ITALY'S** Computerworld Italia, Lotus Magazine, Macworld Italia, Networking Italia, PC Shopping Italy, PC World Italia; **JAPAN'S** Computerworld Today, Information Systems World, Macworld Japan, Nikkei Personal Computing, SunWorld Japan, Windows World; **KENYA'S** East African Computer News; **KOREA'S** Computerworld Korea, Macworld Korea, PC World Korea; **LATIN AMERICA'S** GamePro; **MALAYSIA'S** Computerworld Malaysia, PC World Malaysia; **MEXICO'S** Compu Edicion, Compu Manufactura, Computacion/Punto de Venta, Computerworld Mexico, MacWorld, Mundo Unix, PC World, Windows; **THE NETHERLANDS'** Computer! Totaal, Computable (CW), LAN Magazine, Lotus Magazine, MacWorld; **NEW ZEALAND'S** Computer Buyer, Computerworld New Zealand, Network World, New Zealand PC World; **NIGERIA'S** PC World Africa; **NORWAY'S** Computerworld Norge, Lotusworld Norge, Macworld Norge, Maxi Data, Networld, PC World Ekspress, PC World Nettverk, PC World Norge, PC World's Produktguide, Publish& Multimedia World, Student Data, Unix World, Windowsworld; **PAKISTAN'S** PC World Pakistan; **PANAMA'S** PC World Panama; **PERU'S** Computerworld Peru, PC World; **PEOPLE'S REPUBLIC OF CHINA'S** China Computerworld, China PC Info Magazine, Computer Fan, PC World China, Electronics International, Electronics Today/Multimedia World, Electronic Product World, China Network World, Software World Magazine, Telecom Product World; **PHILIPPINES'** Computerworld Philippines, PC Digest (PCW); **POLAND'S** Computerworld Poland, Computerworld Special Report, Networld, PC World/Komputer, Sunworld; **PORTUGAL'S** Cerebro/PC World, Correio Informatico/Computerworld, MacIn; **ROMANIA'S** Computerworld, PC World, Telecom Romania; **RUSSIA'S** Computerworld-Moscow, Mir - PK (PCW), Sety (Networks); **SINGAPORE'S** Computerworld Southeast Asia, PC World Singapore; **SLOVENIA'S** Monitor Magazine; **SOUTH AFRICA'S** Computer Mail (CIO), Computing S.A., Network World S.A., Software World; **SPAIN'S** Advanced Systems, Amiga World, Computerworld Espana, Communicaciones World, Macworld Espana, NeXTWORLD, Super Juegos Magazine (GamePro), PC World Espana, Publish; **SWEDEN'S** Attack, ComputerSweden, Corporate Computing, Macworld, Mikrodatorn, Natverk & Kommunikation, PC World, CAP & Design, Datalngenjoren, Maxi Data,Windows World; **SWITZERLAND'S** Computerworld Schweiz, Macworld Schweiz, PC Tip; **TAIWAN'S** Computerworld Taiwan, PC World Taiwan; **THAILAND'S** Thai Computerworld; **TURKEY'S** Computerworld Monitor, Macworld Turkiye, PC World Turkiye; **UKRAINE'S** Computerworld, Computers+Software Magazine; **UNITED KINGDOM'S** Computing/Computerworld, Connexion/Network World, Lotus Magazine, Macworld, Open Computing/Sunworld; **UNITED STATES'** Advanced Systems, AmigaWorld, Cable in the Classroom, CD Review, CIO, Computerworld, Computerworld Client/Server Journal, Digital Video, DOS World, Electronic Entertainment Magazine (E2), Federal Computer Week, Game Hits, GamePro, IDG Books Worldwide, Infoworld, Laser Event, Macworld, Maximize, Multimedia World, Network World, PC Letter, PC World, Publish, SWATPro, Video Event; **URUGUAY'S** PC World Uruguay; **VENEZUELA'S** Computerworld Venezuela, PC World; **VIETNAM'S** PC World Vietnam.

08/15/95

Dedication

We want to dedicate this book to many people who have stood behind us.

Thanks, Alberta! You have been the *best* mother anyone could ever ask for! Selita, thank you; you have truly been supportive. Thank you, Dirk, Jason, Jolly, **Mama Kim** (love you!), and Brandy — there can be no friends closer and more understanding than you. Justin, stay bright and on your current path. You are truly a diamond in the rough! Kevin Beetz, wherever you are, I hope you are well. Mrs. Z and Mrs. Chaves, thanks to you both for your support and training; you truly made a difference. (I'm sorry I was so distant during this project.) Finally, thanks to Artie's Place; you made those difficult times not so difficult.

— Derek Sutton II

To Nikki and Jarel, for putting up with this year (and you certainly know from where I speak). To Renee and Norma, for providing an ear closer to my own age. To favored attorney Eugene Jackson, Jr., for your help in the "discovery phase of my case." And this one is also dedicated to everyone that's a member of my extended family, wherever you may be.

— Ed Jones

Credits

Publisher
Karen A. Bluestein

Acquisitions Manager
Gregory Croy

Acquisitions Editor
Ellen L. Camm

Brand Manager
Melisa M. Duffy

Editorial Director
Andy Cummings

Editorial Executive Assistant
Jodi Lynn Semling

Editorial Assistant
Nate Holdread

Production Director
Beth Jenkins

Supervisor of Project Coordination
Cindy L. Phipps

Supervisor of Page Layout
Kathie S. Schnorr

Pre-Press Coordinator
Steve Peake

Associate Pre-Press Coordinator
Tony Augsburger

Media/Archive Coordinator
Paul Belcastro

Editors
Barbara L. Potter
N. Jeannie Smith
Erik Dafforn
Melba D. Hopper
Kerrie Klein
Gregory R. Robertson

Project Editor
Jim Grey

Technical Reviewer
Greg Guntle
Michael Watson

Associate Project Coordinator
J. Tyler Connor

Production Staff
Gina Scott
Carla C. Radzikinas
Patricia R. Reynolds
Melissa D. Buddendeck
Leslie Popplewell
Dwight Ramsey
Robert Springer
Theresa Sánchez-Baker
E. Shawn Aylsworth
Dominique DeFelice
Angela F. Hunckler
Mark C. Owens
Laura Puranen

Proofreader
Jennifer Kaufeld

Indexer
Sharon Hilgenberg

Book Design
Drew Moore

Cover Design
Three 8 Creative Group

Acknowledgments

As with any major work (and trust us, this was a major work!), this book is the combined result of the concerted efforts of many people.

First, the IDG Books Universe: We would like to thank Greg Croy, who entrusted us with this significant project. Sincere and well-deserved thanks to Jim Grey, whose long hours in the editorial process were instrumental in making this book the best guide to Microsoft Office there is. Thanks to Erik Dafforn for leading in the early days of this project. Thanks also to Barb Potter for her comprehensive and thorough work in copy editing, to Jeannie Smith for picking up some copy editing slack, and to Melba Hopper for her developmental comments in several chapters. Thanks to Greg Guntle for his work in producing a thorough technical review. Thanks to everyone in the Production department at IDG Books — they played important roles in helping us bring this work to market. Finally, thanks to Accounting for getting the checks out (no one ever seems to remember the people who help you pay your bills!).

Thanks to King Sittipong for his generous loan of office space and lodging for one of the authors who was in Washington, D.C., during part of the project. Thanks to America Online for making it possible for us to work from most parts of this planet and still manage to stay in contact with friends and family. Thanks to the sysops of the Microsoft Beta Support Team on CompuServe, for their fast answers to the many questions that inevitably arose during the software shakeout process. And finally, thanks to the people of Puerto Rico and the U.S. Virgin Islands, for making the weekends of this year enjoyable while we spent the long days of the weeks huddled over our computer screens.

(The Publisher would like to give special thanks to Patrick J. McGovern, without whom this book would not have been possible.)

Contents at a Glance

Introduction 1

Part 1: Introducing Microsoft Office 9
Chapter 1: About Microsoft Office and the Office Shortcut Bar 11

Part 2: Word 23
Chapter 2: Creating and Working with Documents 25
Chapter 3: Formatting Documents 67
Chapter 4: Previewing and Printing Your Documents 97
Chapter 5: Working with Tables and Outlines 113
Chapter 6: Working with Fields 145
Chapter 7: Building Tables of Contents and Indexes 165
Chapter 8: Working with Styles and Templates 181
Chapter 9: Working with Word Macros 205
Chapter 10: Desktop Publishing with Word 221
Chapter 11: Word for Windows at Work 249
Chapter 12: The Word Top Ten 261

Part 3: Excel 271
Chapter 13: Making the Most of Workbooks 273
Chapter 14: Getting Information into Excel 301
Chapter 15: Excel Formatting 339
Chapter 16: Adding Graphics to Worksheets 365
Chapter 17: Working with Excel Charts 385
Chapter 18: Printing with Excel 411
Chapter 19: Working with Excel Databases 429
Chapter 20: Working with Excel Macros 449
Chapter 21: Excel Analysis 463
Chapter 22: Using Visual Basic for Applications 481
Chapter 23: Excel at Work 493
Chapter 24: The Excel Top Ten 513

Part 4: PowerPoint ... 521
Chapter 25: Working in PowerPoint ... 523
Chapter 26: Enhancing a Presentation ... 549
Chapter 27: Working with Charts in PowerPoint ... 571
Chapter 28: Producing Your Work ... 593
Chapter 29: PowerPoint for Windows at Work ... 607
Chapter 30: The PowerPoint Top Ten ... 619

Part 5: Office Works Together ... 623
Chapter 31: Using Schedule+ ... 625
Chapter 32: Using the Binder ... 651
Chapter 33: Sharing Data between Applications with OLE ... 659

Part 6: Appendixes ... 677
Chapter 34: Installing Microsoft Office ... 679
Chapter 35: Word Basics ... 691
Chapter 36: Excel Basics ... 705
Chapter 37: PowerPoint Basics ... 721
Chapter 38: On the CD-ROM ... 737

Index ... 762

IDG Books Worldwide License Agreement ... 804
CD-ROM Installation Instructions ... 806

Reader Response Card ... Back of Book

Table of Contents

Introduction 1
Is This Book for You? 1
Hey! There's a CD-ROM Stuck to the Back Cover! 2
How This Book is Organized 2
    Part I: Introducing Microsoft Office 2
    Part II: Word 2
    Part III: Excel 4
    Part IV: PowerPoint 5
    Part V: Office Works Together 6
    Appendixes 6
Conventions This Book Uses 7
Where Should I Start? 8

Part 1: Introducing Microsoft Office   9

Chapter 1: About Microsoft Office and the Office Shortcut Bar 11
Getting to Know Microsoft Office 11
Understanding the Office Shortcut Bar 12
    Using the Office Shortcut Bar versus the Start menu 13
    Getting Help with the Answer Wizard 13
    Sizing and docking the Office Shortcut Bar 14
Customizing the Office Shortcut Bar 14
    The Buttons tab 14
    The View tab 16
    The Toolbars tab 17
    The Settings tab 18
Closing the Office Shortcut Bar 19
Adding and Removing Office Programs 19
Summary 21
    Where to go next 21

Part 2: Word   23

Chapter 2: Creating and Working with Documents 25
Creating New Documents 25
Understanding Templates 25
    Exploring template categories 27

Looking at template wizards 28
Editing templates 34
Working with Text 34
Deleting text 34
Inserting text from the Clipboard 35
Inserting graphics 35
Navigating within a document 36
Selecting text 37
Looking at Word's Views 38
Examining the Vital Three: Margins, Tabs, and Line Spacing 40
Changing margins 40
Applying tabs 40
Line spacing 43
Paragraph spacing 45
Moving and Copying Text 45
Using Search and Replace 46
Searching for regular text 46
Searching for special characters 47
Replacing text 48
Using the Spelling Checker 50
Checking spelling as you type 52
Using the Thesaurus 53
Using the Grammar Checker 53
Using Hyphenation 56
Adding Bullets or Paragraph Numbers 57
Using AutoText Entries 57
Creating Annotations 60
Finding annotations 62
Locking the document 62
Document Summaries 63
Summary 66
Where to go next 66

Chapter 3: Formatting Documents 67

Formatting Levels 67
Character Formatting 69
Using character formatting options 69
Using character formatting shortcuts 72
Changing character fonts and point sizes 73
Applying superscript and subscript 74
Adjusting kerning 75
Copying character formatting 75
Paragraph Formatting 75
Applying paragraph formatting 76
Indenting paragraphs 78

Aligning paragraphs 80
Applying line spacing 81
Applying paragraph spacing 81
Applying borders to paragraphs 82
Page Formatting... 83
The Margins tab 84
The Paper Size tab 85
The Paper Source tab 85
Section Formatting 86
Headers and Footers 88
Deleting a header or footer 89
Adjusting margin settings 89
Positioning headers and footers 89
Page Numbers 90
Footnotes 91
Editing existing footnotes 93
Moving and deleting footnotes 93
Exploring footnote options 94
Changing footnotes to endnotes 94
Summary 95
Where to go next 95

Chapter 4: Previewing and Printing Your Documents 97

Printing in the Background 97
Previewing Documents 98
Understanding the Print Preview toolbar 99
Adjusting margins and object locations 100
Printing a Document 101
Printing a portion of a document 104
Printing more than documents 105
Printing sideways 106
Using the Print Options 106
Changing Your Printer Setup 108
Printing Envelopes 110
Summary 112
Where to go next 112

Chapter 5: Working with Tables and Outlines 113

Understanding Tables in Word for Windows 113
Creating Tables 114
Navigating with the mouse 116
Navigating with the keyboard 117
Creating your own table..118
Editing Tables 119
Inserting and deleting cells 120

   Merging cells 123
   Splitting a table 123
  Formatting Tables 124
   Setting column widths 124
   Adjusting the space between columns 125
   Making row adjustments 126
   Applying borders 127
  Exploring Other Uses for Tables 128
   Creating side-by-side paragraphs 128
   Converting text to tables 128
   Sorting information 129
  Understanding Outlines in Word for Windows 130
   Selecting text 132
   Changing the structure of an outline 132
  Changing Outline Headings 134
   Converting body text 134
   Expanding or collapsing outline headings 135
   Moving headings 136
   Applying numbering to outlines 136
  Creating Your Own Outline 137
   Collapsing and expanding the sample outline 139
   Changing headings in the sample outline 140
  Creating a Table of Contents from an Outline 141
  Printing Outlines 142
  Summary 143
   Where to go next 143

Chapter 6: Working with Fields 145

  How to Use Fields 146
   Inserting fields 146
   Viewing field codes 148
   Updating fields 148
   Moving between fields 148
   Formatting fields 148
   Locking a field's contents 150
   Using fields in an example 150
  How to Create a Mail Merge 152
   How to finish your mail merge 152
   Specifying a main document 152
   Creating a data source 153
   Adding merge fields to the main document 154
   Merging data 155
  How to Print Envelopes and Mailing Labels 155
   Printing envelopes 156
   Printing mailing labels 157

How to Use Other Software to Create Data Documents 159
    Working with Excel worksheets 159
    Embedding data 160
Summary 164
    Where to go next. 164

Chapter 7: Building Tables of Contents and Indexes 165

Building Tables of Contents 165
    Using style and outline headings 166
    Using nonstandard styles 168
    Using TC entries 168
Creating Your Own Table of Contents 170
Building Tables of Figures 172
Building Indexes 173
    Marking the index entries 173
    Inserting the index 174
    Creating multilevel index entries 175
    Using page number ranges in indexes 176
    Using additional index options 177
Building Large Indexes 177
Summary 179
    Where to go next 179

Chapter 8: Working with Styles and Templates 181

What Are Styles and Templates? 181
Applying Styles 183
    Using the Formatting toolbar 183
    Using the keyboard 184
Defining a Style 185
    Using the Style command 186
    Defining styles by example 187
    Assigning a shortcut key to a style 188
    Basing a style on another style 189
    Copying, deleting, and renaming styles 191
Finding Styles When You Need Them 192
    Displaying style names as you work 192
    Using the Style Gallery 193
Defining and Applying Styles: An Exercise 194
Understanding Templates 196
Working with Templates 198
    Applying templates 199
    Creating a template 199
    Basing a new template on an existing template 199
    Modifying an existing template 199
    Changing the default template 200

Creating and Applying a Template: An Exercise 201
Summary 203
　　Where to go next 203

Chapter 9: Working with Word Macros 205

Defining Macros 205
Introducing the Macro Toolbar 207
Storing Macros 208
Creating Macros 209
　　Preparing to create your macro 209
　　Recording the macro 210
Running Macros 214
Understanding the Macro Dialog Box 215
Using Macros in an Example 216
Creating Macros That Run Automatically 217
Summary 219
　　Where to go next 219

Chapter 10: Desktop Publishing with Word 221

Using Columns 221
Using the AutoFormat Command 223
Understanding Graphic Images 226
　　Bitmapped images 227
　　Object images 228
Using Graphic Images 230
　　Inserting images into Word 230
　　Changing the look of the image 232
　　Editing images 234
Inserting Graphs into Word 235
Working with Frames 237
　　Inserting a frame around an existing object 238
　　Inserting an empty frame into a document 238
　　Understanding the Frame dialog box 239
　　Moving frames 240
　　Sizing frames 241
　　Wrapping text around frames 241
　　Removing frames 242
Using the Organizational Tools of Desktop Publishing 243
　　Columns and margins 243
　　Headlines and subheads 244
　　Graphic images 244
　　Graphs and tables 245
Using the Newsletter Wizard 245
Summary 247
　　Where to go next 247

Chapter 11: Word for Windows at Work ... 249
Creating a Time Sheet ... 249
Designing a Fax Cover Sheet ... 251
Writing an Interoffice Memo ... 255
Producing an Invoice ... 257
Summary ... 259
    Where to go next ... 259

Chapter 12: The Word Top Ten ... 261
I have a document that was created with another word processing program. Can I work on this file in Word? ... 261
Why do addresses print on envelopes in the wrong position? ... 262
How can I prevent page breaks from appearing in my document where I don't want them? ... 263
Why doesn't Word print the gridlines in my table? ... 264
Can I run Word for Windows 95 and an earlier version of Word on the same computer, or do I need to remove my earlier version in order to run Word for Windows 95? ... 266
Can I delete Word documents without leaving Word? ... 266
Why can't a computer that runs Word 2.0 read files from a computer that runs Word for Windows 95? ... 266
Why aren't all my changes saved in a document, even with AutoSave turned on? ... 267
How can I set a different font (or font size or style) as the default? ... 268
How can I create a bulleted or numbered list? ... 268
Summary ... 269
    Where to go next ... 269

Part 3: Excel   271

Chapter 13: Making the Most of Workbooks ... 273
Understanding Excel Workbooks ... 273
    Opening a new workbook ... 275
    Opening an existing workbook ... 275
Working with Worksheets ... 276
    Navigating within your worksheet ... 277
    Moving among worksheets ... 279
    Renaming the worksheet tabs ... 280
    Selecting multiple worksheets ... 280
    Selecting a range of cells ... 281
    Adding and deleting worksheets ... 283
    Moving and copying information in worksheets ... 284
    Splitting the worksheet window ... 285

Working with Excel's Toolbars 286
Saving and Closing a Workbook 288
    Adding summary information to your workbook 289
    Using the AutoSave feature 290
    Saving in other file formats 293
    Saving a workspace file 293
    Closing a workbook and exiting Excel 294
Finding Workbooks 295
    Using the Open dialog box 295
    Performing advanced searches 297
    Organizing your files 299
Summary 300
    Where to go next 300

Chapter 14: Getting Information into Excel 301

Entering Data 301
    Entering numbers 303
    Entering text 305
    Entering dates and times 305
    Displayed values versus underlying values 307
Adding Notes to Cells 308
    Adding sound notes 309
Editing Data 310
    Editing using the Formula bar 310
    Using In-Cell Editing 311
Clearing Data from Cells 311
Copying and Moving Cells 312
    Copying and moving data with Cut, Copy, and Paste 312
    Copying and moving data with drag-and-drop 313
    Copying data with Fill and AutoFill 314
    Building series 316
    Using Paste Special 318
Inserting and Deleting Cells, Rows, and Columns 319
    Inserting cells, rows, and columns 319
    Deleting cells, rows, and columns 320
Working with Named Ranges 321
Working with Formulas 323
    Creating formulas in the Formula bar or with Edit Directly in Cell 323
    Creating formulas by pointing 324
    Allowed elements 324
    Displaying and editing formulas 326
    Changing the recalculation options 327
Using Functions 328
    Average, Maximum, Minimum, and Sum 329
    Using AutoSum 330
    Using the Function Wizard 331

Using Find and Replace	332
Finding data	332
Finding and replacing data	333
Checking Spelling	334
Adding a custom dictionary	335
Summary	337
Where to go next	337

Chapter 15: Excel Formatting 339

Using the AutoFormat Feature	339
Changing Column Widths and Row Heights	343
Column widths	343
Row heights	344
Hiding and Unhiding Columns, Rows, and Gridlines	345
Hiding columns	345
Hiding rows	345
Hiding gridlines	345
Changing Alignments	346
Centering, Wrapping, and Justifying Text	347
Centering text	347
Wrapping text	348
Justifying text	348
Applying Fonts and Style Formats	349
Applying Borders, Patterns, and Colors	351
Working with Number Formats	353
Working with Date and Time Formats	355
Using Custom Number Formats	356
Copying Formats with the Format Painter	359
Creating Your Own Styles	360
Protecting Your Formatting Changes	361
Summary	364
Where to go next.	364

Chapter 16: Adding Graphics to Worksheets 365

Why Bother with Graphics in Excel?	365
Inserting Graphics into a Worksheet	366
Working with Graphic Objects	368
Drawing lines, arcs, ellipses, and rectangles	370
Using the Freehand and Freeform tools	371
Selecting and grouping objects	372
Using the Bring To Front and Send To Back tools	373
Moving and copying objects	373
Resizing objects	374
Formatting objects	374
Adding Text Boxes	376

Word Art 379
Adding Macro Buttons 382
Summary 384
    Where to go next 384

Chapter 17: Working with Excel Charts 385

What Is a Chart? 385
About Embedded Charts and Chart Sheets 387
    Creating an embedded chart 388
    Creating a chart sheet 388
Creating a Sample Chart 391
Saving and Printing Charts 393
Understanding the Parts of a Chart 393
Working with Charts 396
    Selecting parts of a chart 396
    Working with the Chart toolbar 397
    Adding titles 398
    Adding unattached text 399
    Formatting text 399
    Adding legends 400
    Formatting chart axes 400
    Adding gridlines 401
    Customizing a chart's area 401
Working with Chart Types 402
Working with AutoFormat 405
Understanding How Excel Plots a Chart 406
Summary 410
    Where to go next 410

Chapter 18: Printing with Excel 411

The Basics of Printing 411
    About the Print dialog box 412
    About the Page Setup dialog box 413
Setting the Print Range 416
    Specifying multiple print ranges 417
Previewing Print Jobs 417
Controlling Aspects of Printing 418
    Printing titles 420
    Controlling page breaks 420
    Turning the gridlines on and off 421
    Printing nonconsecutive sheets 421
    Inserting headers and footers 421
Changing the Printer Properties 423
Sending a File on a Network 425

Summary 427
    Where to go next 427

Chapter 19: Working with Excel Databases 429

What is a Database? 429
Creating a Database 431
Working with Database Records 432
    Adding new records 433
    Editing records 433
    Deleting records 433
    Finding data by using criteria 434
Using the AutoFormat Command on Your Database 436
Sorting a Database 436
Using the AutoFilter Command 440
    Printing a report based on specific data 442
    Using complex criteria with AutoFilter 442
    Turning off the effects of AutoFilter 443
Performing a Mail Merge with Excel Data 445
Designing Databases 445
    About data and attributes 446
    Steps in database design 446
Summary 448
    Where to go next 448

Chapter 20: Working with Excel Macros 449

Understanding the Types of Macros 450
Creating a Macro 451
Stopping the Macro Recorder 452
Assigning Macros to Buttons 454
Assigning a Macro to a Graphic Object 456
Running the Macro 457
Changing Your Macro Options 458
Making Macros Available to All Worksheets 459
Summary 461
    Where to go next 461

Chapter 21: Excel Analysis 463

What's Involved in What-If Analysis? 463
Using the Goal Seek Command 464
Using Solver 466
Projecting Figures with Data Tables 469
Working with Pivot Tables 472
Summary 479
    Where to go next 479

Chapter 22: Using Visual Basic for Applications 481

Using Macros to Learn Visual Basic for Applications 481
Understanding Visual Basic for Applications Code 484
    About comments 485
    About headers and footers 485
    About selecting and entering data 486
    About control statements 486
    About displaying dialog boxes 487
    About user input 487
Editing Visual Basic for Applications Code 489
Printing Visual Basic Code 489
About the Visual Basic Toolbar 489
Just A Beginning 490
Summary 491
    Where to go next 491

Chapter 23: Excel at Work 493

Cash-Flow Management 493
Break-Even Analysis 495
IRA Calculator 500
Mortgage Analysis and Amortization Schedule 507
Summary 512
    Where to go next 512

Chapter 24: The Excel Top Ten 513

Can I set up a workbook so that it opens each time I start
    Microsoft Excel? 513
How do I change the default working directory or the standard
    font in Microsoft Excel? 513
How can I display more than one workbook at a time? 514
I'm an accomplished Excel 4.0 user, and I'm having trouble
    getting used to the new menu structure of Excel 95. Does
    Excel 95 offer any help for Excel 4.0 users? 514
How can I prevent a slash (/) or a hyphen (-) from being formatted as a
    date when it is entered? 515
What are some shortcuts for selecting cells and ranges? 515
How do I format characters in a cell that I want to be superscript,
    subscript, or in a different font? 516
How can I combine the contents of two cells into
    one cell? 517
How can I define an area on my worksheet for printing? 517
How can I make my titles print on each page? 518
Summary 519
    Where to go next 519

Part 4: PowerPoint — 521

Chapter 25: Working in PowerPoint — 523

Learning About the Presentation Window — 523
Working with Shortcuts and Toolbars — 527
    Using shortcut menus — 527
    Using shortcut buttons — 527
    Using the toolbars — 528
Using PowerPoint's Default Presentations — 528
Working with Presentations — 531
    Opening a new presentation — 532
    Saving a presentation — 533
    Entering summary information — 533
Working with Text — 535
    Editing in Outline view — 535
    Editing in Slide view — 536
Working with Slides — 536
    Moving between slides — 536
    Inserting slides — 537
    Deleting slides — 538
    Copying and moving slides — 538
    Rearranging slides — 539
    Changing the slide layout — 539
Working with Objects — 540
    Selecting and grouping objects — 540
    Moving and copying objects — 540
    Cropping objects — 541
    Aligning objects — 542
    Stacking objects — 543
Working with Shapes — 544
    Drawing shapes — 544
    Drawing freeform shapes — 545
    Changing the color and style of shapes — 545
    Rotating and sizing shapes — 546
Using AutoShapes and Clip Art — 546
Summary — 548
    Where to go next — 548

Chapter 26: Enhancing a Presentation — 549

Using the AutoContent Wizard — 549
Using the AutoLayout feature — 553
Using the Slide Master — 554
Working with Lists and Columns — 557
    Creating bulleted lists — 557
    Creating columns — 559

Working with Fonts, Styles, and Colors 560
    Applying shadowing and embossing 560
    Applying superscript and subscript 561
Creating Special Effects with WordArt 561
Adding Excel Worksheets and Word Tables 564
    Inserting Excel worksheets into PowerPoint 565
    Inserting Word tables into PowerPoint 566
Adding Sound to Presentations 567
Summary 569
    Where to go next 569

Chapter 27: Working with Charts in PowerPoint 571

Chart Types 573
Inserting Charts 574
    Entering and editing data in the Datasheet window 575
Editing Charts 576
    Changing the data series 577
    Changing the chart type 579
    Using AutoFormat to select a chart design 581
Enhancing a Chart's Appearance 582
    Changing fonts 582
    Changing chart colors 583
    Adding titles 584
    Changing axes 585
    Changing borders 586
Changing the Appearance of 3-D Charts 586
Creating Organizational Charts 589
Summary 591
    Where to go next 591

Chapter 28: Producing Your Work 593

Printing Presentations 593
    Setting up your slides for printing 593
    Printing parts of your presentation 595
Producing On-Screen Slide Shows 596
    Creating build slides 597
    Hiding and unhiding slides 599
Adding Speaker's Notes and Audience Handouts to a Presentation 599
Using the PowerPoint Viewer 602
Using the Pack & Go Wizard 603
Using the Send Command 605
Summary 606
    Where to go next 606

Chapter 29: PowerPoint for Windows at Work ... 607

Creating an Organization Chart ... 607
Creating a Travel Presentation ... 611
    Applying a template to the presentation ... 611
    Applying a background to the slides ... 612
    Adding notes and handouts to the presentation ... 613
    Adding headers and footers to your presentation ... 614
    Printing your notes pages ... 615
    Adding transitions to your presentation ... 615
Summary ... 617
    Where to go next ... 617

Chapter 30: The PowerPoint Top Ten ... 619

How can I format the title and text for an entire presentation? ... 619
How can I group and edit objects as one? ... 619
How can I copy the formatting of one object to another? ... 619
How can I apply a PowerPoint presentation as a template? ... 620
How can I change the layout of my slide without losing my existing work? ... 620
How can I preview all my slide transitions? ... 620
How can I view my presentations on a business trip without installing PowerPoint? ... 620
How can I print slides in reverse order? ... 620
How can I add and erase on-screen annotations in a slide show? ... 621
How can I create new slides without using the New Slide dialog box? ... 621
Summary ... 622
    Where to go next ... 622

Part 5: Office Works Together   623

Chapter 31: Using Schedule+ ... 625

Starting Schedule+ ... 625
Understanding the Schedule+ Window ... 627
    The Daily tab ... 629
    The Weekly tab ... 629
    The Monthly tab ... 631
    The Planner tab ... 632
    The To Do tab ... 634
    The Contacts tab ... 635
Making Appointments ... 636
    The General tab ... 636
    The Attendees tab ... 638

The Notes tab	638
The Planner tab	639
Recurring meetings	640
Changing and deleting appointments	640
Using the To Do List	641
Adding, Editing, and Deleting Contacts	642
Sending and Receiving Meeting Requests	642
Printing in Schedule+	643
Using the Timex Data Link Watch Wizard	645
Summary	649

Chapter 32: Using the Binder 651

What Is the Binder?	651
Using the Binder	652
Adding existing documents to a binder	653
Adding new documents to a binder	654
Saving a binder	655
Opening an existing binder	656
Working with Documents in the Binder	656
Moving and copying documents within a binder	656
Renaming documents	656
Deleting documents	656
Printing binder documents	657
Summary	658
Where to go next	658

Chapter 33: Sharing Data between Applications with OLE 659

Defining OLE	659
I have a document that was created with another word processor. Can I work on this file in Word?	659
Linking Versus Embedding	662
Linking	662
Embedding	662
When to use linking and when to use embedding	663
Establishing Links in Your Documents	664
Linking with the Paste Special command	664
Linking with the Object command	665
Changing a link's update settings	667
Breaking and restoring links	668
Embedding Objects in Your Documents	669
Embedding with the Paste Special command	669
Embedding with the Object command	670
Editing embedded OLE objects	671
Converting file formats of embedded objects	672

Adding Sound and Video to Office Documents 673
Creating an OLE Example 673
Summary 675
    Where to go next 675

Part 6: Appendixes — 677

Appendix A: Installing Microsoft Office — 679

Beginning the Installation 679
About the Custom Installation Options 683
    Office Binder and Shortcut Bar options 684
    Excel options 685
    Word options 686
    PowerPoint options 687
    Schedule+ options 688
    Office Tools options 689
    Converters, Filters, and Data Access options 690
    Completing the installation process 690

Appendix B: Word Basics — 691

Starting Word 691
About the Screen 691
Opening New or Existing Documents 695
Basic Navigation 696
Basic Text Editing 697
Saving 697
    Saving a document 698
    Using File⇨Save As 699
    Allow Fast Saves 700
    Prompt for Document Properties 700
    Automatic Save Every x Minutes 700
    Using File⇨Save All 700
Printing 701
    Printing part of a document 702
Opening Existing Documents 702
Summary 703
    Where to go next 703

Appendix C: Excel Basics — 705

Understanding Spreadsheets 705
Understanding the Excel Screen 706
Understanding the Workbook Concept 709
Opening an Existing Workbook 710

Workbook and Worksheet Navigation 710
    Navigating in the workbook window 710
    Navigating in a worksheet 711
Entering and Editing Data 712
    Numbers 714
    Times and dates 714
    Text entry 715
Building Formulas 716
Printing the Worksheet 716
Saving the Worksheet 717
Summary 719
    Where to go next 719

Appendix D: PowerPoint Basics 721

Understanding PowerPoint Terminology 721
Creating Presentations 722
    Using the AutoContent Wizard 723
    Using a template 725
    Starting a blank presentation 725
Opening a Presentation 726
Saving and Closing a Presentation 726
Understanding PowerPoint's Views 727
Adding Slides 730
Moving Among Slides 730
Editing a Slide's Contents 731
    Editing text in Slide view 731
    Editing text in Outline view 731
Adding Clip Art to a Presentation 733
Printing Your Presentation 734
Summary 735
    Where to go next 735

Appendix E: On the CD-ROM 737

Using the CD-ROM 737
About Shareware 739
Excel 739
    The Power Utility Pak 739
    Amort.xlm version 4.1 744
    Deprec8.xlm version 1.0 745
Fonts 747
    Fonts from the 35HEADS collection 747
Utilities 749
    Jasc Media Center 749
    Paint Shop Pro 750
    NoteWorthy Composer 752
    WinZip95 755

Word 757
    TypeRodent 758
    APA Style Templates 758
    Carrier Pigeon 760
Book Examples 761

Index 762

IDG Books Worldwide License Agreement 804
    CD-ROM Installation Instructions 806

Reader Response Card .... Back of Book

Introduction

Welcome to *The Microsoft Office for Windows 95 Bible, Standard Edition*. This is your personal guide to the applications that make up the standard edition of Microsoft Office: Microsoft Word, Microsoft Excel, Microsoft PowerPoint, Microsoft Schedule+, and Microsoft Binder. This book tells you everything that you need to learn any or all of the Microsoft Office applications, regardless of how much you already know about Office. This book is first and foremost a comprehensive reference — but it also helps you learn by example, and it gives you special tips and techniques to get the most out of the Office applications. *The Microsoft Office for Windows 95 Bible, Standard Edition* also tells you how to make the Office applications work in concert for maximum results. Using the techniques outlined in this book, you'll be able to integrate the use of the Office applications for maximum efficiency and share information between the applications to produce impressive documents and presentations.

Although each chapter is an integral part of the book as a whole, each chapter can also stand on its own. You can read the book in any order you want, skipping from chapter to chapter and from topic to topic. (Note that this book's index is particularly thorough — rely on the index to find the topics you're interested in.)

For each of the major applications (Word, Excel, and PowerPoint), we've included chapters that answer the ten most common user questions, based on user feedback to Microsoft and support discussions on CompuServe and America Online. We've also included "At Work" chapters that show you how to accomplish common, everyday office tasks with Office. And, if you've never touched Word, Excel, or PowerPoint, we've included appendixes that tell you the basics for each application.

Is This Book for You?

If you use (or will soon use) Microsoft Office, *this book is for you.*

As we'll describe fully in just a minute, this book is divided into parts; each part describes one of the Office applications. If you're an Office beginner, start with the first chapter in each part and work to the end. (If you've never used *any* kind of word processor, spreadsheet, or presentation creator before, start with the appendixes!) If you have some Office experience, be sure to breeze through the chapters that cover topics you already know — we've added special tips and techniques throughout that will help you work better with Office.

Hey! There's a CD-ROM Stuck to the Back Cover!

We've made a thorough search for various shareware packages and files that you may find useful when working with Microsoft Office or with Windows 95. We made a conscious effort to look for useful additions that will appeal to the typical user of Microsoft Office. You'll find a complete listing of what's on the CD-ROM in Appendix E.

How This Book is Organized

This book has been divided into five parts: one that gives an overview of Office; one each for Word, Excel, and PowerPoint; and one that describes Schedule+ (a time management application) and tools you can use to make Office applications work together.

Part I: Introducing Microsoft Office

This tiny, one-chapter part tells you about tools Office gives you to work more efficiently.

Chapter 1: About Microsoft Office gets you started. You'll learn about starting the Office Manager, launching applications, getting Office Manager tips, making appointments, adding tasks, adding contacts, and exiting the Office Manager.

Part II: Word

Ah, Word: the 800-pound gorilla of word processors. This part tells you what Word can do for you.

Chapter 2: Creating and Working with Documents is where you'll create your first document. You'll also be introduced to templates, Clipboard insertions, and Word's multiple views. This chapter also helps you tackle some everyday word-processing tasks: changing margins, setting tabs and line spacing, and moving and copying text. You'll also learn about using search and replace; using the thesaurus; using the spelling and grammar checkers; changing your hyphenation options; adding bullets and paragraph numbering; and creating and editing glossaries.

Chapter 3: Formatting Documents tells you the hows and whys of formatting, which is the way you specify what your document will look like. It helps you apply *character* and *paragraph* formatting, as well as *page* and *section* formatting. It tells you how to deal with tabs; create document summaries; make headers, footers, and page numbers; and handle complex documents.

Chapter 4: Previewing and Printing Your Documents discusses previewing documents; adjusting margins and objects in preview mode; printing documents; printing multiple documents; printing parts of a document; printing sideways; printing envelopes; and changing the printer setup.

Chapter 5: Working with Tables and Outlines tells you how to create, edit, and format tables; work with side-by-side paragraphs; and convert text to tables. It also describes Word outlines, telling you how to create and organize outlines; promote and demote headings; convert headings to body text and vice versa; and move headings.

Chapter 6: Working with Fields tells you all about working with fields and with Word's mail merge facility. It gives you great tips on embedding Excel data into a mail merge, and you'll also find information that helps you work with data from other programs, such as dBASE and Paradox.

Chapter 7: Building Tables of Contents and Indexes helps you create tables of contents. You can do this in two ways: by using existing headings in your document, or by embedding special codes called *TC fields*. The chapter also helps you add multiple levels to a table of contents. In addition, this chapter tells you how to build indexes, including creating multilevel index entries, and how to use page number ranges. It gives special tips for handling large indexes.

Chapter 8: Working with Styles and Templates helps you make your documents look better. You can use styles to format your documents. Word comes with some predefined styles, but you can create and apply your own, and even use styles from other documents. Templates are a way to collect styles you want to reuse — for example, creating a *memorandum* template that includes all the styles you typically use when you write a memo. The chapter tells you how to use templates to create documents; how to create and apply a template; and how to customize Word's default template.

Chapter 9: Working with Macros helps you reduce tedious tasks to a single keystroke (or toolbar button or menu choice). This chapter tells you how to record and play macros, and how to assign shortcut keys to macros. It even tells you how to create macros that run automatically. And you'll also find suggestions for real-world uses of macros in your work.

Chapter 10: Desktop Publishing with Word describes ways you can add desktop publishing-style flair to your documents. It discusses using columns and adding graphics. It tells you about Word's brochure and newsletter wizards — fast ways to look professional. It also tells you about Word's AutoFormat feature, which can make your plain-text document look pretty.

Chapter 11: Word for Windows At Work provides step-by-step details of how you can perform various common office tasks with Word. It helps you create brochures, fax cover sheets, interoffice memos, invoices, office newsletters, and weekly time sheets.

Chapter 12: The Word for Windows Top Ten answers the ten most burning questions Word users have.

Part III: Excel

This part describes Office's spreadsheet application, Excel.

Chapter 13: Making the Most of Workbooks tells you all about workbooks, which are collections of individual Excel spreadsheets. It tells you how to create, open, save, and close workbooks. It tells you how add, delete, rename, move, and copy sheets within a workbook. It also tells you about selecting cells and sheets, and about moving and copying data between sheets.

Chapter 14: Getting Information into Excel tells you how to get data into Excel. It describes entering numbers, dates, and times; text entry; building series; handling trends as a part of data entry; editing, moving, and copying cells; and adding and deleting rows and columns. It also details using and customizing AutoFill, a great way to make Excel do some work for you.

Chapter 15: Excel Formatting tells you how to customize the look of your spreadsheets. It details changing row heights and column widths; changing alignments and fonts; changing borders, patterns, and colors; modifying cell shading; working with number formats; using custom formats; using styles with formats; and using AutoFormat.

Chapter 16: Adding Graphics to Worksheets tells you how to embed graphics into your spreadsheets. (And you thought spreadsheets were only for crunching numbers!) It discusses drawing objects, adding text, selecting and grouping objects, and sizing and moving objects.

Chapter 17: Working with Excel Charts discusses Excel's chart feature, a quick way to turn your spreadsheet data into an easily understandable graphic. It tells you how to add *embedded, separate,* and *freestanding* charts. It helps you add titles and labels to your charts, change a chart's type after you've created it, and format charts.

Chapter 18: Printing with Excel tells you about the choices you have when printing your work in Excel. It describes working with printer setup and margins, using headers and footers, previewing print jobs, specifying what to print, dealing with complex print jobs, working with title layouts, working with fonts, and general printing tips.

Chapter 19: Working with Excel Databases tells you about using information from a database in Excel. It tells you how to create databases in Excel, how to find the information that you need, and how to print reports. You'll also find tips here on designing your databases for maximum efficiency, importing data, how to use Microsoft Query and ODBC, and how to work with query results.

Chapter 20: Working with Macros helps you reduce tedious tasks to a single keystroke (or toolbar button or menu choice). It tells you how to make and use macros and use the macro toolbar, and it gives useful examples of Excel macros.

Chapter 21: Excel Analysis helps you make Excel help you make decisions. It covers tools and techniques that you can use to perform "what-if" scenarios, to work backwards from a desired goal to find the underlying data that you need to reach these goals. This chapter also discusses data consolidation, statistical analysis, forecasting with the goal seeker, finding solutions through the use of the Solver, summarizing data using pivot tables, modifying the pivot tables, and working with the analysis toolpack.

Chapter 22: Using Visual Basic for Applications introduces you to Visual Basic for Applications, a programming language you can use to make Excel do more for you. Macros are a key to learning Visual Basic for Applications; this chapter tells you how. It also helps you understand Visual Basic for Applications code; tells you how to use comments, cell selection techniques, and control statements; tells you how to display input boxes and dialog boxes; and describes the editor you use to create Visual Basic for Applications programs.

Chapter 23: Excel for Windows at Work helps you use Excel in the office to create employee pay sheets, sales projections, and a check register.

Chapter 24: The Excel Top Ten answers the ten most problematic questions Excel users have.

Part IV: PowerPoint

This part tells you how to use PowerPoint to create great presentations.

Chapter 25: Working in PowerPoint introduces you to PowerPoint basics: selecting and grouping objects; moving and copying objects; resizing, scaling, and aligning objects; use of the grid; drawing lines, shapes, and curves; and drawing freeform shapes.

Chapter 26: Enhancing a Presentation tells you how to make your presentations look better. You can use AutoLayouts, which makes PowerPoint format the presentation for you. You can also use slides from other presentations. This chapter tells you how to do both. It also describes working with columns and lists; working with fonts, styles, and colors; working with color schemes; working with shading and fill; and adding sound to your presentation. Finally, it tells you how to add Excel worksheets and Word tables.

Chapter 27: Working with Charts in PowerPoint describes PowerPoint's chart feature. It tells you how to insert and edit graphs, and discusses using AutoFormat to choose a graph's design. It helps you enhance a chart's appearance by giving tips on formatting; on sizing and positioning of objects; and on working with shadows, colors, and backgrounds.

Chapter 28: Producing Your Work tells you how to print presentations, produce on-screen slide shows, create speaker's notes, and create audience handouts.

Chapter 29: PowerPoint for Windows at Work tells you how to create an organization chart and a sales presentation using PowerPoint's AutoContent wizard.

Chapter 30: The PowerPoint Top Ten solves the ten most frustrating problems users have with PowerPoint.

Part V: Office Works Together

This part tells you about Schedule+, Office's time management application. It also describes the OLE and the Office Binder, two ways that you can make Office applications work together.

Chapter 31: Working with Schedule+ helps you create appointments and tasks, schedule meetings, and respond to meeting requests. Using Schedule+ as your planning assistant, you can track appointments, projects, meetings, personal and business contacts, and events.

Chapter 32: Using the Binder tells you how to group documents from the various Office applications into *binders,* which are collections of Word, Excel, and PowerPoint documents. Binders provide you with a central place to edit and print documents related to a single project.

Chapter 33: Sharing Data Between Applications with OLE tells you how OLE (Object Linking and Embedding) lets you place data from one Office application into another — and have the data automatically stay up to date.

Appendixes

If you haven't installed Office on your computer yet, or if you've never used any of the Office applications, then bury your nose in the appendixes. They'll get you going.

Appendix A: Installing Office tells you how to install Microsoft Office.

Appendix B: Word Basics tells the new Word user how to start Word, how to create a document, how to open an existing document, how to navigate a document, how to enter and edit text, how to print a document, and how to save a document.

Appendix C: Excel Basics tells the new Excel user how to start Excel, what a *workbook* is, how to navigate a workbook, how to enter and edit data and formulas, how to do basic formatting, how to print your work, and how to save your work.

Appendix D: PowerPoint Basics tells the new PowerPoint user how to start PowerPoint; how to create, move around in, and save presentations; and how to enter text and graphics into presentations.

Appendix E: On the CD tells you how to use the CD-ROM included with this book, and gives some information about the software and files it includes.

Conventions This Book Uses

We've written a thick book — there's a lot to say about Office! So, we've used several devices that help you find your way.

You'll see eye-catching icons in the margin from time to time. They'll alert you to critical information, warn you about problems, tell you where to go for more information, and highlight useful tips.

Note This icon highlights a special point of interest about the current topic.

Hot Stuff This icon helps you work faster by pointing out shortcuts and killer techniques. If you've worked with the Office applications before, and want to quickly expand your knowledge, skim the book for these icons.

Danger Zone Sometimes, bad things can happen when you work in Office. This icon points out all of them that we found.

More Info This icon sends you to other places in the book for more information about something we mention.

Working Together The whole *point* of Office is that its applications work together. This icon highlights examples where we've used more than one Office application to accomplish a task.

> ### Sidebars
>
> We use sidebars to highlight related information, give an example, or discuss an item in greater detail. For example, one sidebar tells you where to get graphics you can add to documents, spreadsheets, and presentations — cool information, but not critical. If you don't want to delve too deeply into a subject, stick to the body of the text and skip the sidebars.

When we write command names, we use a convention that shows you the menus you need to use to execute the command. So, when we want you to execute the Print command from the File menu, we've written File➪Print. Or, when we want you to execute the Define command from the Name submenu of the Insert menu, we've written Insert➪Name➪Define.

Finally, we've taken great (tedious) pains to underline every single hotkey in this book. You can use hotkeys to execute menu commands from the keyboard. For example, you can execute File➪Print by pressing Alt+F+P — that is, press and hold the Alt key, press F, press P, then release Alt. *F* and *P* are the Print command's hotkeys, and you use the Alt key to activate them. Remembering hotkeys isn't easy because they're not always the first letter of each command. So, from here on out, it's File➪Print, and it's Edit➪Paste Special, and it's Format➪Sheet➪Hide.

Where Should I Start?

If you want to learn about Word, start with Chapter 2. If you've never used a word processor before, read Appendix B first.

If you want to work with Excel, go to Chapter 13. Appendix C teaches the basics of Excel, if you've never used a spreadsheet program.

If you want to create presentations in PowerPoint, start with Chapter 25 (or Appendix D, if you don't know the first thing about presentation creation software).

If you want to use Schedule+, go to Chapter 31.

If you're fairly familiar with Office, but want to know how to make its applications work together, go to Chapters 32 and 33.

❖   ❖   ❖

Introducing Microsoft Office

PART 1

In This Part

Chapter 1
About Microsoft Office and the Office Shortcut Bar

About Microsoft Office and the Office Shortcut Bar

CHAPTER 1

◆ ◆ ◆ ◆

In This Chapter

Getting to know Microsoft Office

Working with the Office Shortcut Bar

Customizing the Office Shortcut Bar

Running Office Setup and Uninstall

◆ ◆ ◆ ◆

This chapter introduces Microsoft Office and the Office Shortcut Bar, giving you an overview of the parts of Microsoft Office. It details how you can work with the Office Shortcut Bar, a toolbar that provides easy access to the applications in Microsoft Office and to other applications and files that you can add by customizing the toolbar.

Getting to Know Microsoft Office

Microsoft Office consists of a group of applications developed over time by Microsoft to work together, both in terms of accomplishing things in a similar way and in terms of providing easy access to data shared between the individual applications. Office is designed to make you more productive with less hassle. With Microsoft Office, you can create business documents to meet virtually any need, handle complex financial analysis, and produce professional presentations. Microsoft Office includes the following applications:

- ◆ **Word:** Arguably the most popular Windows word processor on the market, Microsoft Word provides all the power you need in a word processor along with a range of tools that make complex formatting tasks easier.

- ◆ **Excel:** In Microsoft Excel, you have a spreadsheet that is powerful yet simple to use. Besides offering powerful spreadsheet capabilities and the ability to work with multiple pages in the same spreadsheet file (the *workbook* concept), Excel provides powerful charting and graphing features, and can readily use spreadsheets you have saved in other popular spreadsheet formats, such as Lotus 1-2-3.

- ✦ **PowerPoint:** PowerPoint is a presentation graphics program that can provide you with overheads for team meetings, slides for sales meetings, animated special effects for video presentations, and more. PowerPoint's tools combined with its simple approach make it easy for you to create presentations that clearly emphasize what you are trying to say.
- ✦ **Access:** With Microsoft Access (provided with the Professional edition of Microsoft Office), you get a database manager that provides all the power of a fully relational product with the ability to produce complex applications. At the same time, Access's design tools enable you to design databases that are easy for end users to work with. Access was designed from the ground up to make use of a wide variety of data from existing database sources.
- ✦ **Schedule+:** Schedule+ is a time management system you can use to manage your appointments, meetings, tasks, contacts, and events. Schedule+ even works over a network, letting your entire office share scheduling information. Schedule+ includes an appointment book, a to-do list, a meeting planner, a contact manager, and an event tracker.

Understanding the Office Shortcut Bar

When you install Microsoft Office, one of the default options causes the Office Manager to be installed. The Office Manager is automatically added to Windows setup routines — an option for Microsoft Office is added to the Windows Programs menu. Choose the Programs command from the Start menu at the lower-left corner of your screen and then choose the Microsoft Office Shortcut Bar option from the Microsoft Office pop-up menu. After you choose these commands, the Office Shortcut Bar appears as a toolbar at the upper-right corner of the screen. Figure 1-1 shows the Office Shortcut Bar. In the figure, the toolbar is arranged horizontally. However, you can change the location and shape of the toolbar, as detailed in "Customizing the Office Shortcut Bar" later in this chapter.

Figure 1-1: The Microsoft Office Shortcut Bar.

The Office Shortcut Bar is designed to provide you with fast access to any of the Office Manager applications. Just click on the application's button to start the program. You can also start any of the applications by choosing Programs from the Start menu, selecting Microsoft Office, and then clicking on the desired application from the pop-up menu that appears.

Hot Stuff: By default, the Office Shortcut Bar does not contain buttons for Word, Excel, PowerPoint, or Access. You can easily add buttons for these applications, though. You do this by right-clicking on any blank space in the toolbar, choosing Customize from the menu that appears, clicking on the Buttons tab in the resulting dialog box, and turning on the desired buttons. For more details on adding buttons, see "Customizing the Office Shortcut Bar" later in this chapter.

Using the Office Shortcut Bar versus the Start menu

There can be a significant difference between launching one of the Office applications with the Office Shortcut Bar and launching that same application through the Windows 95 Start menu. The difference exists when a copy of the application is already running. When an application is running and you use the Office Shortcut Bar to start one of the Office applications, Windows switches to the application that is already running. When an application is running and you use the Start menu to start that same application again, you launch a second instance of the same Office application, one that now runs in Windows memory.

Danger Zone: Be warned: running two instances of the same application uses Windows resources and slows overall system response time. If all you want to do is switch from one Microsoft Office application to another, use the Office Shortcut Bar (or the Alt+Tab key combination) instead of the Programs command on the Start menu.

Getting Help with the Answer Wizard

If you've used earlier versions of any Office applications, you may remember Cue Cards, those help screens that remained visible while you performed a particular task. These always-visible help screens have been implemented for many Windows 95 applications. In Microsoft Office, these screens aren't called Cue Cards anymore. Now you get help in the form of answers to your questions by using the *Answer Wizard*. To start the Answer Wizard, click on the Answer Wizard button in the Office Shortcut Bar. When you do, the Answer Wizard dialog box (Figure 1-2) appears.

In the "Type your request, and then click Search" field, type a phrase that describes the task you need directions for, and then click on the Search button. (For example, if you want to know how to create a new document, you might enter the phrase **create a new document**.) When you click on the Search button, the lower portion of the dialog box displays a list of topics related to your request. Click on any item in the list to select it. Then click on the Display button to show a help screen for that topic. The help screen remains visible above any windows you have open, so you can refer to it as you perform tasks in Office. When you're done with the help screen, click on the Close box (in the upper-right corner of the help screen's window) to put it away.

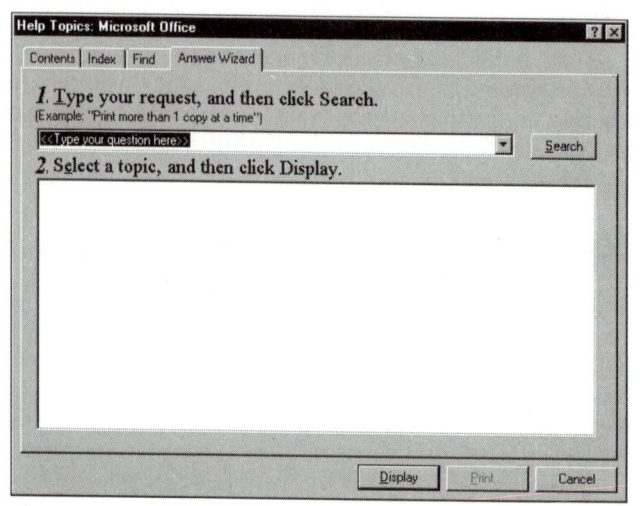

Figure 1-2: The Answer Wizard dialog box.

Sizing and docking the Office Shortcut Bar

You can click on and drag any side of the Office Shortcut Bar to change its size and shape, and you can click on and drag the toolbar to a different location on-screen. When you drag the toolbar against any of the edges (the top, bottom, left, or right sides of the window), the bar takes on a narrow, rectangular shape and appears docked against the chosen edge. When the toolbar is not dragged against an edge, you can change the size of the rectangle that contains the toolbar by clicking on and dragging any corner of the toolbar.

Customizing the Office Shortcut Bar

You can customize the Office Shortcut Bar — or any toolbar, for that matter — by adding and deleting buttons, changing the size of the buttons, changing the toolbar's position on-screen, and making all sorts of adjustments. To customize the Office Shortcut Bar, right-click in any blank spot on the Office Shortcut Bar. From the menu that opens, choose Customize. The Customize dialog box appears. Notice its four tabs. You can make all sorts of changes to the toolbars by using these tabs.

The Buttons tab

If you regularly use other applications (such as Microsoft FoxPro) or other common Windows tools (such as Windows Paint), you can add buttons for these applications to the toolbar. You aren't limited to applications produced by Microsoft, either; you can add any Windows application to the Office Shortcut Bar. You may want to consider adding buttons for Explorer, My Computer, or for the MS-DOS prompt, if you regularly use any of these aspects of Windows. If the Buttons tab isn't already selected in your Customize dialog box, click on its tab to bring it to the front, as shown in Figure 1-3.

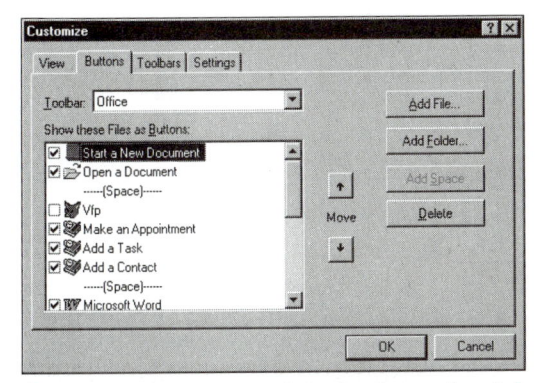

Figure 1-3: The Buttons tab in the Customize dialog box.

Moving buttons

To move the location of a button within the toolbar, first choose the toolbar that you want to change in the Toolbar list box. Then select the application that you want to move in the Show these Files as Buttons list box. Click on the up or down Move arrows to move the order of the selected application. (Moving it up places it closer to the left side or top of the toolbar; moving it down places it closer to the right side or bottom of the toolbar.)

Adding new buttons

To add a button to the toolbar for an existing item in the Toolbar list, select the item in the list and click on its check box. When you click in the check box, the item is added to the toolbar.

To add Windows software that isn't already in the Show these Files as Buttons list, click on the Add File button. The Add File dialog box appears, as shown in Figure 1-4.

In the Look in list box, you can select the drive or folder that contains the desired program. When you locate the desired program, click on it to select it and then click on the Add button in the dialog box. If you know the program's exact name and path, you can type it in the File name text box and then click on the Add button. After you click on Add, the icon for the new program is added to the Office Shortcut Bar.

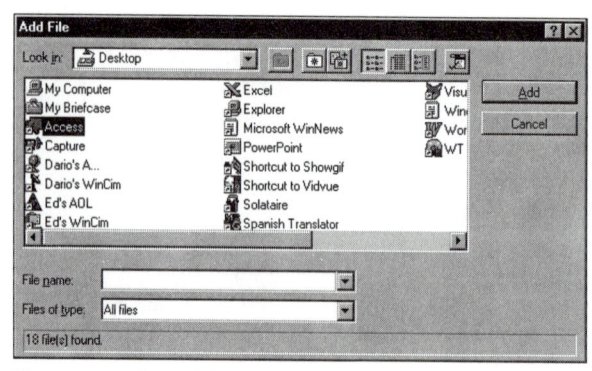

Figure 1-4: The Add File dialog box.

Removing buttons

To remove a button from the toolbar, first select the unwanted application in the applications list in the Buttons tab of the Customize dialog box. Then uncheck the option to remove it from the toolbar and from the applications list.

The View tab

To see the View tab, click on its tab to bring it to the front of the Customize dialog box, as shown in Figure 1-5. In this tab, you can do many things to make the toolbar stand out.

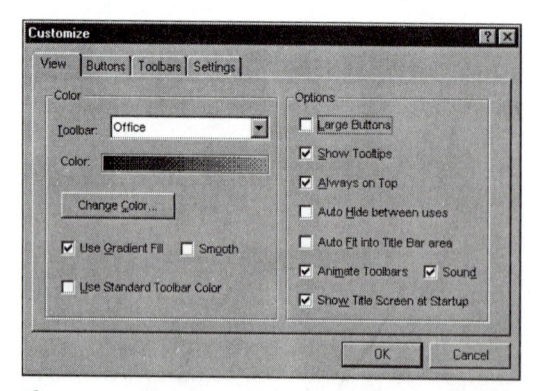

Figure 1-5: The View tab in the Customize dialog box.

In the Color section of the dialog box, you can change the color for the Office Shortcut Bar. Click on the Change Color button to display a Color dialog box, where you can select a desired color and click on OK. Checking the Use Gradient Fill option causes the chosen color to use a gradient fill pattern, and checking the Use Standard Toolbar Color option causes the Office Shortcut Bar to take on the default Windows color.

In the Options area of the View tab, you can turn on or off any of the options shown. Large Buttons switches between small and large toolbar buttons; Show Tooltips turns on the Tooltips feature; and Always on Top specifies that the toolbar should remain above other applications. When turned on, Auto Hide between uses hides the toolbar when it isn't in use (you can redisplay it by holding the mouse pointer over the side of the screen where the toolbar is docked). The Auto Fit into Title Bar area causes the toolbar to automatically fit into an area the width of the title bar when you drag the toolbar to resize it. Turn on Animate Toolbars if you want the toolbars to appear to grow and shrink as you open and close them, or turn on Sound to hear a noise when Office applications are launched.

The Toolbars tab

Click the Toolbars tab to bring it to the front of the Customize dialog box (see Figure 1-6). You can use the Toolbars tab to add other folders or programs to the screen as separate toolbars. In the Show these Folders as Toolbars list box, you can check the folders that you want to appear as toolbars. You can move the folders in the list so that the toolbars produced by the folders that you add appear in a certain order on screen. To do this, click on a desired folder and use the up or down Move arrows to move the folder to the desired location in the list of checked folders.

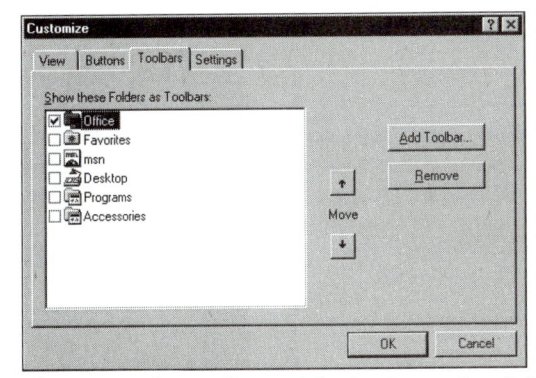

Figure 1-6: The Toolbars tab in the Customize dialog box.

For example, Figure 1-7 shows three toolbars that have been enabled in the Toolbars tab of the Customize dialog box. In addition to the Office Shortcut Bar, toolbars for the Favorites folder and for all programs have been enabled. If you look at the top of the resulting toolbar arrangement (at the right edge of the screen), you see three toolbar icons at the top. The first icon displays the Office Shortcut Bar; the second displays the Favorites folder toolbar; and the third displays the Programs toolbar. The three toolbars appear layered in this order because they were placed in the Customize dialog box in that order. If you choose one toolbar that hides the others, you always see icons for the hidden toolbars at the bottom or right edge of the visible toolbar. You can click on any of those icons to display the other toolbars.

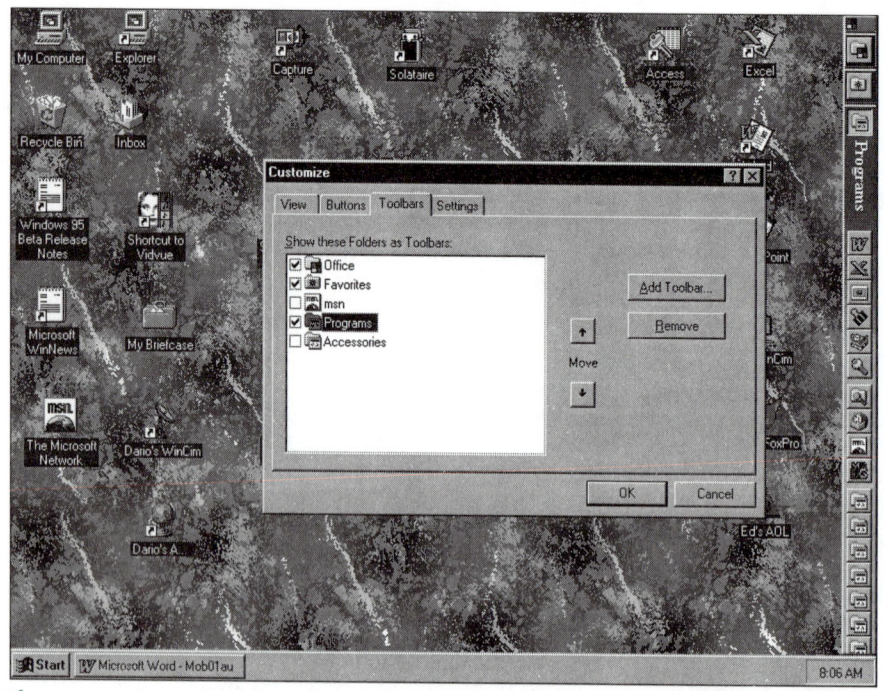

Figure 1-7: The Customize dialog box toolbar settings and three resulting toolbars.

You can create a new toolbar based on an existing folder. Click on the Add Toolbar button. An Add Toolbar dialog box appears. Use it to make a toolbar for a folder that you choose, or to create a new, blank toolbar. (If you create a blank toolbar, you can then add buttons to that toolbar by using the steps shown under "Adding new buttons" earlier in the chapter.)

The Settings tab

Click on the Settings tab to bring it to the front of the Customize dialog box (see Figure 1-8). In this tab, you can change the default folder that stores the templates used by Microsoft Office or the default folder that stores the templates used by workgroups (on a local-area network). To change any of the settings, click on the desired setting in the dialog box and then click on the Modify button. If you are changing one of the file folder options, clicking on Modify displays a Templates Location dialog box, in which you can choose the desired folder that is to contain the templates.

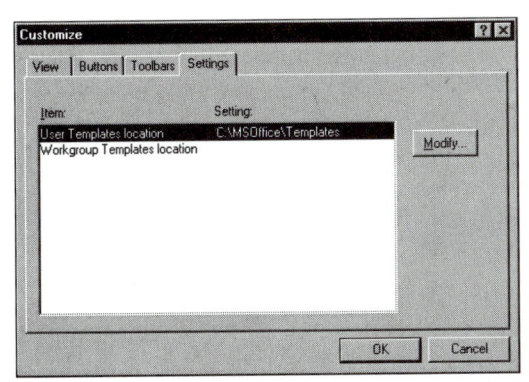

Figure 1-8: The Settings tab in the Customize dialog box.

Closing the Office Shortcut Bar

If you don't want the Office Shortcut Bar on-screen all the time, and you seldom switch between applications, go ahead and close the Office Shortcut Bar. You can still use the Microsoft Office applications, but you have to launch them from the Windows Start menu or by using shortcuts that you've added to your Windows environment. You can close the Office Shortcut Bar by performing these steps:

1. Right-click on the title bar of the Office Shortcut Bar.
2. From the menu that appears, choose Exit.

You can redisplay the Office Shortcut Bar at any time by choosing the Programs command from the Start menu. Then choose the Microsoft Office Shortcut Bar option from the Microsoft Office pop-up menu.

Adding and Removing Office Programs

After you've installed Microsoft Office, you can add or remove one of the applications or a part of an application. You can also remove any previously installed Office applications and their components. For example, you may want to add text converters for Word if you didn't originally install them with Word, or you may want to remove clip art if you're running short on hard disk space. You can add and remove Office programs by performing the following steps:

1. On the Office Shortcut Bar, right-click on the title bar to open the Office menu.

2. From the menu, choose Add/Remove Office Programs. You will next see the Office Setup and Uninstall dialog box. Select the application that you want to modify, reinstall, or remove and then click on OK.

3. The Welcome screen for the Setup program appears. The screen contains choices that enable you to add or remove parts of the application, repeat the previous installation, or remove all installed applications and their parts. Follow the instructions that appear on-screen to add or remove the desired parts of Microsoft Office.

Summary

This chapter showed how you can work with the Office Shortcut Bar to provide fast access to the Microsoft Office applications. The Office Shortcut Bar is easily customizable — you can add your favorite programs and files to this toolbar to make performing your tasks much easier. This chapter covered these points:

- Microsoft Office includes Word (for word processing), Excel (for spreadsheets), PowerPoint (for presentations), and Schedule+ (for tracking time-related tasks). The Professional version of Office includes all these applications and Access (for database management).
- You can use the Office Shortcut Bar to quickly launch different Microsoft Office applications.
- You can customize the Office Shortcut Bar by adding applications and files to the toolbar, changing the position of the toolbar, enlarging its buttons, and doing other things to the toolbar to make it stand out.

The remainder of this book will detail how you can get the most out of the different applications of Microsoft Office.

Where to go next...

- If you want to work in Word, go to Chapter 2. If you're a Word neophyte, Appendix B gets you started.
- If you want to use Excel, go to Chapter 13. Appendix C gives you Excel basics, if you've never used a spreadsheet before.
- If you want to create presentations in PowerPoint, see Chapter 25. Rank beginners, see Appendix D.
- If you've yet to install Office, hie thee directly to Appendix A.

✦ ✦ ✦

Word

PART II

In This Part

Chapter 2
Creating and Working with Documents

Chapter 3
Formatting Documents

Chapter 4
Previewing and Printing Your Documents

Chapter 5
Working with Tables and Outlines

Chapter 6
Working with Fields and Form Letters

Chapter 7
Building Tables of Contents and Indexes

Chapter 8
Working with Styles and Templates

Chapter 9
Working with Macros

Chapter 10
Desktop Publishing with Word

Chapter 11
Word for Windows at Work

Chapter 12
The Word Top Ten

Creating and Working with Documents

CHAPTER 2

In This Chapter

Creating a new document

Defining templates

Moving around in your document

Understanding the multiple views in Word

Changing margins, tabs, and line spacing

Moving and copying text

Using the Search and Replace commands

Using the spelling checker, thesaurus, and grammar checker

Using the Hyphenation command

Adding bullets and paragraph numbers

Using AutoText entries

Creating document summaries

Because the first thing you will do in Word is create documents, it makes sense to cover creating documents in the first Word chapter. You also need to know about the many techniques that you can use to edit the documents that you create. These techniques will help you find mistakes in your documents so that you can create the best documents possible.

Creating New Documents

You can start Word by opening the Windows 95 Start menu and then choosing Programs. Choose Microsoft Office and then Microsoft Word from the submenus that pop up. A blank document screen appears, in which you can begin typing your new document.

Hot Stuff If you already have some documents created and saved, you can launch Word and open a document simultaneously by finding the document in My Computer or in the Windows Explorer and double-clicking on the document.

Understanding Templates

Word gives you two ways to create your documents: you can use the `Normal.dot` template or a template of your choosing. You will probably use both methods in your work. *Templates,* or document models, help you streamline the creation of documents that you produce on a regular basis.

Making Word easier to start

If you regularly start Word by choosing Word from the Windows 95 menus, you can save yourself considerable time by adding an icon to your Windows desktop. This icon represents a shortcut to the program. To add the icon to the desktop, open My Computer under the Windows 95 menu, double-click on the icon representing your hard drive, and open the folder that contains Word for Windows. (If you accepted the default settings during installation, Word is in the `Winword` folder within the `MSOffice` folder on your hard drive.)

In the `Winword` folder, find the `Winword` icon. Right-click on the icon and choose Create Shortcut from the menu that appears. After this step, the Shortcut to Winword icon appears, and it is already selected in the folder. Click on and drag this icon onto your desktop and close all the folders that you had to open by using My Computer.

From now on, you can start Word by double-clicking on the Shortcut to Winword icon on your desktop. If you don't like the icon's default name, you can change it by right-clicking on the icon, choosing Rename from the menu that appears, and entering a new name. Alternately, you can click on the icon, click on the name portion of the icon to select it, and type a new name.

Do *not* be tempted to skip the creation of a shortcut by simply dragging the `Winword` icon from the `Winword` folder onto the desktop. If you do this, you are literally moving the program file from the `Winword` folder (where it is designed to work well) into a folder called `Desktop`, which Windows 95 uses to manage the desktop. The result is that Word suddenly has a hard time finding its files.

When Word is first opened, it contains a document with default settings ready for you to use. This is the `Normal.dot` template (stored as `Normal.dot` in the Templates folder), which contains a set of standard margins and no formatting. Keep in mind that clicking on the New button in the Standard toolbar always creates a new document based on the Normal template. After you begin to enter text, you can change all these settings to anything you want.

If you do not want to use the default `Normal.dot` template, you can use one of the other templates in Word that may be better suited to your needs. To open one of these templates, choose New from the File menu. The New dialog box appears, in which you can make the selection that is best for your needs (see Figure 2-1). The dialog box is divided by a series of tabs, and each tab contains one or more templates appropriate to a specific task. For example, if most of the documents that you create are memos, you can click on the Memos tab to display a group of templates appropriate for creating memos. (The tab also lists one wizard; see the heading "Looking at template wizards" a little later in this chapter for information about using wizards.) After you create a document based on a template, the template controls the appearance of the document.

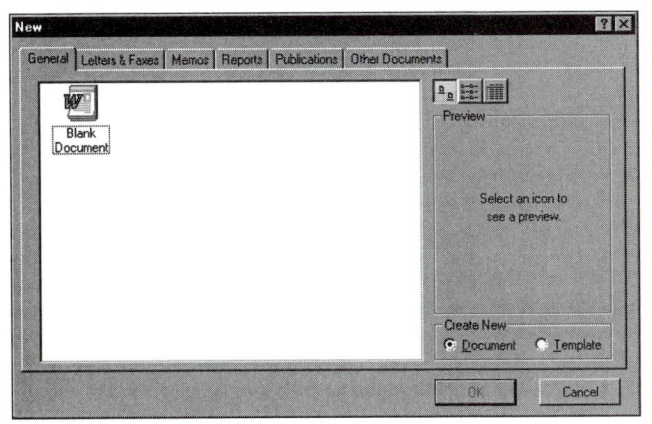

Figure 2-1: The New dialog box.

Many documents are made up of standard parts. For example, an interoffice memo often contains a company name and address heading; To, From, Date, and Subject headings; and closing information, such as a routing list of persons receiving the memo. Assuming that a template is designed for your interoffice memos, you can let the template fill in the *boilerplate,* or standard text, for you. Templates can also be designed to prompt you for the specific information (such as the recipient's name) needed each time the template is used. The information you enter is automatically inserted into the proper place in the document, based on the template.

Exploring template categories

Table 2-1 lists the template categories that the New dialog box contains, and the templates in each category. The names of the templates explain their functions.

Table 2-1
Templates available in Microsoft Word

Template Category	*Name of Template*
General	Blank Document (uses Normal template)
Publications	Elegant Press Release
	Manual
	Newsletter
	Professional Press Release
	Thesis

(continued)

Table 2-1 *(continued)*

Template Category	Name of Template
Publications	Brochure
	Contemporary Press Release
	Directory
Reports	Contemporary Report
	Elegant Report
	Professional Report
Memos	Contemporary Memo
	Elegant Memo
	Professional Memo
Letters & Faxes	Contemporary Letter
	Elegant Letter
	Professional Letter
	Contemporary Fax
	Elegant Fax
	Professional Fax
Other Documents	Invoice
	Purchase Order
	Weekly Time Sheet
	Contemporary Resume
	Elegant Resume
	Professional Resume

Looking at template wizards

Word for Windows 95 also includes template wizards, which help you create a document when you may not be sure of its layout or even its content. To activate any one of these wizards, choose New from the File menu. Scroll through the Template list and click on the wizard that best fits the document that you want to create. Then click on OK.

For example, the Agenda Wizard, found in the Other Documents tab, creates an agenda for any type of meeting. As you step through the dialog boxes in the Agenda Wizard, you are prompted to add elements to the agenda that may be included in a meeting of an organization. For example, you are prompted to add a date, time, and location for the meeting. You can also enter a main topic for the meeting and include information about what the attendees should bring with them. You can include a list of the names of people who will have responsibilities in the organization, such as the caller of the meeting, the notetaker, the timekeeper, and the resource person. The first entry is made as an overview of the meeting, and you can continue to add entries from this point. Finally, you can create a page on which the notetaker can take notes. Figure 2-2 shows what a document that has been created with the Agenda Wizard may look like; an agenda you may create may look different, based on the selections that you make in the Agenda Wizard dialog boxes.

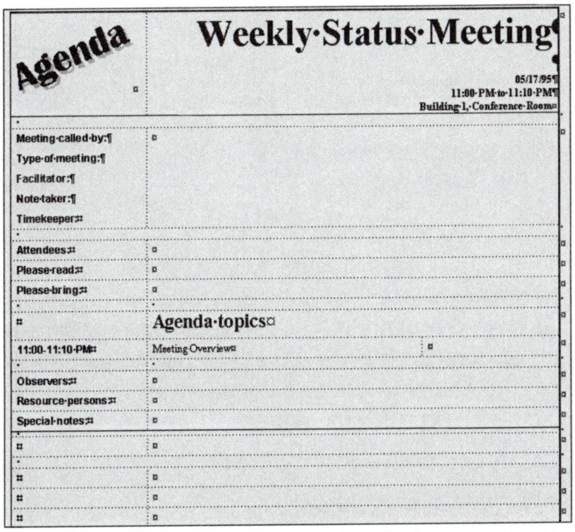

Figure 2-2: A document created with the Agenda Wizard.

The Award Wizard, also found under the Other Documents tab, creates a customized award for any occasion by providing the art for the award certificate (which avoids the annoyance of finding clip art and then appropriately inserting it). The wizard lets you choose award certificates of a more modern, formal, or decorative manner. Each one of the styles has corresponding art for the certificate. Figure 2-3 shows a document created with the Award Wizard.

Figure 2-3: A document created with the Award Wizard.

The Calendar Wizard, also found under the Other Documents tab, creates a monthly calendar in various styles, such as the one shown in Figure 2-4. You can design the calendar in either a portrait or a landscape orientation. You can show the month name in different formats, such as a banner or box-and-border. You can add pictures to the calendar if you want. Finally, one of the Calendar Wizard's most impressive features is that it can create a calendar that starts and ends with the months that you specify.

Figure 2-4: A calendar created with the Calendar Wizard.

The Fax Wizard, found under the Letters & Faxes tab, creates a fax sheet that you can customize. The fax sheet can be a contemporary, modern, or jazzy fax sheet. In the Fax Wizard you also have the luxury of not having to look for your names and addresses. If they are stored in Microsoft Exchange (a feature of Windows 95 — see Alan Simpson's *Windows 95 Uncut,* IDG Books Worldwide[1995], for details), you can click on Address book and pull the name of the person to which you want to send the fax into the address and phone number boxes. Figure 2-5 shows a fax sheet created by the Fax Wizard.

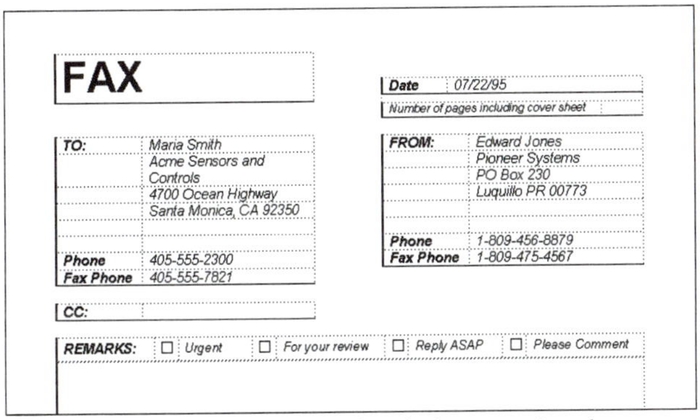

Figure 2-5: A fax sheet created with the Fax Wizard.

The Letter Wizard, also found under the Letters & Faxes tab, can create prewritten letters or help you design you own. The Letter Wizard includes prewritten business letters that you can send to collection firms for late payments or bounced checks. (But you'd never need letters like *those,* would you?) You also have the opportunity to select the layout for any personal letters that you need to write. Again, you can use Microsoft Exchange to enter addresses from the Address book. Figure 2-6 shows a letter created with the Letter Wizard.

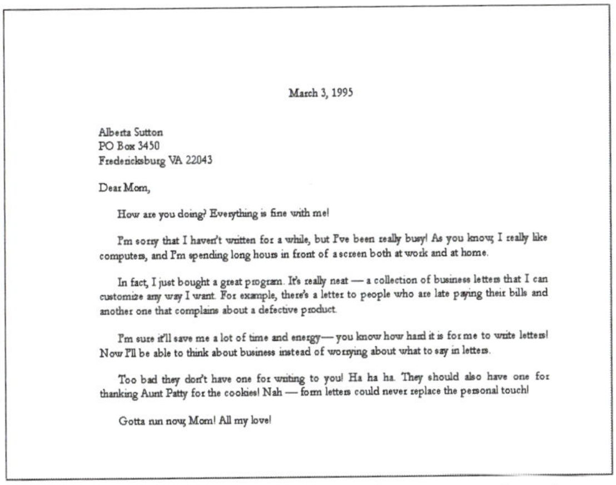

Figure 2-6: A letter created with the Letter Wizard.

The Memo Wizard, found under the Memos tab, helps you create customized memos (see Figure 2-7). You can create office memos (the default setting) or any other kind of memo. Addresses here can also be drawn from the Address book in Microsoft Exchange.

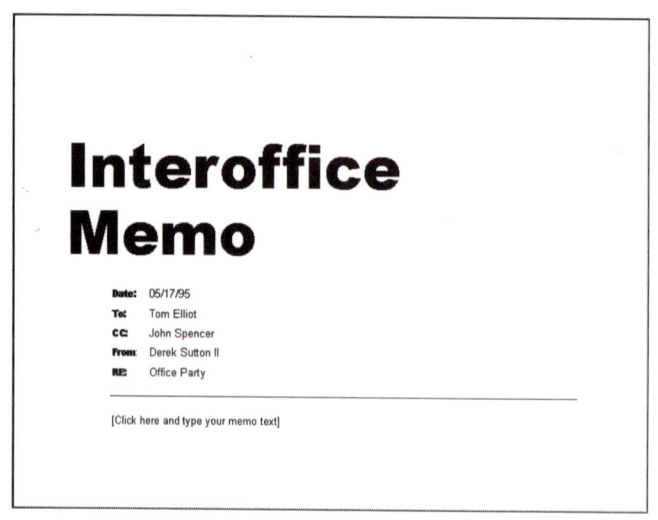

Figure 2-7: An office memo created with the Memo Wizard.

The Newsletter Wizard, found under the Publications tab, helps you create an attractive newsletter. You can create the newsletter in a classic or modern style with the number of columns and pages that you specify. You can also include the date, table of contents, and volume number. Figure 2-8 shows a newsletter created with the Newsletter Wizard. As you can see, the wizard handles what would manually be a challenging task by creating a professional-looking newsletter in a short amount of time.

Figure 2-8: A newsletter created with the Newsletter Wizard.

Chapter 2 ♦ Creating and Working with Documents

The Pleading Wizard, also found under the Other Documents tab, provides a quick and easy way to create a legal pleading (see Figure 2-9). The legal pleading that results includes the name of the court, inserted in the correct location in the document for the style you choose. The alignment and style can all be modified by using the various options presented as you move through the Pleading Wizard. Footnotes can also be added to the pleading.

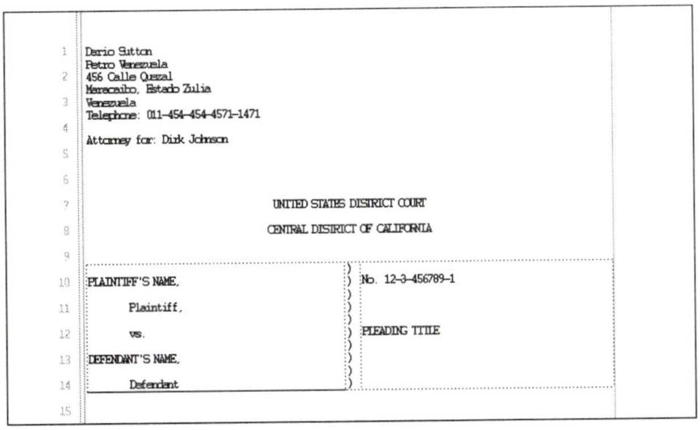

Figure 2-9: A legal pleading created with the Pleading Wizard.

Use the Resume Wizard, also found under the Other Documents tab, to create resumes in record time, tailored to your experience (see Figure 2-10). The Resume Wizard can create a resume in various forms. You may need a contemporary, classic, or professional resume. The Resume Wizard also provides some tips on the best way to lay out a resume. You can choose to create a professional, chronological, entry-level, or functional resume. Finally, you can omit any elements you don't want to include.

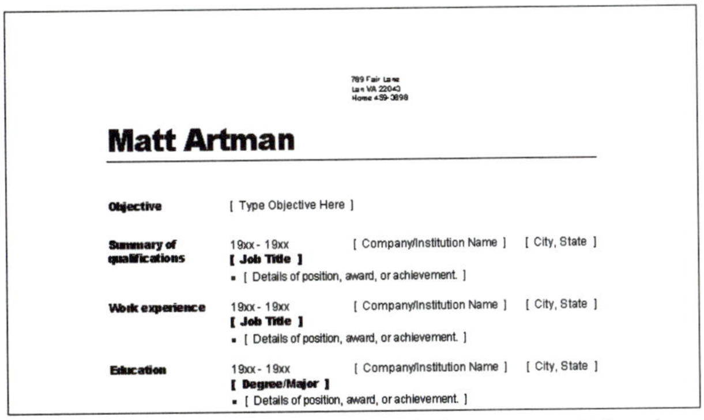

Figure 2-10: A resume created with the Resume Wizard.

Editing templates

You can change the different templates so that they can better fit your needs. To change the templates, choose the File➪Open menu to get to the Open dialog box. Move to the `Templates` directory and in the Files of type drop-down menu, select Document Templates. Select the folder that continues the template. Then type or select the name of the template that you want to modify and click on OK. Edit the template as though it were a document. When you have finished the modifications, choose Save from the File menu to save the template and give it the name of your choice.

More Info You'll find additional information on working with templates in Chapter 8.

Working with Text

To create text, type on the keyboard. The text is then entered at the insertion point. You shouldn't press Enter at the end of each line — Word automatically moves from line to line as you type. This feature is called *word wrap*. Press the Enter key only when you want to create a new paragraph. After you press Enter, previously entered text is moved up to keep the insertion point visible. (The insertion point is that flashing solid line that marks the spot where the characters you type appear. Some people call this thing a cursor, a term that's a holdover from the early days of computers.)

Deleting text

You can delete text in several ways. One method is by using the Backspace key. When you use the Backspace key, the text to the left of the insertion point is removed. Another method is using the Delete key. Use the Delete key to delete text that appears to the right of the insertion point.

You can also delete blocks of text in Word. First you should highlight the block of text that you want to delete. (You can click on and drag across a desired selection with the mouse, or you can hold the Shift key down and use the arrow keys to highlight a section of text.) After selecting the text, press the Delete key to remove the text from the document.

> ### Avoiding bad typing habits
>
> If you are upgrading to the world of Word from a very old environment (such as a typewriter or a very early generation word processor), you may have accumulated some habits that won't do you any good in Word. First, and probably the most obvious, is that you don't have to press Enter at the end of every line because of Word's automatic word wrap feature. Second, don't use spaces (inserted with the Spacebar) to center or indent text. To center text, use the Center button on the Formatting toolbar (discussed in Chapter 3). To indent, use tabs or indented paragraphs (also discussed in Chapter 3). If you need to create columns, don't use spaces or tabs — use Word's *columns* feature (see Chapter 3), or use tables (see Chapter 5).

Inserting text from the Clipboard

You can paste text or graphics from the Clipboard into a document. The Clipboard, a standard Windows 95 feature, is an area of memory that stores temporary information (see your Windows 95 documentation for additional information about the Clipboard). Edit⇨Paste, or Ctrl+V, pastes whatever is in the Clipboard into the current document at the insertion point. (Of course, the Clipboard must contain something before you can paste it into your document.)

To insert text into the Clipboard, select the desired text and choose the Edit⇨Copy command (Ctrl+C), or click on the Copy button on the Standard toolbar. Then move the insertion point to the desired position for the text and choose Edit⇨Paste (Ctrl+V) or click on the Paste button on the Standard toolbar. The text stored in the Clipboard appears at the insertion point.

You can also use the Clipboard to move text from one place in a document to another. To move text, use Edit⇨Cut (Ctrl+X). First, highlight the text that you want to move. Next, click on the Cut button on the Standard toolbar or press Ctrl+X. This action places the selected text on the Clipboard. Move the insertion point to the desired location and click on the Paste button on the Standard toolbar or press Ctrl+V. The text is then inserted at the insertion point location.

Inserting graphics

If you want to paste graphics, first get into the drawing or graphics program (such as Paint) that contains the image you want to use in your Word document. Use the selection tool within the drawing or graphics program to select the desired image; then choose Edit⇨Copy (or press Ctrl+C) to copy the selection into the Clipboard. Exit from the drawing or graphics program and get into your document. With the insertion point at the desired location, choose Edit⇨Paste (or press Ctrl+V). The graphic appears at the insertion point.

Hot Stuff: If you are running Word and your graphics program simultaneously, you can easily switch from the graphics program to Word by pressing Alt+Tab or by clicking on the desired program's name in the Windows 95 Taskbar.

You can also add graphics to your documents by means of clip art. Word for Windows 95 includes a great deal of clip art that can be added to documents. Simply choose Picture from the Insert menu to open the Insert Picture dialog box, as shown in Figure 2-11. After you select one of the clip art files, you can see it in the Preview box. To insert the selected clip art into your document, position the insertion point where you want the clip art to go and click on OK. The clip art appears at the insertion point in your document.

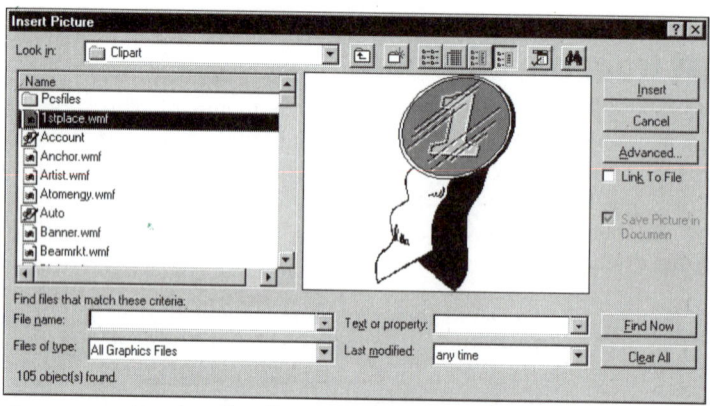

Figure 2-11: Preview the clip art file before you insert it into your document.

Navigating within a document

For basic navigation within a Word document, you can use the arrow keys and the navigation keys on the keyboard. Table 2-2 lists the keyboard combinations that help you move around in your document.

Table 2-2
Navigation shortcuts

Keyboard Combination	What it Does
Ctrl+Up Arrow key	Moves the cursor up one paragraph
Ctrl+Down Arrow key	Moves the cursor down one paragraph
Alt+Left Arrow key	Moves the cursor one word to the left

Keyboard Combination	What it Does
Alt+Right Arrow key	Moves the cursor one word to the right
Page Up key	Moves the cursor up one screen page
Page Down key	Moves the cursor down one screen page
Home key	Moves the cursor to the beginning of the current line of text
Ctrl+Home key	Moves the cursor to the beginning of the document
End key	Moves the cursor to the end of the current line of text
Ctrl+End key	Moves the cursor to the end of the document

You can also use the scroll bars to move through a document. Click on the scroll box (scroll boxes are the square boxes that appear inside the scroll bars) and drag it up or down or left or right to move in the direction that you want to go in your document. Or click the arrow blocks at either end of the scroll bars to move a preset amount of space in the direction that you want to go. You can also click within the shaded areas of the scroll bars to scroll roughly one screen's worth of document. Clicking on the shaded area above the scroll box moves you upward in the document, and clicking on the shaded area below the scroll box moves you downward in the document.

Hot Stuff If you click on the scroll box, drag it, and hold the mouse button down for roughly a half-second or more, a small window will appear showing the page number of the document represented by that position of the scroll box. In a large document, this can provide an easy way to quickly reach a desired page.

Hot Stuff If you want to jump to a specific page number in a document, press F5 and enter a page number in the dialog box that appears.

Selecting text

After you've typed large amounts of text, you need ways to select it so that you can work with it. For most users, clicking and dragging with the mouse is the most common way to select text. If you're not proficient with a mouse, spend time practicing. In the long run, the time that you spend practicing with the mouse will regularly save you hours of time at the keyboard. The following list contains practical techniques for selecting text:

- ✦ To select entire words, double-click anywhere in the word. You can then select adjacent words by holding down the mouse key after the second click and dragging through the additional words.
- ✦ To select entire lines, move the mouse pointer to the left of the line (where it changes into the shape of an arrow) and click on it once.

- To select entire sentences, hold down the Control key while you click anywhere in the sentence.
- To select entire paragraphs, triple-click anywhere within the paragraph.
- To select the entire document, press Ctrl+A.
- To select a large portion of a document, click on the start of the portion that you want to select. Then move to the end of the desired portion, hold down the Shift key, and click again.

Looking at Word's Views

Word lets you view a document as you edit it in one of four possible views: Normal, Outline, Page Layout, and Master Document. You can access these views by clicking on the appropriate command on the View menu. These commands work like toggle switches, so you can turn the view on and off by clicking on the command. A bullet appears beside the command in the View menu if it is turned on. If you don't see a bullet by Outline, Page Layout, or Master Document in the View menu, then you are in Normal view (the default view).You can also switch among all views except Outline Document by clicking on the View buttons at the bottom left of the screen. (At the bottom left corner, the leftmost button is Normal View, the center button is Page Layout View, and the rightmost button is Outline View.) Master Document view must be activated by the View menu.

Use Normal view for basic typing and editing. Normal view shows a simple version of the document and is the best all-purpose view for typing in Word. Normal view is the default setting for Word for Windows 95. After you change views, you can return to Normal view any time by clicking on the Normal View button in the lower-left corner of the screen.

> **More Info**
> If line numbering is on, you must be in Page Layout view to see the line numbers. See Chapter 3.

> **More Info**
> Use Outline View for outlining and organizing a document. Outline View lets you see only the main headings of a document or the entire document. In this view, you can easily move text over long distances or change the order of your topics, as detailed in Chapter 5. To change to Outline View, choose View➪Outline.

> **More Info**
> You control how much you see of the document in Outline View by clicking on the plus signs located next to the headings for each section. When you double-click on the plus sign, the text under the heading is hidden to show only the heading. Chapter 5 discusses outlines in detail.

Chapter 2 ♦ Creating and Working with Documents

Use Page Layout View to "see the printed page," while still allowing for editing. This view lets you see how the different elements of the document will appear when they are printed. This view is very useful in checking the final appearance of your document. (This differs from Print Preview in that you can't edit a document in Print Preview.) To switch to Page Layout View, click on the Page Layout View button on the lower-left corner of the screen.

Use Master Document View to work with long documents. This view helps you divide long documents into several shorter documents to make them easier to work with, because you can see all the components of a document when you are in Master Document View. To switch to Master Document View, click the Master Document View button at the lower left corner of the screen.

Word for Windows 95 also lets you change options in each of the views. To change the default settings, choose Options from the Tools menu. An Options dialog box appears, from which you can change options for the current view. The Options dialog box contains 12 tabs, each with its own set of options, as shown in Figure 2-12. Click on a tab to bring it to the front of the dialog box so that you can view and make changes to its options. Make whatever changes that you want in the tabs. The new settings take effect in all the tabs that you have changed after you click on the OK button.

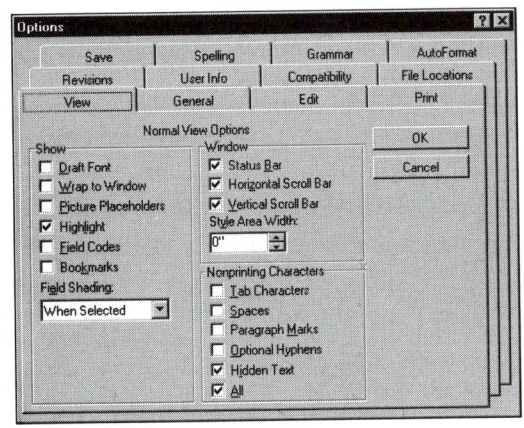

Figure 2-12: The Options dialog box.

Examining the Vital Three: Margins, Tabs, and Line Spacing

The three most elementary aspects of formatting — margins, tabs, and line spacing — can be found even on the most basic typewriters. These elements are very important to setting up your pages appropriately in Word for Windows. This section shows you how to apply these formatting elements to all or part of a document. To control page margins, you use the Page Setup command from the File menu; to set default tab stops, you use the Tabs command from the Format menu; and to change line spacing, you use the Paragraph command from the Format menu. Keep in mind, however, that these commands are not the only ways to change parameters that affect margins, tabs, and line spacing in Word, as you'll discover shortly.

Changing margins

When you start a new document in Word for Windows 95, default margins are already set at 1 inch for the top and bottom margins and 1.25 inches for the left and right margins. If you want to change the default settings, choose File⇨Page Setup. The Page Setup dialog box appears, with its four tabs. The Margins tab lets you set the top, bottom, right, and left margins to your desired measurements. You also can click on the Mirror Margins check box to force the left-facing and right-facing pages to have the same margins between the edge of the text and the center of the binding.

Applying tabs

Using tabs is a common method for aligning text in columns; therefore, Word has tab stops set to every 0.5 inch by default. You can identify these tab stops by looking for the gray tick marks that appear at the bottom of the ruler. To turn on the ruler, click on the Ruler command on the View menu so that it has a check mark beside it. Use the Tabs command from the Format menu to change the default tab stops. In the Tabs dialog box, change the measurement in the Default Tab Stops box to any desired value in inches or centimeters.

In addition to the default tab stops, Word lets you set custom tab stops for each paragraph. Custom tab stops take precedence over the default tab stops; therefore, whenever you set a custom tab stop, Word clears all default tab stops that occur to the left of the custom tab stop. When you set one or more custom tab stops, these remain in effect until you change the tab setting. Each paragraph in Word can have its own tab settings, so remember to use the newline command (Shift+Enter) between lines of text if you want the same set of tabs to apply to all the lines.

Types of tabs

In Word, you can use any of five types of tabs; left, center, right, decimal, and bar. The type of tab that you choose indicates precisely where the text aligns with the tab. When you use a left tab, the left edge of the text aligns with the tab stop. With right tabs, the right edge of the text aligns with the tab stop. When you use centered tabs, the text centers at the tab stop. Decimal tabs are used when the decimal point in numbers must align with the tab stop. Finally, bar tabs are thin vertical bars that can be used to separate columns created by tabs within a document.

Setting custom tabs

You can set custom tabs with the mouse and the Tab button on the ruler (the easier method) or with the Tabs command on the Format menu. To set tabs with the mouse, first click on the Tab button on the ruler (the button to the far left of the ruler) until you get the tab alignment that you want and then click just under the ruler at the desired location. For example, to set a center tab at the 2-inch location on the ruler, you would first click on the Tab button until the one for the center tab appears and then click just under or on the 2-inch marker on the ruler. To verify the position of the tab stop, double-click on the tab stop on the ruler to open the Tabs dialog box (see Figure 2-13).

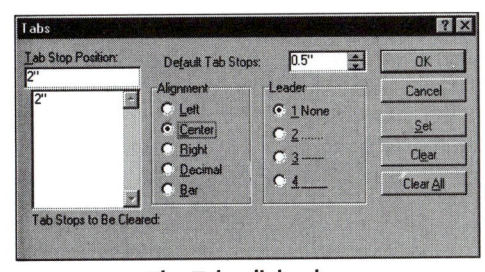

Figure 2-13: The Tabs dialog box.

If the 2-inch tab stop isn't in the exact position that you want, you can click on it and drag it to whatever position you want on the ruler. After you drag it to its new location, verify the new position of the tab stop by opening the Tabs dialog box again. If you are still not satisfied with the position of the tab stop, you can manually enter a measurement in the Tab Stop Position text box. The Tabs dialog box gives you unlimited control of how you want to position the tabs in your documents.

Figure 2-14 shows some of the different tab alignments in Word. In the figure, a left tab stop has been set at the 1.0 inch position, a center tab at the 2.0 inch position, a right tab at the 4.0 inch position, and a decimal tab stop at the 5.0 inch position.

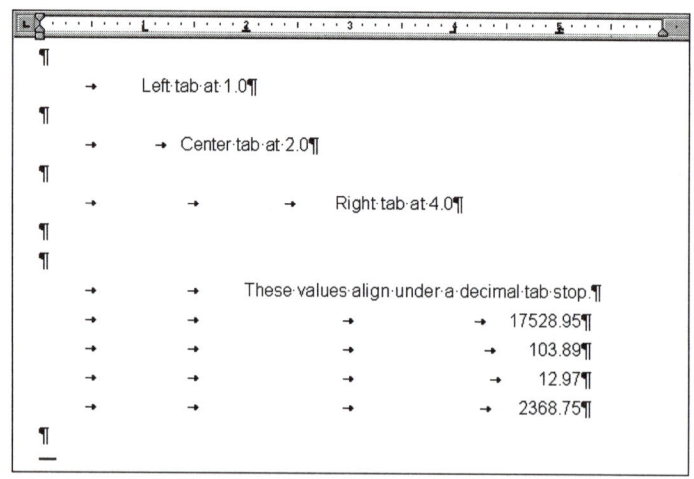

Figure 2-14: The different Tab alignments shown in Word.

To set tabs with the Tabs command, choose Format⇨Tabs. The Tabs dialog box (Figure 2-13) appears. In this dialog box, you can enter or clear tab stops. Enter the desired location for the tab stop in the Tab Stop Position text box and then choose the type of tab that you want (Left, Center, Right, Decimal, or Bar) from the Alignment options. If you have additional tabs to set, click on the Set button to set the tab and then go back to the Tab Stop Position box to enter the location for the next tab and to choose its alignment. After you finish setting the tabs, click on the OK button.

Try experimenting with the tab stop techniques to find the one that suits you best. You can use the following steps to see the effects of the different tab stops that you can set in Word:

1. Create a new document with a left tab at 1 inch, a center tab at 2.5 inches, a right tab at 3.5 inches, and a decimal tab at 5.0 inches.

2. Press the tab key once (to reach the left-aligned tab at the one-inch mark), and type the words **left-aligned**. Then, press Enter.

3. Press the tab key twice (to reach the center tab at the 2.5-inch mark), and type the word **centered**. Notice that as you type, the word remains centered at the tab stop. When done, press Enter.

4. Press the tab key three times (to reach the right-aligned tab at the 3.5-inch mark), and type the words **right-aligned**. Notice that as you type, the words remain right aligned with the tab stop. When done, press Enter.

5. Press the tab key four times (to reach the decimal tab), type the value **103.87**, and press Enter.

6. Press the tab key four times (to reach the decimal tab), type the value **1242.23**, and press Enter. Notice that the second number correctly aligns with the first, based on the location of the decimal point.

Figure 2-15 shows the results of this exercise.

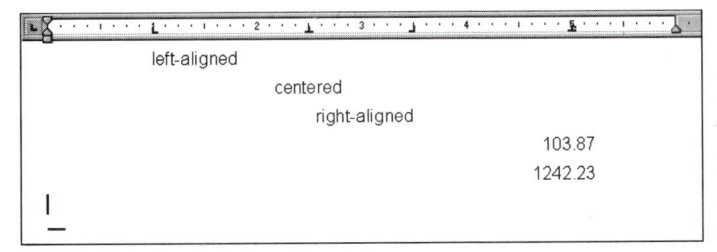

```
left-aligned
            centered
                right-aligned
                                    103.87
                                    1242.23
```

Figure 2-15: A document showing different tab stops.

Moving and clearing tabs

As with setting tabs, you can move tabs and clear tabs with the ruler and the mouse or with the Tabs command on the Format menu. Again, the mouse excels in ease of use. To move a tab, simply click on the tab and drag it to the desired location. To clear a tab, simply drag the tab up or down off the ruler.

You can also use the Tabs command from the Format menu to move or clear tabs. The Tab Stop Position area of the Tabs dialog box displays all tab settings for custom tabs in the document. From the list of tab positions, select the tab that you want to delete and then click on Clear. To clear all custom tabs, click on Clear All and then click on OK. To move a tab stop, select it in the dialog box, click on Clear, and then enter a new location for the tab.

Creating leader tabs

Some documents, such as tables of contents, make use of *leader tabs,* characters that fill the space left by the tab. To set a leader tab, set the tab as you normally would and then open the Tabs dialog box with the Tabs command. Word offers three kinds of leader tabs: periods, hyphens, and underlines. After you select the desired type of leader, click on OK to set the tab.

Line spacing

Line spacing affects the amount of space between lines of a paragraph. You can also change the spacing between paragraphs. To change the line spacing, place the insertion point anywhere within the desired paragraph and then choose Format⇨Paragraph. The Paragraph dialog box appears, with the Indents and Spacing tab visible, as shown in Figure 2-16. Use the options in this tab to enter the desired line and paragraph spacing. In the Line Spacing list box, select the kind of spacing that you desire: Single, Double, 1.5, At Least, Exactly, and Multiple. You can adjust the preset spacing of these options by clicking on the arrows in the At box. The Exactly option makes the spacing only the specified amount. The At Least choice can be used to set the spacing to be a specified amount or greater.

In the Indentation area, you can specify the amount of indentation that you want to apply to the left and right margins of the document. The Special box also allows for the addition of a hanging indent or other custom indent.

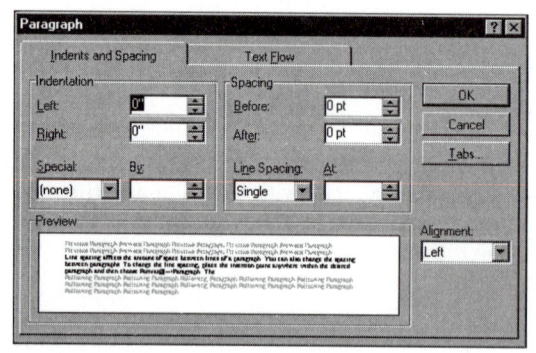

Figure 2-16: The Indents and Spacing tab of the Paragraph dialog box.

If you don't want to use the default measurements, be sure that you enter one of the abbreviations. In the At box to the right of the Line Spacing list box, enter any value that Word understands: inches (in.), centimeters (cm.), picas (pi.), points (pt.), or lines (li.). Picas and points are units of measurement used by typesetters — 6 picas equals 1 inch, and 72 points equals 1 inch. If you enter a numeric value alone, Word assumes that the value is in points.

You can use various Control key combinations to set the three commonly used variations of line spacing. With the insertion point anywhere in the desired paragraph, press Ctrl+1 for single line spacing, Ctrl+2 for double line spacing, or Ctrl+5 for one-and-a-half line spacing.

If you want to apply spacing to a specific paragraph only, first select the paragraph and then choose Paragraph from the Format menu. In the Paragraph dialog box, select the desired spacing and click on OK. You may also use the Control key combinations to change the spacing in the paragraph.

Paragraph spacing

Word also lets you control the amount of space that appears before or after paragraphs. In the Paragraph dialog box, you may have noticed the Before and After text boxes in the Spacing area of the dialog box. You can enter numeric values in the Before or After boxes to indicate a desired additional spacing before or after a paragraph. As with line spacing, you can enter any value for paragraph spacing that Word understands: inches (in.), centimeters (cm.), picas (pi.), points (pt.), or lines (li.). Word assumes points as a default value of measurement (one point being $1/72$ of an inch).

Moving and Copying Text

Word for Windows 95 provides a way to move and copy information without using the Clipboard if you want to save what you may have stored there. You can use the drag-and-drop method to move text: after you select the text, click on it and drag it with the mouse to the desired position.

If you want to copy information without using the Clipboard, simply select the text that you want to copy, hold down the Control key, click on the selected text, and drag it to the new location where it is copied.

You can also use the Clipboard to copy and move information. If you want to make a copy of information to place in another application or in another section in Word, select the text that you want to copy and click on the Copy button on the Standard toolbar, or choose Edit⇨Copy. Then move the cursor to the desired position and click on the Paste button, or choose Edit⇨Paste, to copy the information.

You can also use the Clipboard to move information. Select the desired text and click on the Cut button on the Standard toolbar, or choose the Cut command from the Edit menu. The text is then placed in the Clipboard. Then move the cursor to the desired position and click the Paste button, or choose Edit⇨Paste, to place the text in the desired position.

Because Word lets you work on multiple documents at the same time, it is easy to move or copy text from one document to another. If you use the Open command from the File menu to open more than one document, you can then open the Window menu and choose Arrange All to see all your open documents in multiple windows. Then you can select the desired text in one document and choose the Move or Copy command. Place the insertion point at the desired location in the other document and choose the Paste command.

Hot Stuff: Word also lets you move text from one location to another by using a feature called *drag and drop*. With drag and drop, you select the desired text and then you click on and drag it to the desired location by holding down the mouse button as you drag. As you drag the selection, the mouse pointer consists of the usual pointer arrow and a small rectangle; the rectangle indicates that you are dragging text. After you release the mouse button, the selected text appears in the new location. You can also copy text with drag and drop; just hold down the Control key as you perform the drag-and-drop operation.

Using Search and Replace

Like all full-featured word processors, Word for Windows 95 offers a search-and-replace capability through the Find (Ctrl+F) and Replace (Ctrl+H) commands from the Edit menu. These commands may offer more search capability than you are accustomed to because you can look for more than just text. You can search for specific formatting as well as for special characters, such as paragraph marks, newline characters, and tabs.

Searching for regular text

To search for text, choose Edit⇨Find. In the Find dialog box (see Figure 2-17), enter the desired word or phrase in the Find What text box. Click on the Find Next button or press Enter. Word finds the first occurrence of the text. You may continue the search for subsequent occurrences by pressing Enter or the Find Next button.

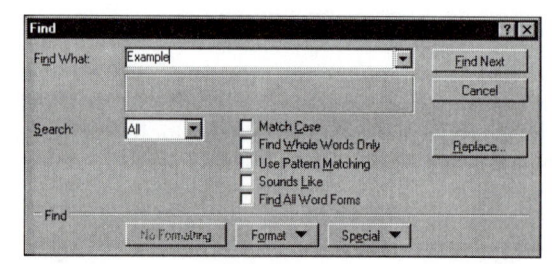

Figure 2-17: The Find dialog box.

The choices in the dialog box are fairly self-explanatory. The Match Case option tells Word whether you want the search to be case sensitive. If the option is checked, Word searches for a match that uses the same case as the letters you entered. When the option is not checked, case does not matter during the search. The Use Pattern Matching option tells Word to let you use wildcards, such as a question mark, for any single character and an asterisk for any combination of characters within the search text.

The Find Whole Words Only option specifies that only whole words matching the search text will be found. For example, if you search for the word *move* in the sample document and the Find Whole Words Only option is not checked, Word finds occurrences of *move, moves,* and *moved* in the document. If Find Whole Words Only is checked, only occurrences of the word *move* are found. The Sounds Like option finds words that sound like the word entered but are spelled differently. The Find All Word Forms option, when checked, tells Word to locate all matching noun forms or verb tenses. (Word is able to do this based on logic built into its grammar checking.) The Search list box lets you set the direction of the search. The default choice is All, which tells Word to search through the entire document. If you select Up or Down from this list box, Word begins its search at the current insertion point location and searches up or down in the document for the desired search term. If the end of the document is reached and the search term has not been found, Word displays an alert box telling you that a match has not been found.

If you have text stored in the Clipboard, you can search for that text by pressing Shift+Insert when the Find dialog box appears. First select the desired search text and use the Copy command to copy it into the Clipboard. Then choose Edit⇨Find, press Shift+Insert, and click on the Find Next button to begin the search.

Searching for special characters

If you want to find special characters, such as paragraph marks or tab characters, you can also use the Find dialog box. Click on the Special button to open a pop-up menu (see Figure 2-18) for special characters that you want to search for and select the desired character from the menu.

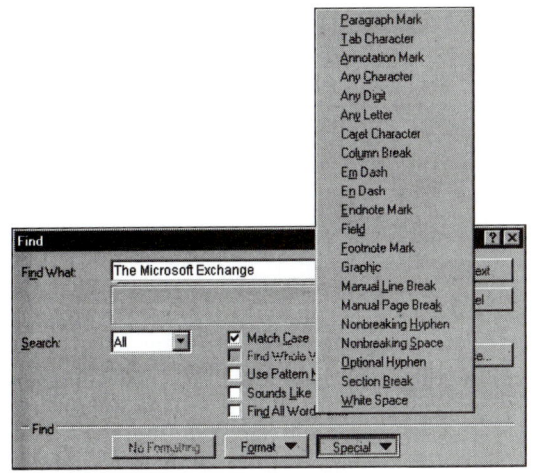

Figure 2-18: The pop-up menu for special characters.

If you want to search for a format, click the Format button and select the format that you want to find. This option lets you search for fonts, paragraph formats, languages, styles, tabs, frames, and highlighting.

Replacing text

You can use the same search techniques to replace the search text with other text, as well. For example, you may want to replace every occurrence of the word *version* with the word *level* throughout a document. Or perhaps a certain word has been underlined at every occurrence in a document, and you want to replace it with the same word without the underline. To replace text, you use Edit⇨Replace (Ctrl+H), which displays the Replace dialog box, as shown in Figure 2-19.

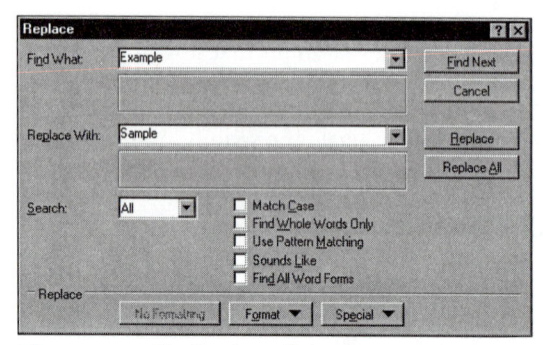

Figure 2-19: The Replace dialog box.

As with searches, you enter the search text in the Find What text box. You can also use the Format and Special buttons to find special characters or formats that you want to replace. In the Replace With text box, you enter the text that should replace the search text when it is found. The Find Whole Words Only and Match Case options can also be used. Turn on the Find Whole Words Only option if you want the search to find only complete words, and turn on the Match Case option if the case of the letters found must match that of the search text. The Use Pattern Matching and Sounds Like options work just as they do in the Find dialog box.

After you click on the Find Next button, Word stops and asks for confirmation when the search term is located. Click on the Replace button to make only the change that Word has currently found. Click on the Replace All button if you want Word to make automatically all the subsequent changes for you without asking for confirmation. After the changes are made, Word tells you the number of replacements it made.

Chapter 2 ✦ Creating and Working with Documents 49

Danger Zone Be careful when using the Replace All button because it may cause you to make some replacements that you do not care to make. For example, if you want to replace the word *Figure,* as in *Figure* 2-18 with the word *Item,* and you choose Replace All, then the phrase "Figure out the answer" also gets changed, to "Item out the answer." Oops! Not exactly what you intended. Therefore, if you are not sure that the word is used only in the one context that you want to replace, click on the Replace button to make the first replacement and then use the Find Next button to find the next occurrence of the word and decide if you want to replace it.

If you choose the Replace button, the replacement of the word is then made. If you do not care to replace that particular word, skip it by using the Find Next button. Word then finds the next occurrence of the word and again you have the option of replacing it if you want.

More Info In Chapter 3, you will learn more about formatting documents, so you should know that you can search for and replace formatting in the Replace dialog box. For example, you can replace all instances of a word in bold formatting with the same word in italic formatting. With the cursor in the Find What text box, press Ctrl+B (for Bold formatting). Then tab to the Replace With text box and press Ctrl+I (for Italic formatting). Figure 2-20 shows an example of this search procedure. After you click on Find Next, Word finds the first occurrence of the word *Figure* in Bold formatting. You can click on Replace or Replace All to make the change to Italic formatting.

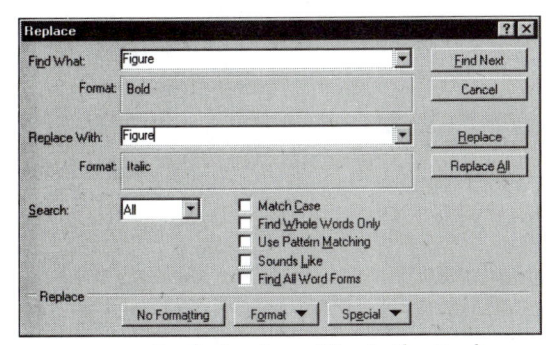

Figure 2-20: Replacing formatting in the Replace dialog box.

If you are searching for an occurrence of a word or format by using the Find dialog box, and you decide to change the word or format, Word provides an easy way to make the change. Simply click on the Replace button, which brings up the Replace dialog box. In the Replace dialog box, you can replace what you are looking for in your search by entering text in the Replace With text box.

Using the Spelling Checker

You can use Word's Spelling Checker to check your documents for spelling errors. Word offers multiple dictionaries, allows you to create your own custom dictionaries, and permits you to use different dictionaries for special uses. You can check the spelling of a single word or of entire documents.

Word's Spelling Checker uses a main dictionary and a custom dictionary. The main dictionary is supplied with the program and cannot be changed. The custom dictionary, called Custom.dic, is the default supplemental dictionary. When you add new words to the dictionary (which you can do when the Spelling Checker finds a word it does not know, but you know is spelled correctly), you are adding them to Custom.dic unless you specify a different dictionary.

The Spelling Checker in Word lets you check a selected portion of a document or the entire document. To check the spelling in only part of a document, first select the part that you want checked and then choose the Spelling command from the Tools menu. If no selection has been made, Word assumes that you want to check the entire document.

After you choose the Spelling command from the Tools menu, or you click on the Spelling button on the Standard toolbar, Word checks all words against those in the dictionaries. If a suspected misspelled word is found, Word stops, and the Spelling dialog box shown in Figure 2-21 appears. After Word finds a misspelling, it tries to provide a number of options for a correct spelling of the word.

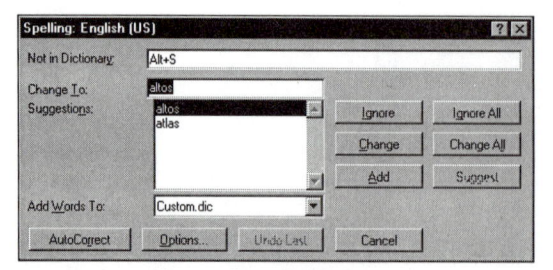

Figure 2-21: The Spelling dialog box.

Often, Word offers suggestions for the misspelled word in the Suggestions list. If one of the suggestions is the desired spelling, select it in the list box and then click on the Change button. The Ignore button lets you leave a word as is; the Cancel button cancels the entire spell-checking operation. The Add button lets you add a word to the selected user dictionary (Custom.dic by default).

Chapter 2 ✦ **Creating and Working with Documents**　51

Hot Stuff You can use the Spelling key (F7) to start checking the spelling of a selection or a document. Pressing F7 is the equivalent of choosing the Spelling command from the Tools menu or clicking on the Spelling button on the Standard toolbar.

Hot Stuff When checking large documents, you can increase the speed of the Spelling Checker by reducing the overhead needed by Windows for other operations. To improve performance, close any other documents that are open under Word and close any other Windows applications that you are not using. Make sure that you are in Normal View and turn off the Formatting toolbar (Alt+V+T and click on the Formatting toolbar check box), ruler (Alt+V+R), and status bar (Alt+T+O and click on the Status Bar check box in the Window section of the View tab).

As mentioned, Word always uses the main dictionary and at least one supplemental dictionary. You normally add words to the Custom.dic supplemental dictionary when you click on the Add button in the Spelling dialog box, but you can add words to any supplemental dictionary that you have created or intend to create.

To change supplemental dictionaries, click on the Options button in the Spelling dialog box. The Spelling tab of the Options dialog box appears, as shown in Figure 2-22. In the Custom Dictionaries area, you should see CUSTOM.DIC, the default custom dictionary, already chosen. After you click on the Custom Dictionaries button, click on the New button to create a new custom dictionary. For example, if you work with medical documents that use many medical terms that are not found in your regular custom dictionary, you can create a medical dictionary, called Med.dic. Then you can add the medical words to this new dictionary as they are found in the Spelling Checker. But remember to tell Word to use that dictionary via the Options button in the Spelling dialog box.

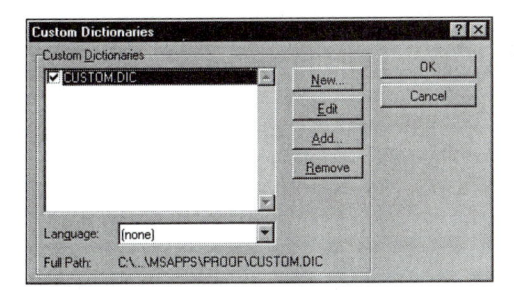

Figure 2-22: The Custom Dictionaries dialog box.

Click on the Add button in the Custom Dictionaries dialog box to add a custom dictionary that you have on a disk. The Add Custom Dictionary dialog box opens (see Figure 2-23), where you can enter the name and location of the dictionary that you want to install. Select the dictionary that you want to add, and then click on the OK button.

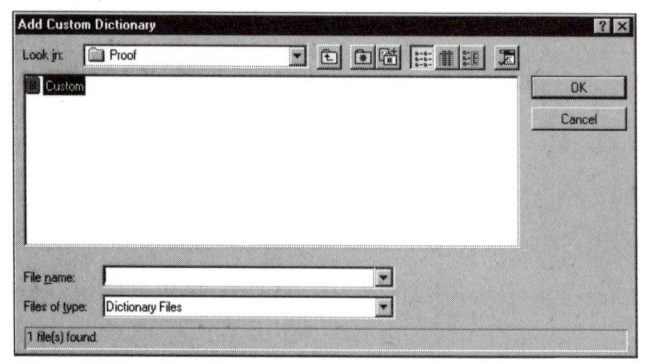

Figure 2-23: The Add Custom Dictionary dialog box.

Checking spelling as you type

One new feature of Word is its ability to do automatic or "on-the-fly" spell checking; you can check spelling as you type. You can turn on automatic spell checking with these steps:

1. Choose Tools⇨Options.
2. In the Options dialog box that opens, click on the Spelling tab.
3. Turn on the Automatic Spell Checking check box, and then click on OK.

When Word checks spelling as you type, red wavy lines appear underneath any words that Word thinks you have misspelled. You can get help correcting your mistakes by right-clicking on any word so underlined. A pop-up menu appears, containing alternate spellings (assuming Word can find any in its dictionaries). You can choose the desired word from the list. In addition to a list of alternate words, the pop-up menu also contains three options: Ignore All, Add, and Spelling. Use Ignore All to tell Word to ignore all occurrences of the word, or use Add to add the word to the default custom dictionary. Use Spelling to open the Spelling dialog box, discussed earlier.

Why should you use more than one custom dictionary?

Many Word users leave Word set to the default custom dictionary, called CUSTOM.DIC. But, depending on your needs, you may have good reason to create and use more than one custom dictionary. If you tend to bounce back and forth between projects that involve a good deal of technical lingo or other nonstandard terms, you can make the overall process of spell checking a bit faster by using different custom dictionaries, with each one specific to the task you are working on. Word spends less time searching a smaller, specific custom dictionary than a large custom dictionary that contains terms for lots of subjects. Just remember to turn on the custom dictionary of your choice when it's needed by using the Spelling tab available through the Tools⇨Options command.

Using the Thesaurus

Word's Thesaurus lets you find synonyms for specific words in your documents. To find a synonym, first select the desired word (remember, you can double-click on anywhere in a word to select it) and then choose Tools⇨Thesaurus (Shift+F7). The Thesaurus dialog box appears, as shown in Figure 2-24.

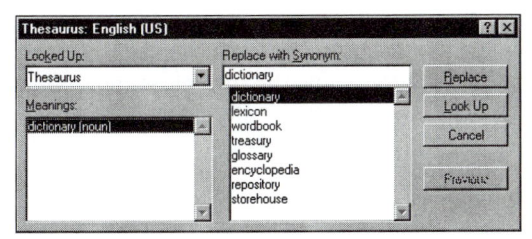

Figure 2-24: The Thesaurus dialog box.

The dialog box shows any synonyms found for the selected word in the Replace with Synonym list box. To replace the selected word with a synonym, select the desired synonym from the list box and then click on the Replace button.

In the Meanings list box, you can find one or more definitions for the selected word. The list of available synonyms changes when you select a different meaning. You can use the mouse to move between the Replace with Synonym and the Meanings list boxes. If you want to look up one of the words in the Meanings list box, simply select the word and click on the Look Up button.

Using the Grammar Checker

To check your documents for proper grammar and style, Word provides the Grammar command from the Tools menu. When this command is activated, Word checks the selected section or the entire document for grammatical errors. If Word finds an error, it often suggests ways to correct the sentence containing the error. You can make changes based on Word's suggestions; you can make changes based on your own preferences; or you can bypass the error altogether (the "error" may be okay as is).

Hot Stuff When you use the Grammar command, Word simultaneously checks your spelling, so you may see the Spelling dialog box overlay the Grammar dialog box during a grammar check.

To check grammar in a document, first select a passage of text, or make no selection to check the entire document. Then choose Grammar from the Tools menu. If an error is found, Word displays the Grammar dialog box. There may be a suggestion that explains the error or that offers a way to fix it. If you agree with the suggestion to fix the error, click on the Change button. You can ignore the error by clicking on the Ignore button. Sometimes you may want to edit the sentence yourself. Click in the Sentence text box and edit the sentence as you normally would. Then click on the Change button.

If the Suggestions box contains an explanation about the error, you can get more detail about the error by clicking on the Explain button. The Grammar Explanation window appears, as shown in Figure 2-25. After reading the rule, close the Grammar Explanation window by double-clicking on the close box in the upper-left corner of the window. You can ignore this rule in the rest of the grammar check by clicking on the Ignore Rule button in the Grammar dialog box.

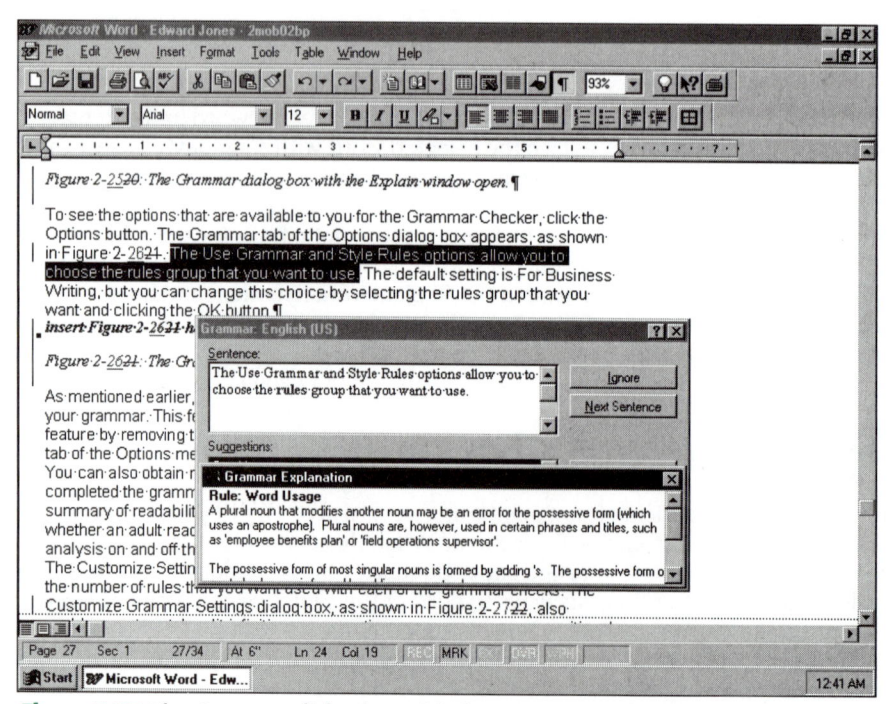

Figure 2-25: The Grammar dialog box with the Grammar Explanation window open.

To see the options that are available to you for the Grammar Checker, click on the Options button. The Grammar tab of the Options dialog box appears, as shown in Figure 2-26. The Use Grammar and Style Rules options allow you to choose the rules group that you want to use. The default setting is For Business Writing, but you can change this choice by selecting the rules group that you want and clicking on the OK button.

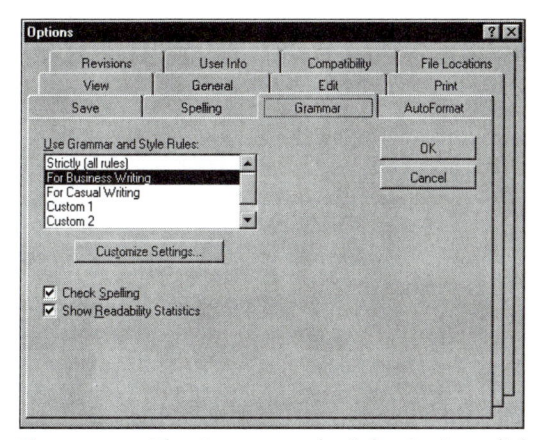

Chapter 2 ✦ **Creating and Working with Documents** 55

Figure 2-26: The Grammar tab of the Options dialog box.

Hot Stuff As mentioned earlier, Word for Windows 95 also checks your spelling as it checks your grammar. This feature slows down Word, however. You can turn off this feature by removing the check mark from the Check Spelling box on the Grammar tab of the Options menu to increase the speed of your grammar checking.

You can also obtain readability statistics on your document. After Word has completed the grammar check, it analyzes the document and provides a summary of readability statistics. These statistics let you evaluate whether an adult reader can easily understand your document. You can turn this analysis on and off through the Grammar tab of the Options menu.

The Customize Settings button on the Grammar tab lets you customize the number of rules that you want used with each of the grammar checks. The Customize Grammar Settings dialog box, as shown in Figure 2-27, also lets you catch split infinitives, consecutive nouns, numerous prepositional phases, and run-on sentences. These rules can be adjusted by clicking on the check boxes next to them or by typing in the numbers required for the rule (see the Sentences Containing More Words Than option).

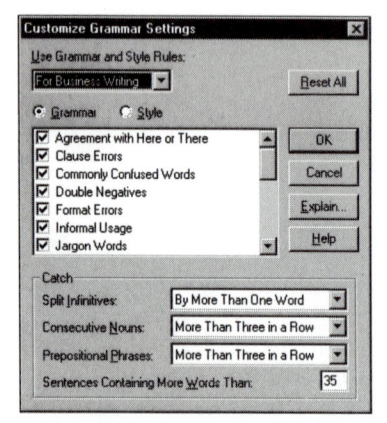

Figure 2-27: The Customize Grammar Settings dialog box.

Using Hyphenation

Word provides different ways to handle *hyphenation,* the process of adding hyphens to reduce the ragged appearance of a document's right margin. If the text is justified, hyphens reduce the space between words to fill out a line. In Word, you can add hyphens manually or automatically.

To enter hyphens manually, you must use the Hyphenation command from the Tools menu, which displays the Hyphenation dialog box (see Figure 2-28). After you click on the Manual button, Word switches to Page Layout View and stops to let you confirm the desired location for each hyphen. If you don't want to add a hyphen to the word, or you want to skip it, click on No, and the word is skipped.

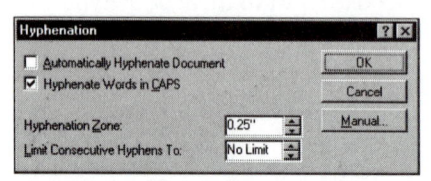

Figure 2-28: The Hyphenation dialog box.

With automatic hyphenation, Word adds hyphens automatically, making its best guess as to where hyphenation should occur. In the Hyphenation dialog box, click on the Automatically Hyphenate Document check box to activate automatic hyphenation.

If you choose to hyphenate as you type, you can use one of two types of hyphens: optional or nonbreaking. Optional hyphens appear only if the word is at the end of the line. Word also inserts an optional hyphen when you use semiautomatic or automatic hyphenation. To insert an optional hyphen, press Ctrl+Hyphen. Use nonbreaking hyphens (also called *hard hyphens*) when you do not want a hyphenated word to be broken at the end of a line. To insert a nonbreaking hyphen, press Ctrl+Shift+Hyphen.

Adding Bullets or Paragraph Numbers

With Word, you can automatically add paragraph numbers to your documents or bullets to each paragraph. This feature can be very useful when you are working with legal documents. Also, documents that are numbered are easy to edit and revise. As you add or delete paragraphs, Word maintains the correct numbering for the paragraphs.

To add paragraph numbering or bullets, open the document and select the paragraphs or section to which you want to apply the numbering or bullets. Next, choose Format⇨Bullets and Numbering. The Bullets and Numbering dialog box appears, from which you can choose from six different bullet layouts on the Bulleted tab. On the Numbered tab, you can choose from six different numbering layouts. The Multilevel tab lets you create outline style numbering with numbers and letters. Each of the tabs contains diagrams of the different layouts.

If you want to add bullets or numbers to the paragraphs as you type, use the buttons on the Formatting toolbar. Select the paragraphs or section to which you want to add numbers or bullets and then click on the Bullets button to add bullets or the Numbering button to add numbers. When you want to add numbers, Word automatically checks the preceding paragraph for its numbering style. If it is numbered, Word uses the same style of numbering for the selected paragraph. If the paragraph is not numbered, Word applies the style of numbering that you selected last.

Using AutoText Entries

AutoText entries are stored entries of text that you frequently use but that you don't want Word to insert automatically. For example, closings to business or personal letters can be stored as an AutoText entry. To store an AutoText entry, type the text that you want or import the graphics and then select it. Next, click on the Edit AutoText button on the Standard toolbar to open the AutoText dialog box. In the AutoText dialog box, Word suggests a name for the AutoText entry. If you want to keep the suggested name, click on the Add button to create an AutoText entry. If you want to change the name, type the name that you want to give the entry in the Name text box.

To insert an AutoText entry, put your cursor in the place where you want the entry to go and then select AutoText from the Edit menu. The AutoText dialog box is then displayed, as shown in Figure 2-29. From the Name list, choose the entry that you want to insert, and in the Insert As area, decide whether you want the text to be plain or formatted. Click on the Insert button to insert the entry to the left of the insertion point.

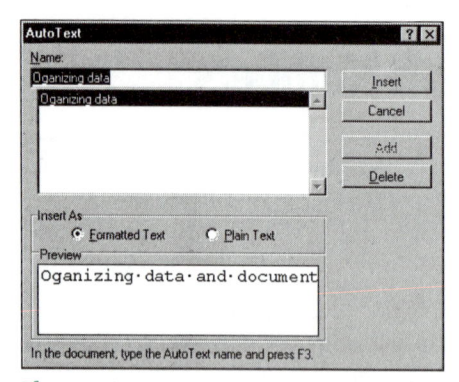

Figure 2-29: The AutoText dialog box.

Word also gives you the option of assigning an AutoText entry to a toolbar, which allows you to insert the AutoText entry by clicking on that toolbar button. If you want to assign an AutoText entry to a toolbar, perform the following steps:

1. From the View menu, choose Toolbars.

2. In the Toolbars dialog box, click on the Customize button. The Toolbars tab of the Customize dialog box appears (see Figure 2-30).

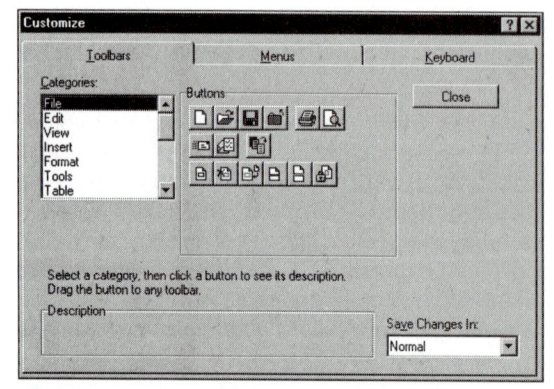

Figure 2-30: The Toolbars tab of the Customize dialog box.

Chapter 2 ✦ **Creating and Working with Documents** 59

3. In the Categories list box, scroll down to the AutoText entry. When you click on this category, the adjacent box becomes the AutoText box, which displays the name of all AutoText entries that you have stored.

4. Click on the name of the entry to which you want to assign a button. You will see the outline of a toolbar button appear.

5. Next, drag the button to the toolbar to which you want to assign the AutoText button. The Custom Button dialog box appears, as shown in Figure 2-31.

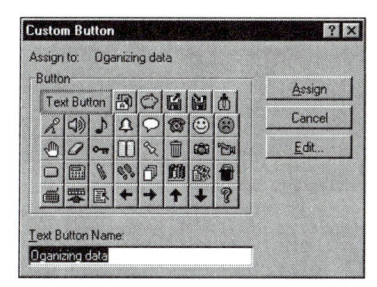

Figure 2-31: The Custom Button dialog box.

6. Select the button that you want for the AutoText entry or enter a name for the button in the Text Button Name text box. Word suggests a name by default, but you can change the name to whatever you want. Click the Assign button or click on the Edit button to create your own button for the entry.

7. If you choose to create your own button, the Button Editor dialog box opens (see Figure 2-32), where you can use the grid to draw a text button as you desire.

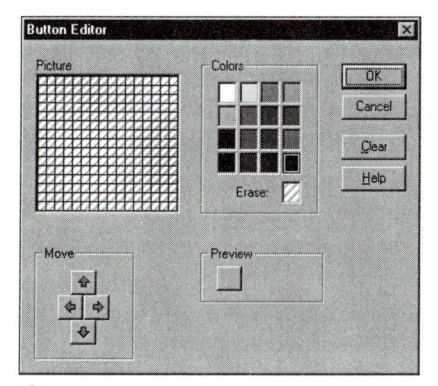

Figure 2-32: The Button Editor dialog box.

Changes can be made to an AutoText entry at any time. Type the name of the AutoText entry and make the revisions. After making the revisions, select the entry and, in effect, redefine it by giving it the same name.

If you no longer need an AutoText entry, you can delete it. Open the AutoText dialog box by selecting any word in the document and then clicking on the Edit AutoText button on the Standard toolbar. Select the name of the AutoText entry that you want to delete and click on the Delete button. The entry is removed.

You can also print your AutoText entries. To print them, select Print from the File menu. The Print dialog box appears. Next, select AutoText Entries from the Print what list box. After you click on OK, the AutoText entries will be printed.

Creating Annotations

You can easily create and edit *annotations,* a form of notes regarding your document, as a part of a Word document. Think of annotations as comments added to a document; they are not normally visible in the document, but they can easily be seen by using the Annotations command from the View menu. Annotations are very useful when multiple Word users want to make comments on a proposed document. Because each annotation includes the initials of the person making the comment, you can view the annotations and contact the persons who have made the comments for help in incorporating the changes. Even when you are working on documents alone, you may find annotations useful for reminding yourself about revisions that you plan to make to the document.

To create an annotation, place the insertion point at the desired location for the annotation and choose the Annotation command from the Insert menu (Alt+I+A). Word splits the current window and inserts your initials within a bracket at the annotation point, as shown in Figure 2-33. In addition to your initials, Word provides an annotation number so that you can add more annotations later. Each annotation is assigned a number in sequential order.

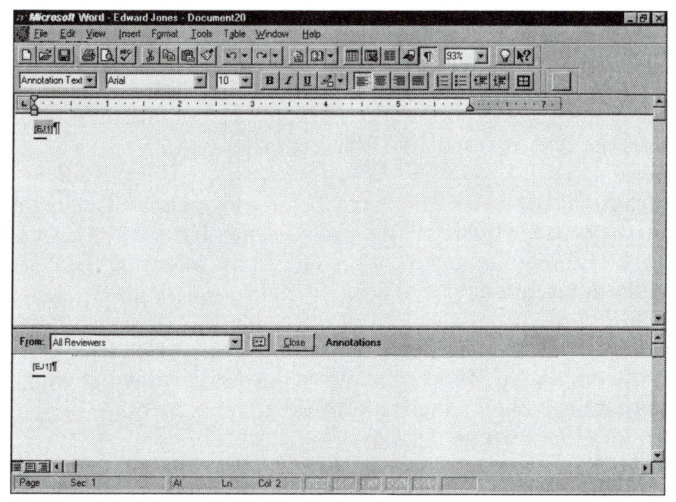

Figure 2-33: The Annotations window.

The active insertion point is automatically placed in the Annotations pane, which is the lower half of the split window. You can type your desired comments here — there is no limit to the length of an annotation. Figure 2-34 shows the sample document with two annotations added. When you finish writing the annotations, close the Annotations pane of the window by choosing the Annotations command from the View menu or by dragging the split bar within the right scroll bar to the bottom of the window.

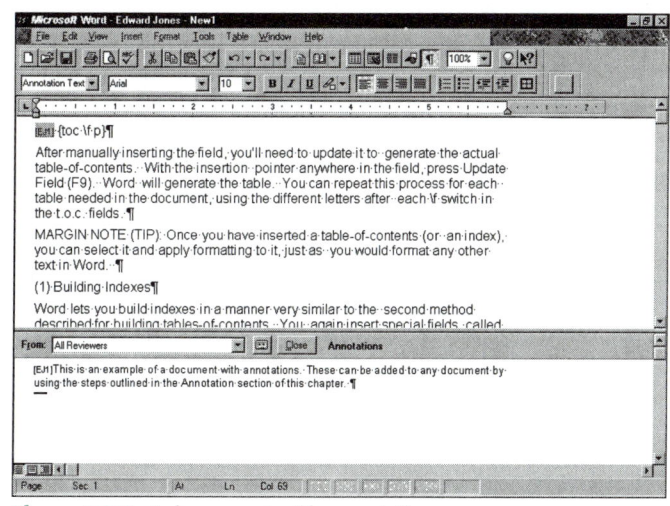

Figure 2-34: A document with annotations.

To view annotations that you have added to a document, use the Annotations command from the View menu. The command is a toggle, so choosing it repeatedly will turn annotations viewing on or off. To edit the text of an existing annotation if the Annotations pane is not already open, choose the Annotations command from the View menu and then edit the text as you would edit any other text.

To delete an annotation, go to that annotation's marker in the document, select it, and press the Delete button on your keyboard. You can also print all the annotations in a document by choosing the Print command from the File menu, selecting the Options button, and turning on the Annotations check box.

Hot Stuff: Remember that you can use the Cut and Paste commands to move text from the Annotations pane into the document. This technique is particularly helpful when some of the comments that have been added to your documents by other people should be incorporated into the document itself.

Finding annotations

In a large document, you can quickly get to a desired annotation with the Go To command from the Edit menu (F5 or Ctrl+G). In the Go To dialog box, choose Annotation in the Go to What list box, followed by the name of the reviewer, or Any Reviewer if that is not known. For example, to go to the second annotation in the document, press the Next button. You are then moved to the next annotation in the document by the specified reviewer or any reviewer based on what was entered in the Enter Reviewer's Name box.

Locking the document

When multiple persons are commenting on a document, you may find it helpful to lock the document so that no one but the author can change the document itself — others can only add or edit annotations. If you lock a document for annotations only, you can then safely pass the file around for comments, while ensuring that others cannot make any changes to the document.

To lock a file for annotations only, choose the Save As command from the File menu when you next save the file and then click on the Options button in the Save As dialog box. In the Save tab, you can enter a Write Reservation Password that prevents changes from being made to a document. You can also restrict the editing of your document by clicking on the Read-Only Recommended box.

Chapter 2 ✦ **Creating and Working with Documents**   63

Document Summaries

While not directly related to the formats of your document, document summaries are an important aid to the editing process. If you customarily press Enter to bypass the document summary screen every time you are creating a new document, you are missing out on a flexible way of storing information relating to a document. And you can use the information stored in the document summaries as a way to search for desired documents.

Hot Stuff If you can't recall a filename, you can find the file by searching document summaries. Choose File⇨Open, click on the Advanced button in the Open dialog box that appears, set the desired search criteria for the document summaries, and click on the Find Now button.

To view or edit the document summary, make sure that the document is open, choose File⇨Properties, and then click on the Summary tab in the dialog box that opens. The Summary tab is shown in Figure 2-35.

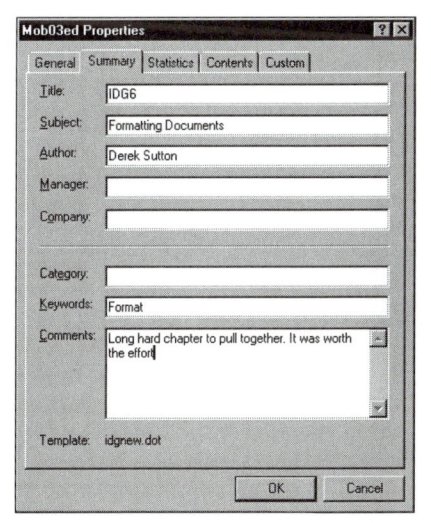

Figure 2-35: The Summary tab of the Properties dialog box.

The fields are self-explanatory — you can enter the desired document title, subject, and keywords that may help you identify the document later. Word inserts the author's name, based on the name that is stored in the dialog box on the User Info tab of the Options dialog box (accessed from the Tools menu). When you change the author's name in the Summary dialog box, the change takes effect only for the current document.

The Statistics tab in the Properties dialog box can be useful for getting information about the productivity of the document. After you click on this tab, you see all sorts of useful information regarding your document (see Figure 2-36).

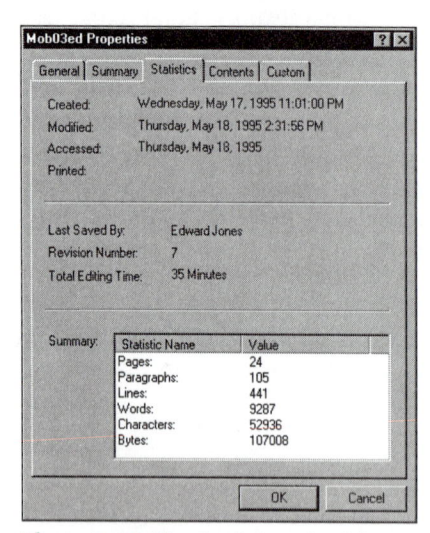

Figure 2-36: The Statistics tab of the Properties dialog box.

The Statistics tab shows the document's creation date, when it was last saved, how many times it has been revised, the total time you have spent editing it, and how many characters, words, and pages are in the document.

If you fill in the fields of the Summary tab of the Properties dialog box for all your documents, you can later find documents based on those fields. This is often helpful when you need to retrieve a document but can't remember the filename. To search for a document based on the summary information, choose File➪Open. From the Open dialog box that appears, choose Advanced. From the Property portion of the dialog box, choose the summary information that you want to use in the search. The Advanced Find dialog box, used for advanced searches, is shown in Figure 2-37.

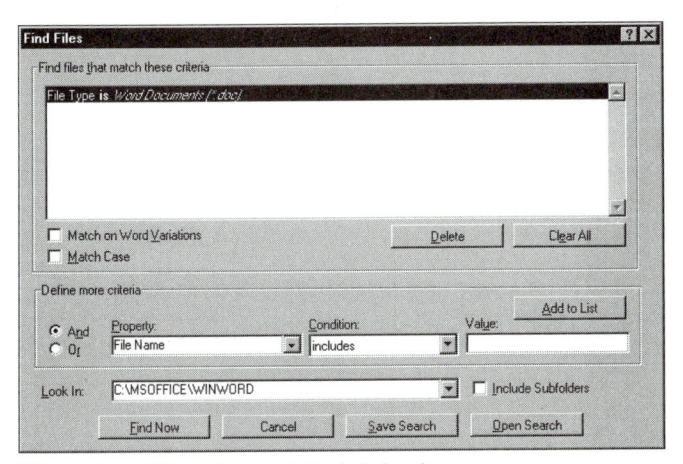

Figure 2-37: The Advanced Find dialog box.

After specifying the location of your search, use the condition and value portions of the dialog box to specify the information that you want Word to use in the search. Special characters may also be used to create approximate criteria (see "Searching for special characters" earlier in this chapter). After you have entered the information, click on Find Now to carry out the search.

Summary

This chapter provided you with techniques that are useful in your start with Word. The following points were covered:

- ◆ Word's File⇨New command displays a dialog box containing tabs that you can use to create new documents. New documents are based on a blank document or on one of Word's predefined templates. In Word, you can base your documents on different templates containing certain formatting and, in many cases, boilerplate text.

- ◆ Word includes a number of wizards that ask you a series of questions and then create a basic document based on your responses.

- ◆ You can work with text in Word through one of four possible views: Normal, Outline, Page Layout, and Master Document.

- ◆ You can change your margin settings with the File⇨Page Setup command; your tabs with the Format⇨Tabs command; and your line spacing with the Format⇨Paragraph command.

- ◆ You can search for text with the Edit⇨Find command, and you can search for and replace text with the Edit⇨Replace command. Word provides a full-featured search-and-replace capability that lets you search for text, formatting, and special characters such as paragraph marks and tabs.

- ◆ You can use Word's spell-checking feature to find and fix misspellings, and you can have Word check spelling as you type. And Word also provides a grammar checker that can check your documents for proper grammar and style.

- ◆ You can use the Insert⇨Annotations command to add annotations to a document.

Chapter 3 takes you to the next step: Formatting Documents.

Where to go next . . .

- ◆ If you're ready to print your work, Chapter 4 tells you how.
- ◆ If you need to create tables, outlines, tables of contents, or indexes, see Chapters 5 and 7 for help.

◆ ◆ ◆

CHAPTER 3

Formatting Documents

♦ ♦ ♦ ♦

In This Chapter

Applying character formatting

Applying paragraph formatting

Working with document summaries

Applying page formatting

Applying section formatting

Adding headers and footers

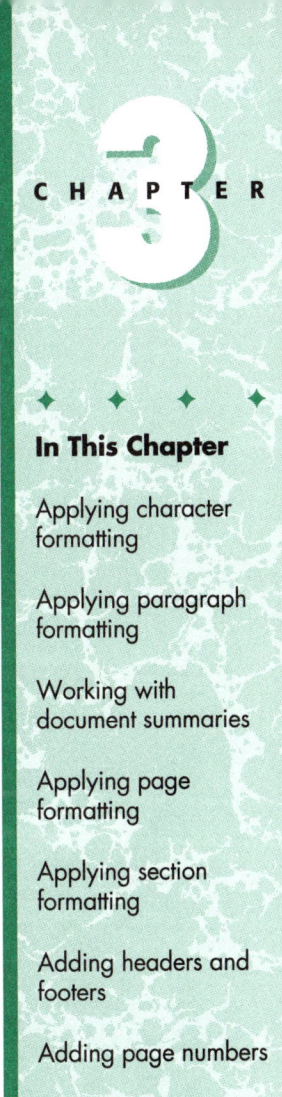

Adding page numbers

Using footnotes

♦ ♦ ♦ ♦

As you create and refine your text, you will need to control the appearance of the document. You can do so by using Word's formatting features. In Chapter 2, you were introduced to some of the basic ways of formatting your text. This chapter will detail formatting as it applies to characters, paragraphs, pages, and sections of a document.

Formatting Levels

Word provides formatting options for different levels of text, including characters, paragraphs, sections, and documents. Later in this chapter, you'll use many of the options on Word's Format menu, which offers many of the features that control Word's formatting.

♦ The smallest unit of formatting is the character. With *character formatting,* any formatting that you apply affects all the characters within a selected area of text or all the characters that you type after you select the formatting. Here's a case where you're applying character formatting and you may not even realize it: when you select a sentence and then click on the Bold button in the Formatting toolbar to transform the sentence into bold text. Character formatting is often used to make a word or group of words in your document stand out.

- The next size up in the formatting arena is *paragraph formatting*. With paragraph formatting, the formatting that you apply controls the appearance of the text from one paragraph mark to the next. Paragraph marks appear whenever you press the Enter key. If you press Enter once, type seven lines of text, and then press Enter again, those seven lines of text are one paragraph. After you select a paragraph, you can change the formatting for that particular paragraph. For example, you can change its alignment or its line spacing.

  Because paragraphs are made up of characters, it is easy to confuse character and paragraph formatting. It may help to remember that paragraph formatting generally controls the appearance of lines because a group of lines typically makes up a paragraph. Paragraph formatting controls the alignment of lines, the spacing between lines, the indents in lines, and borders around the paragraph.

- Next, there is *page formatting*. With page formatting, you control the appearance of every page for the entire document. Page formatting affects such settings as page size, default tab stops, and margins for the document.

- Optionally, you can apply *section formatting* to entire sections of a document. (A document can be made up of a single section, or you can divide a document into multiple sections.) When you format a section of a document, you change certain formatting aspects for pages within that section. For example, you may want to change the number of columns in a portion of the document, or you may want to change the look of the headers and footers in another section. After you divide a document into sections, you can use many formatting commands to format each section individually.

Choosing your weapon

Although Word divides formatting into four levels that control Word's behavior, these levels do not need to control your formatting choices. Where you start and end a particular type of formatting depends entirely on how you want the document to appear. For example, suppose that you want to display all the text of two paragraphs in italic. Even though you are applying formatting to two *paragraphs*, you can select these paragraphs and click on the Italic button on the Formatting toolbar to apply *character* formatting. Remember that *you* are in control of formatting options. This chapter explains the levels of formatting in Word for Windows because that is how Word provides access to the formatting options within its menus. You can, however, choose to apply formatting by using any combination of methods that suits your needs.

Character Formatting

As mentioned earlier, character formatting is the smallest level of formatting. Character formatting governs how your characters look on-screen and in print. When you apply character formatting, the most common type of formatting, you are changing the format for each character. When you look at a newspaper or a book, character formatting is evident. Headlines appear in boldfaced characters and in large fonts. Secondary headlines, however, are in smaller fonts and may not be in bold print. The role of character formatting, therefore, is to emphasize text.

Characters and lines

can be produced

in a number of ways,

even in combination,

TO HELP MAKE

a different point.

Also, you can add color formatting to the characters in your document. Whether you can view or print the colors that you select depends on the type of printer you have and the display hardware.

Using character formatting options

Character formatting can be further divided into specific areas that are controlled by the options in the Font dialog box, which appears after you choose the Font command from the Format menu. Table 3-1 explains the formatting options available in the Font dialog box.

Table 3-1
Formatting options

Option	Description
Font	A character set with a consistent and identifiable typeface, such as Times New Roman, Courier, or Arial.
Font Style	Defines a style for the chosen font, such as regular text, italic, bold, or bold italic.
Size	Specifies what *point size* to use — essentially, how big the text should be. Strictly speaking, point size measures character height, but characters proportionally increase in width as they increase in height. A point is $1/72$ of an inch, so a 72-point font can take up an inch from top to bottom. (Not counting *descenders,* which dangle from the bottom of y, g, q, and so on.) This does not mean, however, that a 72-point P is always an inch tall. Each font has other characteristics that determine its actual size. (This is why a P in one font may look bigger than a P in another font, even when they're at the same point size.)
Color	Offers 16 possible colors that can be viewed in the list box.
Underline	Specifies a type of underlining (single, double, dotted).
Effects	Specifies appearance attributes such as strikethrough, hidden (which means the text does not appear, but is actually still there), ^{superscript}, $_{subscript}$, SMALL CAPS, and ALL CAPS.
Spacing	Controls the amount of space that appears between characters (found on the Character Spacing tab of the Font dialog box). Word allows a default amount of space between characters, but you can expand or condense this allowance.
Position	The position of the characters on a line, such as normal, raised (the characters appearing above the baseline by half a line), or lowered (the characters appearing below the baseline by half a line).

The quickest way to apply character formatting is to use the Formatting toolbar. You can choose the font and point size that you want to use, and apply bold, italics, and underlining. These choices are the most frequently used character formats in documents.

If you need to make adjustments or change several formats at one time, choose the Format⇨Font command. The Font dialog box appears. Click on the Font tab to reveal the options available in Figure 3-1. Here you can choose from the many fonts, select a style, change text color, specify the type of underlining you desire, and add effects such as strikethrough, all caps, or small caps.

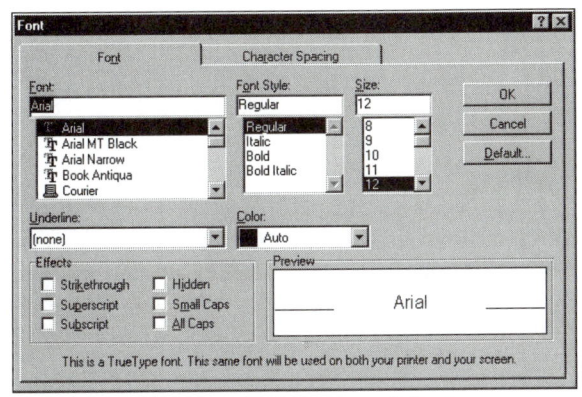

Figure 3-1: The Font tab of the Font dialog box.

You can use the options in the Font and Font Style list boxes to choose a desired font and font style, and you can choose a desired size in the Size list box. You can select a type of underlining (Single, Words Only, Double, or Dotted) in the Underline list box, and you can select a color for the text in the Color list box. In the Effects portion of the tab, you can turn on as many of the special effects at one time as you want.

The Character Spacing tab of the Font dialog box (Figure 3-2) provides options for changing the amount of spacing between characters (Normal, Expanded, or Condensed), the position (whether text appears raised or lowered relative to the baseline of normal text), and *kerning* (the precise amount of space between characters, as detailed shortly).

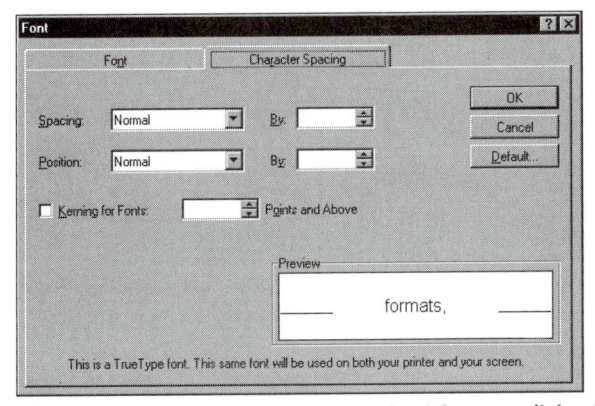

Figure 3-2: The Character Spacing tab of the Font dialog box.

To remove or apply character formats, simply select the text that you want to format, or position the cursor where you want to begin typing the formatted characters. Then, using the Formatting toolbar, click on the formatting option that you want to apply to the characters.

Using character formatting shortcuts

You can apply most of these character formats with shortcut keys, which are easier to use when you are typing than removing your hands from the keyboard to use the mouse. The shortcut keys act as switches to turn the various Format commands on and off. Table 3-2 contains several shortcut keys that you can use to apply character formatting.

Table 3-2
Shortcut keys for character formatting

Format	Shortcut Key
Bold	Ctrl+B
Italic	Ctrl+I
Underline	Ctrl+U
Word underline	Ctrl+Shift+W
Double underline	Ctrl+Shift+O
Subscript (H_2O)	Ctrl+Equal Sign
Superscript (X^2)	Ctrl+Shift+Equal Sign
Small caps	Ctrl+Shift+K
All caps	Ctrl+Shift+A
Change case of letters	Shift+F3
Hidden text	Ctrl+Shift+H
Copy formats	Ctrl+Shift+C
Paste formats	Ctrl+Shift+V
Remove formats	Ctrl+Spacebar
Font	Ctrl+Shift+F
Symbol font	Ctrl+Shift+Q
Point size	Ctrl+Shift+P

Format	Shortcut Key
Next larger size	Ctrl+>
Next smaller size	Ctrl+<
Up one point	Ctrl+]
Down one point	Ctrl+[

Hot Stuff You can turn off all character formatting for a selection by pressing Ctrl+Spacebar. This is especially useful when you've used several key combinations to turn on various formatting features for a selection, and you want to turn them all off.

Changing character fonts and point sizes

One significant advantage of using Word for Windows is your ability to see and use various fonts within your document. The font used as the default is initially Times New Roman, but you can change this to whatever you wish. The fonts available to you depend on the type of printer that you are using and the fonts that were installed as a part of your Windows installation. You can use the following steps to change the default font used for your documents:

1. From the menus, choose Format⇨Font.
2. Click on the Font tab in the Font dialog box (if it isn't already visible).

The hows and whens of formatting

Word provides a great deal of flexibility by offering many formatting options. You can apply formatting as you are creating a document, which changes the appearance of the document as you go along. Or you can enter all the new text in a single format and then change the formatting in selected areas of the document. Or you can use both methods in combination.

If you choose to format as you go along, remember that many options of formatting (particularly for characters and paragraphs) can be turned on and off as you work. For example, when you turn on underlining, everything that you type from that point is underlined. To stop underlining, turn underlining off. This is true whether you apply formatting with commands, shortcut keys, or buttons on the toolbars.

If you want to enter the text of a document first and then apply formatting to specific areas later, you can use the "select and act" technique common to Word for Windows. That is, you first select the affected text and then you execute an action (by choosing a formatting command or button) that applies to the selection.

3. Choose the desired font, font style, and size you want to use as the default.
4. Click on the Default button in the dialog box.
5. When asked for confirmation that you want to change the default font, click on Yes.

In addition to choosing appropriate fonts, you can also select various point sizes with the Formatting toolbar or the Font dialog box. Each point is $1/72$ of an inch, so in a 10-point font size, the characters would be roughly 10/72 of an inch high. The following lines demonstrate the effects of various point sizes:

This is 12-point Times New Roman.

This is 14-point Times New Roman.

This is 16-point Times New Roman.

This is 18-point Times New Roman.

With varied fonts and font sizes, it is all too easy to get carried away. A document with too many different fonts and font sizes can take on a busy look and be visually distracting to the reader.

Applying superscript and subscript

You can create raised, or *superscripted,* text, and lowered, or *subscripted,* text, by selecting the Superscript or Subscript options on the Font tab of the Font dialog box. Most formatting of this type is applied while you type the information, although as with other formatting in Word, you can apply the formatting later by selecting the desired characters and then choosing the Superscript or Subscript options. Examples of both types of text are as follows:

This is $^{\text{superscripted text}}$. And this is back to normal.

This is $_{\text{subscripted text}}$. And this is back to normal.

You can apply super- or subscripting to text by using either the Font dialog box or the shortcut keys (see Table 3-2). One advantage of using the Font dialog box is that you can change the measurement amount that you use for the superscript or the subscript. Click on the Font tab, and turn on the Superscript or the Subscript option as desired for the selected text.

Adjusting kerning

Kerning can also be controlled from the Character Spacing tab of the Font dialog box. Kerning is the adjusting of the space between characters, relative to the specific type of font used. Kerning can be useful in giving a document a better appearance, although you need a high-resolution printer (a 600-dpi laser printer or better) for the effects of minor changes in kerning to be noticeable. Kerning can be used only with proportionally spaced TrueType fonts or with similar scalable fonts that are larger than a minimum size you specify.

Copying character formatting

If you are using a particular type of formatting often in a document (but not in all places), you can save time by copying the format from one place in the document to another. Word for Windows makes this a simple task when you use the Format Painter button on the Standard toolbar. To copy a character format, first select the characters with the format that you want to copy. Next click on the Format Painter button on the toolbar. (It's the button with the small brush.) Then choose the characters or section to which you want to apply the format. The formatting is automatically applied to the new characters.

Paragraph Formatting

Word lets you apply paragraph formatting to any area that is considered a paragraph. Word considers any amount of text that you enter between one paragraph mark and the next to be a single paragraph. If you want to see the paragraph marks in a document (see Figure 3-3), press the Show/Hide button on the Standard toolbar (it's the button containing the paragraph symbol, which looks sort of like a backwards P).

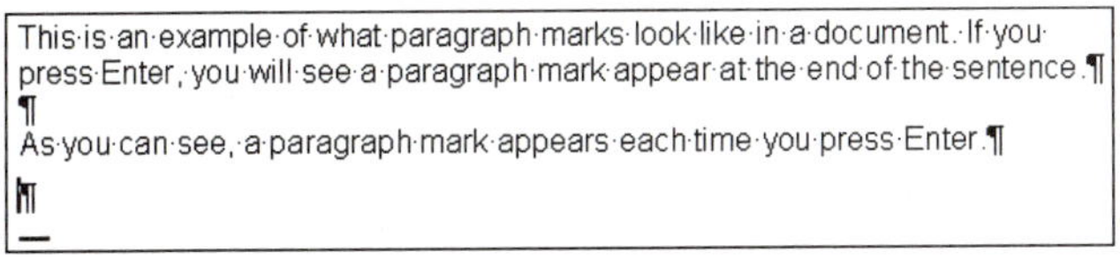

```
This is an example of what paragraph marks look like in a document. If you
press Enter, you will see a paragraph mark appear at the end of the sentence.¶
¶
As you can see, a paragraph mark appears each time you press Enter.¶
¶
```

Figure 3-3: Paragraph marks in a document.

When deciding where paragraph formatting is necessary, it helps to remember that paragraphs are basically collections of lines. Paragraph formatting affects the appearance of a collection of one or more lines that end with a paragraph marker, which appears when you press Enter. Paragraph formatting lets you control the length of lines, the alignment of lines at the left and right edges, the space between lines, and the space between paragraphs. You can also control the placement of tab stops and how text is aligned at the tab stops.

Hot Stuff: Using the newline command (Shift+Enter) rather than pressing the Enter key can make paragraph formatting easier because Word does not consider the newline character (a left-pointing arrow) to be the start of a paragraph.

Applying paragraph formatting

As with character formatting, you can apply paragraph formatting in different ways. You can use the Format⇨Paragraph to bring up the Paragraph dialog box shown in Figure 3-4. Or you can use the buttons that apply to paragraphs on the Formatting toolbar. The Formatting toolbar also displays important information regarding the existing formats for the current paragraph. Look at the alignment buttons (Align Left, Center, Align Right, and Justify). The one that looks pressed in reflects the alignment of the paragraph that contains the cursor.

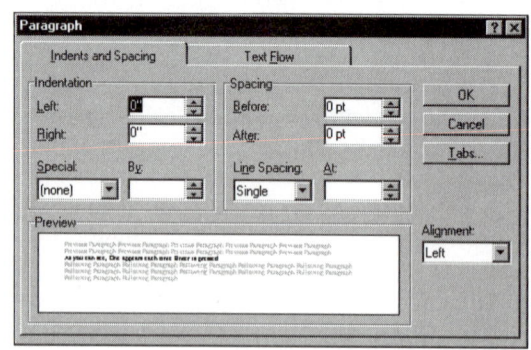

Figure 3-4: The Indents and Spacing tab of the Paragraph dialog box.

The Paragraph dialog box contains two tabs. On the Indents and Spacing tab, you can choose the amount of left and right indentation and whether there should be a first-line or a hanging indent (and the corresponding amount of indentation). In the Spacing area, you can choose the amount of spacing before and after each line and the line spacing for the line itself.

The Text Flow tab of the Paragraph dialog box (see Figure 3-5) contains options that control how text flows within a paragraph. You can turn on the following options:

- ✦ The Widow/Orphan Control option prevents a *widow* (a single line at the bottom of the page) from appearing by itself at the bottom of the page, and it prevents an *orphan* (a single line at the top of a page) from appearing by itself at the top of the page.

- ✦ The Keep Lines Together option prevents a page break within the paragraph.

- ✦ The Keep with Next option prevents a page break between the paragraph and the one that follows.

Chapter 3 ✦ **Formatting Documents**   77

- ✦ The Page Break Before option inserts a page break before the paragraph.
- ✦ The Suppress Line Numbers option suppresses line numbers for the selected paragraph when line numbering is turned on in a document.
- ✦ The Don't Hyphenate option excludes the paragraph from automatic hyphenation.

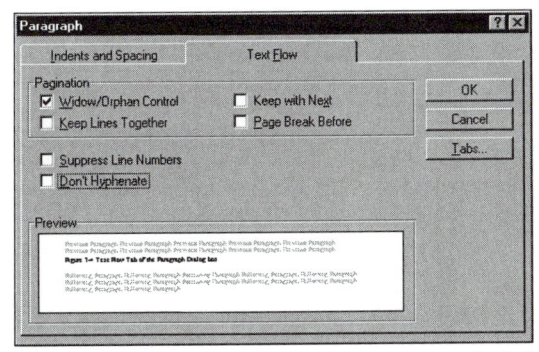

Figure 3-5: The Text Flow tab of the Paragraph dialog box.

You can also click on buttons on the Formatting toolbar and drag items on the ruler to indent paragraphs, align text, or set tab stops in a document. Many of these paragraph formats can also be applied by using shortcut keys. Table 3-3 provides a list of the paragraph formatting shortcut keys.

What are first-line indents and hanging indents?

In some paragraphs, you might want to align the first line of the paragraph differently than the remaining lines.

A *first-line indent* begins a paragraph's first line to the right of the paragraph's margin. You probably remember the "two-finger" first-line indent you learned in elementary school; this is the high-tech version.

A *hanging indent,* sometimes called an *outdent,* begins a paragraph's first line to the *left* of the paragraph's margin. You can use a hanging indent to create a bulleted list, for example. Use Format➪Paragraph to bring up the Paragraph dialog box. In the Special list box of the Indents and Spacing tab, choose Hanging. In the By entry, type **.25"**. Click on OK. Now, type a bullet symbol, a tab, and then type the text of the bullet item. The text wraps cleanly along that quarter-inch margin.

Table 3-3
Shortcut keys for paragraph formatting

Format	Shortcut Key
Left align text	Ctrl+L
Center text	Ctrl+E
Right align text	Ctrl+R
Justify text	Ctrl+J
Indent from left margin	Ctrl+M
Decrease indent	Ctrl+Shift+M
Create a hanging indent	Ctrl+T
Decrease a hanging indent	Ctrl+Shift+T
Single space lines	Ctrl+1
Create 1.5-line spacing	Ctrl+5
Double space lines	Ctrl+2
Add or remove 12 points of space before a paragraph	Ctrl+0 (zero)
Remove paragraph formats not applied by a style	Ctrl+Q
Restore default formatting (reapply the Normal style)	Ctrl+Shift+N
Display or hide nonprinting characters	Ctrl+*(asterisk)

Word for Windows also provides a shortcut menu to do character and paragraph formatting. You can open this menu by clicking on the right mouse button over any location in your paragraph. Figure 3-6 shows the formatting shortcut menu that appears. Here you can choose Cut, Copy, Paste, Font, Paragraph, or Bullets and Numbering to accomplish their different formatting tasks.

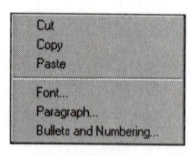

Figure 3-6: The formatting shortcut menu.

Indenting paragraphs

A common change to paragraphs involves setting the indents. When indenting paragraphs, it is important to remember that all paragraph indents are relative to any page indents that you may also have specified. Word lets you indent paragraphs from the left or right sides. You can also indent the first line of a paragraph. For practice, type the following text (or use text from a paragraph of your own devising) and follow the steps for applying different kinds of paragraph formatting:

1. Type the following text:

   Chess

   Chess is a very old game of strategy in which players try to capture, or checkmate, their opponent's king. Players alternate turns and make one move at a time. Each player has 16 playing pieces.

   The pawn usually moves first. It can be moved forward, one square at a time, except for its first move (when it can go one or two squares) or when it is capturing, at which time it advances diagonally one square. The rook can move in a straight line forward, backward, or to either side. The bishop moves and captures diagonally. The queen can move in a straight line or diagonally any number of spaces. The king can move in any direction but only one space at a time.

2. Place the insertion point anywhere on the first line, and click on the Center button in the Formatting Toolbar. When you do this, the first paragraph (containing just the word Chess) takes on a centered alignment.

3. Place the insertion point anywhere within the first full paragraph of text. Choose Format⇨Paragraph. The Paragraph dialog box appears. You will use the Indentation area on the Indents and Spacing tab to control the paragraph indents.

4. Enter **0.5** as a value in the Left box, and then enter **0.5** as a value in the Right box. Click on OK. The paragraph appears indented by one-half inch on both sides.

5. In the Paragraph dialog box, choose the Indents and Spacing tab. In the Special list box, select the First Line option. Enter **1** in the By entry. Click on OK. The first line of the paragraph is now indented by 1 inch.

   Figure 3-7 shows the results of all this paragraph formatting.

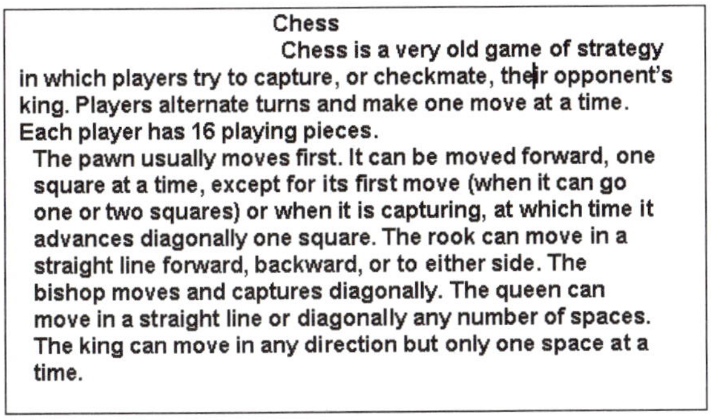

Chess
Chess is a very old game of strategy in which players try to capture, or checkmate, their opponent's king. Players alternate turns and make one move at a time. Each player has 16 playing pieces.
The pawn usually moves first. It can be moved forward, one square at a time, except for its first move (when it can go one or two squares) or when it is capturing, at which time it advances diagonally one square. The rook can move in a straight line forward, backward, or to either side. The bishop moves and captures diagonally. The queen can move in a straight line or diagonally any number of spaces. The king can move in any direction but only one space at a time.

Figure 3-7: Paragraphs after formatting has been applied.

Mouse users can also use the ruler to set the left indent, right indent, and first line indent values. You may have noticed that when you changed the values by using the Paragraph command, the triangle-shaped symbols on the ruler moved accordingly. You can set the indentations by dragging the appropriate symbol on the ruler to the desired location. If you drag the left-indent symbol (the lower of the two triangles) of the first full paragraph back to the zero mark on the ruler, the left edge of the paragraph realigns with the zero marker on the ruler. Now the paragraph is no longer indented from the left, although the first line remains indented by one inch. Next, drag the first-line indent symbol back to the zero mark on the ruler and drag the right-indent symbol $^1/_2$ inch to the right. The paragraph now takes on the appearance it had before you changed any of the indentations.

When you set indentations by dragging the symbols in the ruler, keep in mind that the measurement set by the first-line symbol is always relative to that set by the left-indent symbol. Therefore, if you want to indent an entire paragraph by $^1/_2$ inch and the first line by another $^1/_2$ inch, you should drag the left-indent symbol to the right by $^1/_2$ inch and then drag the first-line symbol to the right another $^1/_2$ inch past the left-indent symbol. To drag the first-line symbol without dragging the left-indent symbol, be sure that the mouse pointer is on the top of the two triangles.

Aligning paragraphs

Paragraphs in Word can be aligned in four ways: left, right, centered, and *justified* (aligned on both sides). Most of the text that you typed in the exercise has been left aligned, meaning that the left edge of the paragraph is even and the right edge is ragged. By comparison, there may be times that you need justified text (where both edges of the paragraph are aligned), or centered paragraphs (as in titles or headings). In rare instances, you may need to right align a paragraph; in such cases, the right side aligns flush, and the left edge of the paragraph is ragged. You can change these settings in the Alignment box of the Indents and Spacing tab in the Paragraph dialog box or by clicking on the alignment buttons on the Formatting toolbar.

To see an example of the available paragraph alignments, open any existing document, place the insertion point anywhere within a paragraph, and click on each alignment button. Watch how the text moves from left to center to right to justified.

Books and magazines usually use justified text for a neater appearance. Word justifies your text by adding extra space between words where necessary to make the right edge of the line even with the edge of the paragraph.

Note Depending on the type of document, the appearance of justified text may be improved by hyphenation. To enable Word to hyphenate automatically, choose Tools⇨Hyphenation, turn on the Automatically Hyphenate Document option in the Hyphenation dialog box, and then click on OK.

> **To justify, or not to justify?**
>
> Many people consider the look that results from fully justified text (that is, justified both left and right) to have a professional and "typeset" quality. Justification also provides an appearance of formality. And in multicolumn text, the justified right edge creates a line that serves as a clear delimiter between columns. On the other hand, if you want your document to appear more "friendly," avoid full justification. Also, bear in mind that full justification can cause uneven spacing and vertical "rivers" of white space in paragraphs. If you don't allow hyphenation, full justification creates some lines that are excessively "loose" (lots of space between words), and some lines that are excessively "tight" (too little space between words). If you allow hyphenation when you use full justification, Word hyphenates lots of words to create evenly spaced lines — far more than if you left the right margin ragged.

Applying line spacing

Line spacing affects the amount of space between lines in a paragraph. To change the line spacing, place the insertion point anywhere within the desired paragraph and then choose the desired line spacing by using shortcut keys (see Table 3-3) or by setting the Line Spacing option in the Indents and Spacing tab of the Paragraph dialog box.

The common choices for line spacing are Single, 1.5 Lines (for $1^1/_2$ times single spacing), and Double. You can also select At Least, Exactly, or Multiple. (When you choose any of the last three options, you must enter or select a corresponding amount in the At box.) The At Least choice sets a minimum line spacing that Word adjusts when needed to allow for larger font sizes or graphics. The Exactly choice sets a fixed line spacing that Word cannot adjust. The Multiple choice lets you enter incremental values (such as 1.2) to increase or decrease spacing by a fractional amount. For example, choosing Multiple and entering 1.2 in the At box results in line spacing that is 120 percent of single spacing.

Applying paragraph spacing

Word also lets you control the amount of space that appears before or after paragraphs in the Spacing area on the Indents and Spacing tab of the Paragraph dialog box. You can enter numeric values in the Before or After boxes to indicate the additional space that you want. As with line spacing, you can enter the value in points (pt.), each point being $^1/_{72}$ of an inch.

Applying borders to paragraphs

You may find borders useful for emphasizing a particular portion of text. Borders are also commonly used in newsletter layout. You can apply a border to paragraphs by using the Paragraph Borders and Shading command from the Format menu. If you apply borders often, click on the Show Toolbar button in the Paragraph Borders and Shading dialog box. (Alternatively, you can right-click in any blank area of the toolbar, and choose Borders from the shortcut menu that appears.) The Borders toolbar that appears makes adding borders to your documents much easier.

Word offers seven border choices:

- **Top Border** — a line above the paragraph
- **Bottom Border** — a line below the paragraph
- **Left Border** — a line to the left of the paragraph
- **Right Border** — a line to the right of the paragraph
- **Inside Border** — a line within the paragraph
- **Outside Border** — lines that surround the paragraph
- **No Border**

You can even change the line size that you use for the different borders in your document. Click on the down-pointing arrow in the Border toolbar to drop down the line-size options. Or you can select these same options in the Style section of the Borders tab of the Paragraph Borders and Shading dialog box (see Figure 3-8).

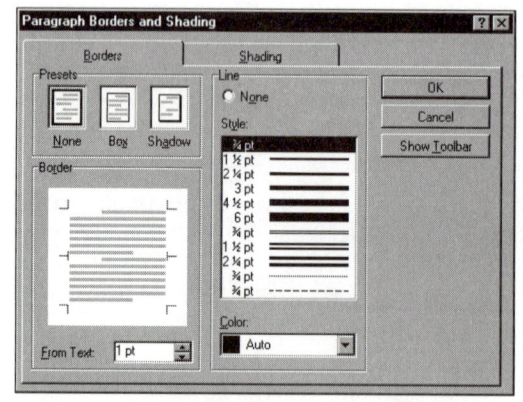

Figure 3-8: The Borders tab of the Paragraph Borders and Shading dialog box.

The Shading tab of the Paragraph Borders and Shading dialog box (Figure 3-9) lets you add various kinds of shading to your text. The shading can range from a light gray to a solid black. Click on the Custom radio button to apply a shading and then select the desired level of shading from the list box. The color options in the Foreground and Background boxes can be used to select desired colors for the shading. You can also choose the shading that you want from the Borders toolbar.

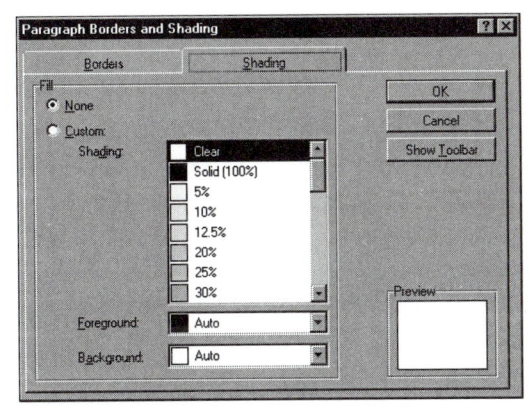

Figure 3-9: The Shading tab of the Paragraph Borders and Shading dialog box.

Page Formatting

In Word, you use page formatting to control the appearance of each page for the entire document. Page formatting controls such settings as page size, orientation, and page margins. To change most aspects of page formatting, you use the File⇨Page Setup command, which produces the Page Setup dialog box with its four tabs: Margins, Paper Size, Paper Source, and Layout. All tabs have a Default button, an Apply To list box, and a Preview window.

The Default button can be used to apply your changes to Word's default settings. (If you are using a template other than the default Normal.dot template, the changes are applied to the template that you are using.) The remaining choices you make apply to the rest of your document as you specify in the Apply To list box. You can choose Whole Document (applies your changes to the entire document) or This Point Forward (applies your changes to the current page and all pages that follow). The Preview window provides a visual representation of how the formatting changes appear when applied to the printed page.

The options that appear in the Layout tab of the Page Setup dialog box are covered in detail in the "Section Formatting" section. The next few sections describe the other tabs in this dialog box.

The Margins tab

In the Margins tab (see Figure 3-10), you can enter a numeric value to determine the distance between the top of the page and the first printed line or between the bottom of the page and the last printed line. You can also enter a numeric value to determine the distance between the left edge of the paper and the left edge of the printed lines, or between the right edge of the paper and the right edge of the printed lines. (Remember that any indents that you give paragraphs will be added to this amount.) Note that when you turn on the Mirror Margins option, the names of these options change to Inside and Outside.

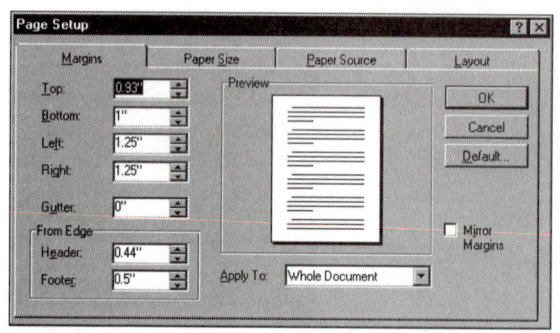

Figure 3-10: The Margins tab of the Page Setup dialog box.

Turn on Mirror Margins to force margins on facing pages to mirror each other. You should use this option when you want to print on both sides of a page. With this option turned on, inside margins will have the same width as outside margins. You can also enter a numeric value to determine the width of an optional *gutter,* an additional white space that is allowed when a document is to be bound.

If you choose the From Edge option, you can enter or choose the distance from the top and bottom edge of the page to the header and footer. Word measures the distance from the top edge of the header and the bottom edge of the footer to the page edges.

In the Apply To list box, you can choose Whole Document to apply the changes to the entire document, or you can choose This Point Forward to apply the changes to all text following the current location of the insertion point.

The Paper Size tab

In the Paper Size tab (see Figure 3-11), you can select a desired paper size from the list box. The available choices are Letter, Legal, Executive, A4 (European), No. 10, DL, six different envelope sizes, or Custom Size. When you use Custom Size as a paper size, you can enter the desired width and height for the paper size in the Width and Height boxes, or you can use the arrow buttons at the right edge of the text boxes to dial in the desired values. In the Orientation list box, you can choose the orientation desired (Portrait or Landscape).

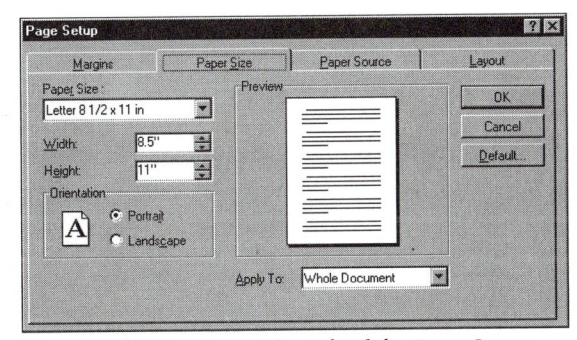

Figure 3-11: The Paper Size tab of the Page Setup dialog box.

The Paper Source tab

The options that appear in the Paper Source tab of the Page Setup dialog box are First Page and Other Pages (see Figure 3-12). Use either of these options to determine which bin of your printer is used to supply paper for the first printed page and for remaining pages. (If your printer does not support multiple-bin printing, you will not be able to select these options.)

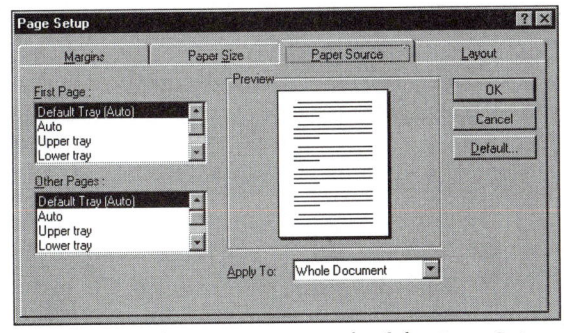

Figure 3-12: The Paper Source tab of the Page Setup dialog box.

> ### A word about styles
>
> Like most programs under Windows, Word gives you more than one way to accomplish the same task. Character, paragraph, and page formatting are known as *direct formatting* options. Another way to control formatting is with *styles*. When you use styles, you apply a group of formatting settings to an entire document. As an example, if a certain style defines indented paragraphs, and you apply that style to a document, that document's paragraphs will be indented. Chapter 8 explores the use of styles.

Section Formatting

Sections are portions of documents that carry formatting characteristics independent of other sections in the same document. Section formatting isn't required; by default, Word treats an entire document as a single section. But by giving you the power to add multiple sections to a document, Word gives you a way to apply different formatting settings to each section. At first, the concept of sections may be difficult to understand because so many word processors apply formatting to characters, lines, or entire pages. But knowledge of how sections operate in Word is worth the effort because sections add flexibility to how a document can be formatted. If you have used older versions of Word for DOS or powerful desktop publishing software such as Corel's Ventura Publisher or Aldus's PageMaker, the concept of formatting in sections will be more familiar to you. (Older versions of Word for DOS use *divisions,* which are equivalent to sections under Word for Windows. Like Word for Windows, the last versions of Word for DOS use sections.)

Typically, you use section formatting when you want to change the number of columns or the style of page numbering for a section of the document. Changes that affect all pages of a document, such as page margins, are part of page formatting.

Even in a very short document, you are still using sections, although you may not give them any thought. In a short document (such as a one-page memo), the entire document consists of a single section, so you can use Word's section formatting commands to control certain elements of its layout.

If you want to apply a specific set of formatting to a section, select the text and choose File➪Page Setup. In the Page Setup dialog box, click on the Layout tab (see Figure 3-13). In the Apply To list box, you can see Selected Text, the default option. In this tab, you can control the section breaks for a document, headers and footers, and vertical alignment.

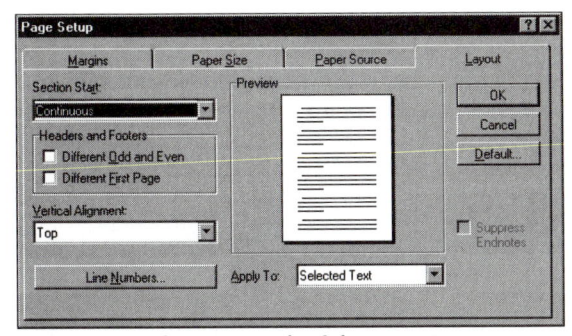

Figure 3-13: The Layout tab of the Page Setup dialog box.

To control the section breaks in a document, select an option in the Section Start list box. Here, you can control where you want the section to begin and where the preceding section should end.

- ✦ **Continuous** — This option causes the selected section to immediately follow the preceding section, without a page break.
- ✦ **New Column** — This option starts printing the selected section's text at the top of the next column.
- ✦ **New Page** — This option breaks the page at the section break.
- ✦ **Even Page** — This option starts the selected section at the next even-numbered page.
- ✦ **Odd Page** — This option starts the selected section at the next odd-numbered page.

The Layout tab also lets you control vertical alignment. *Vertical alignment* is the spacing of a document from the top to the bottom of the page. The document can be vertically centered to the top, centered, or justified. Line numbers can also be added by clicking on the Line Numbers button and turning on the Add Line Numbering option in the dialog box that appears (see Figure 3-14). Line numbers can be applied to the whole document or only to a selected section.

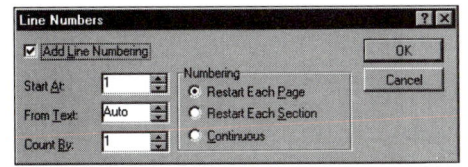

Figure 3-14: The Line Numbers dialog box.

You can apply line numbers in various ways: they can start at the beginning of the document and go to the end; they can start at a specified line or section; they can begin from line 1 at the start of each new page; or they can begin at a specified number on the selected page. Line numbers are useful in legal documents where you may need to examine a specific line of a contract or other legal document.

Headers and Footers

Word for Windows also makes it easy to add headers and footers to a document. A *header* is text or a graphic that is printed at the top of every page in a document; a *footer* is text or a graphic that is printed at the bottom of every page. Headers and footers can also be different for odd and even pages.

You can create headers and footers by choosing the View⇨Header and Footer command. Word switches to Page Layout view, and the Header and Footer toolbar appears, as shown in Figure 3-15. You can switch between headers and footers by clicking on the Switch Between Header and Footer button (the first button) on the toolbar, or you can scroll up or down the document with the vertical scroll bar.

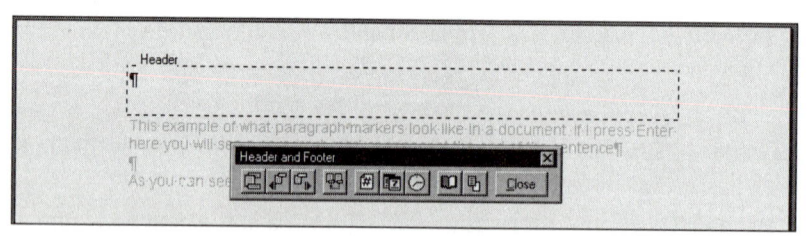

Figure 3-15: The Header and Footer toolbar in Page Layout view.

You type and format text in headers and footers the same way you type text in a normal document. After entering the characters that you want for your header or footer, click on the Close button, and Word displays the dimmed entry in Page Layout view.

You can also enter page numbers, the date, and the time as a header or footer in a document. Click on the Page Numbers, Date, and Time buttons on the Header and Footer toolbar. Remember, you can format the header or footer the same way you format normal text; therefore, if you want the time, page number, or date centered, you can do so just the way you center text in a document.

You may also want to use a different header or footer for the first page and for the odd and even pages. On the Layout tab of the Page Setup dialog box, click on the Different Odd and Even check box if you want to create different headers and footers for the odd and even pages of a document. If you want to create a different header or footer for the first page in a document, click on the Different First Page check box.

Deleting a header or footer

Deleting a header or footer is also a simple task. Choose the Header and Footer command from the View menu and then select the text that you want to delete in the header or footer. Press Delete or the Backspace key to remove the text. If you want to delete other headers or footers, click on the Show Next button on the Header and Footer toolbar to display the next header or footer. Then follow the steps to delete the text.

Adjusting margin settings

Headers and footers are printed in the top and bottom margins. If the header or footer is too large to fit in the margin, Word adjusts the top or bottom margin so that the header or footer will fit. If you don't want Word to adjust the margins, choose the Page Setup command from the File menu. In the Margins tab of the Page Setup dialog box, enter a hyphen before the Top or Bottom margin setting. If the header or footer is too large, it may overwrite the main document.

Positioning headers and footers

You may want to adjust the position of your headers and footers in your document. You can adjust the horizontal position by centering it, running it into the left or right margin, or aligning it with the left or right margin. There are two preset tabs in the header and footer areas. One is centered between the left and right margins, and one is right aligned at the default right margin. You can use these tabs to place a page number flush right and to center text in the headers and footers. (If you change the margins, you may also want to adjust the tab stops.)

For a left-aligned header or footer, type the text where the cursor first appears in the text box. For a centered header or footer, tab once to the center and begin typing. You may also use the alignment buttons on the Formatting toolbar to center, left align, right align, or justify your headers or footers. If you want to add a negative indent to your header or footer, drag the indent markers on the ruler or use the Paragraph command from the Format menu to place a negative indent in your header or footer. (Remember, you need to select the header or footer before using the Paragraph command.)

You can adjust the vertical position of the header or footer by adjusting the distance of the footer from the top or bottom of the page. Simply click on the Page Setup button on the Headers and Footers toolbar. Then select the Margins tab and make the necessary changes by typing or selecting the distance that you want from the edge of the paper.

You can also adjust the space between the header or footer and the main document. Go to the header or footer that you want to adjust. Move your pointer to the vertical ruler at the left of your screen and point to the top or bottom margin boundary. The pointer becomes a double-headed arrow. If you want to reduce the space between the top of the document text and the header, simply drag the top margin boundary up or down. To adjust the space between the bottom of the document text and the footer, drag the bottom margin boundary up or down.

Page Numbers

Inserting page numbers is one of the easiest of all formatting jobs. Choose Insert⇨Page Numbers to bring up the Page Numbers dialog box shown in Figure 3-16.

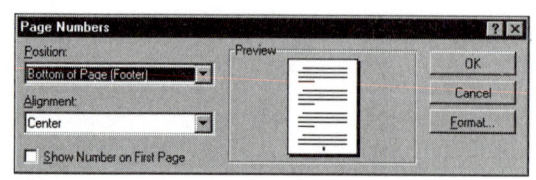

Figure 3-16: The Page Numbers dialog box.

In this dialog box, you can change the position and the alignment of page numbers by using the corresponding list boxes. If you press the Format button, you open the Page Number Format dialog box. This dialog box lets you change the number format. For example, you may want to use letters instead of numbers or roman numerals. You also can add chapter numbers to your document, but you have to tell Word where a new chapter begins. To indicate where a new chapter begins, use the Chapter Starts With Style list box, which causes Word to look for the style that is designated as the chapter heading for each chapter. You also have the option of numbering from a previous section if you don't want to number the entire document. And finally, you can ask Word to start numbering from a specific page.

Footnotes

Word's capability to display multiple portions of a document simultaneously makes adding footnotes to a Word document a simple matter. You can look at and work with the text of a footnote in a separate pane, while the related portion of your document remains visible. Word, like most word processors, lets you position footnotes either at the bottom of each page or collectively at the end of the document. (When footnotes are placed at the end of a document, they are called *endnotes*.) However, in Word you can also put a footnote directly beneath the text to which it applies or at the end of a section.

To add a footnote, first place the insertion point where the footnote reference mark (such as a superscript number) is to appear in the text. Then choose the Insert⇨Footnote command to bring up the Footnote and Endnote dialog box shown in Figure 3-17.

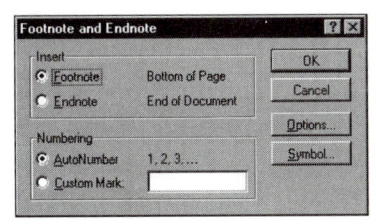

Figure 3-17: The Footnote and Endnote dialog box.

In this dialog box, you can specify whether you want the footnote to be automatically numbered by Word (the default), or you can enter a reference mark of your own choosing, such as an asterisk or a number in parentheses. The Options button displays another dialog box that lets you control the placement of footnotes and the number format that you want.

After you click on OK, a footnote pane opens in the bottom portion of the screen (Figure 3-18) where you type the desired footnote. When the footnote pane is open, a split bar appears in the vertical scroll bar. Mouse users can drag the split bar up or down to change the size of the pane. At any time when you are working with footnotes, you can return to the main part of the document while leaving the footnote pane open. Press F6 (Next Pane). When you are finished typing the footnote, you can drag the split bar to close the footnote pane or click on the Close button. You can see footnotes in your document only if you are in Page Layout view.

Part II ✦ Word

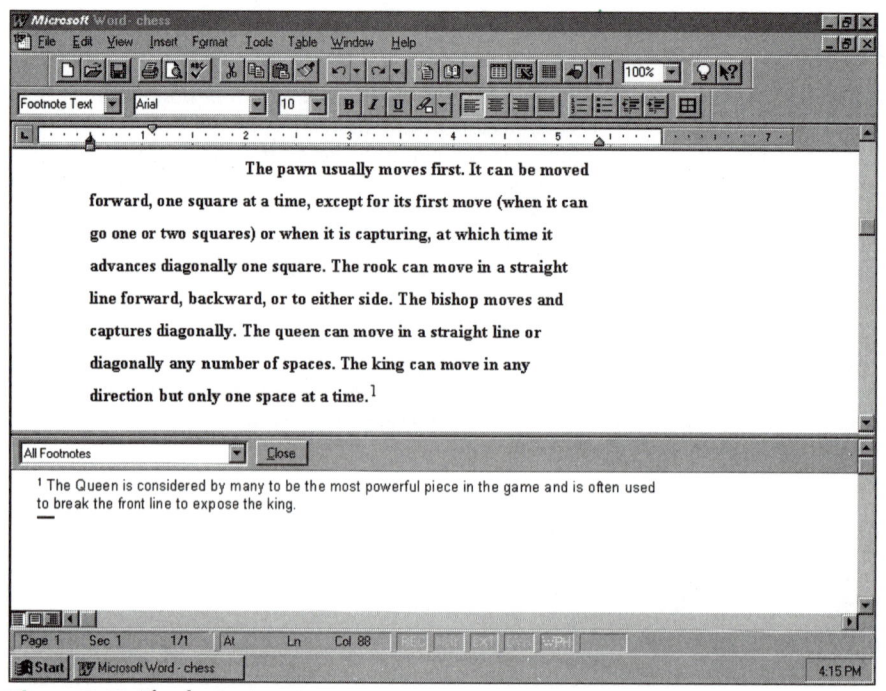

Figure 3-18: The footnote pane.

Try adding a footnote to the sample document that you created earlier in the chapter or to a paragraph of your own choosing. After you create the footnote, the following sections will show you how to edit and delete the footnote text, position both the reference marks and the footnotes themselves, and define the separator line at the bottom of the page. Follow these steps to add a footnote to a document:

1. Switch to Normal view and put the insertion point at the end of a paragraph. You can use the chess document you created earlier, or you can use a document of your own choosing. If you use the chess document, place the insertion point at the end of the second full paragraph of text.

2. Choose Insert➪Footnote.

3. To accept automatic numbering for footnotes, choose OK from the dialog box. Word places a superscript reference number at the end of the paragraph in the document and opens the footnote pane for the footnote text.

4. Type the following text in the footnote pane:

    The Queen is considered by many to be the most powerful piece in the game and is often used to break the front line to expose the king.

5. Click on the Close button or use the Alt+V+F shortcut to close the footnote pane. (This shortcut acts like a toggle switch to open and close the footnote window.)

If you have used the sample document for your exercise, your footnote should look like the one in Figure 3-19.

Hot Stuff: You can return to the document and keep the footnote pane open by pressing F3.

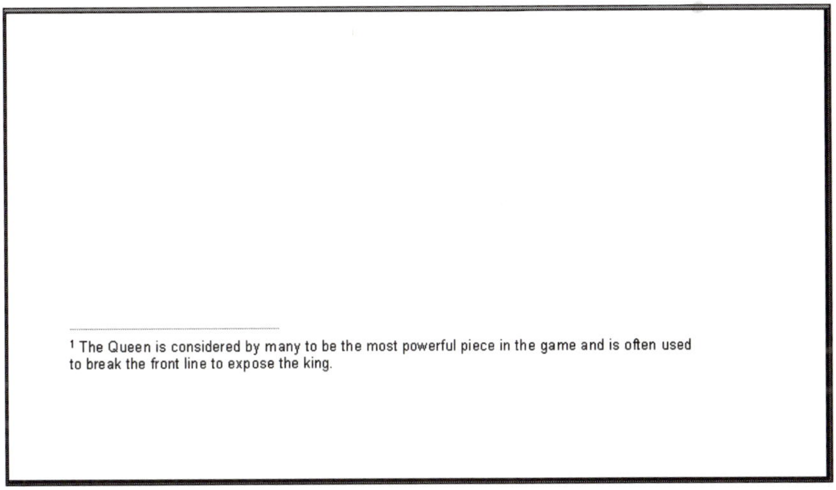

[1] The Queen is considered by many to be the most powerful piece in the game and is often used to break the front line to expose the king.

Figure 3-19: A footnote added to end of a sample document in Page Layout view.

Editing existing footnotes

To edit an existing footnote, open the footnote pane with the View⇨Footnotes command. Scroll within the footnote pane to find the desired footnote and edit it as you would regular text.

Hot Stuff: You can quickly jump from footnote to footnote with the Go To key (F5). Press F5 and click on Footnote in the Go to What list box. Then use the Next and Previous buttons to jump through the footnotes until you find the one that you want, or enter the footnote number in the Footnote Number box and click on OK to go to that footnote.

Moving and deleting footnotes

Footnotes are indicated by the reference marks in the document, so moving or deleting a footnote is as easy as moving or deleting the reference mark.

- ✦ To move a footnote, select the reference mark within the document and move it to the desired new location.
- ✦ To delete a footnote, select the reference mark and press Delete or use Edit⇨Cut. If you used Word's automatic footnote numbering, the footnotes are renumbered accordingly. If you numbered footnotes manually, you need to renumber them yourself as necessary.

Exploring footnote options

In the Footnote and Endnote dialog box is the Options button. After you click on this button, the Note Options dialog box appears, as shown in Figure 3-20. Click on the All Footnotes tab to choose options that apply to footnotes, or click on the All Endnotes tab to choose options that apply to endnotes.

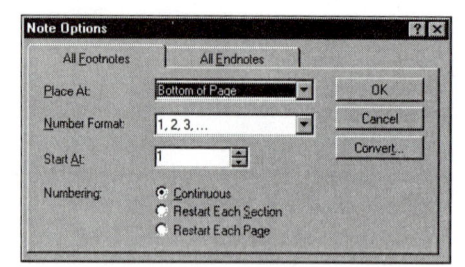

Figure 3-20: The Note Options dialog box.

The Place At list box in the All Footnotes tab lets you determine the placement of the footnotes. You can choose between Bottom of Page or Beneath Text. Select Bottom of Page to place the footnotes for a given page at the bottom of that page. The Beneath Text choice places the footnote directly after the text containing the footnote reference mark.

The Number Format list box lets you choose the type of numbers that you want to use for the footnotes. The Start At box lets you change the starting number for automatically numbered footnotes. If you want Word to restart the automatic numbering each time a new section begins, turn on the Restart Each Section option in the Numbering area.

Changing footnotes to endnotes

Changing all your footnotes (or just one footnote) to endnotes is easy. Activate the footnote window by choosing the Footnotes command from the View menu. Select the footnotes that you want to convert to endnotes by moving the cursor to the beginning of each. Right-click in the footnote pane to open the shortcut menu. You will notice two new menu options: Go to Footnote and Convert to Endnote. Choose Convert to Endnote to convert the footnote to an endnote. Now, to see the kind of note you want, choose it from the Notes box in the footnote window.

You can also copy and move a footnote by using the regular Cut, Copy, and Paste commands or by clicking and dragging it to its new location. You can delete a footnote by highlighting the reference mark and pressing Delete.

Summary

In this chapter, you have read about all sorts of formatting techniques that you will use often if you work in Word on a regular basis. The chapter covered these points:

- ✦ In Word, you can apply formatting to characters, paragraphs, pages, or sections of a document.
- ✦ To apply formatting to characters, you can use the various buttons of the Formatting toolbar that apply to character formatting, or you can use the Format⇨Font command.
- ✦ To apply formatting to paragraphs, you can use the various buttons of the Formatting toolbar that apply to paragraph formatting, or you can use the Format⇨Paragraph command.
- ✦ You can apply borders and shadings to paragraphs by using the Format⇨Borders and Shading command.
- ✦ You can change most aspects of page formatting through the various tabs of the Page Setup dialog box. To display the dialog box, use the File⇨Page Setup command.
- ✦ Section formatting can also be applied through the use of the File⇨Page Setup command, by using the options that appear under the Layout tab of the resulting Page Setup dialog box.
- ✦ You can add headers and footers to a document with the View⇨Header and Footer command.
- ✦ You can add footnotes and endnotes to a document with the Insert⇨Footnote command.

Where to go next...

- ✦ Now that you've explored so many aspects of document formatting, you're probably anxious to try printing some examples of your work. Chapter 4 will set you right up.
- ✦ You can make many common formatting tasks easier by applying *styles* to portions of your document. You'll find details in Chapter 8.

✦ ✦ ✦

CHAPTER 4

Previewing and Printing Your Documents

In This Chapter

Printing in the background

Previewing documents

Adjusting margins in Print Preview mode

Multiple printings

Changing print orientation

Changing the printer setup

Printing envelopes

This chapter details how you print your documents and how you can preview them prior to printing. Keep in mind that your printer must be set up and ready before you can print documents — an obvious point, maybe, but many printer problems can be traced to an incorrect printer setup or to a printer that was never turned on.

Printing in the Background

If you just have one printer connected to your computer (and you know it works with other Windows applications), you can print a single copy of any document in Word with one simple action: a mouse click on the Print button on the Standard toolbar. (The Print button is ridiculously easy to find — it's the only one with a picture of a printer on it.) When you open any document and click on the Print button, Word sends one copy of the document to the printer. As the document is processed by the built-in Windows Print Manager, the status bar in Word displays the progress of the printing process. Note that by default, Word prints in the background and creates an image of the document on disk that can be sent to the printer when the printer is ready to receive data. So unless you're printing to a network laser printer that is the size of a compact car (one of those big, *fast* models), Word is likely to finish the printing process long before your printer does.

If your system doesn't print in the background — instead, it waits until the printing is finished before it frees Word to do something else — you can change the system. Choose Tools⇨Options, click on the Print tab, turn on the Background Printing option, and click on the OK button. Your system will print in the background.

Previewing Documents

The Print Preview command from the File menu (and the Print Preview button on the Standard toolbar) lets you see on your screen what a document will look like when you print it (see Figure 4-1). Print Preview saves trees: you don't waste paper printing draft copies before printing a final copy. Print Preview shows footnotes, headers, footers, page numbers, multiple columns, and graphics. You can view more than one page at a time by clicking on the Multiple Pages button on the Print Preview toolbar and selecting the number of pages that you want to see at one time. You can easily move between pages, but you cannot edit a document while in Print Preview mode.

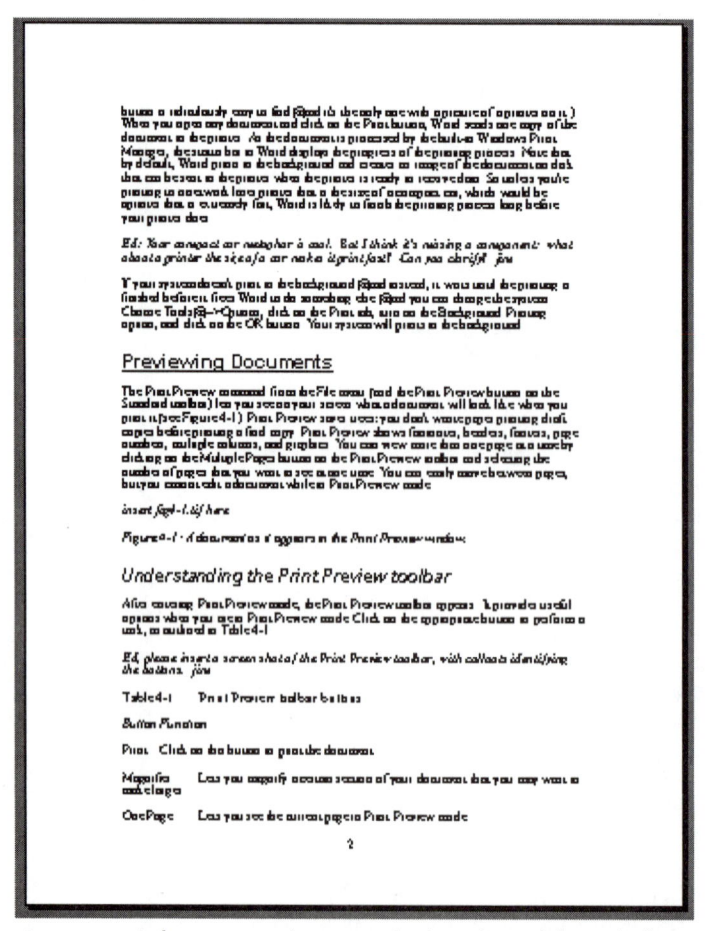

Figure 4-1: A document as it appears in the Print Preview window.

Understanding the Print Preview toolbar

After entering Print Preview mode, the Print Preview toolbar (Figure 4-2) appears. It provides useful options when you are in Print Preview mode. Click on the appropriate button to perform a task, as outlined in Table 4-1.

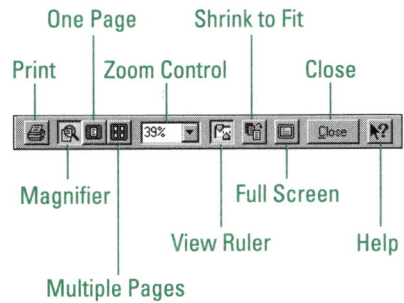

Figure 4-2: The Print Preview toolbar.

Table 4-1
Print Preview toolbar buttons

Button	Function
Print	Click on this button to print the document.
Magnifier	Lets you magnify a certain section of your document that you may want to make larger.
One Page	Lets you see the current page in Print Preview mode.
Multiple Pages	Lets you see up to six pages at once on-screen. These pages appear so that you can see the layout of each page.
Zoom Control	Lets you control the distance at which you see the pages on the Print Preview window.
View Ruler	Lets you see a ruler for each of the pages that you have on-screen so that you can move the margins in Print Preview mode.
Shrink to Fit	Lets you shrink information so that it will all fit on one page. This feature helps you keep paragraphs together.
Full Screen	Lets you see your document in Full Screen mode.
Close	Returns you to Normal view.
Help	Provides online help for your printing questions.

Hot Stuff A quick way out of Print Preview mode is to press the Esc key.

Many commands from the normal Word menus are not available when you are in Print Preview mode. These commands appear dimmed on the menus. Remember that you cannot open files or change windows while you are in Print Preview mode.

Adjusting margins and object locations

Although you cannot edit documents in Print Preview mode, you can make changes to some aspects of the document, such as the location of page margins, headers, and footers. You can easily make changes to page margins by turning on the ruler. Choose View⇨Ruler. Then select the text by clicking on the Magnifier icon to change to the arrow. Next click and drag to select the text you wish to highlight. Now, move the triangles on the ruler until the document takes on the appearance that you want. You can also use clicking and dragging techniques to move graphics in your document while you are in Print Preview mode.

If you inserted an object, such as a picture, into your document, you may want to frame it so that you can drag it to any location while you are in Print Preview. To frame the object while you are in Print Preview, first click on the Magnifier button to turn off the magnifier. Then right-click on the picture that you want to frame. Choose Frame Picture from the shortcut menu to add a frame to the graphic. When you do this, the frame appears around the graphic.

To format the lines of the frame or perform other maintenance to the lines, right-click on the lines of the frame. From the shortcut menu, choose Borders and Shading. This opens the Picture Borders and Shading dialog box shown in Figure 4-3.

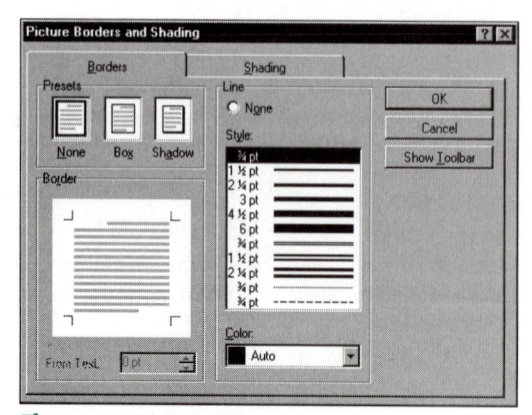

Figure 4-3: The Picture Borders and Shading dialog box.

The Borders tab of this dialog box lets you choose what kind of border to use, as well as the thickness of the border's line. You can also choose how far to place the border from the text. The Borders tab also contains some spacing presets.

The Shading tab of the Picture Borders and Shading dialog box is used to choose shading for the area inside the frame. You can choose from the different available shading percentages shown in Figure 4-4. You can also choose the frame's foreground and background colors.

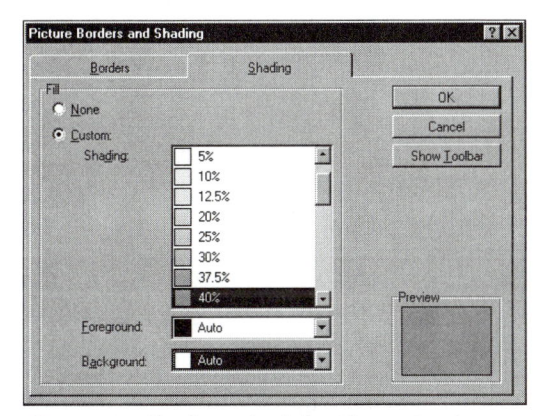

Figure 4-4: Shading tab of the Picture Borders and Shading dialog box.

If the text does not wrap around the frame, it means that text wrapping is not turned on. Right-click on the frame and choose Format⇨Frame. In the Text Wrapping section of the Frame dialog box, select the Around option so that the text will wrap.

You can use the Horizontal area of the Frame dialog box to control the alignment of the insertion. You can also center the entry relative to the margins, page, or columns on the page by making the corresponding choice from the Relative To box in the Horizontal and Vertical boxes. Using the Horizontal and Vertical boxes, you can also distance the text from the entry to your liking.

Printing a Document

Any word processor lets you print a document. But Word gives you more — you can print selected portions of a document; multiple copies of a document; and other information related to a document, such as summary information, annotations, AutoText entries, or style sheets. You can print documents by choosing File⇨Print. The Print dialog box appears, as shown in Figure 4-5.

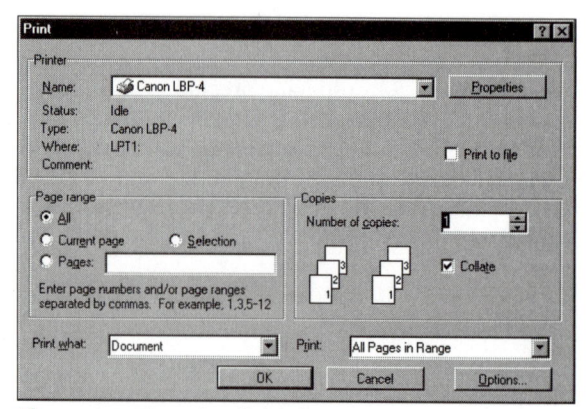

Figure 4-5: The Print dialog box.

The available options in the Print dialog box include:

- ✦ **Printer** — The Printer list box lets you choose the default printer that you want to use by selecting it from the entries. After making a selection, Word provides you with the status and location of the printer.

  Note: If you don't see the printer that you want to use in the list box, you need to install it. Consult your Windows documentation for the steps.

- ✦ **Copies** — In the Copies area, you can enter the number of copies that you want printed in the Number of copies list box (the default is 1). This area also lets you collate copies. When you check the Collate option for more than one copy of a document, Word prints all the pages of each document before it goes on to the next set. If you do not check this option, Word prints all needed copies of page 1, followed by all copies of page 2, followed by all copies of page 3, and so on.

- ✦ **Page range** — In the Page range area, you can choose which portion of the document should be printed. Choose All to print the entire document; choose Selection to print a selection of text; choose Current page to print just the current page; or to print selected pages of a document, choose Pages to print.

  Hot Stuff: You can print a range of pages by separating the starting and ending pages with a hyphen. For example, entering 7-12 in the box will print pages 7 through 12 of the document. You can also separate numbers by commas to print individual pages. For example, entering 3,5,8,10-12 in the box will cause pages 3, 5, 8, and 10 through 12 to be printed.

- ✦ **Print** — In the Print list box, you can choose All Pages in Range to print all the pages in the chosen print range (as selected in the Page range area of the dialog box). Or you can choose to print only the odd pages or only the even pages in the range.

✦ **Options** — You can click on the Options button to display additional options relating to printing (see the "Using the Print Options" section later in this chapter).

✦ **Properties** — The Properties button opens the Printer Properties dialog box shown in Figure 4-6 (the dialog box in this figure will look a little different from yours, unless you have the same printer we do). In this dialog box, you can set different options for your printer. The properties in this dialog box will be different for each printer.

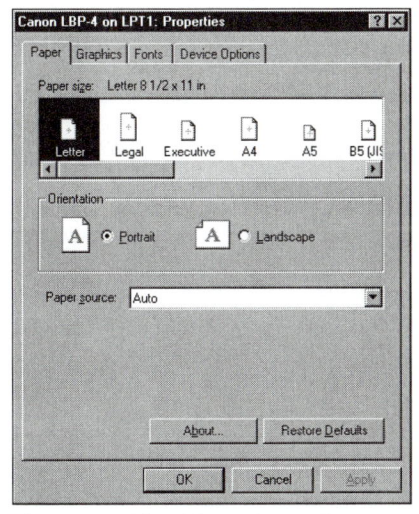

Figure 4-6: The Printer Properties dialog box for Canon LBP-4 Printer.

✦ **Print what** — Use this box to choose what to print. You can print key assignments, summary information, annotations, AutoText entries, and other items related to your documents.

Note You can use the Print key combination (Ctrl+Shift+F12) rather than File➪Print to open the Print dialog box and to make your printing selections. You can also press Ctrl+P to activate the Print dialog box; this is a useful time-saver if you wish to print quickly.

After you have chosen your desired options in the Print dialog box, click on the OK button to start printing.

If you have problems . . .

If you have difficulty printing, or if the printer name in the dialog box doesn't match the printer that is connected to your computer, choose File⇨Print and click on the name list box in the Printer field of the dialog box that appears. This opens the list of printers installed under Windows 95. Select the troublesome printer and then click on the OK button. Try the Print command again. If the correct printer is selected and you still can't print, the problem is either inside the printer itself, with how Windows 95 is set up on your system, or that the printer you wish to use is not installed under Windows 95.

If the printer you wish to use is not installed under Windows 95, perform the following steps:

1. From the Taskbar's Start menu, choose Settings, and then Printers.

2. In the window that appears, double-click on the Add Printers icon and follow the instructions from the Add Printer Wizard.

Word uses the Windows 95 Print Manager to manage all printing. If you can't print from another Windows application (such as WordPad), you can't print from Word, either. If you can't print from Windows, refer to your Windows documentation or the *Microsoft Word for Windows Printer Guide* (supplied with your Word documentation). Also, be sure to check the obvious — make sure that the printer is properly connected, turned on, and online. If you still can't find the source of the problem, you can find many helpful troubleshooting tips in the *Printer Guide*.

Printing a portion of a document

You will encounter times when you want to print only a section of a document. You can choose between two methods to print a section of text. First, you can choose a starting and ending page number to print and enter the page numbers in the Pages text box in the Page range area of the Print dialog box. Word prints the starting and ending page and all pages in between. Or, you can first select a portion of text and then turn on the Selection option in the Page range area of the Print dialog box to print just that selection.

For a more detailed look at the steps involved in printing a section of a document, take a look at the steps that follow. To print selected pages of a document, perform the following steps:

1. With the document open, choose File⇨Print.

2. In the Page range area, click on the Current page radio button to print the current page. Or click on the Pages radio button and enter the starting page number that you want to print. If you want to print consecutive page numbers, separate them with a hyphen. Nonconsecutive page numbers should be separated by a comma.

3. Click on the OK button. The selected pages of the document print.

To print a selection of text, perform the following steps.

1. Select the text that you want to print by using the usual methods for selecting text.
2. With the document open, choose File➪Print.
3. Click on the Selection radio button.
4. Click on the OK button to print the selected text.

Printing more than documents

To print something other than the document itself, click on the down arrow of the Print what list box in the Print dialog box to reveal the list of options that you can print (see Figure 4-7). If you choose Document (the default), Word prints the document. If you choose Summary Info, Word prints just the summary information for the document. If you choose Annotations, Word prints all annotations stored in a document. If you choose Styles, Word prints the style sheet for the document. If you choose AutoText Entries, Word prints the template AutoText entries. If you choose Key Assignments, Word prints the names of macros and the keys to which they are assigned.

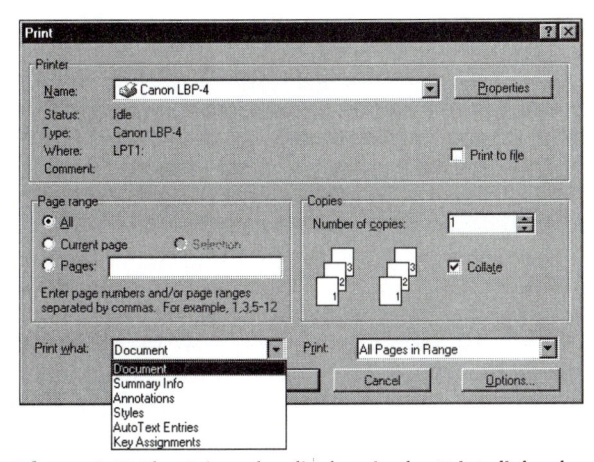

Figure 4-7: The Print what list box in the Print dialog box.

Note You can print summary information or annotations simultaneously with the printing of the document. See the "Using the Print Options" section later in this chapter for more information on how to print these items simultaneously.

Printing sideways

On occasion, you may want to print a document sideways, or in what is known as *landscape orientation*. Such a technique is particularly useful with very wide documents, such as those that contain a table of numbers or documents containing pictures. If your printer supports landscape printing, you can easily print documents that use landscape orientation.

To print a document in landscape orientation, choose File⇨Page Setup and click on the Paper Size tab of the Page Setup dialog box. In the Orientation area, click on the Landscape radio button and then click on the OK button. Now you can print the document by choosing File⇨Print. If there is no Landscape option in the Page Setup dialog box, then your printer does not support landscape printing, and you cannot print sideways under Windows.

Hot Stuff

When you are finished printing in landscape orientation, be sure to change your paper orientation back to normal (portrait) mode. If you do not make the change, all successive printings will be in landscape mode. To change back to portrait mode, choose File⇨Page Setup and click on the Paper Size tab. Then click on the Portrait radio button in the Orientation area of the dialog box.

Using the Print Options

You can find additional printing options in the Print dialog box. These options enable you to include annotations or summary information with documents, to print in reverse order, and to print draft versions of documents. To use these options, choose File⇨Print and then click on the Options button. The Options dialog box appears with the Print tab activated, as shown in Figure 4-8. To choose any of the desired options, click on the option or press the Alt key plus the underlined letter of the option name.

The Print tab options include the following:

✦ **Draft Output** — When you choose the Draft Output option, Word prints a draft of your document. A *draft* is a document that is printed with minimal formatting. This would be a document where the character formatting is removed. This allows you to print your documents faster.

✦ **Reverse Print Order** — The Reverse Print Order option causes the document to be printed last page first. This option is helpful with laser printers that are based on the first-generation Canon engine (like the original Hewlett-Packard LaserJet). The design of such printers causes printed pages to come out face up, so a multiple-page document would be stacked with the last page on top (which is usually not where you want it). If you turn on the Reverse Print Order option, however, the print run starts with the last page and ends with the first page so that the printed document ends up in the proper order.

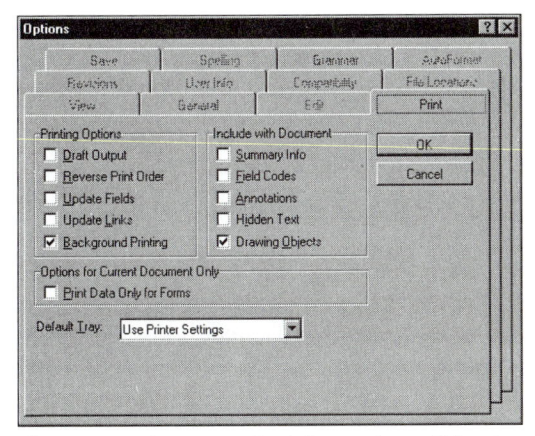

Figure 4-8: The Print tab of the Options dialog box.

- ✦ **Update Fields** — The Update Fields option makes Word update any fields that are in a document before it is printed.

- ✦ **Update Links** — When you choose the Update Links option, Word updates any fields that are in a document before it is printed.

- ✦ **Background Printing** — The Background Printing option lets you work in Word while you're printing. However, this option uses memory, so you may want to turn it off to speed up printing.

- ✦ **Include with Document** — Use the Include with Document options to specify which information should be included with the printed document. If you turn on Summary Info, a summary information sheet is printed along with the document. Turn on Field Codes to print field codes instead of the results of the fields. If you turn on Annotations, Word prints the document and any annotations added to the document. Turn on Hidden Text to print the document and any text that you hid with the Hidden option from the Character dialog box. Also, you will see the Drawing Objects check box. This will print the drawing objects you may have included in your document.

- ✦ **Default Tray** — The Default Tray list box lets you select different paper feed bins (assuming that your printer allows feeding from different paper bins). Actual choices depend upon the printer you have installed. Typical choices are:

    - **Manual** — Choose Manual to make the printer draw paper from its manual bin.
    - **Auto** — Choose Auto for automatic paper feed.
    - **Bin 1, Bin 2, Bin 3** — Choose Bin 1, 2, or 3 to draw paper from a specific bin.

- **Mixed** — Choose Mixed to feed the first sheet from bin 1 and successive sheets from bin 2. Mixed feeding is a common technique with high-production office laser printers, which may have company letterhead stored in one bin and bond paper stored in another bin.

If the Default Tray option appears dimmed in your dialog box, then your printer does not support feeding from multiple paper bins. From Print Manager is the default setting for this option. If you wish to change it, click on the arrow and choose one of the feeding options from the list.

✦ **Options for Current Document Only** — This area applies the options that you select to the current document, but returns to the default options for the next print job. Print Data Only for Forms is used to print just the data for forms that may be in your documents.

Changing Your Printer Setup

Word provides access to the printer setup facility of Windows through File➪Print. You can choose the default printer from among different printers. The Print dialog box lets you select a printer that is already installed under Windows in the name list box; however, you cannot use this dialog box to choose a printer that is not yet installed under Windows. (See your Windows documentation if you need to add a new printer to your Windows configuration.)

Note Only one printer can use the same connection (*printer port*) at a time. If you change printers and the new printer is connected to the same printer port, you must use the Windows Control Panel to change the printer connection. To change the setting, choose Settings from the Start menu and then choose Control Panel. Double-click on the Printers icon. Right-click on the printer for which you want to change the port. Then choose Properties from the shortcut menu and select the Details tab (see Figure 4-9). In this tab, you can change the port for the printer. See your Windows documentation for more details (Remember that the actual appearance of this dialog box depends upon the printer you're using.)

If you want only to change printers, you can do so from the Print dialog box if the printer is already installed. Choose File➪Print. In the Print dialog box, click on the arrow in the Name list box to open the menu of available printers. Choose the printer that you want and then click on the OK button to print the document. If you click on the Properties button in the Print dialog box, you will see the printing options for the new printer. Figure 4-10 shows the printing options for a Canon LBP-4 printer. These options vary, depending on the type of printer that you have installed. Because there are literally hundreds of printers on the market, it is impossible to explain all the possible settings here. Each printer's dialog box contains the options that are applicable to that particular printer. What's more, most dialog boxes contain buttons for choosing between portrait (the default) and landscape printing.

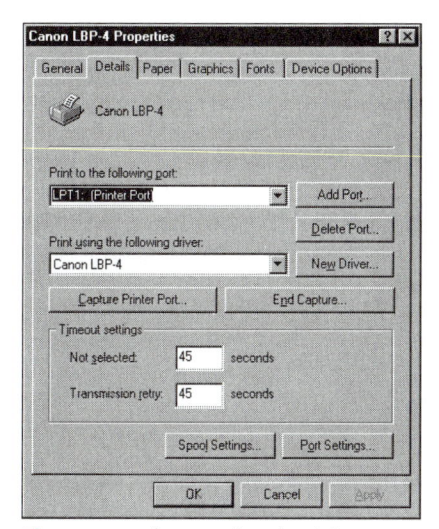

Figure 4-9: The Details tab of the Printer Properties dialog box.

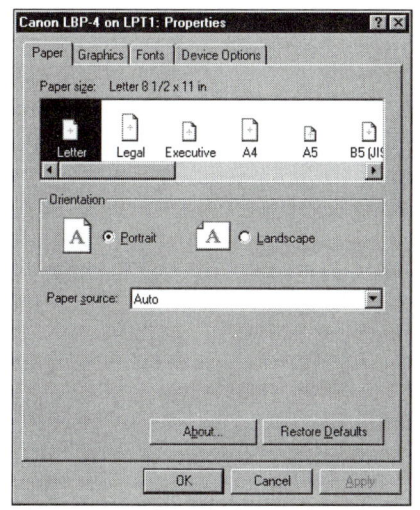

Figure 4-10: The printing options for a Canon LBP-4 printer.

If you are using a laser printer that employs font cartridges, you can select the fonts from a list box in the Print Setup dialog box. Refer to the *Microsoft Word for Windows Printer Guide* to determine the fonts that can be used with your particular laser printer.

Printing Envelopes

Word has an envelope-printing feature that makes printing envelopes a very simple matter if your printer is able to handle envelopes. Choose Tools⇨Envelopes and Labels to open the Envelopes and Labels dialog box (see Figure 4-11). In this dialog box, you are provided with two text boxes where you can enter a delivery and return address. In the Return Address text box, Word enters, by default, the name stored under the User Info tab of the Options dialog box. If you want to change the kind of envelope that you are printing, click on the envelope in the Preview window or click on the Options button to open the Envelope Options dialog box shown in Figure 4-12.

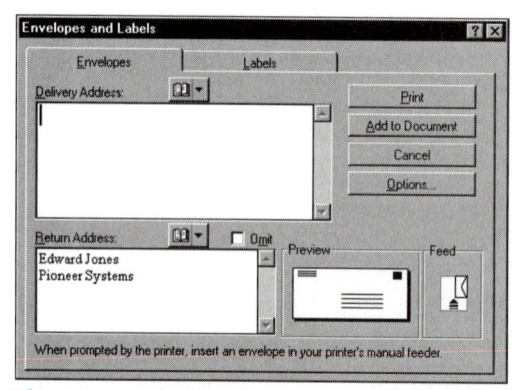

Figure 4-11: The Envelopes and Labels dialog box.

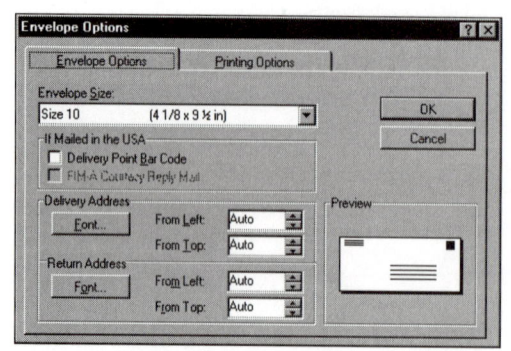

Figure 4-12: The Envelope Options dialog box.

The Envelope Options dialog box contains two tabs. The Envelope Options tab lets you change the kind of envelope that you are printing, to add delivery point bar codes and courtesy facing ID marks, to format the delivery and return addresses, and to control the positioning of the text on the envelope. The Printing Options tab of the Envelope Options dialog box lets you control the way envelopes are printed (see Figure 4-13). You can choose either a horizontal or a vertical feed method. You can also change the way envelopes are fed into your printer, whether you use a manual tractor, an upper or lower tray, and so on.

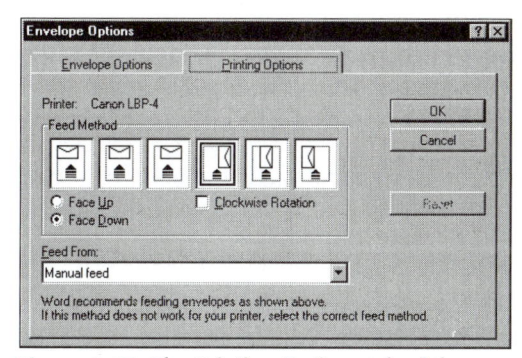

Figure 4-13: The Printing Options tab of the Envelope Options dialog box.

After you have made all the necessary formatting changes, and you have specified the size of the envelope that you want to print, you are ready to print the envelope. Click on the Print button in the Envelopes and Labels dialog box, and your envelope prints.

Summary

In this chapter, you learned how to examine the appearance of documents before you print them and then how you can print the documents in Word. The following points were covered:

- ✦ Choosing File➪Print Preview provides a useful way to see what a document will look like before it is printed.
- ✦ You can quickly print one copy of any document by clicking on the Print button on the Standard toolbar.
- ✦ Using the options shown in the Print dialog box, you can print portions of the document, and you can print other items (such as annotations, styles, macros, and keyboard assignments).

In the next chapter, you will learn how to work with tables and outlines in Word.

Where to go next...

- ✦ Macros let you automate the printing of documents you print regularly. Chapter 9 gives you the lowdown on macros.
- ✦ The appearance of your printed document depends on how your document is formatted. Chapter 3 helps you format your documents.

✦ ✦ ✦

CHAPTER 5

Working with Tables and Outlines

In This Chapter

Creating, editing, and formatting tables

Creating side-by-side paragraphs

Converting text to tables

Sorting information

Understanding outlines

Changing outline headings

Creating a table of contents from an outline

Editing outlines

Printing outlines

Tables are a common feature of business correspondence, but tables in word processing documents have had a reputation for being hard to implement and extremely difficult to modify. These negative characteristics of tables are no longer true with Word's Table feature. Word's Table feature makes it a simple matter to insert tables containing varying amounts of text or graphics.

Outlines are also an important organizational aid in Word. For many who work with words, creating an outline is the first step in getting their thoughts on paper. If you've been working with something less than the power of Word in the past, you may be accustomed to creating outlines by means of tabs and manually typed headings. With Word, there's no need to stay in the Stone Age — Word's automatic outlining enables you automatically to number headings and create tables of contents based on the outline headings.

Understanding Tables in Word for Windows

A *table* is any grouping of information arranged in rows and columns, as illustrated in Figure 5-1. Tables have two or more columns and one or more rows. Each intersection of a row and a column is a *cell* of the table. If you are familiar with computer spreadsheets, such as Excel, you should easily understand the concept of a cell.

Group1	Group2	Group3
Justin Dodd	Kim Dodd	Anne Edheart
Mark Few	Chrissy Laviena	Marino Umana
Tom Elliot	Debbie Carrol	Jose Tellado

Figure 5-1: A sample table.

Before Word's Table feature came along, people typically set up tables by using tabs or indented paragraphs. Although this method works, it is very cumbersome and, well, just awkward. A table set up with tabs can be tricky to design when some cells in the table contain more than one line of text. You have to add all sorts of manual tabs to get the information to line up on-screen, and then there are no guarantees that the table will line up when you print it! Worse, any changes that you make to the table's text will also throw off the alignment of the tabs so that you have to constantly rework the table. Manually creating a table is more trouble than it is worth.

In comparison, Word's Table feature creates a group of cells that expands as needed to fit all your required text or graphics. The only limit to the size of your table is that a single cell cannot be larger than a page. You can resize columns and cells, and you can add rows, columns, and cells. Word also provides useful commands that make life easier when you need to edit the tables. All in all, Word's Table feature is the best way for you to create a table.

By default, a table appears with gridlines surrounding the cells. If you do not see the gridlines surrounding the tables that you create, choose Table⇨Gridlines to turn on the gridlines. Gridlines do not print in your document — they are simply an aid for entering and editing text in tables. You can also add borders (which do appear when printed) to cells or to an entire table (see "Formatting Tables" later in the chapter).

Creating Tables

You can add a table to a document by choosing Table⇨Insert Table or by clicking on the Insert Table button on the Standard toolbar. When you choose the Insert Table command, the Insert Table dialog box appears, as shown in Figure 5-2.

In the Number of Columns text box, you enter the desired number of columns for the table. Word proposes 2, but you can enter any value up to 31. If you are not sure how many columns you will need, don't worry. You can add columns at any time by selecting the column to the right of the table and then choosing the Insert Columns command from the Table menu or clicking on the Insert Columns button on the Standard toolbar.

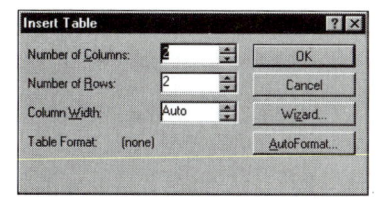

Figure 5-2: The Insert Table dialog box.

In the Number of Rows text box, enter the desired number of rows for the table. It is very easy to add rows as you need them by choosing Table➪Insert Rows or by clicking on the Insert Rows button on the Standard toolbar. (When the insertion point is in a table, the Insert Table button on the toolbar changes to an Insert Rows button. When a column is selected, the button changes to an Insert Columns button.) So if you are not sure how many rows you need, you should enter the minimum number of rows because you can always add more later.

In the Column Width text box, you can leave the setting at Auto, which is the default, or you can enter a decimal measurement for the width of the columns. If you use Auto, Word makes all columns an equal width. How to make columns of differing widths is discussed later.

You may have noticed that this dialog box contains a Wizard button. The Table Wizard takes you through a series of dialog boxes that help determine the table that you need. The wizard then adds the table to your document. Using the Table Wizard is a nice, quick, and easy way to make standard tables with attractive formatting in them.

You can create a table by following these steps:

1. Place the insertion point at the desired location for the table in your document.
2. Choose Table➪Insert Table or click on the Insert Table button on the Standard toolbar.
3. Enter the number of columns desired in the Number of Columns text box and enter the number of rows desired in the Number of Rows text box.
4. Enter the desired column width in the Column Width text box (or accept the Auto default).
5. If you want to have borders or other formatting added to your table, you can click on the AutoFormat button in the dialog box. In the Table AutoFormat dialog box, you can choose from a wide range of effects for your chart (see "Formatting Tables" later in this chapter). You can apply predefined lines, borders, and shading to different sections of the table.
6. When you are finished making your selections, click on the OK button in the dialog box to add the table at the insertion point location.

After you have created a table, you can type the desired data into each cell. You can move forward from cell to cell in the table by using the Tab key; you can move in reverse by using the Shift+Tab combination. If you reach the end of a table and press Tab, you add a new row to the table. The arrow keys will also move the insertion point within the table, and you can use these keys to move into and out of a table. With the mouse, you can click in any cell to place the insertion point in that cell. For a complete summary of the keys used for navigation in tables, see the section "Navigating with the keyboard."

If you use the Insert Table button on the Standard toolbar to add a table, you won't see the dialog box presented in Figure 5-2. Instead, you see a small drop-down table from the menu bar. You can then click and drag across the squares in this box to designate the size of the table that you want to add. For example, if you drag across three rows and five columns of the squares, you will insert a table measuring three rows by five columns. When you release the mouse, the table appears at the insertion point location in your document. The drop-down table defaults to a size of 4×5, but you can size it from a minimum of 1×2 to a maximum of 20×15.

Navigating with the mouse

Navigating inside a table with the mouse works in the same way as navigating in regular text: you point and click at the location where you want the insertion point to be. However, you need to know some additional mouse techniques beyond the obvious. Tables provide special selection areas for mouse use. At the left edge of each cell is a selection bar, an area where the mouse pointer changes to an arrow pointing upward and to the right. If you click on the left edge of a cell while the pointer is shaped like this arrow, you will select the entire cell. You can also double-click in any cell's selection bar to select the entire row of the table. You can also click and drag across cell boundaries to select a group of cells.

At the top of a table is a column selection area. If you place the mouse pointer above the border at the top of the table, the pointer changes to the shape of a downward-pointing arrow, which indicates the column selection mode. If you click while the pointer is shaped like the downward-pointing arrow, you select the entire column below the pointer.

So, how can I type a tab?

Because you use the Tab key to move around within a table, you can't use the Tab key to enter a Tab character. In some ways, this is good because tabs inside tables are dangerous. In the first place, you don't have much horizontal space in the cells to play with. In the second place, the tabs may mess up your overall formatting for the table. Nevertheless, if you must have a tab character inside a table, you can add one by pressing Ctrl+Tab.

Hot Stuff Easily selecting rows and columns with the mouse is a handy technique to know when you have to format portions of your table. You can select the desired cells, rows, or columns and then use Format➪Font and Format➪Paragraph to format your text in those selected cells as desired.

Navigating with the keyboard

To move from cell to cell within a table, you can click on the desired cell with the mouse, or you can use the Tab key (to move forward through cells) or the Shift+Tab combination (to move in reverse). Within a single cell, you can use the same keys that you use to navigate in any Word document. Table 5-1 summarizes the keys that you use to navigate within a table.

Table 5-1
Navigation keys to use within tables

Key	Purpose
Tab	Moves the cursor to the next cell in the table. If the cursor is in the last cell in the table, the Tab key adds a new row and moves the cursor to the first cell of the new row.
Shift+Tab	Moves the cursor to the preceding cell.
Alt+Home	Moves the cursor to the first cell in a row.
Alt+End	Moves the cursor to the last cell in a row.
Alt+PgUp	Moves the cursor to the top cell in a column.
Alt+PgDn	Moves the cursor to the bottom cell in a column.
Alt+NumLock+5	Selects the entire table.
Arrow keys	Moves the cursor within the text in a cell and between cells. If the insertion point is at the edge of a table, you can use the arrow keys to move in or out of the table.

If you press Tab while the insertion point is in the last cell of a table, a new row is automatically added and Word places the insertion point in the first cell of the new row. You can add new rows by choosing Table➪Insert Rows or by clicking on the Insert Rows button on the Standard tool bar, but it is generally easier to add new rows as needed by using the Tab key.

> ### Cells can contain mucho texto . . .
>
> One useful aspect of cells that may not be readily apparent is that you can have more than a single paragraph of text in a cell. At the end of any paragraph in a cell, you can press Enter and keep right on typing. The cell expands as needed to accommodate the text. Longtime users of Word for Windows have often taken advantage of this design trait to create side-by-side columns of unequal size, even though newer versions of Word (like yours) offer specific commands for handling multiple-column documents. And every paragraph in a table can be formatted just like paragraphs that are not in cells of a table; you can assign your paragraphs indentation settings, alignments, line spacing, and the like.

Creating your own table

To get some practice in setting up a table, entering information, and revising a table, follow along with this next exercise. You can also create your own table with your own data, if you want. Follow these steps to create a sample table:

1. Begin a new document by clicking on the New button on the Standard toolbar. Type the following phrase and press Enter to begin a new paragraph:

   Food arrangements for Harin's visit with us

2. Choose Table⇨Insert Table.

3. In the Number of Columns text box, enter **4**.

4. Tab to or click in the Number of Rows text box and enter **6**. For now, you can leave the remaining options as they are.

5. Click on the OK button. The new table, containing six rows and four columns, appears. The insertion point is in the first cell.

6. Enter the information shown in Figure 5-3. Use the Tab key to advance to each new cell. (Do not press the Enter key to advance to a new cell because the Enter key cannot move you out of a cell.)

   Notice that as you enter the information shown in the table, the text in the rightmost column will often be too long to fit on a single line. When this happens, the cell expands in size automatically. This example illustrates one advantage of Word's Table feature: You do not need to calculate the space that you need between rows of a table because Word does this automatically. You can enter as little or as much text as you want in a cell (up to the limit of one page in size).

DAY	WHO	WHAT	WHERE
Monday	Alberta & Kitty	Salads	Garden Oasis of Mill Valley
Tuesday	Brandy & Dirk	Mexican	Las Casas Grandes
Wednesday	Derek	Chinese	N.Aida's Steak House
Thursday	Selita	Pizza	Programmer's Pub
Friday	Chrissy	Health	Mother Nature's Bar and Grill

Figure 5-3: A sample table containing lunch arrangements.

7. After you have finished entering the information in Step 6, move your cursor into the cell containing the text "Programmer's Pub." Use the End key to get to the end of the existing text and then press Enter to begin a new paragraph. Type the following text:

   (reservations will need to be made in advance if we want to obtain the best seating)

   Notice how Word expands the table as necessary to accommodate all the necessary information (see Figure 5-4).

> **More Info** Remember that you can insert graphics into the cells of a table. To do so, use the cut-and-paste technique for graphic images that is detailed in Chapter 10.

Editing Tables

You can edit a table in many ways after you have created it and added text. You can add or delete columns and rows, you can merge the information from more than one cell, and you can split your table into more than one part. This section looks at how to do all these things in a table.

But before you can edit a table, you must learn how to select the cells in a table. To select cells in a table, use the same selection methods that you use in regular text. Briefly, you can click and drag across text in one or more cells with the mouse, or you can hold down the Shift key while you use the arrow keys. You can also use any of the Alt key combinations shown in Table 5-1. While selecting, as you move the insertion point past the end of text in a particular cell, text in the adjacent cell is selected. If there is no text in a cell, the entire cell is selected as you move through it while dragging.

DAY	WHO	WHAT	WHERE
Monday	Alberta & Kitty	Salads	Garden Oasis of Mill Valley
Tuesday	Brandy & Dirk	Mexican	Las Casas Grandes
Wednesday	Derek	Chinese	N.Aida's Steak House
Thursday	Selita	Pizza	Programmer's Pub (reservations will need to be made in advance if we want to obtain the best seating)
Friday	Chrissy	Health	Mother Nature's Bar and Grill

Figure 5-4: Word expands the table to accommodate more information.

Inserting and deleting cells

When you need to remove rows, columns, or cells from a table, first select the cells that you want to delete and then choose Table⇨Delete Cells. The Delete Cells dialog box (see Figure 5-5) lets you shift the cells left after deletion, shift the cells up after deletion, or delete entire rows or columns.

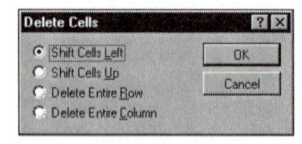

Figure 5-5: The Delete Cells dialog box.

You can use the Insert Cells command to insert a cell or a group of cells. First select the cell next to where you want to insert the cell or group of cells. Then choose Table⇨Insert Cells or click on the Insert Cells button on the Standard toolbar. The Insert Cells dialog box shown in Figure 5-6 asks whether you want to insert a row of cells or whether you want the cells to shift after you add them to the table.

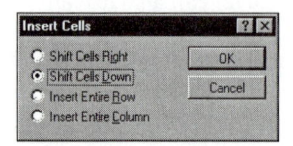

Figure 5-6: The Insert Cells dialog box.

How the insertion or deletion of cells affects the table depends on what you delete or add and whether you choose to shift the cells horizontally or vertically. As an example, Figure 5-7 shows a table measuring 5 rows by 2 columns — ten cells.

FIRST	SECOND
THIRD	FOURTH
FIFTH	SIXTH
SEVENTH	EIGHTH
NINTH	TENTH

Figure 5-7: A 5 × 2 table.

If you select a cell or a group of cells (in the examples that follow, the third and fourth cells are selected), choose Table⇨Insert Cells, and then choose Shift Cells Right in the dialog box, the new cell or cells are inserted at the selection location, and the existing cells are moved to the right, as shown in Figure 5-8.

FIRST	SECOND		
		THIRD	FOURTH
FIFTH	SIXTH		
SEVENTH	EIGHTH		
NINTH	TENTH		

Figure 5-8: The table from Figure 5-7 after choosing Shift Cells Right from the Insert Cells dialog box.

If you select a cell or a group of cells, choose Table⇨Insert Cells, and then choose Shift Cells Down in the dialog box, the new cell or cells are inserted at the selection location, and the existing cells are moved down, as illustrated in Figure 5-9.

FIRST	SECOND
THIRD	FOURTH
FIFTH	SIXTH
SEVENTH	EIGHTH
NINTH	TENTH

Figure 5-9: The table from Figure 5-7 after choosing Shift Cells Down from the Insert Cells dialog box.

If you select a cell or a group of cells and choose Table➪Delete Cells, you again have the choice of choosing to shift the cells up or to the left. Figure 5-10 shows the example table if the fifth and seventh cells were selected and the Shift Cells Left option was chosen.

FIRST	SECOND
THIRD	FOURTH
SIXTH	
EIGHTH	
NINTH	TENTH

Figure 5-10: The table from Figure 5-7 after choosing Shift Cells Left from the Insert Cells dialog box.

Merging cells

Once in a while, you may need to merge information from one group of cells into one cell. You can merge a group of horizontally adjacent cells into a single cell by first selecting the cells that you want to merge and then choosing Table➪Merge Cells. After choosing the command, the information merges into one cell. As an example, consider the simple table shown in Figure 5-11.

Group 1	Group 2	Group 3	Group 4
Alberta Sutton	Selita Sutton	Epey White	Felton White
Alice Royals	Jim Royals	Ricky Stephens	Kirk Stephens
Leona Sutton	Michael Whitfield	Eric Whitfield	Vanessa Williams

Figure 5-11: A table before cells are merged.

If you were to select the two cells at the right end of the top row of the table, and choose Table➪Merge Cells, the result would resemble that shown in Figure 5-12, where the adjoining cells are merged into one cell. Note that any text in the cells is also merged into a single entry, as demonstrated in the example.

Group 1	Group 2	Group 3 Group 4	
Alberta Sutton	Selita Sutton	Epey White	Felton White
Alice Royals	Jim Royals	Ricky Stephens	Kirk Stephens
Leona Sutton	Michael Whitfield	Eric Whitfield	Vanessa Williams

Figure 5-12: The same table after cells are merged.

Note If you merge cells and you don't like the result, keep in mind that you can undo the operation by immediately choosing Edit➪Undo Merge Cells.

Splitting a table

You can also split a table in two horizontally at a point between any given rows. When you choose Table➪Split Table, the table is split in two just above the insertion point. (You can also use the Ctrl+Shift+Enter key combination to split a table.) This option is very useful in cases where you need to separate groups in a table. Splitting the table makes the groups more visible. Splitting a table is also useful if you want to insert text between the rows of an existing table, and you do not want the text to be a part of the table.

Formatting Tables

More Info In Word, you can format the contents of your tables (usually text), and you can format the tables themselves. Formatting can be applied to the contents of tables in the same way that you apply formatting to characters or paragraphs in Word. (See Chapter 3 for more on character and paragraph formatting.) For example, if you want to apply bold character formatting to a portion of text in a table, you can select the desired text and then click on the Bold button in the Standard toolbar or press Ctrl+B to apply the formatting.

If you want to format aspects of the table itself (as opposed to its contents), you use Table➪Table AutoFormat to open the Table AutoFormat dialog box (see Figure 5-13). In this dialog box, you see a selection of various formats that you can apply to your table. Choose the format that you want to use and select the areas to which you want to apply the format by clicking on as many check boxes as you want. The Preview box lets you see what the table will look like after the formatting is done. When you are finished making your selections in the dialog box, click on the OK button to apply the formatting to the table.

Setting column widths

Choose Table➪Cell Height and Width to open the Cell Height and Width dialog box (see Figure 5-14), where you can specify the width of one or more cells of the table. In the Row tab of the dialog box, you can change the row height, the indentation from the left, and the alignment. You can also tell Word whether to allow rows to break across the ends of pages. In the Column tab, you can set the width of the columns and the amount of space between columns.

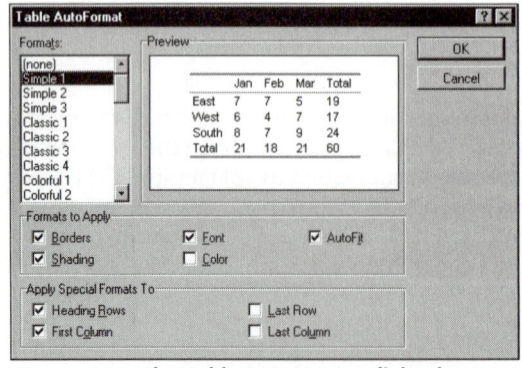

Figure 5-13: The Table AutoFormat dialog box.

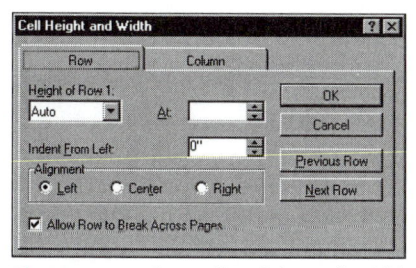

Figure 5-14: The Cell Height and Width dialog box.

You can also adjust column and cell width by placing the mouse pointer on the gridline of the desired cell or column. When you do so, the pointer changes into a two-sided arrow that you can click and drag to the desired width.

After you have adjusted the column width, all the columns to the right of the adjusted column are resized in proportion to their previous widths, but the overall width of the table is not changed when you drag the gridline or the column marker. The following list contains the options that you have for adjusting your current column:

✦ To adjust the current column and one column to the right (the overall table width remains unchanged), hold down the Shift key while you drag.

✦ To adjust the current column and make all columns to the right equal in width, hold down the Ctrl key while you drag.

✦ To adjust the current column without changing the width of the other columns (the overall table width changes), hold down the Ctrl and Shift keys while you drag.

Adjusting the space between columns

You can adjust the spacing between columns by choosing the Cell Height and Width command from the Table menu and clicking on the Column tab in the Cell Height and Width dialog box (see Figure 5-15). In this tab, you can use the Space Between Columns box to adjust the horizontal space that Word places between the text of adjacent cells. (The default value is 0.15 inches.) If you click on the AutoFit button, Word automatically sizes the columns to best fit the text contained in them.

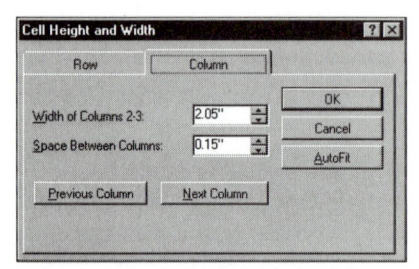

Figure 5-15: The Column tab of the Cell Height and Width dialog box.

Making row adjustments

To set the height of a row, choose Table➪Cell Height and Width and click on the Row tab in the dialog box. Use the Height of Rows list box to set the minimum height of one or more rows. By default, this value is set to Auto, which means that the row will be high enough to contain any text in the row. If you choose the At Least option from the Height of Rows list box, Word makes the row at least as tall as the value that you enter. If any text within a cell is larger than the minimum height, Word increases the height as needed to accommodate the text. You can also choose the Exactly option from the list box, which causes Word to make the cell exactly the height that you enter in the box.

To add indents to your cells, click on the Indent From Left box on the Row tab. The row will be indented from the left page margin by the decimal amount that you enter. For example, if you enter **0.5 in.**, the row will be indented one-half inch from the left page margin. You can enter a negative value to shift the row to the left, past the left margin. If you want to apply the indent to one row, select the entire row or just one cell in the row before you open the dialog box. Then after you make your entries on the Row tab of the Cell Height and Width dialog box, they are applied to the entire row. If you don't make a selection first, the changes are applied to the entire table.

To determine the alignment of rows with respect to the page margins, choose from among the Left, Center, or Right options in the Alignment area of the Row tab. These options are comparable to the ones found in the Paragraph dialog box from Format➪Paragraph. As with paragraphs, you can left-align, center, or right-align rows horizontally on a page. By default, the selected row is left-aligned, which causes the left edge of the row to be aligned with the left margin (assuming that you have not specified an indentation). Choose Center to center the row or choose Right to align the right edge of the row with the right page margin.

Note For the Row Alignment options to have any visible effect, your table must be smaller than the width of the page margins. If you used the default options in the Insert Table dialog box when you created the table, then the table is already as wide as the page margins, and choosing an alignment option will have no visible effect. The alignment options are useful when you specify your own widths for the table columns rather than letting Word automatically size the table.

Remember that adjusting the Alignment options in the dialog box moves the horizontal position of the entire row, not the text within the row. If, for example, you choose the Center option from the Alignment area, Word will center the row within the page margins, but individual text within the cells will not be centered. If you want to left-align, center, or right-align text within a cell, you have to select the desired text and then use the alignment options of the Format➪Paragraph command (or the alignment buttons on the Formatting toolbar).

If you don't select any text to which to apply the text alignment, then the alignment that you choose applies to the specific cell that contains the insertion point. To apply the alignment to the current row, select the row and then choose one of the alignment buttons on the Formatting toolbar.

Applying borders

You can use the various options within the Cell Borders and Shading dialog box (see Figure 5-16) to place borders around a cell or a group of cells in the table. You select one or more cells, then open this dialog box by choosing Format➪Borders and Shading while the insertion point is in a table. The borders that you insert by using this dialog box will be printed, unlike the table gridlines that are visible by default. The borders that you specify are added directly on top of the table gridlines.

How Word applies the borders depends on the selections that you make in the Cell Borders and Shading dialog box. As with other options in this dialog box, Word applies borders and shading according to the cell or cells that you select in the table.

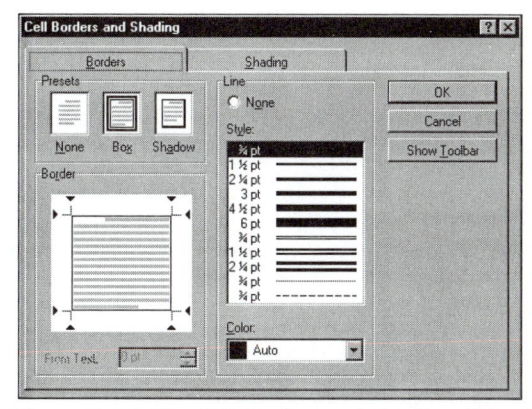

Figure 5-16: The Cell Borders and Shading dialog box.

You can also use Table⇨Table AutoFormat to add borders and shading to a table. When you choose this command, Word provides you with a list of different formats for shading and borders that you can use (see "Formatting Tables" earlier in this chapter). Simply select the format that you want in the Table AutoFormat dialog box and click on the OK button.

Besides specifying the presence of a border, Word lets you select from among different types of borders. After you choose the desired option (Outline, Inside, Top, Bottom, Left, or Right) in the Cell Borders and Shading dialog box, you can select the style of borders that you want and the colors to be used for the border.

Exploring Other Uses for Tables

You can do more with tables than just create them and type in text. You can use tables to lay out large amounts of textual data in the form of side-by-side paragraphs. You can also convert existing text to table form, and you can sort information stored in your tables.

Creating side-by-side paragraphs

More Info

Word's capability to store up to one page length of text in any column of a table makes it easy to set up side-by-side paragraphs by using the Table feature. (Side-by-side paragraphs are one way to create newspaper-style columns. You can create side-by-side paragraphs in other ways as well, and Chapter 10 provides additional details regarding this and other desktop publishing topics.) To create side-by-side paragraphs, simply insert a table with two or more columns into your document and use the Cell Height and Width dialog box to size the columns as desired. Remember that you can use the mouse to set the column widths by clicking on the gridlines and dragging them to the appropriate width. Then type as much text as you want in the columns, but keep in mind the rule that a table cannot extend beyond the length of a single page. The table will automatically display the paragraphs of text side-by-side on-screen. You can add borders to differentiate the text.

Converting text to tables

Rest easy. Word lets you convert all the old tables that you created — by inserting tabs, spaces, and other characters to separate your columns — into brand new, usable, and up-to-date Word tables. Therefore, if you have old tables that you still need, you can "clean them up" by using Table⇨Convert Text to Table.

This feature is also helpful if someone else has created an old-fashioned table, and you want to work with it in the new table format. You can also use this feature to convert data from databases in a comma-delimited format into the table form in Word. (See your database management software documentation for directions on creating comma-delimited files.) Text that is separated either by tabs, by commas, or by paragraph marks can be converted into a table.

To convert text into a table, first select the text and then choose Table⇨Convert Text to Table. When the Convert Text to Table dialog box appears, choose the Paragraph, Tabs, or Comma option (as appropriate, based on the text to be converted) from the Separate Text At area of the dialog box. Then click on the OK button. Word will recommend a number of columns and a number of rows, based on the appearance of the text that you are converting to table form. (You can change the recommendations by entering any desired values in the Number of Columns and Number of Rows text boxes.) To complete the conversion of the text to a table, click on the OK button.

For example, consider the text shown in Figure 5-17. (You can easily duplicate this example by opening a new document, typing the text shown, pressing tab once between columns, and pressing Enter at the end of each line.)

```
¶
¶
¶
¶
Alberta·Sutton  →  Selita·Sutton  →  Epey·White      →  Felton·White¶
Alice·Royals    →  Jim·Royals     →  Ricky·Stephens  →  Kirk·Stevens¶
Leona·Sutton    →  Michael·Whitfield → Erick·Witfield →  Dirk·Johnson¶
¶
```

Figure 5-17: Text separated by tab marks can form the basis of a table.

To convert this text into a table, select all three rows of text. Then choose the Convert Text to Table command from the Table menu. In the Convert Text to Table dialog box, accept Word's suggestions for a table measuring 4 columns by 3 rows by clicking on the OK button. The table shown in Figure 5-18 is the result of Word's efforts. (In the figure, we've added borders to the table to make the effects of the table more visible.)

Alberta Sutton	Selita Sutton	Epey White	Felton White
Alice Royals	Jim Royals	Ricky Stephens	Kirk Stevens
Leona Sutton	Michael Whitfield	Erick Witfield	Dirk Johnson

Figure 5-18: A newly created table based on the text in Figure 5-17.

Sorting information

You may encounter times when you want to arrange a list of data (often within a table) in alphabetical or numerical order. You can use Word's Sort command for this task.

Keep in mind, however, that the Sort command is by no means limited to tables. You can use the Sort command to sort any list of data, whether the information is in a table or in a simple list with paragraph marks separating the lines.

Hot Stuff

When Word sorts a list, it rearranges the list entries in alphabetic or numerical order. You can choose whether to sort in ascending or descending order or whether to sort by date text or number. Follow these steps to sort the data in a table:

1. Select the column or row or the items in the table that you want to sort.
2. Choose Table⇨Sort. (If the selected information is not a table, the command is Sort Text.) The Sort dialog box appears, as shown in Figure 5-19.
3. If you have headings that you do not want sorted, click on the Header Row radio button in the My List Has area of the dialog box.
4. In the Sort By area, make your selection for the column that you want to sort by.
5. In the Type list box of the Sort By area, choose the Text, Number, or Date option and then click on either the Ascending or the Descending radio button. To choose additional columns to sort by, repeat Steps 4 and 5.
6. Click on the OK button to sort the data.

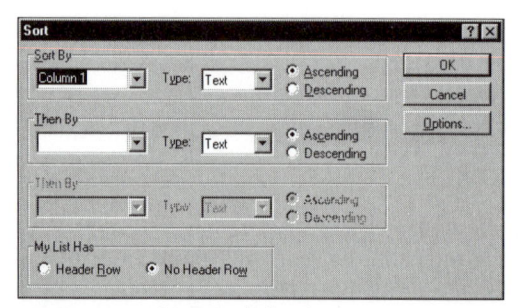

Figure 5-19: The Sort dialog box.

Understanding Outlines in Word for Windows

For many who work with words, an outline is the first step to getting cohesive thoughts down on paper. With even the earliest of word processors, simple outlining was possible with the use of tabs and manually typed headings. Word, however, offers automatic outlining and its significant advantages. In addition to aiding the organizing process, Word's outlining lets you number headings automatically and create tables of contents based on an outline. And when you create an outline in Word, you can easily rearrange parts of the outlining without giving thought to precise formatting.

In Word, outlining is built into a document. As you create a document, you can create an outline at the same time. With Word, the only difference between a normal document and an outline is the view that you use to examine the document. When you are in Normal view, Draft view, or Page Layout view, you are looking at the document in its normal (nonoutline) form. When you turn on Outline view, however, you look at the document in the form of an outline. Figure 5-20 shows an example of a document in outline form (you will duplicate this document later in an exercise).

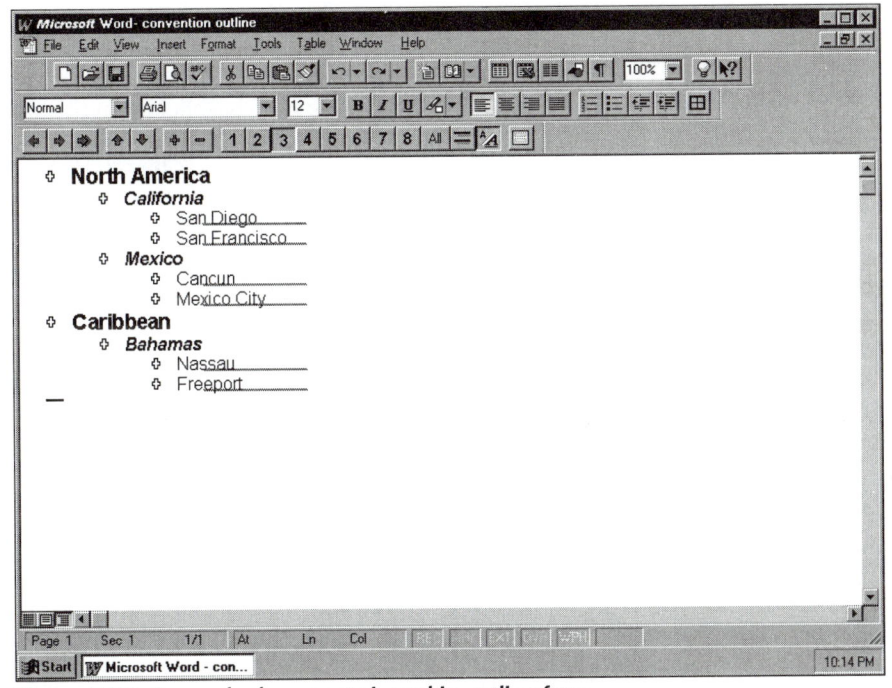

Figure 5-20: A sample document viewed in outline form.

Outlines are made up of headings and body text. A *heading* is any paragraph that has been assigned a special paragraph style. Word provides these styles specifically for the creation of outlines. There are eight of these predefined styles, from Heading 1 through Heading 8. The numbers define the importance of headings in an outline — a top-level heading is assigned the Heading 1 style; the next level heading is assigned the Heading 2 style; and so on. Word automatically places all top-level headings at the left margin by default, and each lower-level heading style is successively indented (placed farther to the right than the preceding heading level).

Body text is any text within an outline that hasn't been given a heading style. Word also uses the term *subtext* to refer to all headings and body text that appear below a particular heading.

Selecting text

When you are in Outline view, selecting text is basically the same as selecting text in other areas of Word. However, there are some differences that you should be aware of. The most significant one is that you lose the capability to select a full paragraph along with only part of another paragraph. If you use the mouse or keyboard methods to select past the boundary of a paragraph and into the following paragraph, the entire second paragraph becomes selected. As you drag across additional paragraphs, each paragraph becomes selected in its entirety. This feature makes editing more difficult in Outline view. (You can, of course, get around this by turning off Outline view while you do your editing.)

You can select a heading and all the subtext below it by double-clicking in the selection bar area beside the heading. Unfortunately, there is no equivalent for this mouse action from the keyboard, but you can accomplish the same result by selecting the desired heading and subtext with a combination of the Shift and arrow keys.

Changing the structure of an outline

To work with a document in Outline view, choose View⇨Outline. In Outline view, Word gives you additional tools to help structure the outline. A different toolbar, called the Outlining toolbar, appears at the top of the screen when you choose the Outline command. Figure 5-21 shows the Outlining toolbar. In addition to the Outlining toolbar, small icons appear to the left of each paragraph.

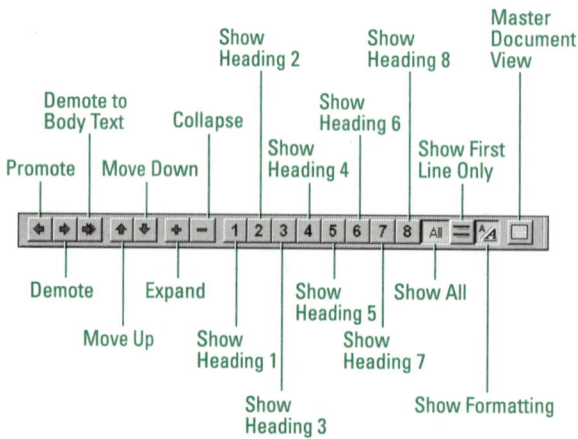

Figure 5-21: The Outlining toolbar.

A flexible feature of Word's outlining is that you can use it with a document at any time. You can create a document and later come back to it and structure the document in outline form. Or you can create the document in outline form as you go along. You can add additional portions of a document, whether they are headings or body text, to the document at any time.

You can change the structure of the outline by promoting a paragraph to a higher level or by demoting it to a lower level of importance. When changing the structure of an outline in Word, you generally select the desired paragraph and then click on a button from the Outlining toolbar to change a feature of the outline. Table 5-2 explains the function of the Outlining toolbar's buttons.

Table 5-2
The Outlining toolbar's buttons and their functions

Button	Function
Promote	Promotes a paragraph to a higher level
Demote	Demotes a paragraph to a lower level
Demote to Body Text	Demotes a heading to body text
Move Up and Move Down	Moves a heading up or down to a new location in the outline
Expand	Expands all text within a heading
Collapse	Collapses a paragraph so that only the heading shows
Show Heading	Controls how many levels of the outline are displayed
All	Expands or collapses entire outline
Show First Line Only	When All is selected, shows just the first line of body text
Show Formatting	Shows or hides character formatting
Master Document View	Switches to Master Document view

Keyboard users should note that there are keyboard equivalents for every button on the Outlining toolbar. Table 5-3 summarizes the keyboard equivalents.

Table 5-3
Keyboard equivalents for the Outlining toolbar

Keyboard combination	Function
Alt+Shift+left arrow or Tab	Promotes a paragraph
Alt+Shift+right arrow or Tab	Demotes a paragraph
Alt+Shift+up arrow	Moves a paragraph up
Alt+Shift+down arrow	Moves a paragraph down
Alt+Shift+plus sign	Expands body text

(continued)

Table 5-3 *(continued)*

Keyboard combination	Function
Alt+Shift+minus sign	Collapses body text
Alt+Shift+5 (on numeric keypad)	Converts heading to body text
Alt+Shift+1 through Alt+Shift+9 (on numeric keypad)	Expands or collapses headings to specified levels (1 through 8), or to show body text (9)
Alt+Shift+A	Shows all headings and body text
Alt+Shift+L	When All is selected, shows just the first line of body text
Slash (/ on numeric keypad)	Shows or hides character formatting

Although Alt+Shift+5 on the numeric keypad is specified as the keyboard equivalent for converting headings to body text, laptop users should note that this keyboard combination does not work on many laptop keyboards (or other keyboards, too) because of the compromises made in designing laptop keyboards. These keyboards often give up the numeric keypad and combine all numbers with the character keys. If you are using a laptop, and you plan on doing a lot of work with outlines, consider adding a mouse so that you can use the Outlining toolbar.

Changing Outline Headings

You can use the Promote and Demote buttons, or the equivalent keyboard combinations, to change heading levels, to convert body text to headings, or to convert headings to body text. To promote a heading level with the mouse, select the heading and click on the Promote button on the Outlining toolbar or drag the heading's icon to the left. To demote a heading level, select the heading and click on the Demote button on the Outlining toolbar or drag the heading's icon to the right.

When you promote a heading, it is assigned the next highest heading level, and it is outdented farther to the left. The opposite happens when you demote a heading; it is assigned the next lower level, and it is indented farther to the right.

Converting body text

To demote a heading to body text, click on the double-right arrow in the Outlining toolbar. This action causes the selected text to appear as body text in the document rather than as a heading.

You can convert body text to a heading simply by promoting the body text. Select the body text and click on the Promote button. When body text is promoted, it is converted to a heading that has the same level as the heading above it.

Expanding or collapsing outline headings

As an aid in organizing your thoughts, Word lets you expand or collapse outline headings. When you expand a heading, all the subtext (lower-level headings and body text) below the heading are made visible. On the other hand, when you collapse a heading, all subtext below the heading is hidden from view. Figure 5-22 shows an outline with its body text collapsed; it then shows the same outline with its body text expanded.

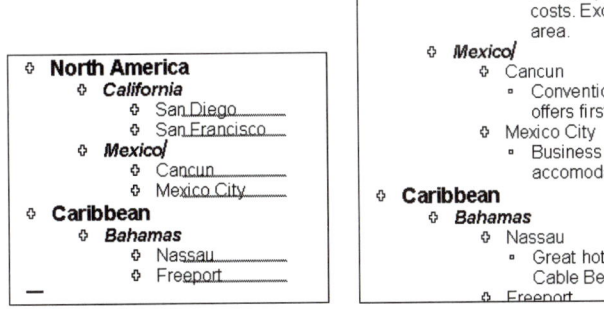

Figure 5-22: At left: An outline with collapsed body text. At right: the same outline with body text expanded.

To expand a heading, select the desired heading and then click on the Expand button on the Outlining toolbar. To collapse a heading, select the heading and then click on the Collapse button.

Hot Stuff: Many keyboards have two minus keys and two plus keys (one set located on the numeric keypad). Word recognizes either set — it doesn't matter which set you use with the Alt+Shift keyboard combinations.

You can also use the Show buttons on the Outlining toolbar to collapse or expand an entire outline. The numbered buttons correspond to the possible heading levels within an outline; clicking on the 1 button causes level 1 headings to be visible; clicking on the 2 button causes all headings that are level 1 or level 2 to be visible; clicking on the 3 button causes all heading levels of 1, 2, or 3 to be visible; and so on. Clicking on the All button causes all headings and all body text in an outline to be visible.

Moving headings

Word provides considerable flexibility regarding the movement of headings and associated subtext. You can move headings around in an outline, and you can move associated subtext with or without the headings. And you can move multiple headings and associated subtext by selecting more than one heading prior to the move operation.

To move a heading, first select it. This is not quite as simple as it sounds, however. If you select only a heading in an expanded outline (the subtext is visible), then Word moves only the heading and leaves the subtext in its current position. If the heading is collapsed, however, any movement of the heading causes the associated subtext to be moved, even if only the heading is selected.

After you have selected the heading that you want to move, click on the up arrow or down arrow on the Outlining toolbar to move the heading up or down in the outline. You can also use the click-and-drag method to move the headings. Simply click on the heading that you want to move and drag it to its new location.

Applying numbering to outlines

You may want to apply numbering to the headings of an outline. Of course, you could manually number an outline by typing the numbers as you type the headings. But a major drawback to this technique is evident if you later rearrange the outline by adding, deleting, or moving headings. If you make these changes, you must then manually renumber the headings. You can avoid this problem if you use Word's Format⇨Bullets and Numbering command to apply numbering to your outline headings.

To number an outline, perform the following steps:

1. Collapse or expand the outline so that only those headings that you want to number are visible. Word will number any visible paragraphs, so if all headings and body text are visible, the entire contents of the outline will be numbered, which is probably not what you want.

2. Select the paragraphs that you want to number. If you want to number the entire document, select the entire document by pressing Ctrl+A.

3. Choose Format⇨Bullets and Numbering to open the Bullets and Numbering dialog box. (See Chapter 3 for a more detailed discussion of this dialog box.)

4. Leave the default settings as they are.

5. Click on the Numbered tab and then click on one of the six possible number formats shown in the tab.

6. Click on the OK button. Paragraph numbers will appear beside each visible topic in your outline.

Hot Stuff: Remember that you can remove paragraph numbering from the outline at any time by choosing Format⇨Bullets and Numbering and clicking on the Remove button on the Numbered tab.

Creating Your Own Outline

To demonstrate the concepts that you can use in building outlines, you need to create an outline of your own on which to experiment. Follow along with this exercise to create an outline:

1. Choose File⇨New and click on the OK button in the New dialog box to create a new document.
2. Choose View⇨Outline to switch to Outline view.
3. To form the headings for your outline, type the following text and press Enter after each line:

   North America

   California

   San Diego

   San Francisco

   Mexico

   Cancun

   Mexico City

   Caribbean

   Bahamas

   Nassau

   Freeport

4. To create a second level in your outline, move the cursor to the California heading and click on the Demote button. Repeat this step for the Mexico and Bahamas headings.
5. To create a third level in your outline, move the cursor to the San Diego heading and demote this line twice by clicking on the Demote button twice. Repeat this step for the San Francisco, Cancun, Mexico City, Nassau, and Freeport headings.

   At this point, the structure of the sample outline is apparent. If you have been following the directions, your outline should resemble the example shown in Figure 5-23.

```
○ North America
    ○ California
        ○ San Diego
        ○ San Francisco
    ○ Mexico
        ○ Cancun
        ○ Mexico City
○ Caribbean
    ○ Bahamas
        ○ Nassau
        ○ Freeport
```

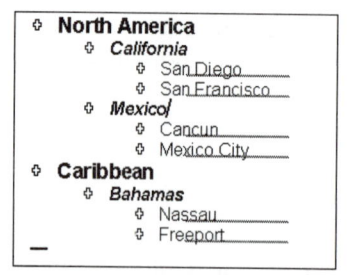

Figure 5-23: The structure of the sample outline.

Now you can begin adding body text to the various parts of the outline. Keep in mind that Word's flexibility means that you do not necessarily have to create your outlines in this same manner. This example follows the common technique of creating outline headings first and then filling in the details; however, you can create headings and body text as you go along. To add some body text to the sample outline, perform the following steps:

1. Move the cursor to the end of the San Diego line. Press Enter to begin a new line. Note that the icon aligns with the existing lines; hence, the new line is initially a heading. Before you begin typing, convert this new line to body text.

2. Click on the Demote to Body Text button on the Outlining toolbar and then type the following text:

   Great meeting facilities, accommodations, and restaurants all centrally located in downtown area.

3. Move the cursor to the end of the San Francisco line. Press Enter to begin a new line and click on the Demote to Body Text button on the Outlining toolbar. Then type the following text:

   Proximity to company offices will reduce transportation costs. Excellent dining and attractions in Fisherman's Wharf area.

4. Move the cursor to the end of the Cancun line. Press Enter to begin a new line and click on the Demote to Body Text button on the Outlining toolbar. Then type the following text:

   Convention center and hotels located on the beach. Cancun offers first-rate water sports all year.

5. Move the cursor to the end of the Mexico City line. Press Enter to begin a new line and click on the Demote to Body Text button on the Outlining toolbar. Then type the following text:

   Business hotels near Chapultepec Park provide meeting accommodations and computer fax lines.

6. Move the cursor to the end of the Nassau line. Press Enter to begin a new line and click on the Demote to Body Text button on the Outlining toolbar. Then type the following text:

   Great hotels with meeting facilities located on the beach, in Cable Beach area.

7. Finally, move the cursor to the end of the Freeport line. Press Enter to begin a new line and click on the Demote to Body Text button on the Outlining toolbar. Then type the following text:

   Shopping, excellent golf, and water sports readily available.

8. Choose File⇨Save to save the document with the name Sample Outline #1. At this point, your outline should resemble the one shown in Figure 5-24.

```
✧ North America
    ✧ California
        ✧ San Diego
            ▫ Great meeting facilities, accommodations, and restaurants
              all centrally located in downtown area.
        ✧ San Francisco
            ▫ Proximity to company offices will reduce transportation
              costs. Excellent dining and attractions in Fisherman's Wharf
              area.
    ✧ Mexico
        ✧ Cancun
            ▫ Convention center and hotels located on the beach. Cancun
              offers first-rate water sports all year.
        ✧ Mexico City
            ▫ Business hotels near Chapultepec Park provide meeting
              accomodations and computer and fax lines.
✧ Caribbean
    ✧ Bahamas
        ✧ Nassau
            ▫ Great hotels with meeting facilities located on the beach, in
              Cable Beach area.
        ✧ Freeport
```

Figure 5-24: Adding body text to the sample outline.

Collapsing and expanding the sample outline

As mentioned earlier, it's often helpful to collapse an outline so that you can look at the major points without being distracted by the less important points or by the body text. An easy way to collapse an entire outline is by using the numbered Show buttons on the Outlining toolbar or their keyboard equivalents.

To experiment with collapsing your own outline, open the Sample Outline #1. Click on the 1 button on the Outlining toolbar to show only level-1 headings in your outline. At this point, only the North America and Caribbean lines should be visible. To expose the next level of headings, click on the 2 button. Now you should also be able to see the California, Mexico, and Bahamas lines. When you click on the 3 button, the level 3 headings (the names of the cities) become visible beneath the level 2 headings. Finally, click on the All button. The body text becomes visible along with all headings of the outline.

Of course, you can also individually expand or collapse headings by using the Expand and Collapse buttons on the Outlining toolbar. To see how these buttons work, place the cursor anywhere in the Mexico heading and click on the Collapse button. Notice that the Cancun and Mexico City headings collapse underneath and hide the body text. If you click on the Expand button, the subheadings expand to reveal the body text underneath.

Changing headings in the sample outline

You can use the Promote and Demote buttons on the Outlining toolbar to promote and demote headings. Remember that body text for a heading gets promoted or demoted along with the heading, but subheadings do not. To see how this concept works, select the San Francisco heading and the subtext below the heading and then click on the Promote button. Notice that the San Francisco heading is promoted to the same level as the California and Mexico headings. While the heading and subtext remain selected, click on the Demote button to demote the heading and subtext back to its original level.

Use the Move Up and Move Down buttons on the Outlining toolbar (or their keyboard equivalents) to move headings up or down within an outline. Remember, if any subtext is collapsed, subtext moves with the heading. If subtext is not collapsed, it moves with the heading only if you have selected it with the heading. To demonstrate this concept, place the cursor in the Mexico City heading and click on the Move Up button (or press Alt+Shift+up arrow). The Mexico City heading moves up in the outline. However, the body text associated with the heading remains in its original location. While Mexico City is still the selected paragraph, click on the Move Down button (or press Alt+Shift+down arrow) to restore the heading to its proper location.

Next, select the Mexico City heading and the subtext underneath the heading. Click on the Move Up button twice. This step moves the heading and its subtext above the Cancun heading and its subtext, as shown in Figure 5-25.

In most cases you'll want the body text to move with the headings. To make this move easier, first collapse the outline to the level of the heading to be moved (with the numbered Show buttons or their keyboard equivalents). After you have collapsed the outline, you can move headings without worrying about selecting the subtext because the subtext will automatically follow the headings.

```
○ North America
    ○ California
        ○ San Diego
            ▫ Great meeting facilities, accomodations, and restauraunts
              all centrally located in downtown area.
        ○ San Francisco
            ▫ Proximity to company's offices will reduce transportation
              costs. Excellent dining and attractions in Fisherman's Wharf
              area.
    ○ Mexico
        ○ Mexico City
            ▫ Business hotels near Chapultepec Park provide meeting
              accomodations and computer and fax lines.
        ○ Cancun
            ▫ Convention center and hotels located on the beach. Cancun
              offers first-rate water sports all year.
○ Caribbean
    ○ Bahamas
        ○ Nassau
            ▫ Great hotels with meeting facilities located on the beach, in
              Cable Beach area.
        ○ Freeport
```

Figure 5-25: Moving the Mexico City heading and subtext.

Creating a Table of Contents from an Outline

One powerful feature that Word provides is the capability to quickly generate a table of contents based on the headings within an outline. Use Insert⇨Index and Tables command to insert a table of contents at the location of the insertion point.

After your document exists in outline form, perform the following steps to create a table of contents:

1. Place the insertion point where you want to insert the table of contents.
2. Choose Insert⇨Index and Tables command to open the Index and Tables dialog box.
3. Click on the Table of Contents tab and then choose the type of format that you want for the table of contents from the Formats list box. The Preview box gives you an idea of how the format will look before you apply the style.
4. Click on the OK button. Word inserts a table of contents at the insertion point.

You can see how easy it is to create a table of contents by using the sample outline that you created earlier. Perform the following steps to add a table of contents to the sample outline or to any existing outline that you have created.

1. Choose View⇨Normal to turn off the Outline view. (You want to turn off Outline view so that you can add a page break to put the table of contents on the first page. You cannot add page breaks while you are in Outline view.) Otherwise, it doesn't matter whether you are in Outline view or not if you want to insert a table of contents, as long as the headings are in the document.

2. Press Ctrl+Home to get to the start of the document. Press Enter once to add a new line and then press Ctrl+Enter to insert a page break. Press Ctrl+Home again to get back to the start of the document. You will add the table of contents on what is now page 1 of the document, with the remainder of the document appearing on page 2.

3. Choose Insert⇨Index and Tables, and click on the Table of Contents tab.

4. Leave the default options set as they are.

5. Click on the OK button. Word creates your table of contents.

> **More Info** Because the entire outline is on page 2, all topics of the outline are shown in the table of contents as being on page 2. If your sample document were longer, Word would assign the proper page numbers automatically. Note that if you later change the contents of the outline so that page numbers change, the table of contents is not updated automatically. You must update the table of contents by selecting the entire document and then pressing F9 (Update Fields) because the entries in the table of contents are based on fields. (For more information on fields, see Chapter 6.) Note that Word can do a lot more when it comes to tables of contents and indexes. See chapter 7 for additional details on these subjects.

Printing Outlines

Although you print outlines in the same way that you print any other document, keep in mind that what you get will vary depending on what view you are using when you print. Just as the document looks different on-screen in the various views, the document also prints differently in the different views. If you are in Outline view, the document prints much like it appears on-screen in Outline view. The only items that don't appear on the printed copy are the outline icons. Word uses whatever tabs are in effect for the document to indent the headings and body text.

If you are not in Outline view, Word prints the document somewhat differently. The headings are still indented, but they are indented by a smaller amount. And body text is printed at the left margin, without any indentation. You may want to try printing the sample outline that you created with Outline view turned on and then with it turned off so that you can examine the differences in appearance of the printed copy.

Summary

This chapter covered topics related to tables and outlines. The following topics were covered:

- You learned how to create tables by using Word's Table feature.
- You learned how to edit the contents of a table and how to delete, insert, and merge cells.
- You were armed with the tools needed to add borders, control table alignment, and sort table contents.
- You learned how to convert text to a table.
- You were introduced to the Outlining toolbar.
- You learned how to promote, demote, and move headings in an outline.
- Finally, you learned how to create a table of contents from your outline.

In the next chapter, you will learn how to work with fields and form letters in Word.

Where to go next...

- Tables are a routine part of documents that demand a "desktop-published" appearance. For more tips and techniques on performing desktop publishing tasks, you'll find Chapter 10 devoted to the topic.
- If you regularly use outlining in complex documents, keep in mind that you can quickly create tables of contents based on your outline. For details on using an outline to create a table of contents, see Chapter 7.

✦ ✦ ✦

Working with Fields

CHAPTER 6

♦ ♦ ♦ ♦
In This Chapter

Inserting, viewing, updating, formatting, and printing fields

Creating main documents for a form letter

Creating data documents to use in a mail merge

Printing envelopes and mailing labels

Creating data documents with other software

Embedding data

♦ ♦ ♦ ♦

This chapter covers topics that are related to working with fields. You will learn some of the common uses for fields when working in Word and how to create form letters.

In Word, a *field* is a special set of instructions that tells Word to insert certain information at a given location in a document. The basic difference between fields and normal text is that with fields, the computer provides the information for you. However, using fields does more than just save the effort of typing in the information. Fields are *dynamic* — they can change as circumstances change. You already may have used fields at various times in your work with Word for Windows; for example, when you insert the current date or page numbers in a document, you are inserting a certain kind of field.

Think of fields as special codes that you include in documents. The codes tell Word to insert information at the location where the code appears. The codes can automatically update the text of your document, or you can tell Word to update the information produced by the fields only when you want it to. Typically, you will use fields to add text or graphics to a document, to update information that changes on a regular basis, and to perform calculations.

Word has dozens of types of fields. Some, like page numbers and the current date, are simple to understand and use. Others are more complex and are beyond the scope of this book. But all fields can be inserted into a document and updated by using the same procedures, and this chapter will detail those procedures.

You can effectively work with fields after you learn four skills: how to insert fields in a document, how to update fields so that they show the most current results, how to view fields, and how to move between fields.

How to Use Fields

A field is made up of three parts: field characters, a field type, and instructions. As an example, consider the following date field.

```
{ Date \@ M/d/yy }
```

The *field characters* are the curly braces that enclose the field. The curly braces indicate the presence of a field in Word to the user. Inside the curly braces you find the special code or instruction that tells Word what is to appear in this area. Note that although curly braces are used to indicate the presence of a field, you cannot insert a field in a document by typing curly braces. You must use a command or a key combination specifically designed to insert fields, such as the Insert⇨Field command.

The *field type* is the first word that appears after the left field character. In the preceding example, the word *date* is the field type; this particular field type tells Word to insert the current date — based on the computer's clock — into the document.

The *instructions* follow the field type. Instructions are optional, depending on the field type, but most field types have instructions. The instructions tell Word exactly how the information specified by the field type will be displayed. In this example, \@ M/d/yy is an instruction that tells Word to display the current date in the American numeric format with the month, day, and year separated by slashes. The contents of the instructions may appear somewhat cryptic, but you need not be concerned with what they mean, because Word inserts the proper instructions for you automatically.

Inserting fields

Many commands in Word insert fields indirectly. When you insert page numbers or a table of contents, for example, you are inserting fields to produce the page numbers or the table of contents. But when you specifically want to insert fields into a document, you use a special command or key combination that is designed to insert fields, such as Insert⇨Field. Follow these steps to use the Field command to insert a field into your document:

1. After placing the insertion point where you want to insert the field, choose Insert⇨Field. The Field dialog box appears, as shown in Figure 6-1.

2. From the Categories list box, select the field category that you want to insert. The All category enables you to see all the fields in alphabetic order in the Field Names list box. You can use the scroll bars or the arrow keys to navigate among the possible field types.

3. From the Field Names list box, select the field that you want to insert. The Field Codes text box at the bottom of the dialog box displays whatever field you have selected. (You can also use this text box to enter the name of the desired field; however, it's generally easier to pick the field by name from the Field Names list box.)

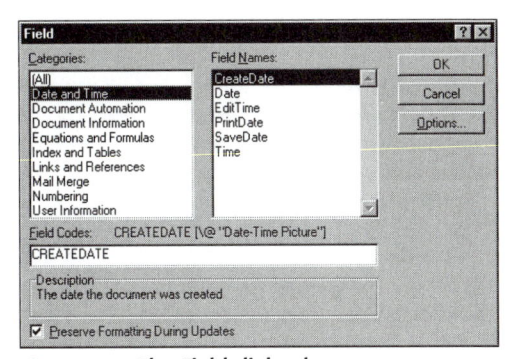

Figure 6-1: The Field dialog box.

   4. Click on the Options button if you want to add switches or formatting to the field. When the Options button is clicked, the Field Options dialog box opens, as shown in Figure 6-2. To add switches or formatting, click on the Add to Field button. If you change your mind and decide to remove the formatting or switches, click on the Undo Add button.

   5. Click on the OK button to insert the field into the document.

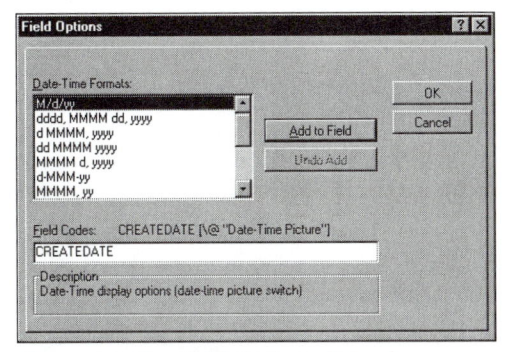

Figure 6-2: The Field Options dialog box.

> **Hot Stuff**
> Word also provides an Insert Field shortcut key combination (Ctrl+F9). This shortcut inserts the field characters (curly braces) into the document, which enables you to type the field name and instructions manually. This method for entering fields is typically used by programmers who are familiar with the Visual Basic programming language that is built into Word. Unless you are very familiar with field types and their instructions, you will probably find it much easier to add fields with Insert➪Field.

Viewing field codes

By default, when you insert a field, you see the results of that field. For example, when you insert a date field, you see the current date. When you are editing documents, however, you may find it useful to see the actual contents of the fields rather than the results. Here's how to see a field's contents, instead of its results:

1. Place the pointer in the field and right-click with the mouse. Word displays a shortcut menu.
2. Choose Toggle Field Codes to turn on the codes for the field. Perform the same steps if you want to turn off the codes again.

Note that you can also view an individual field by using the Toggle Field shortcut key combination (Shift+F9). This shortcut switches between a field's results and its actual contents. Place the insertion point anywhere in the desired field and press Shift+F9. If you are working with a large document that contains a number of fields, you may find it helpful to split the document into two panes. You can then turn on Field Codes in one pane by selecting the entire document and right-clicking to open the shortcut menu. From the shortcut menu, choose Toggle Field Codes.

Updating fields

You can update fields by selecting the text containing the field, right-clicking the text, and choosing Update Field from the shortcut menu that appears. Some fields, like those used in page numbering, are automatically updated whenever you print or repaginate a document; others are not updated until you tell Word to update the fields.

To update fields in the entire document, select the entire document (Ctrl+A) and then right-click anywhere in the document. Choose Update Field from the shortcut menu that appears.

Moving between fields

To move to the next field, use F11 or Alt+F1. To move to a previous field in a document, use Shift+F11 or Alt+Shift+F1. If you're more comfortable with the mouse, just click on the field that you want to move to.

Formatting fields

You can format the field results or the field codes, and you can add switches to the field codes. To format the field when it displays its result, right-click the field and choose the desired formatting option from the shortcut menu. (Choose Font to format the fonts used or Paragraph to apply paragraph formatting.)

To format the field when it displays its code, perform the following steps:

1. Choose Tools⇨Options, click on the View tab of the Options dialog box that appears, and check the Field Codes option. Then click on OK. (If you just need to see the field codes for one field, place the insertion point in the field and right-click the field to open the shortcut menu. Then choose Toggle Field Codes.)

2. After the fields are displayed, right-click the field and choose the appropriate option (Font or Paragraph) from the shortcut menu. Fill in the options in the dialog box that appears to apply the desired formatting.

Adding switches to field codes so that you can format the fields is not a "user-friendly" process, to say the least. You can add switches to the field codes by typing them into the code. Switches are options that change certain characteristics of the field results, such as displaying characters as uppercase, or converting numbers to roman numerals. For example, a simple DATE field looks like this:

```
{ DATE }
```

However, a field with the DATE code and a switch that tells Word how to display the date looks like this:

```
{ DATE \@ d-M-yy }
```

Table 6-1 lists some of the general switches and their functions.

Table 6-1
Commonly used switches and their functions

Switch	Function
* caps	Capitalizes the initial letter of each word in the result.
* firstcap	Capitalizes the initial letter of the first word in the result.
* lower	All letters in the result appear as lowercase.
* upper	All letters in the result appear as uppercase.
* arabic	Converts a number to Arabic (standard) format, overriding any default set elsewhere in Windows.
* dollartext	Spells out a number with two decimal places as words with initial capital letters, the word *and*, and the numbers that follow the decimal places (suitable for producing checks with currency amounts spelled out).
* roman	Converts a number to lowercase roman numerals.
* Roman	Converts a number to uppercase roman numerals.

(continued)

Table 6-1 *(continued)*

Switch	Function
\@ dddd, MMMM, d, yyyy	Displays a date as spelled out, as in Wednesday, May 24, 1995.
* mergeformat	Preserves manual formatting in the fields, such as character and paragraph formatting in text, and scaling and cropping dimensions in graphics.
* charformat	Applies the formatting on the first character of the field name to the entire field result.

Locking a field's contents

At times, you may want to prevent the results of a field from being updated. You can *lock* a field to prevent it from being updated until you unlock it. To lock a field, place the cursor anywhere in the desired field and press Ctrl+F11. To unlock the field, place the cursor anywhere in the field and press Ctrl+Shift+F11.

Using fields in an example

To see how fields can be used within a document, first open a new document in the usual manner and then perform the following steps:

1. Choose Insert⇨Field to display the Field dialog box. In the Categories list box, choose Date and Time. Then click on Date in the Field Names list box and click on OK. The current date, as measured by your PC's clock, appears at the insertion point. (If you see the actual field type and instructions for the field instead of the current date, choose Tools⇨Options, click on the View tab in the Options dialog box, turn off the Field Codes option, and then click on OK).

2. Press Enter twice and then type the following words:

    This document was written by:

    Add a space after the colon and then choose Insert⇨Field. In the Categories list of the Field dialog box, choose Document Information. In the Field Names list box, choose Author. Click on OK to insert the author's name into the document. (The name that appears is based on what you entered for a user name when Word was installed; you can change the author's name by choosing the Options command from the Tools menu and clicking the User Info tab of the dialog box.)

> ### Printing field codes
>
> When you print a document containing fields, Word prints the results of the fields by default and does not print the actual field codes themselves. At times, you may want to print the field codes themselves so that you can get a concrete idea of what codes are actually in your documents. You can print the field codes by choosing File➪Print and then clicking the Options button in the Print dialog box that appears. In the Print tab of the Options dialog box, turn on the Field Codes check box and click OK. Then click OK in the Print dialog box to begin printing.

   3. Add a period after the author's name and then start a new sentence by typing the following:

      The document contains

      Add a space after the last letter and then choose Insert➪Field. In the Categories list box, choose Document Information. In the Field Names list box, choose NumChars (an abbreviation for "number of characters") and click on OK.

   4. Add a space after the number that was just inserted and then finish the sentence by typing the following:

      words, and the time of day is now:

   5. Add a space after the colon and choose Insert➪Field. In the Insert Categories list box, choose Date and Time. In the Field Names list box, choose Time. Then click on OK to place the field.

At this point, your document should resemble the one shown in Figure 6-3. Of course, the date and time will be different from the date and time in the figure, and if you have varied the example text, the word count may differ, as well.

```
07/27/95¶
¶
This document was written by: Edward Jones.¶
The document contains 71 words, and the time of day is now: 12:54 PM¶
```

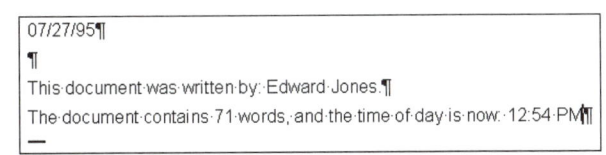

Figure 6-3: The sample document containing fields.

How to Create a Mail Merge

One way to take advantage of fields in your documents is to use them in mail merges to create personalized form letters. You can also create mailing labels and put together legal documents, data sheets, catalogs, and other documents of this kind. Mail merges let you print multiple copies of a document, where certain information (such as a name or address) changes for each document. The form letters that you receive from businesses are examples of mail merges at work.

Mail merges combine two kinds of documents: a *main document,* which contains the text that is identical for each printed copy, and a *data source,* which contains the text that is specific to each copy printed. The main document also contains fields that tell Word where to find the information that is stored in the data source. These fields are referred to as *merge fields*. As you type the main document, you can insert the fields at any desired location.

In the data source, you type the information that Word needs to fill in the fields inserted in the main document. For example, if your main document contains a name field and an address field, your data document should have names and addresses of all the people who should receive the letter. The first line of a data document normally contains a *header record*, a single line that identifies the order in which you place the data in the data document.

Hot Stuff The easiest way to store the information in a data source is to set up a table. If you do not use a table, the data must be separated either by tabs or by commas. A data source can be created by typing the desired information into a Word document. You can also create a data source by using information stored in database form within spreadsheet programs (such as Excel or Lotus 1-2-3) or database management software (such as dBASE or Paradox). In the next section of this chapter, under "Creating a data document," you'll learn how to create a data source by using data stored in a spreadsheet or in a database.

How to finish your mail merge

After the data source and the main document both exist, you can print multiple copies of the main document, based on the data contained in the data source. When you print the file, Word reads the first record in the data source, inserts the fields of that record into the main document, and prints a copy. It repeats this process for as many records as are contained in the data source; therefore, if a data source has five entries that contain the name and address for five individuals, a mail merge operation would print five copies of the document, each addressed to a different individual.

Specifying a main document

In the process of creating a form letter, the first step is to choose the main document that you intend to use. To choose the main document, perform the following steps:

1. Choose Tools⇨Mail Merge to activate the Mail Merge Helper dialog box shown in Figure 6-4.
2. Click on the Create button and choose Form Letters from the list box that appears. Word then asks you whether you want to use the active document or to create a new document as your main document, click on the Active Window button to use the active document.

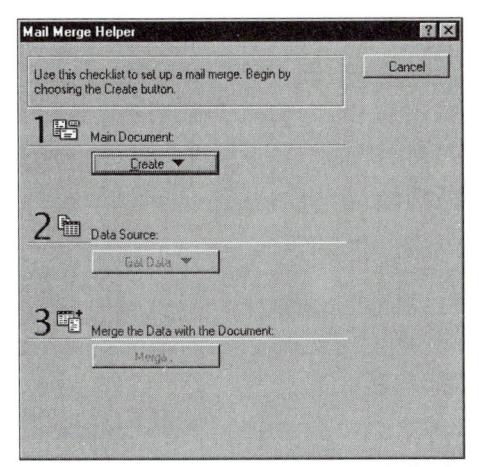

Figure 6-4: The Mail Merge Helper dialog box.

Creating a data source

Now that you have created your main document (the document that will be your actual form letter), you need to create a source from which you will get the data to use in the form letter's fields.

Follow these steps to create a data source:

1. After opening the main document or creating it, choose Tools⇨Mail Merge to activate the Mail Merge Helper dialog box (see Figure 6-4).
2. Now click on the Get Data button and choose Create Data Source. This activates the Create Data Source dialog box shown in Figure 6-5. This dialog box aids you in the creation of the fields that you are going to use in your form letter. The Field Names in Header Row box lists commonly used fields for form letters.

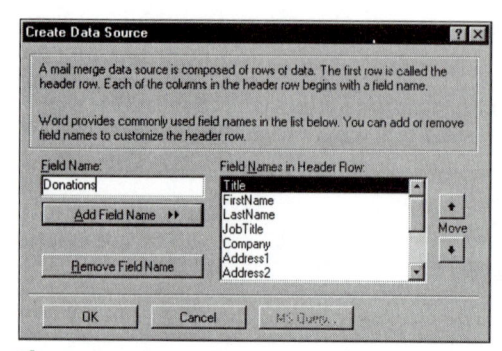

Figure 6-5: Create Data Source dialog box.

3. In the Field Names in Header Row box, highlight the names of the fields you do not need. Remember Word includes all data fields by default. One by one, you click on the Remove Field Name box to get rid of the fields that you don't need. If you have a field that you want to use that is not included in the list, type the name in the Field name entry and click on the Add Field Name button. Click on the OK button. The Save as dialog box then opens. Enter a name for your data source and save it.

4. Word then displays a message telling you that your data source has no data. Click on the Edit Data Source button to open a data source in which you can enter information for your mail merge. If you have no information for one of the fields, press Enter to skip it. Don't enter any spaces in the boxes. To add a new record, click on the Add New button. Do this until you have entered all the information needed in your data source.

5. Now that you have created your data source, return to your main document by clicking on OK.

6. If you later decide that you want to add information to your data source, click on the Mail Merge Helper button on the Mail Merge toolbar. You will then see the Mail Merge Helper. Under Data Source, click on the Edit button and choose the data source that you created. You will then see the Data Form used to enter information in you data source. Click on the Add New button to add a new record.

Adding merge fields to the main document

After finishing the process of creating a data document or opening the one that you want to use, you can finish the main document.

First, add any text or graphics that you want to complete your document. Then add the fields. Insert a merge field where you want each category of information to appear in printed form. You can format the information in any way you want by using the Formatting toolbar. When the information is placed in the main document, the formatting that you applied appears.

To add merge fields to your main document, follow these steps:

1. Enter the graphics and text that you want in each version of the form letter.
2. Click on the Insert Merge Field button on the Mail Merge toolbar and choose the appropriate merge field. Be sure to add any spaces or punctuation that you want to include between merge fields. (A merge field cannot be typed directly into a document.)
3. Save the main document to complete your work.

Merging data

Now you come to the part where you actually merge the data with the main document. Before continuing, be sure that you have completed the following:

✦ You have entered all the information into the data document.

✦ You have inserted all the merge fields into the main document.

You can use the Mail Merge toolbar to see the form letter on-screen so that you can be sure that the records contain everything you want to have in the form letter. This is done by clicking on the View Merged Data button on the Mail Merge Toolbar. When you have completed your inspection, you can print each letter by using the Print command from the File menu.

Follow these steps to merge the data document with the main document:

1. Be sure that the main document is active and click on the View Merged Data button on the Mail Merge toolbar. You see the information from the first data record inserted into the fields in the main document. Click on the Next Record button on the Mail Merge toolbar to see the information inserted from the next records. You can print the current form letter by choosing File⇨Print.
2. Merge the data document into the main document by doing one of the following:

    If you want to place the resulting form letters or other merged documents into a new document, click on the Merge to New Document button on the Mail Merge toolbar.

    To print the form letters, click on the Merge to Printer button.

How to Print Envelopes and Mailing Labels

Word also provides a way to print mailing labels and envelopes by using the Mail Merge command. You can either create a new data document or use an existing one. This feature can prove invaluable — it prevents you from having to address lots of envelopes by hand.

Printing envelopes

The steps for printing envelopes and mailing labels are similar to the steps used to create a form letter. Follow these steps for printing envelopes:

1. First you need to set up the main document, the one that represents the face of the envelope. Keep in mind that Word uses the information from the currently selected printer. If you want to print on a different printer, you need to know which type of envelope and feeder the printer uses so that you can size the envelope correctly.

2. Choose Tools⇨Mail Merge and click on the Create button in the Main Document area. Select the Envelopes option.

3. In the Microsoft Word message box, click on the Active Window button.

4. You have an option for this step. In the Data Source area, you can click on the Get Data button and choose Open Data Source. Select the data document that you want and click on OK. Then click on the Set Up Main Document button.

   Your other option is to choose Create Data Source from the Get Data menu. Be sure that all the field names you want to include are listed in the Field Names in Header Row list box and then click on OK. Next, you need to provide a file name to save the data source under and click Save.

5. The Envelope Options tab then appears; select the envelope size that you want from the Envelope Options tab. You can format the appearance of the address by using the font buttons on the Formatting toolbar. You can also adjust the position of the address. Then select the Printing Options tab.

6. Click on the OK button to close the dialog box. The Envelope Address dialog box appears (Figure 6-6).

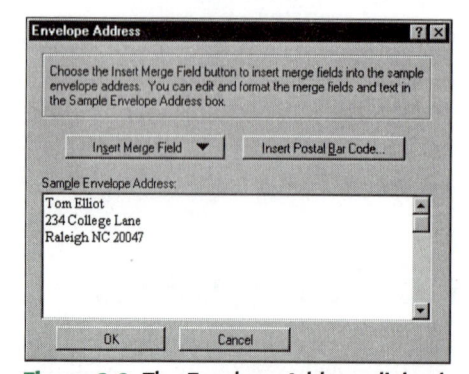

Figure 6-6: The Envelope Address dialog box.

7. In the Envelope Address dialog box, place the insertion point in the Sample Envelope Address box and insert the appropriate merge fields by clicking on the Insert Merge Field button on the Mail Merge toolbar. Enter all the punctuation that you want and press Enter at the end of each line. You can add a postal bar code to identify the delivery address by clicking the Insert Postal Bar Code button.

8. Click on OK to close the Envelope Address dialog box.

9. Click on the Edit button in the Main Document area and select the envelope document from the list of envelope documents.

10. The envelope is now displayed in Page Layout view in a frame. If an address is specified in the mailing address area, check the printer to be sure it is ready to print. Click on the Merge to Printer button.

After all of the steps have been performed, the envelope should zip right through your printer.

Printing mailing labels

You can also use Word to print mailing labels. If you have used the Merge command from the Print menu in earlier versions of Word, you can reuse your main document. If this is the first time you are printing labels, or you want to change the size of the labels, use Tools⇨Mail Merge and set up a new main document. A document is automatically set up for most Avery brand labels. If you need to use another brand, specify an Avery label of the same size or specify a custom label. Keep in mind that it is important to know what printer you are using. Each printer feeds labels differently; therefore, you may need to look at your printer's documentation to see how to feed the mailing labels to the printer.

To print mailing labels, perform the following steps:

1. Choose Tools⇨Mail Merge and click on the Create button.

2. Choose the Mailing Labels option. In the Microsoft Word message box, click on the Active Window button.

3. The Mail Merge Helper dialog box appears. In the Data Source area, click on the Get Data button.

4. In this step, you have four options. You can choose Open Data Source, select the desired file in the dialog box, and click on Open. When the Word message is displayed, choose the Set Up Main Document button.

   Or you can create your own data document by choosing Create Data Source. In the dialog box that is displayed, save the new data document. When the next message is displayed, click on the Edit Data Source button. Enter the address information in the Data Form dialog box. Click on the OK button and then click the Mail Merge Helper button on the Mail Merge toolbar. Then click on the Setup button in the Main Document area.

When you choose Use Address Book, the Use Address Book dialog box appears. Choose which address book you want to use.

You can also choose Header Options. When you do, the Header Options dialog box appears. Choose the Create button to create a header. You can also use a current data source as a header if you want by clicking on the Open button and choosing the file you want to use.

5. Select the printer type and label feed method in the Label Options dialog box. Before choosing OK, enter the type of label and label product number you are using.

6. Enter the merge fields in the Sample Label text box, as shown in Figure 6-7. Simply move the cursor to the text box, click on the Insert Merge Field button, and select the fields that you want to include. Again, enter any spaces or punctuation that you want between the fields. Press Enter at the end of each line.

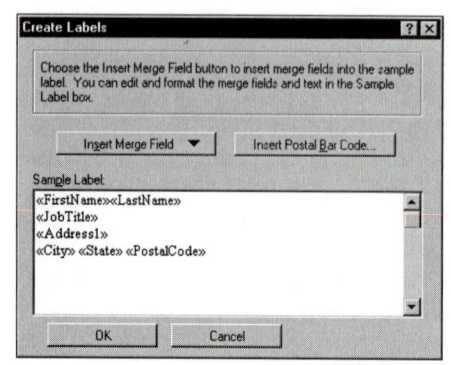

Figure 6-7: The Create Labels dialog box.

7. You can insert a postal bar code by clicking on the Insert Postal Bar Code button, selecting the fields that contain the ZIP code and delivery address, and clicking on OK.

8. Click on OK to close the Create Labels dialog box after you have inserted the merge fields.

9. Be sure that the printer is ready to print and then click on the Merge to Printer button on the Mail Merge toolbar.

How to Use Other Software to Create Data Documents

So far in this chapter, you've used data documents that were created by typing the data directly into a Word table. While this method has its advantages, you may want to set up a data document by using tabs or commas, especially when the data is already stored in another software package, such as in a spreadsheet or in a database manager. Most spreadsheets and nearly all database managers can export a file in a file format known as *comma-delimited*. This common file format can be imported as text into a Word document, and the document can then be used as the data document in a mail merge operation. (See your spreadsheet or database manager documentation for details on how to create a comma-delimited file.)

When setting up a data document where the data is not stored in table form, you must use either tabs or commas to separate the fields. A paragraph mark (at the end of the line) indicates the end of each record. If you use commas as field separators, you can also include quotation marks around each field. The quotation marks are not required, but many database managers automatically add quotation marks around each field when they produce comma-delimited files. All versions of dBASE and most dBASE-compatible database managers, for example, produce comma-delimited files resembling the following example:

```
"Johnson","Linda",2890.30,"Carrollton","TX"
"Ford","Brandon",2495.00,"Fort Worth","TX"
"Fairfield","Jason",2075.40,"Dallas","TX"
"Johnson","Mark",1890.50,"Arlington","TX"
"Sutton","Alberta",1775.00,"Carrollton","TX"
"Laveina","Chrissy",1740.00,"Dallas","TX"
"Carrol","Sarita",1534.60,"Garland","TX"
"Tellado","Carlos",1390.00,"Fort Worth","TX"
"Tatiem","Ryan",1170.20,"Dallas","TX"
```

In this database, all character fields are surrounded by quotation marks. Word can work with this file as a data document with no modifications, other than the addition of a header to indicate the names of the fields.

Working with Excel worksheets

Working Together

Excel can be used to create data documents, which is useful when you want to pull information from Excel for your mail merge. If you have a database stored as an Excel worksheet, you can easily create a table in Word based on that data. The process is much easier with Excel than with most other software. When a portion of an Excel worksheet is selected and copied to the insertion point in a Word document, the Excel data appears in the form of a table. You can then add a header and save the table as a Word document. Then you use the Mail Merge commands to do the merge.

To transfer data from an Excel worksheet into a Word document, perform the following steps:

1. Start Excel and open the desired worksheet.
2. Using the selection techniques common to Excel, select the worksheet range that contains the desired data.
3. Choose Edit⇨Copy to copy the selection to the Clipboard.
4. Start Word (if it's not already running) and open a new document.
5. Choose Edit⇨Paste. The data that was selected in the Excel document appears as a table in Word.
6. Choose Table⇨Insert Rows to add a new row to the start of the table and enter the header information into this row. (This step may not be necessary if the worksheet range you copied had column names in the first row. You can use the existing column names as the header.)

After the data exists in table form in Word, you can use the techniques outlined earlier in this chapter to complete the mail merge process.

Embedding data

Working Together

There will be times when you want to use data that already exists in Access or Excel for your merge. By establishing an OLE link to existing data in Access or Excel, you gain the advantage of having your mail merge information automatically updated when the data in Access or Excel changes. You can use this data by choosing between two methods: You can insert field codes that provide a link from your data document to the database file, or you can use the less complicated way and insert the data directly into the data document.

More Info

For more information about OLE (Object Linking and Embedding), see Chapter 33.

If you think you will regularly update the information in your data document, then you will want to use the field code method. If you won't be updating the information, then insert it directly into the data document. In both cases, choose the Database command from the Insert menu or click on the Insert Database button on the Database toolbar to open the Database dialog box shown in Figure 6-8.

Next click on the Get Data button to open the Open Data Source dialog box shown in Figure 6-9. This box looks like the Open dialog box from the File menu. Choose the data document that you want to use from the list by clicking on the Files of type list box. You can choose an Excel worksheet, an Access database, another Word document or a number of other types.

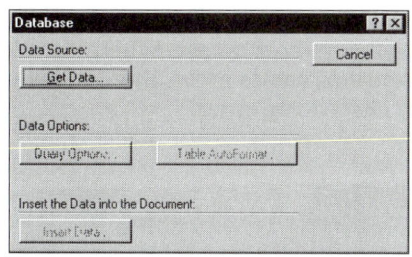

Figure 6-8: The Database dialog box.

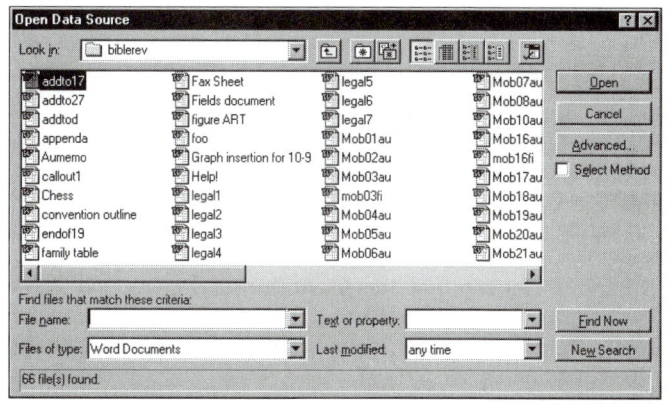

Figure 6-9: The Open Data Source dialog box.

The application corresponding to the file that you have opened is launched. For example, if you open an Excel file, Excel is launched in the background. You now see a dialog box that allows for the selection of a range if you are importing a worksheet. (You will learn how to import selected records for a database file later.) If you want to enter a range, press the Backspace key and enter a range. If not, choose OK.

After you have selected the range or the entire worksheet, you have the option of performing a query on the information that you are importing. Click on the Query Options button in the Database dialog box to open the Query Options dialog box, where you can filter records by entering conditions in the Filter Records tab, or you can sort records by choosing the desired sort fields in the Sort Records tab.

If your goal is to limit the number of imported records, click on the Filter Records tab and choose a field from the drop-down list. Next, move to the Comparison box and enter a comparison, such as equal to, not equal to, greater than, less than, and so forth. The final part of the query is to enter a value to which the field can be compared in the Compare to box. If you care to enter additional conditions for the query, accept And as the relationship and enter the rest of the conditions that you want to use in the query on successive lines of the dialog box.

The records can also be sorted. Click on the Sort Records tab of the Query Options dialog box (see Figure 6-10). You can choose a field to sort by, and if there are additional conditions to your sort, you can enter the field names in the Then By boxes. Then choose between sorting in ascending or descending order.

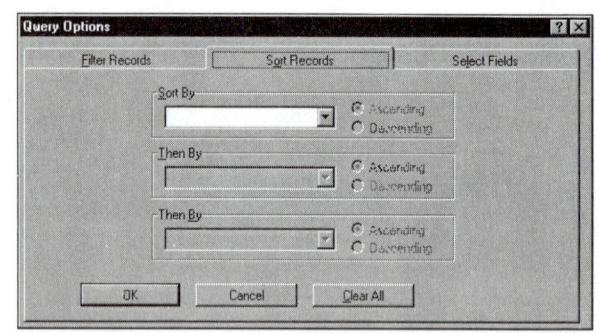

Figure 6-10: The Sort Records tab of the Query Options dialog box.

You can also click on the Select Fields tab of the Query Options dialing box to reveal the options shown in Figure 6-11. Use these options to select the fields that you want to import. By default, all the fields are chosen. If you want to remove any, select the name and click on the Remove button.

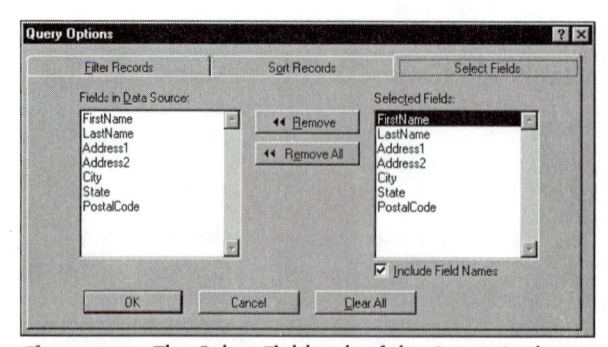

Figure 6-11: The Select Fields tab of the Query Options dialog box.

After you have finished, click on OK, and you are returned to the Database dialog box. Before you click on the Insert Data button, you can format the table by choosing the Table AutoFormat command from the Table menu. The Preview window lets you see what the data will look like after the formatting is applied.

After choosing the format that you want for the table, click on OK and then click on the Insert Data button in the Database dialog box. The Insert Data dialog box appears, as shown in Figure 6-12. This dialog box gives you one more opportunity to choose a range for the information being imported. If you want to choose the entire worksheet, click on OK to import the information.

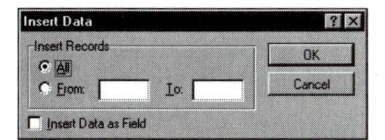

Figure 6-12: The Insert Data dialog box.

If you want the information to be linked, activate the Insert Data as a Field check box in the Insert Data dialog box. The information can be updated by selecting the text containing the fields, right-clicking the selected text, and choosing Update Fields from the shortcut menu that appears.

Summary

This chapter has detailed the following topics related to working with fields:

✦ Fields are instructions that Word uses to insert certain information, such as the current date, into a document.

✦ You can insert fields by choosing Insert➪Field, or by using the Insert Field shortcut key combination.

✦ You can update a field's results by right-clicking on the field and choosing Update Fields from the shortcut menu.

✦ Fields can be formatted like other text.

✦ A major use of fields in Word is in the creation of form letters, which can be handled with the Mail Merge Helper built into Word.

✦ Fields can also be used in the creation of envelopes.

✦ We also covered the creation of data sources in other software applications. This is very useful for large mailing lists or other cases where you need to work with large amounts of data that would be better handled in Access.

Where to go next...

✦ Embedding data in a document makes use of OLE. For more information on OLE, see Chapter 33.

✦ After you have created your form letters, you will want them to look the best that they can. This will require some formatting work. For more information on formatting, see Chapter 3.

✦ ✦ ✦

Building Tables of Contents and Indexes

CHAPTER 7

In This Chapter

Building tables of contents by using default styles

Building tables of contents by using nonstandard styles

Building tables of contents by using TC fields

Building tables of figures

Creating indexes

Creating multilevel indexes

This chapter covers two elements of a document that are similar in many ways: tables of contents and indexes. Both are essentially lists that are arranged in slightly different ways. A table of contents is a list of the major portions of a document (such as sections of a report), including the page numbers for each section. By comparison, an index is a list of important words or subjects in a document, with page numbers where the subjects can be found.

Word lets you avoid much of the work in preparing both tables of contents and indexes. With the Index and Tables command from the Insert menu, you can automatically create tables of contents and similar lists or indexes based on special fields that you insert while writing your document. Besides saving you all that typing and formatting time and labor, you can easily update the table of contents and index to reflect changes that you make to the document.

Building Tables of Contents

You can use several methods for building a table of contents: You can base the table of contents on built-in Heading styles or outline headings; you can change the default styles so that Word creates the tables of contents based on your chosen styles; or you can build the table of contents by using *TC fields*, a special type of field that you insert into a document by using the steps outlined in this chapter. The easiest method for creating a table of contents requires that you structure your document in outline form. Figure 7-1 shows an example of a typical table of contents in Word. In this case, the table of contents was generated on the default Heading styles used throughout the document.

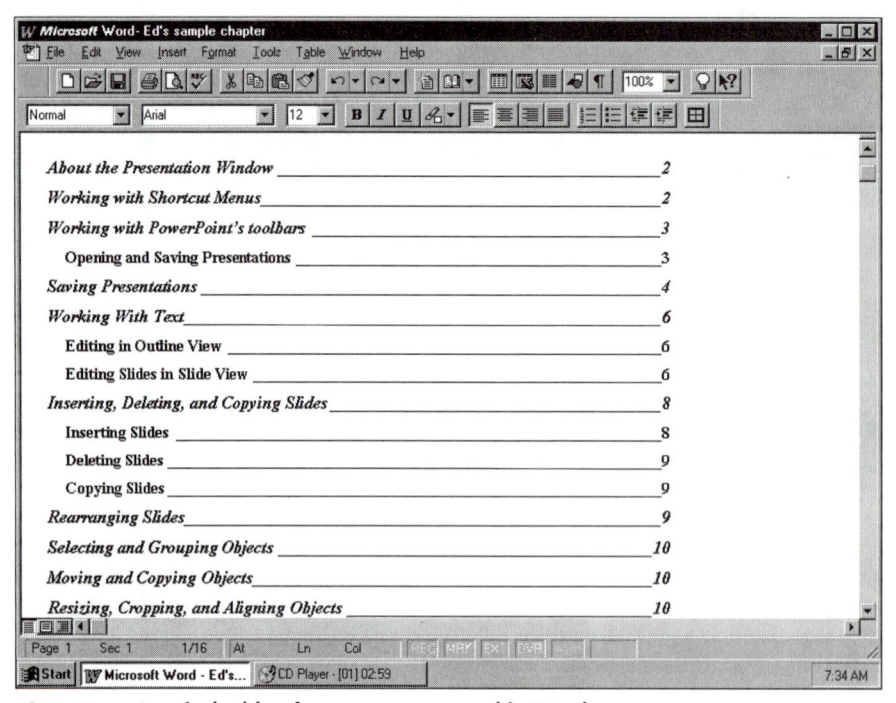

Figure 7-1: A typical table of contents generated in Word.

If you need both a table of contents and an index in the same document, create the index first (use the techniques discussed in the second part of this chapter). In this way, you can include an entry for the index in your table of contents.

Using style and outline headings

In any document, Word includes the default styles of Normal, Heading 1, Heading 2, Heading 3, and Heading 4. You can apply these styles (or outline headings, if you've added these to your documents) to lines of text in your document to make the creation of tables of contents a simple matter. Follow these steps:

1. Check the headings of your document to be sure that they are formatted in one of the Heading styles. To apply a Heading style, place the insertion point anywhere within the heading, open the Style list box at the left side of the Formatting toolbar, and choose one of the Heading styles. (For more about the use of styles, see Chapter 8.)

2. Move the insertion point to the place where you want the table of contents.

3. Choose InsertIndex and Tables and then click on the Table of Contents tab in the Index and Tables dialog box (see Figure 7-2).

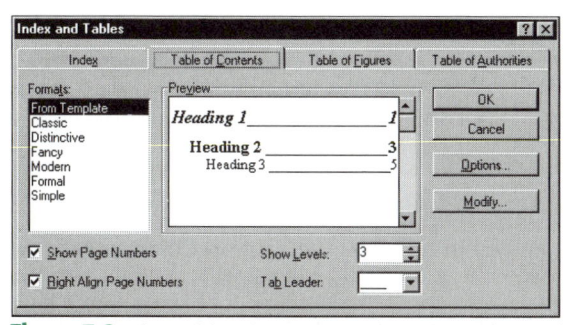

Figure 7-2: The Table of Contents tab of the Index and Tables dialog box.

4. In the Formats list box, select the format that you want to use in your table of contents. As you click on the different formats, a representative sample of what the table of contents will look like appears in the Preview area of the dialog box.

   Along with the format, you can include page numbers by leaving the Show Page Numbers check box turned on. You can also specify the number of heading levels by entering the desired value in the Show Levels box. (When you select 1, only Heading 1 styles are included in the table of contents; when you select 2, Heading 1 and Heading 2 styles are included in the table of contents; and so on.) Clicking on the Options button displays the Options dialog box that lets you designate styles (other than Word's default Heading styles) that Word should use to build the table of contents.

5. After you select the options that you want, click on the OK button. Word constructs the table of contents at the insertion point location.

Why does my table of contents contain funny codes instead of real text entries?

If you see a series of codes, such as {TOC}, rather than actual text after you generate your table of contents, then your table of contents is displaying field codes. If you want to see the actual text of the table of contents, place the cursor in the field code and press Shift+F9. You can also choose Tools⇨Options, select the View tab in the Options dialog box, and then clear the Field Codes check box in the Show area.

Using nonstandard styles

Sometimes you may find that the heading styles that are built into Word are not the styles that you want to use to build your table of contents. If you want to base the table of contents on different styles, you can do so by performing these steps:

1. Position the cursor in the area that you want to insert the table of contents.
2. Choose Insert⇨Index and Tables and click on the Table of Contents tab in the Index and Tables dialog box.
3. In the Formats list box, select the format that you want to use. Then click on the Options button to open the Table of Contents Options dialog box (see Figure 7-3).

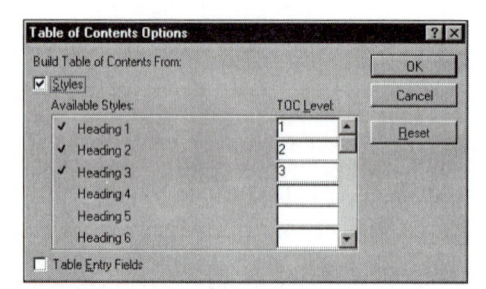

Figure 7-3: The Table of Contents Options dialog box.

4. Type a number from 1 to 9 in the TOC Levels entry to the right of the style name. This number is the level in the table of contents that you want headings that use this style to represent.
5. Scroll down in the Available Styles list box to find the style that you want to use for the table of contents. Click on the check box beside the name to turn it on. Repeat Steps 4 and 5 for all styles that you want to compile in the table of contents. Delete all level numbers that you will not use in your table of contents.
6. Click on the OK button in the Table of Contents Options dialog box to see the preview of what the table of contents will look like in the Index and Tables dialog box.
7. Click on the OK button in the Index and Tables dialog box. Word compiles the table of contents at the insertion point location.

Using TC entries

Another method for building a table of contents involves adding fields called *TC entries* (an abbreviation for table of contents entries) to your document. You can use the Ctrl+F9 (Insert Field) key combination because it takes fewer mouse actions than its equivalent of using Insert⇨Field. The overall technique involves two main steps: identifying and marking the items that should be included in the table of contents and then generating the table of contents itself.

How can I make the strange codes go away?

By default, TC entries are stored as hidden text. If you cannot see them, however, they become difficult to enter because you cannot see what you're typing. If you do see the codes, they may become annoying to look at when you are trying to proof your text. You need a way to turn these codes on and off easily. You can make hidden text visible while you are entering the TC entries by clicking on the Show/Hide button on the Standard toolbar. After you have finished inserting the TC entries, you can turn them into hidden text by clicking on the Show/Hide button again.

You can insert TC entries in a document and generate the table of contents by performing the following steps:

1. Be sure that hidden text is showing on the screen. (If you can see paragraph markers at the end of your paragraphs, then hidden text is showing.) If, not, click on the Show/Hide button on the Standard toolbar.

2. Place the insertion point at the location in the document where you want to insert a TC entry. (A good place for TC entries is right after the section titles or headings in your document.)

3. Press Ctrl+F9 to insert an empty field. You will see the field braces with the insertion point placed between them. The field code resembles the following: { | }

4. Type the letters **TC** and then a space. Then type a quotation mark and then the entry that you want to appear in the table of contents and then another quotation mark. (The letters *TC* can be either uppercase or lowercase.) For example, if you want to add a table of contents entry that reads *Unpacking your new lawn mower*, your entry would resemble the following:

   {tc "**Unpacking your new lawn mower**"}

5. Repeat Steps 2 through 4 for each table of contents entry that you want to add.

6. When all the TC entry fields have been placed in the document, move the insertion point to the desired location in your document for the table of contents.

7. Choose Insert⇨Index and Tables and click on the Table of Contents tab. Next click on the Options button and, in the dialog box that appears, turn on the Table Entry Fields check box. This action tells Word to base the table of contents on the TC entries that you have added to the document. Click on the OK button.

8. Click on the OK button in the Index and Tables dialog box. Word builds the table of contents at the insertion point location.

If the Field Codes option is turned on, you will see field codes in the table of contents rather than text. You can turn off the field codes by choosing Tools⇨Options, clicking on the View tab in the Options dialog box, and turning off the Field Codes option. (Another easy way to turn off the field codes is to right-click in the field code, and choose Toggle Field Codes from the shortcut menu that appears.)

Remember that the table of contents is based on a Word field. If you make changes to the document that changes the page count, you need to update the table of contents if it is to reflect those changes. To update a table of contents, place the insertion point anywhere within the table of contents and right-click. Choose Update Field from the shortcut menu that appears.

Hot Stuff Remember that TC entries are fields. If you want to delete or move a TC entry to another location, select the entire field and move it or delete it as you would move or delete any text in Word.

Creating Your Own Table of Contents

To see how to build a table of contents by inserting TC fields, you can follow the steps in the next exercise. Or if you have a sizable document of your own, you may want to apply these steps to create a table of contents based on your own document.

1. Choose File⇨New and then click on the OK button to create a new document.
2. Type the following lines (press Enter after each one) and press Ctrl+Enter after each line to insert a page break between each line:

    Principles of Flight

    Aircraft and Engines

    Flight Instruments

    Navigation

Formatting your table of contents and indexes on the fly

Probably the easiest way to make a quick format change to your table of contents or index is to right-click anywhere within the table of contents or index. Then choose the Font, Paragraph, or Bullets and Numbering command from the shortcut menu that appears. Depending on which menu option you select, you can then make appropriate changes in the dialog box that appears.

3. If the hidden text option is not turned on, click on the Show/Hide button on the Standard toolbar (it's the button containing the paragraph symbol, which sort of looks like a backwards letter "P") to show the hidden characters.

4. Place the insertion point at the end of the first line of text. Press Ctrl+F9 and then type the following inside the braces:

   tc "Principles of Flight"

5. Move the insertion point to the end of the next line of text. Press Ctrl+F9 and then type the following inside the braces:

   tc "Aircraft and Engines"

6. Move the insertion point to the end of the next line of text. Press Ctrl+F9 and then type the following inside the braces:

   tc "Flight Instruments"

7. Move the insertion point to the end of the next line of text. Press Ctrl+F9 and then type the following inside the braces:

   tc "Navigation"

8. Press Ctrl+Home to get back to the start of the document. Press Enter once to add a new line and then press Ctrl+Enter to insert a page break. Press Ctrl+Home again to get back to the start of the document. You will add the table of contents on what is now page 1 of the document, with the remainder of the document appearing on the following four pages.

9. Choose Insert⇨Index and Tables. Then click on the Table of Contents tab in the Index and Tables dialog box.

10. Click on the Options button to open the Table of Contents Options dialog box and turn on the Table Entry Fields check box. Click on the OK button.

11. Click on the OK button in the Index and Tables dialog box. Figure 7-4 shows the resulting table of contents that is inserted into the document.

Principles of Flight .... 2¶
Aircraft and Engines .... 3¶
Flight Instruments .... 4¶
Navigation .... 5¶
¶
―――――――― Page Break ――――――――
Principles of Flight{ tc:"Principles of Flight" }
―――――――― Page Break ――――――――
Aircraft and Engines{ tc:"Aircraft and Engines" }
―――――――― Page Break ――――――――
Flight Instruments{ tc:"Flight Instruments" }
―――――――― Page Break ――――――――
Navigation{ tc:"Navigation" }
―――――――― Page Break ――――――――
¶

Figure 7-4: The sample table of contents.

Building Tables of Figures

A table of figures is another type of list that you can easily create in Word. Like a table of contents and an index, a table of figures is a list of items. In this case, the items are figure captions, shown in the order in which the figures appear in the document. A table of figures can include such items as illustrations, figures, charts, or graphs. Examples of figure captions appear throughout this book — every figure in this book includes a caption that describes the figure. You can do the same kind of thing in your Word for Windows documents.

All the captions that you create in your documents can be easily included in a table of figures that you can place at any location within your document. You first create the document, and then you insert the captions in your document by choosing Insert⇨Caption. In the Caption dialog box, you type the name of the caption. You repeat this process for every caption that you want to insert.

After inserting all your captions, you can perform the following steps to insert the table of figures:

1. Position the cursor where you want to place the table of figures.
2. Choose Insert⇨Index and Table and click on the Table of Figures tab in the Index and Tables dialog box (see Figure 7-5).

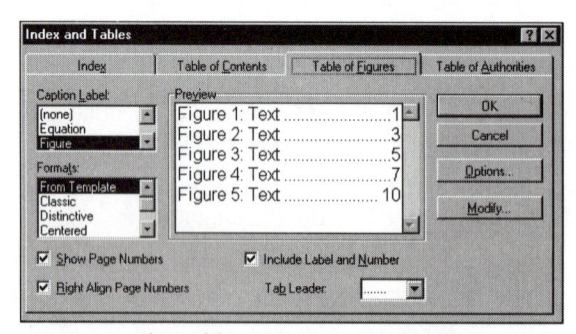

Figure 7-5: The Table of Figures tab in the Index and Tables dialog box.

3. Choose the kind of caption label that you want for your table of figures.
4. Select the format that you want for your table. As with tables of contents, you can choose from Classic, Distinctive, Centered, Formal, and Simple. (These formats are displayed in the Preview portion of the dialog box.) The Show Page Numbers option, when checked, causes page numbers to be included with the table of figures. The Right Align Page Numbers option, when checked, causes the page numbers to be aligned with the right margin.

5. After making your choices, click on the OK button to insert the table of figures at the insertion point.

Building Indexes

Word lets you build indexes in a manner very similar to the one for building tables of contents. You again insert special fields, called *index entries*, into the document at locations where you mention the indexed topics. In the case of index entries, Word provides a command just for this purpose, or you can use the Insert Field key (Ctrl+F9). After you mark all the index entries, you use Insert⇨Index and Tables to place the index at the insertion point. As with a table of contents, the index that Word generates is based on a field, which you can easily change by updating the field as the document changes.

Word offers considerable control over the index. You can generate an index for the entire document or for a range of letters in the alphabet. Index entries can all appear flush left in the index, or they can be indented to multiple levels. And you can easily add bold or italics to the page numbers of the index entries.

Marking the index entries

Every item that is to appear in the index must have an index entry. You can mark index entries by performing the following steps:

1. Select the text in the document that you want to use for an index entry or place the insertion point immediately after the text.

2. Choose Insert⇨Index and Tables and then click on the Index tab in the Index and Tables dialog box. Click on the Mark Entry button to reveal the Mark Index Entry dialog box (see Figure 7-6). By default, any selected text appears in the Main Entry text box. If you want the text to appear in the index as a subentry (a secondary-level index heading), delete any entry in the Main Entry text box and enter the entry in the Subentry text box.

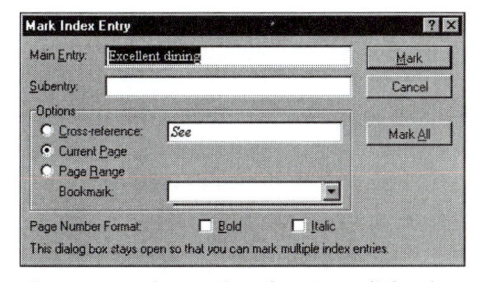

Figure 7-6: The Mark Index Entry dialog box.

3. After entering the desired entry, click on the Mark button. Word inserts the index entry at the insertion point location. (Like the fields that you use to insert tables of contents, index entries are stored as hidden text. You will not see them in the document unless you click on the Show/Hide button on the Standard toolbar.

The Mark Index Entry dialog box contains various options that you can use to determine how Word should handle the index entries. In the Cross-reference text box, you can type the text that you want to use as a cross-reference for the index entry. You can also specify a range of pages in an index entry by turning on the Page Range option and typing or selecting a bookmark name that you used to mark a range of pages. And you can use the Page Number Format options to apply bold or italic formatting to page numbers in the index.

For those who despise menus and dialog boxes, an alternative way of inserting index entries exists. Because an index entry is a field, you can use the Insert Field key (Ctrl+F9) to insert an index entry. To do so, press Insert Field (Ctrl+F9), type the letters **xe** and then a space, and then type the index entry surrounded by quotation marks. If you want the page number of the index entry to be in bold or italic, you must also add a \b or \i switch; type **\b** for bold or **\i** for italic (you can add both options in the same field). With hidden text showing, a sample index entry may resemble the following:

{xe "Adding Oil to the Lawn Mower" \b}

One important note: index entries should follow the topic to which it refers in the text; that is, the index entry should be placed immediately *after* the sentence that concludes the subject that is indexed. (If you select the text before you use the Index and Tables command — rather than typing the index entry yourself — Word automatically places the index entry immediately after the selection.) This rule of thumb is important because if you place the index entry before the subject being indexed, and the subject is near the bottom of the page, Word may add a page break between the index entry and the text. The result would be an index with an incorrect page number.

Inserting the index

After you mark all the index entries, you can use Insert⇨Index and Tables to place the index in the document. To insert the index, perform the following steps:

1. Place the insertion point at the desired location for the index. (With most documents, indexes are customarily placed at the end of the document.)
2. Choose Insert⇨Index and Tables and click on the Index tab of the Index and Tables dialog box, as shown in Figure 7-7.

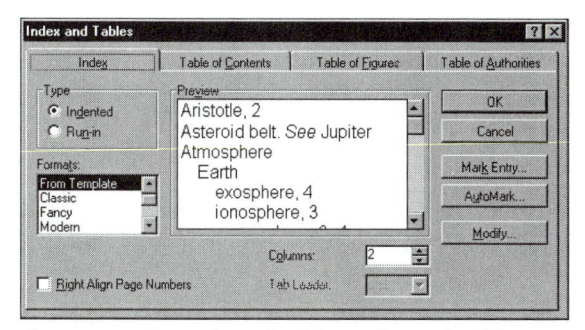

Chapter 7 ✦ **Building Tables of Contents and Indexes** 175

Figure 7-7: The Index tab of the Index and Tables dialog box.

3. Choose the type of index (Indented or Run-in) that you want and choose the desired format for the index. As you select among the available formats, a preview of each format appears in the Preview area of the dialog box.

4. After you click on the OK button, Word generates the index. Note that if Field Codes is turned on, you will see the fields that built the index and not the index itself. You can turn off the field codes by choosing the Options command from the Tools menu and clicking on the View tab of the Options dialog box. Then turn off the Field Codes option in the Show area of the tab.

Creating multilevel index entries

You can insert index entries that indicate multiple levels. As an example, the following part of an index is designed with two levels:

> Data
> > Copying, 104
> > Definition, 251
> > Deleting, 92
> > Editing, 91
> > Linking, 216
> > Reporting, 251
>
> Data Menu, 64, 216
>
> Database
> > Attributes of, 251
> > Creating, 216
> > Criteria, 230

To create an index based on multiple levels, you enter the text of the secondary entry in the Subentry text box rather than in the Main Entry text box of the Mark Entry dialog box. If you are typing the entries manually, you simply add a colon (:) when you type the index entry into the dialog box to separate the levels. You can create a multilevel index by performing the following steps to mark your index entries:

1. Place the insertion point at the desired location for the index.
2. Choose Insert⇨Index and Tables and click on the Index tab of the Index and Tables dialog box. Then click on the Mark Entry button.
3. In the Main Entry text box, type the first-level entry. In the Subentry text box, type the second-level entry.
4. Click on the Mark button to place the index entry.

When you specify multiple levels, keep in mind that you now have a choice of how Word structures a multilevel index when you use the Index and Tables command. You can choose either the Indented or the Run-in type of Index on the Index tab. The default option is the Indented type of index, which results in an index where sublevel entries are indented, as shown in the following example:

> Database
>   Attributes of, 251
>   Creating, 216
>   Criteria, 230

On the other hand, if you choose the Run-in option in the dialog box, Word inserts all sublevel entries in the same paragraph as the main entry in the index. The main entry is separated from the subentries with a colon, and all remaining subentries are separated by semicolons. The preceding indented example now appears as a run-in example in the following:

> Database; Attributes of, 251; Creating, 216; Criteria, 230

Using page number ranges in indexes

In those cases where a subject covered by an index entry spans several pages in a document, you may want the reference in the index to include the range of pages in the document. In the following example, the entries for the Go To command and Hardware both contain a range of pages:

> Get Info command, 41
>
> Go To command, 62-65
>
> Gridlines command, 145
>
> Hardware, 19-20
>
> Help menu, 12

With the methods described so far for inserting index entries, you get only the first page of the subject referred to by the index, even if you make a selection that spans multiple pages. If you want page numbers that span a range of pages, you must do things a little differently. First you must select the range of text and insert a bookmark that refers to the selection by following these steps:

1. Use your preferred selection method to select the range of text that you want to index.
2. Choose Edit⇨Bookmark. In the Bookmark dialog box, type a name for the bookmark and then click on the Add button.
3. Choose Insert⇨Index and Tables, click the Index tab, and click on the Mark Entry button. In the Mark Index Entry dialog box, click on the Page Range Bookmark radio button and enter the bookmark name in the list box. When you create the index using the steps described earlier in this chapter, your entry includes your specified range of pages.

Using additional index options

Additional switches are available for you to use in index fields in Word to add sophistication to your indexes. These features include changing the separator character that is used between ranges of page numbers (normally a hyphen) and restricting an index to include only index items that begin with a certain letter. These special index switches are beyond the scope of this book, but you can find out more about them in your *Microsoft Word User's Reference*.

Building Large Indexes

If you are generating a large index (one with 4,000 entries or more), Word may run out of memory when you attempt to use the Index and Tables command. Microsoft recommends that you generate indexes for very large documents in multiple steps. For example, first you build an index that contains entries only for the letters A through L; then you build an index for the letters M through Z. You choose the Field command from the Insert menu rather than the Index and Tables to insert a separate field for each portion of the index after you have marked all the entries that you want in the document.

To create a separate field for each portion of the index, do the following:

1. Place the insertion point at the location in the document where the index is to appear.
2. Choose Insert⇨Field.
3. Type the word **index** followed by a space, a backslash, the letter **p**, a space, and a range of letters (such as A – L).

4. Click on the OK button to insert the first index field into the document. If the hidden text option is turned on, the field may resemble the following:

   {index \p A – L}

5. Move the insertion point to the right of the existing index field and press Enter to start a new line.

6. Repeat Steps 2 through 5 for each additional range of letters that you need.

Summary

In this chapter, you learned how to use Word's capabilities to generate tables of contents and indexes. The chapter covered the following topics:

- Tables of contents can be based on heading styles, on outline headings, or on TC fields (a special kind of field inserted into a document).

- If you use Word's default heading styles or outlining in your document, you can quickly generate a table of contents by choosing Insert⇨Index and Tables, clicking the Table of Contents tab, and selecting the desired format in the dialog box.

- You can create tables of contents based on any text in your document by adding fields called TC Fields to your document. After adding the fields, you can generate a table of contents with the Table of Contents tab which appears in the dialog box when you choose Insert⇨Index and Tables from the menus.

- You can create indexes by adding fields called Index Entries to your document. After adding the Index Entries, you can generate an index with the Index tab which appears in the dialog box when you choose Insert⇨Index and Tables from the menus.

In the next chapter, you'll learn how to work effectively with styles and templates to govern the overall appearance of your document in Word.

Where to go next...

- If you make full use of Word's predefined styles or of outlines in your documents, the creation of tables of contents becomes an easy task. You can find more information on working with Word's predefined styles in Chapter 8. For the lowdown on using outlines in Word, see Chapter 5.

- Also, an important part of any complex document will be page number formatting, and possibly the inclusion of headers and footers. These topics are detailed in Chapter 3.

✦ ✦ ✦

CHAPTER 8

Working with Styles and Templates

In This Chapter

What are styles and templates?

Applying styles with the Formatting toolbar

Applying styles with the keyboard

Defining styles

Basing styles on styles

Viewing style information

Copying, deleting, and renaming styles

Creating and applying templates

Changing the default template

Word provides *styles* and *templates* — tools that you can use to easily mold the appearance of routinely produced documents. The first part of the chapter deals with styles; the second part of the chapter deals with templates. As you will learn, the two concepts are closely related.

What Are Styles and Templates?

Too many users of Word find styles and templates to be an esoteric subject, and they avoid it. It is quite possible to use Word for Windows day after day and never learn about the flexibility of styles or about any templates other than the default template Word uses. You're doing yourself a disservice if you avoid these tools — styles and templates can be major time-savers.

If you're a new Word user, you might be confused about what a style is and what a template is and how the two concepts are different. A *style* is a collection of character formatting and paragraph formatting settings that are stored under different names. Word already has a number of built-in styles, but you can also create your own. Figure 8-1 shows a letter that contains a number of different styles (notice the names of the styles to the left of the document). You can use the drop-down Style list on the left side of the Formatting toolbar to view all the available styles as you are creating a document.

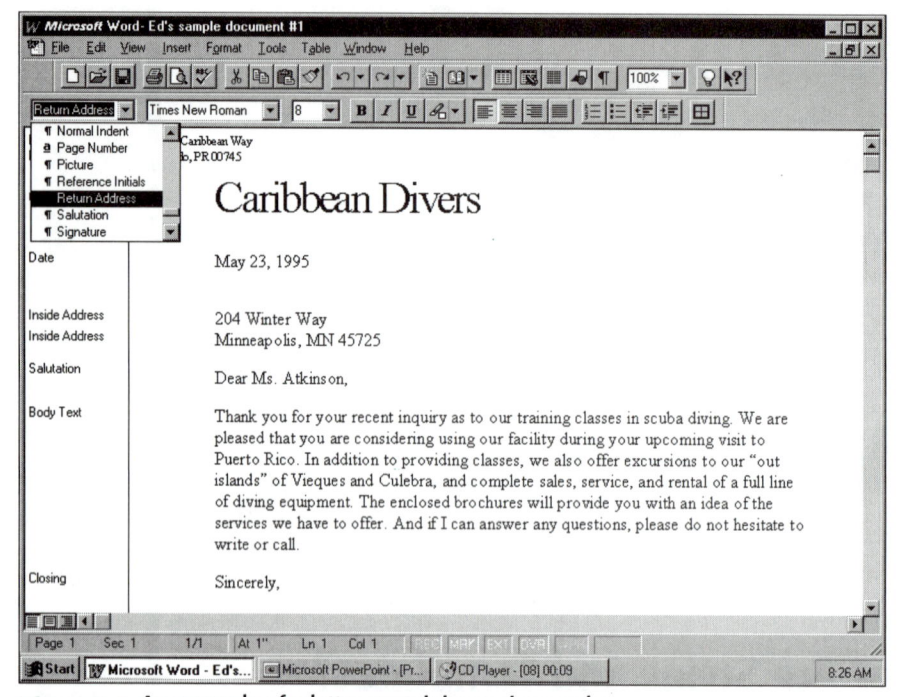

Figure 8-1: An example of a letter containing various styles.

If you use styles, you can save time that you might otherwise spend formatting your documents, and you can give your documents a consistent look. For example, you may routinely apply a 1/2-inch left indent, a first-line indent, and Times Roman font to paragraphs in a document. You can define this set of formatting aspects to a style. After the style has been defined, you then can apply all these formatting aspects to any paragraphs in a document with a single operation.

Besides making formatting easier to apply, styles also offer an advantage when you revise document formats. When you change the formatting in the style, all paragraphs that are formatted with this style will automatically change. For example, you may decide to apply a border and shading to all paragraphs with a particular style. By changing the definition of the style to include the border and shading, you automatically add the border and shading to all paragraphs in all documents that use that particular style.

Word offers two overall kinds of styles that you can use to format your documents: *character styles* and *paragraph styles*. Character styles apply a variety of formatting to the individual letters and punctuation in a document. You apply character styles with the Font command from the Format menu. In the Font dialog box, you can choose formatting that includes font size and style; bold, italics, or underlining; small caps;

and other text-related settings. Paragraph styles govern the overall appearance of the paragraph. You apply paragraph styles with the Paragraph command from the Format menu. In the Paragraph dialog box, you can choose formatting that includes indentation, line spacing, and paragraph alignment.

Word normally saves styles along with the active document, but you can easily copy styles that you create to a specific template. A *template* is a collection of styles, keyboard and toolbar assignments, and macros that have been saved to a file with a .DOT extension. By storing styles in templates, you can make these styles available for use whenever you are using that template. When you click on the drop-down arrow in the Style list on the Formatting toolbar, the different styles that you see are all stored in the template that you are using at the present time.

Templates also provide a way to tailor a document quickly, but templates can encompass much more than just character and paragraph formatting. Think of a template as a model that governs the overall format of the document that you create. Templates can contain any boilerplate text that you want included in each variation of a document that you create. For example, in the case of an interoffice memo, you can create a template that has the same text for a company name, date, to, from, and subject headings. In addition to boilerplate text, templates can also contain styles, macros, and custom keyboard, menu, or toolbar assignments.

You select a template whenever you create a new document, as the second part of this chapter explains in more detail. Because templates include collections of styles, it's important to understand styles before you begin working with templates.

Applying Styles

You can apply styles throughout your Word documents in two ways. You can use the drop-down Style list that's in the Formatting toolbar. Or, you can use keyboard shortcuts.

Using the Formatting toolbar

Because Word comes with a number of default styles, putting them to work is as easy as choosing the desired style from the Style list on the Formatting toolbar. Follow these steps to apply any of the available styles to paragraphs in your document:

1. If the Formatting toolbar isn't already available, choose View➪Toolbars and click on the Formatting option in the Toolbars dialog box.
2. If you want to apply the style an entire paragraph, place the insertion point anywhere in that paragraph. To apply the style to a specific portion of a paragraph, select the desired portion of text. To apply the style to more than one paragraph, select all the desired text.

3. Click on the arrow to the right of the Style list in the Formatting toolbar to open the list of available styles (see Figure 8-2).

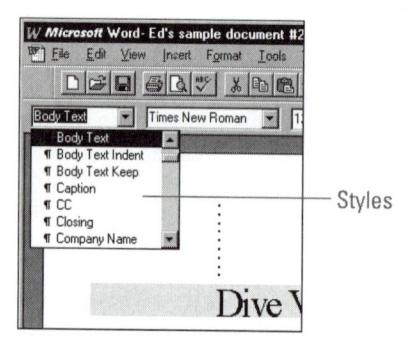

Figure 8-2: The drop-down Style list on the Formatting toolbar.

4. Click on the desired style to apply it to the selected paragraphs.

Hot Stuff: If you don't like the effects of any style that you apply, remember that you can undo its effects by immediately choosing Edit⇨Undo Style.

Using the keyboard

If you are using a document that is based on Word's default or Normal template, you can use keyboard shortcuts to apply the available styles. Table 8-1 shows the available styles in the Normal template and the keyboard shortcuts that you can use to apply the styles.

Why don't I see all the styles that you show here?

If you look at the available styles shown in Figure 8-2 and compare them to the styles shown in your own Style list, you may find that the lists don't exactly match. "Where are all these styles?" you may ask. Remember that a template is a collection of styles. When you look in the Style list, the styles that you see are part of the template that you are using. I may be using a different template, so my styles will be different. For now, keep in mind that you can choose different templates in the New dialog box that appears when you start a new document. Each template in the New dialog box has its own list of styles that are useful for that particular type of document.

Table 8-1
Styles that have keyboard shortcuts

Style name	Formatting applied	Keyboard shortcut
Normal	Font: Times New Roman 10 point; Language: English (US); Flush Left	Ctrl+Shift+N
Heading 1	Normal; Arial 14 point; Bold; Space Before 12 pts; After 3 pts	Alt+Ctrl+1
Heading 2	Normal; Arial 12 point; Bold; Italic; Space Before 12 pts; After 3 pts	Alt+Ctrl+2
Heading 3	Normal; Arial 12 point; Space Before 12 pts; After 3 pts	Alt+Ctrl+3

Hot Stuff: You can quickly apply the same style to a number of items in your document. After applying the style to the first selection, select the additional text that you want formatted with the same style and press Ctrl+Y.

I applied a style, and my italicized words are now normal text. Why?

If you apply a style that includes bold or italics to selected text that already contains bold or italic formatting, the existing bold or italicized text in the selection will change back to normal text. This change happens because in Word, bold and italic character formatting is a "switch" that is either on or off for a given selection. So any bold or italic formatting applied by a style will toggle that switch, which will remove any bold or italic formatting that was previously applied to the selection.

Defining a Style

Word provides two overall methods for creating, or defining, styles. In the first method, you choose Format⇨Style and then click on the New button in the Style dialog box. In the New Style dialog box that appears, you enter a name for the new style and then click on the Format button to define the style. Then you can choose any of the choices from the Format menu to lay out the aspects of the style. (Yes, this is a lot to describe in one paragraph, but the next section gives you the complete scoop.)

Styles can also be defined by example. In plain English, this means that you can define a style based on an existing paragraph that already has all the desired formatting. This method is easier, but you can be sure of exactly what you are getting only if you use the first method.

Using the Style command

The more powerful (and, yes, more complicated) method of defining a style is using Format⇨Style. This command opens the Style dialog box, as shown in Figure 8-3. Click on the New button in the dialog box to reveal the New Style dialog box, as shown in Figure 8-4.

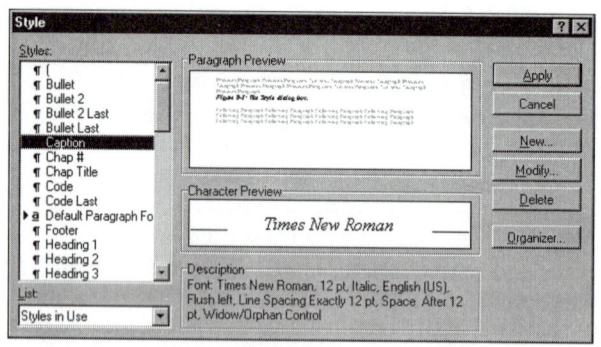

Figure 8-3: The Style dialog box.

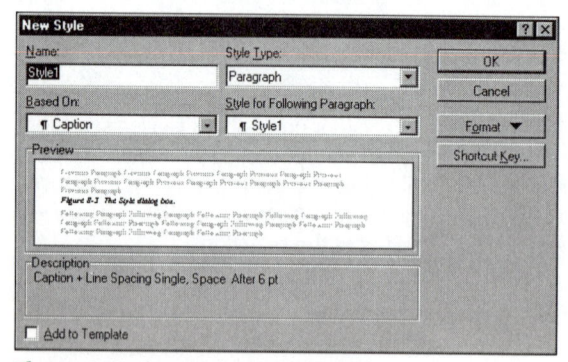

Figure 8-4: The New Style dialog box.

You can change the formatting for the style by clicking on the Format button and selecting the appropriate area that you want to format. Each of the menu choices displayed by the Format button (Font, Paragraph, Tabs, Border, Language, Frame, and Numbering) takes you directly to the dialog box that the particular formatting command uses. For example, choosing Font displays the Font dialog box that is displayed with Format⇨Font; choosing Paragraph displays the Paragraph dialog box that is displayed with Format⇨Paragraph; and so on. The Style Type list box offers two choices — Character or Paragraph — where you indicate whether your new style is a character style or a paragraph style.

Make the desired changes in the respective dialog boxes and then click on the OK button to get back to the New Style dialog box. (The only formatting option not covered elsewhere in this text is the one provided by the Language option. This menu option brings up a dialog box that lets you change the language used by the Spelling Checker, Thesaurus, and Grammar Checker.)

You can use the Based On list box in the New Style dialog box to base a style that you are creating on an existing style. (If the style that you are defining is not based on any other style, this box will be blank.) To base a new style on an existing one, type the name of the existing style into this text box or choose an existing style name. (This technique is covered in more detail in the "Basing a style on another style" section later in the chapter.)

You can turn on the Add to Template check box at the bottom of the New Styles dialog box if you want to add the style that you've defined to the current template. (If you are using the default Normal template, the style will be added to that template and will therefore be available in all documents that you create in Word.)

After you have made all the desired changes to the formatting, you enter a name for the style in the Name box. Remember that each style name must be unique. Because it doesn't make sense to have two styles with the same name, Word doesn't let you make this mistake. Style names are case sensitive, however, so you can use "Figures" and "figures" as two different style names (although to do so would be terribly confusing to most people). Style names can be up to 253 characters in length, and they can use any combination of characters except for the backslash (\), the curly braces ({ }), or the semicolon (;).

After giving your style a name, click on the OK button to return to the Style dialog box. From here you can apply the style to the current paragraph or selection by clicking on the Apply button. When you do, the dialog box closes and you are back in your document. After the style has been defined, you can apply that style to the desired paragraphs of the document by using the techniques covered under the "Using the Formatting toolbar" section earlier in this chapter.

The Style dialog box also contains other interesting buttons in addition to the Apply button. Use the Modify button to change the formatting of an existing style that you have selected in the Styles list box. Use the Delete button to remove an unwanted style from the Styles list box. Click on the Organizer button to display the Organizer dialog box, which lets you rename and copy a style (see the "Copying, deleting, and renaming styles" section later in this chapter for more information).

Defining styles by example

The easy way to define a new style is to base it on an existing paragraph and then use the buttons on the Formatting toolbar. You can create a new style based on an existing paragraph by performing these steps:

1. Be sure that the Formatting toolbar is displayed. Then place the insertion point anywhere in the paragraph on which you want to base the style.
2. Click *once* in the Style list box on the Formatting toolbar to display the current style of the paragraph. The style is highlighted (see Figure 8-5), indicating that you can type a new name.

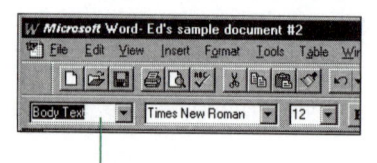

Style list box

Figure 8-5: A highlighted entry in the Style list box.

3. Type a name for the style and press Enter. Word will add the new style name to the list of styles for the document.

Assigning a shortcut key to a style

As a time-saving feature, Word lets you assign shortcut keys to styles. Then anytime you want to apply a style that you use regularly, all you have to do is press a key combination to apply the style to the selected paragraphs. To assign a shortcut key to a style, perform the following steps:

1. Choose Format⇨Style.
2. In the Style dialog box (refer to Figure 8-3), select the desired style and then click on the Modify button to open the Modify Style dialog box.
3. Click on the Shortcut Key button to open the Customize dialog box (see Figure 8-6). In this dialog box, you can assign a shortcut key to the style that you have created.
4. Press the desired shortcut key combination. The Currently Assigned To prompt appears in the dialog box.
5. The Currently Assigned To area tells you whether the key combination that you have chosen is currently selected for another use in Word. If you see an existing description for that particular key combination, you can overwrite the existing key assignment or choose another.
6. Click on the Assign button to assign the shortcut key to the style.

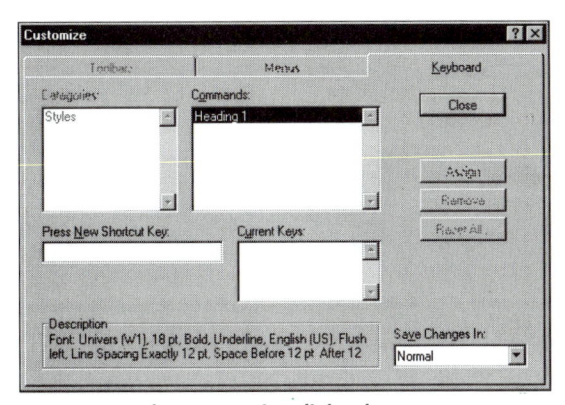

Figure 8-6: The Customize dialog box.

Before you create a large number of styles on your own, first take the time to become familiar with the styles that are already built into Word's templates. Word may already have a style that will accomplish what you want.

Basing a style on another style

In Word, you can base a new style on an existing style. Suppose that you have an existing paragraph of text that uses the Normal style. If you indent that paragraph by $1/2$-inch, click once in the Style list box, and type a new name (to define a new style based on the way that the paragraph now appears). The new style that you have just created is based on the Normal style. If you then change the font used for the Normal style, the font used for your new style would also change. In such a case, the Normal style would be the *base style* for the new style that you created.

You can see which (if any) style is used as a base style by opening the Style dialog box (by choosing Format⇨Style). As you select any style in the Styles list box at the left, the Description area at the bottom of the dialog box shows whether that style is based on another style. For example, Figure 8-7 shows the Style dialog box with the Body Text style selected. The Description area tells you that the Body Text style is based on the Normal style with 6-point line spacing after paragraphs are added.

Be aware that this capability to base a style on another style can create quite a chain of interdependencies. For example, in a document that is based on Word's built-in Letter1 template, the Signature Name style is based on the Signature style, which is based on the Body Text style, which is based on the Normal style. A change to the paragraph indentation used by the Normal style would affect all the other styles named.

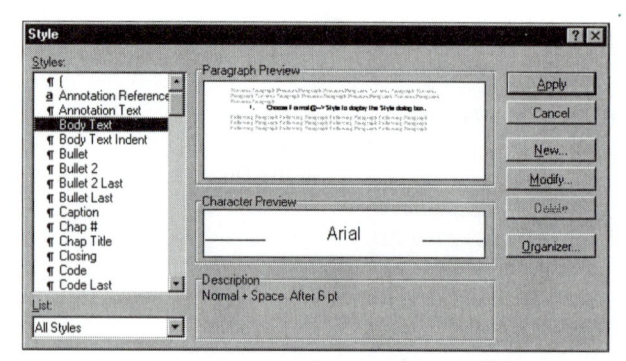

Figure 8-7: The Body Text style is based on the Normal style, according to the Description area in this dialog box.

You can change the base style for any style by using the options found in the Modify Style dialog box. To change a style's base style, follow these steps:

1. Choose Format⇨Style to display the Style dialog box.

2. In the Styles list box, select the style for which you want to change the base style.

3. Click on the Modify button to reveal the Modify Style dialog box, as shown in Figure 8-8. In the Name text box, you should see the name of the style that you want to change. In the Based On list box, you should see the base style that is currently used.

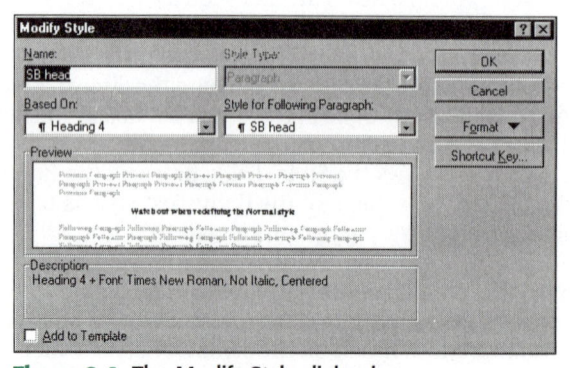

Figure 8-8: The Modify Style dialog box.

4. Click on the arrow at the right side of the Based On list box to display all available styles in the document.

Watch out when redefining the Normal style

Word takes advantage of the fact that styles can be based on styles by basing many of its built-in styles on the Normal style. Therefore, redefining the Normal style can cause major repercussions elsewhere, some of which may prove undesirable. For example, if you redefine the Normal style to use 12-point Arial font, every style based on the Normal style will use 12-point Arial, whether you like it or not. (In your headers and footers, 12-point Arial will look pretty silly.)

5. Choose a desired style to serve as the base style and then click on the OK button.

Note If you turn on the Add to Template check box before clicking on the OK button, the changes to the base style are recorded in the template that you used to create the document.

Copying, deleting, and renaming styles

Word lets you copy styles from one document to another. In many cases, this capability helps you to avoid the work necessary in creating the same style twice. You can copy styles from one document to another — and you can delete and rename styles — by performing the following steps:

1. Choose Format⇨Style.
2. In the Style dialog box, click on the Organizer button. Word displays the Organizer dialog box, as shown in Figure 8-9.

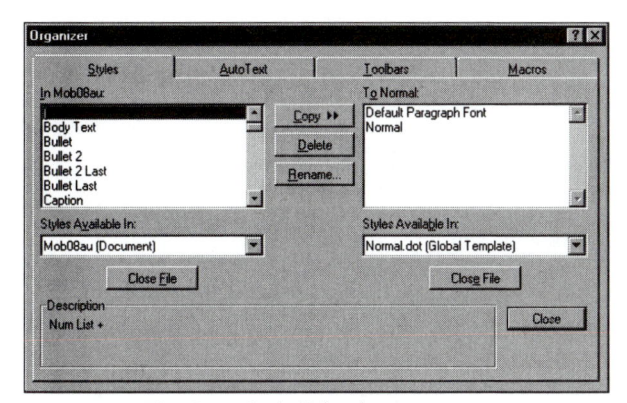

Figure 8-9: The Organizer dialog box.

3. To copy a style to or from a different document or template, click on the Close File button and then click on the Open File button to open the desired document or template that contains the style. Select the desired style in the list box to the left and click on the Copy button to copy the style to the other document or template.

4. To delete a style, click on the desired style in the list box to the left and then click on the Delete button. (Note that Word will not let you delete its built-in styles; you can delete only custom styles that you or others have created.)

5. To rename a style, click on the desired style in the list box to the left and then click on the Rename button and enter a new name in the dialog box that appears. Then click on Close.

Finding Styles When You Need Them

Word provides two different ways in which you can find and use the various styles. You can display information about your styles as you work, using Word's Help feature. And you can use Format⇨Style Gallery.

Displaying style names as you work

You can see which styles are in effect in your documents in two ways. One surprisingly simple way is to use the context-sensitive help that is built into Word to display a dialog box that shows the style information for any text in the document. First click on the Help button on the Standard toolbar. The mouse pointer now includes a question mark along with the usual arrow. Then click on any place within the text that you are curious about. After you click, a balloon appears that contains the style and formatting information (see Figure 8-10).

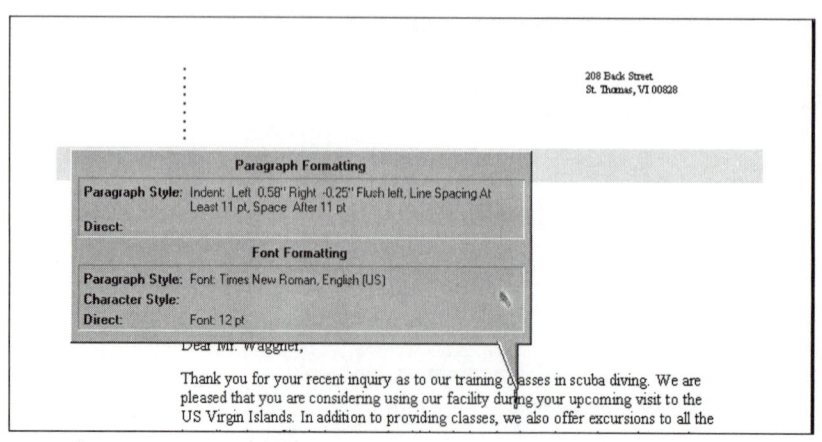

Figure 8-10: A balloon that displays formatting and style information.

The information in the dialog box includes the styles that are applied to the paragraph and the paragraph and font settings. As long as the mouse pointer includes the question mark, you can click on any other text in the document to see its formatting. To turn off the help, again click on the Help button on the Standard toolbar.

Another way to see the styles that you have used in your document is to display them on-screen in the left margin area. In Figure 8-1, you can see the styles displayed in such a manner. To see your styles to the left of the screen, first make sure that you are in either Normal or Outline View (you can't show styles in the margin in any of the other views of Word). Then perform the following steps:

1. Choose Tools⇨Options.
2. Click on the View tab in the Options dialog box.
3. In the Style Area Width box, enter or select a desired width. (One inch works well for showing the names of most styles, unless you've added very long style names to your document.)
4. Click on the OK button. After you do so, the style names in your document appear to the left of the document. You can remove the style names from view by opening the Options dialog box again and changing the Style Area Width setting to zero.

Using the Style Gallery

With Word's plethora of built-in styles scattered across numerous templates, it can be challenging to find where a useful style is located. To help you find the styles that you are looking for, use Word's Style Gallery dialog box (see Figure 8-11). To open this dialog box, choose the Style Gallery command from the Format menu.

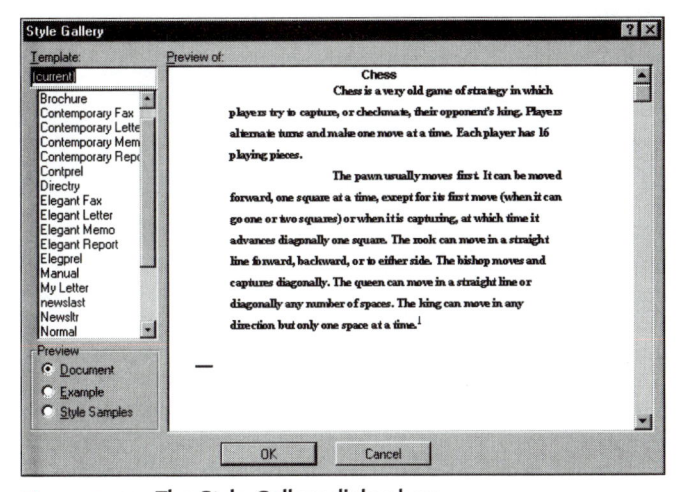

Figure 8-11: The Style Gallery dialog box.

The Template list box contains all the available templates. You can click on any template name in the list box to see a preview of the existing document that uses the styles contained in that particular template. At the lower-left corner of the dialog box, you can click on the Style Samples radio button to view samples of the different styles instead of viewing a preview of the document. And you can click on the Example radio button to see an example document formatted with the various available styles. The Style Gallery is often helpful when you're trying to locate a style that will work in a given situation.

Defining and Applying Styles: An Exercise

Try your hand at creating new styles and applying them to a document by performing the following exercise:

1. Open any existing document that contains two or more paragraphs and place the insertion point anywhere in the first paragraph.

2. From the Format menu, choose the Style command. When the Style dialog box appears, click on the New button.

3. In the Name text box, type **My Style** as a name for the new style.

4. Click on the Format button and choose Font from the list to display the Font dialog box (see Figure 8-12). In the Font list box, choose any font other than the one you are currently using and then click on the OK button.

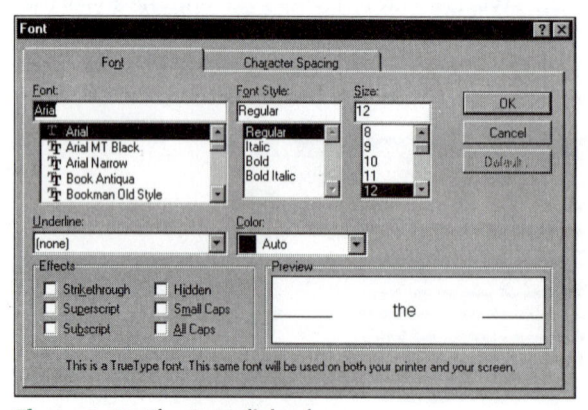

Figure 8-12: The Font dialog box.

5. Press the Format button again and choose Paragraph to display the Paragraph dialog box (see Figure 8-13). In the Indentation area, set the Left value to 0.5 inches; then click on the Special list box, choose First Line, and set the First Line indentation to 0.5 inches. Set the Line Spacing to 1.5 lines and then click on the OK button.

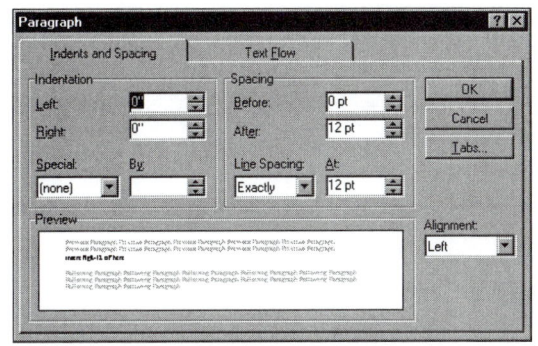

Figure 8-13: The Paragraph dialog box.

Note that the Preview box lists the formatting changes that you have made, including your selected font, the new paragraph indentations, and the new line spacing.

6. Click on the OK button to add the new style to the list.

7. To apply the style and close the Style dialog box, click on the Apply button.

Perform the following steps to apply the new style to another paragraph in the document.

1. Place the insertion point anywhere in a different paragraph of the document.

2. If the Formatting toolbar is not visible, turn it on by choosing the Toolbars command from the View menu and turning on the Formatting check box.

3. Click on the arrow to the right of the Styles list box and choose My Style from the list. When you choose the style, the paragraph assumes the style's formatting, as shown in Figure 8-14.

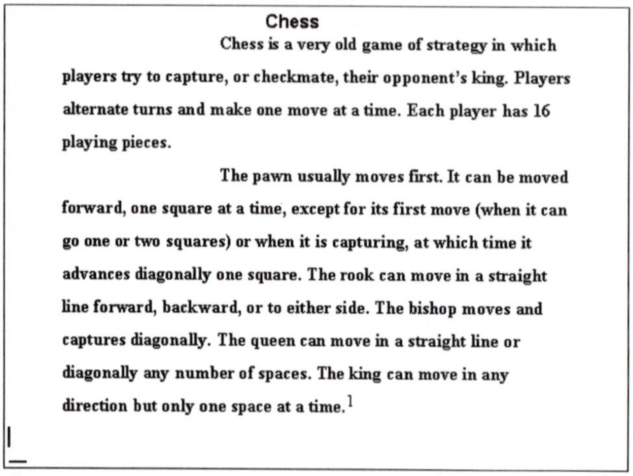

> **Chess**
> Chess is a very old game of strategy in which players try to capture, or checkmate, their opponent's king. Players alternate turns and make one move at a time. Each player has 16 playing pieces.
>
> The pawn usually moves first. It can be moved forward, one square at a time, except for its first move (when it can go one or two squares) or when it is capturing, at which time it advances diagonally one square. The rook can move in a straight line forward, backward, or to either side. The bishop moves and captures diagonally. The queen can move in a straight line or diagonally any number of spaces. The king can move in any direction but only one space at a time.[1]

Figure 8-14: The results of applying the styles to sample paragraphs.

Understanding Templates

If you want to carry your consistency of document design even further than character and paragraph formatting, you'll want to make use of templates. As mentioned earlier in the chapter, templates are collections of styles that are saved to a file. They are models that serve as molds for your documents.

When you create a new document with the New command from the File menu, Word always asks which template you want to use by displaying the available templates on several tabs in the New dialog box (see Figure 8-15). The tabs group Word's pre-defined templates according to their styles. Any new templates that you create appear under the General tab. If you click on the OK button in this dialog box without making a selection, Word uses the default Normal template to create the new document.

When you select a template from this dialog box, your new document takes on all the features belonging to that template — including any text stored in the template; any character, paragraph, and page layout formatting; any preset styles; and any new styles that you have added to the document. Any macros, AutoText entries, or keyboard, menu, or toolbar definitions stored in the template are also available to the document.

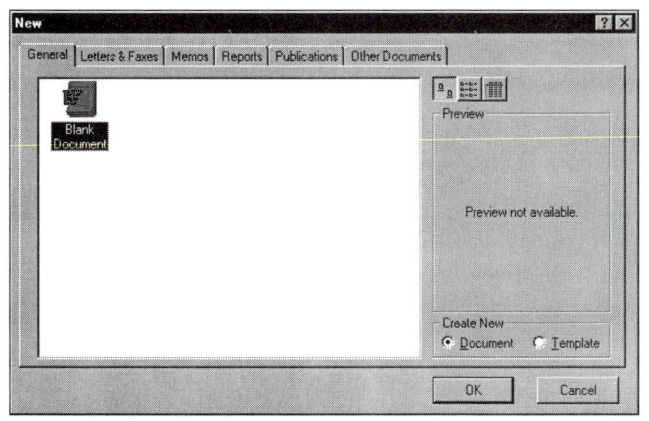

Figure 8-15: The New dialog box.

You can use any of Word's predefined templates, or you can create and save your own templates. If you take the time to examine the templates provided with Word, you may find many that can be useful in your work. Word comes with 37 templates, including

- ◆ Contemporary fax
- ◆ Contemporary letter
- ◆ Elegant fax
- ◆ Elegant letter
- ◆ Professional fax
- ◆ Professional letter
- ◆ Contemporary memo
- ◆ Elegant memo
- ◆ Professional memo
- ◆ Contemporary report
- ◆ Elegant report
- ◆ Professional report
- ◆ Agenda
- ◆ Award

- Calendar
- Newsletter
- Pleading
- Resume

Because a template is a document, you use the same procedure to create and save a template as you use for a document. Word lets you specify whether you want to create a document or a template when you use the New command from the File menu. At the lower-right corner of the New dialog box, simply click on the Template radio button to make the new document a template and then click on the OK button. When the new document appears on-screen, you can add whatever boilerplate text, formatting, and styles that you want and then save the file with the Save command from the File menu.

You can also specify that a file be saved as a template after you have created it. For example, if you have created a boilerplate document, and you want to store that document as a template, you can do so with the Save As command from the File menu. In the Save As dialog box, choose Document Template from the Save as Type list box. The file will be saved as a template with the .DOT extension.

Working with Templates

When you need to set standards for more than just the character and paragraph formatting of your documents, you can use templates. As mentioned earlier in this chapter, templates can contain styles, and they can also contain boilerplate text or graphics, macros, and even custom menu, keyboard, and toolbar assignments.

What's "Normal"?

Some new users of Word get confused about what "Normal" refers to. Word has both a Normal *style* and a normal *template*, and the two don't mean the same thing. The Normal style refers to one particular style (available in all Word's default templates) that defines the character and paragraph formatting for ordinary text. The Normal template, on the other hand, is a template file (saved as `Normal.dot`) that contains Word's default styles along with the default keyboard, menu, and toolbar macro assignments. All styles and default keyboard, menu, and toolbar macro assignments that are saved to the Normal template are available for use from anywhere within Word.

Applying templates

To apply a template, you simply choose that template by name when you use Word's New command from the File menu. Any template (with a .DOT extension) that you create will appear in the General tab of the New dialog box.

Creating a template

You can create a new template for use with Word by performing the following steps:

1. From the File menu, choose the New command.
2. In the New dialog box, click on the Template radio button and then click on the OK button.
3. Design your template as desired. Word will automatically insert the text and graphics in the same location whenever a new document is created based on that template.
4. Add any desired character, paragraph, section, or page layout formatting and create any desired styles. Define any desired AutoText entries or desired macros.
5. From the File menu, choose the Save command.
6. In the File Name text box, enter a name for the template. By default, Word saves all template files to a folder named `Templates`, which is stored in the `Msoffice` folder.
7. Click on the Save button to save the template.

Basing a new template on an existing template

You can use a simple variation of the steps in the preceding section to create a new template based on an existing template. In the New dialog box, click on the Template radio button. Then, click on the desired tab under which the existing template is stored, or choose the name of the template on which you want to base the new template, and then click on the OK button. When you save the template, be sure to save it under a different name than the original template.

Modifying an existing template

To modify an existing template, you simply open the template in a way similar to the way you open a document. From the File menu, choose the Open command. In the Open dialog box, select Document Template from the List Files of Type list box. The list box then shows only those files with a .DOT extension, and you can choose the desired template by name, or you can enter the name in the File Name text box. Make the desired changes to the template and save the template with the Save command from the File menu.

Changing the default template

Word uses its default template, `Normal.dot`, to store all its *global settings,* those settings that are available no matter what document you are using. Because `Normal.dot` is the default template, it is worth the time you may need to spend to customize it so that it meets the needs of the work that you do. And because the Normal template is a template like all other templates, you can modify it (and save the changes) as you would any other template. Keep in mind that the Default button present in some dialog boxes also lets you change the default settings in the Normal template. You can change the defaults for the character font, the page setup, and the language used by the proofing tools.

To open the Normal template, choose the Open command from the File menu and select Document Templates from the List Files of Type list box. Then look in the `Templates` folder (by default, it's stored in the `Msoffice` folder, unless you have customized the storage locations during Office installation). Select the Normal template.

To change the default font, choose the Font command from the Format menu, select the desired font and point size in the Font dialog box, and then click on the Default button. Click on the Yes button in the next dialog box to verify that the changes should be stored in `Normal.dot`.

To change the default page setup, choose File⇨Page Setup and select the desired options in the Page Setup dialog box. You will have a choice of four tabs: Margins, Paper Size, Paper Source, and Layout. Click on the desired tab and make the appropriate choices in that tab. Click on the Default button and then click on the Yes button in the next dialog box to verify that the changes should be stored in `Normal.dot`. Click on the OK button to close the Page Setup dialog box.

To change the default language used by the proofing tools, choose the Language command from the Tools menu to open the Language dialog box shown in Figure 8-16. Select the desired language in the dialog box and then click on the Default button. Then click on the Yes button in the next dialog box to verify that the changes should be stored in `Normal.dot`. Click on the OK button to close the Language dialog box.

Note You may need to purchase optional dictionaries to use a language other than the one supplied with the version of Word for your country.

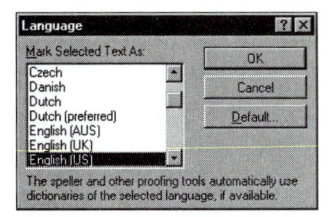

Figure 8-16: The Language dialog box.

When you are finished making changes to the Normal template, save the changes by using the Save command from the File menu.

Creating and Applying a Template: An Exercise

To give you practice in creating templates, create your own business letterhead as a template. You can later create documents based on that template, and the documents will automatically include your letterhead. Perform the following steps to create your own template:

1. Choose File➪New.
2. In the New dialog box, click on the Template radio button and then click on the OK button. A blank document appears with the title Template1.
3. On the first three lines of the document, type your name and address. Add a blank line after the last line of your address.
4. Select all three lines and press Ctrl+E to center the text.
5. With the three lines still selected, choose the Font command from the Format menu. In the Font dialog box, select a font that you like and a larger point size (our example uses Century Gothic, 14 point). Click on Bold in the Font Style list box and then click on the OK button.
6. Press Ctrl+End to move to the end of the document and press Enter twice.
7. From the File menu, choose the Save command. When the Save As dialog box appears, you will notice that any filenames shown are all existing template files.
8. Enter **My Letter** in the File Name text box and then click on the Save button to save the template.
9. Close the document by choosing File➪Close.

You can now create documents based on the template that you saved. Choose File➪New, select My Letter from the General tab of the New dialog box, and then click on the OK button. The result will be a new document that already contains your letterhead, such as the example shown in Figure 8-17.

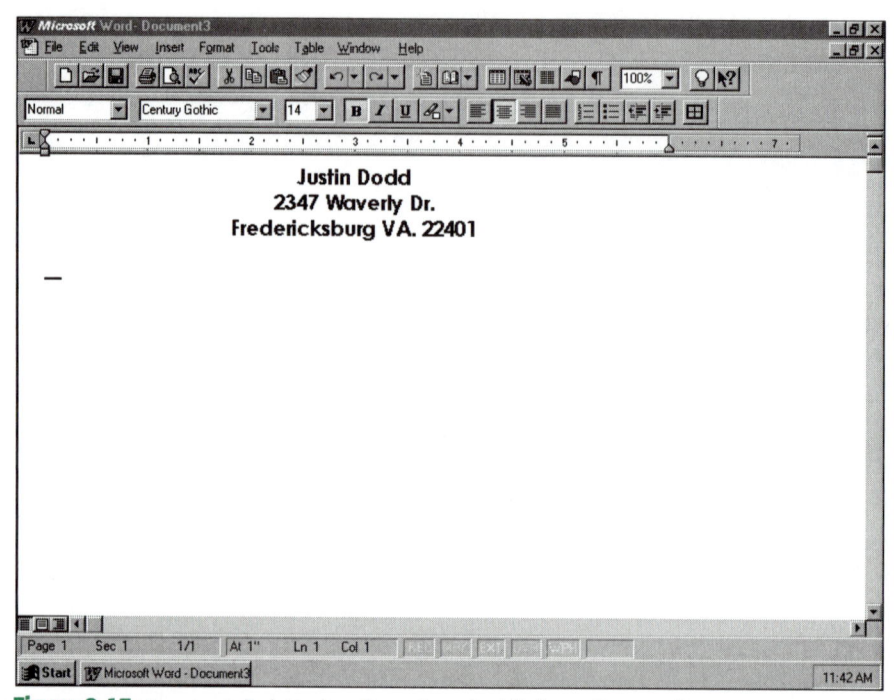

Figure 8-17: An example letterhead produced with the new template.

This chapter gives you an idea of what you can do with styles and templates — a detailed discussion of the possibilities could fill a book of its own. You can obtain more ideas about creating styles and templates of your own by examining the sample templates provided with Word.

Summary

In this chapter, you learned how you can use styles and templates to mold the appearance of your documents to suit your needs. The following points were covered:

- Styles are collections of character and paragraph formatting decisions; templates are collections of styles, macros, and keyboard and toolbar assignments.
- You can choose a variety of styles from the Style list on the Formatting toolbar.
- You can base new styles on existing styles.
- You can copy styles between documents and between templates.
- Word provides a number of predefined templates that contain different collections of styles.
- All of Word's global settings regarding formatting are stored in the Normal template and saved under the name `Normal.dot`.

In the next chapter, you'll learn how you can use macros to automate many of the tasks that you normally perform in Word.

Where to go next...

- Because styles are, in effect, collections of character and paragraph formatting, it makes sense to be familiar with the mechanics of formatting when you want to put styles to work in your Word documents. You can find more details about those formatting specifics in Chapter 3.
- The complexities offered by styles and templates are naturals to use when you want to do desktop publishing in Word. Chapter 10 has the lowdown on desktop publishing.

✦ ✦ ✦

Working with Word Macros

CHAPTER 9

In This Chapter

Defining a macro

Introducing the Macro toolbar

Creating a macro

Running a macro

Copying macros to different templates

Macros have always had a bad reputation. Macros were first made popular in DOS-based spreadsheet programs — where you had to be a borderline programmer to use them. Because things are no longer that dismal from an ease-of-use point of view, there is no need to fear macros in Word. Macros are easy to create, and they can accomplish a great deal by saving you time in your everyday work. In this chapter, you will learn what macros are and how you can create them. You can then take a look at step-by-step examples that illustrate how you use macros to automate your common tasks in Word.

Defining Macros

Macros are recorded combinations of keystrokes and certain mouse actions. Macros can automate many of the tasks that you normally perform manually, keystroke by keystroke, within Word. In a macro, you can record a sequence of keyboard and mouse entries and link them to a single key combination or to a menu option or to a toolbar button. Later, you can "play back" the recorded sequence by pressing the assigned key combination or clicking the toolbar button or choosing the menu option. When the macro is played back, Word performs as if you had manually executed the operations contained within the macro. When your work involves highly repetitive tasks, such as the production of daily reports or the repeating of certain formatting tasks, you can often save many keystrokes by creating a few macros.

More Info At first glance, macros may seem similar to AutoText entries (see Chapter 2), but there are significant differences. AutoText entries can reproduce text at any location in a document. Macros can do much more than simulate typing. Macros can perform menu and dialog box selections, something that you cannot do with AutoText entries. For example, if you routinely print two copies of a certain weekly report, you can create a macro that opens the document, chooses File, prints from the menus, and marks the dialog box options needed to send two copies of the report to the printer.

Word records your macros as instructions in the programming language used by the Microsoft Office applications: Visual Basic for Applications (or VBA for short). Don't panic at the sound of the name (or the implication that you need to learn programming). You can create macros in Word without knowing an iota about Visual Basic for Applications. You can create macros in the following two ways in Word:

- ✦ You can record a series of keyboard and mouse actions, the most commonly used method. This method requires no knowledge of Word's programming language.
- ✦ You can type a macro directly into a macro window. This method enables you to accomplish some advanced tricks by means of VBA commands that you can't do by recording actions, but it requires you to "get your hands dirty" to some extent with VBA.

Not only can you use a macro to combine a sequence of commands that you use regularly, but you can also use a macro to perform routine editing and formatting tasks faster. You can also create a macro to get to those well-buried Word features more quickly, such as the dialog box that you use to change printer options.

Macros are especially useful when you format documents. You may have to change a document's font and spacing, enter heading styles, change margins, and check spelling and grammar. If you make these changes regularly, create a macro so that you don't have to invoke the same commands over and over again. The following sections show you how to make your life easier with macros.

Alternatives to macros

After spending this much time touting the benefits of macros, you should know that sometimes a macro may not be the most effective solution to a specific need. Before you jump into the task of designing macros for any task that you handle often, consider whether another feature of Word can handle the task with less effort on your part. If you want to use a macro to apply many character or paragraph formatting options to selected text, consider using a style sheet instead. If you want to use a macro to type long, repetitive phrases, note that you can use AutoCorrect instead to designate an abbreviation of your choices to serve as the phrase. And if you are trying to use a macro to automate the process of filling out a form, you can use fields to make this task easier.

Introducing the Macro Toolbar

When you are working with macros, Word puts the Macro Record toolbar on the screen. Before continuing, be aware that you use the Macro toolbar only when you create your macros in Visual Basic or edit the macros after you create them. Unless you are into creating your macros in Visual Basic, you may want to just file this information away for later use.

This toolbar is different from other Word toolbars because you can't view it by choosing View➪Toolbars and turning on its check box. The Macro toolbar is available only when you are creating a macro in Visual Basic or editing a macro. Figure 9-1 shows the Macro Record toolbar.

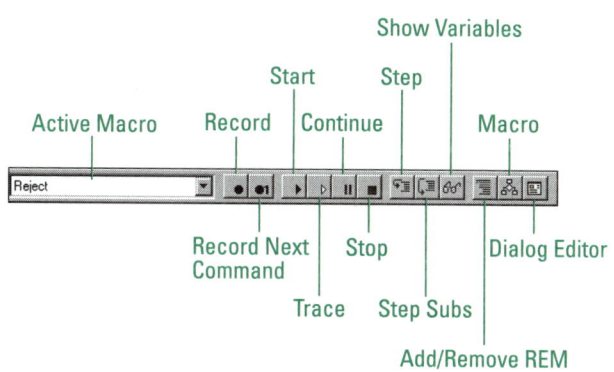

Figure 9-1: The Macro Record toolbar.

Table 9-1 describes the function of the Macro toolbar items.

	Table 9-1
	Macro toolbar items
Toolbar item	***Function***
Active Macro box	Contains the name of the macro
Record	Turns macro recording off or on
Record Next Command	Records only the next command chosen by the user
Start	Starts the macro currently selected in the Macro Name box
Trace	Highlights each statement in the active macro as it runs

(continued)

Table 9-1 *(continued)*

Toolbar item	Function
Continue	Continues the running of the macro
Stop	Stops running the macro
Step	Runs the active macro a single step (or macro operation) at a time
Step Subs	Runs the active macro a single step at a time and considers all the steps within the subroutine to be a single step
Show Variables	Provides a list of all variables used in the active macro
Add/Remove REM	Adds or removes a remark (REM) statement at the start of the selected line in the macro
Macro	Displays the Macro dialog box, which you can use to delete, create, run, or edit a macro
Dialog Editor	Starts the Dialog Editor, which can be used to create dialog boxes

Storing Macros

Where you store macros depends on two things: the settings in the Template and Add-ins dialog box (which appears when you choose File⇨Templates) and whether you are using the default template (`Normal.dot`). If you are using the default template, macros are stored in `Normal.dot`. When you exit Word, you are asked whether you want to store the macros you've created during a session to the `Normal.dot` template; you can answer Yes to store the macros or No to discard the macros.

If you are using a template different from `Normal.dot`, the storage location for new macros depends on the settings in the Templates and Add-ins dialog box. If you turn on the check box for the template you are using, Word saves macros in that template. You can click on the Add button to display all your templates, and double-click on any template to add it to the list in the Templates and Add-ins dialog box. In addition to saving Macros to templates you've checked in the Templates and Add-ins dialog box, on exit Word will ask if you want to save the new macros to the `Normal.dot` template file. All macros saved to `Normal.dot` are *global* in nature, which means that they are available from any document in Word.

Creating Macros

The easiest way to record a macro is to turn on Word's macro recorder with Tools⇨Macro and then follow the steps in the dialog boxes that appear. You then perform the desired actions with your keyboard and mouse and tell Word to stop recording.

Note You can also create macros manually by using Visual Basic for Applications, the programming language used with Word. Using Visual Basic for Applications to write and edit macros is beyond the scope of this chapter, but in short, you open a macro-editing window and type macro instructions.

Hot Stuff The macro recorder is limited in an important way: You cannot record mouse actions within a document, such as selecting text with the mouse. If you try to use the mouse within a document, Word just beeps. You *can* use the mouse to select menu options and choose dialog box settings, however. If you want to select text as part of a macro, use the keyboard. (You can hold down the Shift key and use the arrow keys to select large amounts of text, and you can use the Ctrl+A key combination to select all text in a document.)

Preparing to create your macro

Before you record your macro, you need to make some decisions about how you will invoke your macro, in what kinds of documents you will use your macro, and so on. Keep the following points in mind:

- ✦ Give some thought to the overall workspace and how it should appear when the macro runs. You want to organize the workspace in the same manner as it should appear when the macro runs. For example, if you will use the macro in a blank document, you should have a blank document on-screen before you begin recording the macro.

- ✦ Think about all the steps you need to take to accomplish the task for which you are creating the macro. Write the steps down if this will help you remember them. You don't want to forget an important step as you are recording the macro.

- ✦ If you want the macro to apply to a selected piece of text, select the text before you begin to record the macro.

- ✦ Think of a name for the macro that reminds you of the macro's function. For example, if you have a bad habit of typing two periods at the end of a sentence, and you want a macro that deletes the extra period, you can call the macro DELETE_PERIOD.

- ✦ Decide how you want to invoke your macro. You can assign a shortcut keystroke to your macro, place it in a menu in the menu bar, or create a button for it in a toolbar.

- When you choose to assign a shortcut keystroke to a macro, you can use Shift keys, Ctrl keys, or a combination of Ctrl and Shift keys along with all letters, numbers, and function keys F2 through F12. Word also lets you use the Insert and Delete keys alone or with the Ctrl or Shift keys. When you assign the keystroke, simply press it to execute the macro. So if you assign Ctrl+Alt+P to a macro that prints two copies of the document that's currently open, and then you open a document and press Ctrl+Alt+P, the document prints twice.

> **Danger Zone**
>
> It's not a good idea to assign a macro to the Insert or Delete key because doing so disables the normal editing function of these keys. Also, be aware that Word has several shortcut keys that have already been assigned to execute other functions. You can assign a macro to these pre-assigned keystrokes, but if you do, their pre-assigned function will be lost. For example, Ctrl+B makes typed or selected text appear in bold font. If you assign Ctrl+B to a macro, you would not be able to use that key combination to apply bold to any text. Don't worry about accidentally overwriting a keystroke, however, because Word tells you whether it's already assigned to another function.

Recording the macro

To record a macro, follow these steps.

1. When a document is open, choose Tools⇨Macro. When no document is open, choose File⇨Macro. With either method, the Macro dialog box appears, as shown in Figure 9-2.

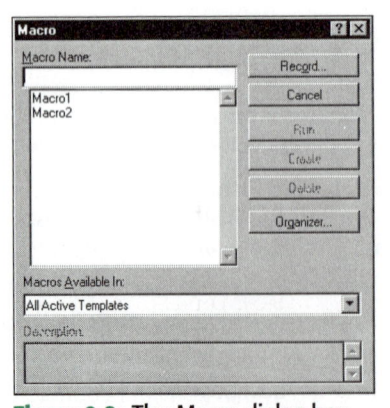

Figure 9-2: The Macro dialog box.

2. Type a name for your macro in the Macro Name text box or select an existing name to replace an existing macro. (Macro names cannot contain spaces, commas, or periods.) If you enter a new name, Word creates a new macro, saves it in the `Normal.dot` template, and makes the macro available to all active templates unless you choose a different template in the Macros Available In list box.

3. If desired, add an optional description in the Description text box.

4. Click on the Record button. The Record Macro dialog box appears (see Figure 9-3). Click on the appropriate button (Toolbars, Menus, or Keyboard) to associate the macro with a toolbar, menu, or keyboard shortcut to activate the macro.

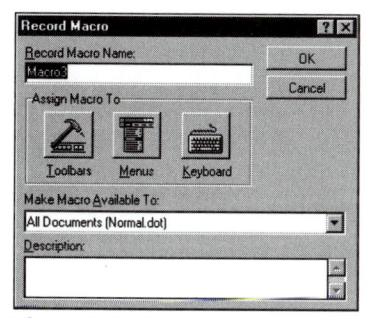

Figure 9-3: The Record Macro dialog box.

Hot Stuff: If you know Visual Basic for Applications and want to manually create your macro, click on the Create button *instead* of the Record button. A macro-editing window appears. You're on your own from here, though: this kind of programming is outside the scope of this book.

5. After you choose how you want to activate the macro, the Customize dialog box appears with the tab of your chosen method selected.

If you choose to add the macro to a toolbar, for example, the Toolbars tab of the Customize dialog box appears (see Figure 9-4). Drag the name of the macro to the area on the toolbar where you want to place the button. After you do this, the Custom Button dialog box appears (see Figure 9-5). You can assign any of the existing buttons to your macro by clicking on the desired button and then clicking on Assign. You can also create custom buttons by clicking on Edit to display a Button Editor dialog box, where you can design your own buttons. (Designing custom buttons is beyond the scope of this text, but you can click on the Help button in the Button Editor to get details on the use of the Button Editor.)

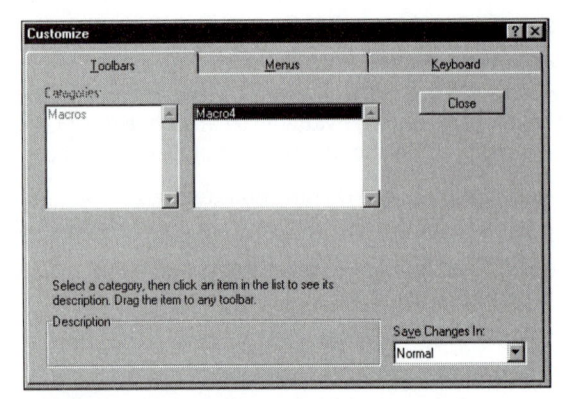

Figure 9-4: The Toolbars tab of the Customize dialog box.

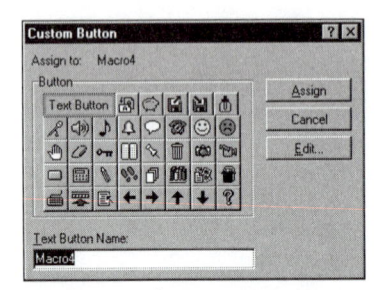

Figure 9-5: The Custom Button dialog box.

If you choose to add your macro to a menu, the Menus tab appears in the Customize dialog box (see Figure 9-6). To create a new menu, click on the Menu Bar button and enter the name that you want to appear on the custom menu bar. If you want the macro to appear on an existing menu, choose the menu in the Change What Menu list box and choose a menu item's name in the Position on Menu list box. Then click on the Add button. Your macro appears under this item in the menu.

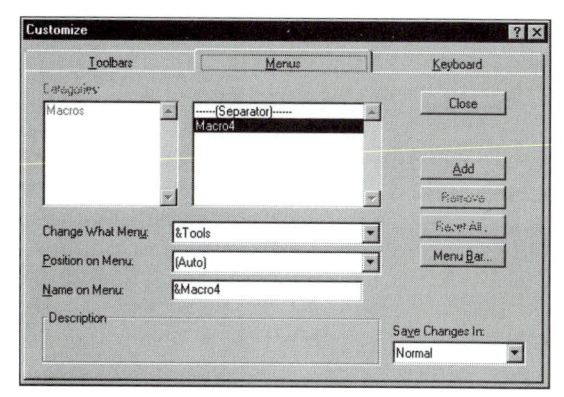

Figure 9-6: The Menus tab of the Customize dialog box.

If you choose to assign your macro to a shortcut keystroke, the Keyboard tab of the Customize dialog box appears (see Figure 9-7). Click in the Press New Shortcut Key text box and press the keystroke that you want to assign to the macro.

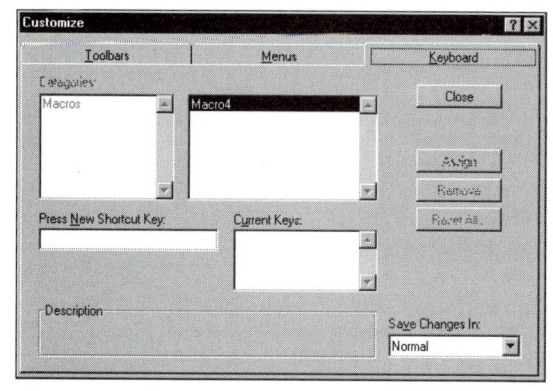

Figure 9-7: The Keyboard tab of the Customize dialog box.

6. When you have finished, click on the Close button to implement the changes and start recording the macro.

7. The Macro Recorder toolbar appears (see Figure 9-8). This toolbar contains just two buttons: a Stop button (the one on the left) and a Pause button (the one on the right). Perform the steps that you want to record in the macro.

If you want to pause the recording of the macro while you carry out actions that you don't want recorded, click on the Pause button. When you want to start recording again, click on the Pause button again.

What's recorded? What isn't?

Word's Macro Recorder doesn't actually record your *actions*; instead, it records the commands and the keystrokes that you enter. Remember that the Macro Recorder doesn't record mouse movements. If you want to create a macro that depends on selecting text, select the text by using the keyboard and not the mouse. Clicking the OK button in a dialog box — while you are recording a macro — records the state of every option in the tab that is visible in the dialog box. If you want to select options in another tab of the same dialog box, you must click OK to accept the options in the first tab and then reopen the dialog box. Click the new tab, select the options on it, and click OK to accept the options in the second tab. You do all these steps while you are recording the macro.

Figure 9-8: The Macro Recorder toolbar.

Stop

Pause

8. After you finish recording, click on the Stop button on the Macro Recorder toolbar.

Now you can activate the macro in the way you chose in Step 4: from the toolbar, from a menu, or by pressing the shortcut keystroke.

Running Macros

If you assigned your macro to a shortcut keystroke, a menu, or a toolbar, you can execute the macro by using the appropriate method. You can also run macros with Tools➪Macro. Follow these steps:

1. Choose Tools➪Macro. The Macro dialog box appears.

2. Type the name of the macro in the Macro Name text box or choose a macro from the list.

    If the macro you want to execute isn't listed, Word may not be configured to run macros from all active templates. If the Macros Available In list box does not contain either All Active Templates or the name of the template in which you created the macro, select either of those values. This list box controls available macros based on the templates in which they were created.

3. Click on the Run button. Word executes the chosen macro.

> **Hot Stuff:** If you try to run a macro and you can't find it, chances are that your document is using a different template from the one to which your macro was originally saved.

Understanding the Macro Dialog Box

As noted earlier, you enter the name of the desired macro in the Macro Name text box. After a name has been entered (or chosen from the list box), all the buttons at the right side of the dialog box are made available. Also, if you entered a description when you created the macro, the description appears in the Description text box at the bottom of the dialog box. The buttons in the dialog box perform the functions shown in Table 9-2.

Table 9-2
Macro dialog box buttons

Button	Purpose
Record	Begins recording the macro
Cancel	Closes the dialog box without running the macro
Run	Runs the selected macro
Create	Creates a macro by using the Visual Basic for Applications program code
Delete	Deletes the selected macro
Organizer	Displays the Organizer dialog box, which can be used to copy macros between templates

After you click on the Organizer button in the Macro dialog box, you can use the Macros tab of the Organizer dialog box to copy macros from one template to another. This dialog box is very useful when you have created a macro in one template that you want to use in another template. Follow these steps to copy a macro from one template to another:

1. Choose Tools⇨Macro to bring up the Macro dialog box.

2. Click on the Organizer button to bring up the Organizer dialog box, as shown in Figure 9-9. The Macros tab should be in the front of the dialog box.

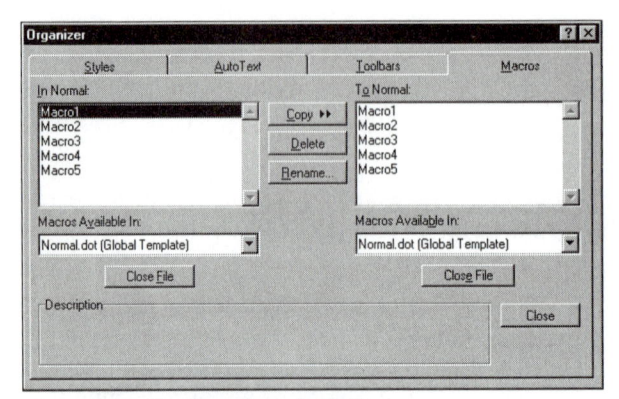

Figure 9-9: The Organizer dialog box.

3. You may need to close the open file. If so, click on the Close File button on the left side of the dialog box. Then click on the Open File button and choose the template in which you created the macro that you want to copy. On the right side of the dialog box, do these steps again: Click on the Close File button, click on the Open File button, and then choose the template to which you want to copy the macro.

4. The Copy button now appears active so that you can copy the macro to the other template. You can also rename the macro by clicking on the Rename button and entering a new name in the Rename dialog box.

Note Word stores your macros in the `Normal.dot` default template so that you can use them with every document. You can use the Organizer dialog box to sort out your macros by putting them into the templates in which you will use the macros most often.

Using Macros in an Example

To show you that macros aren't intimidating, try your hand at creating the following example. After following these steps to create the macro, you can then try one of your own that will help you speed up operations at work or at home.

In this example, let's assume that you regularly switch to Page Layout view from Normal view so that you can see as much of your document as possible. You routinely choose View➪Page Layout menu and then turn off the ruler. These steps are time-consuming if you do them a lot during a day, so you can save time by creating a macro to carry out the commands for you. To set the stage, first turn on your ruler, if it is not already on, by choosing the Ruler command from the View menu and be sure that you are in Normal view. Now you can record the macro by following these steps:

1. Choose Tools➪Macro to bring up the Macro dialog box.

2. In the Macro Name text box, enter **MoreSpace** as the name for this macro. Then click on the Record button to open the Record Macro dialog box.

3. Click on the Keyboard button to assign the macro to a keyboard combination. The Customize dialog box appears, with the Keyboard tab selected.

4. Because Word doesn't use Ctrl+Period for anything, it makes a good shortcut key. Press Ctrl+Period and then click on the Assign button to assign this key combination to the MoreSpace macro.

5. Click on the Close button to begin recording the macro.

6. Choose on the Ruler command from the View menu to turn off the ruler.

7. Choose View⇨Page Layout to activate this view.

8. End the recording by clicking on the Stop button (the one on the left) on the Macro Recorder toolbar.

To try out the macro, go back to the Normal view and redisplay the ruler. Then run the macro by pressing Ctrl+Period. Word turns off the ruler and switches to Page Layout view. Now you can create a macro that switches it back!

Creating Macros That Run Automatically

You can assign specific names to macros that cause them to run automatically when you perform a certain action. For example, if you want a macro to run whenever you start Word, you would name that macro AutoExec. If you want a macro to run each time you open a new document, you would name that macro AutoNew. Table 9-3 lists the names that you can assign macros to make them run when you perform the related action.

Table 9-3
Macros that run automatically on their related actions

Macro name	Action that triggers the macro
AutoExec	Runs when you start Word
AutoExit	Runs when you quit Word
AutoOpen	Runs when you choose File⇨Open
AutoNew	Runs when you choose File⇨New
AutoClose	Runs when you close the current document

You can have only one AutoExec macro for your copy of Word. However, you can have a different AutoOpen macro for each template. For example, a good use of an AutoOpen macro would be to activate a special toolbar that you need in that template or to add a special message to the screen. Note that an AutoClose macro, which runs whenever you close a document, will also run whenever you exit Word or exit Windows before closing a Word document (because Word automatically closes documents when you attempt to quit Word or Windows).

Hot Stuff
An excellent use for an AutoOpen macro is one that automatically changes to your favorite subdirectory for your Word files. When you create this macro, name it AutoOpen, and while recording, use the usual selections in the Open dialog box from the File menu to switch to your favorite directory. After switching directories, click on Stop to stop recording the macro.

Summary

In this chapter, you've learned how to use macros in Word.

- ✦ Macros are actually Visual Basic for Applications programs, but you don't need to know programming to create a macro. You can *record* a series of keystrokes and mouse actions as a macro.
- ✦ You can assign macros to toolbar buttons, menu options, and key combinations.
- ✦ Some macros can be associated with starting Word, exiting Word, creating a file, opening a file, or closing a file. Such macros execute automatically when the event occurs.

Where to go next...

- ✦ Macros can be used to perform a number of tasks. Printing is one of them. Chapter 4 has the details.
- ✦ You may also create macros for formatting that you do on a regular basis. For some ideas on the different formatting options you have and how you can go about implementing them, see Chapter 3.

✦ ✦ ✦

CHAPTER 10

Desktop Publishing with Word

In This Chapter

Adding columns to a document

Using Word's AutoFormat command

Importing graphics into a document

Adding business graphs to a document

Adding and working with frames

Understanding the organizational tools of desktop publishing

Using the Newsletter Wizard

This chapter explains how you can use several different techniques to take advantage of Word's desktop publishing capabilities. You will learn to create documents that contain graphic images, text boxes, frames, columns, newsletters, and other documents that contain headlines.

Word also provides significant drawing and charting tools that you can use to create business graphs (also called charts). You can easily insert the graphs you create — with such built-in Microsoft programs as Microsoft Graph or with many other programs, such as Harvard Graphics or CorelDRAW! — into a Word document.

Using Columns

When you get into desktop publishing, you will often want to insert columns into your documents, so this section explains just how to do that. You can add columns to only a section of your document, or you can set up the entire document in newspaper-style columns. To insert columns into a document, follow these steps:

1. Select the text that you want to place in columns.
2. Click on the Columns button on the Standard toolbar and choose the number of columns that you want for your text, or choose Format⇨Columns. The Columns dialog box (Figure 10-1) appears.

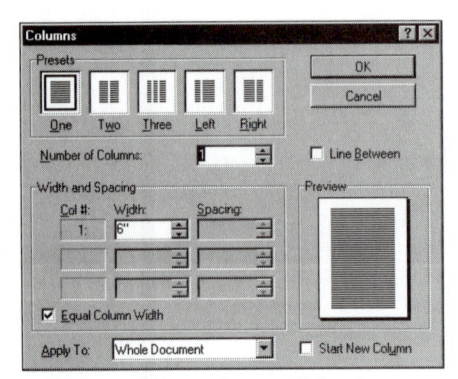

Figure 10-1: The Columns dialog box.

In this dialog box, you can choose one, two, or three columns for your document. You can also choose to have two columns, one smaller than the other, with the smaller column on the left or the right side of the page. You can also control width and spacing for the columns by adjusting the settings in the Width and Spacing area of the dialog box. The Preview area lets you see the layout of the document with the settings that you have chosen.

When you click on the Columns button on the Standard toolbar, a drop-down box lets you choose the number of columns that you want in your document. These columns are preset in width, but they can be adjusted, as explained in the next section.

After you have chosen the number of columns that you want for your document, you may need to change the preset column widths. There are two ways of changing the width of the columns. If you want to adjust the column width by using the Columns dialog box, you must first select the text that you have formatted for columns and then choose Format⇨Columns to open the Columns dialog box. In the Width and Spacing area, choose the desired width for the columns and click on the OK button to make the changes to your document.

You can also adjust the column width in the document itself. This method is very useful if you are not sure of the width that you want your column to be. To change the column width in the document, move your mouse pointer to the column marker on the ruler until the pointer turns into a double-sided arrow. Then click and drag to make the columns the width that you want.

> **So where are my columns?**
>
> If you add columns to a document and they aren't visible, don't think that you've done something horribly wrong. You are probably in Normal view. Columns aren't visible side-by-side in Normal view. To see your columns in a side-by-side format — the way they will actually appear when printed — you have to switch to Page Layout view (choose View⇨Page Layout). Keep in mind that many desktop publishing features of Word are not really evident unless you are in Page Layout view. So if you are doing a lot of desktop publishing work in Word, you may want to switch to Page Layout view after you have entered the basic text.

Using the AutoFormat Command

Automatic formatting is a relatively new feature, first introduced to Word with version 6.0. Word's AutoFormat command provides a quick and easy way to format a document that you have created. AutoFormat makes Word analyze each of the paragraphs in your document to determine how the paragraph is used. Even though you may have formatted the text, the AutoFormat command may change the formatting to improve the overall appearance of the document. The styles that you have applied while formatting the document are not changed unless you permit Word to do so. To accept the changes that Word makes, choose Accept from the AutoFormat dialog box.

AutoFormat removes extra returns or paragraph marks at the end of each line of body text. AutoFormat also replaces straight quotes and apostrophes with "smart" (curly) quotation marks and apostrophes. You can program AutoFormat so that it adds copyright (©), trademark (™), and registered trademark (®) symbols to a document.

AutoFormat can also replace hyphens, asterisks, or other characters that you have used in a bulleted list with another kind of bullet character. Finally, AutoFormat indents your paragraphs to replace horizontal spacing that you have inserted with the Tab key or the Spacebar.

To use AutoFormat, open the desired document and then choose Format⇨AutoFormat, or click on the AutoFormat button on the Standard toolbar. Before moving on, keep this in mind: if you use the AutoFormat button, you will not have the opportunity to review your changes. When you use this button it makes the changes; if you don't agree with any of them, you will need to go back and manually change them. Click on the OK button in the AutoFormat dialog box to begin the formatting process. When Word is finished formatting the document, it presents another dialog box that gives you the opportunity to accept all changes, reject all changes, or review the changes. You simply select the option that you want.

Some people may not be comfortable with permitting Word to make such global changes to their documents. However, you can control the changes that the AutoFormat command makes by adjusting the options on the AutoFormat tab of the Options dialog box (see Figure 10-2). To open this dialog box, choose Format➪AutoFormat➪Options. The AutoFormat tab lets you control the changes that Word makes to your document when you select the AutoFormat command. You can control whether Word preserves the styles that you apply or whether Word applies styles to lists, headings, and other paragraphs. You can also control whether Word makes adjustments to paragraph marks, spaces, tabs, and empty paragraphs. And in the Replace area of the AutoFormat tab, you can control the replacements that Word makes as it formats. It is a good idea to review these options before you begin the AutoFormat process to prevent unwanted changes.

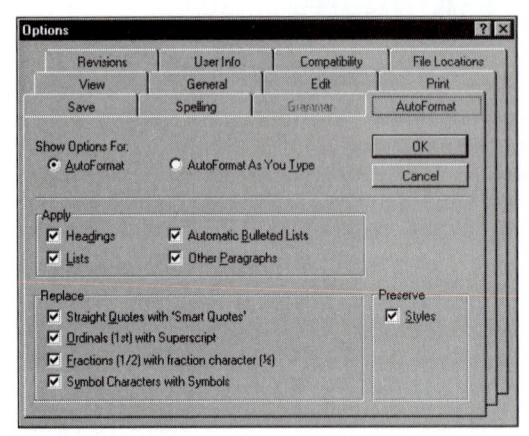

Figure 10-2: The AutoFormat tab of the Options dialog box.

You also have the option of reviewing the formatting results. When the formatting is complete, the second AutoFormat dialog box (Figure 10-3) appears. It contains the Review Changes button. Click on this button to review the changes made. Next you will see the Review AutoFormat Changes dialog box. In this box you can make changes one by one by clicking on the Find right arrow button to move forward, or clicking on the Find left arrow button to move back, to make changes. Each change is explained in the description area of the AutoFormat dialog box.

Hot Stuff: Keep in mind the differences between the AutoFormat button and Format➪AutoFormat. If you wish to quickly format your document, you can click on the AutoFormat button and review the changes after they are made. Remember, though, that if you use this method, you must review the changes manually. If you're at all worried about having Word wantonly reformat your text, and you wish to review each of the changes that AutoFormat makes, you will want to use Format➪AutoFormat. This will give you the chance to review each of the changes that you were made to your document.

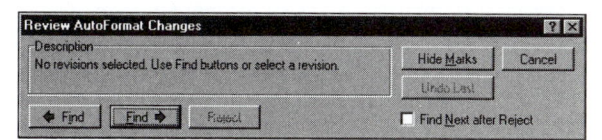

Figure 10-3: The Review AutoFormat Changes dialog box.

Word uses temporary revision marks and color to indicate the changes that it has made in the document. You can turn off these marks by clicking on the Show/Hide button on the Standard toolbar.

More Info: The AutoFormat command is very valuable. It can take the monotony out of formatting documents for those of you who don't do it along the way. If you want more information about the styles that Word uses as it formats your documents, see Chapter 8.

When *not* to use AutoFormat

Word's AutoFormat command shares an interesting trait with that of Excel's — they both work well with documents (in Excel's case, *worksheets*) that follow a conventional format. If your document is very unusual in terms of how it is structured, you may not like the kind of changes that AutoFormat applies. If you happen to click on the Accept button in the AutoFormat dialog box, and you don't like what Word does to your document, remember that you can reverse the changes by choosing Edit➪Undo.

Understanding Graphic Images

Word's capability to import graphic images from other software adds much to your desktop publishing capabilities. Word can import any of the image types in Table 10-1.

Table 10-1
Image types that you can import into Word

File type	Extension
AutoCAD 2-D Format	.DXF
CompuServe GIF	.GIF
Computer Graphics Metafile	.CGM
WordPerfect Graphics	.WPG
Encapsulated PostScript	.EPS
Hewlett-Packard Graphics Language	.HGL
JPEG	.JPG
Macintosh PICT	.PCT
Micrografx Designer/Draw	.DRW
PC Paintbrush	.PCX
Tagged Image Format	.TIF
TARGA	.TGA
Windows Bitmap	.BMP
Windows Metafile	.WMF

Word uses *graphic filters* to convert these image file formats to an image that appears in your document. When you install Word, it is possible to omit graphic filters that you don't need to save disk space. If you try to import a picture (with Insert⇨Picture) that has been captured in a file format that you don't have on your list, you have to run Word's installation program to re-install the graphic filter for that image file format. See your Word documentation for details.

Hot Stuff: As programs grow in popularity, new graphic filters are added to Word, so your version of Word may be able to import more file types than those shown here. Refer to your Word documentation to see which file types your version of Word can import.

In Windows, there are two kinds of graphic images: *bitmapped images*, which are created in painting programs, and *object images*, which are created in drawing programs. Because both types of images have definite advantages and disadvantages, you should be familiar with both.

Bitmapped images

Bitmapped images are images that are composed of a collection of dots, or *pixels,* on-screen. These images are called bitmaps because the image is literally defined within the computer by assigning each pixel on-screen to a storage bit (location) within the computer's memory. You can use painting programs to create bitmapped images. Your copy of Windows comes with a painting program called Paint. (See your Windows documentation for information about how you can use Paint to create your own bitmapped images.) You can purchase bitmapped images from various software suppliers, or you can find them on computer bulletin boards. Disks of bitmapped images typically contain collections of useful graphics, such as business cartoons, sports illustrations, or images of animals and nature settings. You can import bitmapped images that are stored under any of the file formats into a Word document. Figure 10-4 shows an example of ready-to-use bitmapped images from a clip art collection.

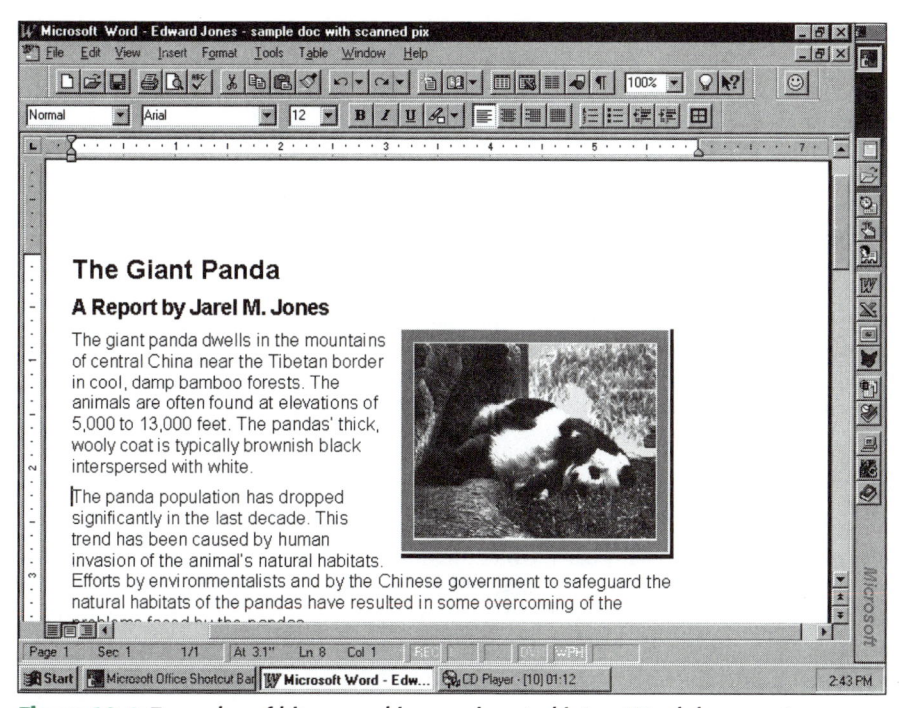

Figure 10-4: Examples of bitmapped images inserted into a Word document.

Some clip art is provided free with Paint. The art files have .BMP extensions and are stored in the same directory as your Windows program files. Computer bulletin boards and PC users groups are also excellent sources for clip art collections on disk.

Photographs are also stored as bitmapped images. If you have access to a scanner, you can scan photographs and store them on disk as bitmapped images by using the directions supplied with your scanner. You can then import the bitmapped image of the photo into your Word document. Note that black-and-white photos typically scan with greater clarity than color photos. Figure 10-5 shows an example of a photograph scanned into a bitmapped image.

Figure 10-5: A scanned photo inserted as a bitmapped image in a Word document.

Bitmapped images have one major advantage and one major disadvantage. The strength of bitmapped images is that you can easily modify them. Most painting programs (including Paint) enable you to modify existing parts of a bitmapped image by selectively adding or deleting bits. You can "zoom in" on the image as if it were under a magnifying glass, and you can turn individual pixels black, white, or any one of a range of colors. The disadvantage of bitmapped images is that you typically cannot modify their size by *scaling* (stretching or shrinking the image in one or more directions).

Object images

Object images are images that are based on a collection of geometric objects, such as lines, arcs, circles, or rectangles. Object images are created by drawing packages. Some of the popular drawing packages that run under Windows include CorelDRAW! and Micrografx Draw (you may be using one of these). Drawing programs work better than painting programs for creating line drawings, such as company logos, maps, and images of constructed objects (houses, cars, planes, bridges, and so on). Painting programs work better than drawing programs for projects where you would sketch on a piece of paper without using a ruler, such as drawing a portrait of a person's face.

The disadvantage of painting programs becomes the advantage of drawing programs, and vice versa. For example, object images can easily be scaled, which means that you can change the size of the object by stretching it or shrinking it in one or more directions. Because the object is based on a collection of straight or curved lines, the software simply expands or contracts the lines to expand or contract the entire image. The disadvantage of object images, however, is that you cannot modify them as easily as you can a bitmapped image. You can select any of the objects that make up the image (such as one line in a drawing of a building) and individually stretch, shrink, or redraw that line. But this is a tedious process, and with complex drawings, it may be difficult to get the results that you want when you are modifying an existing image.

Note that most drawing programs have the capability to load a bitmapped image and convert it to an object image. However, the differences between the way the images are stored means that the results of the conversion may be less than spectacular. Curved lines in a bitmapped image are stored as jagged or "stepped" patterns of light and dark pixels, and if you bring a bitmapped image into a drawing program and then try to scale the image, the jagged patterns will change disproportionately. The result is often an image with some distortion.

Where can I get some of those neat stock pictures and graphics?

You've probably seen documents created in Windows word processors (such as Word) that contain snazzy graphics and clip art. Many users who haven't done much work with graphics want to know where artwork like this can be found. There's no shortage of artwork available, and you may need to look no further than your own PC. If you performed a complete installation of Office (or if you at least included the ClipArt files in the options list when you installed the program), you can find many clip art files in the ClipArt folder that is stored inside the MSOffice folder. In addition to these files, you can find clip art and stock photos in many inexpensive commercial disk packages that are available through computer and software retailers. You can also use mail-order libraries of photos and art — there are plenty of advertisements in the back pages of magazines such as *PC World*. And you can find clip art in the libraries of online services such as America Online and CompuServe.

Using Graphic Images

As you begin your work in desktop publishing, you will find the addition of graphic images to your documents very useful. After you have inserted the images, you will need to perform various tasks to make the object look presentable in your document. This would include tasks such as cropping, adding borders, or even callouts to your graphic image.

Inserting images into Word

To import images from a wide range of software, you need to use Insert⇨Picture. To insert a picture into your document, perform the following steps:

1. Place the insertion point where the image is to appear.
2. Choose Insert⇨Picture to open the Insert Picture dialog box, as shown in Figure 10-6.

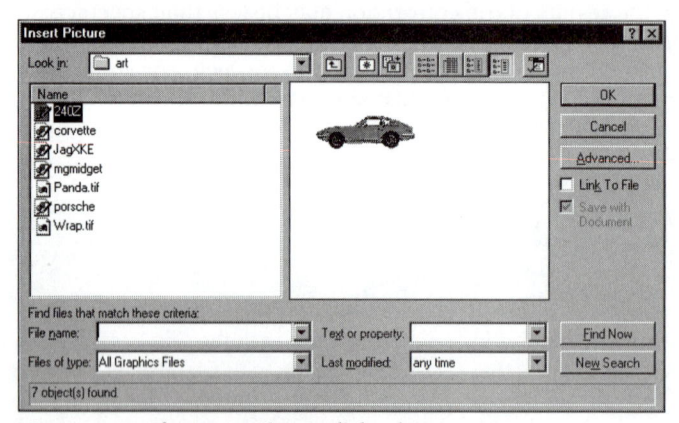

Figure 10-6: The Insert Picture dialog box.

3. In the File name list box, you can enter the name of the image file, or you can select the desired filename from the list. To see files of a particular type, click on the arrow to the right of the Files of type list box and choose your image file format from the list. Use the Look in list box and the Up One Level button to change to a different folder or to a different drive.

After you select a file in the Name list box, you can click on the Preview button at the top of the dialog box to see the image in the Preview box of the Insert Picture dialog box. The Preview box provides a handy way to examine collections of clip art. You can highlight each filename in the File name list box and click on the Preview button to see the image that's stored in the file.

> **Hot Stuff**
>
> If you want to link the image in Word to the original graphic file, turn on the Link To File check box. Word then inserts the image as a field, and you can later use the Update Field key (F9) to update the picture if you later change the picture in the program that was used to create the image.

4. Click on the OK button (or press Enter) to close the dialog box and to insert the image into your Word document. The image appears at the insertion point location. Figure 10-7 shows an example of a clip art image pasted into a Word document by using this technique.

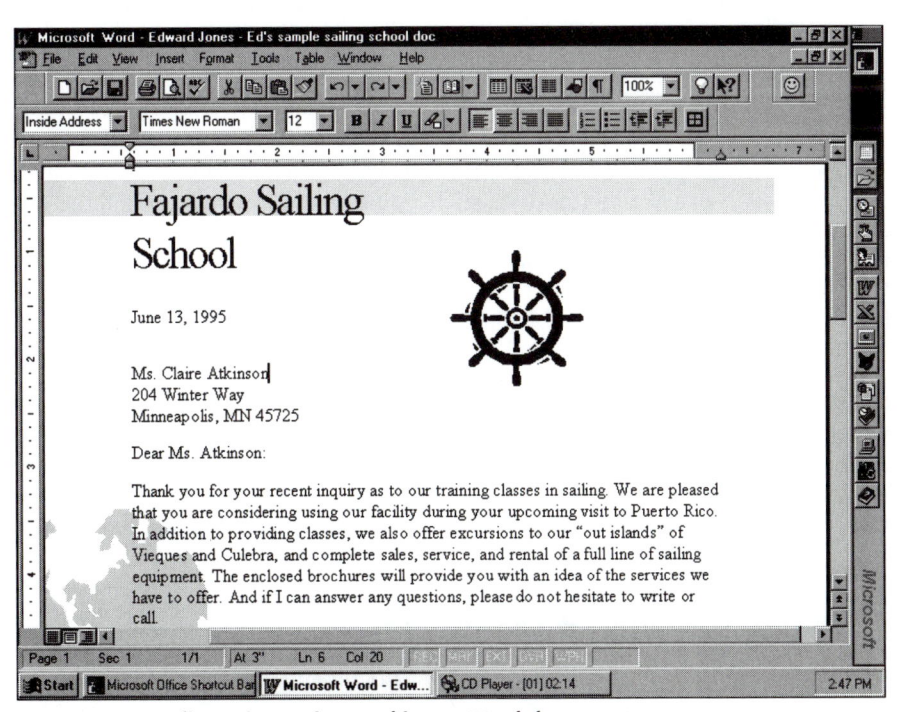

Figure 10-7: A clip art image inserted into a Word document.

> ### Don't forget your trusty Clipboard
>
> If the software that you are using to produce the image runs under Windows, remember that you can also use the Windows Clipboard to copy images into a Word document. You can do so by performing the following steps:
>
> 1. Use the Start menu of Windows 95 to start your painting or drawing program under Windows in the usual manner.
>
> 2. After you have the desired image within your program, use whatever selection tool is provided by your program to select the desired portion of the image.
>
> 3. Choose Edit⇨Copy (all programs that conform to Windows standards will have this command).
>
> 4. Press Alt+Tab to switch back to Word.
>
> 5. Open your desired document, place the insertion point at the desired location, and choose Edit⇨Paste. The image from the other program is inserted into your Word document at the insertion point location.

Normally, you can think of an image that you insert into a document as a single large character, such as a giant letter *A*. As such, you cannot place text around the image because the image takes up one giant line of text. However, you can insert a frame that surrounds the image, and then you can position the frame containing the image anywhere in your document. Text will then automatically reposition itself around the frame (although this will be visible only in Page Layout view). See "Working with Frames" later in this chapter for details about using frames in Word.

In addition to importing graphics, you can also create graphics directly from Word. Word includes a Drawing toolbar that you can use to create graphics. If the Drawing toolbar isn't visible, choose View⇨Toolbars, click on the Drawing check box in the Toolbars dialog box, and click on the OK button. After the Drawing toolbar is visible, you can click on any of the toolbar buttons or you can use the mouse to draw the shapes that you want to add to your document.

Changing the look of the image

After you have inserted an image into a Word document, you can change the size of the image by *scaling* (resizing) and *cropping* (trimming) the images. It is easier to use the mouse than the keyboard to change the size of the image. Mouse users scale images by selecting the image and dragging the sizing handles that appear; keyboard users must use Format⇨Picture and then enter dimensions in the dialog box that appears.

You can also apply borders to an image by using Format⇨Borders and Shading or by clicking on the Borders button on the Formatting toolbar. You cannot apply shading to an image as you can to a paragraph. Notice that when you select a picture and then choose Format⇨Borders and Shading, the Shading tab is dimmed in the dialog box.

Scaling an image

To scale an image, you must first select it. When you click on an image, Word selects the image and displays sizing handles. Keyboard users can select an image by placing the insertion point anywhere inside the image, holding down the Shift key, and pressing the right-arrow key once.

To scale (resize) a graphic with the mouse, you drag one of the handles until the image reaches the desired size. Dragging a handle on either center side resizes the width of the image. Dragging a handle on the center top or the center bottom resizes the height of the image. Dragging any of the corner handles resizes both the width and height of the image. To scale an image with the keyboard, select the image and choose Format⇨Picture to open the Picture dialog box, as shown in Figure 10-8.

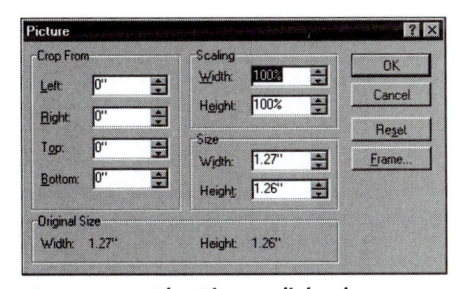

Figure 10-8: The Picture dialog box.

You can change the scaling in one of two ways: either you can enter a percentage in the Width and Height text boxes in the Scaling area (in which case the Size measurements change accordingly), or you can enter a measurement in the Width and Height boxes in the Size area (in which case the Scaling percentages change accordingly). Use the Reset button to restore an image that you have scaled to its original size. (Word remembers the original size of an image, regardless of how you scale or crop it, so that you can later undo your modifications with the Reset button.) After you have made your desired changes, click on the OK button or press Enter.

Cropping an image

To crop a graphic by using the mouse, hold down the Shift key while you drag one of the handles. Dragging a handle on either center side crops the image on that side; dragging a handle on the center top or the center bottom crops the image from the top or the bottom; and dragging any of the corner handles crops from both the side nearest that corner and the top or bottom nearest that corner.

To crop a graphic by using the keyboard, select the image and choose Format⇨Picture. In the Picture dialog box, use the measurement boxes in the Crop From area to enter the amounts by which you want to crop the image. A measurement in the Left and Right text boxes specifies how much the image should be cropped on the left and right sides, and a measurement in the Top and Bottom text boxes specifies how much the image should be cropped on the top and bottom. Use the Reset button to restore an image that you have cropped to its original size. After you have made your desired changes, click on the OK button or press Enter.

Adding borders

To apply a border to an image, first select the image and then choose Format⇨Borders and Shading. In the dialog box that appears, select the type of border that you want. (You can also add borders by using the Borders toolbar.)

Editing images

After you have placed an image into Word, you can edit it. To edit an image, double-click on that image or right-click and choose Open Picture from the shortcut menu. Then you can edit the picture by using the Drawing toolbar.

After you are finished editing the image, click on the Close Picture button on the Picture toolbar located in the upper-left corner of the screen.

Note Remember that the drawing capabilities of Word are object based, so you may get unsatisfactory results if you import a bitmapped image into a Word document and then modify it with the Drawing toolbar.

You can add callouts to your art, too!

You may want to add callouts to the images that you insert into your documents. You can insert callouts in several ways, but one easy way is to use Word's Table feature. Add a table with the Table⇨Insert Table command and insert the image into one cell of the table. Then type the text of your callout into an adjacent cell of the table and format the table so that the text appears where you want it. You can also use the Drawing toolbar. After you select the image, click on the Format Callout button and then click and drag to place a callout of the desired size and type the desired text into the callout.

Inserting Graphs into Word

You can insert graphs (charts) into Word by using Microsoft Graph, a program designed for creating business graphs. You can also insert graphs from spreadsheets, such as Lotus 1-2-3, Excel, and the spreadsheet module of Microsoft Works. To insert a graph from Microsoft Graph into a Word document, perform the following steps:

1. Choose Insert⇨Object to open the Object dialog box and click on the Create New tab. In the Object Type list box, select Microsoft Graph 5.0 and click on the OK button to add a default graph and a Datasheet window. When you do this, you will see a new set of menus appear for your work with the chart. In the data sheet, you can type the values that you want to use for the graph. Figure 10-9 shows the graph and the Datasheet window in a document.

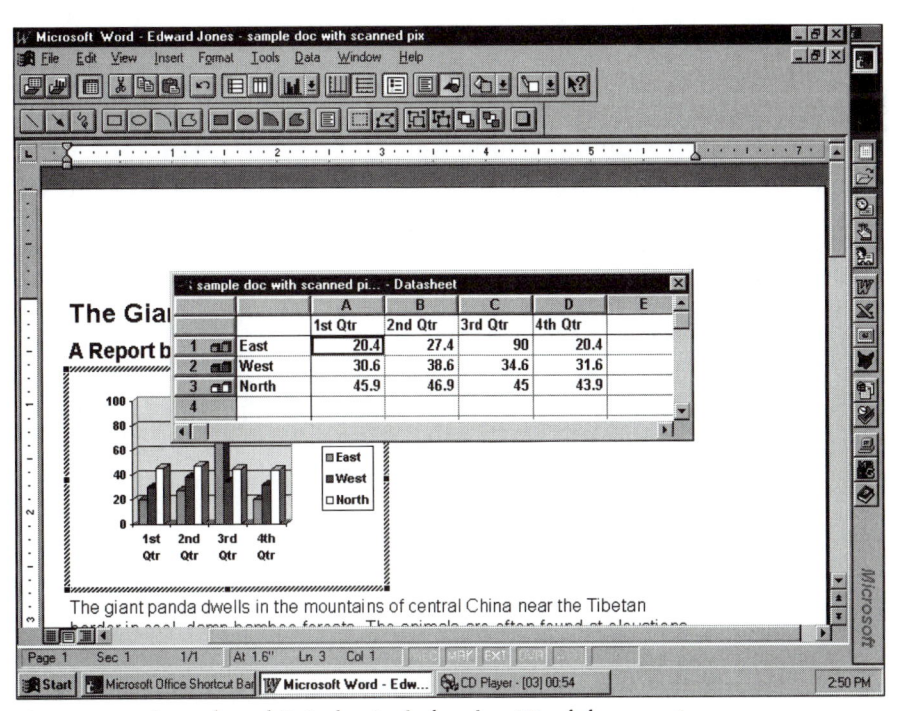

Figure 10-9: A graph and Datasheet window in a Word document.

2. Enter the numeric data into the Datasheet window and close it.

3. Choose Format⇨Chart Type to select the type of chart that you want.

4. From the Insert menu, use the various commands to add any desired titles, legends, gridlines, or other items to the chart.

5. When you are finished making the desired refinements to the chart, click anywhere outside the chart. The chart then appears inside your presentation, and the menus and toolbars revert back to those of Word for Windows.

If you are using Microsoft Excel, Microsoft Works, or another Windows program that conforms to the Windows design standards, you can use the Copy and Paste commands with the Clipboard to copy graphs from those programs into your Word documents. In Excel or in Works, display the graph in a window. Then select the graph and choose Edit⇨Copy. Exit the program and switch to Word in the usual manner. Place the insertion point at the desired location and choose Edit⇨Paste to insert the graph into your document.

Hot Stuff: You can use the Clipboard techniques to copy information from any Windows software into a Word document.

Because Microsoft Graph shows a simple bar graph by default whenever it is started, you can easily use the program to insert a graph into a document. For practice, perform the following steps as an exercise in using Microsoft Graph to place a graph in a document:

1. Open a new document and enter the following text:

    This is a test of my skills in inserting a graph in my document. Word makes inserting graphs very easy. There are many options provided for the formatting of my chart that will be discussed more as we move along in the chapter.

2. Place the insertion point at the end of the paragraph and press Enter to begin a new line.

3. Choose Insert⇨Object and then choose Microsoft Graph from the dialog box that appears. Click on the OK button to open the Microsoft Graph 5.0 window. A default bar graph appears in the document.

4. Click on the cell that contains East. Enter the name Johnathan and then press Enter. For the cell that contains West, enter Dirk; and for the cell containing North, enter Kevin. Change a few of the numbers using the same methods. After you click anywhere outside the graph, the graph will appear in the sample document, as shown in Figure 10-10.

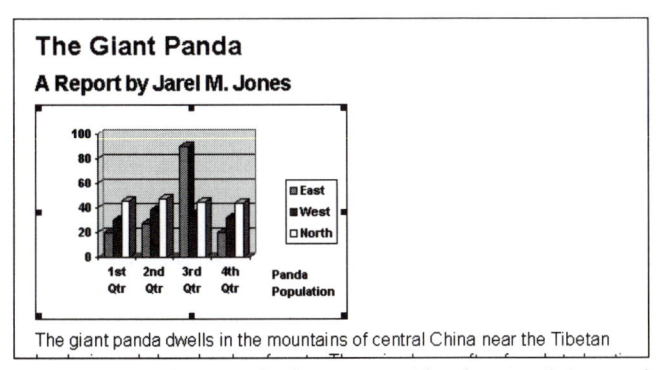

Figure 10-10: The sample document with a bar graph inserted from Microsoft Graph.

If you later want to make more changes to the graph's design, you can double-click on the graph to switch back to the menus and toolbar of Microsoft Graph. For now, leave the document open on-screen because you will use it in an upcoming exercise involving frames.

Working with Frames

At times, you may want certain objects in a document to appear at a specific location on a page. With Word, you can change the position of the object by inserting it into a frame. The object that you insert into a frame can be a graphic image, a table, or other text. After the object is surrounded by a frame, you can position the frame anywhere you want within the document. When you move a frame, everything within the frame moves as a single unit.

Those familiar with desktop publishing software may think of frames only as places to insert graphic images, but you can use frames in other ways, too. In addition to serving as placeholders for graphics, you can use frames to place *absolutely positioned paragraphs*, which are paragraphs that must occupy a specific location in a document.

After you place a frame in the desired location, you can decide how you want text outside the frame to wrap around it. As you work with frames, it is a good idea to use Word's Page Layout view because you can see how your frames relate to other text or objects on the page. Text wrap (around a frame) is visible only in Page Layout view.

Inserting a frame around an existing object

You can place a frame around an existing object by selecting the object and then choosing Insert⇨Frame. Or you can right-click on the object and choose the Frame Picture command from the shortcut menu.

After Word inserts the frame, the framed object remains selected. You can proceed to resize or move the frame as desired. Note that by default, Word places a single-line border around frames. If you remove the frame, the border will remain as a single-line border around the object. You can remove the border by using Format⇨Borders and Shading.

If you created the sample document by working through the exercise earlier in this chapter, you can insert a frame around the graph by performing the following steps:

1. Select the graph by clicking on it or by placing the insertion point to the immediate left of the graph, holding down the Shift key, and pressing the right-arrow key. After you select the graph, it will be enclosed in a visible border, and sizing handles (the small black squares) will appear at the edges.

2. Right-click on the graph and choose Frame Picture from the shortcut menu to place a frame around the graph. You can try dragging the frame containing the graph to another location in the document. You could not reposition the graph if it were not surrounded by the frame.

Inserting an empty frame into a document

At times you may need to insert an empty frame into a document. An empty frame can function as a placeholder for a future graph or text. After you insert an empty frame, you can type within it, and your text will wrap within the frame. To insert an empty frame, perform the following steps:

1. Make sure that no text or object is selected.
2. At the far right side of the Formatting toolbar, click on the Borders button to activate the Borders toolbar.
3. Click on the Outside Border button to create a frame in which you can add text. You can move this frame to the desired position by using the normal methods for moving objects. This frame extends across a line in your document, and you can type the desired text within it.

If you want to create a frame that does not extend across a line in your document, you can use the following steps:

1. Choose Insert⇨Frame.

2. Click and drag to make the frame the size that you want.

3. Type the text that you want in the frame of the document.

4. If you need to add more space to the frame, hold down the left mouse button, drag the frame to the desired size, and then release the mouse button. Or with the keyboard, use the arrow keys to drag the frame to the desired size and then press Enter.

Understanding the Frame dialog box

After you have placed frames in a document, you may need to control various aspects of the frame, such as its location, its size, and whether adjacent text should be permitted to wrap around the frame. Mouse users can accomplish most of these tasks with the mouse, but for the few tasks that can't be done with a mouse (or if your laptop is on an airline tray table, and your mouse is packed in the cargo hold), Word provides the Frame dialog box (see Figure 10-11). When a frame is the selected object, you can open the Frame dialog box by choosing the Frame command from the Format menu.

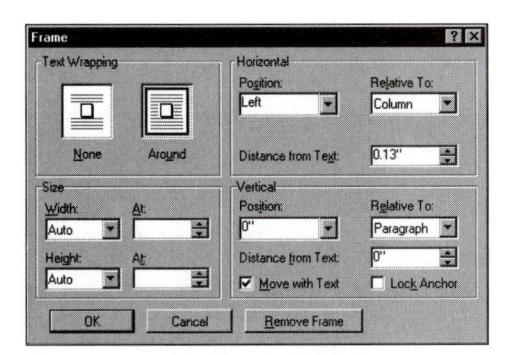

Figure 10-11: The Frame dialog box.

The Horizontal and Vertical areas of the dialog box contain list boxes that you can use to enter measurements that specify the location of the frame. In the Relative To list boxes, you tell Word what the measurement is relative to: a margin, a page, a column, or a paragraph of adjacent text. In the Vertical area, you can turn on the Move with Text option to move text that is adjacent to a frame to another location in a document (the frame moves along with the text).

The Text Wrapping area of the dialog box lets you specify whether adjacent text can wrap around a frame. If you select the None option, the adjacent text will not wrap around the frame. If you select the Around option, the adjacent text will wrap around the frame.

The Size area of the dialog box lets you change the size of a frame. In the Width and Height list boxes, you can choose Auto, At Least (in the Height list box only), or Exactly. If you use At Least or Exactly, you can then enter a measurement in the adjacent At boxes. Using Auto causes the frame to make itself as large as needed to hold the contents. Using Exactly forces the frame to assume the exact measurements that you enter in the At boxes. Using At Least sets the frame to a minimum size specified by the measurements in the At boxes. You can then add information to the frame, and it will expand as needed beyond the minimum size.

Use the Remove Frame button in the dialog box to remove a frame while leaving the contents of the frame intact.

As you will see in the exercises that follow, mouse users can avoid dealing with the Frame dialog box because it is easier to locate or size a frame by dragging the frame around in the document with the mouse.

Moving frames

After you have inserted a frame, you can easily move it to any location in a document. (As with most tasks of this nature, using the mouse is easier than using the keyboard.) Mouse users can move a frame by performing the following steps:

1. Turn on Page Layout view by choosing View⇨Page Layout.
2. Place the insertion point on the border of the frame. The mouse pointer will change into a four-headed arrow.
3. Click and drag the frame to the new location. As you drag the frame, a dotted line will indicate its position. The contents of the frame will move to the new location after you release the mouse button.

Keyboard users can move a frame by performing the following steps:

1. Turn on Page Layout view by choosing View⇨Page Layout.
2. Using the arrow keys, position the insertion point inside the frame that you want to move.
3. Choose Format⇨Frame.
4. In the Frame dialog box, enter the horizontal location that you want for the frame in the Horizontal Position box. (Use the Relative To list box to choose whether the measurement that you enter is relative to the margin, the page, or a column.)
5. Enter the vertical location that you want for the frame in the Vertical Position box. (Use the Relative To list box to choose whether the measurement that you enter is relative to the margin, the page, or a paragraph.)
6. Click on the OK button (or press Enter).

For practice, you can try moving the frame in your sample document to a different location.

Sizing frames

You can resize frames by using the mouse or the keyboard. Mouse users can select the frame and drag one of the sizing handles to resize the frame. Keyboard users can select the frame, use Format⇨Frame, and then enter the desired height and width in the dialog box that appears.

To resize a frame with the mouse, perform the following steps:

1. Turn on Page Layout view by choosing View⇨Page Layout.
2. Click anywhere in the frame that you want to resize. Eight black sizing handles appear on the edges of the frame.
3. Point to one of the sizing handles. The mouse pointer changes shape into a two-headed arrow.
4. Drag the handle to resize the frame as desired.

Keyboard users can resize a frame by performing the following steps:

1. Turn on Page Layout view by choosing View⇨Page Layout.
2. Using the arrow keys, position the insertion point inside the frame that you want to resize.
3. Choose Format⇨Frame to open the Frame dialog box.
4. In the Size area, choose Exactly in the Width list box and enter the desired width for the frame in the At box. (To make the width as wide as the object within the frame, choose Auto in the Width box.)
5. In the Size area, choose Exactly in the Height list box and enter the desired height for the frame in the At box. (To make the height as tall as the object within the frame, choose Auto in the Height box.)
6. Click on the OK button or press Enter.

For practice, you can try resizing the frame in your sample document.

Wrapping text around frames

By default, Word wraps adjacent text around frames. You can turn this trait on or off for a particular frame with the Text Wrapping option in the Frame dialog box. To turn on (or off) text wrapping around a frame, perform the following steps:

1. Turn on Page Layout view by choosing View⇨Page Layout.
2. Using the mouse or the arrow keys, place the insertion point inside the frame.
3. Choose Format⇨Frame to open the Frame dialog box.
4. In the Text Wrapping area, choose Around if you want text to wrap around the frame or choose None if you do not want text to wrap around the frame.
5. Click on the OK button or press Enter.

Figure 10-12 shows the difference between text wrapping that is on and text wrapping that is off. On the left, the frame containing the graph has been placed in the center of the paragraph and the Around option in the Text Wrapping area is turned on. Notice how the text wraps around the frame in this figure. On the right, the frame is at the same location, but the Text Wrapping option has been set to None, so the text does not wrap around the frame that contains the graph. Note that the option applies to the *selected* frame.

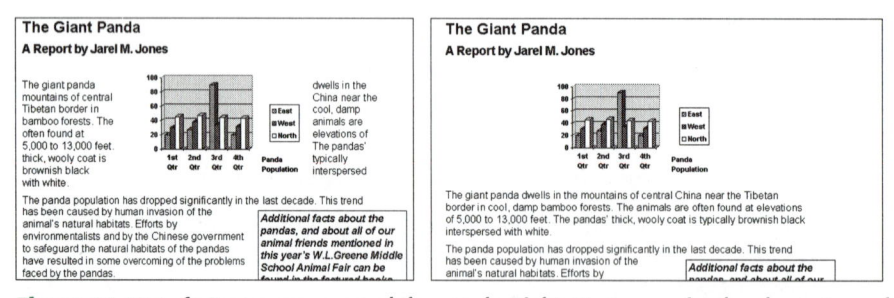

Figure 10-12: Left: Text wraps around the graph. Right: Text wrapping has been turned off.

Removing frames

You can remove a frame and leave the contents of the frame intact, or you can delete both a frame and its contents. To remove a frame while leaving the contents of the frame intact, perform the following steps:

1. Click in the frame or use the arrow keys to place the insertion point within the frame.
2. Choose Format⇨Frame to open the Frame dialog box.
3. Click on the Remove Frame button.

When you remove a frame while leaving its contents intact, note that any borders applied to the frame will remain around the object after the frame has been removed.

To delete both the frame and its contents, perform the following steps:

1. Use your preferred selection method to select the frame to be deleted.
2. Press the Delete key.

You may want to experiment further with the use of frames within the sample document. When you are finished experimenting, you can close the document without saving the changes because you will not need this document elsewhere in this book.

Using the Organizational Tools of Desktop Publishing

When you need to create a document with a professionally published appearance, you can use different organizational tools and techniques that Word provides. The combination of these techniques and the use of graphics turns an ordinary document into a professional one. These organizational tools include such things as columns, gutter margins, headlines and subheads, headers and footers, and the integration of graphics. Later in this chapter you will learn how to use the Newsletter Wizard to create newsletters, another form of desktop publishing.

Before you attempt to apply desktop publishing techniques to any document, you should first sketch out, on paper, exactly how you want the document to look. It is much easier to pattern a document in Word after one that you've already outlined on paper. This step also helps you avoid mistakes that may detract from the appearance of the finished document. Mistakes in overall layout are often apparent from a paper-based sketch.

Columns and margins

With many documents, the way in which you lay out your columns comprises a significant part of desktop publishing design. One- and two-column layouts are the most popular, although you can have many more than two columns. With text, there is a "visual" limit to keep in mind. As the number of columns increases, you reach a point where readability suffers. Readers don't read individual words; they read phrases, or groups of words. Therefore, column width has a direct impact on readability. Overly wide columns make it difficult for the reader to follow phrases from line to line. Overly narrow columns can also be hard to read because the eyes must often jump lines before absorbing a complete phrase. Page margins, number of columns, and the width between columns all have an impact here. Point size also has an impact on readability, with regard to the number of columns. Small point sizes tend to work better in narrow columns; wide columns generally need larger point sizes. Also, keep in mind that hyphenation helps reduce that jagged-text look that is often prevalent with narrow columns.

When working with columns in Word, remember that not all columns need be the same width if you set up the columns as side-by-side paragraphs by using Word's Table feature.

Keep in mind the effects that page margins will have on the space available for your columns and on the overall design of your document. Larger margins result in a "lighter" document; smaller margins result in a "denser" appearance to the document.

Headlines and subheads

Headlines are vital in calling attention to your message. For this reason, they are commonly used throughout newsletters, magazines, advertisements, and brochures. You can differentiate your headlines from your body text by setting the headlines in different point sizes or type styles. You can also block headlines with borders or shading, or you can separate them from the normal text by means of white space or with rules (vertical or horizontal lines drawn with Format➪Borders and Shading or the Borders toolbar). You should avoid headlines that are all uppercase letters or ones that contain more than three lines (both tend to be hard to read).

You can use subheads to add clarification to a headline. You may also want to use subheads within your text as a way of breaking up large expanses of text into smaller groups. The smaller groups tend to be visually easier to follow. Figure 10-13 shows an example.

Laser Printers: The Latest and Greatest
PCWorld Tests 20 Laser Printers All Priced Under $1,000

Figure 10-13: A headline with a subheadline.

Hot Stuff Avoid a common blunder with your subheads: make sure that the subheads are visually tied to the text that follows the subhead. To position the subhead accurately, use Format➪Paragraph and click on the Indents and Spacing tab of the Paragraph dialog box. In the Spacing area, set the value of the Before measurement to one that is greater than the value in the After measurement. This adjustment results in more space above the subhead than below the subhead. If you don't set the measurements in this way, the subhead may be too close to the prior text and not close enough to the text that follows it. In such cases, the subhead appears disconnected from the text that follows.

Graphic images

Word's capability to place graphics into frames means that you have a great deal of flexibility when you integrate graphics into the text. Remember that you can also place a graphic image into a cell of a table and then use the formatting commands that apply to tables to control the location of the graphic. There is no "correct" method to place graphics; use whichever method feels the most comfortable and achieves the desired results.

You can use the sizing (scaling) and cropping techniques covered earlier in the chapter to add visual interest to many graphics. In some cases, you may be able to add interest to an illustration by purposely stretching it out of proportion. For example, you can use a stretched image of a dollar bill to convey an increase in buying power.

With graphics, the possibilities are endless. Remember that professionally published documents are often a source of inspiration for effective graphics. You can obtain ideas about graphic design by examining publications with abundant informational graphics, such as *USA Today, Time,* and *Newsweek.*

Graphs and tables

With Microsoft Graph, you can design business graphs that can be inserted into Word documents. With Word's Table feature, you can design tables of data. Use graphs when you want the reader to see a visual representation of the underlying data. Use tables when you want the reader to see the underlying data itself, rather than a visual representation. With tables that display business figures, you should visually set off any headings or column titles within the table from the remaining contents of the table. You can set the headings apart by formatting the headings or titles or by adding borders or shading.

Informational graphics (such as pie and bar charts) can go a long way in getting business information across to an audience of readers. You may want to consider combining clip art or drawings that are done in Paint with business graphs that are done in a spreadsheet like Excel or in Microsoft Graph.

Using the Newsletter Wizard

Creating newsletters is a common task in many organizations. And because of the complexity of newsletters, they have often presented design challenges. Word includes a powerful tool for creating newsletters, a tool that greatly reduces the tedium involved. The Newsletter Wizard is a very useful aid in creating a document that you send out on a regular basis. It also has perfect examples for how to use headings, columns, and graphics in a document.

To create a newsletter, choose File➪New and click on the Publications tab in the New dialog box. Then double-click on the Newsletter Wizard to launch the Newsletter Wizard.

The first Newsletter Wizard dialog box lets you choose between two style options: Classic and Modern. After choosing the style that you want for your newsletter, click on the Next button.

The next Newsletter Wizard dialog box asks you to enter the number of columns that you want for your document. You have a choice of one to four columns. Keep in mind that the formats that you set out in the wizard are not set in stone. If you later want to add another column to the document, you can do so by using Format⇨Columns.

The third dialog box asks you to enter a name for your newsletter. If you can't think of one, you don't have to enter one at this time. You can enter the name later, when you complete the setup of the newsletter.

The fourth Newsletter Wizard dialog box asks you how many pages you want in your newsletter. At the top of each of the newsletter pages, you will find the page number and the title of your newsletter in a shaded bar, which gives the document a professional look.

Use the fifth and final Newsletter Wizard dialog box to choose the elements that you want to include in your newsletter. You can choose none, some, or all of the following options: Table of contents, Fancy first letters, Date, and Volume and issue.

You can turn on or off each of these options by clicking on their check boxes. This flexibility gives you the freedom to include some of the elements from the wizard and exclude some of them. After you are finished selecting the desired options, click on the Finish button, and Word will open the newsletter. You can add the desired text, and then you can save and print the document in the usual manner.

Keep in mind that you can change the formats that you specify in the Newsletter Wizard dialog boxes after you create your document. In many cases, you will find it essential to change them and include or exclude some things. Use the normal formatting techniques in Word to make these changes and customize the newsletter to your own needs.

Summary

This chapter has provided an overall look at how you can combine the various tools of Word to perform desktop publishing tasks. The chapter included the following points:

- Use Format⇨Columns to place columns in a document.
- You can quickly add attractive formatting to a document by using Word's AutoFormat command (from the Format menu).
- In Word, you can import graphic images of various types into a document.
- You can add business graphs to Word documents by pasting them in from other programs or by using Word's Object command from the Insert menu. You can insert a Microsoft Graph object and change Word's menus and toolbars to those of Microsoft Graph.
- You can add frames to your documents, and these frames can contain text or graphics. You can size frames, and you can drag them to any desired location on a page.

The next chapter will outline a number of step-by-step exercises that you can follow to quickly create typical business documents in Word for Windows.

Where to go next...

- Much of what you do in desktop publishing involves the complex use of Word's different formatting tools. You can find out more about these tools in Chapter 3.
- If you desktop publish documents on a regular basis, you'll want to make use of Word's styles and templates. Chapter 8 has the dirt.

✦ ✦ ✦

Word for Windows at Work

CHAPTER 11

♦ ♦ ♦ ♦

In This Chapter

Creating a time sheet

Designing a fax cover sheet

Devising an interoffice memo

Producing an invoice

♦ ♦ ♦ ♦

In this chapter, you'll find a number of step-by-step exercises that you can follow to quickly put Word for Windows to work. These exercises are designed to use some of Word's wizards and templates to make short work of producing professional-looking documents.

Creating a Time Sheet

Figure 11-1 shows an example of an office time sheet that you can quickly create by using Word's Weekly Time Sheet template.

First, you need to customize the template that you use to build the time sheet so that it contains your company name. To customize the template, perform the following steps:

1. Choose File⇨Open. The Open dialog box appears (Figure 11-2).

2. In the Files of type list box at the lower left of the dialog box, select Document Templates.

3. In the Look in portion of the list box, move to the MS Office folder and then double-click on the Templates folder to open it. After you are inside the Templates folder, double-click on the Other Documents folder to open it.

4. Double-click on the file named Weekly Time Sheet.

5. Choose Tools⇨Unprotect Document.

6. In the document, click on and drag the mouse through the words *Your Company Name*. With the words highlighted, type the name of your company to replace the generic name.

7. Repeat Step 6 for the lines containing the slogan, address, and phone number.

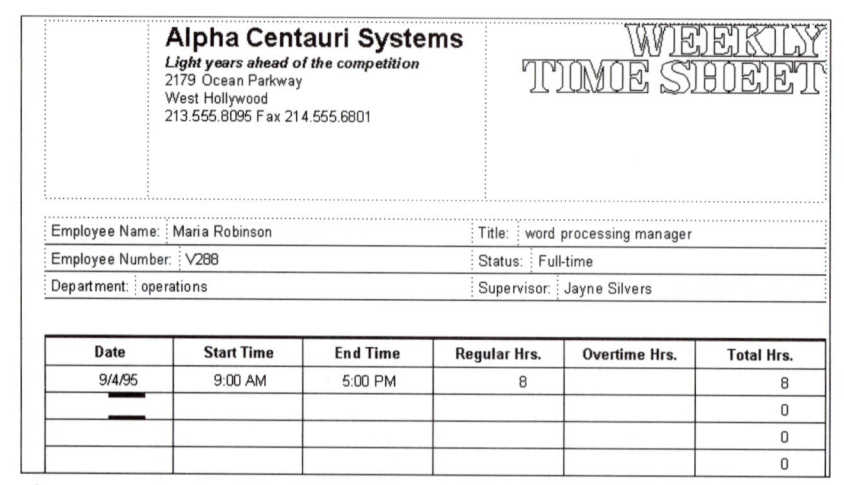

Figure 11-1: An example of a time sheet.

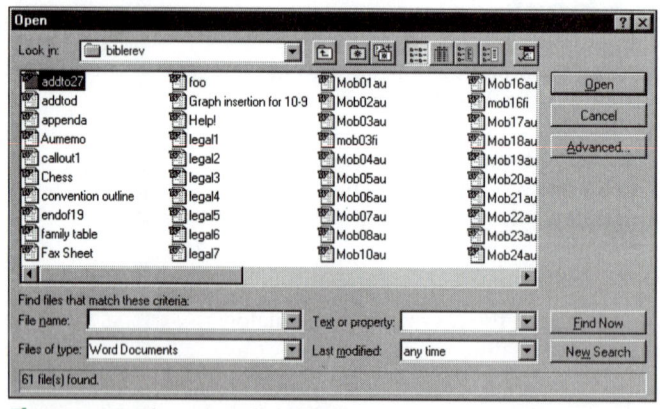

Figure 11-2: The Open dialog box.

   8. Choose Tools⇨Protect Document. In the dialog box that appears, click on Forms and then click on OK.

   9. Choose File⇨Close. Click on Yes in the dialog box that appears to save the changes and put away the template.

With the template customized, you can now perform the following steps whenever you want to produce a time sheet:

   1. Choose File⇨New. The New dialog box appears.

2. Click on the Other Documents tab and double-click on Weekly Time Sheet.

3. Place the cursor in each shaded area and type the appropriate information (such as the employee name, title, status, and hours worked) into each area.

4. After you're finished inserting the entries, choose File⇨Print to print the time sheet.

5. If you are finished using Word, choose File⇨Exit. When asked whether you want to save the document, you can click on Yes and enter a name for the time sheet.

Designing a Fax Cover Sheet

Figure 11-3 shows an example of a fax cover sheet that you can quickly create by using Word's Fax Wizard.

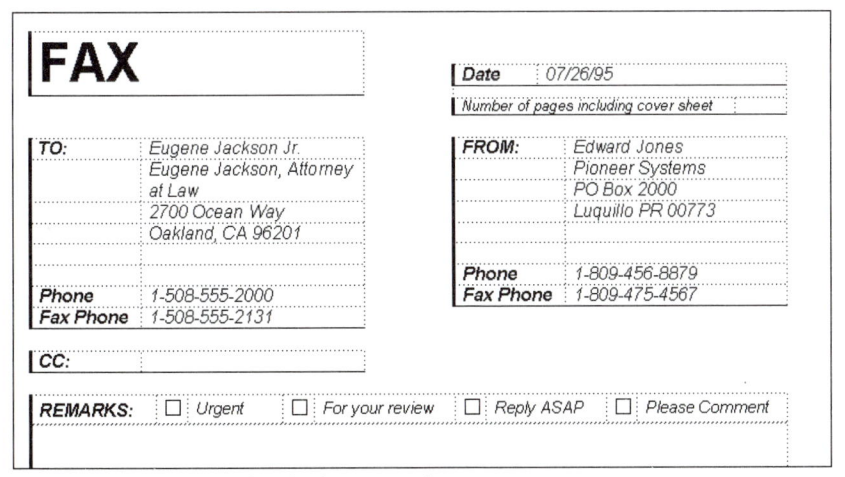

Figure 11-3: An example of a fax cover sheet.

To create a fax cover sheet, perform the following steps:

1. Choose File⇨New. The New dialog box appears.

2. Click on the Letters and Faxes tab and then double-click on Fax Wizard.

3. In the first Fax Wizard dialog box (Figure 11-4), choose either portrait or landscape orientation, as desired, and then click on the Next button. (Portrait lays out the cover sheet in a normal page fashion; landscape prints sideways across the page.)

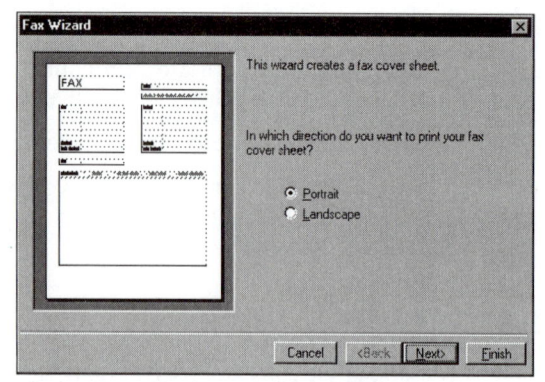

Figure 11-4: The first Fax Wizard dialog box.

4. In the second Fax Wizard dialog box (Figure 11-5), choose the style that you want (your options here are Contemporary, Modern, or Jazzy). As you select from among the possible styles, a representation of that style appears at the left side of the dialog box. After selecting the desired style, click on the Next button.

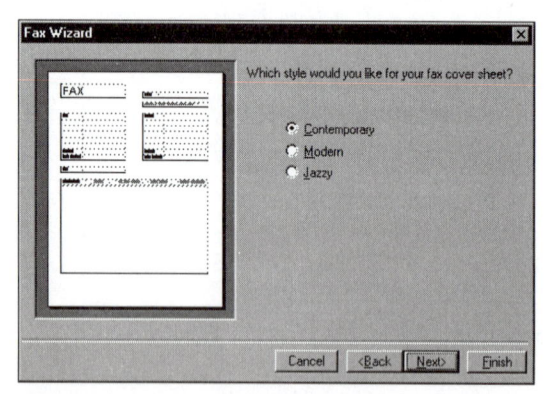

Figure 11-5: The second Fax Wizard dialog box.

5. In the third Fax Wizard dialog box (Figure 11-6), enter your name, the company's name, and the address (or leave the default values) and then click on the Next button.

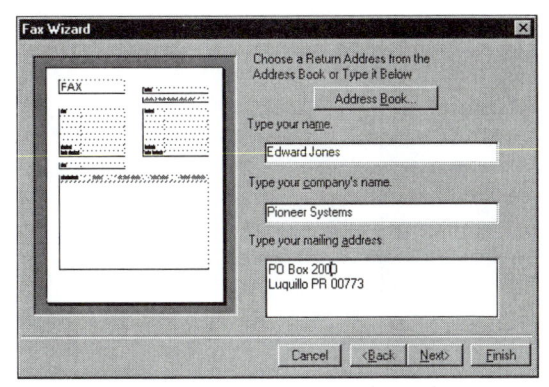

Figure 11-6: The third Fax Wizard dialog box.

6. In the fourth Fax Wizard dialog box (Figure 11-7), enter your phone and fax numbers and then click on the Next button.

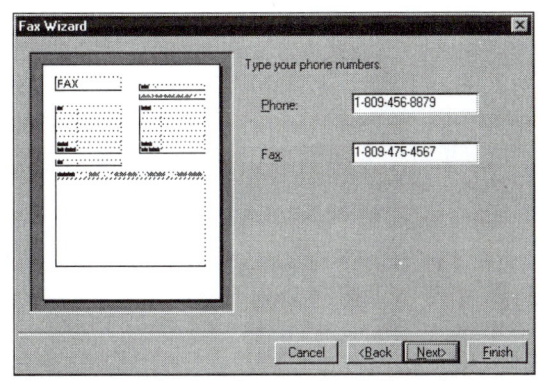

Figure 11-7: The fourth Fax Wizard dialog box.

7. Next you will see the fifth Fax Wizard dialog box (Figure 11-8). This box prompts you to enter the recipient's name, company name, and mailing address.

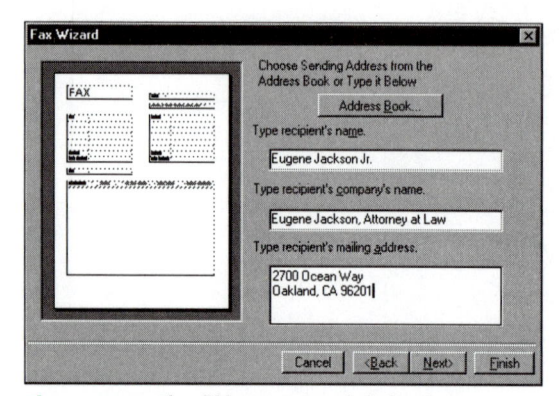

Figure 11-8: The fifth Fax Wizard dialog box.

8. Now you will see the dialog box that allows you to enter the recipient's phone and fax numbers. Figure 11-9 shows the sixth dialog box of the Fax Wizard.

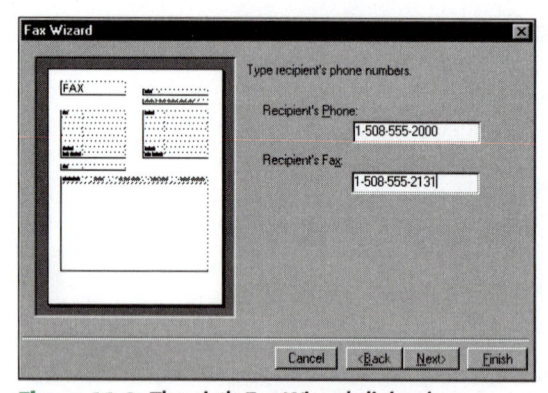

Figure 11-9: The sixth Fax Wizard dialog box.

9. In the last Fax Wizard dialog box, click on Finish to display the fax cover sheet, ready for further editing.

You can now click in the desired area of the fax cover sheet and add your remarks and comments where appropriate. The Wizard creates the cover sheet by adding tables in the appropriate locations. As with all tables, you can click within the desired cell to add or edit text, or you can use the Tab key to move between cells of the table.

Writing an Interoffice Memo

Figure 11-10 shows an example of an interoffice memo. You can easily produce a memo like this with Word's Memo Wizard.

Figure 11-10: An example of an interoffice memo.

To create an interoffice memo, perform the following steps:

1. Choose File⇨New. The New dialog box appears.
2. In the New dialog box, click on the Memos tab and then double-click on Memo Wizard.
3. In the first Memo Wizard dialog box that appears (Figure 11-11), click on the Next button.

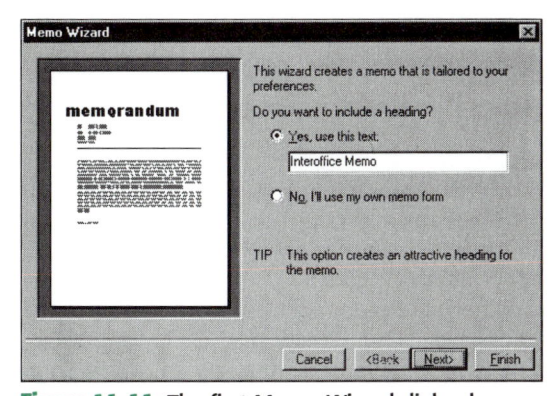

Figure 11-11: The first Memo Wizard dialog box.

4. The second dialog box of the Memo Wizard (Figure 11-12) asks whether you want a separate page for a distribution list. The default option is No. Accept the default option by clicking on the Next button.

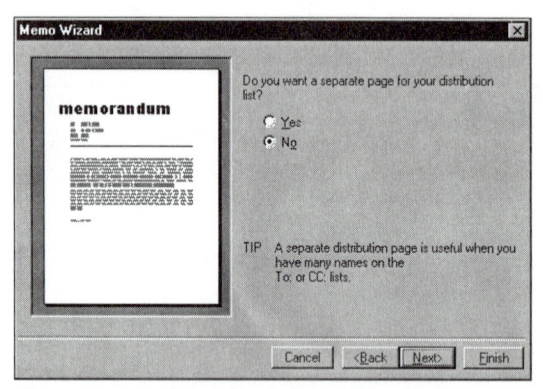

Figure 11-12: The second Memo Wizard dialog box.

5. In the third dialog box of the Memo Wizard (Figure 11-13), change the date and sender name, if desired.

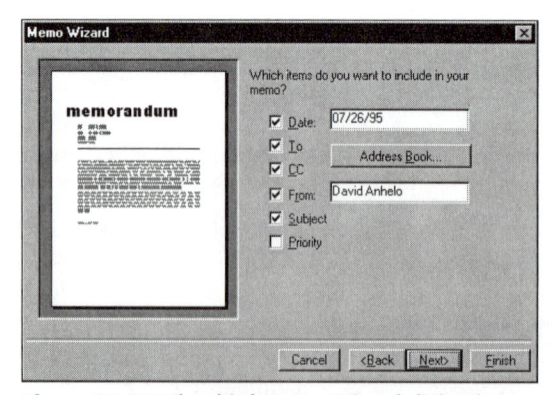

Figure 11-13: The third Memo Wizard dialog box.

6. Click on the Next button three times and then choose a desired style from the dialog box that now appears (your choices are Professional, Contemporary, or Elegant). Then click on the Finish button.

The interoffice memo appears, similar to the layout shown in Figure 11-10. (Yours may look different, depending on which appearance-related options you have chosen.) You can double-click on the entries beside the To, CC, and RE headings and type your text to replace the entries. Then type the memo's body text.

Producing an Invoice

Word has an attractively designed invoice template that serves as a good generic invoice, especially for a small business. Figure 11-14 shows an example of the invoice.

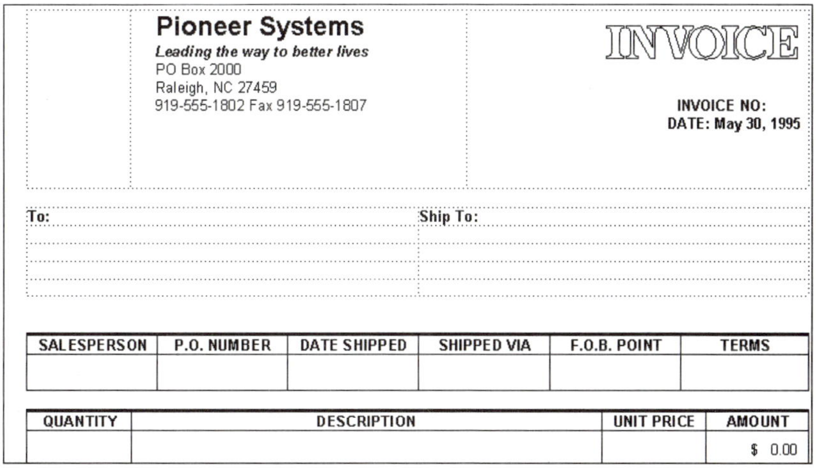

Pioneer Systems
Leading the way to better lives
PO Box 2000
Raleigh, NC 27459
919-555-1802 Fax 919-555-1807

INVOICE

INVOICE NO:
DATE: May 30, 1995

To:

Ship To:

SALESPERSON	P.O. NUMBER	DATE SHIPPED	SHIPPED VIA	F.O.B. POINT	TERMS

QUANTITY	DESCRIPTION	UNIT PRICE	AMOUNT
			$ 0.00

Figure 11-14: Example of an invoice.

As with the time sheet template, you'll need to customize the template that you use to build the invoice so that it contains your company name. To customize the template, perform the following steps:

1. Choose File⇨Open. The Open dialog box appears (see Figure 11-2, near the beginning of the chapter).
2. In the Files of type list box at the lower left of the dialog box, choose Document Templates.
3. In the Look in portion of the list box, move to the `MSOffice` folder and then double-click on the Templates folder to open it. After you are inside the Templates folder, double-click on the Other Documents folder to open it.
4. In the File name list box, double-click on the Invoice template.
5. Choose Tools⇨Unprotect Document.
6. In the document, click on and drag the mouse through the words *Your Company Name*. With the words highlighted, type the name of your company to replace the generic name.
7. Repeat Step 6 for the lines containing the slogan, address, and phone number.

8. Choose Tools⇨Protect Document. In the dialog box that appears, click on the Forms option and then click on OK.

9. Choose File⇨Close. Click on Yes in the dialog box that appears to save the changes and put away the template.

With the template customized, you can now perform the following steps whenever you want to produce a new invoice:

1. Choose File⇨New. The New dialog box appears.
2. Click on the Letters & Faxes tab and then double-click on Invoice.
3. Place the cursor in each shaded area and type the appropriate information (such as the To, Ship To, Quantity, Description, and Unit Price fields) into each area. The Amount, Subtotal, and Total fields are calculated automatically within the form as you make numeric entries into the Quantity and Unit Price fields.
4. After you're finished inserting the entries, choose File⇨Print to print the invoice.
5. If you are finished using Word, choose File⇨Exit. When asked whether you want to save the document, you can click on Yes and enter a name for the invoice.

Summary

This chapter has provided a step-by-step look at what's involved in using Word for Windows to create typical business documents. You can use the different templates and wizards to ease the drudgery of creating many common types of documents.

- ✦ Use the Weekly Time Sheet template to create a time sheet.
- ✦ Use the Fax Wizard to create a fax cover sheet.
- ✦ Use the Memo Wizard to quickly create an attractive memo form, complete with sender, date, recipient(s), and subject, into which you can type your message.
- ✦ Use the Invoice template to create an invoice.

The next chapter answers common questions that arise when you use Word for Windows.

Where to go next...

- ✦ Many of the examples demonstrated in this chapter use the templates that come with Word. Chapter 8 tells the whole story about working with templates.

✦ ✦ ✦

CHAPTER 12

The Word Top Ten

This chapter answers ten common Word for Windows questions. These questions are based on inquiries to Microsoft Technical Support and the Microsoft forums on CompuServe. These questions range from loading documents created in other word processor programs, to making your addresses appear correctly on your envelopes, to deleting documents in Word.

I have a document that was created with another word processing program. Can I work on this file in Word?

For the most part, files that have been created in other programs are converted by Word when you open them. There are, however, some things you should keep in mind. In cases where the file extension differs from the default Word .DOC file extension, you should select All Files (*.*) from the List Files of Type list box to see the files.

Note, too, that Word uses file converters when it opens files created by other programs. If you did a complete installation of Word, then all the converters were installed. If not, you may need to add the converters by running the Word Setup program. Perform these steps to add converters:

1. From the Windows 95 Start menu, choose Programs, and then choose Microsoft Office Shortcut Bar.

2. When the Office Shortcut Bar appears, right-click on its header (the top of the bar if it is arranged vertically, the left side of the bar if it is arranged horizontally) and choose Add/Remove Office Programs from the shortcut menu that appears.

3. The Office Setup and Uninstall dialog box appears. Choose Microsoft Office, then click on OK.

In This Chapter

Using documents created by other word processing programs

Printing envelopes

Preventing unwanted page breaks

Including table gridlines in printed documents

Running Word for Windows 95 and earlier versions of Word on the same computer

Deleting documents without leaving Word

Understanding why Word 2.0 won't open Word for Windows 95 files

Using Word 2.0 templates with Word for Windows 95

Knowing what to realistically expect (and not expect) from AutoSave

4. You next see the Office Setup dialog box. The Add/Remove button enables you to choose different components to add or remove from the Office installation.

5. Click on the line that reads Microsoft Word to select it, then click on the Change Options button in the dialog box. The Word Setup dialog box displays the items that are currently installed for Microsoft Word, including the converters. By clicking on the check boxes, you can select and deselect the items that you want to add or remove from the setup.

Word comes with these converters:

- WordPerfect for DOS 5.x
- WordPerfect for Windows 5.x
- Microsoft Excel BIFF 2.x, 3.0, 4.0, and 5.0 (This can be used only to open files, not to save them.)
- Microsoft Word for Windows 1.x and 2.x
- Word for Macintosh 4.x and 5.x
- Write for Windows
- Lotus 1-2-3
- Text with layout
- WordStar for DOS and Windows
- WordPerfect versions 6.0, 6.1, 5.0, 5.1, and 5.2
- Word for Windows 2.0
- Word for DOS 3.0 to 6.0
- Word for the Macintosh 4.0-5.1
- Microsoft Excel
- Works for Windows 3.0 and 4.0
- RFT-DCA (IBM DisplayWriter)

Why do addresses print on envelopes in the wrong position?

The addresses may print on your envelopes in the wrong position for several reasons. The printer bin may be set incorrectly. In this case, you may need to refer to your printer manual to see what the correct setting is for printing envelopes. You may also have other printer options set incorrectly. One good example is the size of the envelope. Business envelopes and personal letter envelopes are different sizes; therefore, you need to check your printer options to see whether they have been set to the correct size.

If you want to print an envelope, follow these steps:

1. Choose Tools⇨Envelopes and Labels. The Envelopes and Labels dialog box appears, as shown in Figure 12-1. In the Envelopes tab, you will see the Delivery Address text box and the Return Address text box. The Return Address text box contains the name that you entered during setup as the user.

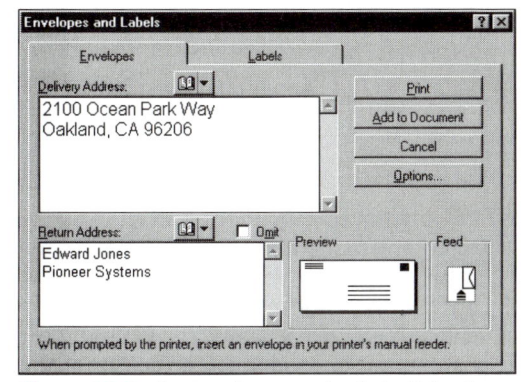

Figure 12-1: The Envelopes and Labels dialog box.

2. To change the envelope size, click in the Preview area to open the Envelope Options tab of the Envelopes Options dialog box. Here you can change the size of the envelope and the position of the delivery and return addresses.

3. To change the type of feed from vertical to horizontal, or vice versa, click on the Printing Options Tab of the Envelopes Options dialog box and choose the appropriate feed method.

4. On the Envelopes tab of the Envelopes and Labels dialog box, you will notice an Add to Document button. Clicking on this button produces a dialog box that enables you to add an envelope to the beginning of a document. Then when you print, you can print the envelope followed by the letter (a convenient feature for writing letters).

5. To print the envelope, click on the Print button.

How can I prevent page breaks from appearing in my document where I don't want them?

Unwanted page breaks can come for any number of sources. For example, you may have applied paragraph formats, such as Page Break Before, Keep with Next, or Keep Lines Together. These formats can produce unwanted page breaks. To remove these formats, highlight the paragraph immediately following the page break and then choose Format⇨Paragraph. In the Text Flow tab of the Paragraph dialog box (Figure 12-2), uncheck the offending format option so that you will not have a page break.

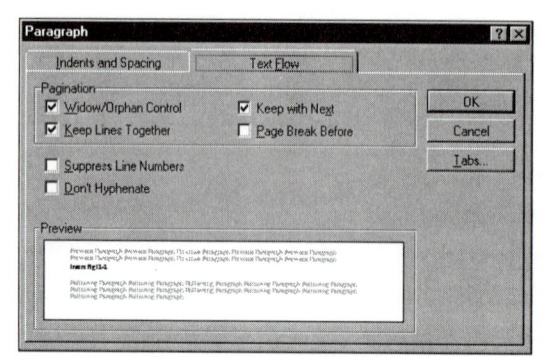

Figure 12-2: The Paragraph dialog box.

Sometimes only a few lines of a paragraph are moved over to the following page in a document. If you want to keep all the lines of the paragraph together on one page, switch to Print Preview and try to adjust the margins to bring the lines back onto the same page. If changing the margins is not effective, choose Format⇔Paragraph and turn on the Keep Lines Together option. In cases where you are trying to move only a small amount of text to the preceding page, try clicking on the Shrink to Fit button on the Print Preview toolbar.

Also, you may have a section break in your document. If you don't want the section break, you can remove it by placing the cursor in the section immediately after the section break. (If you need to see where the section break is, click on the Show/Hide Paragraph button on the Standard toolbar.) Then choose Insert⇔Break. In the Section Breaks area of the Break dialog box, click on the Continuous option. Finally, delete the unwanted Next Page section break.

You may also have a table in Word that is divided in the middle of a cell. If the entire table does not have to be on the same page, your solution is simple. Place your insertion point anywhere on the row that is being split. Choose Table⇔Cell Height and Width. In the dialog box, click on the Row tab and clear the Allow Row to Break Across Pages check box. (If the table does have to all be on one page, you have no choice but to rearrange adjoining text to allow the table to fit.)

Why doesn't Word print the gridlines in my table?

A table's gridlines appear only on-screen. If you want to add lines to your table printouts, you need to apply borders to the table. The Table⇔Table AutoFormat command sets up predefined borders and shading. You select the design that you want from the dialog box that appears. Figure 12-3 shows the Table AutoFormat dialog box.

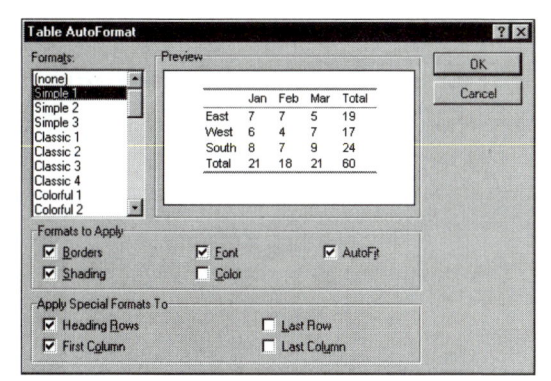

Figure 12-3: The Table AutoFormat dialog box.

If you want to make a custom border, however, choose the Borders and Shading command from the Format menu to bring up the Table Borders and Shading dialog box, as shown in Figure 12-4. In this dialog box, you can apply formatting to the table gridlines or to the text paragraph within a cell. If you want to apply formatting to the gridlines, be sure that you select the end-of-cell mark in the table.

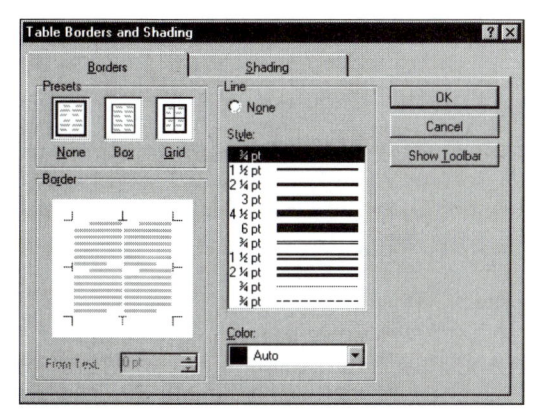

Figure 12-4: The Table Borders and Shading dialog box.

Can I run Word for Windows 95 and an earlier version of Word on the same computer, or do I need to remove my earlier version in order to run Word for Windows 95?

You can run both versions of Word on your computer at the same time. However, you need to do two things to keep the versions separate. First, install Word for Windows 95 in a different directory from the earlier version of Word. You may want to install Word for Windows 95 in a directory called `Winword95` and allow the earlier version of Word to remain in its current directory.

Next, because the main application files for all versions of Word have the same name — `Winword.exe` — you should rename one of the files if you want to run the two versions on the same computer without name conflicts. To rename the program file, start either My Computer or Explorer (double-click on the My Computer or the Explorer icon under Windows 95), find the folder for the earlier version of Word, find the applications file `Winword.exe`, and rename the file. After renaming the Word program file for the earlier version of Word, you will need an easy way to start the program. You can handle this need with the following steps:

1. In My Computer or in Explorer, right-click on the renamed program file.
2. From the shortcut menu that appears, choose Create Shortcut.
3. When the new shortcut icon appears in My Computer or Explorer, click on it and drag it onto the Windows desktop.

You can now start the older version of Word by double-clicking on the shortcut icon on the desktop.

Can I delete Word documents without leaving Word?

Yes, and it's ridiculously easy to do. The method is just not intuitively obvious. You have to use the Open command from the File menu, which is not where most people think of going to delete a file. In the Open dialog box, locate the unwanted file and click on it to select it. Then press the Delete key. A dialog box appears that asks whether you want to move the file to the Windows Recycle Bin. Click on Yes to move the file to the Recycle Bin. To delete the file permanently from your hard disk, open the Recycle Bin and empty it.

Why can't a computer that runs Word 2.0 read files from a computer that runs Word for Windows 95?

Word 2.0 and Word for Windows 95 use different file formats. For a computer that runs Word 2.0 to read Word for Windows 95 files, the files must be saved in Word 2.0 format. Word for Windows 95 comes with a converter that lets you save files in Word

2.0 format. To save a Word for Windows 95 document in the Word 2.0 format, follow these steps:

1. Open the document in Word for Windows 95 that you want to save in 2.0 format.
2. Choose File⇨Save As to open the Save As dialog box.
3. Select Word for Windows 2.0 from the Save File as Type list box. Enter a name for the file and specify the directory in which you want to store the file, then click on the OK button in the dialog box.

Why aren't all my changes saved in a document, even with AutoSave turned on?

The AutoSave feature doesn't work the way most people think it does. This feature periodically makes a copy of your document and adds the .ASD extension to it. As time passes between the saves, you may have added a substantial amount to your document, but the changes are not in the .ASD document. These files are temporary and are erased when your document is saved; they are deleted when you close the file. AutoSave is designed to recover work in the case of a power outage or system crash. You should always save your document by using the Save command when you exit Word.

If you want to turn on the AutoSave feature or just change the time intervals on the saves, choose Tools⇨Options and select the Save tab. Enter the time interval that you want in the Automatic Save Every box, as shown in Figure 12-5.

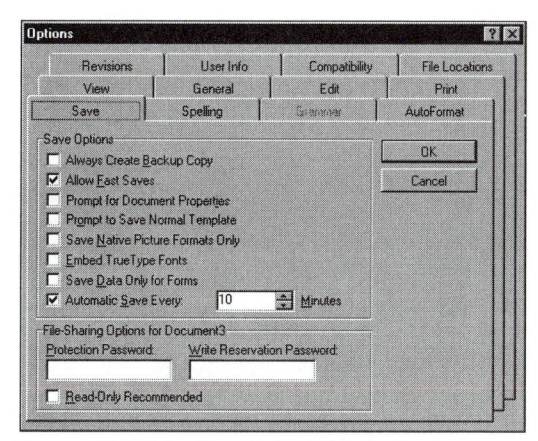

Figure 12-5: The Save Tab of the Options dialog box.

Hot Stuff: Don't put more faith than is deserved in AutoSave. Often it may save you significant amounts of time and work, but power outages, in particular, are difficult situations for Word (or any word processing program) to deal with. We wrote much of this book while on assignment in the Caribbean, where power outages are a way of life. After power failures, Word demonstrated an annoying habit of making open files unrecoverable. We quickly learned that the best defense is to back up important work to another media source (like your floppy drive) regularly.

How can I set a different font (or font size or style) as the default?

You may want to use a font different from the default font Word uses in the `Normal.dot` template. Fortunately, changing that font is a piece of cake. Open the Font dialog box by choosing Format⇨Font. In the dialog box, select the desired font, font style, and font size. Then click on the Default button. Word displays a dialog box asking you to confirm the change to the default font; click on OK in this dialog box to put the change into effect.

How can I create a bulleted or numbered list?

Word offers an easy way to create a bulleted or numbered list, quickly add the bullets or numbers, and apply a hanging indent to each of the paragraphs. To add bullets or numbers to a list, first select all the paragraphs in the list. Then, click on either the Numbering button in the Formatting toolbar (to add numbers), or the Bullets button (to add bullets). If the Formatting toolbar isn't visible, choose View⇨Toolbars and turn on the Formatting option in the dialog box that appears.

Note, too, that Word's AutoFormat technology helps you automatically create bulleted and numbered lists. For this to work, these options must be turned on in the AutoFormat tab of the Tools⇨Options dialog box. Choose Tools⇨Options and click on the AutoFormat tab in the dialog box which appears. Under the AutoFormat tab, turn on the Automatic Bulleted Lists and the Automatic Numbered Lists in the Apply As You Type portion of the dialog box. From then on, whenever you start a paragraph with an asterisk followed by a space or a tab and then a line of text, Word will automatically convert that paragraph and each one that follows to a bulleted paragraph. When you are done typing bulleted paragraphs, start a new paragraph and use the Backspace key to delete the bullet, and Word stops adding the bullets to successive paragraphs. Similarly, whenever you start a paragraph with a number 1 followed by a space and then a line of text, Word automatically converts that paragraph and each one that follows to a numbered paragraph. When you are done typing numbered paragraphs, start a new paragraph and use the Backspace key to delete the number, and Word stops adding the numbers to successive paragraphs.

Summary

This chapter has provided coverage of the top ten Word for Windows questions and their answers. The chapter also concludes the Word for Windows section of this book. The section which follows deals with Microsoft Excel, the spreadsheet package provided with Office 95.

Where to go next...

- ✦ Printing is a task that you will find yourself doing on a regular basis. For more information on the particulars of printing in Word, see Chapter 4.
- ✦ Formatting question are also common in Word. For answers to your formatting questions, see Chapter 3.

✦ ✦ ✦

Excel

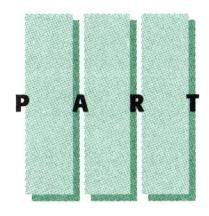

PART III

In This Part

Chapter 13
Making the Most of Workbooks

Chapter 14
Getting Information into Excel

Chapter 15
Excel Formatting

Chapter 16
Adding Graphics to Worksheets

Chapter 17
Working with Excel Charts

Chapter 18
Printing with Excel

Chapter 19
Working with Excel Databases

Chapter 20
Working with Macros

Chapter 21
Excel Analysis

Chapter 22
Using Visual Basic for Applications

Chapter 23
Excel for Windows at Work

Chapter 24
The Excel Top Ten

Making the Most of Workbooks

CHAPTER 13

◆ ◆ ◆ ◆

In This Chapter

Opening workbooks

Moving between workbooks and worksheets

Moving around in a worksheet

Selecting cells and ranges

Adding and moving sheets

Saving workbooks and workspaces in Excel and other file formats

Finding workbooks

Organizing files

◆ ◆ ◆ ◆

This chapter covers topics related to working with Excel workbooks, which are collections of worksheet pages that are saved to the same disk file. Before you can effectively work with Excel, you need to become familiar with the workbook concept.

Understanding Excel Workbooks

For some time, many popular Windows spreadsheets have used the workbook concept, which places multiple pages, each containing a worksheet, inside of a "notebook" of sorts (called *workbook* in Excel lingo). The workbook concept is a case of a computer model imitating real life because Excel's designers assumed that most people who use spreadsheets have different but related groups of number-based data that would best occupy different pages. If, for example, you lived generations before the advent of the computer and you worked with numbers to earn a living, you would have different pieces of paper on your desk, each with related number-based information about a particular project. At the day's end, all the pages would go back into a file folder that was stored in your desk. In Excel, each of these pages becomes a separate worksheet, and the worksheets are identified by tabs at the bottom. All the worksheet pages make up a workbook (the file folder in the analogy).

The workbook concept makes your spreadsheet-related work manageable. Before spreadsheet designers implemented the workbook concept, spreadsheets first accommodated a user's desire for more power by providing larger and larger spreadsheets in the form of a single page. But finding information became quite a challenge as spreadsheet pages approached the physical size of small houses. The next step in spreadsheet design was to give users the ability to base formulas in one spreadsheet on cells of another. This capability partially solved the organizational problem, but you had to remember to open all the spreadsheet files that you needed. The workbook concept overcomes the limitations of earlier spreadsheet designs, however, by placing all your information in an easily accessible notebook.

With the workbook concept, you can easily find information by navigating among the multiple pages of the workbook. And you can name the tabs that indicate each page (worksheet) of the workbook so that they better indicate what is stored in each worksheet. Figure 13-1 shows a typical workbook in Excel, with the House Sales worksheet page of the workbook currently active. (You'll find this worksheet on the CD-ROM).

	A	B	C	D	E	F	G	H
1		January	February	March	April			
2	Walnut Creek	$123,600.00	$137,000.00	$89,900.00	$201,300.00			
3	River Hills	$248,700.00	$256,750.00	$302,500.00	$197,000.00			
4	Spring Gardens	$97,000.00	$102,500.00	$121,500.00	$142,500.00			
5	Lake Newport	$346,300.00	$372,300.00	$502,900.00	$456,800.00			
6								
7	Total Sales	$815,600.00	$868,550.00	$1,016,800.00	$997,600.00			
8								
9								
10								
11	Income							
12								
13	Sublet Office Space	$1,800.00	$1,800.00	$1,800.00	$1,800.00			
14	Misc. Income	$750.00	$750.00	$500.00	$800.00			
15								
16	Total Income	$2,550.00	$2,550.00	$2,300.00	$2,600.00			
17								
18								
19	Gross Receipts	$818,150.00	$871,100.00	$1,019,100.00	$1,000,200.00			

Chart 1 / Chart 2 \ House Sales / House Totals / House Graph / Ho

Figure 13-1: A typical Excel workbook.

In Excel, each workbook can contain up to 255 separate worksheet pages. Each worksheet measures 16,384 rows by 256 columns — realistically, more than you should ever need on a single page. Each intersection of a row and column comprises a *cell,* and cells are identified by their row-and-column coordinates (for example, A1 is the cell in the upper-left corner of the worksheet). In addition to containing worksheet pages, an Excel workbook can also contain chart sheets (used to store charts); modules (collections of program code written in Visual Basic for Applications, the programming language used by Excel); Excel 4.0 macro sheets; and dialog box sheets.

Where are my tabs?

If you don't see tabs for your Excel worksheet pages, someone has turned off the tab display. Choose Tools⇨Options to display the Options dialog box. Click on the View tab and turn on the Sheet Tabs check box. Then click on the OK button to restore the tabs.

Opening a new workbook

When you start Excel, it opens a new workbook, and you can begin entering your information. If you want to create a new workbook at any time, click on the New Workbook button on the Standard toolbar, or choose File➪New.

Opening an existing workbook

To open an existing workbook, choose File➪Open to bring up the Open dialog box, as shown in Figure 13-2. Select the desired file and then click on the Open button to open the file. If the file is in a different folder, you may need to move to that folder by finding the folder in the dialog box and double-clicking on it. You can navigate upward in your PC's folder structure by clicking on the Up One Level button in the dialog box.

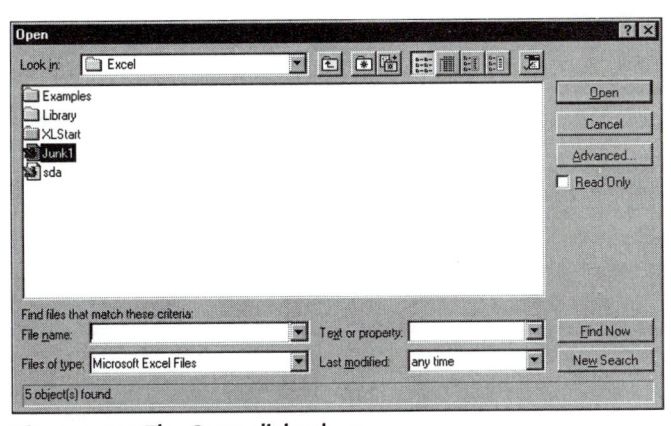

Figure 13-2: The Open dialog box.

If you want to open a workbook that you have recently worked with, open the File menu and choose the file from the bottom of the menu. Excel remembers the last four files that you have worked with, and lists them at the bottom of the File menu. If the list of recently used workbooks is not displayed in your File menu, the option for displaying them has been turned off. To turn it back on, choose Tools➪Options. Click on the General tab in the Options dialog box and turn on the Recently Used File List check box to activate the option. Then click on the OK button.

Hot Stuff
If you cannot find the file that you are looking for, enter the name of the file in the File name box, along with an entry in the Text or property area to perform a simple search. The process of searching is explained in more detail later in this chapter.

The more workbooks, the merrier ...

In Excel, you can have more than one workbook file open at a time. Each workbook that you open is in its own document window. As you need to work with a specific workbook, you bring it to the front by pressing Ctrl+F6 until you see the workbook or by choosing the workbook from the Window menu. You can move and size the windows containing your workbooks by using standard Windows moving and sizing techniques. And if you size the windows so that they don't take up the entire screen, you can then navigate between multiple windows by using the mouse to make any desired window the active window.

Working with Worksheets

As you work with Excel worksheets, you'll use various techniques to move around in the sheet and to select areas of the sheet in which you'll perform common operations. First, though, it makes sense to become familiar with the parts of a worksheet. The parts of a worksheet window are illustrated in Figure 13-3, and Table 13-1 describes them.

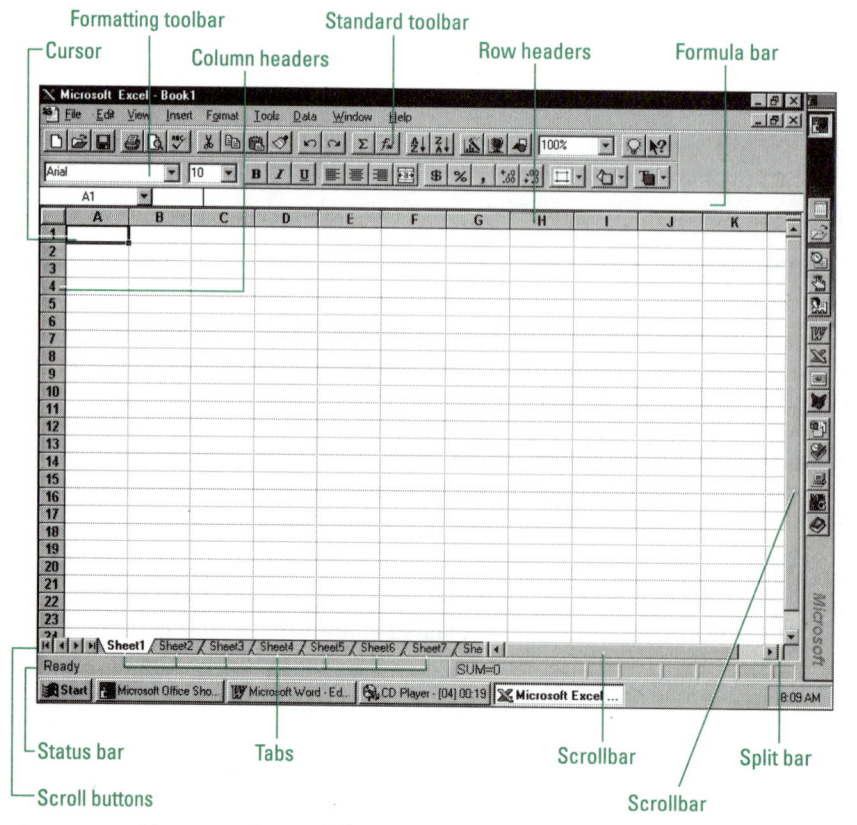

Figure 13-3: The parts of a worksheet.

Table 13-1
Parts of a worksheet

Worksheet part	Purpose
Scrollbars	Use these to view sections of the worksheet that are not currently visible by clicking on the arrows, or by moving the scroll box.
Split bars	Use these to split the worksheet window into two panes to enable you to view different portions of the worksheet. To use the split bars, move the pointer to an area between columns or cells and click and drag to size.
Row headers	Identifies each row and can be used to select rows (by clicking on the headers).
Column headers	Identifies each column and can be used to select columns (by clicking on the headers).
Cursor	Indicates the currently selected (or active) cell.
Tabs	Selects each worksheet in the workbook.
Standard toolbar	Provides buttons to access common operations, such as opening and saving files, and cutting, copying, and pasting data.
Formatting toolbar	Provides buttons to access common formatting tasks, such as changing the fonts and alignments used to display data.
Formula bar	Displays the contents of the active cell.
Status bar	Displays various messages as you use Excel.
Scroll buttons	Scrolls among the worksheet tabs in a workbook.

Navigating within your worksheet

The primary means of navigating within the worksheet is with the mouse. As you move the mouse pointer around the worksheet, the pointer changes shape depending on its location. In most areas of the worksheet, the pointer resembles a plus sign. In most areas outside of the worksheet or over the scrollbars, the pointer changes shape to resemble an arrow. You can scroll the worksheet one row or one column at a time by pointing to the arrows at the ends of the scrollbars and clicking on them with the mouse button.

You can also point to a scroll box, one of the two solid white blocks within the scrollbars, and use the mouse to drag the block to another position on the scrollbar. Dragging a scroll box causes the worksheet to scroll several rows or columns when you release the mouse button. When you use this technique, notice that the row or column reference that appears on-screen in the upper-left corner changes to indicate your position within the worksheet.

The Tab and Return keys, used alone or in combination with the Shift key, also move the cursor. Pressing Tab moves the cursor to the right; pressing Shift+Tab moves the cursor to the left. Pressing Return moves the cursor down; pressing Shift+Return moves the cursor up.

Hot Stuff
If you've lost the cursor and you want to quickly locate it, press Ctrl+Backspace. This action causes the window to scroll as needed to reveal the active cell.

You can also use the Go To key (F5) to move quickly within a worksheet if you know the cell that you want to go to. Press F5 to open the Go To dialog box, as shown in Figure 13-4. In the Reference text box, enter the name of the cell that you want to go to and click on the OK button or press Enter. Excel automatically takes you to that cell. For example, if you enter **AZ400** into the Reference text box and press Enter, the cursor moves to cell AZ400. You can also open the Go To dialog box by choosing Edit➪Go To.

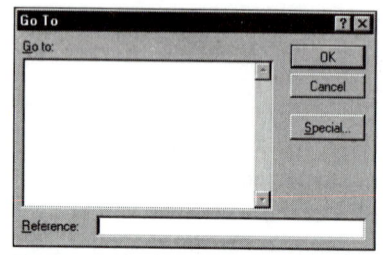

Figure 13-4: The Go To dialog box.

More Info
If you're curious, you can use the Go To list box to select a *named range* to go to in a worksheet. Chapter 14 provides details about working with named ranges.

You can also navigate within your worksheet by using arrow keys. As you reach the right side or the bottom row of the worksheet, pressing the same cursor key once more causes the worksheet to scroll, bringing an additional row or column into view.

Keep in mind that the part of the worksheet that you can see is just a small part of the entire sheet. Table 13-2 shows various other key combinations that you will find useful when moving around in an Excel worksheet.

Table 13-2
Useful keys for worksheet navigation

Keys	Function
Arrow keys	Moves cursor in direction of the arrow
Ctrl+↑ or Ctrl+↓	Moves the cursor to the top or bottom of a region of data
Ctrl+← or Ctrl+→	Moves the cursor to the leftmost or rightmost region of data
PgUp or PgDn	Moves the cursor up or down one screen
Ctrl+PgUp or Ctrl+PgDn	Moves the cursor to the preceding or the following worksheet
Home	Move the cursor to the first cell in a row
Ctrl+Home	Moves the cursor to the upper-left corner of the worksheet
End	Moves the cursor to the last cell in a row
Ctrl+End	Moves the cursor to the first cell of the last row in a worksheet
End+← or End+→	Moves the cursor to the next blank cell in the direction of the arrow when the active cell is blank
End+Enter	Moves the cursor to the last column in a row

Moving among worksheets

With any spreadsheet that uses the workbook concept, you need a fast, easy way to move among the individual worksheets of the workbook. In Excel, you activate a worksheet by clicking on its tab at the bottom of the worksheet. At the lower-left corner of the worksheet (refer to Figure 13-1) are scroll buttons that enable you to scroll among the different worksheet tabs. If a tab that you want to select is not visible, you can click on the buttons to scroll the tab into view. Clicking on the left- or right-arrow button scrolls you by one tab to the left or right. Clicking on the left-end or right-end button (the one with the line to the left or right of the arrow) scrolls you to the first or last tab in the worksheet. By default, new workbooks in Excel have 16 worksheets, but you can add more (up to the limit of 255 worksheets per workbook) by inserting new worksheets, a topic covered later in this chapter.

Hot Stuff Remember that you can use the Ctrl+PgUp and Ctrl+PgDn keys to move between worksheets. Ctrl+PgUp moves to the prior worksheet, and Ctrl+PgDn moves to the next worksheet.

Scrolling among the tabs works well if your workbook contains relatively few worksheets. But if your workbook is fairly large (for example, 4 years worth of projected budgets stored on 48 worksheets), there's an easier way to get around the worksheets: You can use the Go To key (F5). When the Go To dialog box appears, you enter the name of the tab followed by an exclamation point and the cell that you want to go to. Follow these steps to use the Go To key:

1. Press F5 to open the Go To dialog box.

2. In the Reference text box, enter the tab name, an exclamation point, and the cell reference. Then click on the OK button.

   For example, to jump to the first cell in the sixth worksheet, you would press F5 and enter **Sheet6!A1** in the Reference text box.

Unfortunately, this technique doesn't work when you have given your tabs names that include spaces, such as House Sales. With these names, Excel interprets the first word that you type in the Reference text box as a *named range*, and when Excel can't find a range by that name, it displays an error message. The only way around this problem (if you want to be able to jump across pages with the Go To key) is to rename the tab with a name that doesn't include spaces or to create named ranges in the other worksheets so that Excel can find the named range.

Renaming the worksheet tabs

As you work with different worksheets of the workbook, you may find it helpful to rename the tabs to something meaningful. Face it, Sheet4 means a lot less to most people than May 95 Slush Fund. You can easily rename the tabs to whatever you want by right-clicking on the desired tab and choosing Rename from the shortcut menu. In the Rename Sheet dialog box (see Figure 13-5), enter the name for the tab and then click on the OK button. While Excel doesn't limit what you can call your tabs, you should keep the names short so that you can view more tabs at one time at the bottom of the workbook.

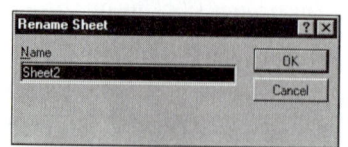

Figure 13-5: The Rename Sheet dialog box.

Selecting multiple worksheets

For many common operations (such as inserting or deleting sheets or applying formatting), you need a way to select more than one worksheet at a time. You can select multiple sheets that are *adjacent* (directly beside one another) by performing these steps:

1. Use the scroll buttons to bring the first tab that you want to select into view and click on the tab to select that worksheet.

2. Use the scroll buttons (if needed) to bring the last tab of the group that you want to select into view. Hold down the Shift key and click on the last tab.

To select multiple sheets that are not adjacent to each other, you can use the following steps:

1. Use the scroll buttons to bring the first tab that you want to select into view and click on the tab to select that worksheet.

2. Use the scroll buttons (if needed) to bring the next tab that you want to select into view. Hold down the Ctrl key and click on the desired tab.

3. Repeat Steps 1 and 2 for each additional tab that you want to select.

Selecting a range of cells

For many operations, you will need to select large areas of cells, or *ranges* of cells. To select all cells from A1 to F6, for example, you would click in cell A1, hold down the mouse button, and drag down to cell F6 (see Figure 13-6). As you select the A1:F6 cell range, the first cell does not appear in reverse video, as the others do; nevertheless, it is one of the selected cells. By placing the cursor at any cell and clicking and dragging the mouse, you can select any range of cells.

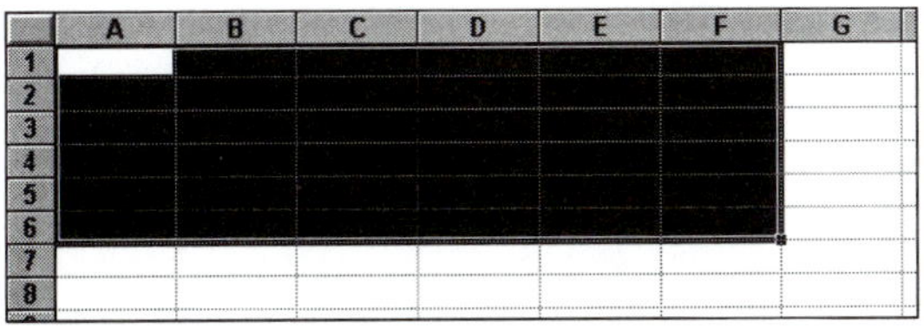

Figure 13-6: Selecting a range of cells in an Excel worksheet.

A similar technique for selecting a range of cells is to use the mouse and the Shift key. Simply click in the first cell of the range and then hold down the Shift key while you click in the last cell of the range. The entire range is then selected, and the active cell is the last cell that you selected. For example, if you click in cell B2, hold down the Shift key, and click in cell E15, the entire range from B2 to E15 is selected, and the active cell becomes cell E15.

If you need to select a very large range of cells, use the Go To key to make your selection process faster. Follow these steps:

1. Select the first cell in the range that you want to select.

2. Press F5 to open the Go To dialog box.

3. In the Reference text box, enter the cell reference for the last cell in the range.

4. Hold down the Shift key while you click on the OK button.

You can also use other methods to select a range of cells. You can select an entire row by clicking on the row header at the left edge of the worksheet, and you can select an entire column by clicking on the column header at the top of the column. To select more than one complete row or column of a worksheet, click on and drag across a series of column headers or down a series of row headers. For example, if you want to select all cells in rows 4, 5, and 6, you click on the row 4 header and drag across rows 5 and 6.

With Excel, you can also select *discontiguous ranges*, or nonadjacent areas. For example, you can select B2:C10 and then select D12:E16. To make this selection, select the first range in the usual manner. Then hold down the Ctrl key and select the second range by clicking and dragging. Excel selects the second area without deselecting the first. Figure 13-7 shows the result of selecting these two ranges.

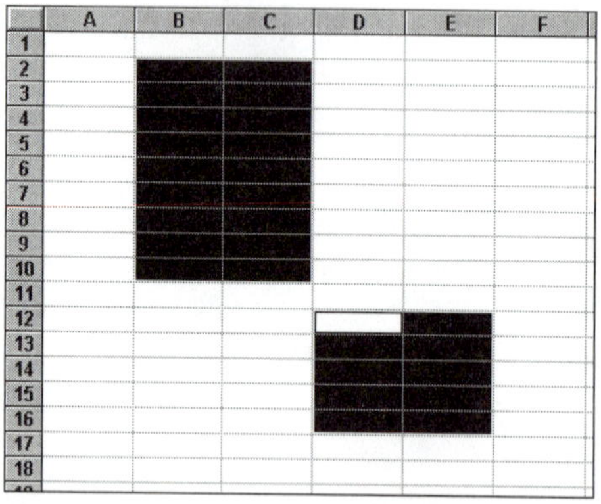

Figure 13-7: Selecting discontiguous ranges of cells.

More Info You may find it helpful to select multiple ranges, such as both rows and columns, as one unit so that you can apply the same formatting to them. (Chapter 15 goes into more detail about formatting your worksheets.) To select rows and columns at the same time, select the first row or column that you want and then hold down the Ctrl key as you select the other rows or columns. Figure 13-8 shows the results of selecting rows 1 and 2 and columns A and B with this technique.

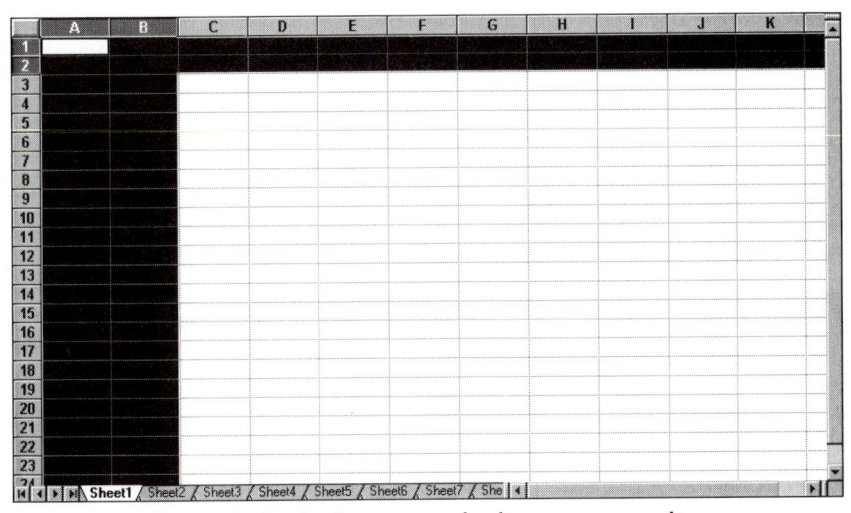

Figure 13-8: The result of selecting rows and columns as one unit.

Adding and deleting worksheets

As you work in an Excel workbook, you may have to rearrange the worksheets in it. Right-clicking on one of the worksheet tabs causes a shortcut menu to open. You can use this shortcut menu to add, delete, and move your worksheets.

Follow these steps to add a worksheet to a workbook:

1. Right-click on the tab of the worksheet that will appear after the worksheet you want to add.
2. Choose Insert from the shortcut menu to open the Insert dialog box with the General tab displayed, as shown in Figure 13-9.

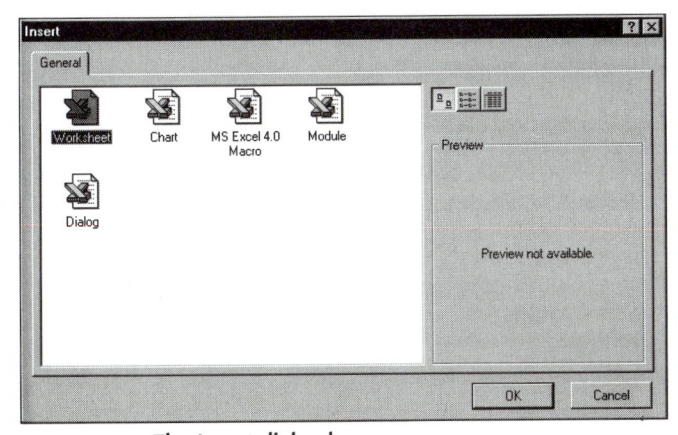

Figure 13-9: The Insert dialog box.

3. Click on the Worksheet icon to insert a new worksheet and then click on the OK button (or double-click on the Worksheet icon).

You can also delete a worksheet by using the shortcut menu. Simply select the tab of the sheet that you want to delete, right-click on it, choose Delete, and click on OK to confirm the deletion.

Moving and copying information in worksheets

You can move or copy information in worksheets and in workbooks in a variety of ways. To copy information from one place to another on a worksheet or to another worksheet, perform the following steps:

1. Select the information that you want to copy.
2. Click on the Copy button in the Standard toolbar or choose Edit➪Copy.
3. Move to the cell in the worksheet in which you want to begin the insertion of the information.
4. Press Enter to place the information in the worksheet.

You can move information in the same worksheet or to another worksheet by following these steps:

1. Select the information that you want to move.
2. Click on the Cut button in the Standard toolbar or choose Edit➪Cut.
3. Move to the cell in the worksheet in which you want to begin entering the information. Be sure that the areas are of the same size so that the move will work without overwriting existing information that you may need.
4. Click on the Paste button in the Standard toolbar or choose Edit➪Paste to insert the information.

Moving and copying information from one workbook to another is almost as easy as moving and copying information in worksheets of the same workbook. To copy information from one workbook to another, follow these steps:

1. Select the cells that you want to copy.
2. Right-click on the tab of the sheet and choose Move or Copy from the shortcut menu to open the Move or Copy dialog box. In the Move Selected Sheets to Book list box, you can select the (new book) option or the last book that was opened. If you choose the (new book) option, the entire sheet is copied to a new workbook; therefore, if you want to copy only a few cells, use the Copy and Paste buttons on the Standard toolbar.

You can also copy information from one workbook to another by using the Copy and Paste buttons on the Standard toolbar. First select the information that you want to copy. Click on the Copy button on the Standard toolbar. Open the workbook in which you want to copy the information, place your cursor in the cell of the appropriate sheet, and click on the Paste button on the Standard toolbar to insert the information.

To move information from one workbook to another, follow these steps:

1. Select the information that you want to move to another workbook.
2. Click on the Cut button on the Standard toolbar.
3. Open the workbook in which you want to move the information. Or if the workbook is already open, press Ctrl+F6 to move to the other workbook.
4. Place the cursor at the desired location for the data and then click on the Paste button on the Standard toolbar to insert the information.

Splitting the worksheet window

With large worksheets, you may find it helpful to view entirely different parts of the worksheet at the same time by splitting the worksheet window into different panes (see Figure 13-10). To split a worksheet window, drag one of the split bars. You can also place the cursor where you want the window to split and choose Window⇨Split.

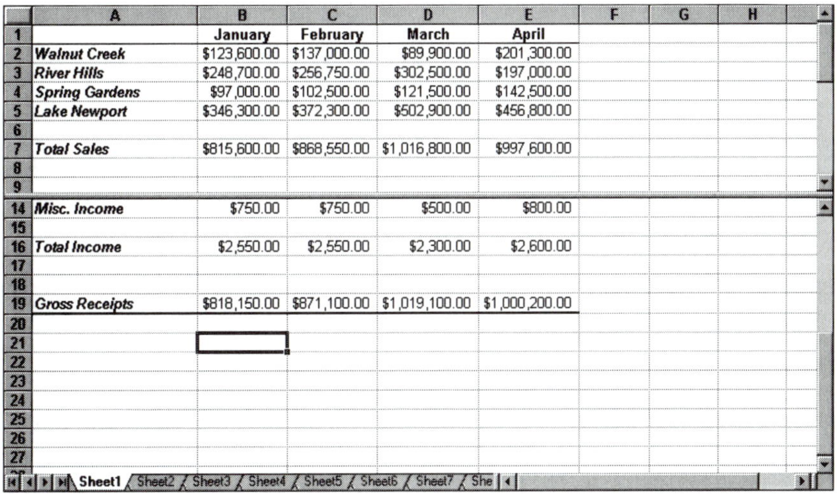

	A	B	C	D	E
1		January	February	March	April
2	Walnut Creek	$123,600.00	$137,000.00	$89,900.00	$201,300.00
3	River Hills	$248,700.00	$256,750.00	$302,500.00	$197,000.00
4	Spring Gardens	$97,000.00	$102,500.00	$121,500.00	$142,500.00
5	Lake Newport	$346,300.00	$372,300.00	$502,900.00	$456,800.00
6					
7	Total Sales	$815,600.00	$868,550.00	$1,016,800.00	$997,600.00
14	Misc. Income	$750.00	$750.00	$500.00	$800.00
16	Total Income	$2,550.00	$2,550.00	$2,300.00	$2,600.00
19	Gross Receipts	$818,150.00	$871,100.00	$1,019,100.00	$1,000,200.00

Figure 13-10: A worksheet window split into multiple panes.

You can drag the split bar at the right side of the window to create a horizontal split, and you can drag the split bar at the bottom of the window to create a vertical split. You can then switch between panes by clicking in the pane that you want to work with. When you are finished using multiple panes, you can close one pane by dragging the split bar back to the right or bottom of the window, or you can choose Window⇨Remove Split.

While a window is split, you can keep the top or left pane from scrolling by choosing Window⇨Freeze Panes. This menu option freezes the window panes above and to the left of the split.

Working with Excel's Toolbars

Like the other Microsoft Office applications, Excel provides several toolbars that you can use to accomplish common tasks. By default, Excel displays the Standard and the Formatting toolbars, shown earlier in Figure 13-3. But Excel has several other toolbars that you may find useful as you work in Excel. Figure 13-11 shows an Excel worksheet with several toolbars turned on. (Obviously, these toolbars use up a lot of screen real estate.)

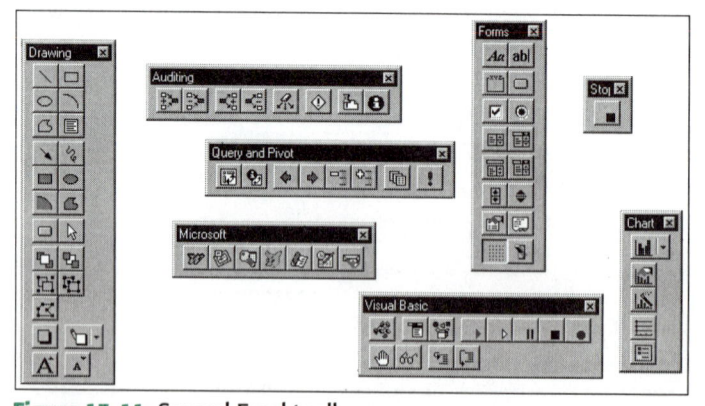

Figure 13-11: Several Excel toolbars.

If you never use the toolbars, you can turn them off to make more space available for viewing your worksheet. And if you want to bring other toolbars into view, you can do so by turning them on. To turn the display of a toolbar on or off, choose View⇨Toolbars to open the Toolbars dialog box (see Figure 13-12). In the dialog box, turn on any toolbar that you want to display, or turn off any toolbar that should not be displayed. (A check mark in the check box indicates that the toolbar will be displayed.)

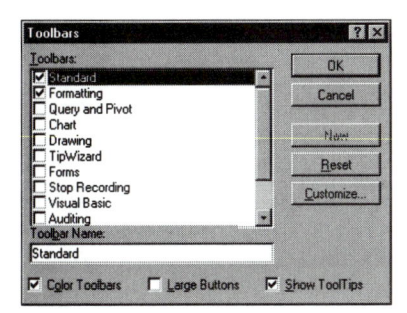

Figure 13-12: The Toolbars dialog box.

The options at the bottom of the Toolbars dialog box enable you to choose whether toolbars are shown with icons in color, whether large buttons should be used, and whether Tooltips (those helpful explanations that appear when you hold the mouse pointer over a toolbar button) should be turned on. When you are finished selecting the desired options, click on the OK button.

Displaying several toolbars at once does use up memory and resources in Excel (OK, not a great deal of memory, but on some machines, every little bit helps). Even if your machine is the latest and greatest with oodles and oodles of memory, turning of toolbars that you are not using gives you more room to see what you're doing.

What's that button do, anyway?

We could have provided a table that would list every toolbar button in Excel, but because there are nearly 300 of them, you would grow tired of seeing the table long before it ended. A better way to find the purpose of any toolbar button is to make use of the Tooltips feature. When you hold the mouse pointer over any toolbar button for more than one second, a Tooltip appears that gives the name of the button, and the purpose of the button also appears in the status bar. If you want a really detailed explanation of any toolbar button, click on the Help button in the Standard toolbar (the one with the arrow and the question mark) and then click on the toolbar button that you want more information about.

> ### Toolbars: Have it your way
>
> If you don't like the toolbars that Excel offers, you can create your own. From the View menu, choose Toolbars to open the Toolbars dialog box. In the Toolbar Name text box, enter your own name for a toolbar. Then click on the New button. Excel creates a floating toolbar and displays a Customize dialog box, which contains all the buttons available for use on a toolbar. You can drag any of the buttons from the dialog box onto your toolbar. When you are finished creating your own toolbar, click on the Close button.

After you turn on a toolbar, you can position it anywhere you want in the window. Toolbars can be *floating* (like most of those shown in Figure 13-11), or they can be *docked* to the sides, top, or bottom of the window. The Standard and Formatting toolbars are usually docked to the top of the screen. You use these steps to move a toolbar:

1. Place the mouse pointer over any blank area of the toolbar.
2. Hold down the mouse button and drag the toolbar to the desired area.

If you want to dock the toolbar, you can dock it to any one of four possible areas: the sides of the window, the bottom of the window above the status bar, and the top of the window between the menu bar and the formula bar. Toolbars that contain drop-down lists cannot be docked to the sides of the window.

Hot Stuff: You can quickly dock a floating toolbar to the top of the window by double-clicking on the title bar of the toolbar.

Saving and Closing a Workbook

You can save a workbook by clicking on the Save button on the Standard toolbar, entering a name for the workbook in the Save dialog box, and clicking on the OK button. If the workbook had been saved earlier, you can save it again under the same filename that you gave it earlier.

You can also protect the workbook with a password if you want. To protect the workbook, choose File⇨Save As. In the Save As dialog box, click on the Options button, as shown in Figure 13-13. The Save Options dialog box appears, as shown in Figure 13-14. In this dialog box, you can add a protection password to the workbook (which you need to open the workbook), or you can add a write reservation password (which you need to change the document). You can also make the workbook a read-only workbook, which means that no edits can be added to the document, This is done by turning on the Read-Only Recommended check box. Turning on the Always Create Backup option tells Excel to save the preceding version of the worksheet to a backup file each time that you save the latest version.

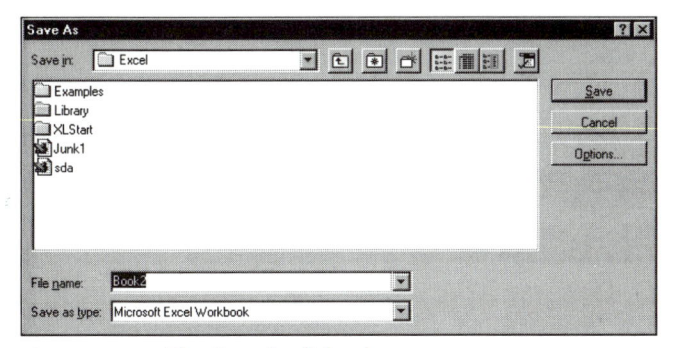

Figure 13-13: The Save As dialog box.

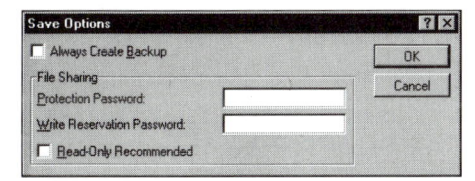

Figure 13-14: The Save Options dialog box.

Adding summary information to your workbook

As part of the information that is saved with your workbook, Excel lets you include specifics about the workbook such as a title, author name, key words, and comments about the workbook. You can view and edit this information by choosing File⇔Properties. In the Properties dialog box, click on the Summary tab (see Figure 13-15). Here you can add any information that you want. The information that you add to the various text boxes can then be used to aid in the file search process. Therefore, give real consideration to entering something in this dialog box that may help you find the workbook at some time in the future.

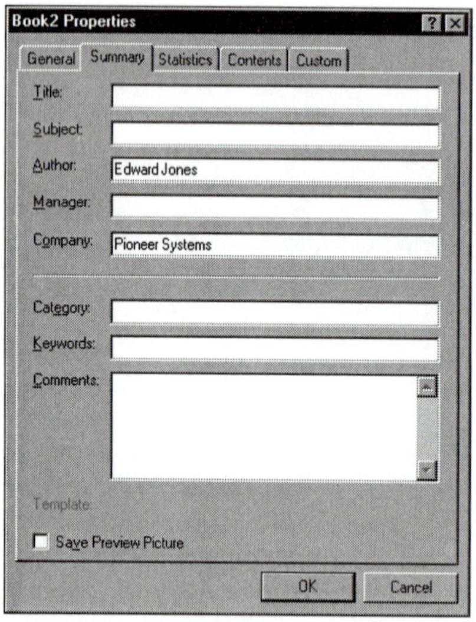

Figure 13-15: The Summary tab of the Properties dialog box.

Using the AutoSave feature

Excel, like other Microsoft products, includes an AutoSave option. The AutoSave option often protects you from losing significant amounts of work in the event of a power failure or system crash (but note that it is *not* infallible).

To enable AutoSave, choose Tools⇨AutoSave. (If you don't see this menu option, read the next paragraph.) In the AutoSave dialog box, turn on the Automatic Save Every check box and enter the time interval that you want Excel to use for the AutoSave. Then choose whether you want to save only the active workbook or all open workbooks with the AutoSave feature and decide whether you want Excel to prompt you before each AutoSave.

If you don't see the AutoSave option on the Tools menu, choose Tools⇨Add-Ins to bring up the Add-Ins dialog box, as shown in Figure 13-16. This dialog box contains different options that you can activate for Excel. After you put a check mark by the AutoSave option, the option becomes available on the Tools menu. Follow the steps in the preceding paragraph to turn on the AutoSave option.

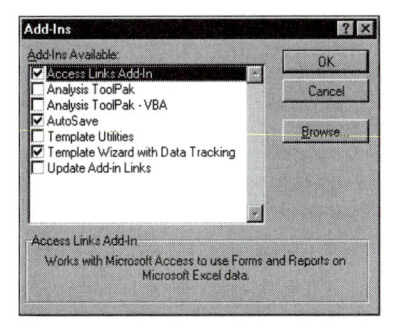

Figure 13-16: The Add-Ins dialog box.

If you still do not see the AutoSave option in the Add-Ins dialog box, you need to install this component of Office 95. To install AutoSave, perform the following steps:

1. Close all other Windows applications.
2. Right-click on the title bar of the Office Shortcut Bar. Figure 13-17 shows the resulting shortcut menu.

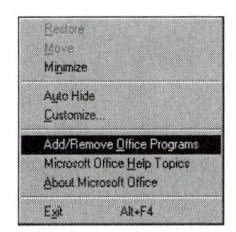

Figure 13-17: The Office Shortcut Bar shortcut menu.

3. From the shortcut menu, choose Add/Remove Office Programs.
4. You are then moved to Office 95 Setup, and you see a Setup dialog box for Office 95.
5. Before you are allowed to proceed, you have to close the Office Shortcut Bar by right-clicking on the title bar and choosing Exit from the shortcut menu.

6. Click on the Add/Remove button in the Setup dialog box. You will then see the Microsoft Office 95 Maintenance window.

7. Select Excel from the list. and click on the Change Options button to the right of the window. The next window you see contains the different installation options for Excel.

8. Choose Add-Ins from the list and click on the Change Options button. You will then see the Microsoft Office 95 – Add-Ins dialog box, as shown in Figure 13-18.

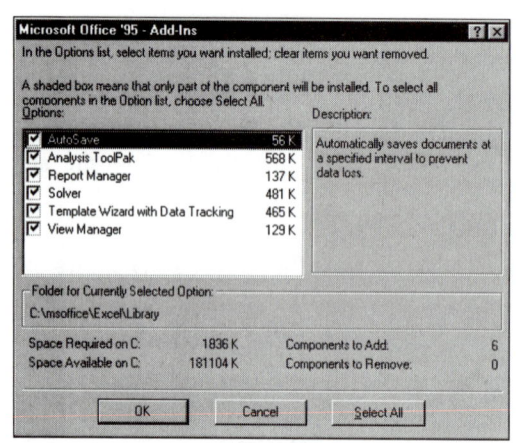

Figure 13-18: The Microsoft Office 95 – Add-Ins dialog box.

9. Click on the check box next to AutoSave to include it as part of the Excel installation. A description is given for each of the options at the right of the dialog box. This description can help you decide whether to include a particular component as part of your setup.

10. Now click on the OK button on the bottom of the dialog box until you see the Continue button on the bottom of the window. When you see the Continue button, place the Office 95 disk in the drive and click on the Continue button. The new components that you chose are then added to your current setup of Office.

Another way to protect your work from being lost in the event of a crash or power failure is to create a backup file for each "parent file" that you are working with. The backup file again minimizes the chances of losing your work in the event of a power outage or other accident.

If you want to take advantage of this option, choose File➪Save As. In the Save As dialog box, choose the Options button. In the Save Options dialog box, check the Always Create Backup check box. After you activate this option, Excel creates a file with the .BAK extension for the workbook with each save.

Saving in other file formats

Often you may need to save files in formats other than that used by the current version of Excel. Other users may be using earlier versions of Excel, or they may be using other spreadsheets, and you need to provide them with spreadsheet data that they can work with. Saving files in other formats is relatively simple if you follow these steps:

1. Choose File➪Save As to open the Save As dialog box.
2. In the Save as type list box, you can select the format in which you want to save the file.
3. After selecting the file type, enter a name for the file (or accept the default).
4. Click on the Save button to save the file.

Danger Zone If you save files in a format that is not the native Excel format, some features of the worksheet may be lost if they are not supported by the other program's file format. For example, if you save a file in an Excel 3.0 format, only the current page of the workbook will be saved to a worksheet file because that version of Excel did not support the concept of workbooks with multiple sheets.

Saving a workspace file

If you work with more than one workbook at the same time on a regular basis, you may get tired of having to open the same workbooks day in and day out. Excel has a nice feature that allows you to avoid this monotony: the *workspace file*. You can use this file to save the workbooks that you are working on, the order that they are in, and the sheets that are open at the time. The next time that you need to work with these same workbooks, you can open the workspace file, and all the workbooks are in the same position that they were in when you created the workspace file. Follow these steps to create a workspace file:

1. Open the workbooks that you want to include in the workspace file and arrange them in the way that you want them to be when you open the workspace file.
2. Choose File➪Save Workspace to open the Save Workspace dialog box, as shown in Figure 13-19.

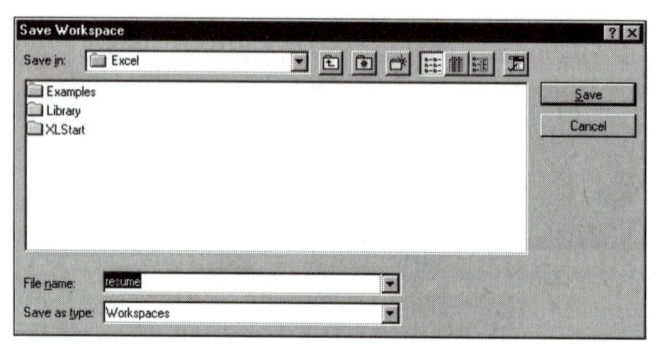

Figure 13-19: The Save Workspace dialog box.

3. Enter a name for the workspace file and click on the OK button.

Danger Zone Remember that the workspace file keeps track of the arrangement of your work area, but it doesn't save changes to your workbook files. If you make changes to the workbooks, you will need to save them before closing them or exiting Excel.

Closing a workbook and exiting Excel

To close a workbook, choose File➪Close or click on the icon at the left edge of the menu bar. If you made any changes to the workbook that were not saved, Excel asks whether you want to save the changes. (This safeguard is provided to avoid your exiting Excel without saving your work.)

Exiting Excel is about as straightforward as exiting any Windows program. Choose File➪Exit. If you have any unsaved work, Excel asks whether you want to save the changes before you are returned to the Windows environment.

Opening a workspace file when you start Excel

If you want to open the workspace file when you start Excel, you will need to move the workspace file to the Startup folder (normally \Excel\Xlstart). You have to transfer only the workspace file, not the workbook files themselves.

Finding Workbooks

Finding files in Excel has been made easier in the latest version. Finding files is now done via File➪Open. In the Open dialog box, you can perform searches based on name, location, author, and other summary information. This is why it is important to enter information in the Summary tab of the Properties dialog box. The information that you enter in the Properties dialog box can be instrumental in helping you find a file that you have forgotten the name of or that you have not worked with in a long time.

You can also do a search for files based on specific text that appears in the workbook. The specific text may be a name of a column, a key number, or anything that may specify the file that you are searching for. The criteria for the searches can be as narrow or as broad as you want it to be.

Using the Open dialog box

Unlike earlier versions of Windows products, you will find the new Open dialog box very different. This dialog box is especially user-friendly; you will find that working with this dialog box is different from your earlier boxes but in many ways easier to use. So don't let the new box give you reservations.

This box allows you to perform simple searches, document maintenance, and create more complex searches. The following section will help familiarize you with the dialog box and make it a little easier to use.

By default, the Open dialog box is in List mode (see Figure 13-20). However, you can change the mode of the dialog box by clicking on the buttons on the Open toolbar. Table 13-3 gives the names of the buttons on the Open toolbar and their functions.

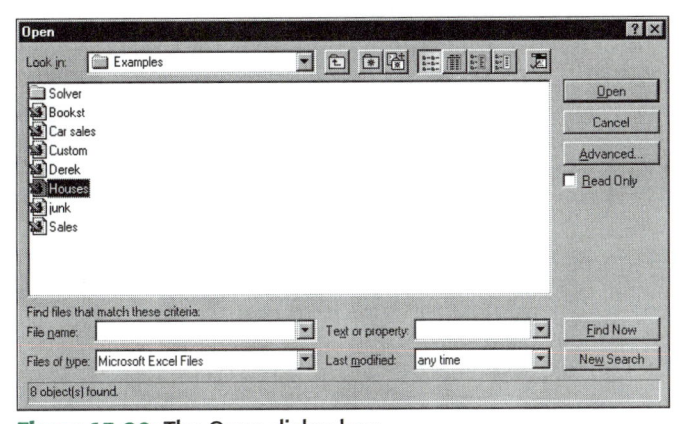

Figure 13-20: The Open dialog box.

Table 13-3
The Open toolbar buttons and their functions

Button	Function
Up One Level	Moves up one folder
Look in Favorites	Looks in the Favorites folder
Add to Favorites	Adds a file to the Favorites folder
List	Places the window in List view
Details	Places the window in Detail view, which lists the size, type, and last modified date
Properties	Lists the author's comments that were entered in the Summary tab of the Properties dialog box
Preview	Previews the files selected in the left half of the window
Commands and Settings	Controls the commands and settings for the Open dialog box (Here you can print, open a file as read-only, sort files, and search subfolders by choosing the corresponding choice from the menu.)

The Open dialog box lets you preview the files when you press the Preview button. This feature can help you remember a file by enabling you to see part of it in a preview. When you press the Preview button, the single window that you see splits into two windows (see Figure 13-21) with the Preview window on the right.

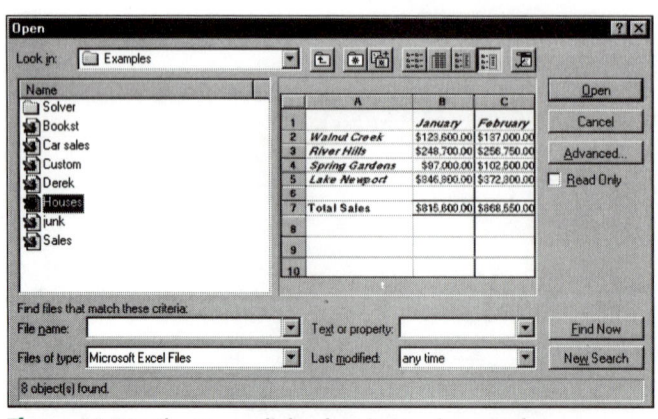

Figure 13-21: The Open dialog box in Preview mode.

You can easily forget where you have stored a file if you have not worked with it for a while; therefore, the features of the Open dialog box come in handy for helping you find a file. By default, you will see all the folders that are contained in the Excel directory when you activate the Open dialog box. Clicking on the folders shows their contents. Remember that, by default, Excel shows only the Excel file types. If you want to see other file types, you must change the file type in the Files of Type list box at the bottom of the Open dialog box.

At the bottom of the Open dialog box are four list boxes that enable you to enter criteria for a search. If you know the name of the file, you can enter it in the File Name list box. Remember that, by default, the program searches in the Excel folder for the filename. If the file is not there, it will not be found. You can use *.*file extension* (such as `Sales.xls`, `Houses.xls`, and so forth), as you did in earlier versions of Excel, if you are not sure what the file's name is.

If you want Excel to look for your file in the subfolders, also, click on the Commands and Settings button on the Open toolbar and then select Search Subfolders. Figure 13-22 shows the Commands and Settings menu.

Figure 13-22: The Commands and Settings menu.

After you have set the criteria for your search and specified the folder that you want to look in, you can click on the Find Now button to find the file that you are looking for.

Performing advanced searches

You can also perform advanced searches for files in Excel. Click on the Advanced button in the Open dialog box to open the Advanced Find dialog box shown in Figure 13-23. This dialog box enables you to set up the criteria for your search.

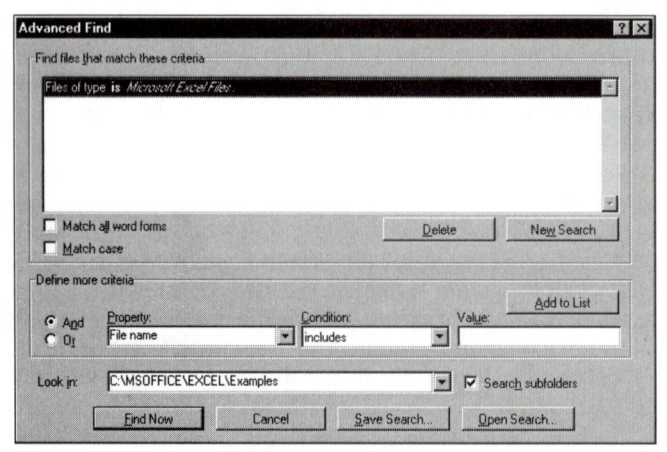

Figure 13-23: The Advanced Find dialog box.

To do an advanced search, follow these steps:

1. Clear any existing searches by clicking on the New Search button.

2. If you want parameters for your search, you can activate the Match All Word Forms option and/or the Match Case option to find the words that are similar to what you are looking for or just the exact word you are looking for.

3. In the Define More Criteria area, you can begin to define your search. Specify a search criterion (which could be a file name if you are just having a problem finding the file but know the name), in the Property list box to tell Excel what to look for. The Property list box enables you to perform searches based on the different sections of the Summary tab of the Properties dialog box. This is the information — filename, author name, or other elements of the document — that you enter when you save a file for the first time.

4. In the Condition list box, choose from Includes, Begins with, or Ends With to look for a search that begins with, includes, or ends with your Value list box entries.

5. Finally, make an entry in the Value text box to work with your property and condition choices. For example, if you choose Ends with in the Conditions list box, enter the ending value in this field.

6. To begin the search, click on the Find Now button.

Note Don't forget that you may need to look in subfolders, also, so be sure that you check the Search Subfolders check box, located just below the Define More Criteria dialog box and to the right. If you do not check this option, you may not find the file that you are looking for because it may be in a folder other than the one in which the search is being performed.

The Advanced Find dialog box also enables you to activate searches that you have previously performed by clicking on the Open Search button. The Open Search dialog box appears, which contains a list of the searches that you have performed. Click on the name of the search that you want to activate and click on the Open button.

As time goes on, your saved searches may become old and you may want to get rid of them. To remove an old search, select the name of the search and click on the Delete button in the Open Search dialog box. The searches can also be renamed by simply clicking on the Rename button. When you do so, the Rename dialog box opens. Now you can use the Backspace key and rename the search.

Organizing your files

The way you organize your files is very important. An organized file management system helps you keep up with your files and helps you find them when you want them. Grouping related files in the same folder is definitely one way to keep your files organized and prevent the loss of a file. For example, you may want to keep all workbook files related to small-business accounting in one folder. Then you can keep all workbook files related to your personal finances in another folder. When you are looking for a workbook file related to your personal finances, you know that you need look only in the folder that you set aside for your own finances.

Summary

This chapter covered topics related to making good use of workbooks. You learned many different techniques that you can use for working with workbooks. This chapter covered the following topics:

- Excel uses the workbook concept, where each file contains a workbook of multiple worksheets occupying different tabbed pages. You can store related information in the different worksheets of the workbook, and they are saved to a single filename.

- You can open one or more workbooks. And in each workbook, you can move among the worksheets by using the worksheet tabs.

- Excel provides a variety of methods for navigating throughout a worksheet and for moving among worksheets.

- You can add and delete sheets in a workbook, and you can move sheets from one location to another in a workbook.

- You can save files to Excel format or to a variety of other file formats.

- Excel has a Find feature that lets you search for a specific workbook based on certain search parameters that you can enter in a dialog box.

The next chapter will cover data entry and editing specifics.

Where to go next...

- Now that you have become familiar with workbooks, an obvious next step is to learn the best ways to handle data entry and editing. See Chapter 14 for more information on entering data.

- If you work with a large number of workbooks and other Microsoft Office documents to produce complex projects, you'll want to become familiar with the Binder. See Chapter 32.

✦ ✦ ✦

CHAPTER 14

Getting Information into Excel

In This Chapter

Entering text, numbers, dates, and times

Clearing cells

Copying data with Fill, AutoFill, and the Series command

Inserting, deleting, copying, and moving cells

Inserting and deleting rows and columns

Working with named ranges

Using formulas and functions

Using Find and Replace

Using Spell Check

This chapter tells you how to get data into your worksheets. It also tells you how to insert cells and add and delete selected ranges, columns, and rows, and describes great features like AutoSum, which sums a row or column of numbers at the click of a button; AutoFill, which can fill a range with successive numbers or dates; and the Function Wizard, which quickly helps you find a needed function. The chapter wraps up by telling you how to use formulas and named ranges in your worksheets.

Entering Data

You won't get anywhere working on a spreadsheet without first taking the time to enter data. You can enter either a *value* or a *formula* in any cell of an Excel worksheet.

Values are exactly that: constant amounts or sets of characters, dates, or times; for example, 234.78, 5/23/95, 9:35 PM, or John Doe. Formulas are combinations of values, cell references, and operators that Excel uses to calculate a result. For more information about formulas, see "Working with Formulas" later in this chapter.

When you place the cursor in a given cell and begin typing, your entry appears in the Formula bar at the top of the window, as shown in Figure 14-1. In the Formula bar, the insertion pointer (the flashing vertical bar) indicates where the characters that you type will appear. As you type an entry, a Check button and an X (Cancel) button appear enabled in the Formula bar. You can click the Check button when you finish typing the entry to accept it, or you can just press Enter. If you decide that you don't want to use an entry, you can either click the X button in the Formula bar or press the Esc key.

Part III ✦ Excel

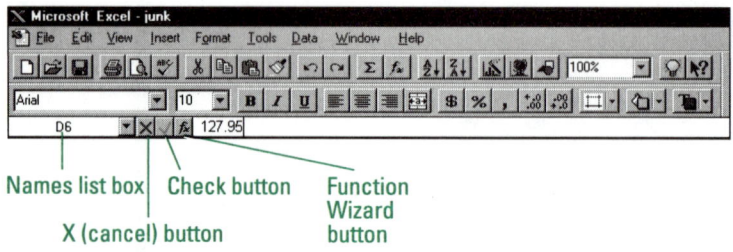

Figure 14-1: Data entered into Excel's Formula bar.

You may notice two additional buttons in the Formula bar: a Names list box (to the left of the X button) and a Function Wizard button (to the right of the Check button). The Names list box displays the name or cell reference of the currently active cell. Use the arrow next to the Names list box to drop a list of named ranges for the current workbook. The Function Wizard button displays the Function Wizard, which helps you construct formulas. See "Working with Named Ranges" and "Using the Function Wizard" later in this chapter for more information.

You can also enter data directly into the cells of a worksheet by turning on Excel's Edit Directly in Cell option. To do this:

1. Choose Tools⇨Options. In the Options dialog box that appears, select the Edit tab (shown in Figure 14-2).

2. Turn on the Edit Directly in Cell check box.

3. Select OK.

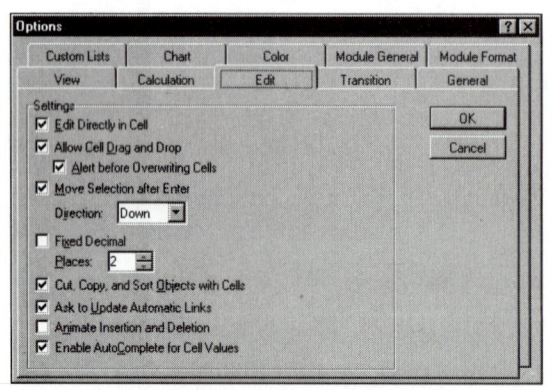

Figure 14-2: The Edit tab of the Options dialog box.

When the Edit Directly in Cell option has been turned on, you can double-click on the cell where you want to enter the data and then begin typing. To abort an entry, press the Esc key.

As many as 255 characters can be entered in one cell at a time. All of them will not be displayed unless you widen the column, which you can do by dragging its right-hand border.

Entering numbers

You can enter numbers into your spreadsheet in several ways. A wonderful feature is that when a number is entered, Excel tries to figure out how the number will be used. This prevents your having to format each cell for each number you want to enter. The worksheet in Figure 14-3 shows some of the ways that you can enter numbers in Excel.

85.80%
$2,995.50
7,345,231
.52
5/8
3 3/4

Figure 14-3: Cells with numbers entered in various formats.

To enter a number, select the cell and then type the number; when finished, press Enter. You can enter numbers as integers, (226), as integer fractions ($1/8$ or $1^3/5$), as decimal fractions (987.326 or 43.65), or in scientific notation (2.5849E+8).

What the heck is ######? Where did my data go?

If you're new to Excel, you're likely to be unpleasantly surprised at some point by the dramatic appearance of the dreaded ####### in one or more of your cells. Don't panic; Excel has not suddenly absorbed all of your data into some mystical black hole. What this means is that the cell is *too narrow* to display your data or your formula's results. You can change the width of the column to see the value; just click and drag the right edge of the column's header. If you don't like the idea of changing the column's width, you can try reducing the size of the font used to display the data. Select the cells containing the data, right-click the selection, and choose Format Cells from the shortcut menu that appears. When the Format Cells dialog box appears, click the Font tab, and choose a smaller font size.

Table 14-1 shows some number entries and how Excel chooses to format them.

Table 14-1
How Excel formats number entries

Number entered	Format chosen by Excel
97.9%	Number, percentage format
9705 Becker Ct.	Text, left aligned
$200.00	Number, currency format
7862	Number, general
144,000	Number, thousands format
-27	Negative number
(27)	Negative number
0 $^{4}/_{5}$	Fraction
2 $^{4}/_{5}$	Fraction

As you can see, even in cases where the numbers are mixed with text, Excel detects what needs to be stored as text. This feature makes a big difference when you're entering database information such as street addresses.

Danger Zone One thing you must remember is that you need to enter an integer in order to enter a fraction. If, as in the next-to-last example in Table 14-1, you need only the fractional part of a number, you must enter a zero and a space before that fraction. Otherwise, the number is interpreted as a date, and you can't use it in calculations.

To format, or not to format?

Since Excel automatically formats a cell upon data entry — when you provide clues by means of how you enter the data — do you want to always use such clues in the data entry process? Maybe, but maybe not, depending on how much data you have to enter. For example, typing a dollar sign in front of an amount does tell Excel to format the entry as currency. But if you're faced with typing in 200 entries, putting a dollar sign in front of each currency amount is a lot of added work. It's easier to just enter all the numbers, letting Excel accept them as a general format, and then go back after data entry to select all the entries and apply a formatting change to the entire range of cells to format them as currency. (Chapter 15 gives details on formatting a range of cells in your worksheet.)

Entering text

Your text entries can be any combination of letters, numbers, or other special characters. To enter text, select the desired cell and start typing. When done with the entry, press Enter or click the Check button in the Formula bar. (A single cell can hold a maximum of 255 characters, so don't get carried away.) By default, Excel aligns text at the left side of the cell. You can change the alignment used for text by selecting the cell and clicking the Center or Align Right buttons in the Formatting toolbar, or you can refer to other formatting techniques covered in the chapter that follows.

Hot Stuff — Sometimes, you may need to enter a number and have Excel accept it as text rather than as a numeric value. You can do so by preceding the value with an apostrophe (') character. For example, if you enter '2758 in a cell of a worksheet, Excel will store the entry as a text string made up of the characters 2758, and not as a numeric value.

Entering dates and times

You can also store dates and times within an Excel worksheet (see an example in Figure 14-4). This can be useful for recording chronological data, such as employee dates of hire or the time spent on billable tasks.

04/30/52
6-Jul-95
July-95
15-Apr-94
7:30 AM
2/5/87 15:15

Figure 14-4: Cells with dates and times entered in various formats.

Dates and times entered in acceptable date and time formats are recognized by Excel as valid date or time values. The times and dates that you enter are converted into serial numbers, with dates being the number of days from the beginning of the century until the date value you entered. Excel see a time entry as a decimal fraction of a 24-hour day. If Excel recognizes the entry as a valid date or time, then it properly displays the date or time on the screen. If you look in the Formula bar for any cell that contains a date you entered, you'll see that all dates appear in the m/dd/yyyy form, regardless of how you entered them. Time entries all appear in the Formula bar in AM/PM format with seconds displayed, regardless of how you enter them.

The following examples show ways that Excel can accept valid date entries. You can use a slash, a hyphen, or a space to separate the different parts of the entry.

> 7/6/97
>
> 6/Jul/97
>
> 6/Jul (the current system year is used)
>
> Jul/97
>
> 07/06/1997

Time values can be entered in forms like the examples shown here:

> 7:50
>
> 7:50 AM
>
> 15:23
>
> 15:23:22
>
> 3:23 PM
>
> 3:23:22 PM
>
> 11/13/97 15:23

Hot Stuff Both the current date and time can be entered using shortcut keys. To enter the current date, press Ctrl+; (semi-colon). To insert the current time, press Ctrl+: (colon).

You can display time using a 12- or 24-hour clock, depending on how you enter your times. If you decide to use a 24-hour format, remember that you do not need to use AM or PM. If you decide to use a 12-hour time entry, be sure to place a space before AM or PM. If you choose to store dates and times within the same cell, the dates and times should be separated by a space.

Excel's ability to handle dates and times as real values is a significant benefit in some applications, because you can use Excel's computational abilities to perform math on dates and times. For example, Excel can subtract one date from another to provide the number of days between the two dates.

Ooops? Whadaya mean, ooops?

As you enter data into Excel, keep in mind how useful Edit⇨Undo is. Undo can get you out of just about anything you can do to a worksheet, as long as you use the command immediately after you've done whatever it is that needs undoing. (Undo can reverse only the most recently completed action.) You can either open the Edit menu and choose Undo or click the Undo button on the Standard Toolbar. And if you undo something in haste, you can use Edit⇨Redo (*still* Alt+E+U, don't ask us why) to correct that, too!

Displayed values versus underlying values

Excel displays values according to precise rules; *which* rules depends on what formats you've applied to the cells in a worksheet.

Here's an example: in a blank worksheet, with no formatting applied, try entering the following data exactly as shown in the cells listed.

In this cell	Enter this
A1	1234567890.1234
A2	$100.5575
A3	2.14159E10

The results appear as displayed values, as shown in the worksheet in Figure 14-5.

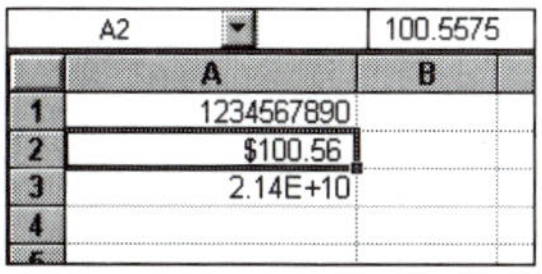

Figure 14-5: A worksheet with displayed values.

If you move the cursor between the cells containing the data and note the contents of each cell in the Formula bar, one fact quickly becomes apparent: Excel may display data differently than it is actually stored.

Excel stores the data as you enter it, but displays the data according to the formatting rules you established (or according to the rules of the *General* format if you applied no formatting). Because the entries in cells A2 and A3 of the example included symbols, Excel formatted those cells and displayed the contents according to those formats. (You can also select formats by using menu commands; Chapter 15 covers this topic in more detail.) In the case of cell A1, because the value is so large, Excel displayed the whole numbers only.

In each case, what appears in the cell is the *displayed value*. What appears in the Formula bar is the *underlying value*. Excel always uses the underlying value when calculating your formulas, unless you tell it otherwise. So be aware of the possible differences between underlying values and displayed values.

Adding Notes to Cells

Excel offers the ability to add *notes* to any cell of a worksheet. Think of notes as being like the little yellow sticky notes that you probably have cluttering your work area — except that notes in Excel are much neater. A cell with a note attached includes a small rectangle in the upper-right corner, but that's the only visible indication of the note. To attach a note, place the cursor in the desired cell and then choose Insert⇨Note. The Cell Note dialog box opens, as shown in Figure 14-6.

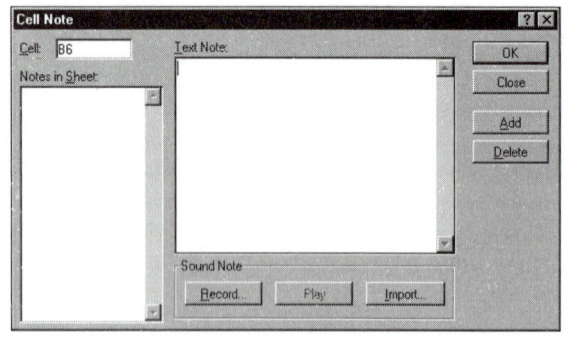

Figure 14-6: The Cell Note dialog box.

The list box at the left side of the dialog box lists all existing notes that are in your worksheet. In the Text Note field at the center of the dialog box, you can type the desired text of your note and then click Add to attach the note to the cell. If you don't want to add any other notes, click OK to close the dialog box.

After you've added a note, you can read the note's contents by moving the mouse pointer over the cell containing the note. When you do this, a window like the one in Figure 14-7 appears with the note's text.

Figure 14-7: The contents of a note displayed within a worksheet.

While you're in the Cell Note dialog box, you can also attach existing notes that are stored elsewhere in the worksheet to the current cell. To do this, select the existing note in the Notes in Sheet list box and then click the Add button. In addition, you can delete notes anywhere in the worksheet: select the unwanted note in the Notes in Sheet list box and click the Delete button.

Adding sound notes

If your hardware supports the playing of sound, you should love Excel's ability to add sound notes to a worksheet's cells. (If *this* doesn't make spreadsheet users run out and buy sound cards for their computers, nothing will.)

When you've added a sound note to a cell, your system plays back the sound whenever you leave the mouse pointer stationary over the cell for one or more seconds. This can be a powerful analytical tool, as you can add spoken comments that describe what's going on in various parts of your worksheet.

Danger Zone Be warned: the sound files that can be recorded with a sound card take up ridiculously large amounts of disk space; a 25-second sound note on one of our systems took 250K of space.

To record the sound, move to the desired cell and choose Insert⇨Note. In the Cell Note dialog box, click the Record button to display Excel's Sound Recorder (shown in Figure 14-8.)

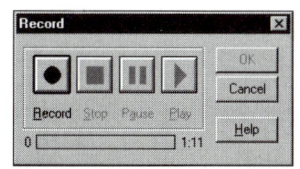

Figure 14-8: Excel's Sound Recorder.

Once your microphone is connected to your sound card's microphone jack (marked MIC on some sound cards), you can click the Record button in the Sound Recorder and record your note. (Excel's Sound Recorder can handle sound notes of up to two minutes in length.) When done, click the Stop button and then click OK in the Sound Recorder to put it away. (You can use the Play button in the Sound Recorder if you want to hear how your note sounds.) If you're satisfied with the note you've recorded, click the OK button in the Cell Note dialog box to add the note to the cell.

Now whenever you hold the mouse pointer over that cell in the worksheet, you'll hear the note you chose played through the speakers connected to your sound card.

You can also attach existing sounds that have already been saved as sound files to cells as notes. To do this: move to the desired cell and choose Insert⇨Note. In the Cell Note dialog box, click the Import button, find the sound file in the Import Sound dialog box that appears, select the file, and click OK.

Hot Stuff If your system is multimedia-ready and you don't have any sound files, you'll find some on the CD-ROM packaged with this book.

> ### Multimedia? Why not?
>
> In adding sound annotations to worksheets, Excel is making use of the multimedia features that are built into Windows. Multimedia is increasingly a feature of business applications — you can drop sound clips into Word documents, into PowerPoint presentations, and into records of an Access table. (Video is a feature of multimedia as well, but it demands a whole new level of hardware capabilities that we don't get into here.)
>
> If your system isn't yet multimedia-capable, you should consider upgrading. For sound, all you'll need is a sound card that supports the MPC-2 standard (and these days, most do). Cards manufactured by the major companies (like Creative Labs' popular Sound Blaster series) come with fairly clear documentation to help you get the card installed. After installing the card, you'll need to run the Windows 95 Hardware Installation Wizard to tell your system about the sound card (see your Windows documentation for details). Then, connect your microphone and speakers to the card, and you're in business.
>
> Oh, and do yourself a favor — run down to Radio Shack and get yourself some nice, amplified speakers. Don't settle for those cheesy little ones that come free with some sound cards.

Editing Data

Excel gives you two ways to make changes to cells. One way is to edit the entry within the Formula bar; the other is to perform editing within the cell itself.

If you're a spreadsheet user from way back, you'll probably prefer to type the entry into the Formula bar, since this is how many spreadsheets have operated for years. But if you have a worksheet that's set up like a database of sorts, with a large amount of data to edit, you may prefer to use the *edit-in-cell* method. (To edit in the cell, you must have turned on Edit Directly in Cell by choosing Tools⇨Options and turning on the option in the Edit tab.) Instructions for both methods follow.

Editing using the Formula bar

When you want to edit using the Formula bar:

1. Move the cursor to the cell containing the data that you want to edit.
2. Move the mouse pointer the area over the Formula bar. (As you do so, the mouse pointer takes on the shape of an I-beam.)
3. Place the mouse pointer at the location where you want to start editing and then click. A flashing insertion pointer in the Formula bar indicates where your editing will occur; you can then proceed to make your edits.

Using In-Cell Editing

If you want to edit using in-cell editing:

1. Double-click the desired cell, or move the cursor to the cell and press F2. When you do this, an insertion pointer appears within the cell itself.
2. Use the arrow keys to place the insertion pointer where you want it.
3. Make your edits and then press Enter.

Clearing Data from Cells

Excel provides different ways to clear, or erase, the contents of existing cells. The most obvious way is to select the cell or range of cells and then press the Delete key. This does indeed clear the cell of its contents — that is, any values or formulas entered into the cell — but there are ways to clear a cell of formatting and notes, as well.

To clear the contents of a cell and remove more than just the data entered, first select the cell or range of cells that you want to clear. Then open the Edit menu, choose Clear, and select the appropriate choice from the submenu. Table 14-2 lists this menu's suboptions.

Table 14-2
Edit⇨Clear submenu options

Option	What it does
All	This clears everything from the selected cells, including formatting, the contents of the cell, and any notes attached to the cell. Formatting for the cell returns to the General format.
Formats	This clears formatting only. Formatting for the cell returns to the General format.
Contents	This clears the formulas or values entered in the cell, but leaves formatting and notes untouched. (This is the functional equivalent of making a selection and pressing the Delete key.)
Notes	This clears any notes that were attached to the cell, but does not change the cell's contents or its formatting.

Hot Stuff: Excel's Edit menu contains two commands that remove the contents of cells: the Clear command and the Delete command. If you want to clear what's in cells, stick with Edit⇨Clear; the Edit⇨Delete command does more than just clear cells. (For specifics, see the sidebar "Edit⇨Clear and Edit⇨Delete: Understanding the Difference," later in this chapter.)

Copying and Moving Cells

As your work with Excel gets more complex, you'll find yourself regularly needing to move and copy entire portions of worksheets from one area to another. (How often does the boss make a request like, "Oh, could we also see last quarter's sales, too?" after you've spent hours getting your worksheet just right?)

Sometimes, you can make the changes you need by inserting or deleting entire blank rows and columns. But in many cases you'll want to leave the overall structure of a worksheet alone and copy or move selected areas of the worksheet around.

Excel lets you copy or move data from place to place using either of two methods. You can use the Cut, Copy, and Paste commands (or their equivalent buttons on the Standard toolbar.) Or, you can use drag-and-drop techniques to move and copy data. The two methods work equally well. Generally, keyboard fans prefer the use of the Cut, Copy, and Paste commands, while mouse fans usually lean toward the drag-and-drop techniques.

Hot Stuff — You can use any of the techniques detailed in the following paragraphs to copy data across worksheets, as well as within the same worksheet. When you want to copy across worksheets, first select the desired data, as detailed in the steps below. Then go to the worksheet where you want to place the copy and continue with the steps outlined below.

Copying and moving data with Cut, Copy, and Paste

To copy cells using the Copy and Paste method, perform these steps:

1. Select the cell or cells that you want to copy and either choose Edit⇨Copy or right-click the selection and then choose Copy (alternatively, you can also use the Copy button in the Standard toolbar). The cells to be copied will be marked with a dotted-line border, as shown in Figure 14-9.

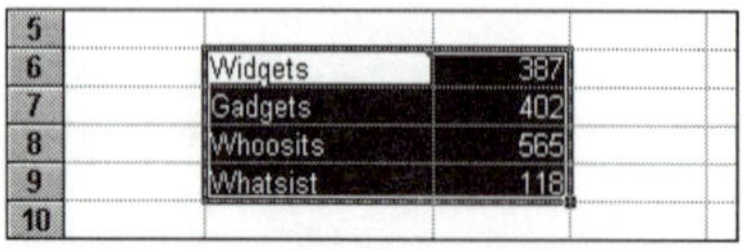

Figure 14-9: Cells in a worksheet marked for copying.

2. Move to the cell or cells in which you want to begin your copying. (You can move to cells in a different worksheet, if you wish.)

3. Choose Edit⇨Paste or right-click in the destination cell or selection and choose Paste from the shortcut menu. (Alternatively, you can also use the Paste button

in the Standard toolbar.) Either method places the copied information into the chosen cell or cells.

While the highlight is still visible around the source cells, you can copy the cells again if you wish by repeating steps 2 and 3, or you can press the Esc key to remove the highlight.

Moving information with Cut and Paste is done in much the same fashion as copying. Use the following steps to move data from one area to another:

1. Select the cells you want to move.
2. Choose Edit⇨Cut or right-click the selection and choose Cut from the shortcut menu. (Alternatively, you can also use the Cut button in the Standard toolbar.) With either method, the selected cells are marked by a moving border.
3. Select the destination cells for the data. (The destination can be either in the same worksheet or in a different one.)
4. Choose Edit⇨Paste or right-click the destination cell and choose Paste from the shortcut menu. (Alternatively, you can also use the Paste button in the Standard toolbar.) If you choose one cell as the destination cell and you selected more than one cell as the source for the information, the selected destination cell becomes the upper-left corner of the paste area.

Copying and moving data with drag-and-drop

Mouse fans can use drag-and-drop techniques to move and copy data between cells or ranges. Here's how:

1. Select the cell or group of cells that you wish to move.
2. Click and drag on the border of the selected cells.
3. Drag the border to the new location. As you drag, an outline of the selected area appears, as shown in Figure 14-10.

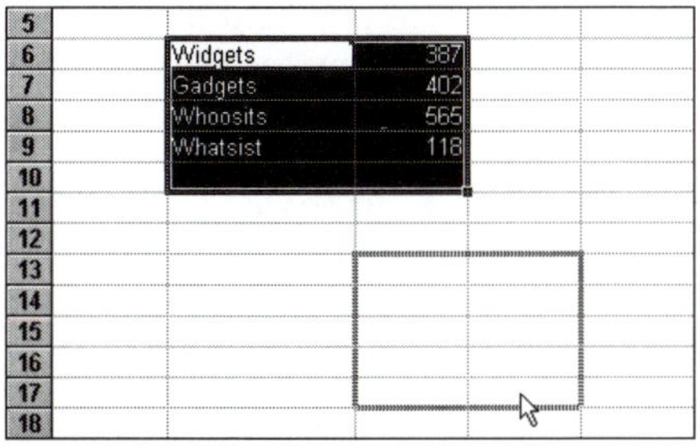

Figure 14-10: The outline of selected cells that appears when moving data using drag-and-drop.

4. Release the mouse button. (Don't forget that if you move cells over others that contain information, those others will be overwritten.)

The same steps can be used to copy a cell or a range of cells. The one difference is that when you want to copy the selection instead of just moving it, you will need to hold down the Ctrl key as you drag and drop.

Copying data with Fill and AutoFill

Excel offers two features that help you quickly fill cells with data: *Fill* and *AutoFill*. The Fill feature fills a range of cells that you select with the data in the original cell. The AutoFill feature fills in a range of cells intelligently, incrementing each successive cell. (For example, if you enter **January** in a cell and then use AutoFill to fill 11 cells to the right of the first cell, Excel fills in the names of the successive months.)

You can copy any existing data from a cell into adjacent cells using the Fill feature. To do so, perform the following steps:

1. Move the cursor into the cell that you want to copy to the adjacent cells.

2. Place the mouse pointer over the selected cell and then click and drag over all the cells that should get a copy of the original cell.

3. Choose Edit⇨Fill. From the submenu that appears, choose the appropriate direction. (Depending on the direction toward which your selection extends, menu choices of Up, Down, Left, or Right may be enabled.) When you make the submenu selection, the data will be copied into the adjacent cells, as in the example shown in Figure 14-11.

Figure 14-11: The results of using the Edit⇨Fill command.

Hot Stuff
You can also use Fill without bothering with any menus. Just drag the *Fill handle* (it's the tiny rectangle at the lower-right corner of the cursor) to highlight the cells where you want to copy the data. When you release the mouse button, the data is copied into the cells.

Hot Stuff
It's possible to copy data across worksheets with Fill, as well. To do this, first select both the worksheet that you want to copy from and the one that you want to copy to by holding down the Shift key while clicking on both worksheet tabs. Next, select the cells to be copied, choose Edit⇨Fill, and choose Across Worksheets from the submenu. In the dialog box that appears, choose what you want to copy (All, Contents, or Formats) and then click OK.

If you want intelligent copying, use the AutoFill feature. By default, AutoFill fills in days of the week and months of the year. But you can also add your own custom lists to AutoFill, so it can handle other requirements that you have on a regular basis.

To use AutoFill to fill in dates, type the desired day of the week or month of the year into a cell. Next, drag the Fill handle (the tiny rectangle at the lower-right corner of the cursor) to highlight the cells where you want AutoFill to add the data. When you release the mouse button, the successive days of the week or months of the year appear. Figure 14-12 shows the results of AutoFill when January is entered into a cell and the Fill Handle is dragged across the next eight cells.

Figure 14-12: The results of using AutoFill.

If you regularly fill in any sort of list of your own, you can add it to the possible lists that AutoFill can generate. To do this, choose Tools➪Options. In the dialog box that appears, click the Custom Lists tab. In the tab that then appears (shown in Figure 14-13), click New List at the left side of the dialog box and then type your own list in the List Entries box, separating each entry with a comma and a space. (In the figure, a custom list of classrooms in a high school has been entered in the List Entries box.) When done, click Add to add the list and then click OK. From then on, you can type any entry in your list into a cell and use AutoFill to fill in the successive entries based on your own list.

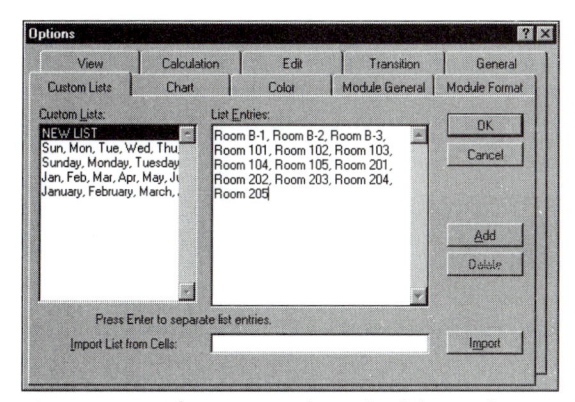

Figure 14-13: The Custom Lists tab of the Options dialog box.

If you choose more cells than the length of the list used by AutoFill, Excel will start the list over until it reaches the end of the selected cells to be filled. To prevent the list from repeating, you may want to count the number of entries that are there and avoid selecting a range that's larger than your possible number of entries.

Making changes to the custom lists used by AutoFill is a simple matter. If you wish to edit one of your custom lists, do the following:

1. Choose Tools⇨Options.
2. From the Custom Lists area of the Custom Lists tab, select the custom list that you want to edit.
3. Click in the List Entries box and make the necessary changes to the list.
4. Click OK.

If you want to delete a custom list that you've created:

1. Choose the name of the custom list from the Custom Lists box of the Custom Lists tab.
2. Choose the Delete button to delete the list from the Custom Lists.

When making your list, remember:

- Error values and formulas are ignored.
- Each list entry can contain up to 80 characters.
- Lists cannot start with a number. (If you want an increasing or decreasing series of numbers, use the Series command, as described in the following section.)
- A custom list can contain a maximum of 2,000 characters.

Building series

While AutoFill does wonders with simple and straightforward lists, there may be times when you need more flexibility in generating a list of values that change across some kind of series. For those occasions, you can use the Edit menu's Fill Series command.

Excel can work with four types of series: *linear* (as in 1, 2, 3, 4, 5, 6, and so on), *growth* (as in 5, 10, 15, 20, 25, and so on), *date-based* (as in 1995, 1996, 1997, 1998, and so on), and *AutoFill* (which is based on the lists entered in the Custom List tab of the Options dialog box). Create a series of values in a range of cells by doing the following:

1. Enter a value in a cell. (The value that you enter will serve as the starting or ending value in the series.)
2. Starting with the cell containing your value, select the cells you want to extend the series into.
3. Choose Edit⇨Fill⇨Series. The Series dialog box, shown in Figure 14-14, appears.

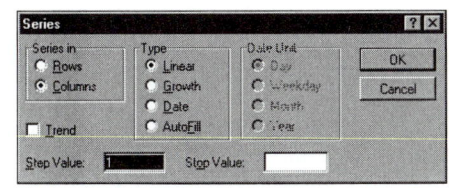

Figure 14-14: The Series dialog box.

4. In the Series In field of the dialog box, make sure that the Rows or Columns selection matches the type of range that you want to fill.

5. If you want the selected values to be replaced by values for a linear or exponential best fit, turn on the Trend check box. (If you do this, your options in Step 6 will be limited to Linear and Growth.)

6. In the Type field of the dialog box, choose the appropriate Type option.

- **Linear** — This option is used to add the step value to the number that preceded the current cell in the series. When you select Trend, the trend values become a linear trend.

- **Growth** — This option multiplies the step value by the number that preceded the current cell in the series.

- **Date** — This option is used with date values; it lets you set the Date Unit options to Day, Week, Month, or Year choices.

- **AutoFill** — This option creates a series automatically, based on entries in the Custom List tab of the Options dialog box (choose Tools⇨Options to get there).

If you choose AutoFill, Excel will fill the selected range based on the entries in the Custom List tab of the Options dialog box.

If you choose Linear or Growth, continue with the following steps up to Step 9 to finish generating your series. (If you chose Date, go to step 10.)

7. Enter a step value (the number by which the entries change from cell to cell).

8. If you don't want the entries to exceed a certain number, you can enter a Stop value. (If you leave this blank, Excel will continue until it fills the selected range.)

9. Click OK.

Excel stops either at the Stop Value or when it reaches the end of the selected cells. Remember that if the step value is negative and you enter a stop value, it will need to be less than your starting value. Dates and times can be entered in any date or time format Excel understands.

If you chose to enter a series of dates by choosing date in step 6, continue with these steps.

10. Choose Day, Weekday, Month, or Year from the Date Unit field of the Series dialog box. This will apply the step value to the chosen entry type in the Date Unit area.

11. Enter the step value to specify an increment. (For example, if you chose month as the date unit, the entries will increase in the month amount by the step value.) Again a stop value may be entered if you think you have chosen too many cells.

12. Choose OK.

Using Paste Special

Sometimes, after copying cells, you may want to invoke special options when you paste the cells. You can do this using the Paste Special command.

To see what these options are, choose any cell in a worksheet, click the copy button on the Standard toolbar, move the cursor to another cell, and choose Edit⇨Paste Special. When you do this, you see the Paste Special dialog box, as shown in Figure 14-15.

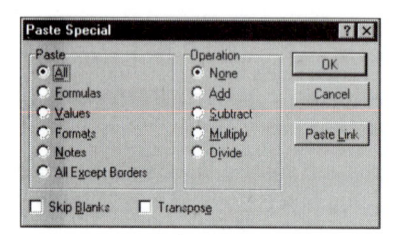

Figure 14-15: The Paste Special dialog box.

You can choose any of the bullets in the Paste portion of the Paste Special dialog box to select the information that is to be pasted. For example, if you wish to copy only a cell's format, you would choose the Formats option. This copies only the cell's format. This keeps you from having to format the new cell.

You can also combine the contents of the copy and paste areas. Do this by first selecting Formulas or Values in the Paste portion of the Paste Special dialog box. Next, under the Operation portion of the dialog box, select the operation you want. This will combine the copy and paste areas by performing the chosen operation. For example, if cell A:6 contains the formula =SUM(A1:A5), and you want to add this formula to the contents of cell D:6, first select cell A:6 and choose the Copy command. Next, choose Edit⇨Paste Special, choose Formulas in the Paste portion of the Paste Special dialog box, and choose Add under the Operation portion of the same dialog box. The result: the formula is copied in the new cell with the new cell references. (Formulas are discussed in "Working with Formulas," later in this chapter.)

The Paste Special dialog box also allows you to transpose copied rows and columns by selecting the Transpose option. This is used to transfer information entered in rows to columns, and vice-versa.

The Skip Blanks option prevents the copying of blank cells from the copy area to the paste area; a blank cell cannot delete existing cell data in the paste area.

The Paste Link button is also a useful option for pasting, establishing a link with the source of the data pasted into the selected cells. (The source has to be a single cell or a range.) In cases where the source is more than one cell, an *array* — a collection of cells that takes on a single value in relation to a formula — is posted. When the paste area is a single cell, the cell becomes the upper-left corner of the paste area with the rest of the range filled in accordingly.

Inserting and Deleting Cells, Rows, and Columns

Another important aspect of manipulating existing data in worksheets is inserting and deleting cells and adding or deleting entire rows and columns. The first three options that Excel provides on the Insert menu let you insert cells, rows, or columns into an existing worksheet.

Danger Zone Before you perform major insertions, be warned that inserting cells in the midst of existing data causes cells in the area of the insertion to be pushed either down or to the right. If your worksheet contains formulas that rely on the location of cells, and you move those cells by inserting new cells, you will create errors in your worksheet's calculations.

Inserting cells, rows, and columns

Insert cells, rows, or columns this way:

1. Select the cell or range of cells where the new cells must be inserted, or select any cells in the rows or columns where the new rows or columns are to be inserted.

    With rows and columns, note that a new row or column is inserted for each row or column cell you select. If you drag across three columns and then choose to insert columns, you insert three new columns.

2. Choose Insert➪Cells, or right-click the selection and then choose Insert from the shortcut menu, to reveal the Insert dialog box (Figure 14-16).

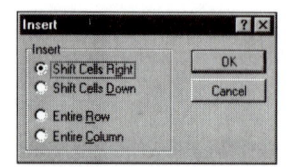

Figure 14-16: The Insert dialog box.

3. If you're inserting cells, choose either Shift Cells Right or Shift Cells Down to move existing cells in the direction you want. If you want to insert entire rows or columns, choose Entire Row or Entire Column.

4. Click OK.

Hot Stuff To insert only rows or columns, just select the number of rows or columns to insert at the point of insertion. For example, say you want to insert two columns ahead of column D. Click and drag across the headers for columns D and E, open the Insert menu, and then choose either Rows or Columns.

Deleting cells, rows, and columns

To delete cells, rows, or columns:

1. Select the cell or range of cells where the cells must be deleted, or select any cells in the rows or columns where the rows or columns are to be deleted.

   Note that a row or column will be deleted for each row or column cell that you select; hence, if you drag across three columns and then choose to delete columns, you will delete three columns.

2. Choose Edit⇔Delete, or right-click the selection and choose Delete from the shortcut menu, to reveal the Delete dialog box, shown in Figure 14-17. (Note that if you select an entire row or column, you won't see this dialog box; Excel assumes that you want to delete the entire row or the entire column, and it does so. If the deletion of a row or column was *not* what you had in mind, choose Edit⇔Undo.)

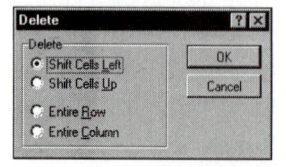

Figure 14-17: The Delete dialog box.

Edit➪Clear and Edit➪Delete: Understanding the Difference

Excel users should understand that there's a fundamental difference between the way Edit➪Clear and Edit➪Delete work. The two commands may appear to do the same thing when applied to a range of blank cells with no adjacent data nearby, but in reality they behave very differently.

Edit➪Clear clears the selected cells of the information in them but does not move cells out of the worksheet. Edit➪Delete, on the other hand, *removes* the cells completely; other cells must take the place of the removed cells, even if the new cells are blank.

Compare the results of Edit➪Delete to pulling out toy blocks from a wall made of those blocks; other blocks must be moved into the empty spaces, or the wall becomes unstable. Likewise, understanding how Edit➪Delete works ensures the stability of the remaining areas of your worksheet.

3. If you're deleting cells, choose either Shift Cells Left or Shift Cells Up; this moves existing cells to fill in the space left by the deletion. If you want to delete entire rows or columns, choose Entire Row or Entire Column.

4. Click OK.

Hot Stuff If you want to delete entire rows or columns, here's the fastest way. First, select the rows or columns by dragging across the row or column headers (rather than selecting cells in the rows or columns). Next, open the Edit menu and choose Delete. Excel annihilates your selections, no questions asked.

Working with Named Ranges

You can refer to a cell or group of cells by a name rather than a cell reference, and you can use these names within your formulas. Many spreadsheet users find it easier to remember the logic behind formulas that are composed of names relating to the type of information stored. For example, you could name row 1 of a worksheet *Income,* and you could name row 3 *Expenses*. A formula in row 5 that computes net profits could then read =Income-Expenses rather than =B1-B3. (Formulas are discussed in "Working with Formulas," later in this chapter.)

To assign a name to a cell or group of cells:

1. Select the range of cells that you want to name. (You can select an entire row or an entire column by clicking the row or column header.)

2. Choose Insert➪Name➪Define. The Define Name dialog box appears, as shown in Figure 14-18.

Part III ♦ Excel

Figure 14-18: The Define Name dialog box.

3. In the text box at the top of the dialog box, either type a name for the range or accept any default. (You can't use spaces in a range name; see the Note at the end of this section.)

    When Excel sees a heading at the top of a row or at the left of a column of cells that you've selected, it uses the text of that heading as a default range name.

4. Click the Add button to add the new name to the list and then click Close.

Figure 14-19 shows an example of named ranges in a worksheet. In this worksheet, columns B, C, D, and E have been assigned the names of the months, at the top of the respective columns, as named ranges. As shown in the Formula bar, column F uses formulas like `=January+February+March+April` to calculate the totals.

	A	B	C	D	E	F
		January	February	March	April	Totals
1						
2	Walnut Creek	$123,600.00	$137,000.00	$89,900.00	$201,300.00	$551,800.00
3	River Hills	$248,700.00	$256,750.00	$302,500.00	$197,000.00	$1,004,950.00
4	Spring Gardens	$97,000.00	$102,500.00	$121,500.00	$142,500.00	$463,500.00
5	Lake Newport	$346,300.00	$372,300.00	$502,900.00	$456,800.00	$1,678,300.00
6						
7	Total Sales	$815,600.00	$868,550.00	$1,016,800.00	$997,600.00	$3,698,550.00

F2: `=January+February+March+April`

Figure 14-19: An example of named ranges in a worksheet.

Once you've performed the preceding steps, you can refer to the range in your formulas by typing its name rather than using its cells' addresses.

> **Note** The names that you use for ranges can be up to 255 characters in length, and they can include letters, numbers, periods, or underscores, but *cannot* include spaces.

Working with Formulas

In addition to entering values, you will use *formulas* throughout your worksheets. Excel uses the formulas that you enter to perform calculations based on the values in other cells of your worksheets. Formulas let you perform common math operations — addition, subtraction, multiplication, and division — using the values in the worksheet cells.

For example, say you want to add the values in cells B1 and B2 and then display the sum in cell B5. You could do so by placing the cursor in cell B5 and entering the simple formula, **=B1+B2**.

With Excel, you build a formula by indicating which values should be used and which calculations should apply to these values. Remember that in Excel, formulas *always* begin with an equal symbol.

Figure 14-20 shows examples of various formulas within a typical worksheet.

	A	B	C	D	E	F
1		January	February	March	April	1st Quarter
2	Walnut Creek	$123,600.00	$137,000.00	$89,900.00	$201,300.00	$551,800.00
3	River Hills	$248,700.00	$256,750.00	$302,500.00	$197,000.00	$1,004,950.00
4	Spring Gardens	$97,000.00	$102,500.00	$121,500.00	$142,500.00	$463,500.00
5	Lake Newport	$346,300.00	$372,300.00	$502,900.00	$456,800.00	$1,678,300.00
6						
7	Total Sales	$815,600.00	$868,550.00	$1,016,800.00	$997,600.00	$3,698,550.00
15	Income					
17	Sublet Office Space	$1,800.00	$1,800.00	$1,800.00	$1,800.00	$7,200.00
18	Misc. Income	$750.00	$750.00	$500.00	$800.00	$2,800.00
20	Total Income	$2,550.00	$2,550.00	$2,300.00	$2,600.00	$10,000.00
23	Gross Receipts	$813,050.00	$866,000.00	$1,014,500.00	$995,000.00	$3,688,550.00

=SUM(B2:E2) is the formula contained in this cell.

=SUM(F2:F6) is the formula contained in this cell.

=B7-B20 is the formula contained in this cell.

Figure 14-20: Examples of formulas within a worksheet.

Creating formulas in the Formula bar or with Edit Directly in Cell

If you place the cursor in any cell and then type an equal symbol, the symbol and a flashing cursor appear in the Formula bar. As you enter the formula, it appears within the Formula bar. When you press Enter, Excel performs the calculation based upon the formula and then displays, in the cell, the results of the calculation. If you've turned on Edit Directly in Cell as described earlier in the chapter, you can double-click the cell and type the formula directly into the cell.

Creating formulas by pointing

One handy way to enter the cell references that make up a major part of formulas is to point at the cells. Typing the entire formula manually invites mistakes that you can avoid by entering the cell references this way:

1. Place the cursor in the cell where you want to enter the formula.
2. Start the formula by typing an equal sign (=).
3. Point to the cell that you want as the first cell reference and then click. (Alternatively, you can move the cursor there with the arrow keys.)
4. Type an operator (such as a plus or minus symbol) or other character to continue the desired formula.
5. Point to the next cell that you want to use as a cell reference and then click (or move the cursor there with the arrow keys).
6. Repeat steps 4 and 5 as needed to complete to formula.

Hot Stuff: While using the pointing technique to create formulas, you can enter cell ranges as references. Just click and drag from the starting cell in the range to the ending cell (or hold down the Shift key as you move the cursor from the starting cell to the ending cell).

Allowed elements

Formulas are used to calculate a value based on a combination of other values. These other values can be numbers, cell references, operators (+, –, *, /), or other formulas. Formulas can also include names of other areas in the worksheet, as well as cell references in other worksheets. Individual cells are referred to by their coordinates (such as *B5*), and ranges of cells are referred to by the starting cell reference, followed by a colon, followed by the ending cell reference (such as *D10:D18*). Cells in other worksheets are referred to by the name of the worksheet, followed by an exclamation point, followed by the cell reference (such as *Sheet2!E5*).

You use math operators within your formulas to produce numeric results. Table 14-3 lists them.

Table 14-3
Arithmetic operators

Operator	Function
+	Addition
–	Subtraction
*	Multiplication
/	Division
^	Exponentiation (for example 3^2 is 3-squared, or 9)
%	Percentage

And in addition to the math operators, Excel accepts an ampersand (&) as a text operator for strings of text. The ampersand is used to combine text strings (this is known as *concatenation*). For example, if cell B12 contains John and cell B13 contains Smith, the formula B12 & B13 would yield the result, John Smith.

Comparison operators are used to compare values and provide a logical value (true or false) based on the comparison. Table 14-4 describes them.

Table 14-4
Comparison operators

Operator	Function
<	less than
>	greater than
=	equal to
<>	not equal to
<=	less than or equal to
>=	greater than or equal to

In a cell, the simple comparison = 6 < 7 would result in a value of True, because 6 is less than 7. The result of = 6 < Number depends on the value of *Number*.

Typically, you use comparison operators with cell references to determine whether a desired result is true or false. For example, consider the worksheet shown in Figure 14-21. In this example, the formulas in cells C2 through C5 are based on a comparison. Cell C2 contains the formula, =B2>48000. Cells C3, C4, and C5 contain similar formulas. The comparison translates to this: If the value in B2 is greater than 48,000, then display a value of True in C2; otherwise, display a value of False in C2.

	A	B	C	D
1				
2		54,050	TRUE	
3		47,999.95	FALSE	
4		48,000.01	TRUE	
5		37	FALSE	
6				

Figure 14-21: Use of comparison operators in formulas of a worksheet.

Excel has the following precise order of precedence in building formulas:

1. – (unary minus or negation)
2. % (percent)
3. ^ (exponentiation)
4. * or / (multiplication or division)
5. + or – (addition or subtraction)
6. & (text operator)
7. < > = (comparison operators)

Depending on how you structure your formulas, you may wish to alter the preceding order of precedence. For example, if you want to add the contents of cells B2 and B3 and divide the resulting total by 5, you cannot use the simple formula =B2 + B3 / 5 because Excel performs division before addition in its order of precedence. If you used the formula above, the value in B3 would be divided by 5, and that value would be added to the value of B2 — producing an erroneous result. To change the order of precedence, insert parenthesis around calculations that are to be performed first. Calculations surrounded by parentheses are always performed first, no matter where they fall in the order of precedence. In our example then, the formula =(B2 + B3) / 5 gets the desired result. Excel would calculate the expression within the parenthesis first and then divide that figure by the constant (in this example, 5).

Displaying and editing formulas

By default, Excel shows the results of the formulas that you enter in cells, and not the actual formulas. (Of course, you can examine any formula by moving the cursor to the cell that contains it and then looking in the Formula bar.) There is a way to see all the formulas in your worksheet, however. Choose Tools⇨Options. When the Options dialog box appears, click the View tab; under Window Options, turn on the Formulas check box and then click OK. The worksheet will show all your formulas in the cells (and Excel will automatically widen the columns to provide room to view the formulas).

You can edit formulas just as you'd edit any other contents of a cell. Select the desired cell, click in the Formula bar, and do your editing there. Or double-click the cell and edit the formula within the cell itself.

What, me make a mistake?

One of the most frustrating aspects of building complex worksheets is the possibility of errors in your formulas. Watching out for common causes of formula errors can help.

Watch out for:

- attempts to divide by zero
- references to blank cells
- leaving out commas between arguments
- deleting cells that are being used by formulas elsewhere in the worksheet

The codes that Excel displays in the cell when an error occurs gives you a clue as to what's wrong. #DIV/0! says your formula is trying to divide by zero. #N/A! means that data needed to perform the calculation is not available, and #NAME? means that Excel thinks you're referring to a name that doesn't exist. #NUM says Excel has a problem with a numeric argument you've supplied, #REF says that a cell reference is incorrect, and #VALUE! indicates that a value supplied isn't the type of value that the formula's argument expected.

Changing the recalculation options

By default, Excel recalculates all dependent formulas in your worksheet each time that you make a change to a cell. In a very large worksheet, this can adversely affect performance, as Excel has to do a lot of calculating every time you change an entry in a cell. You may prefer to turn off Excel's automatic recalculation and let the worksheet recalculate only when you tell it to.

You can change the recalculation options used by Excel through the Calculation tab of the (yes, you guessed it) Tools⇨Options command. Open the Tools menu and choose Options, click the Calculation tab, and choose Manual in the dialog box that appears. From then on, you can force Excel to recalculate your worksheet at any time by pressing the Calc Now key (F9).

Note Try to remember when you turn off automatic recalculation. Otherwise, it's easy to be confused by what appear to be errors in a worksheet but are really changes that were made when automatic recalculation was turned off and left off. Some operations — including opening and printing a worksheet — will force a recalculation, even if automatic recalculation has been turned off.

References: relative vs. absolute

In Excel, you can have *relative* or *absolute* cell references. An absolute cell reference does not change when the cell containing the formula is copied to another location. A relative cell reference changes when the cell containing the formula is copied to another location.

You determine whether a cell reference will be relative or absolute by placing a dollar sign in front of the row or column reference. The presence of a dollar sign tells Excel not to muck around with your cell reference, no matter what. For example, perhaps cell B5 of a worksheet contains the formula =B3+B4. If you copy that cell's contents to cell D5, Excel adjusts the references, and the formula in cell D5 reads =D3+D4.

In most cases, you want Excel to adjust references when you copy formulas elsewhere, but in some cases, you don't. You can make cell references absolute by adding the dollar sign in front of the letter and number that make up the cell address. With the preceding example of a formula in cell B5, if the formula were entered as **=$B$3+$B$4**, then the formula could be copied anywhere in the worksheet — and it would still refer back to cells B3 and B4.

Using Functions

Typing each cell reference is fine when you're adding a short column of numbers, but doing this with larger columns can be time consuming. Fortunately, Excel offers *functions* that can be used in your formulas.

You can think of functions as ready-to-run tools that take a group of values and perform some specialized sort of calculation on those values. For example, the commonly used SUM function adds a range of values. So, instead of having to enter a formula like **=B2+B3+B4+B5+B6+B7+B8**, you could enter the much simpler formula of **=SUM(B2:B8)**.

Besides making for less typing, functions can perform specialized calculations that would take some digging on your part if you needed to duplicate the calculations manually. For example, you can use Excel's PMT function to calculate the monthly principal and interest on a mortgage. (Not many of us carry the logic for that sort of calculation around in our heads.) Excel's functions can make use of range references (like A2:A10), named ranges (like January Sales), or actual numeric values. Figure 14-22 shows examples of the use of functions in a worksheet.

Chapter 14 ♦ Getting Information into Excel

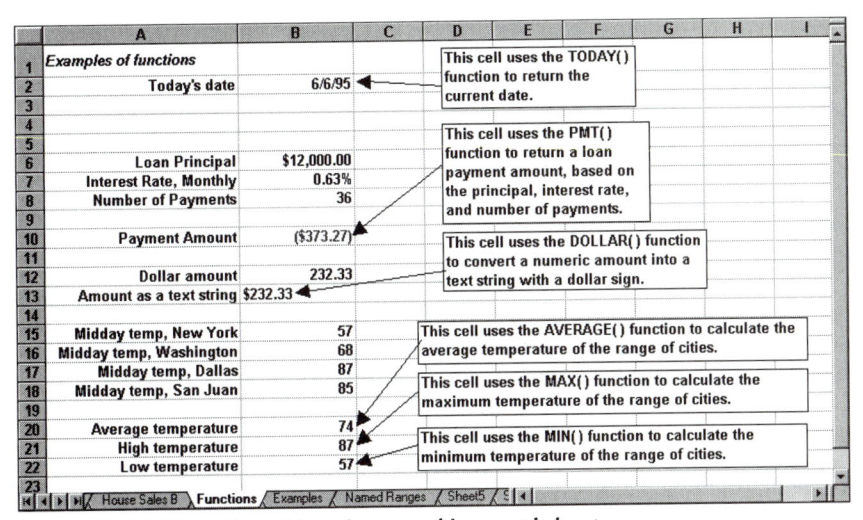

Figure 14-22: Examples of functions used in a worksheet.

Every function is made up of two parts:

- ♦ The function name — such as SUM, PMT, or AVERAGE — which indicates what the function does.

- ♦ The argument — such as B2:B12 — which tells Excel what cell addresses to apply to the function. (Note that in this example, the argument is a range of cells, but arguments may be references to single cells, to a group of single cells, or actual values.)

You can enter functions just as you enter values: by typing them directly into the Formula bar or into the cell. And you can use the AutoSum tool and the Function Wizard (both discussed shortly) to get help with the entry of your functions.

Excel has many different functions for tasks that range from calculating the square root of a number to finding the future value of an investment. You should know about some statistical functions that are commonly used in spreadsheet work: the Average, Maximum, Minimum, and Sum functions.

Average, Maximum, Minimum, and Sum

The Average function calculates the average of a series of values. This function may be expressed as

```
=Average(1st value, 2nd value, 3rd value...last value)
```

As an example, the expression =Average(6,12,15,18) yields 12.75. Similarly, the expression =Average(B10:B15) averages the values from cells B10 through B15.

The Maximum and Minimum functions provide the maximum and minimum values, respectively, of all values in the specified range or list of numbers. These functions may be expressed as:

```
=MAX(1st value, 2nd value, 3rd value...last value)
=MIN(1st value, 2nd value, 3rd value...last value)
```

For example, consider the worksheet shown earlier in Figure 14-19. The formula in cell B22 is =MIN(B15:B18). The value that results from this formula is the smallest value in the range of cells from B15 through B18. The formula in cell B21, which is =MAX(B15:B18), has precisely the opposite effect; the largest value of those found in the specified range of cells is displayed.

The Sum function is used to provide a sum of a list of values, commonly indicated by referencing a range of cells. For example, the Sum function =SUM(5,10,12) would provide a value of 27. The formula =SUM(B5:B60) would provide the sum of all numeric values contained in the range of cells from B5 to B60. The Sum function is an easy way to add a column of numbers; you can most easily use it when using AutoSum, too.

Using AutoSum

Since the Sum function is the most commonly used function in Excel, there is a toolbar button dedicated to the Sum function's use — the AutoSum tool. Using AutoSum is simple:

1. Place the cursor in the cell below or to the right of the column or row that you want to sum.

2. Click the AutoSum button in the Standard toolbar (it's the one containing the Greek letter Σ).

When you do this, Excel makes its best guess about what you would like summed, based on the current cell's location relative to the row or column. (If Excel guesses wrong, you can always edit the formula to your liking.) When you click the AutoSum button, Excel outlines the area that it thinks you want summed and it places the appropriate formula using the Sum function in the current cell, as shown in Figure 14-23. If you don't like the range that Excel selected, you can click and drag to a different range, and Excel will change the formula accordingly. When you're happy with the formula, press Enter to accept it.

Figure 14-23: What happens when you use the AutoSum button.

Using the Function Wizard

One of Excel's most useful features is the Function Wizard. With the Function Wizard's help, it's no longer necessary for serious Excel users to keep a reference dictionary of functions handy, or to be constantly looking in the help screens to see how particular functions should be used.

The Function Wizard steps you through the process of inserting a function into the formula you're building. To use the Function Wizard:

1. Move the insertion pointer into the cell where you want to insert the function. (If you want to insert the function into an existing formula, you can click in the Formula bar at the point where the function should go; this will place the pointer there.)

2. Click the Function Wizard button on the Standard toolbar — the one containing the letters *fx* — or choose Insert⇨Function. The first Function Wizard dialog box appears, as shown in Figure 14-24.

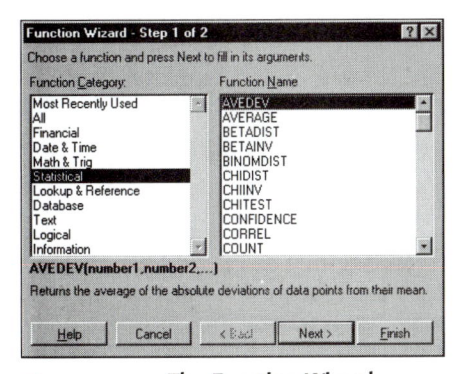

Figure 14-24: The Function Wizard dialog box.

3. In the Function Category list box at the left, choose the category of functions that you want. When you choose a category, the functions in that category appear in the Function Name list box at the right. (You can leave the category set to All to see all the functions, but doing that can make it difficult to find your desired function in the Function Name list, since Excel has hundreds of functions.)

4. From the Function Name list box, select the function that you want to insert into your formula and then click Next.

5. The next dialog box depends on which type of function you chose to add. Enter the necessary values or cell ranges for the arguments needed by the function in the dialog box.

6. Click the Finish button in the dialog box to add the function to your formula.

Using Find and Replace

A useful feature that Excel has borrowed from the word processing world is Edit⇨Find and Edit⇨Replace. Like their counterparts in Word for Windows, these commands search for data and, optionally, replace that data with other data. The data that you search for can be stored as values, as part or all of a formula, or as a cell note.

Finding data

To search for data in a worksheet using Edit⇨Find:

1. Select the cells you wish to search. If you want to search the entire worksheet, select any single cell.

2. Choose Edit⇨Find. You'll see the Find dialog box, as shown in Figure 14-25.

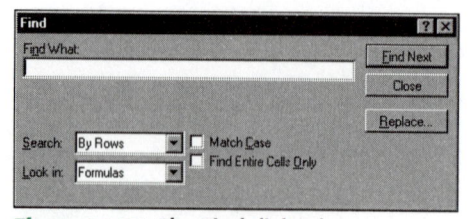

Figure 14-25: The Find dialog box.

3. In the Find What text box, enter your search term. You can include wildcards; the asterisk (*) can be used to indicate any combination of characters, and the question mark can be used to indicate any single character.

4. In the Search list box, choose By Rows if you want to search across rows starting with the current cell, or choose By Columns if you want to search across columns starting at the current cell.

5. In the Look In list box, choose Formulas to search through formulas; Values to search through values stored in cells; or Notes to search all notes that are attached to cells.

6. If you want your search to be case-sensitive, turn on the Match Case check box.

7. Turn on the Find Entire Cells Only check box if you want the entire cell's contents to match your search term. If you leave this option turned off, Excel will find matches where either part or all of the cell's contents matches the search term.

8. Click the Find Next button to find the next occurrence of the search term. (Alternatively, hold down the Shift key and click the Find Next button.) When done searching, click Close.

> **Hot Stuff** Once you have entered the parameters for a search in the Find dialog box, you can repeatedly press F4 to continue searching for the same data.

Finding and replacing data

Use the Replace command of the Edit menu to search for data in a worksheet and replace it with other data. The process is similar to using Edit⇨Find (in fact, the dialog box you see is nearly identical). Here are the steps:

1. Select the cells you wish to search. If you want to search the entire worksheet, select any single cell.

2. Choose Edit⇨Replace. The Replace dialog box (Figure 14-26) appears.

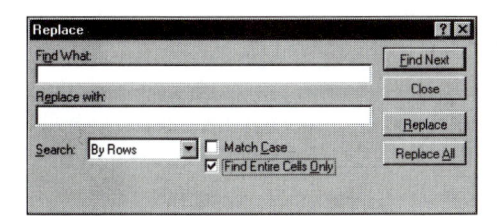

Figure 14-26: The Replace dialog box.

3. In the Find What text box, enter your search term. You can include wildcards; the asterisk (*) can be used to indicate any combination of characters, and the question mark can be used to indicate any single character.

4. In the Replace with text box, type the replacement text.

5. In the Search list box, choose By Rows if you want to search across rows starting with the current cell, or choose By Columns if you want to search across columns starting at the current cell.

6. If you want your search to be case-sensitive, turn on the Match Case check box.

7. Turn on the Find Entire Cells Only check box if you want the entire cell's contents to match your search term. If you leave this option turned off, Excel will replace data where either part or all of the cell's contents matches the search term.

8. Click the Replace All button if you want to find and replace all occurrences of the search term with your new term. Alternatively, click Find Next to find the next match in the worksheet and, after examining it, click the Replace button to replace just that match. When done making your replacements, click Close.

Note: Edit⇨Undo rolls back the effects of a replace operation.

Checking Spelling

Another feature that Excel takes from the word processing realm is its built-in spell checker. You can save yourself from possibly embarrassing blunders in your worksheet's text by checking its spelling — *before* you pass out those copies at the annual board meeting. You can check any part of a selection (even a single word), or you can check the entire worksheet, including any embedded charts that are in the worksheet. You can also add words to custom dictionaries in order to handle specialized words that you use often (like medical and legal terms).

You spell check a worksheet this way:

1. Select the cells you wish to spell check. If you want to check the spelling of the entire worksheet, select any single cell.

2. Choose Tools⇨Spelling, or click the Spelling button on the Standard toolbar. Excel checks the spelling in the worksheet. If it finds what it thinks is a misspelled word, you'll see the Spelling dialog box, as shown in Figure 14-27.

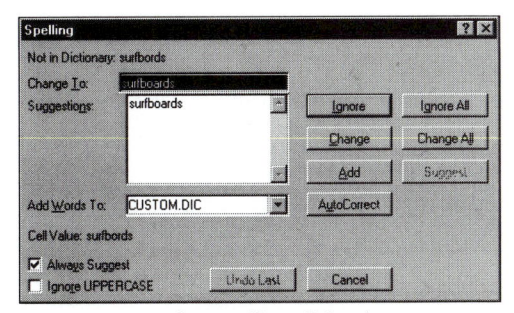

Figure 14-27: The Spelling dialog box.

When Excel finds a misspelling, it tries to provide a number of options for a correct spelling of the word. If the Always Suggest check box is on, Word suggests proper spellings whenever it can. In the Change To text box, you enter the correct spelling — or you can click one of the suggested spellings in the Suggestions list box, which adds that spelling to the Change To box.

If the Always Suggest check box is off, click the Suggest button to see a list of possible spellings in the Suggestions list box. If one of the suggestions is the spelling that you want, select it in the list box and then click Change. The Ignore button lets you leave a word as is, while the Cancel button cancels the entire spell checking operation. Clicking Ignore All tells Excel to ignore all suspected misspellings of the same term; Change All tells Excel to change all misspellings to the entry that you accept in the Change To box. The Add button lets you add a word to the selected custom dictionary (`Custom.dic` by default), and the Ignore UPPERCASE check box, when turned on, tells Excel to skip all words that are all uppercase letters.

Hot Stuff During the spell checking process, it takes a bit of extra time for Excel to suggest corrections to misspelled words. You can speed the process slightly by turning off the Always Suggest check box and using the Suggest button to ask for help when you need it.

Adding a custom dictionary

If you make regular use of specialized terms (such as medical or legal terms) in your worksheets, the spell checking capability will be pretty useless unless it can work with those terms as part Excel's dictionaries. You can add words to Excel's default custom dictionary, but another option is to create additional custom dictionaries this way:

1. Place the cursor in any worksheet containing some of your custom terms; this way, the spell check operation will find them.
2. Choose Tools➪Spelling. When Excel stops at what it thinks is the first misspelled word, the Spelling dialog box appears, as shown earlier in Figure 14-27.

3. Click in the Add Words To list box and then type the name of the new dictionary that you want to create.

4. Click the Add button, to add the current word to the dictionary. Excel will display a dialog box asking if you want to create a new dictionary.

5. Click Yes to create the dictionary. From this point on, you can use the dictionary by choosing it by name in the Add Words To list box.

Summary

This chapter has examined the many different ways in which you can put data into an Excel worksheet, and manipulate that data. The chapter covered the following points:

- You can enter values or formulas into cells of a worksheet. Values can be numbers, text, dates, or times.
- You can attach notes to cells by using the Note command of the Insert menu.
- You can move and copy data from place to place on a worksheet or between worksheets.
- Excel's Fill, AutoFill, and Series features can fill ranges of cells with data.
- You can insert and delete ranges of cells, as well as entire rows and columns.
- Formulas manage the calculations within your worksheets.
- Excel provides hundreds of *functions*, which can be thought of as tools for performing specific types of calculations.
- Excel's Function Wizard can help you quickly find and properly enter the correct function for a specific task.
- You can use the Edit⇨Find and Edit⇨Replace commands to search for data and to replace data with other data.
- You can use the Tools⇨Spelling command to correct the spelling of text in a worksheet.

The next chapter tells you how to format your worksheets so they look good.

Where to go next...

- You'll soon want to print what you've created. You'll find the complete scoop on printing in Chapter 18.

◆ ◆ ◆

Excel Formatting

CHAPTER 15

In This Chapter

Using the AutoFormat feature

Changing row height and column width

Changing fonts, font sizes, and alignment

Formatting text, numbers, dates, and times

Applying borders and patterns to a worksheet

Hiding and unhiding rows and columns

Centering, wrapping, and justifying text

Creating custom formats

Protecting worksheets and workbooks

Most spreadsheet users know all too well that a spreadsheet is usually more than just a collection of raw numbers. Since the days of the first spreadsheets, users have resorted to formatting tricks to enhance the appearance of the numbers presented. (How many seasoned spreadsheet pros can remember filling rows of cells with characters like asterisks or hyphens to enclose information within crude borders?) Excel offers many ways to format your worksheets so that you can give them the most visual impact possible. You can change the fonts, sizes, styles, and colors used by the characters in your worksheets. You can also control the alignment of text within cells, both vertically and horizontally. You can change row heights and column widths, and you can add borders to selected cells. And you can use Excel's powerful AutoFormat feature to quickly enhance the appearance of part or all of a worksheet, without the need to use any formatting commands.

Using the AutoFormat Feature

A significant feature of recent versions of Excel is that it lets you apply automatic formatting to your worksheet data with the AutoFormat feature. You activate the AutoFormat feature by choosing Format⇨AutoFormat. In the AutoFormat dialog box, you can use the sample formats to quickly create a presentation-quality worksheet, even if you know little or nothing about other formatting options. Figures 15-1, 15-2, and 15-3 show some of the different formats that are possible when you use the AutoFormat feature.

In Figure 15-1, the Classic 1 style of AutoFormat uses traditional accounting-style fonts and simple border lines to visually separate the data.

340 Part III ✦ Excel

	A	B	C	D	E	F	G	H
1		January	February	March	April	1st Quarter		
2	Walnut Creek	$123,600.00	$137,000.00	$89,900.00	$201,300.00	$551,800.00		
3	River Hills	$248,700.00	$256,750.00	$302,500.00	$197,000.00	$1,004,950.00		
4	Spring Gardens	$97,000.00	$102,500.00	$121,500.00	$142,500.00	$463,500.00		
5	Lake Newport	$346,300.00	$372,300.00	$502,900.00	$456,800.00	$1,678,300.00		
6								
7	Total Sales	$815,600.00	$868,550.00	$1,016,800.00	$997,600.00	$3,698,550.00		
8								
9								
10								
11	Income							
12								
13	Sublet Office Space	$1,800.00	$1,800.00	$1,800.00	$1,800.00	$7,200.00		
14	Misc. Income	$750.00	$750.00	$500.00	$800.00	$2,800.00		
15								
16	Total Income	$2,550.00	$2,550.00	$2,300.00	$2,600.00	$10,000.00		
17								
18								
19	Gross Receipts	$813,050.00	$866,000.00	$1,014,500.00	$995,000.00	$3,688,550.00		

Figure 15-1: The Classic 1 style AutoFormat.

In Figure 15-2, the Colorful 1 style of AutoFormat makes extensive use of various background choices to highlight the worksheet data.

	A	B	C	D	E	F	G	H
1		January	February	March	April	1st Quarter		
2	Walnut Creek	$123,600.00	$137,000.00	$89,900.00	$201,300.00	$551,800.00		
3	River Hills	$248,700.00	$256,750.00	$302,500.00	$197,000.00	$1,004,950.00		
4	Spring Gardens	$97,000.00	$102,500.00	$121,500.00	$142,500.00	$463,500.00		
5	Lake Newport	$346,300.00	$372,300.00	$502,900.00	$456,800.00	$1,678,300.00		
6								
7	Total Sales	$815,600.00	$868,550.00	$1,016,800.00	$997,600.00	$3,698,550.00		
8								
9								
10								
11	Income							
12								
13	Sublet Office Space	$1,800.00	$1,800.00	$1,800.00	$1,800.00	$7,200.00		
14	Misc. Income	$750.00	$750.00	$500.00	$800.00	$2,800.00		
15								
16	Total Income	$2,550.00	$2,550.00	$2,300.00	$2,600.00	$10,000.00		
17								
18								
19	Gross Receipts	$813,050.00	$866,000.00	$1,014,500.00	$995,000.00	$3,686,550.00		

Figure 15-2: The Colorful 1 style AutoFormat.

In Figure 15-3, the List 1 style of AutoFormat uses shading in alternate rows of the worksheet.

Figure 15-3: The List 1 style AutoFormat.

Excel examines the current range to determine levels of summary and detail. Excel also looks for text, values, and formulas, and then applies formats accordingly. AutoFormats are combinations of several different elements: number, alignment, font, border, pattern, column, and row formats. Perform the following steps to apply AutoFormat to your worksheet:

1. Select the range of cells to which you want to apply the format. If you want to select the entire worksheet, click on the row and column header intersection at the upper-left corner of the worksheet.

2. Choose Format⇨AutoFormat to open the AutoFormat dialog box, as shown in Figure 15-4.

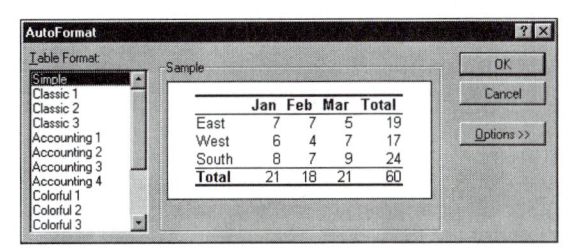

Figure 15-4: The AutoFormat dialog box.

3. From the Table Format list, choose the desired format. When you click on a format, you can see a preview of it in the Sample window.

4. Click on the Options button if you want to choose which formats to apply. Clicking on the Options button expands the dialog box to reveal check boxes for Number, Border, Font, Patterns, Alignment, and Width/Height (see Figure 15-5). By default, all the boxes are turned on.

5. Click on the OK button to apply the formatting to the selection.

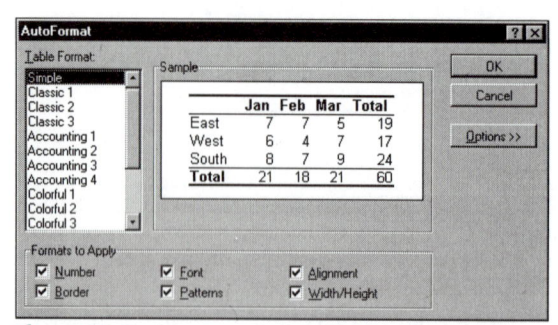

Figure 15-5: The expanded AutoFormat dialog box.

If you don't like the effects of the AutoFormat command, choose Edit⇨Undo. Or, if you have done too many other tasks since applying the AutoFormat to the selection, don't worry. You can simply select the range, choose Format⇨AutoFormat, and select None from the list box of possible styles.

Remember that you don't have to settle for Excel's default formatting selections in its AutoFormats. The Options button in the AutoFormat dialog box lets you accept or reject certain parts of the formatting that Excel would normally apply. For example, you may have spent a great deal of time formatting different ranges of numeric values with different fonts, and you would rather not have Excel's AutoFormat feature mess around with the fonts. Turn off the Font check box in the Formats to Apply area of the AutoFormat dialog box. Then when you apply an AutoFormat to the selection, Excel won't override the fonts that you have already applied.

You can turn off only one formatting option or several formatting options, depending on the selection and the formatting that you want applied. After turning off the desired options, you can choose the format that you want in the Table Format list box and click on the OK button to apply it to your selection. Note that any options that you turn off in this manner *aren't* carried over to the next time that you use the AutoFormat feature. You'll need to turn off any options that you don't want each time that you use AutoFormat.

When to stay away from AutoFormat

As helpful a feature as AutoFormat is, it has its limits. Excel has to make some judgment calls when it applies an AutoFormat to your worksheet. For example, Excel tries to figure out what parts of the selection may contain column headings so that it can apply a pleasing format to those headings. In particular, AutoFormat is designed to work well with worksheets that follow a traditional row-and-column format. If your worksheet doesn't follow tradition — perhaps it contains a large number of scientific formulas laid out more like a flowchart — AutoFormat may not give you the results that you'd like. In these cases, you are probably better off applying your desired formats manually by using the formatting techniques covered later in this chapter.

Changing Column Widths and Row Heights

You can adjust column width and row height in Excel as needed. Excel adjusts row height automatically, however, to accommodate wrapped text and large fonts. So in many cases, you may not need to adjust row height.

Column widths

When you select a new sheet, you can adjust the standard width setting of the columns, or you can change only a few columns. You can choose from two methods to adjust column width. The first method, clicking and dragging the column to size it, is easier to use but is less accurate than the second method. To use the mouse to adjust the size of the columns, follow these steps:

1. Move the mouse pointer to the heading of the column.
2. Double-click on the right edge of the column to size it to the width of the widest entry, or drag the column heading border to size it manually to a width that you want.

The second method is much more accurate but requires the use of commands and dialog boxes. If you know the exact column width that you want, or you are one who likes accuracy, you can choose Format⇨Column and then choose the appropriate command from the submenu that appears. If, for example, you choose the Width command from the submenu, you can enter a numeric value for the width of the column in the Width dialog box. Or if you choose the Standard Width command, you can accept the standard width or height (8.43 points being the default value) that appears in the Standard Width dialog box. Or you can choose the AutoFit Selection command from the submenu, which automatically sizes a column to accommodate the largest entry.

Hot Stuff: The AutoFit Selection command applies its magic only to selected cells, so you must first make a selection for the command to have the desired effect. If you leave the cell cursor in a blank cell, using AutoFit Selection accomplishes nothing. Often, it's a good idea to select the entire column before using AutoFit Selection. (To select a column, click on the header at the top of the column.)

Row heights

Excel also lets you adjust row height. Again, you have two methods to choose between: the click-and-drag method and the Format menu options. To use the click-and-drag method, perform the following steps:

1. Place the pointer over the bottom border of the row heading.
2. Drag the bottom border of the row heading until the row reaches the desired size.

You can also AutoSize a row's height by double-clicking on the bottom border of a row header. This action adjusts the row to fit the tallest entry. If you want to AutoSize a number of rows, first select the desired row and then double-click on the bottom border of any of the selected rows.

As with columns, you can accurately adjust row height by choosing Format⇨Row and then choosing the appropriate command from the submenu. To set the row height, for example, choose the Height command from the submenu and enter a value for the height in the Row Height dialog box (see Figure 15-6). Or you can choose the AutoFit command to adjust the row height to the largest entry in the row.

Figure 15-6: The Row Height dialog box.

Oh, those shortcut menus

Many of the format choices that you may want to apply to rows and columns can be easily accessed from Excel's shortcut menus. If you right-click on a column heading (at the top of the column), you select the entire column and open a shortcut menu with choices that include Column Width, Hide, and Unhide. If you right-click on a row heading (at the far left edge of the row), you select the entire row and open a shortcut menu with choices that include Row Height, Hide, and Unhide.

Hiding and Unhiding Columns, Rows, and Gridlines

You can hide selected columns or rows from view, and you can reveal rows or columns that have been previously hidden. You may want to hide rows or columns so that they don't appear in printed copies of the worksheets, or you may want to hide rows or columns so that a viewer's attention is focused on important parts of the worksheet. For example, you may need to compare the data in columns B and D. With column C between B and D, the data is difficult to analyze. If you hide column C, however, the data now lies side by side and is easy to compare.

Hiding columns

To hide a column, select it and choose Format⇨Column⇨Hide. If you want to bring the column back, choose Edit⇨Go To (F5), enter the address of any cell in that column in the Reference text box, and click on the OK button. Then you choose Format⇨Column⇨Unhide. (Alternatively, you can select the two columns surrounding the hidden column, and choose Format⇨Column⇨Unhide.)

Hiding rows

Hiding rows is similar to hiding columns. Select the desired row and choose Format⇨Row⇨Hide. If you want to bring the row back, choose Edit⇨Go To (F5), enter the address of any cell in that row in the Reference text box, and click on the OK button. Then choose Format⇨Row⇨Unhide. (Alternatively, you can select the two rows surrounding the hidden row, and choose Format⇨Row⇨Unhide.)

Hiding gridlines

With some worksheets, you may not want the gridlines that are normally displayed to appear. To hide the gridlines, you first activate the worksheet page. Then choose Tools⇨Options. In the Options dialog box, click on the View tab and turn off the Gridlines option. Then click on the OK button. As a result, the gridlines disappear from the current worksheet.

The Gridlines option affects only the current worksheet page in a workbook. If you want to turn off gridlines for a different worksheet page, you have to go through all the steps again. If you want to turn off the gridlines for a large number of worksheets, select the worksheets first and then follow the steps to turn off the option. To select several worksheets, hold down the Shift key while you click on each worksheet tab that you want included in the selection.

Changing Alignments

In your quest to give your worksheet a more professional and refined look, you may need to change the alignment of data in your cells. By default, the following alignment applies to cells: right-aligned for numbers, left-aligned for text, and centered for logical and error values. Changing the alignment of text in a cell is especially important because what works with text in one area of your worksheet may not look attractive in another area. You may want to enhance the appearance of certain parts of your worksheet by right-aligning or centering text, for example.

To change the alignment of the cells, first select the range of cells to which you want to apply the new alignment. Then you can choose between two methods to change the alignment. You can use the buttons on the Formatting toolbar, or you can choose Format⇨Cells. In the Format Cells dialog box, you then click on the Alignment tab to bring up the options that you need to change. (You can also open the Format Cells dialog box by right-clicking on the selection and choosing Format Cells from the shortcut menu.) Figure 15-7 shows the Alignment tab of the Format Cells dialog box.

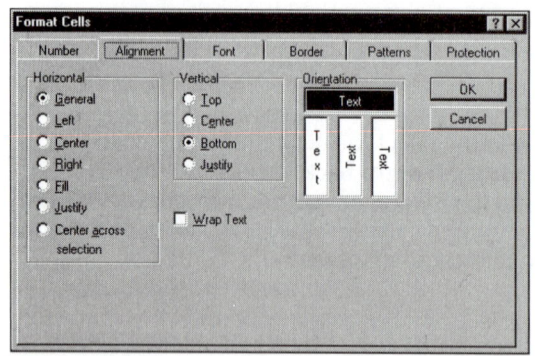

Figure 15-7: The Alignment tab of the Format Cells dialog box.

In the Horizontal area, you can choose the Left, Center, or Right alignment options. (You can also use the Wrap Text and Justify options with text that occupies multiple lines of a cell, as covered in the next section.) If you've changed the row height of a cell so that the cell is much taller than the text entry, the options in the Vertical area of the dialog box become equally useful. You can align the text to the top, bottom, or center of the cell, and you can vertically justify it.

To change the alignment of data in cells by using the Formatting toolbar buttons, follow these steps:

1. Select the cells in which you want to change the alignment.

2. Click on the Align Left button to left-align the selection, the Center button to center entries in the selection, and the Align Right button to right-align the selection.

The disadvantage of using the Formatting toolbar is that it does not offer you the range of options that you get by using the Format Cells dialog box. You can't vertically align text from the toolbar, and you can't use the wrap and justify options. But you can center text across columns, as detailed in the next section.

Centering, Wrapping, and Justifying Text

As you build worksheets with lots of text headings, you'll discover that you need to center headings across a series of multiple cells. Spreadsheet pros from way back routinely center titles across multiple columns through trial and error — they enter the text into a cell where it "looks good" and re-enter the text elsewhere if the results aren't as expected. Excel sends this technique back to the Stone Age, where it belongs, with the Center Across Columns button on the Formatting toolbar and the corresponding Center Across Selection option on the Alignment tab of the Format Cells dialog box. Figure 15-8 shows the Projected Sales title before and after it was centered across the selected range of cells.

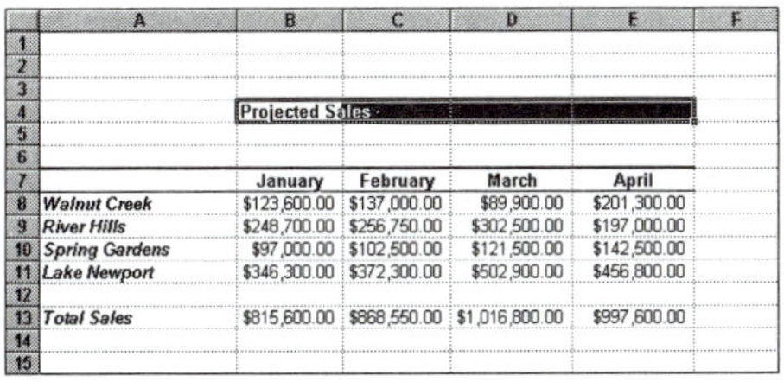

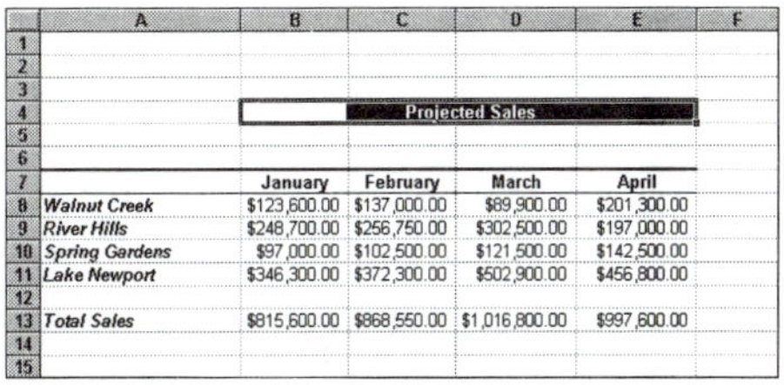

Figure 15-8: Left: A title before centering across a range of cells. Right: The title after centering across a range of cells.

Centering text

You can center the contents of a cell across a selection of blank cells by performing the following steps:

1. Make your selection of cells containing the text that is to be centered across the selection. (For proper results, the leftmost cell in the selection should contain the text that you want centered across the range of cells.)

2. Click on the Center Across Columns button in the Formatting toolbar.

Alternatively, you can make the selection, right-click on it, and choose Format Cells. In the Alignment tab of the Format Cells dialog box, turn on the Center Across Selection option. But unless you've turned off the display of the Formatting toolbar, it's generally easier to use the toolbar button.

Wrapping text

When you make lengthy text entries within cells, you can force Excel to wrap the text so that it fits into an attractive paragraph inside the cell. When you wrap the text, Excel automatically adjusts the row height so that the entry fits within the width of the cell. Figure 15-9 shows the before-and-after effects of using the wrap text option. In the figure, both cells containing text contain the same information. In the upper cell that contains text, the Wrap Text option has not been turned on; in the lower cell that contains text, theWrap Text option has been turned on.

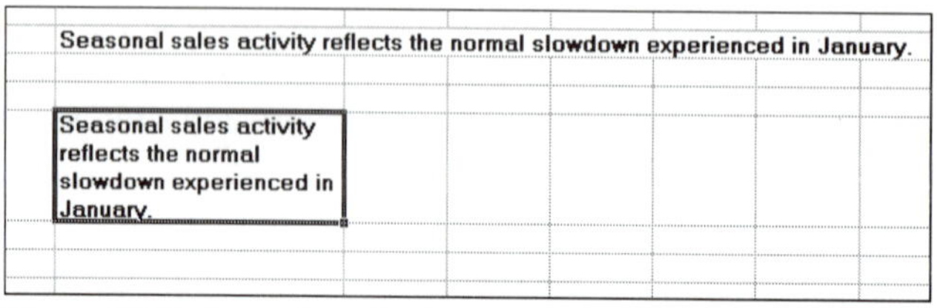

Figure 15-9: Examples of using Wrap Text in a worksheet.

You can wrap text in a cell by performing the following steps:

1. Set the column width as desired.
2. Select the cells containing the text that you want to wrap.
3. Choose Format⇔Cells.
4. Select the Alignment tab in the Format Cells dialog box and turn on the Wrap Text check box.

Justifying text

After you use the Wrap Text option to wrap text, you may also want to justify the text so that every line of the paragraph (except the last, if it is too short to fill a line) is aligned on both sides. (A cell has to contain at least two lines of text for justification to have any effect.) Figure 15-10 shows the before-and-after effects of using text alignment in a worksheet. In the figure, the text in cell D4 is not justified; in cell D7, the Justify option has been applied to the text.

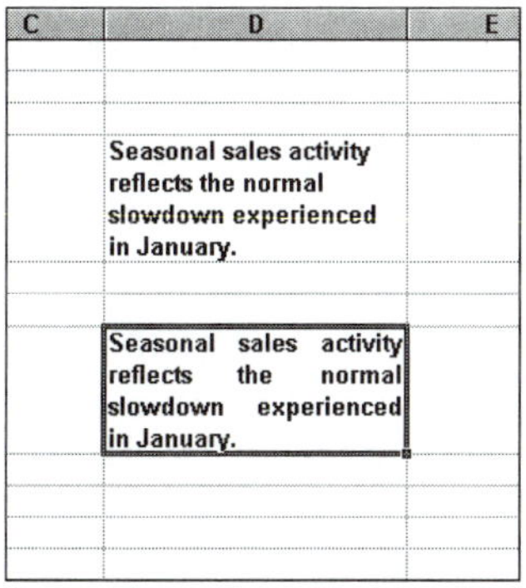

Figure 15-10: Top: Left-justi-
fied, right-ragged text.
Bottom: Left- and right-justi-
fied text.

You can perform the following steps to justify entries in selected cells:

1. Select the text that you want to justify.
2. Choose Format⇨Cells.
3. Select the Alignment tab in the Format Cells dialog box and turn on the Justify option. The text is automatically justified (assuming it contains two or more lines).

Applying Fonts and Style Formats

Just as in Word, you can apply different fonts to your entries in Excel. Applying fonts in Excel is as simple as it is in Word. You select the cells that you want to change, and you choose the font that you want to apply to the selection from the Font list box on the Formatting toolbar. You can also choose a font size from the toolbar, and you can use the Bold, Italic, and Underline buttons to apply these types of formatting to the characters in the selected cells. Alternatively, you can select the cells, right-click on the selection, choose Format Cells from the shortcut menu, and click on the Font tab to display your possible font choices. Figure 15-11 shows the possible font choices in the Font tab of the Format Cells dialog box.

About TrueType fonts and your other fonts

When you work with different fonts in your Excel worksheet, you should understand the difference between TrueType fonts and non-TrueType fonts. Ever since the introduction of Windows 3.1, Windows has included TrueType technology as part of the operating system. TrueType is a technology that enables Windows to use the same fonts that you see on-screen to print documents. Before TrueType, Windows made use of one set of fonts to display data on-screen and another set to print. Windows would try to pick a screen font that closely resembled the printer font, but it wasn't always successful (especially with some of the more unusual printer fonts). Therefore, what you saw on-screen would not always be what you got from your printer. TrueType was designed to solve this problem by providing the same set of fonts for on-screen viewing as for printing. Windows includes a number of different TrueType fonts, and you can purchase more TrueType fonts from software vendors or download them from the software libraries of online services, such as America Online and CompuServe.

The point of all this? If you select a TrueType font when you choose a font from the Format Cells dialog box or from the Font list on the Formatting toolbar, you can be reasonably assured that what you see on-screen is what you get from your printer. You can recognize TrueType fonts by the TT symbol that appears to the left of the font name in the Fonts list box or in the Font tab of the Format Cells dialog box. Printer fonts, by comparison, appear in the lists with a picture of a printer to the left of the font name. The minor disadvantage to using TrueType fonts is that they print more slowly than printer fonts because they must be *rasterized* (converted to a printable character representation) by Windows as it downloads information to the printer.

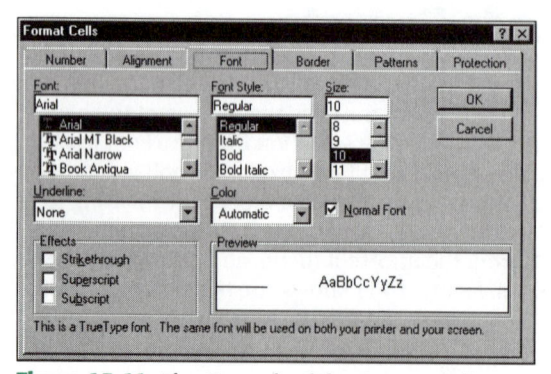

Figure 15-11: The Font tab of the Format Cells dialog box.

On the Font tab, you can use the options in the Font and Font Style list boxes to choose a desired font and font style, and you can choose a point size in the Size list box. You can select a type of underlining (Single, Double, Single Accounting, or Double Accounting) in the Underline list box, and you can select a color for the text in the Color list box. In the Effects area of the tab, you can turn on one of the special effects (Strikethrough, Superscript, or Subscript).

Hot Stuff — You can also apply styles or fonts to only *some of the characters* that are in a cell (yes, we said only *some* of the characters). To accomplish this little known trick, place the cursor in the cell that contains the text that you want to change so that the text appears in the formula bar. In the formula bar, click on and drag to select only the text that you want to change. Next, choose Format⇨Cells. When you make this selection, you see the Format Cells dialog box displaying only the Font tab. Here you can choose the Font that you want to use on the characters, along with the character size and style. Make the desired selections and click on the OK button to apply them.

Applying Borders, Patterns, and Colors

Excel makes lots of border types available. All the border types have different widths, patterns, and even colors. You can use these choices to make your worksheets more attractive and much easier to read. You can apply a border to a selection by performing the following steps:

1. Select the cells to which you want to add the border.
2. Click on the down arrow to the right of the Borders button on the Formatting toolbar.
3. Select the border type that you want from the menu that opens (see Figure 15-12). The border you choose is applied to the selected cells.

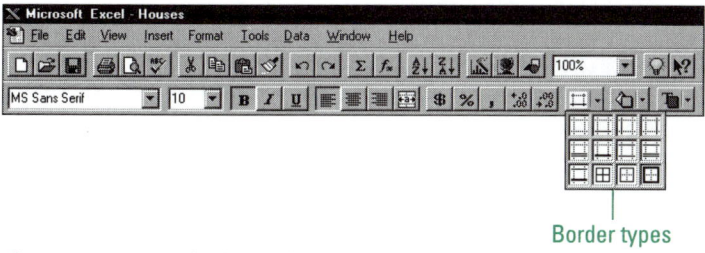

Figure 15-12: Available border types.

You can also choose Format➪Cells to open the Format Cells dialog box. Then click on the Border tab, as shown in Figure 15-13. You can use the options within this tab of the Format Cells dialog box to apply a border to a selected cell or cells. You can also select the style of the border and whether you want the border to appear on all sides or selected sides of the cell.

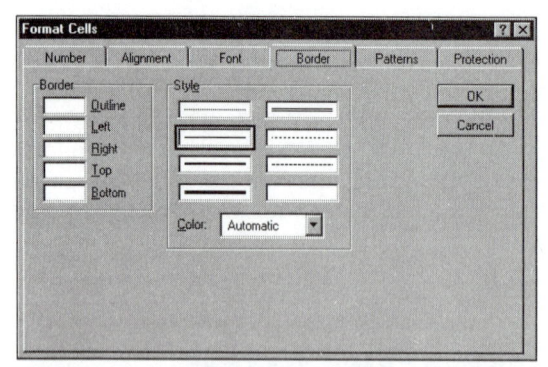

Figure 15-13: The Border tab of the Format Cells dialog box.

You can also add colors and patterns to the cells that you have selected. To apply a color or a pattern, select the desired cells, right-click on the selection, and choose Format Cells from the shortcut menu. When the Format Cells dialog box appears, click on the Patterns tab to bring it to the front, as shown in Figure 15-14.

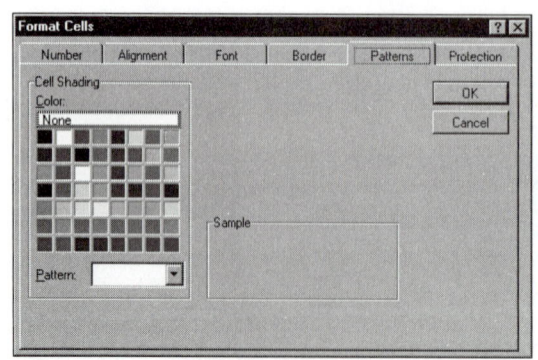

Figure 15-14: The Patterns tab of the Format Cells dialog box.

In the Cell Shading area of the dialog box, you can click on any desired color to apply it. The list of colors also includes some of the grays that are used in shading. Then click on the down arrow in the Pattern list box to reveal a box showing the available background patterns and the remainder of the shading choices that you have. Choose a desired pattern from the list. After you make your desired color and pattern selections, click on the OK button in the Format Cells dialog box to apply them.

You can also apply colors to a selection by clicking on the down arrow to the right of the Color button on the Formatting toolbar and choosing a desired color from the box of colors that appears. And if the Drawing toolbar is turned on, you can apply patterns by making a selection, clicking on the down arrow to the right of the Pattern button in the toolbar, and choosing a desired pattern from the box of patterns that appears.

Hot Stuff: When applied, some patterns can make cell entries very difficult to read. Remember to use Edit⇨Undo if you don't like the looks of a selection that you've chosen.

Sometimes, you may want to apply a color to the characters that you enter rather than to the background of the cell. Applying color to the characters can make a specific number or title stand out. To make the total earnings for the year stand out, for example, you can apply red formatting to the characters in that cell if the earnings were less than the previous year.

To apply a color to the characters in your worksheet, select the characters to which you want to apply the color and then click on the down arrow to the right of the Font Color button on the Formatting toolbar to open a color selection box. Choose a desired color to apply to the characters.

Hot Stuff: With both the Font Color and the regular (cell) Color buttons, you can apply the color that was last chosen to another selection by simply clicking on the button. This is a great shortcut feature.

Working with Number Formats

By default, Excel applies the General format to numbers in a cell. This format displays up to 11 digits if the entry exceeds the cell's width. All the numbers entered in the General format are displayed as integers (such as 21,947 or 12,382), decimal numbers (such as 21.57 or 3.14159), or in scientific notation (such as 9.43E+7 or 21.212E-5).

When you enter a numeric value in a cell, Excel tries to find the number format that is most appropriate for your entry number and assigns that format to the number. If you enter nothing but numbers, and they aren't excessively large or small, Excel is pretty much clueless as to how you want them formatted. In these cases, Excel settles for the General format for the cell.

But you can give Excel clues as to how you want it to format an entry by including symbols with your numeric entries. For example, if you enter a dollar amount and precede it with a dollar sign, Excel automatically formats the entry as a currency value. If you want the entry formatted as a percent, you can follow the entry with a percent sign. You can enter scientific notation directly into the cell. For example, if you enter 17.409E+10 in a cell, Excel stores the value of 174090000000000 in the cell and displays 1.74E+14 in the cell.

If you've already entered the values, and you want to go back and change them, using the Formatting toolbar is the simplest way to apply the most commonly used number formats. After selecting the entry that you want to change, click on one of the number formatting buttons to apply the format. Table 15-1 lists the number formatting buttons and their functions.

Table 15-1
Number formatting buttons on the Formatting toolbar

Button	Function
Currency Style	Changes the cell to a currency format
Percent Style	Changes the cell to a percent format
Comma Style	Changes the cell to a comma format
Increase Decimal	Increases the decimal place of the number
Decrease Decimal	Decreases the decimal place of the number

Number formats can also be applied via the Number tab of the Format Cells dialog box. To activate the Format Cells dialog box, choose Format➪Cells (or right-click on the selection and choose Format Cells from the shortcut menu). Click on the Number tab to display the Format Cells dialog box shown in Figure 15-15.

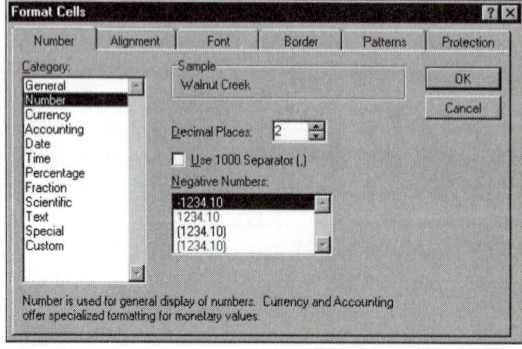

Figure 15-15: The Number tab of the Format Cells dialog box.

To apply number formats by using the Number tab of the Format Cells dialog box, perform the following steps:

1. Select your desired cells.
2. Choose Format➪Cells or right-click on the selection and choose Format Cells from the shortcut menu.
3. Click on the Number tab.
4. In the Category list box, select the category that you want to reformat.
5. If a Type list box appears in the center of the dialog box, choose the way you want the number to appear from the list box. (Some categories, such as Text and Accounting, don't offer a list box of types.)
6. Click on the OK button to apply the formatting.

Remember, there may be occasions when you want to format numbers as text. You can do so while you enter the value in a cell of the worksheet by entering an apostrophe before the number. You can also make a selection, choose the cells command from the Format menu, click on the Number tab in the Format Cells dialog box, and choose the Text option from the Category list box.

Working with Date and Time Formats

More Info If you enter data in an acceptable date or time format, Excel stores the value as a date or time value. For example, if you type 4/30/52 into a cell, Excel stores the entry as a date value of April 30, 1952. Excel also recognizes a value like 22-Jan-95 as a valid date. Similarly, with an entry of 9:45 PM, Excel stores a time value representing that time. (Chapter 14 provides additional specifics on the entry of dates and times in a worksheet.)

You can change the format that Excel uses to display dates and times by performing the following steps:

1. Select the range of cells containing the date or time values.
2. Choose Format➪Cells, or right-click on the selection and choose Format Cells from the shortcut menu.
3. Click on the Number tab.
4. In the Category list, choose Date or Time as desired. Figure 15-16 shows the Date category selected.

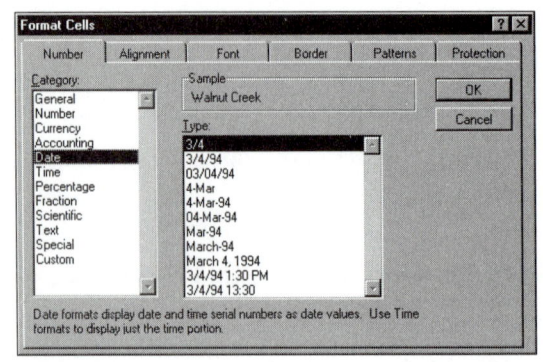

Figure 15-16: Choosing the Date category in the Number tab.

5. In the Type list, choose the desired date or time format and then click on the OK button.

When you enter a date or time in a format that Excel recognizes, Excel displays the value at the right side of the cell by default. If a value appears at the left side of the cell, then Excel has not recognized it as an acceptable date or time value and has formatted the entry as text instead. You should re-enter the value in an acceptable format to get the correct date or time into the cell.

Using Custom Number Formats

Besides using the variety of standard formats built into Excel, you also have the power to design your own custom formats. Custom formats are useful for specialized financial or scientific displays of values or for handling such information as phone numbers, part numbers, or other data that has to appear in a specific format. Figure 15-17 shows some examples of custom formats in columns A, B, and C.

A	B	C
data entered	custom format used	how data appears
1505.99596	0.0000	1505.9960
23562.7678	$#,##0.0000	$23,562.7678
0.15852	0.0000%	15.8520%
3/15/95 14:40	d-mmm-yy h:mm:ss AM/PM	15-Mar-95 2:40:00 PM
2125551212	"(000) 000-0000"	(212) 555-1212
1274542	"Part number " ###-####	Part number 127-4542

Figure 15-17: Examples of custom formats.

In working with custom formats, it helps to understand the number format codes that Excel uses. These number formats are available in all the worksheets when you open the workbook. These formats are automatically stored in the correct number format category. Whenever you want to access them, open the Format Cells dialog box and choose Custom from the Category list in the Number tab. Table 15-2 explains the function of the most common symbols that you use to make custom formats.

Table 15-2
Symbols used in custom formats

Symbol	Function
?	Acts as a placeholder for digits in much the same way as zeros. Zeros that are not important are removed and spaces are inserted to keep alignment together.
/	Denotes that the slash symbol is to be used after the integer portion with fractional custom formats. This causes the number to appear as a fractional value, such as 5 2/3.
0	Acts as a placeholder. This number can be used to display a zero when no number is entered. Also note that decimal fractions are rounded up to the number of zeros that appear to the right of the decimal.
#	Acts as a placeholder for digits, as the zero does. The difference between # and zero as a placeholder is that if a number is not entered, no number is displayed. Decimal fractions are rounded up to the number of #s that appear to the right of the value.
General	Denotes the default format for cells that are not formatted.
, (comma)	Marks the thousands position. (Only one comma is needed to specify the use of commas.)
. (decimal)	Marks the decimal point position. For a leading zero, enter a zero to the left of the decimal.
_ (underscore, followed by character of your choice)	Inserts a space the size of the character that follows the underscore before the character itself appears. As an example, if you enter _) to end a positive format, a blank space is inserted the size of the parenthesis. This lets you align a positive number with a negative one that's surrounded by parentheses.
:$_+()	These characters are displayed in the same positions in which they are entered in the number code.

(continued)

Table 15-2 *(continued)*

Symbol	Function
E_E+e_e+	Displays a number in scientific notation. The zeroes or values to the right of the e denotes the power of the exponent.
%	The entry is multiplied by 100 and displayed as a percentage.
@	Takes the role of a format code to indicate where text typed by the user appears in a custom format.
*character	Fills the remainder of the column width with the character that follows the asterisk.
"text"	Displays the text between the quotation marks.
[color]	The cell is formatted with the specified color.
\ (backslash)	When this precedes an entry, it indicates a single character or symbol.

Format codes include three sections for numbers and one for text. The sections are separated by semicolons. The first section is the format for positive numbers; the second is the format for negative numbers; the third is the format for zeros; and the fourth is the format for text.

The section you include in your custom format determines the format for positive numbers, negative numbers, zeros, and text, in that order. If you include only two sections, the first section is used for positive numbers and zeros, and the second section is used for negative numbers. If you include only one number section, all the numbers use that format.

The text format section, if it is there, is always last. If you have text that you always want to include, enter it in double quotation marks. If your format has no text section, the text you enter in the cell is not affected by the formatting.

To create your own custom format, perform the following steps:

1. Make a selection and choose Format➪Cells, or right-click the selection and choose Format Cells from the shortcut menu.
2. In the Format Cells dialog box, choose the Number tab.
3. Choose Custom from the Category box. From the Type list box (see Figure 15-18), choose a custom format that is closest to the one that you want. You can then modify the chosen format to meet your needs.

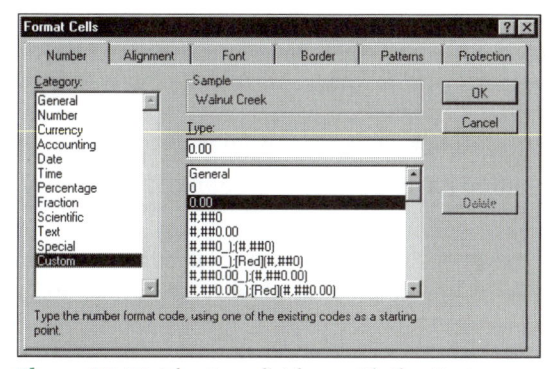

Figure 15-18: The Type list box with the Custom entries.

4. Make the desired changes to the format by editing the entry in the Type text box.
5. Click on the OK button to save the new number format.

Keep the following points in mind when you create custom formats:

- Excel uses zeros and number signs as digit placeholders. If you use a zero, the digit is always displayed, and the number sign suppresses the non-significant zeros.

- If you follow an underscore by a character, Excel creates a space that is the width of the character. If you follow an underscore with a right parenthesis, for example, you can then be assured that positive numbers will line up correctly with negative numbers that are enclosed in parentheses.

- If you want to set a color for a section of the format, type the name of the color in square brackets in the section.

- Add commas to your format to force the displayed numbers to appear in multiples of 1,000. (The commas that are not surrounded by digit placeholders can be used to scale the numbers by thousands.)

Copying Formats with the Format Painter

If you've already spent time and effort creating formats in certain areas of a worksheet, and you want to use them elsewhere, you can easily do so with Excel's Format Painter. As its name implies, the Format Painter lets you take an existing format and literally "paint" that format across any other cells in a worksheet. When you use the Format Painter, you copy all formatting — including text, number, and alignment formats; and cell shading, color, and borders — from the currently active cell to the range of cells that you paint., The Format Painter, the button with the picture of a paintbrush, is accessible on the Formatting toolbar.

Use the Format Painter to copy the formatting information from one cell to a range of cells or from a range of cells to another range of cells. To copy formatting from one cell to a range of cells, follow these steps:

1. Select the cell that contains the formatting that you want to copy.
2. Click on the Format Painter button on the Formatting toolbar. A paintbrush now appears beside the mouse pointer.
3. Click on and drag across the range of cells that should receive the format. When you release the mouse button, the format of the original cell is applied to the selected range.

To copy formatting from a range of cells to another range of cells, use these steps:

1. Select the entire range of cells that contains the formatting you want to copy.
2. Click on the Format Painter button on the Formatting toolbar. A paintbrush now appears beside the usual mouse pointer.
3. Click on the upper-left cell in the range of cells that should receive the format. When you release the mouse button, the format of the original range of cells is applied to a range of cells of the same size as the original range.

Creating Your Own Styles

As this chapter emphasizes, Excel's formatting options give you the power to apply formatting in just about every conceivable manner to your worksheets. If you find yourself applying the same formatting choices repeatedly to different parts of a worksheet, it makes sense to save your formatting choices as a style so that you can easily apply the style over and over again to a selection of cells. In Excel, a *style* is a collection of formatting options that you apply to a cell or a range of cells. The nice thing about styles is that once you apply them to your worksheets and you decide to change some aspect of the style later, all the parts of your worksheet that make use of that style will automatically change accordingly. For example, if you create a style, use it in half a dozen worksheets, and later change the font used by that style, the font will automatically change in those worksheets. (If you are accustomed to working with styles in Word for Windows, you will find the concept of Excel styles to be quite similar.)

You can easily define your own styles by choosing Format⇨Style. To define the style, perform these steps:

1. Choose Format⇨Style. The Style dialog box appears, as shown in Figure 15-19.

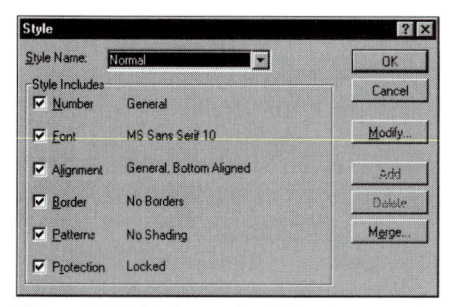

Figure 15-19: The Style dialog box.

2. In the Style Name list box, enter a name for your new style and then click on the Add button to add the new style to the list.

3. Turn off the check boxes for any of the attributes that you don't want included in the style.

4. If you want to change any of the attributes for the format settings shown in the list, click on the Modify button to bring up the Format Cells dialog box.

5. Click on any of the tabs in the Format Cells dialog box and change the settings for the formats.

6. When you are finished setting the formats in the Format Cells dialog box, click on the OK button to go back to the Style dialog box.

7. Click on the OK button to save the new style.

After your custom style exists, using it is a simple matter. Just select the range of cells to which you want to apply the style and choose Format➪Style. In the Style dialog box, click on the down arrow to the right of the Style Name list box and choose the name of your custom style from the list. Then click on the OK button to apply the style to the selected range of cells.

Protecting Your Formatting Changes

You can apply protection to the cells of a worksheet so that the formats and other data cannot be changed. (By default, the cells of a worksheet have protection turned on, but the protection does not take effect until you choose Tools➪Protection and then choose Protect Workbook from the resulting dialog box.) To make sure that the cells of a worksheet will be protected when you turn on overall protection for the workbook, perform these steps:

1. Choose any range of cells that should *not* be protected. Because the default setting for the cells is to be protected, you will want to turn off protection for any cells that you want to retain the ability to change.

2. Choose Format➪Cells.

3. Click on the Protection tab of the Format Cells dialog box (see Figure 15-20).

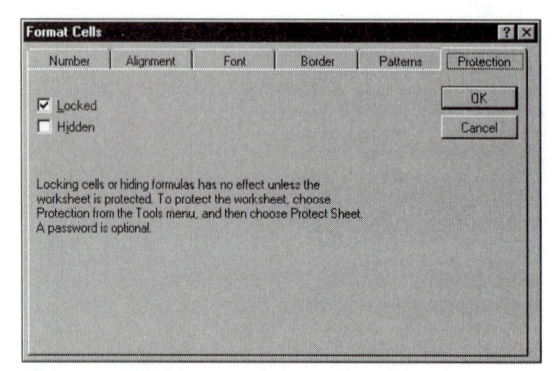

Figure 15-20: The Protection tab of the Format Cells dialog box.

4. Turn off the Locked check box if you want the selected cells to remain unprotected. You can also turn on the Hidden check box to specify that the selected cells' contents do not appear in the formula bar.

5. Click on the OK button and repeat Steps 1 through 4 for every range of cells that should remain unprotected.

6. Choose Tools➪Protection➪Protect Workbook.

7. In the Protect Workbook dialog box, enter a password, if one is desired. If you omit the password, you can still protect the workbook, but others can remove the protection without the use of a password. Also, turn on the Windows check box if you want to protect the windows in the workbook from being moved or resized.

8. Click on the OK button to implement the protection.

Note Passwords that you enter to protect a workbook are case sensitive.

After you have protected the contents of a workbook, you can remove the protection by choosing Protection from the Tools menu and then choosing Unprotect Workbook from the submenu. If you entered a password during the protection process, you are asked for the password before Excel unprotects the document.

Fair warning …

If you protect a workbook with a password, *do not, do not, do not* (did we repeat that enough?) forget the password! If you forget the password, you may as well start re-creating the workbook from scratch. Even the technical support people at Microsoft cannot help you get into a workbook that is password-protected when you don't have the password.

Summary

This chapter covered topics related to formatting in Excel. You learned how to use formatting to give a worksheet a more appealing look and to enhance its appearance. The following topics were covered:

- By selecting a worksheet range, choosing Format⇨AutoFormat, and selecting the desired options in the dialog box that appears, you can quickly give a worksheet a professional look.

- In Excel, you can easily change row heights and column widths to accommodate your entries by clicking and dragging the column or row edges, or by choosing the Column or Row commands (as appropriate) from the Format menu.

- You can apply specific fonts, font sizes and styles, borders, patterns, and colors to a group of cells or to characters within a cell by choosing Format⇨Cells and using the options in various tabs of the Format Cells dialog box.

- In addition to the variety of standard formats provided with Excel, you can create custom formats for the values that you enter in your worksheets.

In the next chapter, you will learn how you can add graphic objects to your worksheets and your charts.

Where to go next...

- After you've formatted your worksheet, you may want to pop in a graphic. Chapter 16 tells you how.

- You can make charts out of the data in your worksheet. Chapter 17 has the details.

♦ ♦ ♦

Adding Graphics to Worksheets

CHAPTER 16

In This Chapter

Inserting graphics in a worksheet

Working with graphic objects

Drawing lines, arcs, ellipses, and rectangles

Using the free-hand and free-form tools

Selecting, grouping, moving, and copying objects

Resizing and aligning objects

Formatting objects

Adding text objects

Inserting illustrations and WordArt

Adding macro buttons

In Excel, worksheets can be far more than just tables of numbers with a chart added here and there. You can emphasize the points expressed by those numbers, add visual information, and (by means of macro buttons) literally make your worksheets easier for others to use. You can do all these things by adding graphics to worksheets. You can draw lines, circles, rectangles, and squares, and you can add text boxes with as little as a short title or as much as multiple paragraphs of text. And you can make use of clip art or professionally drawn artwork from other Windows programs in your Excel worksheets. If you have an artistic personality (or if your worksheets are facing a demanding audience and you need all the help you can get), you can really get carried away with Excel's graphics.

Why Bother with Graphics in Excel?

Many spreadsheet users don't think of Excel and graphics together. Because Excel is a spreadsheet package, many Excel users crunch numbers with it and leave graphics entirely to a drawing program like CorelDRAW!. But if you don't use Excel's graphic capabilities, you miss out on all Excel's power. From its humble origins years ago as a Macintosh product, Excel provided spreadsheet capability with built-in flexible graphics. Microsoft has expanded Excel's capabilities over the years with each release of the product. Excel is now a spreadsheet with the power to add visual oomph to your work. As an example, consider Figure 16-1.

In this worksheet, the gridlines have been turned off, and a text box with an arrow has been added to describe points that the numbers in the worksheet are attempting to get across. Clip art has been added to the worksheet, and a button that runs a macro (to display another worksheet) has been added. You can add all these effects and more by using the Excel's graphics features.

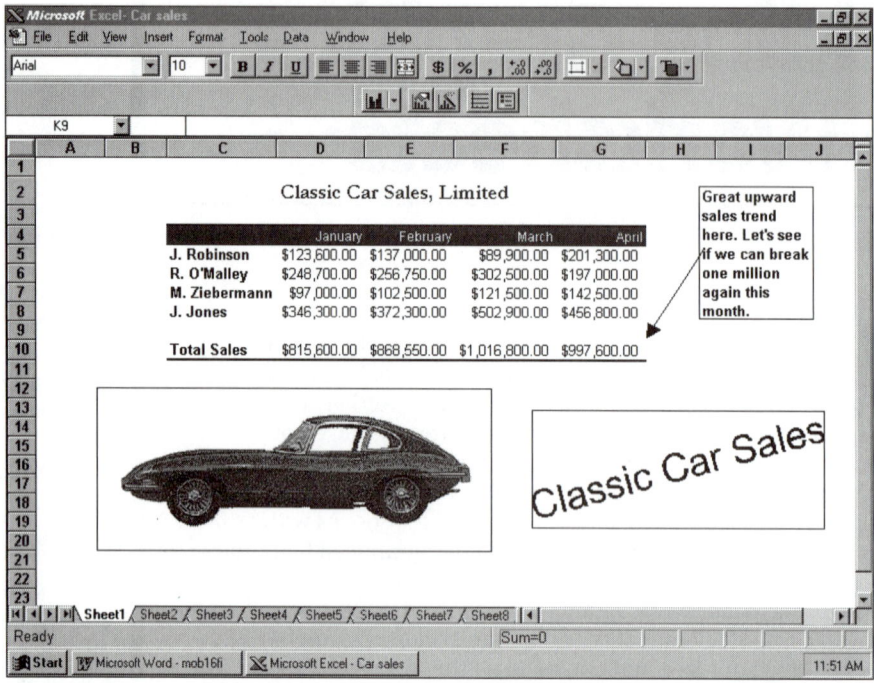

Figure 16-1: A worksheet that makes extensive use of graphics.

Inserting Graphics into a Worksheet

When you want to insert graphic files (such as clip art) into an Excel worksheet, you can use the Picture command from the Insert menu. This command lets you pull graphic pictures from files created in other programs. To insert graphics with the Picture command, do the following:

1. Place the insertion point in the cell where you want the upper-left corner of the picture to appear.
2. Choose Insert⇨Picture. The Picture dialog box appears, as shown in Figure 16-2.
3. In the dialog box, choose the clip art or graphics file that you want to insert into your worksheet.
4. Click on the OK button to insert the graphic into the worksheet.

Another way to insert graphics is to open the graphic in the other Windows program and then use the Copy and Paste commands to copy the graphic into the Excel worksheet. Here's how:

1. Activate the program from which you want to insert the picture. Open the piece of art and select it by using the appropriate Windows selection technique for the program that you are using.

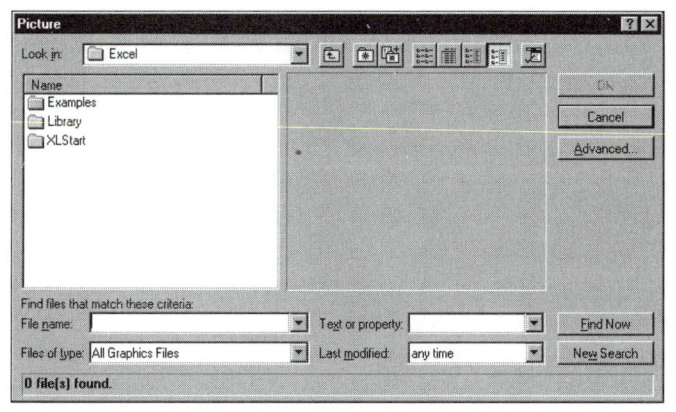

Figure 16-2: The Picture dialog box.

2. Choose Edit⇨Copy.

3. Activate Excel, if it is not already running, and select the cell or the object where you want the upper-left corner of the graphic to appear.

4. Choose Edit⇨Paste. The graphic appears in the worksheet. Remember that your normal sizing and moving methods can be used to change the size or location of the graphic.

Hot Stuff As long as the program from which you inserted the graphic supports OLE, double-clicking on the object activates the menus of that program. This technique lets you perform edits to the graphic without leaving Excel and switching to the other program.

What kinds of graphic files can I import?

Excel's graphic filters let you import graphic files in several file formats, including:

File type	Filename extension
PC Paintbrush	.PCX
Tagged Image File Format	.TIF
Windows Metafile	.WMF
Encapsulated PostScript	.EPS
AutoCAD Format 2-D	.DXF
CorelDRAW!	.CDR
WordPerfect Graphics	.WPG

(continued)

What kinds of graphic files can I import? *(continued)*

File type	Filename extension
CompuServe GIF	.GIF
Kodak PhotoCD	.PCD
JPEG Filter	.JPG
Targa	.TGA
Windows Bitmap	.BMP
Computer Graphics Metafile	.CGM
HP Graphics Language	.HGL
Micrografix Designer Draw	.DRW
Macintosh Picture	.PCT

Working with Graphic Objects

You can use the Drawing toolbar (see Figure 16-3) to create graphic objects right in Excel. If the Drawing toolbar is not displayed, choose View➪Toolbars and select Drawing from the dialog box that appears. You can also right-click on a toolbar to display a shortcut menu and then choose Drawing from the shortcut menu. After the Drawing toolbar is displayed, you can move it as you would move any toolbar, by clicking on any blank area of the toolbar and dragging it to a desired location.

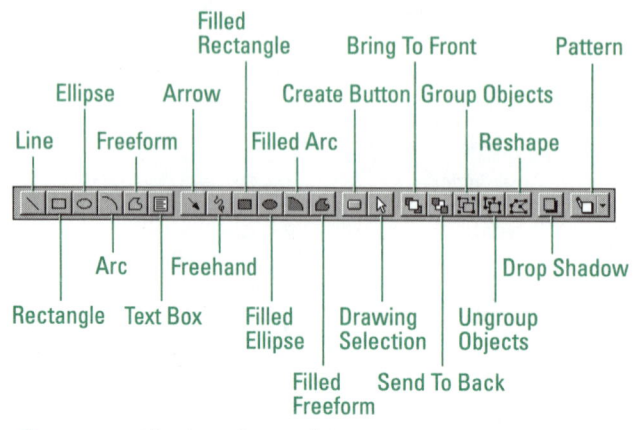

Figure 16-3: The Drawing toolbar.

The Excel Drawing toolbar has a variety of drawing tools that help you enhance your worksheets. This toolbar contains several drawing tools that enable you to create items from lines to polygons. Table 16-1 gives the name of each tool and its function.

Table 16-1
The Drawing toolbar's tools

Tool name	Function
Line	Draws straight lines
Rectangle	Draws rectangles or squares
Ellipse	Draws a circle or ellipse
Arc	Draws an arc
Freeform	Draws a polygon or other freeform shape
Text Box	Creates a text box for word-wrapped text
Arrow	Creates a line with an arrowhead
Freehand	Makes freehand drawings and smooth curves
Filled Rectangle	Creates a filled rectangle or square
Filled Ellipse	Creates a filled ellipse or circle
Filled Arc	Creates a filled arc
Filled Freeform	Creates a filled freeform shape or polygon that closes endpoints
Create Button	Creates a button to which you can assign a macro
Drawing Selection	Selects a group of objects by applying a rectangular marquee
Bring To Front	Brings the selected object to the front of a group of stacked objects
Send To Back	Sends an object to the back of a stacked group of objects
Group Objects	Groups selected objects
Ungroup Objects	Ungroups objects that have been previously grouped
Reshape	Displays the vertexes so you can change the shape of an object
Drop Shadow	Places a shadow to the right and bottom of a shape
Pattern	Applies a pattern to the selected graphic object

Hot Stuff For a real time-saver, use the shortcut menus while you are working with objects. The shortcut menu that is displayed when you right-click on an object is shown in Figure 16-4. These shortcut menus make available the Cut, Copy, and Paste commands as well as other commands related to formatting the object.

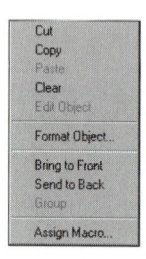

Figure 16-4: An object shortcut menu.

Drawing lines, arcs, ellipses, and rectangles

The Drawing toolbar lets you create lines, arcs, ellipses, and rectangles easily. These are all basic drawing elements, and you can combine these elements to create more complex shapes. You draw an object by first clicking on the desired tool and then clicking on and dragging in the worksheet to place the item.

Hot Stuff

While drawing lines, ellipses, and arcs, hold down the Shift key while you drag to keep the lines vertical, at a 45° angle, or horizontal. You can also hold down the Alt key to align the corners of the object with a cell's gridlines.

Lines

To draw a line, click on the Line tool, click on the beginning location for the line, and then drag to the ending location. To draw a line with an arrowhead, click on the Arrow tool, click on the point where the line should begin, and drag to the point where the arrowhead should appear.

Squares and rectangles

To draw a square or a rectangle, click on the Rectangle tool, click on a corner of the rectangle, and drag to size the rectangle as desired. To draw a square, hold down the Shift key while you drag to size the square.

Don't let others mess with your graphics

If you want to keep others from changing your graphics in your worksheets, you can protect them just as you can protect cells in a worksheet. Right-click on the graphic, choose Format Object from the shortcut menu, click on the Protection tab, and make sure that the Locked option is turned on. Then open the Tools menu, choose Protection/Protect Sheet, enter a password (if desired) in the dialog box that appears, and click on the OK button. If you leave the password text box blank, the worksheet will be protected from changes, but you won't need a password to turn off the protection.

Circles and ellipses

To draw an ellipse, click on the Ellipse tool, click on an edge of the ellipse, and drag to size the ellipse as desired. To draw a circle, hold down the Shift key while you drag to size the circle.

Filled objects

To create filled objects, right-click on the object and choose Format Object from the shortcut menu. This opens the Format Object dialog box. From the Fill area of the Patterns tab, choose the color you want to fill the object and click on the Automatic button to make the fill. After you create different filled objects, you can change the color by right-clicking on the object, choosing Format Object from the shortcut menu to open the Format Object dialog box, and clicking on the Patterns tab in the dialog box. Choose the color that you want to apply to the object from the Fill portion of the Patterns tab.

Arcs

To draw an arc, click on the arc tool on the drawing toolbar. Next, click on and drag to create the arc where you want it on the worksheet. The arc appears. If you need to make more than one arc in the worksheet, then double-click on the arc button before you begin to create the arc.

Using the Freehand and Freeform tools

The Drawing toolbar provides three drawing tools — a Freehand tool, a Freeform tool, and a Filled Freeform tool — that you can use to draw freehand shapes, polygons (shapes having many sides), or filled polygons. Figure 16-5 shows examples of the types of drawings that you can create with the Freehand and Freeform tools.

Using the Freehand tool is like using a pen on a screen (except that a pen is a lot easier to use than a mouse for drawing). First you click on the Freehand tool to select it. Then you click on any desired location in the worksheet and drag to draw a line in any desired shape.

Use the Freeform tool and the Filled Freeform tool in the same manner. First select the desired tool and then click on any point in the worksheet to set a line starting point. Move to where you want the line to end and click. Then move to where you want the next line to end and click again. Repeat these steps to draw all the sides of the polygon. Note that you can draw freehand shapes instead of a line at any point by clicking on and dragging instead of clicking on the line's end points.

Hot Stuff You can reshape existing freeform drawings by using the Reshape tool on the Drawing toolbar. Click on the Reshape tool and then click on and drag any line end point in a freeform shape to its desired new location.

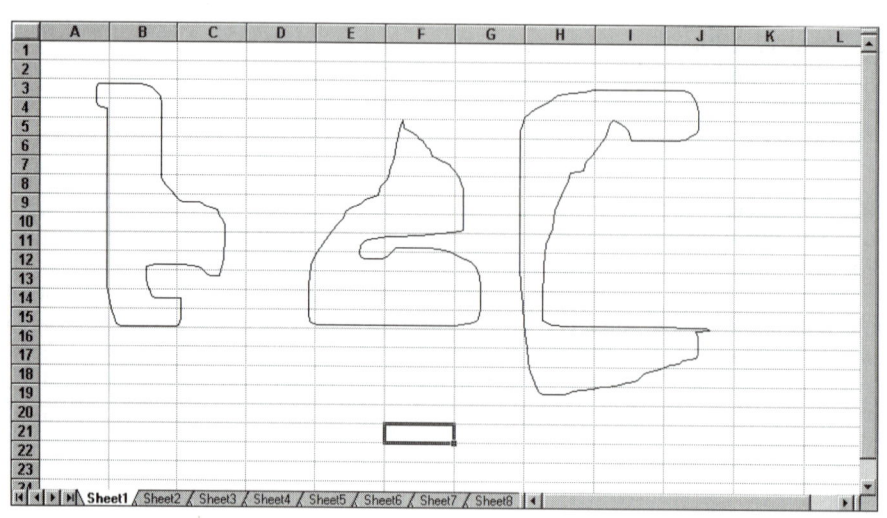

Figure 16-5: Examples of shapes created using Excel's Freehand and Freeform tools.

Selecting and grouping objects

In Excel, most of the items that you add while drawing are considered *objects*. This includes text boxes, graphics brought in from other sources, and the shapes that you draw. You can have as many objects as you want in a worksheet.

To select the object that you want to work with, click on it. You can then change its orientation, shape, color, or pattern by right-clicking on the object. From the shortcut menu that appears, choose Format Object and select the desired choices in the dialog box that appears. You can also select multiple objects by holding down the Shift key while you select the objects. To unselect an object, hold down the Shift key and click on the object again.

You can also group objects together. Grouping objects is useful when you want to change the colors for a group of objects or move or align them as a group. All the objects that you include in the group act as one object; therefore, if you perform an action on one of the items, the action affects all the items in the group. You can group objects by performing the following steps:

1. Select the objects that you want to group. Remember to hold down the Shift key while you select each object.

2. Right-click on any one of the selected objects and choose Group Objects from the shortcut menu that appears.

Using the Bring To Front and Send To Back tools

As you draw and position multiple objects, you may need to place one object on top of another object (for example, a company logo that consists of a circle on top of a rectangle). If the wrong object appears on top, you can adjust the placement by using the Bring To Front or Send To Back tool on the Drawing toolbar. Select any object and then click on the Bring To Front tool to make the object appear on top of another object. Or select the object and then click on the Send To Back tool to make the selected object appear underneath the other object. Figure 16-6 shows the effects of using the Bring To Front and Send To Back tools.

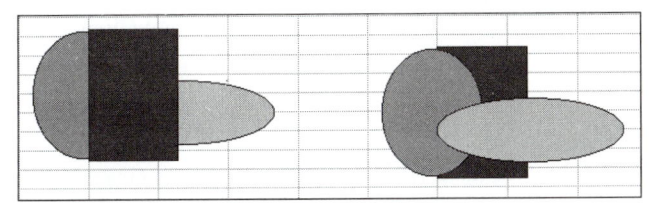

Figure 16-6: Left: Bring To Front brings the rectangle to the front. Right: Send To Back sends the rectangle to the back.

Moving and copying objects

As you work with objects in your worksheet, you may need to move or copy the objects. You have two options to move or copy the objects: you can use the Cut and Copy commands or the click on-and-drag method. To move or copy objects with the Cut and Copy commands, perform the following steps.

1. Select the object(s) that you want to move or copy.

2. Choose Edit⇨Cut or click on the Cut button on the Standard toolbar to remove the object and place it in the Clipboard. Choose Edit⇨Copy instead to leave the existing object intact and place a copy of it in the Clipboard to copy it to a new location.

3. Move the cursor to the location where you want to place the object.

4. Choose Edit⇨Paste or click on the Paste button on the Standard toolbar to place the Clipboard information in the worksheet. The cell that contains the insertion point becomes the upper-left corner of the entry.

The click on-and-drag method for moving objects is equally simple. Simply click on the object and hold down the mouse button. Then drag to the area where you want to place the object. Release the mouse button to place the object. To remove an object, select it and press the Delete key or choose Edit⇨Clear.

Resizing objects

Resizing objects in Excel is done in the same way that you resize objects in other Windows programs. First select the object that you want to resize. You will see small black squares, called *sizing handles,* appear around the object. To resize the object's width, drag one of the side handles to the desired width. To change the height of the object, drag a top or a bottom handle. If you want to resize the length and width of the object simultaneously, drag a corner handle.

Formatting objects

You can apply a variety of formatting options to the object that you have selected by right-clicking on it. In the shortcut menu that appears, choose Format Object. In the Format Object dialog box, you can change the colors, patterns, line styles, and weights of lines. And you can add arrowheads to lines.

Formatting borders and patterns

You can change the pattern, fill color, or border of an object by performing these steps:

1. Right-click on the desired object and choose Format Object from the shortcut menu.

2. In the Format Object dialog box, click on the Patterns tab. Figure 16-7 shows what the Patterns tab looks like when you select an object.

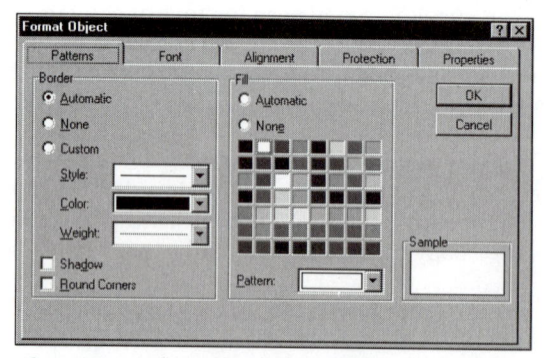

Figure 16-7: The Patterns tab of the Format Object dialog box when you select an object.

3. In the Border area, set the options that you want. The Automatic option specifies the default border format; None specifies no border. Choose Custom to design your own border by using the Style, Color, and Weight list boxes. Turn on the Shadow option if you want the border to have a shadow.

4. In the Fill area of the dialog box, set the desired color and pattern options. Turn on the Automatic option if you want the default fill color; choose None if you want the object to be transparent.

5. Click on the OK button.

Formatting lines

You can change the style, thickness, and color of lines, and you can add arrowheads to lines by performing these steps:

1. Right-click on the desired line and choose Format Object from the shortcut menu.

2. In the Format Object dialog box, click on the Patterns tab. Figure 16-8 shows what the Patterns tab looks like when you select a line.

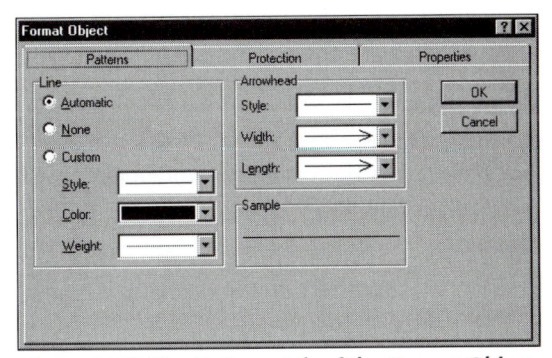

Figure 16-8: The Patterns tab of the Format Object dialog box when you select a line.

3. In the Line area of the dialog box, set the desired options. The Automatic option specifies a default line; None lets you specify an invisible line (although why anyone would want to add invisible lines to a worksheet is an interesting question). Choose Custom to design your own line style by using the Style, Color and Weight list boxes.

4. In the Arrowhead area, choose the options that you want.

5. Click on the OK button.

> ### Hiding objects for better spreadsheet performance
>
> If you have a lot of graphic objects in your worksheet, Excel is forced to redraw the graphics as you scroll within the worksheet. This extra effort can really drag down your system's speed, especially on hardware that meets only the minimum configuration for Windows 95. You can speed up the display of the worksheets by hiding the graphic objects from view or by displaying them as graphic placeholders.
>
> Choose Tools⇨Options and click on the View tab. In the Objects area of the dialog box, turn on the Show Placeholders option to show the graphic objects as placeholders (empty white rectangles) or turn on the Hide All option to hide the graphic objects. When you need to see the objects again, you can go back into this dialog box and turn on the Show All option.

Adding Text Boxes

Excel lets you place text boxes in your worksheets. You can edit and format text in these boxes using typical word processing techniques.

Text boxes make excellent titles for worksheets because they float in a layer over the worksheet. You can position a title of any size without affecting worksheet row or column positions. You can add a text box to your worksheet by performing the following steps:

1. In the Drawing toolbar, click on the Text Box button. Notice that the mouse pointer changes into a crosshair symbol.
2. Click and drag to form the box in which you will enter the text. If you want a square text box, hold down the Shift key while you drag. If you want a box aligned with the grid, hold down the Alt key while you drag.
3. After sizing the text box, release the mouse button. The insertion point now appears inside the text box (see Figure 16-9), which permits you to begin entering text. You can continue typing until the end of the text box. As you type, the text scrolls up so that part of it is hidden. To make all the text visible, select the text box and drag a handle to make the box larger to accommodate the extra text.

Editing text

If you need to edit text in a text box, use the normal Windows navigation methods to do so. To move the cursor, use Ctrl+right arrow or Ctrl+left arrow or use the arrow keys and the mouse. Use the Delete and Backspace keys to delete any unwanted entry and then retype the new entry.

Figure 16-9: A text box added to a worksheet.

Formatting text

You can also format the text boxes that you add. Select the text box, right-click on it, and choose Format Object from the shortcut menu. In the Patterns tab of the Format Object dialog box, you can change the border styles and fill colors used by the text box. You can also click on the Font tab to change the fonts used by the text. Figure 16-10 shows the Font tab that appears when you select a text box. You can choose a desired font, font style, and point size, and you can turn on special effects, such as underlining, bold, italics, strikethrough, superscript, or subscript. Use the Color list box to change the font's color.

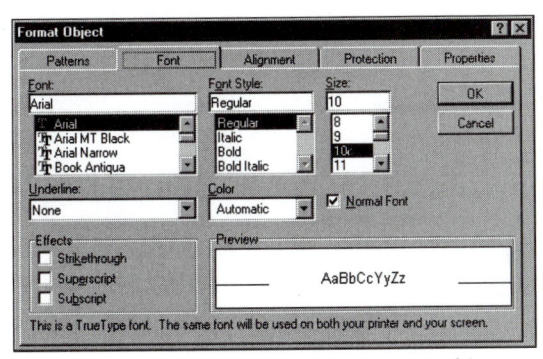

Figure 16-10: The Font tab of the Format Object dialog box when you select a text box.

Rotating text

Excel also lets you rotate text within a text box. Figure 16-11 shows some of the different ways that text in a text box can appear in Excel.

Figure 16-11: Examples of rotated text in text boxes.

To rotate text in a text box, perform the following steps:

1. After creating the text box and entering the text, select the text box and right-click on it.

2. From the shortcut menu that appears, choose Format Object to open the Format Object dialog box.

3. Choose the Alignment tab (see Figure 16-12). The Text Alignment area lets you control both the horizontal and vertical alignment of the text that you enter in the text box.

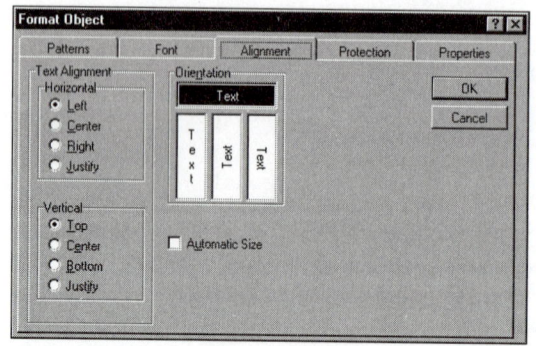

Figure 16-12: The appearance of the Alignment tab when you select a text box.

4. In the Orientation area, choose the desired orientation for the box.

You can use the Automatic Size option in the Alignment tab to size your entries automatically.

Word Art

Microsoft WordArt is a miniapplication that lets you create special effects using text to enhance the appearance of your documents. You can bend and stretch text strings, fit text into a variety of different shapes, add three-dimensional effects — and then insert this twisted text as graphics into your document. Figure 16-13 shows an example of what you can do with WordArt.

Figure 16-13: Example of WordArt in Excel.

WordArt lets you choose from bold, italics, same size, vertical lettering, stretch to fit, alignment of your choice, and make spacing changes between the characters. This is all done by clicking on the buttons on the WordArt toolbar. Figure 16-14 shows the WordArt toolbar and the buttons you can use to activate each of these WordArt features.

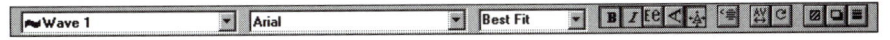

Figure 16-14: The WordArt toolbar.

When you choose the character spacing button, the Spacing Between Characters dialog box (Figure 16-15) appears. It lets you choose from among tight, very tight, normal, very loose, and custom spacing. (The best way to understand this is to play with it.) This box also lets you turn the autokerning on and off by clicking on the Automatically Kern Character Pairs check box. (*Kerning* is the typesetter's way of saying "adjusting the space between letters." Typesetters do this to give text its best appearance.)

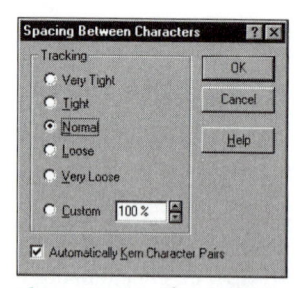

Figure 16-15: The Spacing Between Characters dialog box.

The toolbar's special effects button opens the Special Effects dialog box (Figure 16-16). This box lets you add special effects to your WordArt entries. You can change your text's angle of rotation and the slant of your text's letters. This is all done by clicking on the corresponding arrows in the dialog box.

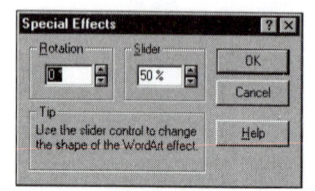

Figure 16-16: The Special Effects dialog box.

The Shading button is also located on the toolbar. You can use this button to add shading and patterns to your entry. Figure 16-17 shows the Shading dialog box. Here, choose the desired shading style and click on OK when done.

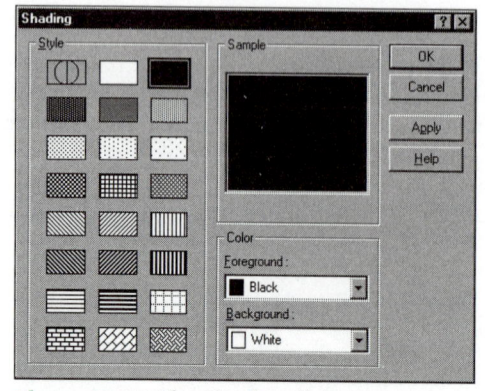

Figure 16-17: The Shading dialog box.

WordArt also offers letter shadowing. You can use this to add background shadowing to the letters of your entry. Click on the letter shadowing button to open the Shadow dialog box, then choose a desired shadow, and click on OK. The Shadow dialog box is shown in Figure 16-18.

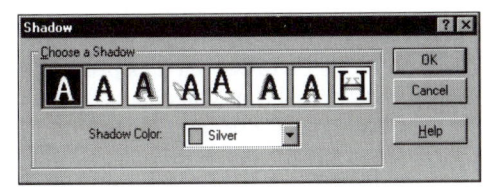

Figure 16-18: The Shadow dialog box.

The final button in the toolbar is the Border button. Use this button to add a border to your entry. When you click on this button, the Border dialog box (Figure 16-19) opens. Use it to choose the border that you want for your entry.

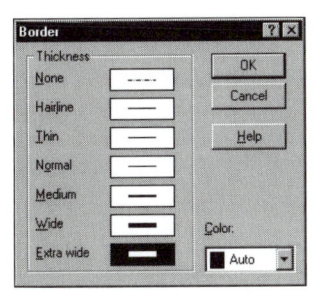

Figure 16-19: The Border dialog box.

The Format list box on the toolbar, shown in Figure 16-20, lets you choose a format for your text entry. The shapes represent the way the text will appear on the worksheet. You can use the Font list box that appears beside the Format list box to choose the desired font. These differ, depending on the fonts that are available on your machine.

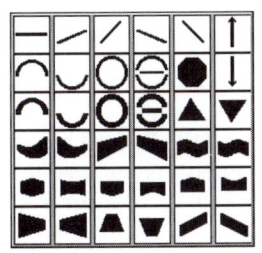

Figure 16-20: The Format list box.

Last of the list boxes on the toolbar is the Best-Fit list box. This box is used to change the font size for your entry. Click on the arrow and select the font you wish to use and begin making your entries.

Adding Macro Buttons

Using macro buttons is an easy way to perform repeated tasks, such as printing a range. The Drawing toolbar contains a Create Button tool that you can use to place a button on your spreadsheet and then attach a macro to it. Pressing the button then activates the macro.

You can add a macro button to a worksheet by performing the following steps:

1. In the Drawing toolbar, click on the Create Button tool. Alternatively, you can choose Tools⇨Macro.

2. In the worksheet, click on and drag to shape the button. You can hold down the Alt key while you drag to create a button the exact size of a cell or a group of cells, or you can hold down the Shift key while you drag to create a button in the shape of a square.

3. The Assign Macro dialog box appears, as shown in Figure 16-21.

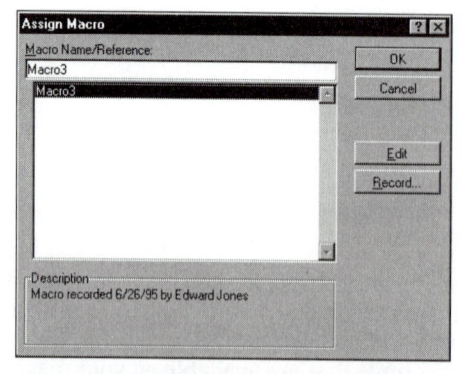

Figure 16-21: The Assign Macro dialog box.

4. From the list of macros, choose the macro that you want to assign to the button.

5. After you click on the OK button, the macro is assigned to the button.

> **More Info** If you want to record a macro to assign to your button, click on the Record button in the Assign Macro dialog box. In the Record New Macro dialog box, enter a name for the macro you are recording and click on the OK button. (See Chapter 20 for a detailed discussion on how macros operate and how you can create them.)

Excel also lets you assign a macro to a completed button or to change the macro that is assigned to the button. This is useful in changing the macros that are assigned to a button. To do these tasks, perform the following steps:

1. Select the button by holding down the Ctrl key while you click on it.
2. Choose Tools⇨Assign Macro or right-click on the button and choose Assign Macro from the shortcut menu. The Assign Macro dialog box appears, as shown in Figure 16-21.
3. If you want to assign an existing macro, choose the name from the list and click on the OK button.
4. If you want to record a macro, type the name of the macro in the name box and click on the Record button. Then use the standard macro recording procedures detailed in Chapter 20.

By default, macro buttons in the worksheet do not print because you normally don't want a useless picture of a button in a worksheet printout. If for some reason you want to include the button in the printout, however, right-click on the button and choose Format Object from the shortcut menu. Click on the Properties tab and turn on the Print Object check box.

Summary

In this chapter, you learned about using Excel's graphics capabilities to add pictures and other graphic objects to a worksheet. The following points were covered:

- ◆ You can insert graphics in a worksheet with Insert menu's Picture command.
- ◆ Excel's Drawing toolbar contains a variety of tools that you can use to draw different shapes in a worksheet.
- ◆ You can select multiple objects to manipulate them as a group and to apply formatting, color, or other design choices.
- ◆ You can add text boxes to worksheets by using the Text Box tool on the Drawing toolbar.
- ◆ You can add macro buttons that cause macros to run when you click on the buttons.

In the next chapter, you'll learn how to work with charts in Excel.

Where to go next...

- ◆ For adding visual oomph to your worksheet-based presentations, graphics and charts often go hand in hand. You'll find full details in Chapter 17.
- ◆ If Excel's graphs are not powerful enough for you, you can add graphics from other drawing programs that support OLE. Chapter 33 has the specifics on adding OLE data to a worksheet.

◆ ◆ ◆

CHAPTER 17

Working with Excel Charts

In This Chapter

Explaining charts

Creating embedded charts

Creating chart sheets

Saving and printing charts

Using the available kinds of charts

Adding titles, text, legends, and gridlines

Working with AutoFormats

Changing the data series used by the chart

This chapter details the powerful capabilities that Excel has for displaying and printing charts. In Excel, you can create charts that emphasize numeric trends, support data analysis, and help supply presentation-quality reports. Excel provides you with a rich assortment of formatting features and options for changing and enhancing the appearance of your charts.

What Is a Chart?

Charts graphically represent worksheet data. A collection of values from worksheet cells that you select are illustrated in charts as columns, lines, bars, pie slices, or other types of markers. Figure 17-1 shows some examples of typical charts. The appearance of the markers that are used to represent the data varies, depending on the type of marker that you choose. In a bar or column chart, the markers appear as columns; in a line chart, the markers appear as lines composed of small symbols. The markers in a pie chart appear as wedges of the pie.

Most charts (with the exception of pie charts) have two axes: a horizontal axis called the *category axis* and a vertical axis called the *value axis*. Three-dimensional charts add a third axis (called the *series axis*). Figure 17-2 shows an example of a three-dimensional chart.

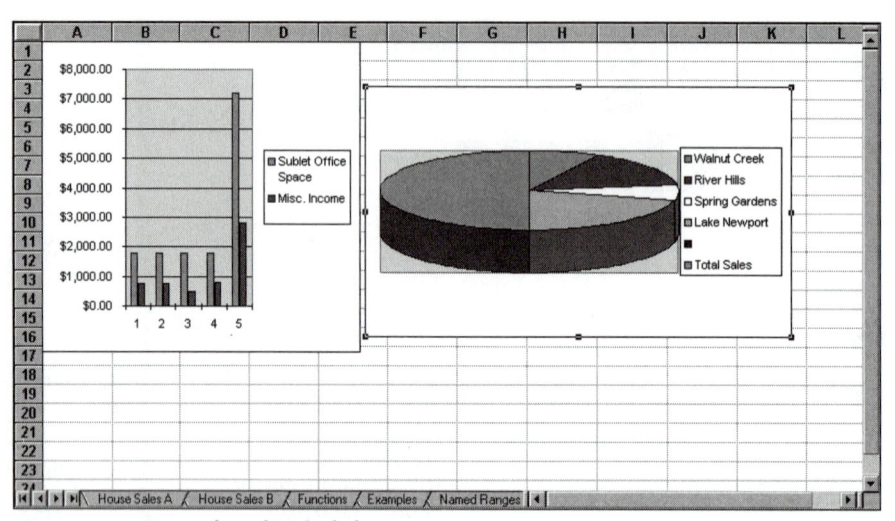

Figure 17-1: Examples of typical charts.

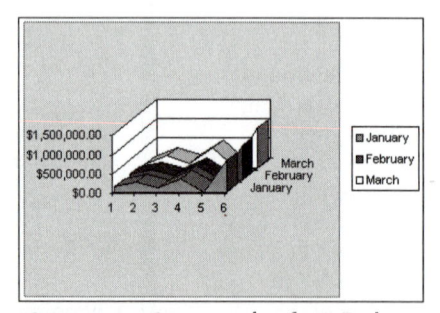

Figure 17-2: An example of a 3-D chart.

Charts also contain gridlines, which provide a frame of reference for the values displayed on the value axis. You can add descriptive text to a chart, such as a title, and you can place the text in different locations. Your charts can also contain legends, which indicate which data is represented by the markers of the chart.

Excel makes adding charts a simple matter by providing a Chart Wizard that automatically appears when you add a new chart to a worksheet. Like all Office wizards, the Chart Wizard produces the desired results by asking a series of questions and producing a desired chart in response to the answers that you provide. During each step of the wizard process, the dialog box displays a sample of the chart so that you can see how your choices in the dialog box will affect the final result.

About Embedded Charts and Chart Sheets

You can add charts to Excel worksheets in one of two ways: as embedded charts or as chart sheets. *Embedded charts* are inserted into an existing worksheet page; hence, the page can show worksheet data with the chart. Figure 17-3 shows an embedded chart.

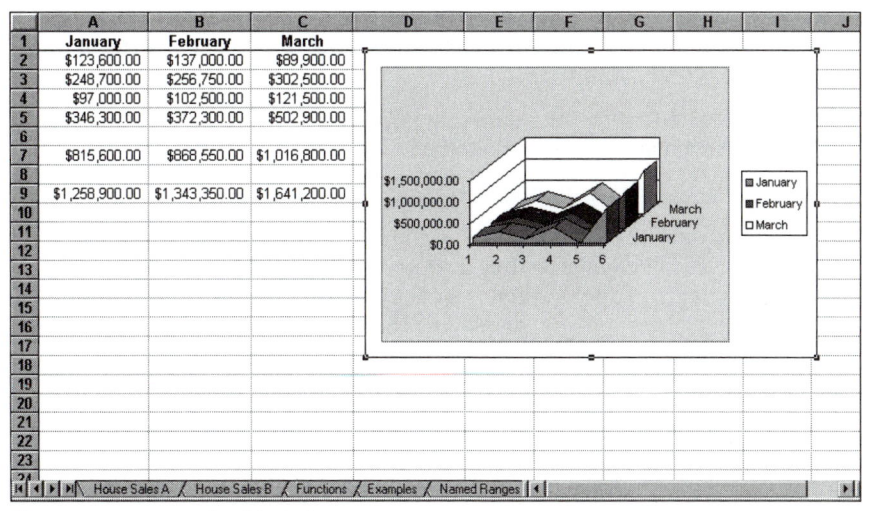

Figure 17-3: An embedded chart.

Chart sheets, on the other hand, are charts that are placed on separate sheets of a workbook, apart from any worksheet data. Figure 17-4 shows a chart added as a chart sheet.

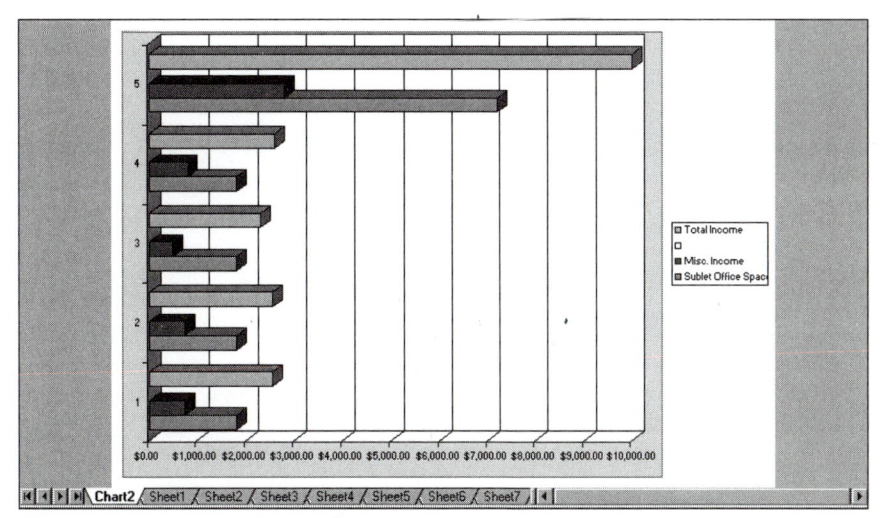

Figure 17-4: An example of a chart sheet.

Embedded charts work best when you need to display or print the chart along with worksheet data; chart sheets work best when all you want to show is the chart. Whether you use embedded charts or chart sheets, the data used to produce the chart is always linked to the worksheet. Therefore, as you change the data in the underlying worksheet, the chart changes to reflect the new data.

Creating an embedded chart

You can add an embedded chart to an existing worksheet page by performing these steps:

1. In the worksheet, select the data that you want to chart. Include any labels that should be used as legends in the chart.

2. Click on the Chart Wizard button on the Standard toolbar.

3. Click on anywhere on the worksheet to have the chart placed and sized to a default size, or click on and drag in the worksheet to place a frame where you want the chart to appear. After you click on the worksheet, the first Chart Wizard dialog box appears, displaying the range of data that you have selected.

4. Click on the Next button and follow the directions in the successive Chart Wizard dialog boxes to specify the type of chart that you want, its format, and the desired options for category labels and for the legend text. (The Chart Wizard dialog boxes are described in detail in a later section of this chapter.)

Alternatively, you can add an embedded chart to a worksheet by selecting the data to chart and choosing Insert⇨Chart⇨On This Sheet. Performing these steps displays the first Chart Wizard dialog box, where you can fill in the desired options to produce the chart.

After you have embedded a chart and then clicked elsewhere in the worksheet, clicking once on the embedded chart won't bring back the chart menus. If you want to use the various chart menu options to make changes, you must double-click on the embedded chart to select it.

Creating a chart sheet

You can create a chart that resides separately on a chart sheet by performing the following steps:

1. In the worksheet, select the data that you want to chart. Include any labels that should be used as legends in the chart.

2. Choose Insert⇨Chart⇨As New Sheet. The first Chart Wizard dialog box appears, displaying the range of data that you have selected.

3. Click on the Next button and follow the directions in the successive Chart Wizard dialog boxes to specify the type of chart that you want, its format, and the desired options for category labels and for the legend text.

With either method of adding a chart, the Chart Wizard displays a series of dialog boxes that help you define precisely how the chart will appear. The first dialog box, shown in Figure 17-5, displays the range of cells that you've selected.

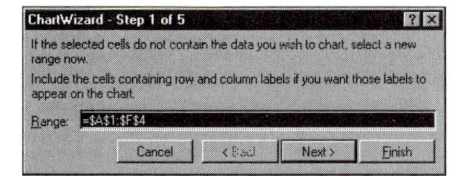

Figure 17-5: The first Chart Wizard dialog box.

You can use this dialog box to define the range of cells within the worksheet that is used as the underlying data for the chart. When you select a range in the worksheet and then start the Chart Wizard, the range automatically appears in the dialog box, as shown in Figure 17-5. If for any reason you want to change the range, you can do so by typing in a different range.

After you enter a range (or accept any default range) and click on the Next button, the dialog box shown in Figure 17-6 appears. In this dialog box, you can select the chart that you want from the 15 available chart types offered by Excel. (For more specifics on the different chart types, see "Working with Chart Types" later in the chapter.) Choose the desired chart type and click on the Next button to move on to the next dialog box.

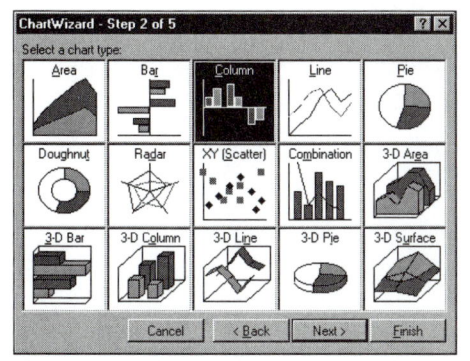

Figure 17-6: The second Chart Wizard dialog box asks for the desired chart type.

The third Chart Wizard dialog box asks you to choose a format for the type of chart that you selected earlier. The contents of this dialog box will vary, depending on which chart type you selected; Figure 17-7 shows the appearance of the dialog box when a column chart is the selected chart type. Choose the desired format for the chart and then click on the Next button.

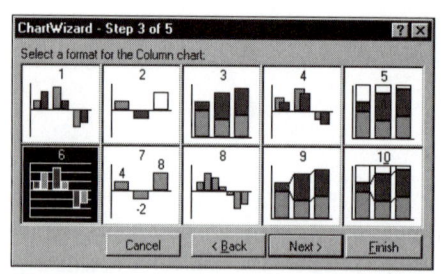

Figure 17-7: The third Chart Wizard dialog box asks for the desired format for your chart selection.

The fourth Chart Wizard dialog box (Figure 17-8) lets you control whether the data series should appear along the rows or along the columns, which rows or columns should be used for the category or x-axis labels, which rows or columns should be used for the value or y-axis labels, and which rows should be used for the text of the legend.

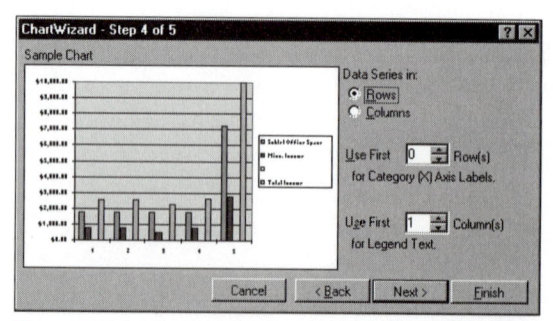

Figure 17-8: The fourth Chart Wizard dialog box.

After you make the desired selections and click on the Next button, the last Chart Wizard dialog box appears, as shown in Figure 17-9. In this dialog box, you can specify whether you want an optional title for the chart, whether a legend should be included, and whether optional titles for the axes should be included. After you specify any desired options, click on the Finish button. The Chart Wizard adds the chart to the worksheet.

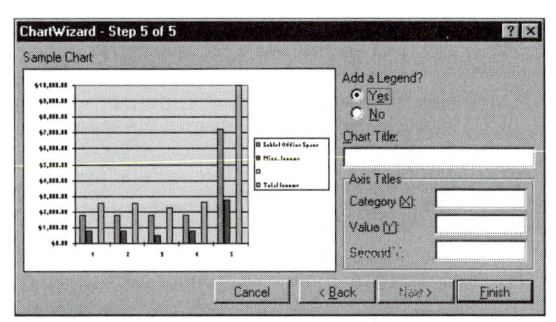

Figure 17-9: The final Chart Wizard dialog box.

After a chart exists and is active, you can run the Chart Wizard on this chart at any time by clicking on the Chart Wizard button on the Chart toolbar. Note, however, that with an existing chart, the Chart Wizard shows only two dialog boxes. The first — identical to the one shown earlier in Figure 17-5 — lets you change the range of worksheet cells used to plot the chart. The second dialog box — identical to the one shown earlier in Figure 17-8 — lets you change the data series and the basis for the labels and the legend of the chart.

Creating a Sample Chart

The examples shown throughout this chapter make use of the `Houses.xls` workbook, which you can find in the Excel directory on the enclosed CD-ROM. You can use the House Totals page to generate the charts shown throughout this chapter, and you can duplicate the examples by opening the House Sales workbook in Excel. Figure 17-10 shows the House Totals page of the `Houses.xls` workbook.

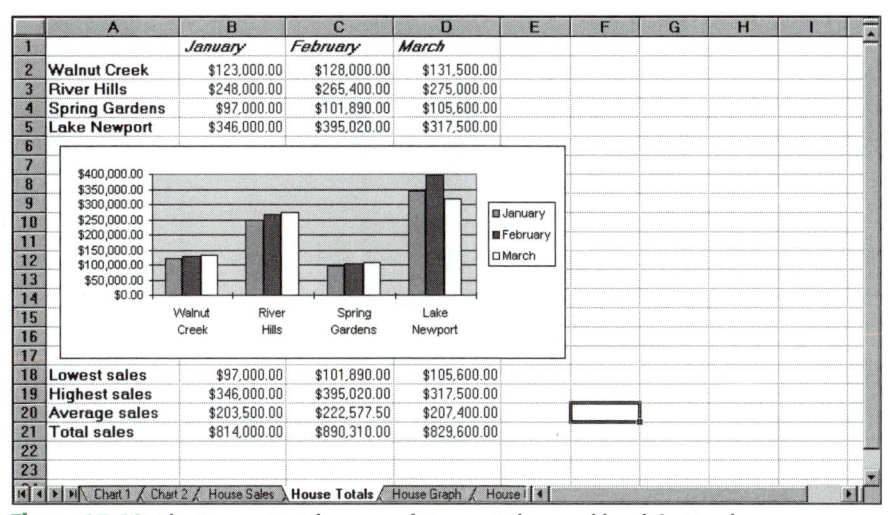

Figure 17-10: The House Totals page of House Sales workbook in Excel.

After you open the workbook and move to the House Totals page, you can perform the following steps to get an idea of how you can easily create charts within Excel:

1. Click in cell A1 and drag to cell E5 to select the range that contains the house sales for all four developments for January, February, March, and April.

2. Choose Insert⇨Chart⇨As New Sheet. (In this case, you'll insert a chart as a separate sheet; you could just as easily have inserted the chart onto the existing worksheet page.) The first Chart Wizard dialog box appears.

3. Because the range matches the cells that you selected in the worksheet, click on the Next button in the dialog box to display the second Chart Wizard dialog box. Choose the Column chart type (if it isn't selected by default) and then click on the Next button.

4. The third Chart Wizard dialog box asks for a desired format for the column chart. Select the first format shown in the dialog box and then click on the Next button.

5. In the fourth dialog box that appears, switch the Data Series option between Rows and Columns and watch the effect of the change in the preview window of the dialog box. With Rows selected, the columns are arranged by months (in four groups, with one group of markers for each month). With Columns selected, the columns are arranged by housing development (in four groups, with one group of markers for each housing development). After you are finished experimenting, choose the Rows option and click on the Next button to proceed.

6. In the last dialog box, enter **House Sales** in the Chart Title text box and then click on the Finish button to create the chart and add it to the workbook. Your sample chart should resemble the one shown in Figure 17-11.

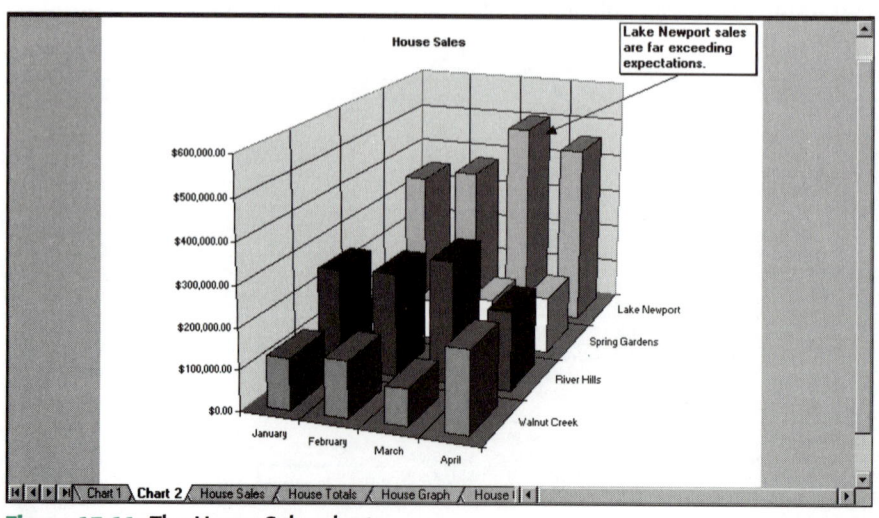

Figure 17-11: The House Sales chart.

Saving and Printing Charts

Because charts are stored with worksheet pages, the tasks of saving and printing charts are no different from saving and printing worksheets. When you save the worksheet by choosing File⇨Save, the chart gets saved along with the worksheet. You can print the chart by activating the page that contains the chart and choosing File⇨Print. The Print dialog box that appears contains the same options that you use for printing worksheets.

Hot Stuff To print pie charts in the proper proportion to fit a single sheet of paper, first choose File⇨Page Setup, and click the Page tab of the dialog box that appears. Then turn on the Fit to One Page Wide by One Tall option.

Understanding the Parts of a Chart

Before you explore the options that Excel offers for creating charts, you should know the parts of a chart and the terminology used to describe these parts. Figure 17-12 shows the parts of a two-dimensional chart.

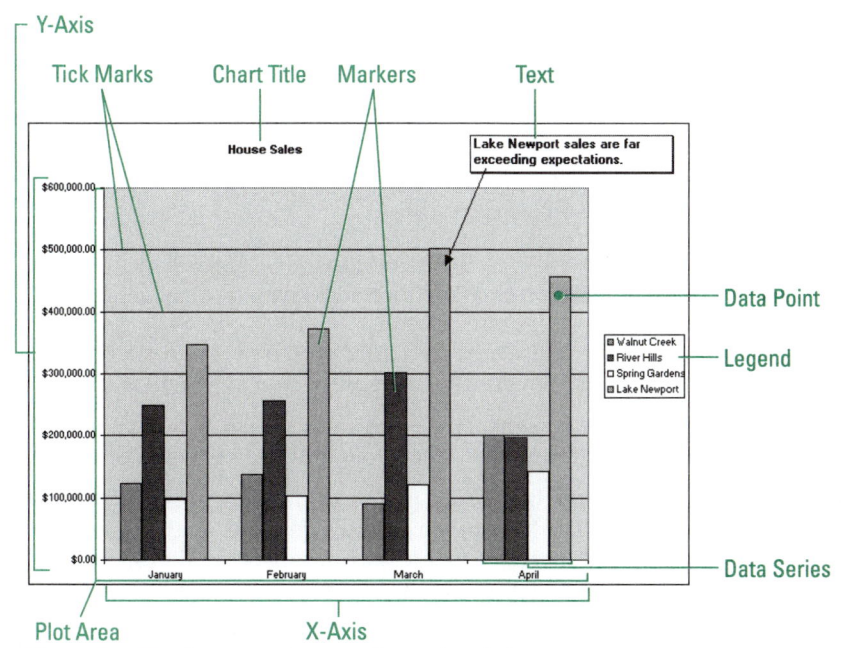

Figure 17-12: The parts of a two-dimensional chart.

Three-dimensional charts have an additional axis that two-dimensional charts do not have. Three-dimensional charts also have a wall, a floor, and corners. The additional parts of a three-dimensional chart are shown in Figure 17-13.

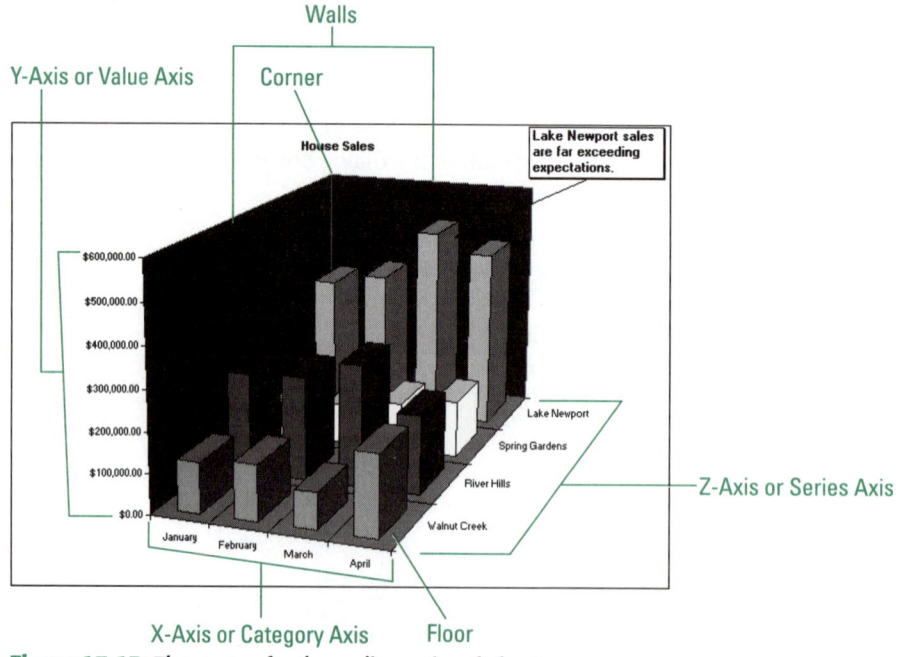

Figure 17-13: The parts of a three-dimensional chart.

The following parts can be found on two- and three-dimensional charts:

- **Chart** — The chart is the entire area contained within the chart sheet (on charts placed in separate sheets) or in the chart frame in an embedded chart.
- **Plot area** — The plot area contains the chart's essential data: the value axis, the category axis, and all the markers that indicate the relative values of your data.
- **Markers** — Markers are the bars, lines, points, or pie wedges that represent the actual data in the chart. The form of the markers depends on the type of chart that you choose. In a pie chart, the markers are wedges, or slices, of the pie. In a line chart, the markers are solid lines, although at some sharp angles, the lines may appear jagged or broken due to the limitations of screen resolution. In a column chart, such as the one shown in Figure 17-11, the markers appear as columns.

Note that each set of markers in the chart represents a set of values within the worksheet. The set of values represented by the markers is referred to as a *data series*. If a chart displays data from more than one data series, each data series will be represented by a different pattern or symbol. In Figure 17-11, for example, the January data is one data series, and the February data is another. Data series are further differentiated by the patterns of shadings of the columns.

If you selected a range in the worksheet that contains just one row or column of data, the resulting chart contains just one data series. In a chart with a single data series, by default Excel takes any label in the extreme left column or top row of the selected range and automatically suggests that name as a title for the chart.

✦ **Chart title** — The title is a text label that Excel places as a title within the chart.

✦ **Axis** — An axis is the horizontal or vertical frame of reference that appears in all types of charts except pie charts. In two-dimensional charts, the horizontal x-axis is called the category axis because categories of data are normally plotted along this line. The vertical y-axis is called the value axis because values are normally shown along this line. With three-dimensional charts, a series axis is added to show multiple data series within the chart.

✦ **Tick marks** — Tick marks are reference marks that separate the scales of the value axis and the categories of the category axis.

✦ **Text** — Excel lets you create text labels as titles and as data labels (associated with data points). You can have *unattached,* or free-floating text, that you can place anywhere in the chart.

✦ **Data series** — A data series is a collection of data points, such as one month's sales for a housing development.

✦ **Data point** — A data point is a single piece of information inside any data series. In the example shown earlier in Figure 17-11, one month's sales for a specific housing development is a single data point.

✦ **Series name** — You can assign a series name to each series of data contained within a chart. Excel automatically assigns default series names based on headings entered within your worksheets.

✦ **Gridlines** — Gridlines are reference lines that extend the tick marks across the entire area of the graph.

✦ **Legends** — A legend defines the patterns or shadings that are used by the chart markers. A legend consists of a sample of the pattern followed by the series name (or the category name, if the chart displays only one data series). If you include labels as series names in the top row or the left column of the selected worksheet range, Excel can use these names in the legend.

✦ **Arrows** — These are lines with arrowheads that can be moved and sized as desired.

> ### Charts and older Excel files
>
> If you open a chart that was originally created in Excel 4.0 or Excel 3.0, the chart appears on a chart sheet in its own workbook. When you save the workbook, Excel warns you that the file is in a file format from an older version of Excel. Excel then asks whether you want to save to the old format or to the current format. If you save to the old format, remember that some formatting options not supported in earlier Excel versions (such as the doughnut chart type) can't be saved.

Working with Charts

Before you can make changes to a chart, the chart must be active. When a chart is active, certain menus (such as the Insert and Format menus) change to reflect options that apply to charts. For example, when a chart is active, you can choose Insert⇨Gridlines to add gridlines to your chart. To activate an embedded chart, double-click on the chart on the worksheet. The chart's border changes from a thin line to a thick border, and Excel's menu options change to reflect the available chart options. After you have selected an embedded chart, you can move it or size it by using the usual Windows techniques for moving and sizing objects, and you can delete the chart by pressing the Delete key. To activate charts that are on chart sheets, just select the worksheet tab for the desired sheet.

Selecting parts of a chart

Before applying menu selections to the parts of a chart, you must first select the desired part. For example, if you want to change the way that text in a legend is displayed, you first must select the legend. You can then right-click on the legend and choose Format Legend from the shortcut menu. In the Format Legend dialog box, you can change options for formatting the legend.

You can select objects with the mouse by clicking on them. You can also use the arrow keys to select objects within a chart. The left-arrow and right-arrow keys first move you among items in the same class of objects (such as markers) and then from class to class (such as from the markers to the legend to the axis and so on). When you select an object, it is marked with squares. While the object is selected, the name of the object also appears on the left side of the formula bar. Figure 17-14 shows a set of markers selected in a chart — note that the marker name appears in the formula bar.

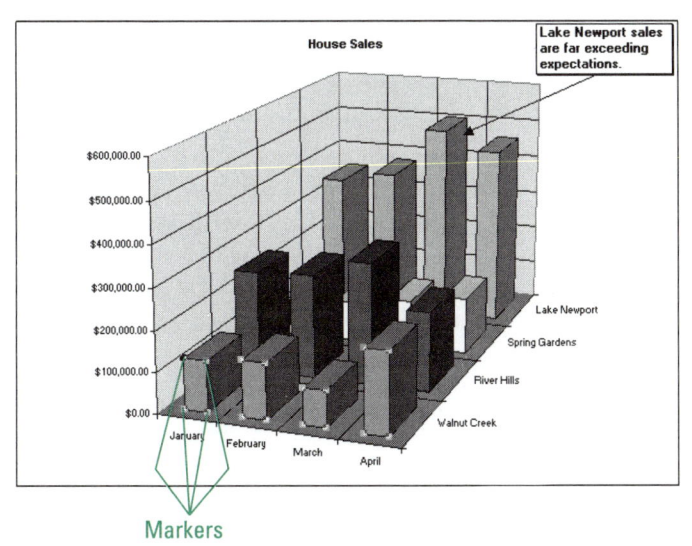

Figure 17-14: A set of markers selected in a chart.

> You can also modify the display properties for objects in charts by double-clicking on the object. When you double-click on an object in a chart, a dialog box for that object opens where you can change settings appropriate to the object.

Working with the Chart toolbar

You can make use of the Chart toolbar to add new charts or to change existing charts. Figure 17-15 shows the Chart toolbar. If the Chart toolbar is not visible, you can bring it into view by choosing View➪Toolbars and turning on the Chart option in the dialog box that appears. Table 17-1 describes this toolbar's buttons.

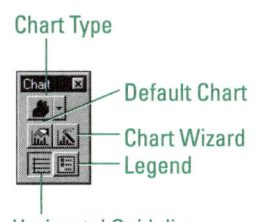

Figure 17-15: The Chart toolbar.

Table 17-1
Chart toolbar buttons

Button	Function
Chart Type	Selects a chart type for the chart.
Default Chart	Changes the chart back to the default chart type (a column chart, unless you've changed this setting).
Chart Wizard	Runs the Chart Wizard, which lets you edit an existing chart or to create a new one.
Horizontal Gridlines	Turns the gridlines on or off.
Legend	Adds or removes the legend from the chart.

Adding titles

Text boxes containing titles are typically used with charts to help describe the purpose of the chart or to clarify the purpose of the various chart axes. You can add titles to a chart by performing the following steps:

1. Activate the chart.

2. Choose Insert⇨Titles or right-click on the chart and choose Insert Titles from the shortcut menu. The Titles dialog box appears, as shown in Figure 17-16.

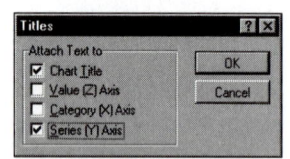

Figure 17-16: The Titles dialog box.

3. In the dialog box, click on each title type that you want to add and then click on the OK button. Excel inserts text boxes for each title that you selected.

4. Click on any text box to select it, click inside the text box, and type the desired text for the title. The text box grows to accommodate the text that you add. And you can format the text by using the steps under "Formatting text" later in the chapter.

Adding unattached text

At times, you may want to add text that is not attached to a title or to a specific axis. Such text is referred to as *unattached text*. You can add unattached text to a chart by displaying the Drawing toolbar, clicking on the Text Box button, and then clicking and dragging in the worksheet to place a text box of the desired size. When you release the mouse, an insertion point appears in the text box, and you can then type the desired text.

Formatting text

With all the text that you can have in text boxes, you may want to change the formatting properties — the fonts and styles used — to something other than the default text formats. You can format the text in your charts by performing the following steps:

1. Right-click on the text that you want to format and choose Format Chart Title (for titles), Format Legend (for legends), or Format Object (for unattached text) from the shortcut menu.

2. In the dialog box that appears, click on the Font tab to reveal the options shown in Figure 17-17.

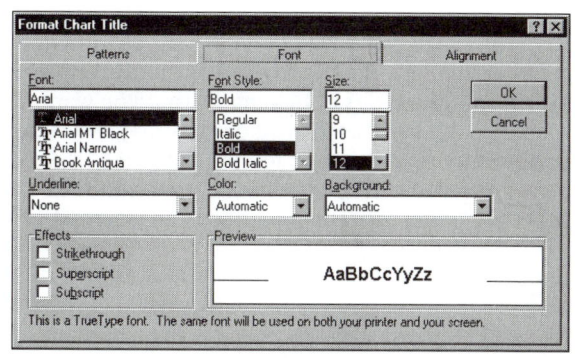

Figure 17-17: The Font tab of the Format Chart Title dialog box.

Choose the desired font, font style, and font size by selecting the options in the dialog box. You can also choose underlining, color, and background, and you can select special effects, such as strikethrough, superscript, and subscript. When you are finished selecting the desired options, click on the OK button to place them into effect.

Formatting chart axes

Excel lets you enhance the appearance of the various axes that you use in your charts. You can change the font, and you can modify the scale. You change the format of any chart axis by right-clicking on the axis that you want to format and choosing Format Axis from the shortcut menu. The Format Axis dialog box appears, as shown in Figure 17-18.

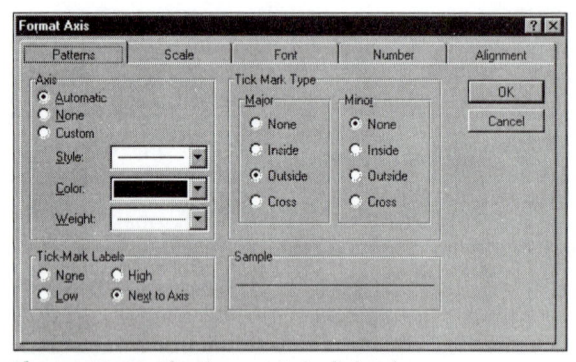

Figure 17-18: The Format Axis dialog box.

The dialog box contains five tabs, which you can use to change various formatting aspects of the axis. Use the options in the Patterns tab to change the patterns that you use for the axis, the tick mark labels, and the types of tick marks that you want. The Scale tab options enable you to change the values that you use to create the axis scale. The Font tab contains the options that you use to modify the font of the axis. The Number tab contains list boxes that you can use to choose the desired formatting for numbers along an axis, and the Alignment tab lets you choose an orientation for the text.

Adding legends

If a chart does not have a legend by default, you can add one at any time by selecting the chart and then choosing Insert⇔Legend. After you add a legend to the chart, you can change its appearance by double-clicking on the legend or by right-clicking on it and choosing Format Legend from the shortcut menu. Either method brings up the Format Legend dialog box, which contains tabs for Patterns, Font, and Placement of the legend. Use the options on the Patterns tab to change the patterns used by the legend to identify the markers in the chart. The Font tab contains the options you use to modify the fonts used by the legend. The Placement tab contains options that specify where in the chart the legend should appear (top, bottom, left, right, center, or corner). Remember that because the legend is just another object in a chart, you can also move the legend by clicking and dragging it to any desired location within the chart.

Adding gridlines

To add gridlines to an existing chart, select the chart to make it active and choose the Gridlines command from the Insert menu. The Gridlines dialog box appears. In this dialog box, you can choose between major or minor gridlines along either the category axis or the value axis. Major gridlines are heavier lines, widely spaced. Minor gridlines are fine lines, closely spaced. After you make the desired options and click on the OK button, the gridlines appear within the selected chart.

Hot Stuff If you want only major gridlines along the value axis, you can click on the Horizontal Gridlines button on the Chart toolbar to add them.

Customizing a chart's area

You can add a lot in terms of visual pizzazz to a chart by customizing the default settings for the chart's area. You can change the background colors, the borders, and the fonts used throughout the chart. After the chart is active, click in any blank area of the chart to make handles appear around the entire chart. Then from the Format menu, choose Selected Chart Area or right-click in any blank area of the chart and choose Format Chart Area from the shortcut menu. The Format Chart Area dialog box appears, as shown in Figure 17-19. The dialog box has two tabs from which you can choose all sorts of options.

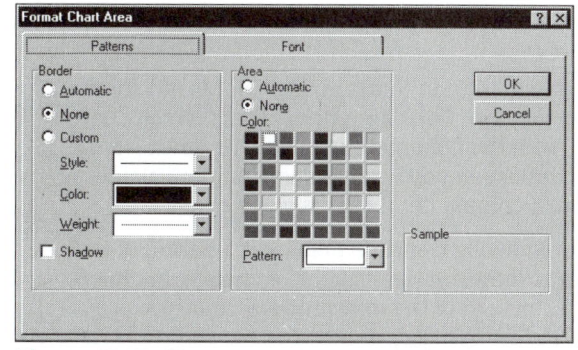

Figure 17-19: The Format Chart Area dialog box.

In the Patterns tab of the Format Chart Area dialog box, you can click on the Custom button to choose your own style, color, and weight for the border. Turning on the Shadow option adds a shadow to the border. In the Area section of the Patterns tab, you can choose a background color. Selecting Automatic sets the color to the Windows default (white, unless you changed it in the Windows Control Panel). Selecting None establishes no background color. In addition to the Automatic and None options, you can click on one of the Color boxes to set a desired color. And you can use the Pattern list box to choose a desired pattern.

On the Font tab, you will find various options that you can use to set the fonts used in the entire chart. Choose the desired font, font style, and font size by selecting the options displayed under the tab. You can also select underlining, color, and background, and you can select special effects, such as strikethrough, superscript, and subscript.

After you finish selecting the desired options, click on the OK button so that the chart takes on the chosen effects.

Working with Chart Types

Excel offers several different chart types. Each of these chart types has subtypes that you can also select when you are choosing the type of chart that you want to create. The following list describes the types of charts, and how they can best be used.

✦ **Area charts** show the significance of change during a given time period. The top line of the chart totals the individual series, so area charts make it visually apparent how each individual series contributes to the overall picture. Area charts emphasize the magnitude of change as opposed to the rate of change. (If you want to emphasize the rate of change, use line charts instead.)

✦ **Bar charts** use horizontal bars to show distinct figures at a specified time. Each horizontal bar in the chart shows a specific amount of change from the base value used in the chart. Bar charts visually emphasize different values, arranged vertically.

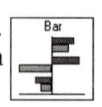

✦ **Column charts** are very much like bar charts, using columns to show distinct figures over a time period. The difference is that column charts are oriented *horizontally*, with the columns running up or down from a base value used in the chart. When you want to show numeric values across a passage of time in the chart, column charts usually work well.

✦ **Line charts** are perfect for showing trends in data over a period of time. Like area charts, line charts show the significance of change, but line charts emphasize the rate, instead of the magnitude of change.

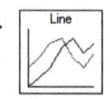

✦ **Pie charts** show relationships between the pieces of a picture. They also can be used to show a relationship between a piece of the picture and the entire picture. A pie chart can be used to display only one series of data at a time, because each piece of a pie chart represents part of a total series. If you have a large number of series to plot, however, you are probably better off with a column chart, because a pie crowded with slices is hard to interpret.

✦ **Doughnut charts** show relationships between pieces of a picture, as are pie charts. The difference is that the doughnut chart has a hollow center.

- **Radar charts** show the changes or frequencies of a data series in relation to a central point and to each other. (Every category has an axis value that radiates from a center point. Lines connect all data in the same series.) Radar charts can be difficult to interpret, unless you're accustomed to working with them.

- **Scatter charts** show relationships between different points of data, to compare trends across uneven time periods, or to show patterns as a set of *x* and *y* coordinates. These charts are commonly used to plot scientific data.

An important decision for you to make is which type of chart will work best to get the desired point across. Excel offers 14 different chart types. All 8 of the types listed above are two-dimensional, and 6 of the eight types listed above are three-dimensional. When you create a chart by using the Chart Wizard, Excel asks you which chart type you want to use.

You also may want to change the chart type of an existing chart. You can do so with Format⇨Chart Type. Follow these steps when you want to change the type of an existing chart:

1. If the chart is on a chart sheet, click on the sheet's tab to make the chart active. If the chart is embedded in a worksheet, double-click on the chart to make it active.

2. Choose Format⇨Chart Type. (Alternatively, you can right-click in an empty space on the chart and choose Chart Type from the shortcut menu.) The Chart Type dialog box appears, as shown in Figure 17-20.

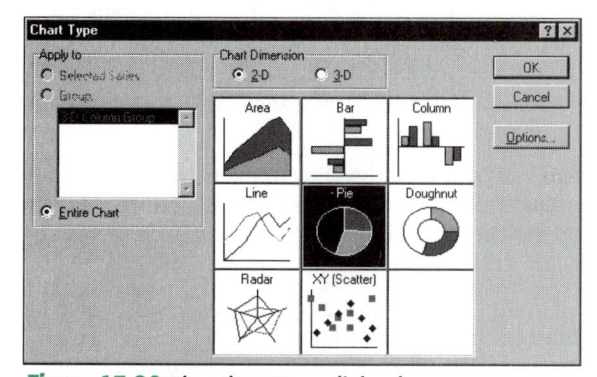

Figure 17-20: The Chart Type dialog box.

3. Choose either 2-D or 3-D as the overall type of chart and then click on the desired type of chart in the dialog box to select it.

4. If you want to change the default subtype for the chosen chart type, click on the Options button and then click on the Subtype tab in the dialog box that appears. Choose a desired subtype and then click on the OK button.

The exact appearance of the Subtype tab will vary, depending on which type you select. Figure 17-21 shows the Subtype tab that appears when you choose a 2-D column chart.

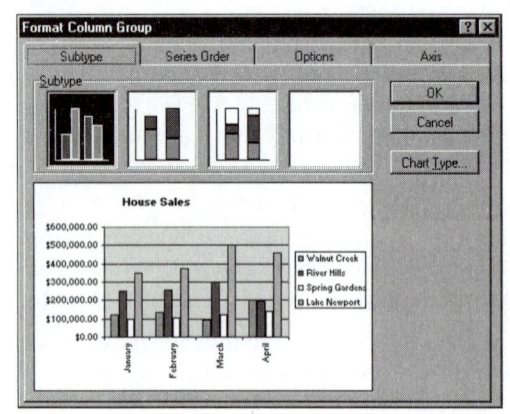

Figure 17-21: The Subtype tab for a 2-D column chart.

In the Chart Type dialog box shown in Figure 17-20, note the presence of the Apply to options in the upper-left corner of the dialog box. By default, the Entire Chart option is selected, meaning that the chart type applies to the entire chart. If you select a single data series before using the Chart Type command, you will have the option of applying the chart type to the selected data series as opposed to the entire chart. You can use the Group option and corresponding Group list box to apply the chart type to a group of data series.

You can create combination charts of your own devising in Excel by applying different chart types to different data series. You can also use the Chart Wizard to select a Combination chart type, but you gain more flexibility by selecting each series and applying the types individually.

If you need to change the type of chart but not the chart subtype, you can also use the Chart toolbar. To display the Chart toolbar, choose View➪Toolbars and turn on the Chart check box. Select the chart and then click on the Chart Type arrow button to drop down a list of chart types. Select a chart type from the list. If you select an individual data series before using the Chart Type list box in the Chart toolbar, your selection gets applied to the individual data series.

> **Changing the default chart format**
>
> If you create the same kind of chart over and over (and it is a type other than the default type), you should change the default chart type from the 2-D column chart, probably the most commonly used type of chart in business applications. To change the default chart type, first select any existing chart that already uses your desired chart type. Then choose Tools⇨Options and click on the Chart tab in the Options dialog box. In the Default Chart Format area, click on the Use the Current Chart button, enter a name for your chart format in the dialog box that appears, and click on the OK button.

Working with AutoFormat

By now, it should be obvious that Excel offers a great deal of flexibility in how you can format the individual parts of your charts. Often, however, doing a lot of design work with the individual aspects of a chart can be very time-consuming. Instead of selecting and formatting individual items one at a time, you can apply an AutoFormat to a chart. If you've worked with templates or styles in Word for Windows, think of AutoFormats as providing the same concepts to charts. You can apply an AutoFormat to any chart that is active, and the AutoFormat will change the appearance of the chart without changing the underlying data in any way. You can apply an AutoFormat to a chart by performing the following steps:

1. Make the desired chart active (click on its tab if it is in a chart sheet, or double-click on the chart if it is an embedded chart).

2. Choose Format⇨AutoFormat. The AutoFormat dialog box appears, as shown in Figure 17-22.

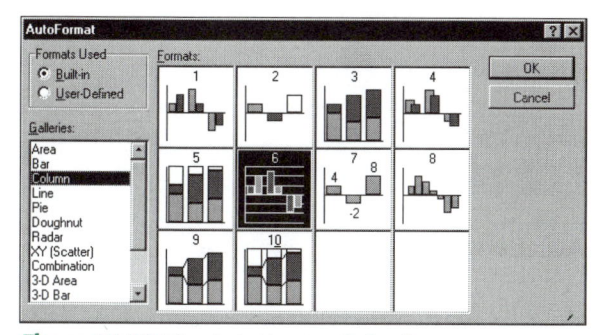

Figure 17-22: The AutoFormat dialog box.

3. In the Galleries list box, choose a chart type. After you choose a type, Excel displays the different available formats for that type of chart.

4. Choose the format that you want from the Formats box.

5. Click on the OK button in the dialog box. Excel automatically reformats the existing chart to match the appearance of the AutoFormat options that you chose.

Understanding How Excel Plots a Chart

When you select a group of cells and create a new chart, Excel follows specific steps to plot the chart. It first organizes the values contained within the selected range into a data series, based on the responses that you gave in the Chart Wizard dialog boxes. It then plots the data series in the chart.

As an example, consider the chart shown in Figure 17-23. In this chart, the light markers are based on one series of data, the sales for January. The dark markers are based on another series of data, the sales for February. In the same chart, dollar amounts are plotted along the value axis, and subdivision names are plotted along the category axis. The chart values appear as dollars because the worksheet values are formatted in dollars. Excel obtains the category axis labels from cells A2 through A5 of the worksheet shown earlier in Figure 17-10, which contains the names of the subdivisions.

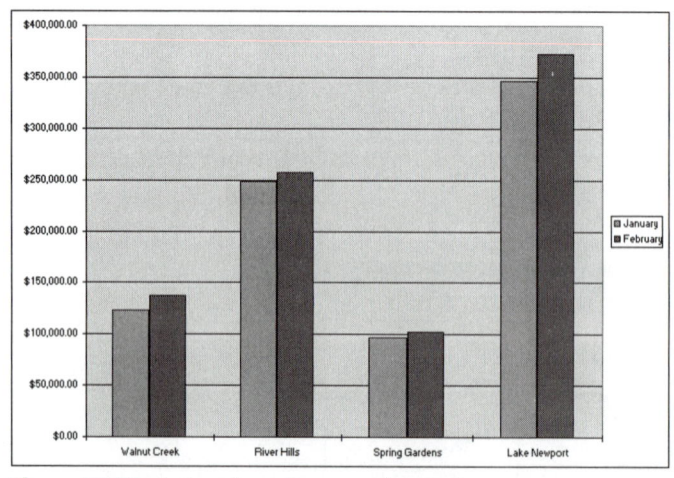

Figure 17-23: A chart based on two data series.

At this point, the column chart that you created earlier (similar to the one shown in Figure 17-11) may still be open on your screen. If it isn't, plot the chart again by selecting cells A1 through D5 in the House Sales worksheet. Then choose Insert⇨Chart and choose As New Sheet from the submenu. Click on the Finish button in the first Chart Wizard dialog box to accept the default options.

The exact points that Excel uses to graph the data are contained in a *series formula* that Excel builds for you. A series formula is similar to other formulas in that it can be edited from within the formula bar. To see the formula, you must first select the chart marker by clicking on the desired group of markers or by pressing the left- or right-arrow key repeatedly until the desired group of markers is selected. When you select a group of markers, Excel places small rectangles inside them.

As an exercise, you can select the markers representing the Lake Newport home sales by clicking on any of the markers for Lake Newport. When the markers are selected, the series formula appears in the formula bar, as shown in Figure 17-24.

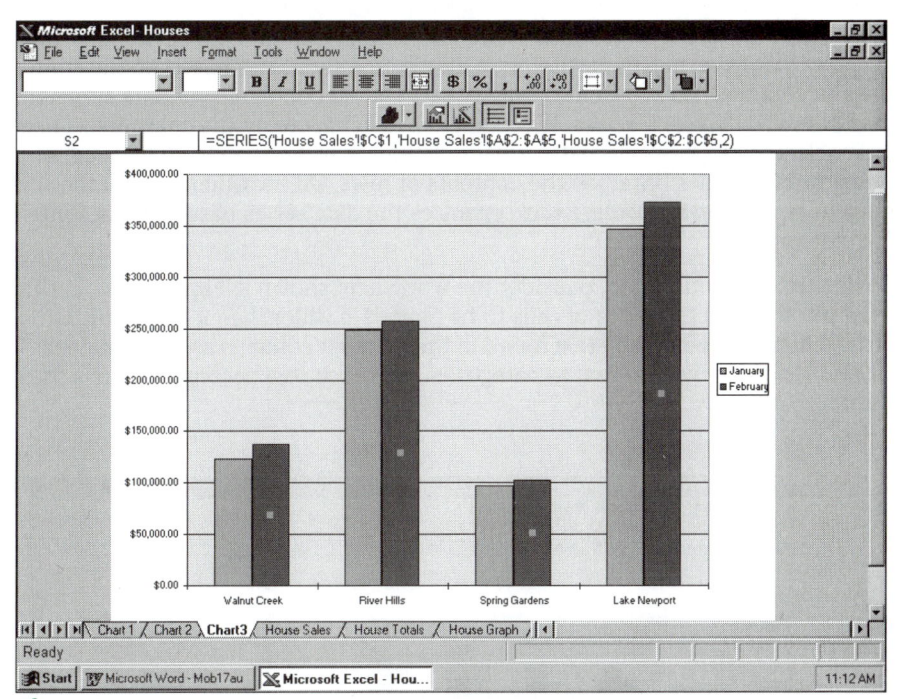

Figure 17-24: The series formula for Lake Newport sales.

Excel uses a special function called the *series function* to build the data series for each set of markers in the chart. If you click on the second set of markers in the chart, the series formula in the formula bar changes to reflect the points that Excel uses for the second data series.

Hot Stuff Excel can use named ranges from a worksheet rather than absolute cell references so that you can make use of named ranges in your worksheets. If you create a chart that uses absolute references and you later insert rows or columns in the worksheet so that the data referred to by the chart is no longer in the same location, the chart will be unable to plot the data. The result will be a chart with zero values, or even worse, a chart with incorrect data. If you use named ranges in the series formula for the chart, Excel can find the data, even if you insert rows or columns in the worksheet.

It is important to understand how Excel builds a chart automatically because, in some cases, Excel's assumptions may not be what you want, and you can make changes to adjust for those assumptions. For example, when you tell Excel to create a chart and you accept the default entries regarding the data series in the Chart Wizard dialog boxes, Excel plots the data based on certain default assumptions. One significant decision that Excel makes is whether a data series should be based on the contents of rows or columns. Excel assumes that a chart should contain fewer data series than data points within each series. When you tell Excel to create the chart, Excel examines your selected range of cells. If the selected range is wider than it is tall, Excel organizes the data series based on the contents of rows. On the other hand, if the selected range is taller than it is wide, Excel organizes the data series based on the contents of the columns.

To illustrate this operation, consider the worksheet shown in Figure 17-25. In this example, the selected range of cells to be plotted is wider than it is tall. With this type of selection, Excel uses any text found in the leftmost columns as series names. Text labels in the top row are used as categories, and each row becomes a data series in the chart.

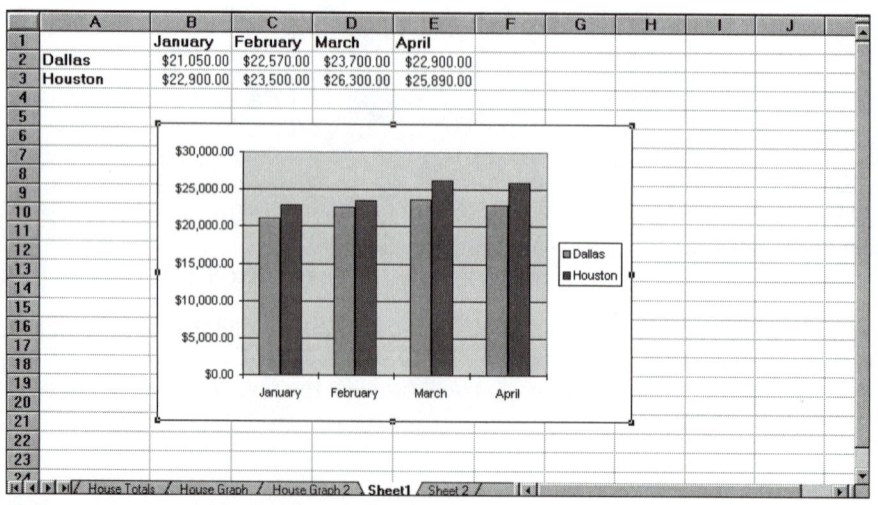

Figure 17-25: A chart oriented by rows.

If the data to be plotted is square (the number of rows is equal to the number of columns) and you accept the default options in the data series dialog box of the Chart Wizard (the fourth dialog box), Excel handles the orientation of the chart in the same manner. On the other hand, if the selected range is taller than it is wide and you accept the default Chart Wizard options, Excel orients the chart differently. In such cases, the text in the top row is used as the series names, text entries appearing in the left columns are used as categories, and each column becomes a data series. This type of worksheet, and the chart resulting from it, are shown in Figure 17-26.

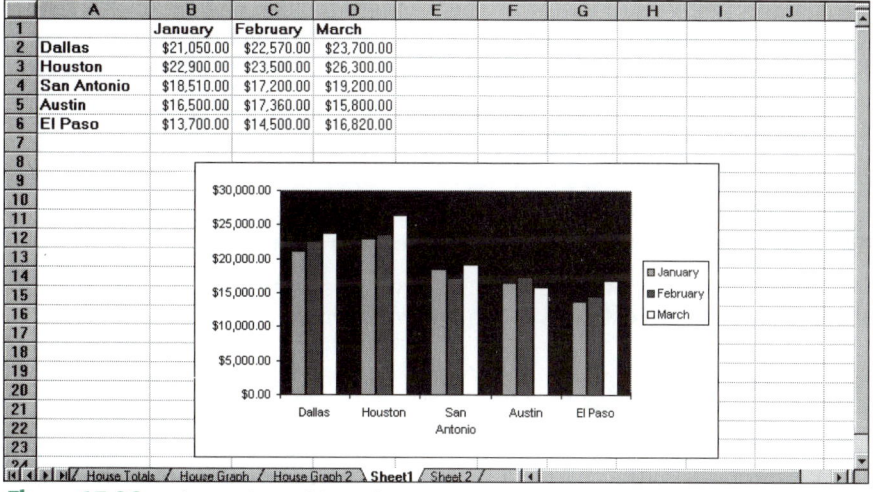

Figure 17-26: A chart oriented by columns.

You can change the method that Excel uses to plot the data series by changing the selection in the data series dialog box of the Chart Wizard (the fourth dialog box). With an existing chart, make the chart active (if it's an embedded chart, you can double-click on it; with a chart that's on a sheet, make that sheet the active worksheet). Then click on the Chart Wizard button on the Chart toolbar to bring up the Chart Wizard dialog box. After you click on the Next button to bypass the Range dialog box, you can then change the data series used by Excel in the data series dialog box that appears.

Summary

In this chapter, you learned how to create charts, how to change the appearance and the basis for the charts, and how to add such items as titles, legends, and text to your charts. The following points were covered:

- ✦ You can add a chart as an embedded chart (included in an existing worksheet page) or as a chart sheet (included on its own worksheet page).
- ✦ You can easily add charts to a worksheet by selecting the range of data, clicking on the Chart Wizard button on the Standard toolbar, and clicking and dragging in the worksheet where the chart should appear. You then follow the instructions in the wizard dialog boxes.
- ✦ You can modify most aspects of a chart by right-clicking on a specific area or object in the chart and the appropriate Format command from the shortcut menu that appears.
- ✦ When a chart is active, you can use the AutoFormat command from the Format menu to apply any one of a variety of formats to the chart.

In the next chapter, you will learn about the various printing options in Excel, which provide you with different ways to produce your work.

Where to go next...

- ✦ Many times you'll find yourself creating your chart in Excel — and then later find you need to use the chart in a Word document. You can do this with Object Linking and Embedding (OLE). See Chapter 33 for the story.
- ✦ Often times you may need to embellish your charts by adding graphics, such as clip art or callouts. For tips on working with graphics, see Chapter 16.

✦ ✦ ✦

CHAPTER 18

Printing with Excel

In This Chapter

Understanding the basic ways to print a worksheet

Working with the Page Setup dialog box options

Choosing which pages to print from a document

Previewing print jobs

Controlling the various aspects of printing

Changing printer properties

Sending a file on a network

With Excel, you can print in several ways with typeset-quality results from most laser printers. You have full control over different aspects of printing that affect the appearance of a worksheet, such as margins, page orientation, horizontal and vertical alignment, and the use of headers and footers. You can also do much more than just print pages from a single workbook. You have the flexibility to print entire workbooks, sheets from a workbook, or a section of a sheet. These options are accessed via the Print button on the Standard toolbar or by choosing File⇨Print. And if you've used Excel under previous versions of Windows, you will also find that printing is considerably faster with Excel 95. (This speed is due more to the improved Windows 95 Print Manager than to Excel itself.)

The Basics of Printing

Because Excel makes a number of assumptions about how you want information printed when you choose File⇨Print or when you click on the Print button on the Standard toolbar, you can perform basic printing with just a few steps. These steps are as follows (you'll learn about each step as you work through this chapter):

1. Select the area that you want to print.
2. Choose File⇨Print to open the Print dialog box, as shown in Figure 18-1.
3. Use the options in the dialog box to decide what you want to print (the current selection, selected sheets, or the entire workbook), a range of pages (the default is All), and the number of copies.
4. Click on the OK button to begin the printing process.

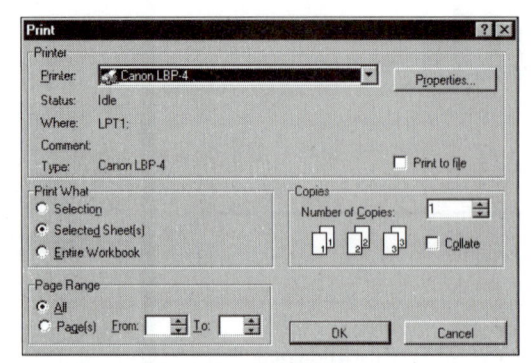

Figure 18-1: The Print dialog box.

If you are sure that you can live with the default options that normally appear in the Print dialog box, you can make the process of printing even faster. Just select the tab of the worksheet that you want printed and click on the Print button on the Standard toolbar.

Hot Stuff If you have multiple sheets that you want to print one after the other in a workbook by clicking on the Print button only once, you can easily do so. Click on the tab of the first worksheet that you want to print and then hold down the Ctrl key while you click on each additional worksheet tab that you want to print. When you have selected all the desired tabs, click on the Print button on the Standard toolbar.

About the Print dialog box

After you choose File⇨Print, the Print dialog box, which provides a number of useful options, appears. In the Printer list box, you can choose any printer that you have installed under Windows. In the Print What area, you can choose Selection to print a selected area of a worksheet, Selected Sheet(s) to print all the selected worksheets in a workbook, or Entire Workbook to print all the data stored in all pages of the workbook.

In the Page Range area of the dialog box, the All option (the default) prints all pages. If you select the Page(s) option instead, enter a range of pages in the from and to boxes. This option works well when you know precisely which pages you want to print. For example, if you know that a worksheet produces a 12-page print run in its entirety, and you know that you need only pages 4 through 8 of that print run, you can turn on the Page(s) option and enter **4** in the from box and **8** in the to box.

In the Copies area, you can enter the number of copies that you want, and you can turn on the Collate option if you want the multiple copies to print in collated order.

About the Page Setup dialog box

You can use Excel's Page Setup dialog box to change a variety of settings that will affect your printing of worksheets. After you choose File➪Page Setup, the Page Setup dialog box appears, as shown in Figure 18-2. This dialog box contains four tabs that affect four different areas of Excel printing: Page, Margins, Header/Footer, and Sheet. In addition to the tabs, the dialog box contains Print and Print Preview buttons. After making the desired changes to the settings, you can click on the Print button to begin printing, or you can click on the Print Preview button to see the worksheet in Print Preview mode.

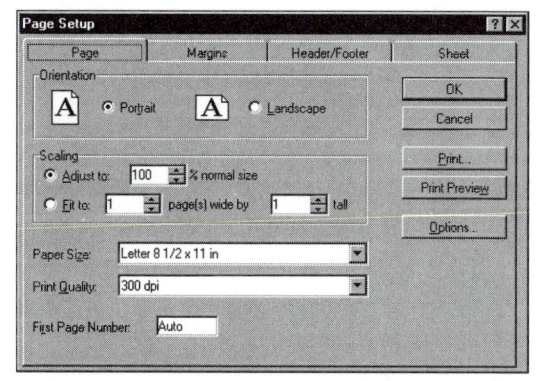

Figure 18-2: The Page tab of the Page Setup dialog box.

The Page tab options

You can use the Page tab's options to control print-related settings that affect all the pages of a print job, such as page orientation and paper size. The Page tab options include:

✦ **Orientation** — In the Orientation area, choose whether to print in *portrait* (default) or *landscape* orientation. Think of a photograph: a portrait is taller than it is wide, while a picture of a beautiful mountain scene is wider than it is tall. So it goes with printing: portrait orientation prints lengthwise (like the pages of this book), while landscape orientation prints "sideways" on the paper.

✦ **Scaling** — Use the options in the Scaling area to reduce or enlarge your worksheets. These options are useful for making a worksheet that is slightly too big for a page fit on a single page. You can choose a percentage in the Adjust To list box, or you can use the Fit To option to fit the printed worksheet to a specific number of pages wide by a specific number of pages tall by entering the dimensions in the boxes to the right of the option.

- **Paper Size** — Use the Paper Size option to set the paper size. By default, the paper size is Letter (8.5x11 inches).
- **Print Quality** — Use the Print Quality option to set the level of print quality. The higher the setting, the nicer the appearance; however, in many cases, your printer takes longer to print documents at higher settings.
- **First Page Number** — Use the First Page Number setting to start printing at a page other than page 1. The Auto default assumes that you want to start at page 1, but you can replace this entry by typing any number that you want into the box.

The Margins tab options

When you click on the Margins tab of the Page Setup dialog box, you see the options shown in Figure 18-3. You can use the Margins tab's options to control the settings that affect each page's margins, such as the size of the margins and whether printing is centered horizontally or vertically between margins.

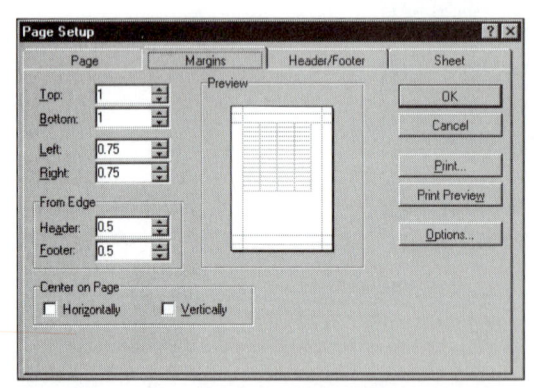

Figure 18-3: The Margins tab of the Page Setup dialog box.

The Margins tab options include the following:

- **Top, Bottom, Left, and Right** — Use the Top, Bottom, Left, and Right options to specify a distance from the edge of the paper for the margins. Note that many laser printers will not print closer than 0.5 inch from the edge of the paper.
- **From Edge** — Use the settings in the From Edge area to indicate how far headers or footers should print from the top or bottom edges.
- **Center on Page** — The Center on Page options determine whether printing should be centered horizontally (between the left and right margins) and vertically (between the top and bottom margins) on the page.

The Header/Footer tab options

If you click on the Header/Footer tab of the Page Setup dialog box, you see the options shown in Figure 18-4. You can use the Header/Footer tab's options to control the appearance and placement of headers and footers printed with your worksheet pages.

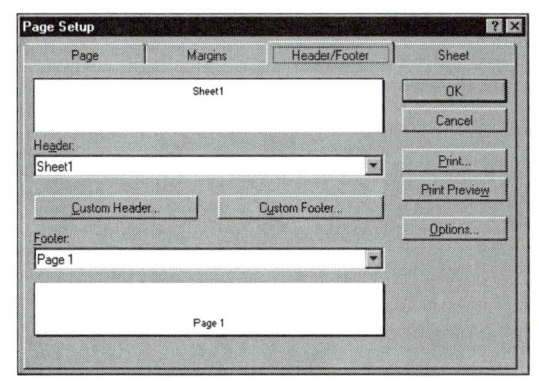

Figure 18-4: The Header/Footer tab of the Page Setup dialog box.

The Header/Footer tab options include the following:

- **Header and Footer** — Use the Header and Footer text boxes to specify a header (for example, a title that appears at the top of every page) or a footer (for example, a page number or the current date that appears at the bottom of every page).

- **Custom Header and Custom Footer** — Use the Custom Header and Custom Footer buttons to open dialog boxes that enable you to design a customized header or footer.

The Sheet tab options

If you click on the Sheet tab of the Page Setup dialog box, you see the options shown in Figure 18-5. You can use the Sheet tab's options to control different print-related settings that affect individual worksheets.

The Sheet tab options include the following:

- **Print Area** — In the Print Area text box, you can enter a range of cells that you want to print, or you can enter the name of a named range. If you leave the entry blank, Excel prints all cells that contain data in the worksheet or workbook.

- **Print Titles** — In the Print Titles area, you can specify rows or columns that you would like to see repeated on every page.

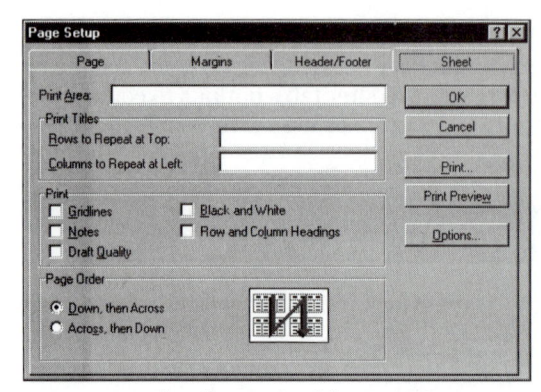

Figure 18-5: The Sheet tab of the Page Setup dialog box.

- ✦ **Print** — Use the options in the Print area to tell Excel how to handle the printing of certain aspects of a worksheet or workbook. You can determine whether gridlines and notes should be included in the printing; whether the printer should use a faster draft-quality printing; whether color printers should print data only in black and white, even if the cells are formatted as colors; and whether row and column headings should be included.

- ✦ **Page Order** — In the Page Order area, you can specify whether printing of multiple-page worksheets should occur from top to bottom and then from left to right, or from left to right and then from top to bottom.

Setting the Print Range

When you tell Excel to print a worksheet, it prints the entire worksheet unless you tell it otherwise. When you want to print a specific portion of a worksheet, you first need to tell Excel what area of the worksheet you want printed. You can specify the portion of the worksheet by choosing File➪Page Setup and using the Print Area option of the Sheet tab. To define a print range, use these steps:

1. Choose File➪Page Setup. In the Page Setup dialog box that appears, click on the Sheet tab.

2. Click in the Print Area text box to place the insertion point there.

3. In the worksheet, select the range of cells that you want to print. (You may have to drag the dialog box out of the way in order to select the range.) As you select the range, a dotted line appears around it, and the coordinates for the range appear in the Print Area text box of the Page Setup dialog box.

4. If you want to change any other options, click on the OK button to close the Page Setup dialog box. Or if you want to begin printing with the other options as they are, click on the Print button in the Page Setup dialog box.

If you want to cancel the effects of the selection and go back to printing the complete worksheet, choose File⇨Page Setup and click on the Sheet tab. In the Print Area text box, delete the coordinates of the selected range and click on the OK button.

Specifying multiple print ranges

Excel lets you select several ranges of pages to print. Each range is printed on its own sheet, and can be printed with titles. You can tell Excel to print multiple worksheet page ranges by performing the following steps:

1. Choose File⇨Page Setup.
2. Select the Sheet tab of the Page Setup dialog box (see Figure 18-5).
3. Click in the Print Area box to place the insertion point there.
4. Click and drag to select the first range that you want to print.
5. Enter a comma in the Print Area text box.
6. Select the next area that you want to print.
7. Repeat Steps 5 and 6 until you select all the areas that you want to print. The areas are printed in the order that you selected them, and they are printed on separate pages.

Another method to do the same thing is to select the ranges that you want to print by using the Ctrl key to move to additional ranges. Then choose File⇨Print. In the Print dialog box, click on the Selection option in the Print What area and then click on the OK button to print your selection.

Previewing Print Jobs

Previewing your work before you print it is very useful because you can find mistakes in the layout of your document before you print it, and it helps you to avoid wasting paper. You can also use the Zoom feature that allows you to take a closer look at the document and its contents.

To preview a worksheet, click on the Print Preview button on the Standard toolbar or choose File⇨Print Preview to put Excel in Print Preview mode, as shown in Figure 18-6. In Print Preview mode, you can make modifications to the worksheet to further improve its appearance by clicking on the Setup button at the top of the screen to activate the Page Setup dialog box.

Part III ♦ Excel

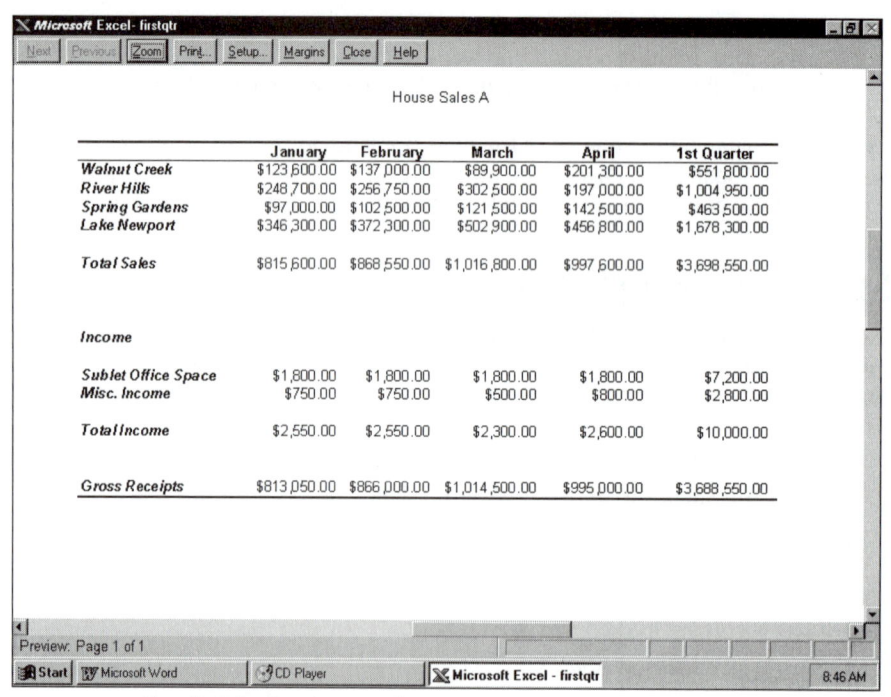

Figure 18-6: Excel's Print Preview mode.

You can also modify the margins of your document in Print Preview by clicking on the Margins button at the top of the screen. Clicking on the Margins button activates the "margin grid" (see Figure 18-7). You can move the margin lines by using the mouse. The margin grid feature is very helpful because it lets you see the document as it is being adjusted, and you can also get an idea as to whether the document will fit on a single page. If you intend to set margins in Print Preview, you may want to use the Zoom feature by clicking on the Zoom button at the top of the Print Preview window. The Zoom feature helps you get a better look at what the margins will look like.

Controlling Aspects of Printing

As you learned in the description of the Page Setup dialog box, many different settings are available to control margins, add titles to your worksheets, and insert headers and footers. You can also control page breaks and specify whether gridlines are included in your printed worksheets.

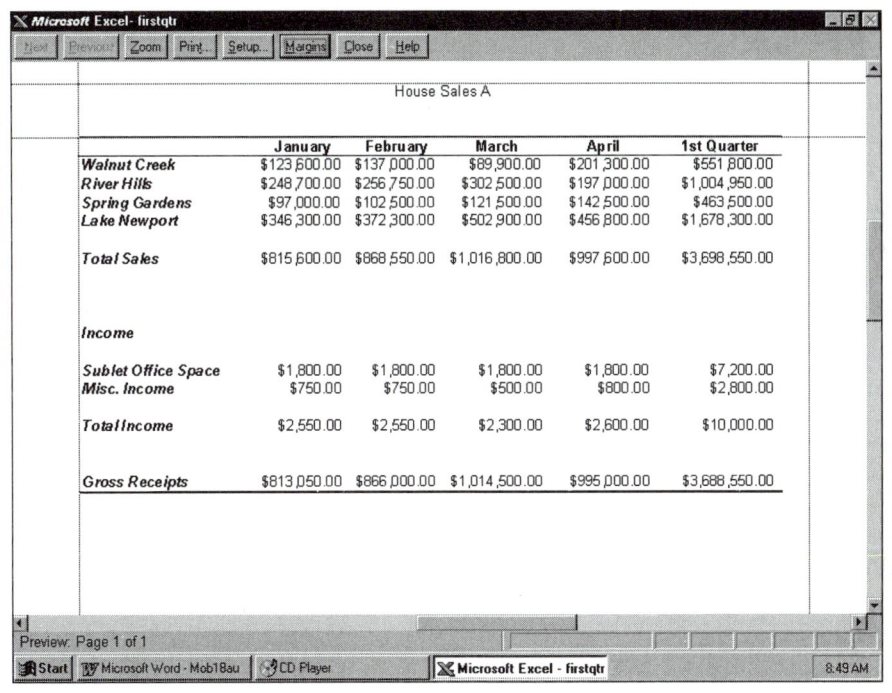

Figure 18-7: The margin grid in Print Preview mode.

Before you print, you should specify the margins for the selected item that you want to print because spreadsheets have many columns and rows that often exceed the screen. Also, it is important to remember that many laser and inkjet printers cannot print to the edge of the paper; therefore, you cannot set margins less than 0.25 inch. Also keep in mind that if you have headers or footers, they will automatically print 0.5 inch from the bottom or top of the page unless you change that distance when you add them.

To change the margins for your document, perform the following steps:

1. Choose File⇨Page Setup.
2. Choose the Margins tab of the Page Setup dialog box (see Figure 18-3).
3. Enter the measurements that you want in the Top, Bottom, Left, and Right text boxes. Remember to keep in mind the header, footer, and printer limitations. You can change the distance that the headers and footers appear from the edge of the page. And you can center the information on the page vertically and horizontally by clicking on the corresponding choice in the Center on Page area.

Printing titles

Printing titles on the worksheets make them easier to read. Titles can prove to be very beneficial when you work with long worksheets. The Print Titles options are available on the Sheet tab of the Page Setup dialog box. To print a title on each page of a sheet, perform the following steps:

1. Choose File➪Page Setup.
2. Choose the Sheet tab from the Page Setup dialog box.
3. Place the insertion point in the Rows to Repeat at Top text box or the Columns to Repeat at Left text box.
4. With the mouse, select the rows or columns that you want to repeat. Move the dialog box, if necessary. (Remember that multiple rows and columns must be adjacent.)
5. Click on the OK button.

If you change your mind and you want to delete the entries that you have made as titles, simply return to the Sheet tab of the Page Setup dialog box and delete the entries that you made in the Rows to Repeat at Top and Columns to Repeat as Left text boxes.

Controlling page breaks

Sometimes automatic page breaks — which are based on paper size, margins, and other settings in the Page Setup dialog box — come at inconvenient places, especially in larger worksheets. When a page breaks at a bad location, you can fix the break by inserting a manual page break instead. Manual page breaks are especially useful when you want to print one section per page. To insert manual page breaks, perform the following steps:

1. Place the insertion point below and to the right of the place where you want to insert the page break.
2. Choose Insert➪Page Break. The page break appears on-screen and is indicated by lines with dashes.

The page breaks that you insert remain in the same location until you remove them. The automatic page breaks are also repositioned after the insertion of a manual page break. If you want to remove a page break that you inserted, choose Insert➪Remove Page Break. This option is available only when you return to the cell in which you entered the page break. Selecting the entire document and choosing Insert➪Remove Page Break removes all the manual page breaks in the worksheet.

Page breaks can also be set horizontally and vertically. To do so, select the column or row at which you want the page break to appear and click in its header. Next choose Insert⇨Page Break. The page break is set horizontally or vertically as you specified.

Turning the gridlines on and off

When printing a worksheet, you may need to insert manual page breaks. Sometimes these page breaks are difficult to see because of the gridlines on an Excel worksheet. To turn off the gridlines so that you can see the manual page breaks, choose Tools⇨Options. Click on the View tab and then turn off the Gridlines check box. Click on the OK button to remove the gridlines.

Printing nonconsecutive sheets

You may often have to print nonconsecutive worksheets. This is a task that Excel can easily handle in a few simple steps. First select the tab of the first sheet that you want to print. Then press the Ctrl key while you select the tabs of all the other worksheets that you want to print. Then choose File⇨Print and select the number of copies that you want to print.

Inserting headers and footers

When you use the Page Setup dialog box, Excel lets you enter headers and footers into a worksheet or workbook that you print. Adding headers and footers is relatively simple and painless. They can be very effective in giving a document a more refined look and making it appear more professional.

To add a header or footer to a worksheet, perform the following steps:

1. Choose File⇨Page Setup.
2. Choose the Header/Footer tab from the Page Setup dialog box (refer to Figure 18-4).
3. Decide whether you want to add a header or a footer to your worksheet.
4. Click on the corresponding Custom button: click the Custom Header button for headers, or click the Custom Footers button for footers. Once you click either button, another dialog box opens (similar to Figure 18-8 and titled "Header" or "Footer" depending on your choice), where you can enter your header or footer text.

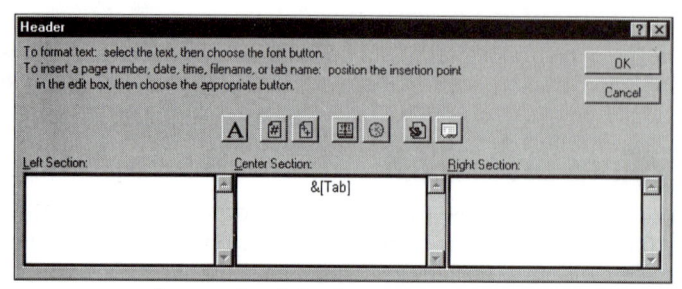

Figure 18-8: The Header dialog box.

5. In the Left Section, Center Section, or Right Section portion of the dialog box, enter the desired text of your header or footer. Use the buttons in the dialog box to add items, page numbers, insert the system date or time, or change the fonts used.

6. Click on OK.

Table 18-1 explains the custom header and footer buttons that appear in the dialog box after you click on either the Custom Header or Custom Footer button on the Header/Footer tab.

Table 18-1
Header/Footer buttons and their functions

Button	Function
Font	Opens the Font dialog box, from which you can change the header or footer's font.
Page Number	Inserts the page number.
Total Pages	Inserts the total number of pages in the active worksheet.
Date	Inserts the system date.
Time	Inserts the system time.
Filename	Inserts the active workbook's filename.
Sheet Name	Inserts the active worksheet's name.

Changing the Printer Properties

Selecting a printer is a simple matter in Excel, thanks to the Properties menu that now exists in Excel and other Windows 95 products. To change the printer that you use in Excel, click on the Print button and select the printer that you want to use from the list of printers that are there. If you do not see the printer that you want to use, you will need to install it. To install the printer, open the Printers folder under Windows 95 and click on the Add Printer icon to activate the Add Printer Wizard. The wizard guides you through the steps that you need to perform to add the new printer.

You can also change the options that are in effect for your printer by choosing File⇨Print. In the Print dialog box, click on the Properties button to open the Printer Properties dialog box, as shown in Figure 18-9. This dialog box has four tabs. Use the Paper tab to select the paper size, the orientation, and the source of the paper. Again, keep in mind that these options vary based on the printer that you have installed.

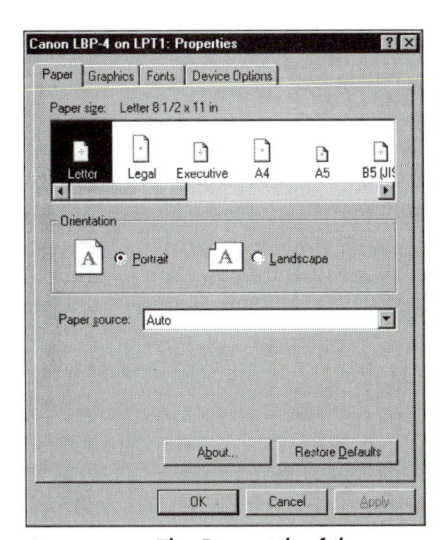

Figure 18-9: The Paper tab of the Printer Properties dialog box.

Use the Graphics tab (see Figure 18-10) to change the intensity of the graphics that you print by adjusting the shading bar to control how dark the shadows will be when an item is printed. Making this adjustment also affects the speed with which the item is printed — the darker the shading, the slower the printing. You also use this tab when you want to speed up printing with graphics. To print graphics faster, decrease the resolution in the Resolution list box. Use the Dithering area to control the amount of space that appears between the dots in a printed item. With printers that support dithering, you can make adjustments in this area to smooth the otherwise jagged appearance of printed characters.

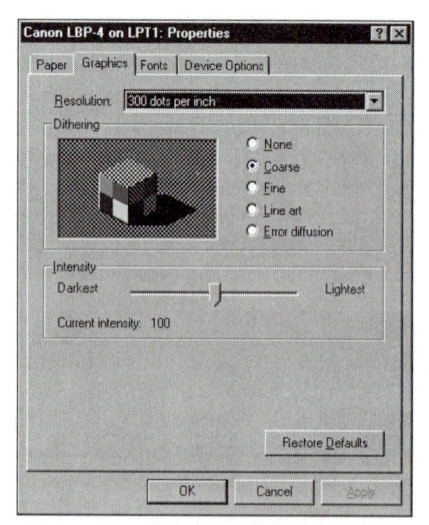

Figure 18-10: The Graphics tab of the Printer Properties dialog box.

The Fonts tab lets you control how your TrueType fonts are printed, as shown in Figure 18-11. To speed up the printing process, select the Download TrueType fonts as bitmap soft fonts option. But in cases where the document contains graphics and some text not repeating frequently on a page, you should use the Print TrueType as graphics option instead. This option is useful in cases where you want to print graphics over text so that only the exposed part of the characters are printed (that is, the graphics partially cover the characters.)

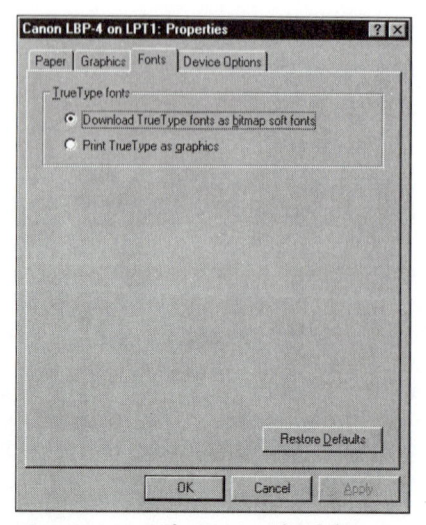

Figure 18-11: The Fonts tab of the Printer Properties dialog box.

Choose the Device Options tab to control printer memory tracking (see Figure 18-12). When a document is printed, the printer driver compares the amount of memory that will be used in the printing of the document and the memory that is available in the printer. Then the printer driver decides whether there is sufficient memory to print a complex document. The nearer the tracking bar marker is to the Conservative side, the less likely it is that the printer driver will overcommit the printer and exceed its memory. In most cases you should keep the marker in the middle. If your printer starts giving you errors when you print more complex documents, try moving the marker toward the Conservative side.

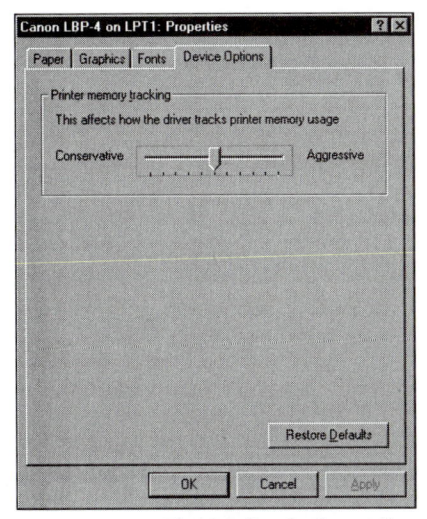

Figure 18-12: The Device Options tab of the Printer Properties dialog box.

Sending a File on a Network

One other common option you have for "producing" your workbook is File➪Send. With this command, you can send the workbook to another person on a network to which your computer is attached or to another person on an online service. This option makes use of Microsoft Exchange, which is provided with Windows 95. (The complete use of Microsoft Exchange is a subject that is beyond the scope of this book, but you can find details about it in your Windows documentation or in a book on Windows, such as *Windows 95 For Dummies,* IDG Books, 1995.)

To send a workbook by using Microsoft Exchange, choose File➪Send. In the Choose Profile dialog box, click on the OK button to accept the default setting of Microsoft Exchange. Excel first saves the presentation to a temporary file, and then it launches Microsoft Exchange and transfers the temporary file containing the workbook to the New Message window of Microsoft Exchange, as shown in Figure 18-13. From here, you can use the techniques that apply to Microsoft Exchange to send the worksheet to the desired recipient.

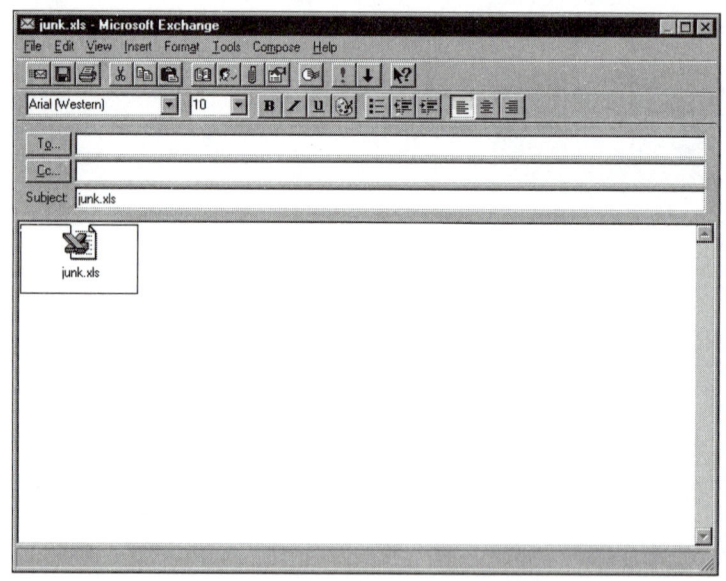

Figure 18-13: The New Message window of Microsoft Exchange.

Summary

This chapter has detailed the different features that Excel offers to help you get your facts and figures on paper. The chapter covered the following points:

- ✦ You can print a selected area of the current worksheet, selected sheets, or the entire workbook by choosing File⇨Print.

- ✦ By choosing File⇨Page Setup, you reveal the Page Setup dialog box, which lets you change various settings for printing, such as orientation, paper size, margins, headers, and footers.

- ✦ Excel's Print Preview feature can be very useful in helping you find errors in a document's layout before printing occurs.

- ✦ You can change printer properties by choosing File⇨Print and clicking the Properties button in the dialog box that appears.

- ✦ You can use the File⇨Send command to send a workbook to another person on a local area network.

The next chapter will explain how you can create and work with databases in Excel.

Where to go next...

- ✦ If you find yourself doing a lot of repetitive printing on a regular basis, you'll want to automate your printing by putting the power of macros to work. Chapter 20 tells you how.

- ✦ Your document's printed appearance is greatly affected by how you format that document. Formatting specifics are covered in Chapter 15.

✦ ✦ ✦

Working with Excel Databases

CHAPTER 19

In This Chapter

Creating a database

Adding, editing, and deleting records from the database

Finding data

Sorting data

Using the AutoFilter command to filter data

Using complex criteria with the AutoFilter command

Designing databases

This chapter details the use of databases (also called *lists*) that are stored in Excel worksheets. Whether you are aware of it or not, you have probably used databases on numerous occasions. Any time you reference a list of business contacts or a Rolodex file or something as familiar as the Yellow Pages, you are working with a database. You can use Excel to manage data in a database, and this chapter will show you how.

What is a Database?

Although the term *database* is often used in reference to computers, it also applies to any system in which information is cataloged, stored, and used. A database is a collection of related information that is grouped as a single item. Figure 19-1 shows an example of a simple database. Metal filing cabinets containing customer records, a card file of names and phone numbers, and a notebook filled with a handwritten list of store inventory are all databases. The physical container — the filing cabinet or the notebook, for example — is not the database. The database is the contents of the container and the way the information is organized. Objects, such as cabinets and notebooks, are only tools for organizing information. Excel is one such tool for storing information.

Information in a database is usually organized and stored in a table by rows and columns. Figure 19-1, for example, is a mailing list in database form. Each row contains a name, a street address, a city, state, and a zip code. Because the mailing list is a collection of information arranged in a specific order — a column of names, a column of addresses, a column of cities, and so on — it is a database.

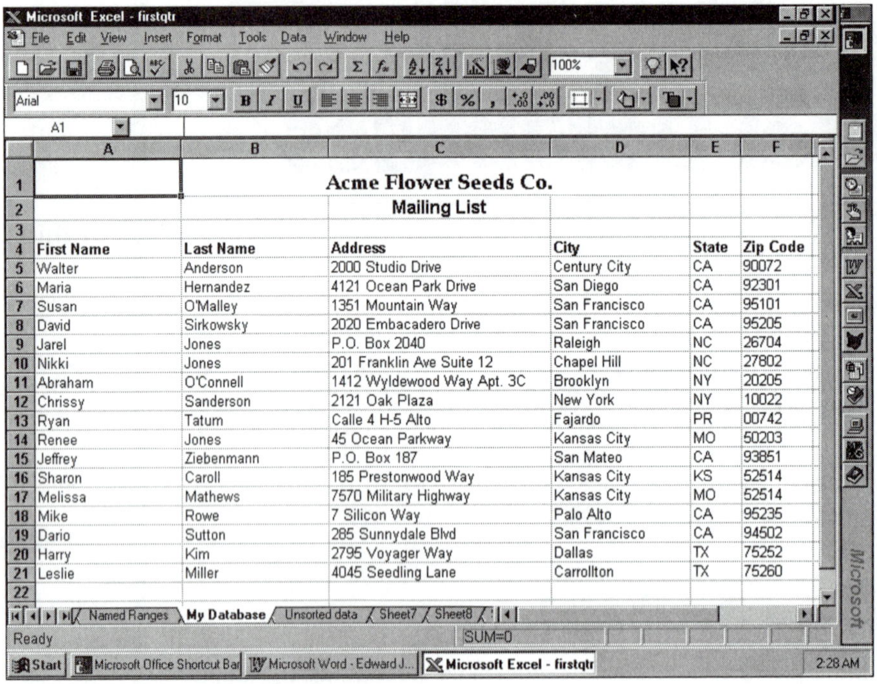

Figure 19-1: A typical database in Excel.

Rows in a database file are called *records*, and columns are called *fields*. Figure 19-2 illustrates this idea by showing an address filing system kept on file cards. Each card in the box is a single record, and each category of information on that card is a field. Fields can contain any type of information that can be categorized. In the card box, each record contains five fields: name, address, city, state, and zip code. Because every card in the box contains the same type of information, the information in the card box is a database.

In Excel, you design a database by following this row-and-column analogy, where each column of the spreadsheet contains a different field, and each row contains an additional record. You keep your data organized by devoting a specific column to each specific category (field) of data. You must enter each specific chunk of data in a separate cell of the worksheet. For example, in the worksheet shown earlier in Figure 19-1, a person's first name goes into a cell of the First Name column, the person's last name goes into a cell of the Last Name column, and so on. You can begin the design of any database by placing the cursor at the top of the worksheet and entering labels for the names of your fields in successive columns.

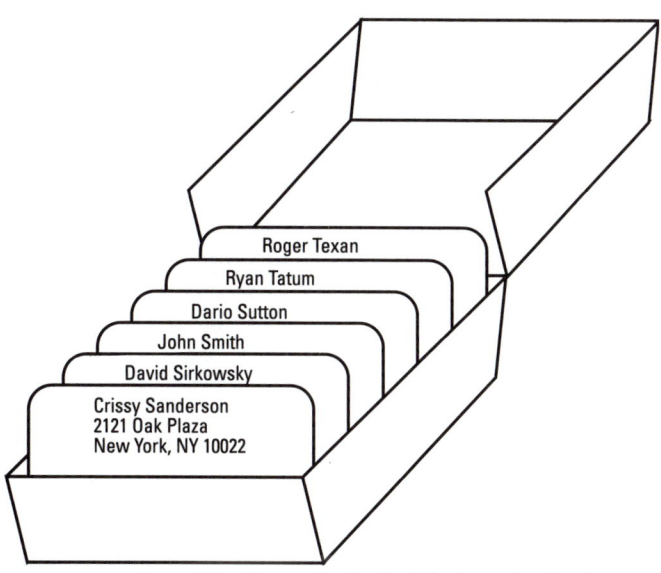

Figure 19-2: A card file shows the logical design of a database.

Creating a Database

You can create a database in an Excel worksheet by performing these steps:

1. In a blank row of the worksheet, enter the desired names of the fields.
2. In each cell of a row directly underneath the field names, type the desired entries for that field into the cell. Don't leave an empty row between the field names and the data because Excel will have problems recognizing where your database begins.
3. To add entries made up of numbers that really should be stored as text (such as zip codes), begin the entry with an apostrophe.

When you finish adding records to your database, you'll have an organized collection of row-and-column data in a format somewhat like our example shown earlier in Figure 19-1.

Hot Stuff — If you need to enter a large number of entries that are composed of numbers that should be stored as text (such as zip codes or phone numbers), first format that column containing that field as text. Select the entire column (click on this column header), right-click on the column, and choose Format Cells from the shortcut menu that appears. Click on the Number tab of the Format Cells dialog box. Then click on theTextoption in the Category list box and click on the Number tab of the Format cells on the OK button. If you don't use this trick, or if you begin each entry with an apostrophe instead, zip codes that begin with zeroes (such as is 00742) will appear without the zeroes, which is probably not how you want the data to appear.

> ### Creating Databases was a lot harder in my old version of Excel …
>
> If you've upgraded from Excel 4.0, and you have worked with databases in the older version, you'll recall things being considerably more complicated. In Excel 4.0 and earlier versions, you had to define a specific range for your data to occupy (called a *database range*). And when you wanted to retrieve specific data, you had to tell Excel what data you wanted by setting up a *criteria range* and an *extract range*. You can still use these old methods in the current version of Excel, but the new approach is much easier to use. Excel now makes intelligent guesses regarding your database range (the size of the database) and provides a data form and an AutoFilter capability that you can use to enter criteria and retrieve desired data.

Your database work will be easier for you to handle if you have only one database per worksheet. To store more than one database in a single worksheet, you would need to define database ranges for each database, a topic that adds an unnecessary layer of complexity. Because each Excel worksheet can contain up to 255 tabs, you can conveniently manage your multiple databases by placing each database on a different worksheet tab. You'll also avoid long-term organizational problems if you don't put other data below your database in the same worksheet. As the database grows, new rows will be added to the bottom of the list. If other spreadsheet data exists below the list, you'll run the risk of overwriting the existing data.

As you work with databases in Excel, keep in mind these points regarding the names of the fields. The database must have its row of field names at the top of the list, and you can't have any blank lines between the row containing the field names and the data. Also, each field name should be unique (for example, it would be confusing to have two fields named Date). You can have other rows above the list if you want, but only the row immediately above the data is recognized by Excel as the row containing field names. Field names can include up to 255 characters, although for readability reasons you'll probably want to keep your field names relatively short.

Avoid putting other important data (such as formulas) to the left or to the right of your database. If you later use Excel's AutoFilter capability to filter the data in the database, the other data may be hidden.

Working with Database Records

You can add and edit records by typing the desired data directly into the cells, and you can delete rows from your database by selecting the unwanted row and choosing Edit➪Delete. However, most users find basic data entry and editing easier when they use a *data form*, a convenient form that Excel provides for you to enter and display data. To display a data form on-screen, place the cursor in any cell of your database and choose Data⇨Form. A data form that contains the fields of your database appears, such as the one in Figure 19-3.

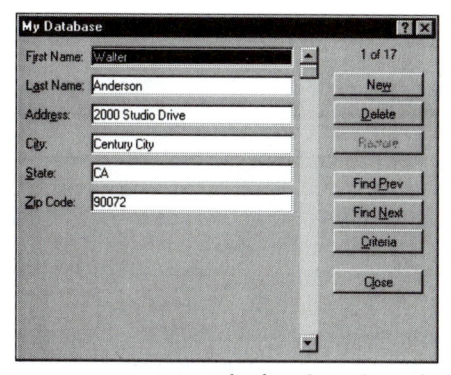

Figure 19-3: A sample data form for a database.

Adding new records

To add a record, click on the New button in the data form. When you do so, the entries in the fields of the form appear blank, and you can type the desired data into each field. Repeat this process for each record that you want to add to the database.

Hot Stuff — If you're adding new records to an existing database, don't be concerned about the order of the records in the database. You can always sort the database to put the records in any order that you want (see "Sorting a Database" later in the chapter).

Editing records

To edit a record by using the data form, first use the Find Next or Find Prev(ious) buttons to locate the desired record. Or you can use the scrollbars or the up- and down-arrow keys to find the appropriate record. In a large database, you can also use the Criteria button to perform a search. When the desired record appears, click in the appropriate fields and make the desired edits.

Deleting records

To delete a record by using the data form, first use the Find Next or Find Prev(ious) buttons to locate the desired record. When the record appears, click on the Delete button in the data form.

Hot Stuff: If you have a large number of records to delete, it may be faster *not* to use a data form. Instead, you can use Excel's AutoFilter capability (discussed later in this chapter) to display all the records that you want to delete. Then you drag across the row headers to select the records. With all the desired rows selected, choose the Delete command from the Edit menu.

Finding data by using criteria

Another way to locate data in a database is to specify *criteria* in a data form. The criteria identifies the specific data that you want to find. For example, in a large database of names and addresses, you may want to locate all records in a particular city. Excel also lets you make use of *computed criteria* to find records that pass certain tests based on the contents of a formula. By using computed criteria with a database of expenses, for example, you can find all expenses that exceed $500 by entering **>500**. When you specify computed criteria in a data form, you make use of Excel's *comparison operators* (the same ones that you can use as part of formulas in the cells of a worksheet). Table 19-1 lists the comparison operators that you can use.

Table 19-1
Comparison operators

Operator	Function
<	Less than
>	Greater than
=	Equal to
<>	Not equal to
<=	Less than or equal to
>=	Greater than or equal to

Follow these steps to find individual records in a database by using criteria:

1. Place the cursor anywhere in the database

2. Choose Data⇨Form to bring up a data form on-screen.

3. Click on the Criteria button in the data form. When you do this, the data form changes in appearance to resemble the one shown in Figure 19-4. The data form now says Criteria in the upper-right corner, and the Criteria button on the data form changes into the Form button.

4. Enter the desired criteria in the appropriate fields. You need to fill in only the fields on which you want to base the search. For example, if you want to search for all San Francisco records, you would enter **San Francisco** in the City field of the form.

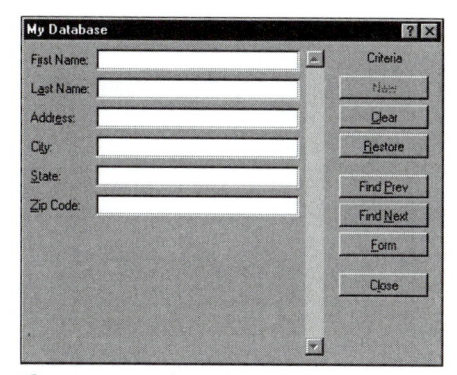

Figure 19-4: The Criteria mode of the data form.

5. Press Enter or click on the Form button to get back to the original data form.
6. Use the Find Next and Find Prev(ious) buttons in the data form to locate the records that match the desired criteria.
7. When you are finished examining the records, click on the Close button.

You can also use *wildcards* to represent characters in your criteria. You can use the question mark to represent a single character, and you can use the asterisk (*) to represent multiple characters. As an example, the criteria **H?ll** in a Name field would locate names such as *Hall*, *Hill*, and *Hull*. The criteria entry ***der** would locate all strings of text ending with the letters *der* such as *chowder* and *loader*.

> **Hot Stuff** If you're familiar with databases in general, you may be wondering how you can perform searches based on multiple criteria, where you find records based on more than a single argument. In some cases, you'll want to find records by using *and-based criteria*, where one condition *and* another condition meet certain requirements. You can easily search on multiple criteria by entering multiple conditions in the different fields of the data form while in Criteria mode. For example, in a table of names and addresses, you may want to find a record that contains the last name Sanderson *and* the city New York. Figure 19-5 shows a data form that is set up to search on these criteria.

This data form business is nice, but how do I get a report?

How can you get a printed copy of all records that meet a certain criteria? You can't use the data form to isolate and print a group of records, but you can filter the data in a database by using Excel's AutoFilter command. After you filter the records to show the ones that you want, you can just print the worksheet to produce a report. For details, see "Using the AutoFilter Command" later in this chapter.

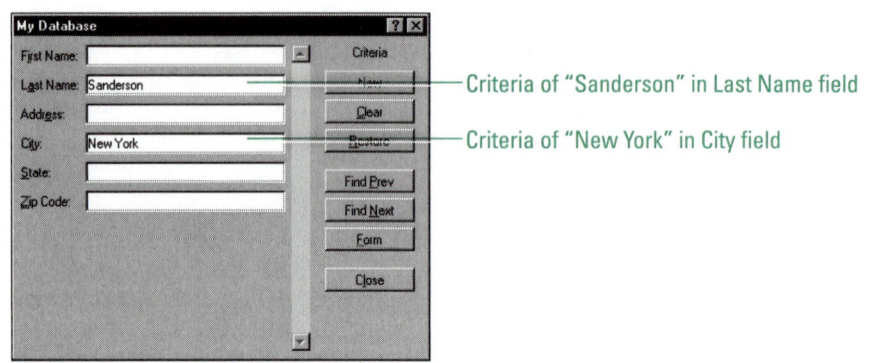

Figure 19-5: The data form set up in Criteria mode to search for multiple criteria.

— Criteria of "Sanderson" in Last Name field
— Criteria of "New York" in City field

When you use *or-based criteria*, things get a little more complex. Or-based criteria describes those cases where the contents of a field meets one criteria *or* another criteria. For example, you may want to find records where the City field contains San Francisco *or* San Diego. Unfortunately, you can't do searches with or-based criteria by using a data form; however, you can use Excel's AutoFilter command.

Using the AutoFormat Command on Your Database

You can quickly improve the appearance of your database by using Excel's AutoFormat command. As detailed in Chapter 15, AutoFormat applies automatic formatting to parts or all of your worksheet to quickly give the worksheet a presentation-quality appearance.

To apply automatic formatting to a database, place the cursor anywhere within the database. Then choose Format⇨AutoFormat. In the AutoFormat dialog box, choose one of the available formats in the list box and then click on the OK button to apply the formatting. If you don't like the effects of the formatting, you can always choose the Undo AutoFormat command from the Edit menu to reverse the effects.

Sorting a Database

After you compile a database, you may need to arrange it in various ways. You can arrange a database by sorting, which changes the order of the records. When Excel sorts a database, it rearranges all records in the database according to a specified new order. If you sorted a database of names alphabetically, the sorted database would contain all the records that were in the old database, but the names would be arranged in alphabetic order.

Danger Zone When you sort fields that contain dates or times, Excel sorts correctly if the data is in an acceptable date or time format. If you use some format of your own devising that Excel doesn't recognize to store dates or times, Excel will sort the data as text, and you probably won't get the results that you want.

When Excel sorts a database in ascending order, it sorts by numbers first, followed by text, and then the logical values True or False. Excel is not case-sensitive; it ignores both case and accent marks while sorting. Blank cells appear at the end of the sort, whether you are sorting in ascending or descending order. You must choose a field, called the *key field*, on which to sort. In some cases, you may need to sort a database on more than one field. For example, if you sort a database alphabetically by using Last Name as the key field, you get groups of records with the last names arranged alphabetically but with the first names in random order. In such a case, you can sort the database by using Last Name as the first key field and First Name as the second key field. To sort a database, use Data➪Sort.

You can sort your database by performing these steps:

1. If you just want to sort a specific number of rows in your database, select those rows by dragging across the row headers. If you want to sort the entire database, place the cursor anywhere within the database.

2. Choose Data➪Sort to open the Sort dialog box, as shown in Figure 19-6.

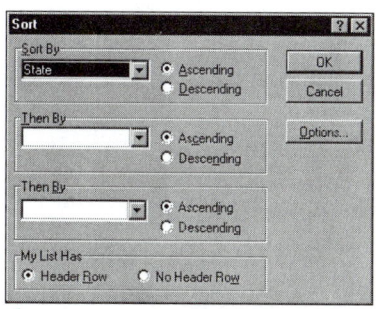

Figure 19-6: The Sort dialog box.

3. In the Sort By area of the dialog box, choose a desired field to sort on from the list and select the Ascending or Descending option to specify the direction of the sort.

4. If you want to use additional fields as the basis for the sort, fill in the Then By area of the dialog box as indicated in Step 3. When you sort on multiple fields, the Sort By list box takes first priority in the sort followed by the first Then By list box and then the second Then By list box.

5. If you did not select a range of rows to sort, make sure that the Header Row option at the bottom of the dialog box remains selected. This option tells Excel not to include the header row, which contains the field names, in the sort.

6. Click on the OK button to perform the sort.

Figure 19-7 shows the effects of sorting. At top, you see a database that contains records entered in random order. At bottom, you see the same database that has been sorted by State and, where State values are equal, by City fields.

	A	B	C	D	E	F
1			Acme Flower Seeds Co.			
2			Mailing List			
3						
4	First Name	Last Name	Address	City	State	Zip Code
5	Walter	Anderson	2000 Studio Drive	Century City	CA	90072
6	Maria	Hernandez	4121 Ocean Park Drive	San Diego	CA	92301
7	David	Sirkowsky	2020 Embacadero Drive	San Francisco	CA	95205
8	Nikki	Jones	201 Franklin Ave Suite 12	Chapel Hill	NC	27802
9	Abraham	O'Connell	1412 Wyldewood Way Apt. 3C	Brooklyn	NY	20205
10	Susan	O'Malley	1351 Mountain Way	San Francisco	CA	95101
11	Jarel	Jones	P.O. Box 2040	Raleigh	NC	26704
12	Chrissy	Sanderson	2121 Oak Plaza	New York	NY	10022
13	Ryan	Tatum	Calle 4 H-5 Alto	Fajardo	PR	00742
14	Renee	Jones	45 Ocean Parkway	Kansas City	MO	50203
15	Jeffrey	Ziebenmann	P.O. Box 187	San Mateo	CA	93851
16	Sharon	Caroll	185 Prestonwood Way	Kansas City	KS	52514
17	Melissa	Mathews	7570 Military Highway	Kansas City	MO	52514
18	Mike	Rowe	7 Silicon Way	Palo Alto	CA	95235
19	Dario	Sutton	285 Sunnydale Blvd	San Francisco	CA	94502
20	Harry	Kim	2795 Voyager Way	Dallas	TX	75252
21	Leslie	Miller	4045 Seedling Lane	Carrollton	TX	75260
22						

	A	B	C	D	E	F
1			Acme Flower Seeds Co.			
2			Mailing List			
3						
4	First Name	Last Name	Address	City	State	Zip Code
5	Walter	Anderson	2000 Studio Drive	Century City	CA	90072
6	Mike	Rowe	7 Silicon Way	Palo Alto	CA	95235
7	Maria	Hernandez	4121 Ocean Park Drive	San Diego	CA	92301
8	David	Sirkowsky	2020 Embacadero Drive	San Francisco	CA	95205
9	Susan	O'Malley	1351 Mountain Way	San Francisco	CA	95101
10	Dario	Sutton	285 Sunnydale Blvd	San Francisco	CA	94502
11	Jeffrey	Ziebenmann	P.O. Box 187	San Mateo	CA	93851
12	Sharon	Caroll	185 Prestonwood Way	Kansas City	KS	52514
13	Renee	Jones	45 Ocean Parkway	Kansas City	MO	50203
14	Melissa	Mathews	7570 Military Highway	Kansas City	MO	52514
15	Nikki	Jones	201 Franklin Ave Suite 12	Chapel Hill	NC	27802
16	Jarel	Jones	P.O. Box 2040	Raleigh	NC	26704
17	Abraham	O'Connell	1412 Wyldewood Way Apt. 3C	Brooklyn	NY	20205
18	Chrissy	Sanderson	2121 Oak Plaza	New York	NY	10022
19	Ryan	Tatum	Calle 4 H-5 Alto	Fajardo	PR	00742
20	Leslie	Miller	4045 Seedling Lane	Carrollton	TX	75260
21	Harry	Kim	2795 Voyager Way	Dallas	TX	75252
22						

Figure 19-7: Top: A database containing records in random order. Bottom: The same database containing records sorted by State and City fields.

Danger Zone: Excel users have been known to get less than desirable results from a sort because sorting involves a major rearrangement of data, and there's always a possibility that you'll make a selection that causes Excel to sort your data in a way that you didn't expect. If you have any doubts about how a sort will turn out, it may be a wise idea to save the workbook under a different name. (Choose File➪Save As and enter a different name for the workbook file in the Save As dialog box.) If you later perform a sort that produces undesirable results, and you're unable to undo the sort, you can always load the original file to get your unchanged data back.

Hot Stuff: You can quickly sort a database on any single field in ascending or descending order by placing the cursor in any desired field and clicking on the Sort Ascending or Sort Descending button on the Standard toolbar.

If you make a selection before sorting (as opposed to sorting the entire list by just placing the cursor anywhere within the list), make sure that you select all the data that you want sorted. If you select most columns and leave some adjacent columns containing data unselected, the sort will affect only the data in the selected columns. The result will be a seriously garbled database. When selecting data for sorting purposes, the safest method is to drag across row headings. In this way, you're assured of selecting all data in the rows.

Sorting bizarre numbers

Many years ago, one of the authors worked as a service technician for a copier manufacturer, and that company used part numbers made up of alphanumeric combinations of varying widths. A list of such part numbers contained entries like the following:

1R9

4R32

12P182

67S2024

109P182

If you have a database that contains alphanumeric records like this one, and you do a sort based on the value, you get results that aren't what you really want. Using the preceding list, Excel puts 12P182 above 1R9, even though in the company's grand scheme of things, 1R9 is a lower part number than 12P182. This is because, in this case, the part numbers are actually made up of three component parts: a number of one or more digits, followed by a letter, followed by another multi-digit number. In such a list, all parts beginning with the number 1 would appear first in the sorted list, followed by all parts beginning with the number 2, then all parts beginning with the number 3, and so on.

You can correctly sort this type of a list by breaking the codes into their component parts and using a separate cell for each part. Storing each of these components in a separate cell and sorting based on all three cells would solve the problem.

Occasionally you may need to sort a database on more than three fields. Suppose that you have a large mailing list in Excel, and you want to sort the database by State, and then by City within each state, and then by Last Name within each city, and then by First Name within each group of last names. Because Excel provides only three fields from which to select in the Sort dialog box, this type of sort appears to be impossible. In fact, Excel can handle such a task if you break down the job into multiple sorts. Begin with the least important group of sorts and progress towards the most important group of sorts. Put the most important field first within each group of sorts. In the example, you would first sort by using the Last Name field as the first field and the First Name field as the second field. Then you would perform another sort by using the State field as the first field, the City field as the second field, and the Last Name field as the third field.

Using the AutoFilter Command

For setting more complex retrieval criteria than is possible with the data form (and for printing reports based on selected data), you can make use of Excel's AutoFilter capability. The AutoFilter command lets you define criteria to filter your database so that only records meeting the specified criteria appear.

Hot Stuff — The AutoFilter command is a *toggle*, which means that after you turn it on, it's on until you turn it off. If you see a drop-down list box next to each field name, or if you see a check mark next to the AutoFilter command after you choose Data⇨Filter, then you know that the AutoFilter command is still on. Turn the option off to clear the previous filters and then turn it on again to use AutoFilter on your database.

Can you undo the effects of a sort? Maybe.

If you sort a database and then go on to do other things with the data, you cannot later undo the effects of the sort. (The Undo command works only if you perform it as the first action after the sort.) If you want to retain your database in the manner in which the records were originally entered, you have two options. You can save the database elsewhere (under another worksheet tab or under another filename) and recall that worksheet if you want to see how the database was originally organized. This approach has problems, however, because it is difficult to keep two databases containing the same data updated. A better approach is to add a column of record numbers to the database. The first record entered becomes record 1; the second record entered becomes record 2, and so on. If you ever want to reorganize the database in the order that the records were originally entered, simply sort on the field that contains the record numbers. You can choose Edit⇨Fill⇨Series to fill a column with sequential numbers, as detailed in Chapter 14.

You can put an AutoFilter into effect on a database by performing these steps:

1. Place the cursor anywhere in the database.
2. Choose Data➪Filter➪AutoFilter.
3. A drop-down list box appears next to each field name in the database (see Figure 19-8). You can use these list boxes to filter out rows of the database that don't match specified criteria.

	A	B	C	D	E	F
1			Acme Flower Seeds Co.			
2			Mailing List			
3						
4	First Name	Last Name	Address	City	State	Zip Cod
5	Walter	Anderson	2000 Studio Drive	Century City	CA	90072
6	Maria	Hernandez	4121 Ocean Park Drive	San Diego	CA	92301
7	Susan	O'Malley	1351 Mountain Way	San Francisco	CA	95101

List box buttons

Figure 19-8: List boxes made visible by using the AutoFilter command.

4. Click on the drop-down list box for the field that you want to filter and choose the entry that you want to use as the filter. You can also select the Custom option from the drop-down list box to create more complex criteria, as described later in this section.

As you make your desired selections from the drop-down list boxes, Excel filters the records according to your selections. You can create and-based criteria by choosing filters from more than one field. For example, in Figure 19-9, an MO filter is used in the State field, and a Kansas City filter is used in the City field. In this case, choosing Kansas City in the City field is not enough because records would appear from both Kansas and Missouri. If you choose multiple conditions, records must meet all of the conditions before they will be visible in the database after the AutoFilter is in effect.

	A	B	C	D	E	F
1			Acme Flower Seeds Co.			
2			Mailing List			
3						
4	First Name	Last Name	Address	City	State	Zip Cod
14	Renee	Jones	45 Ocean Parkway	Kansas City	MO	50203
17	Melissa	Mathews	7570 Military Highway	Kansas City	MO	52514
22						

Figure 19-9: An example of AutoFilter used on two fields of a database.

> ### Keeping a filtered copy of data handy
>
> You may find it useful to keep a copy of data that you filter from a database. For example, perhaps you'll want to refer often during the week to a listing of records that meet a certain condition. First use AutoFilter to filter the desired records. Then select all the records and choose Edit⇨Copy. Move to another worksheet where you want to place a copy of the data and choose Edit⇨Paste to place a copy of the filtered data there.

Printing a report based on specific data

The AutoFilter capability makes it easy to get a report of records from your database that meet a specified condition. After you have filtered your database using the AutoFilter command, and the records are visible, you can print them by choosing File⇨Print or by clicking on the Print button on the Standard toolbar. The printout contains the filtered records. Before the addition of Excel's AutoFilter command, you would have had to use some of Excel's advanced database features to declare a criteria range and an extract range to manage the same sort of task. And because that process is no longer necessary (except in very specialized cases), we won't bore you with the sordid details here. If you're curious, you can find specifics in the Excel Help files.

Using complex criteria with AutoFilter

You can also make use of complex criteria (such as records falling within a certain range, records that use computed criteria, or records meeting or-based conditions) with AutoFilter. You can use complex criteria by clicking on the Custom option that appears in the drop-down list boxes in the filtered database. After clicking on the Custom option, the Custom AutoFilter dialog box appears, as shown in Figure 19-10.

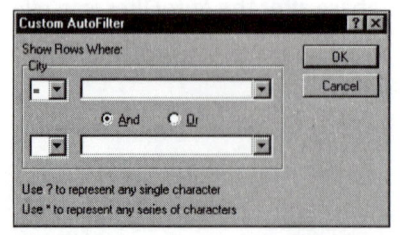

Figure 19-10: The Custom AutoFilter dialog box.

You can use the options in this dialog box to specify ranges of acceptable data and to specify or-based criteria (such as all records with a State value of CA or TX). Choose a desired comparison operator from the first drop-down list box and then enter a desired value in the text box to its right. To add a second comparison, click on the And or the Or button as desired, and use the second drop-down list box and the second text box for the other desired value.

You can see examples of the use of complex criteria by examining the dialog boxes shown in Figure 19-11. At right, the expressions >=M and <=Zz are used to retrieve all last names that start with M through Z. Note the addition of the second z. If this z were omitted, the criteria would actually find all names beginning with M through the letter Z alone, but the criteria would find no names of more than one character beginning with Z. In the middle dialog box, the expression >=40 retrieves all records with a value equal to or over 40 in the Amount field of an Expenses database. And at left, the expressions =San Francisco or =San Diego retrieve all entries with either of these city names.

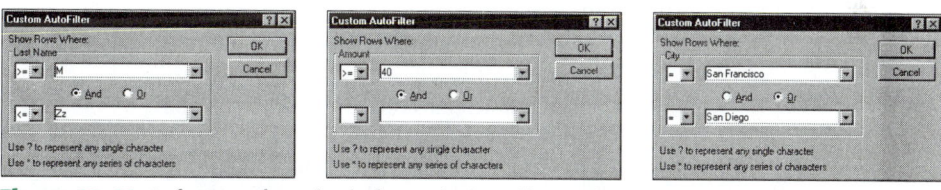

Figure 19-11: Left: Complex criteria for retrieving all records with last names starting with letters from M through Z. Middle: Complex criteria for retrieving all records with a value over 40 in the Amount field. Right: Complex criteria for retrieving all records with San Francisco or San Diego in the City field.

Keep in mind that you can use the Custom option in more than one field. By specifying Custom options in multiple fields, you can filter data based on complex criteria. To clear the effects of a Custom option, choose the All option from the drop-down list.

Turning off the effects of AutoFilter

When you're finished working with a filtered subset of records, remember to turn off the AutoFilter command by choosing Data⇨Filter⇨AutoFilter. Alternatively, you can also open the drop-down list boxes for any filters that you have set and choose the All option from each of the lists.

When is Excel's database power not enough?

Years ago, computer pundits would occasionally make light of the fact that the world's most popular database manager, Lotus 1-2-3, wasn't a database management software package at all. In today's Windows-dominated world, Excel may reign as the most popular spreadsheet, but one fact hasn't changed: thousands of spreadsheet users still get by with spreadsheet packages as their preferred database managers. A thought worth considering is at what point do your database needs outgrow Excel? If you cross that point and you stick with Excel as a database manager, you're making unnecessary work for yourself. As an obvious example, take this simple list of sales data for a small mail-order operation:

Date	Name	Phone	Item	Cost
6/15/95	Smith, R.	723-1020	calendar	18.00
6/15/95	Williams, E.	853-6723	calendar	18.00
6/16/95	Smith, R.	723-1020	padfolio	21.00
6/16/95	Smith, R.	723-1020	organizer	16.50

What may look like a simple, effective list is in reality (to a professional database developer's eye) the beginnings of a logistical nightmare. This kind of data cries out for *normalization*, or the separation of data into individual tables, with relationships established between the tables. This is something that isn't possible with Excel but falls right in line with the power of a relational database manager, such as Microsoft Access. If you find yourself regularly entering any kind of data entry in your Excel databases — the same employee names, customer names, item numbers, or descriptions — over and over, trust us. You're using the wrong product for your database management needs.

Another qualification is if your database grows into thousands of records. Such a massive amount of data puts unusual demands on the database power of a spreadsheet. If you need to use a relational database manager, Microsoft Access is an excellent choice — Access is designed to work well with the other Microsoft Office applications. You can move your existing Excel data directly into a table of an Access database. You can then split the table into two or more tables, and establish relationships between the tables (that pesky *normalization* process again). As a database developer for over a decade, I can tell you that Access is one outstanding product (and no, Microsoft isn't paying me to say this).

Performing a Mail Merge with Excel Data

More Info If you have names and addresses stored in an Excel database, you can combine the power of Excel and Word to create a mail merge document that you can use to generate form letters and envelopes. Much of what you do to handle this task is specific to Word, so it is given much more detail in the Word section of this book (see Chapter 6). However, in a nutshell, you use the following steps to generate form letters by using a mailing list stored in Excel:

1. Use Excel's AutoFilter command, if necessary, to show only those records for which you want to print form letters.
2. Select the entire range of data that contains the records.
3. Choose Edit⇨Copy.
4. Use the usual Windows technique to switch to Word for Windows and open a new document.
5. Choose Edit⇨Paste. When you do this, the data from Excel appears in a table in the Word document.
6. Save the Word document under any desired filename.
7. Open the document that is the basis for the mail merge (or create a new document with the desired text).
8. Choose Tools⇨Mail Merge to display the Mail Merge Helper dialog box.
9. Follow the instructions that appear in the dialog box. When you are asked for a data source, choose the Word document that contains the data from Excel.

Designing Databases

Planning is vital to effective database management. Many users create a database and store data in that database only to discover later that the database doesn't provide all the necessary information. It can become a tedious job to correct mistakes that you make during the design of a database. To avoid such time-consuming mistakes, you should give some thought to how you design your database within Excel.

Database design requires that you think about how the data should be stored and about how you and others will ask for data from the database file. During this design process, your business need (which Excel's database capabilities can help solve) should be outlined on paper. Just as you would not haphazardly toss a bunch of files into a filing cabinet without designing some type of filing system, you should not place information into a database without first designing the database. As you do so, you must define the kinds of information that should be stored in the database.

About data and attributes

Data and attributes are two important terms in database design. *Data* is the information that goes into your database. *Attributes* are the types of data that make up the database. For example, an individual's last name is data. An attribute, on the other hand, is another name for a field, so an entire group of last names is considered to be an attribute. Names, phone numbers, customer numbers, descriptions, locations, and stock numbers are all common examples of attributes that your database file may contain.

In addition to thinking about what kinds of information should go into the database, you must give careful consideration to the ways in which Excel will retrieve information from the database. Information comes from a database in the form of reports. A report is a summary of information. Whether Excel displays a single row of data through a data form or dozens of rows by means of the AutoFilter capability, Excel is providing a report based on the data contained within the database file.

Steps in database design

Designing a database in Excel, regardless of its purpose, involves two major parts:

- Data definition (analyzing existing data)
- Data refinement (refining necessary data)

During the first phase, data definition, you should list on paper all the important attributes that are involved in your application. To do this, you must examine your needs in detail to determine exactly what kind of information must be stored in the database. You should list all possible attributes of your database even though they may not actually be needed by your particular application. You can eliminate unnecessary attributes during the data refinement stage.

During data refinement, you refine the list of attributes on your initial list so that the attributes form an accurate description of the types of data that you will need in the database. At this stage, it is vital to include suggestions from as many other users of the database as possible. The people who use the database are likely to know what kinds of information they will need from the database. What kinds of reports do they need? What kinds of queries will employees ask of the database? By continually asking these types of questions, you begin to think in terms of your database, and this thought process should help you determine what is important and what is unimportant.

Keep in mind that even after the database design phases, you can make changes to the design. But if you follow the systematic approach of database design for your specific application, the chances are better that you won't create a database that fails to provide much of the information you need, and you will avoid extensive redesign.

By inserting rows and columns as needed, you can change the design of a database at any time. However, such changes are often inconvenient to make after the database is designed. For example, if you created a database to handle a customer mailing list, you might include fields for names, addresses, cities, states, and zip codes. At first glance, these fields may seem sufficient. Then you begin entering customer information into the database and gradually build a sizable mailing list. But if your company later decides to begin telemarketing by using the same mailing list, you suddenly realize that you have not included a field for telephone numbers. Although you can easily change the design to include a field for telephone numbers by inserting a new column, you would still face the formidable task of going back and adding a telephone number for every name currently in the mailing list. If this information had been entered as you developed the mailing list, you would not face the inconvenience of having to enter the phone numbers as a separate operation. Careful planning during the database design process can help avoid such pitfalls.

Summary

In this chapter, you learned how to work with databases stored within Excel worksheets. The chapter covered the following topics:

- In Excel, a database is a list of data that is organized into columns of data directly underneath a row of field names.
- You can add data to a database by typing it directly into the cells below the field names or by using a data form.
- In addition to adding data, you can use data forms to find specific records and to edit or delete records.
- Data⇨Sort lets you sort the data in a database.
- You can use Excel's AutoFilter command to filter a database so that only records meeting certain criteria appear. You can then copy these records to a different area of the worksheet or to a different worksheet, or you can print the records.

In the next chapter, you'll learn how you can put macros to work to automate many routine tasks within Excel.

Where to go next...

- A major part of setting up and maintaining a database is the tedious but necessary task of *data entry*. You'll find some tips and techniques that you can use to make data entry easier in Chapter 14.
- When you've entered data into your database, you'll want to make the most of Excel's printing capabilities to generate reports. Chapter 18 has the story.

✦ ✦ ✦

Working with Excel Macros

CHAPTER 20

♦ ♦ ♦ ♦

In This Chapter

Creating macros with the Macro Recorder

Stopping the Macro Recorder

Running macros

Assigning macros to buttons and graphic objects

Making macros available to all worksheets

♦ ♦ ♦ ♦

Macros are combinations of keystrokes that automate many of the tasks you normally perform with a program. Macros enable you to record a sequence of characters that you can then assign to a keystroke combination, a menu choice, a button on a toolbar, or a button on the screen. Later, you can play back the character sequence by entering the keystroke, clicking on the button, or selecting the menu option assigned to the macro. When you run the macro, Excel performs the steps as if you had just typed the characters, made the menu choices, or done whatever actions that you recorded for that macro. If you must produce daily reports or perform similar repetitive tasks, you can save many keystrokes with macros.

Excel's macros can also be very complex programs that make decisions based on user input. The macros can also call other programs outside Excel. For example, you can open the Windows Calculator with a macro attached to a command button in an Excel worksheet.

Even though you may have no interest in becoming a programmer, you can still use macros. Unlike some older DOS-based spreadsheets that forced you to create macros by typing obscure codes into cells, Excel provides a Macro Recorder feature. You can turn on the Macro Recorder and perform the same steps in your worksheet as you normally do manually. When you are finished with the task, you can simply turn off the Macro Recorder, and you have a complete macro that performs those steps for you.

Understanding the Types of Macros

Excel provides two types of macros: command macros and function macros.

Command macros carry out a series of commands. For example, you can create a command macro that marks a specific range of worksheet and chooses File⇨Print to begin printing. You can also create a macro that applies a preferred format to an entire worksheet. Command macros can range from the very simple to the extremely complex.

Function macros are very similar to Excel's functions in that they act upon values by performing calculations and returning a value. For example, you can create a macro that takes the dimensions of an area in feet and returns the area in square yards.

More Info You can remember the difference between the two types of macros if you keep in mind these points: Command macros are similar to commands because they do tasks. Function macros are similar to functions because they are stored in formulas and accept and return a value. You can create command macros by using the Macro Recorder. To create function macros, you must write Visual Basic for Applications code (see Chapter 22).

But when do I really need macros?

The kinds of macros that can be recorded with Excel's Macro Recorder are best at eliminating any kind of redundant work that you perform regularly. The following list contains the kinds of tasks for which you can create macros to save yourself time and effort:

- Selecting several ranges on one or more sheets of a workbook and printing those selected ranges

- Opening a new workbook, entering titles, formatting different ranges in the worksheet, and adjusting row heights and column widths

- Opening a database, sorting it in a desired order, applying a filter to the data, and printing the result

Creating a Macro

When you decide that you want to create a macro, you must first do everything that you do not want to include in the macro — such as opening a worksheet or moving to a specific location in the worksheet — because you don't want any unnecessary steps to be included in the macro. Remember that after you begin recording the macro, everything that you do will be included in it.

To begin creating a macro, choose Tools⇨Record Macro⇨Record New Macro. The Record New Macro dialog box prompts you for the name and description of your new macro (see Figure 20-1).

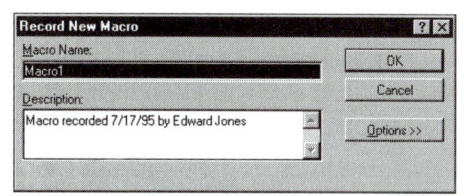

Figure 20-1: The Record New Macro dialog box.

In the Description area, you can enter a description of the macro. A description of the macro can be important if you plan on keeping the macro for some time because you may not remember what it does. If you click on the Options button, you will see different options that you can assign to a macro (see Figure 20-2).

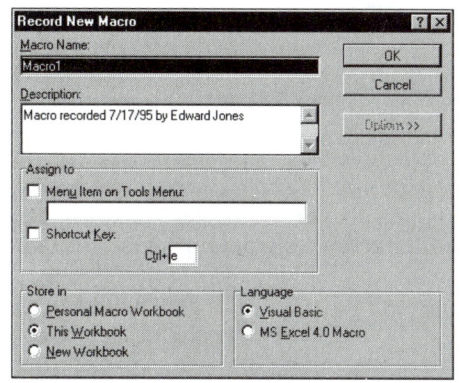

Figure 20-2: The Record New Macro dialog box after clicking on Options.

In the Assign To area, you can assign the macro to the Tools menu or to a keystroke combination by clicking on the corresponding check boxes. If you want to add the macro to the Tools menu, you then enter the menu item that you want the macro to use. If you want to assign the macro to a keystroke combination, you then type the combination. By default, you use the Ctrl key as part of the keystroke combination.

The Store in area gives you the opportunity to specify the place where you want to store the new macro. The Personal Macro Workbook option makes the macro available to all open worksheets by attaching the macro to a hidden notebook that is opened each time you start Excel. If you need to see the macro sheet, choose Window⇨Unhide. The This Workbook option places the macro in a module sheet that appears at the end of the workbook. Finally, the New Workbook option opens a new workbook and attaches the new module sheet to it.

The Language area lets you choose between Visual Basic and MS Excel 4.0 Macro as the macro language that you want. The default option is Visual Basic because the only time you will need to use MS Excel 4.0 Macro language is for backward compatibility with Excel 4.0.

More Info
You can also use another method to record macros in Excel: the Visual Basic toolbar. You can activate the Visual Basic toolbar by right-clicking in the toolbar area and then choosing the Visual Basic option from the shortcut menu. You can then click on the Record button on the Visual Basic toolbar to begin recording a macro. For everyday use of macros outside the world of programming, only two buttons on the Visual Basic toolbar will be of any interest to you: the Record Macro Button and the Run Macro button. For an explanation of the remaining buttons, see Chapter 22, which provides details on programming in Visual Basic for Applications.

Stopping the Macro Recorder

Stopping the Macro Recorder isn't too difficult — you click on the Stop Macro button. This button appears on-screen when you begin to record a macro.

You can resume recording the macro later by choosing Tools⇨Record Macro⇨Record at Mark. This option is good for building on a macro if you need to add more steps to it. The Record at Mark option also prevents you from having to perform all the steps over again if you want to record a similar but separate macro.

If you want to continue recording a macro, select the module that contains the macro and click on the last line of the macro. Then choose Tools⇨Record Macro⇨Record at Mark. The Macro Recorder begins to record at this point. Now switch back to the worksheet and start the tasks you wish to do for your macro.

Now that you have had a general look at creating macros, you need to see how the specifics work. The following steps show you how to create a macro that selects a range in one of you worksheets and prints that range:

1. Open the worksheet to which you want to apply the macro.

2. Choose Tools➪Record Macro➪Record New Macro.
3. In the Record New Macro dialog box, enter **Reportit** in the Macro Name text box.
4. Click on the Options button and select the Shortcut Key option in the Assign To area. Select any keystroke combination that you want to activate the macro.
5. After you click on the OK button, you are ready to make the choices that you need to print the range.
6. Select a range of data from your worksheet and then choose File➪Print to open the Print dialog box, as shown in Figure 20-3.

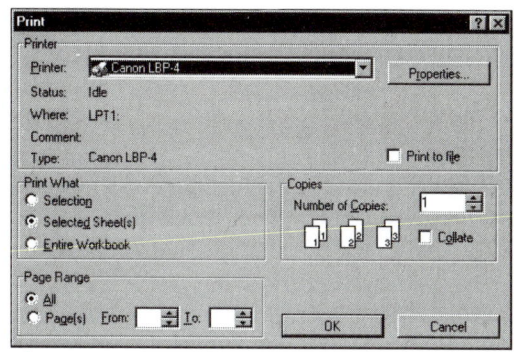

Figure 20-3: The Print dialog box.

7. In the Print What area, choose Selection.
8. Click on the OK button. This prints the selected part of your worksheet.
9. Click on the Stop Macro button to stop recording.

From this point on you can repeatedly select and print the same range of worksheets just by running the macro. To see how this process works, press the keystroke combination that you assigned to the macro or choose Tools➪Macro. In the Macro dialog box, click on the Reportit macro name and then click on the Run button. With either method, the macro runs, and the worksheet range is again printed. That's the beauty of macros — you can automate any task that you perform regularly, such as printing a worksheet range.

The macros that you create will differ because you will have different tasks that you need to automate with a macro.

Assigning Macros to Buttons

Another method that you can use to place a macro is to assign it to a button on a worksheet. This technique lets you access the macro by clicking on its button. A good example of why you would want to do this is if you have set up a macro to open another worksheet page from the current worksheet page. This is useful when there are two worksheets and while a user looks at one, you want to provide an easy way for the user to look at the other.

Macro buttons are an easy way to perform repeated tasks, such as printing a range. You can use the Create Button tool on the Drawing toolbar to place a button in your spreadsheet and attach a macro to it. You activate the macro by pressing the button.

You can add a macro button to a worksheet by performing the following steps:

1. In the Drawing toolbar, click on the Create button.
2. Move to the worksheet and then click and drag to shape the macro button. If you hold down the Alt key as you drag, you can create a button the exact size of a cell or a group of cells. If you hold down the Shift key as you drag, you create a button in the exact shape of a square.
3. After you create the button, the Assign Macro dialog box appears, as shown in Figure 20-4.

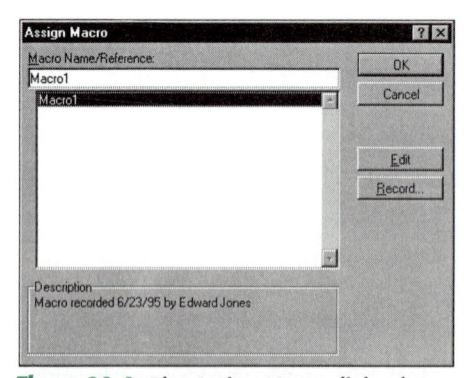

Figure 20-4: The Assign Macro dialog box.

4. From the Macro Name/Reference list box, choose the macro that you want to assign to the button.
5. After you click on the OK button, the macro is assigned to the button.

If you want to record a macro to assign to your button, click on the Record button in the Assign Macro dialog box. In the Record New Macro dialog box, enter a name for the macro that you are recording and click on the OK button.

Excel also lets you assign a macro to a completed button or change the macro that you have assigned to the button. You can do these tasks by performing the following steps:

1. Hold down the Ctrl key as you select the button.
2. Choose Tools⇨Assign Macro or right-click on the button and choose Assign Macro from the shortcut menu. With either method, you will see the Assign Macro dialog box.
3. If you want to assign an existing macro, choose the name from the Macro Name/ Reference text box and click on the OK button.
4. If you want to record a macro, type the name of the macro in the Macro Name/ Reference text box and click on the Record button. Then use the standard macro recording procedures detailed earlier in the chapter.

Macros can also be assigned to buttons on the toolbar. This can prove very useful if there are tasks that you perform on a regular basis. The macro button that the macro is assigned to is usually a custom button. But you also have the option of assigning the macro to an existing button on the toolbar, which will cancel the previous function.

After you have created the macro and assigned it to a button, you can assign the button to any toolbar that you want. This gives you the flexibility to move the button as you use different toolbars.

To assign a macro to a custom button and to place the button on a toolbar of your choice, perform the following steps:

1. Choose View⇨Toolbars.
2. In the Toolbars dialog box, click on the Customize button.
3. In the Categories list box, choose the Custom option, which displays the custom buttons available in Excel.
4. Click on the button that you want to use and drag it to the toolbar to which you want to add it.
5. After you choose the button and drag it to the toolbar, the Assign Macro dialog box appears.
6. Choose the macro that you want the button to activate from the Macro Name/ Reference list box. The macro is then assigned to that particular button.

> ### The old way versus the new way
>
> If you've upgraded to this version of Excel from version 4.0, and you've made extensive use of macros and the Excel macro language in Excel 4.0, you'll discover that many things have changed. In Excel 4.0 (and in earlier versions), you recorded macros in Excel's macro language, a language with some similarities to (and a lot of differences from) Visual Basic for Applications.
>
> Programs were known as macros, and they were recorded on macro sheets. In this version of Excel, each individual program (written in Visual Basic for Applications) is a *procedure*, and procedures are stored in *modules*. Each workbook can have an unlimited number of modules and procedures. And there are differences in the languages. For example, Visual Basic for Applications brings object-oriented techniques into the picture, something that just didn't exist in the old Excel 4.0 macro language.
>
> Keep in mind that you don't have to throw away all those macros that you wrote in Excel 4.0 just because you upgraded. You can run an Excel 4.0 macro from the current version of Excel by using the following Visual Basic for Applications statement in the Module tab of the macro:
>
> `RUN("macrosheetname!macroname")`
>
> In this statement, *macrosheetname* is the name of the Excel 4.0 macro sheet, and *macroname* is the name of the macro that you want to run. For more specifics on using Visual Basic for Applications code in your macros, refer to Chapter 22.

Assigning a Macro to a Graphic Object

Assigning a macro to a graphic object is also something that you may need to do from time to time in order to make your macro easier to remember. If you use many macros, this technique may not be a bad idea because pictures often help you remember things. The procedure for adding a macro to a graphic object is much the same as the procedure for adding a macro to a toolbar button.

For example, consider Figure 20-5. In the figure, a macro that prints a report is attached to a picture of a car. To print the report, the user clicks on the car.

Follow these steps to assign a macro to a graphic object:

1. Add the graphic object to your worksheet by using the steps outlined in Chapter 16. If the object currently has another macro assigned to it, hold down the Ctrl key and then select the object to avoid running the currently-assigned macro.

2. Choose Tools⇨Assign Macro.

3. If you want to assign a macro that you have already created to the object, type or select the name of the macro in the Macro Name/Reference list box and then click on the OK button.

4. You also have the option of assigning a new macro to the graphic object by clicking on the Record button and then following the steps for recording a macro.

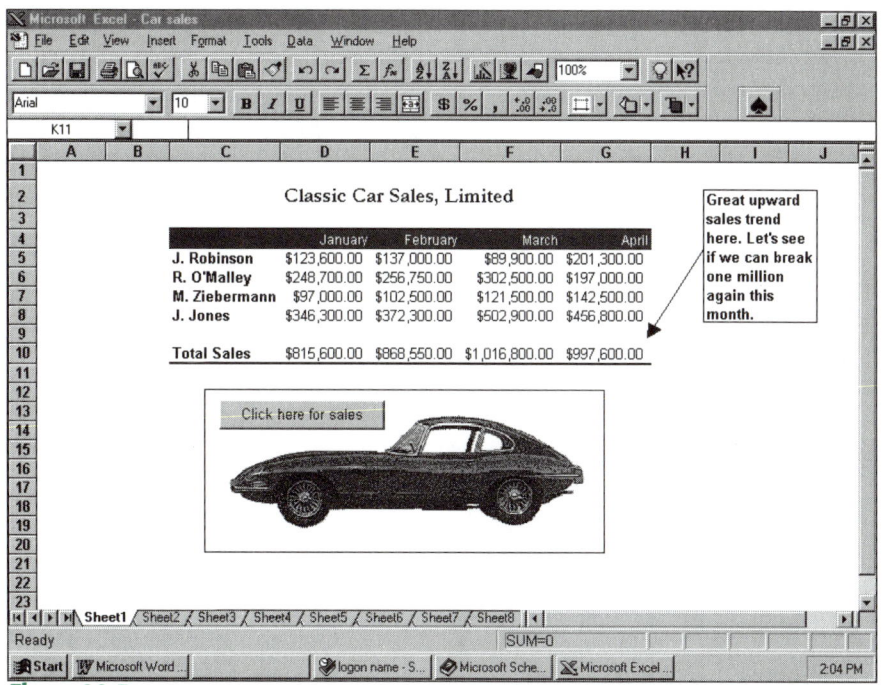

Figure 20-5: A macro attached to a graphic object in a worksheet.

Running the Macro

After you create a macro, you will discover that you can run it in different ways. After reading this section, you can decide for yourself which method is best for your needs.

One obvious way to run a macro is choose Tools⇨Macro. In the Macro dialog box, you click on the name of the macro that you want and then click on the Run button.

Another method for running macros is to use the keyboard combination that you assigned to the macro in the Record New Macro dialog box.

Changing Your Macro Options

After recording a macro, you may have to change some of the options, including the description of the macro, the keyboard combination that runs the macro, or the name of the macro as it appears on the Tools menu. In addition, you can assign the macro to a topic in a Help file.

Perform these steps to change the options for an existing macro:

1. Choose Tools⇔Macro to open the Macro dialog box.
2. In the Macro Name/Reference list box, select the name of the macro with the options that you want to change.
3. Click on the Options button to open the Macro Options dialog box, as shown in Figure 20-6.
4. Make the changes that you want for the different options and click on the OK button.

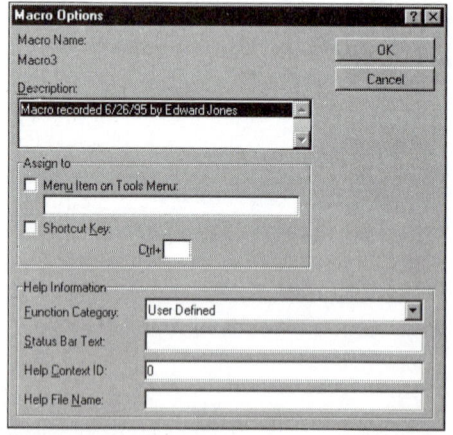

Figure 20-6: The Macro Options dialog box.

> ### About relative versus absolute cell references
>
> When you choose Tools⇨Record Macro, the submenu that appears contains a *toggle* named Use Relative References. Choosing this option turns on (or off) the use of relative references when you record a macro. The difference between relative and absolute references in worksheets is detailed in Chapter 14. But in a nutshell, with *relative references*, Excel locates worksheet cells by locating the relative locations of cells, such as three cells down and two cells to the right of the insertion point. With *absolute references*, Excel locates worksheet cells by locating the exact addresses, such as D12.
>
> If you leave the Use Relative References option turned on when you record macros, all recorded movements of the cursor will be recorded by using relative references. If you turn off the option, cursor movements will be recorded by using absolute references. There may be times when you want to use relative references during recording, and there may be times when you want to use absolute references during recording. Just be sure to understand which is which and to make the appropriate choices accordingly.

Making Macros Available to All Worksheets

You can store macros in many different places, which will directly affect the availability of the macro. You can store a macro in the Personal Macro Workbook, in the active workbook, or in a new workbook.

If you need to make a macro available at all times, then you should store it in the Personal Macro Workbook, which is an invisible workbook that is always open, unless you specify otherwise. The Personal Macro Workbook is like the depository for workbooks that you use in a variety of areas throughout Excel. Because this workbook is always open, the macros are all always available, which lets you use them with all the worksheets that you have open.

To control where you store your macro, choose Tools⇨Record Macro⇨Record New Macro. Click on the Options button in the Record New Macro dialog box to open the expanded version of this dialog box. In the Store in area, click on the Personal Macro Workbook radio button to store this and all successive macros in that workbook. This option remains in effect for all macros until you change it. In addition to placing the macros in the Personal Macro Workbook, you can also put them in the current workbook or in a new workbook.

The Personal Macro Workbook is similar to other workbooks with the exception that it begins with one worksheet where all the macros that you specify are stored. For those who are into Visual Basic, you may want to add other Visual Basic modules items to the Personal Macro Workbook.

To display the Personal Macro Workbook, choose the Unhide command from the Window Menu. Figure 20-7 shows what the Personal Macro Workbook looks like. Remember that the Unhide menu option is visible only if a worksheet has been hidden (as the Personal Macro Workbook normally is).

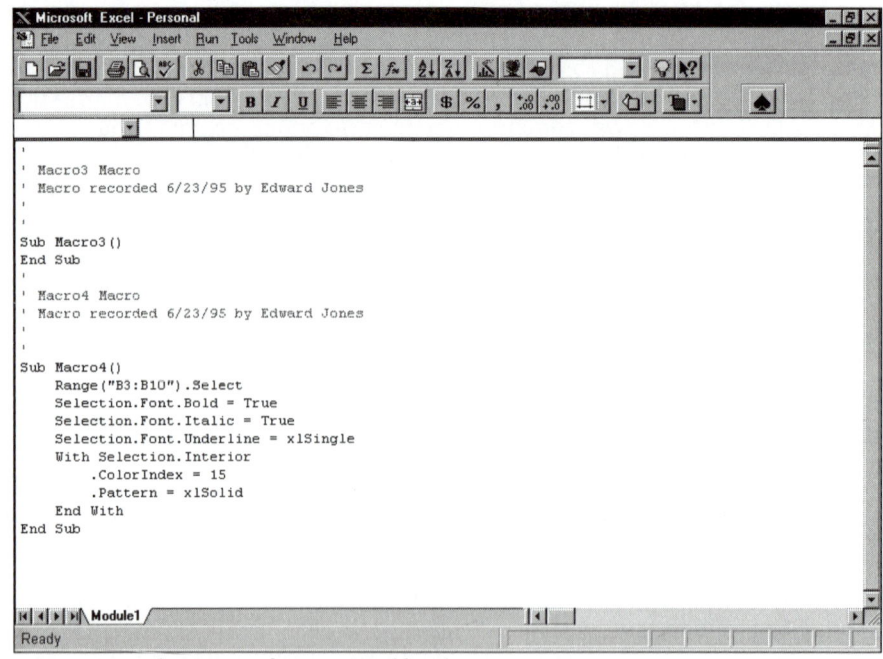

```
' Macro3 Macro
' Macro recorded 6/23/95 by Edward Jones


Sub Macro3()
End Sub

' Macro4 Macro
' Macro recorded 6/23/95 by Edward Jones


Sub Macro4()
    Range("B3:B10").Select
    Selection.Font.Bold = True
    Selection.Font.Italic = True
    Selection.Font.Underline = xlSingle
    With Selection.Interior
        .ColorIndex = 15
        .Pattern = xlSolid
    End With
End Sub
```

Figure 20-7: The Personal Macro Workbook.

Summary

This chapter covered different topics related to macros. Now you have the tools that you need to record macros efficiently and to put them in use for yourself. The following areas related to macros were covered:

- You learned about the different types of macros.
- You can create macros with Excel's Macro Recorder.
- You can run macros by choosing the Macro command from the Tools menu and selecting the desired macro in the dialog box that appears.
- You can attach macros to keyboard combinations, menu options, toolbar buttons, custom buttons, and graphic images.
- Macros are recorded in Visual Basic for Applications (VBA) code, the underlying programming language of Excel.

The next chapter will discuss the use of various analysis tools that you can use within Excel.

Where to go next...

- Macros can take much of the repetitive drudgery out of formatting and printing tasks. For an explanation of the kinds of formatting tasks that you can consider automating, see Chapter 15. For specifics on printing in Excel, you can refer to Chapter 18.
- Excel macros are the key to learning Visual Basic for Applications. Chapter 22 delves more deeply into Visual Basic for Applications programming.

✦ ✦ ✦

Excel Analysis

CHAPTER 21

This chapter details the use of analysis techniques, which can prove useful in dealing with what-if exercises and in providing a flexible "big picture" of Excel data through the use of dynamic cross tabulations called pivot tables.

What's Involved in What-If Analysis?

In some cases, you know which answer you want a worksheet's formula to provide, but you're not sure which value needs to be supplied to the formula to produce the desired result. In such cases, you have to work backwards by supplying different input values until the formula gives you the precise results that you're seeking. With early spreadsheet programs, the only way to accomplish this goal was by trial-and-error — entering different values until it came out right. But recent versions of Excel provide three ways that you can perform this kind of *what-if analysis*. In a nutshell, what-if analysis means exactly what its name implies: You produce values that provide an analysis of your spreadsheet information based on manipulation of dependent values within the worksheet. What if third-quarter sales drop by a certain percentage, but manufacturing overhead remains constant? Can administrative costs be cut, and to what level, to maintain a certain profit margin? These are the kinds of questions that you can answer by using what-if analysis. Excel offers a variety of tools suited for what-if analysis; these include goal-seeking, the use of data tables, and an add-in utility called Solver.

You can use *goal-seeking* in cases where you want to find a value for a specific cell by adjusting the value of one (and only one) other cell. You can use data tables to test how changing certain values in formulas will affect the results of those formulas. And you can use Excel's Solver to find a specific value for a cell by adjusting the value of more than one input cell. All these methods can save you significant amounts of time in experimenting with different values to produce a desired result.

In This Chapter

Using goal-seeking

Using Solver

Using data tables

Using pivot tables

Using the Goal Seek Command

In Excel, goal seeking is a tool that helps you discover what input value you need in a cell in order to provide a given result in another cell. In cases where you're seeking a value, and you can adjust the input value in another cell to provide the desired result, use Tools⇨Goal Seek. Take a real-world scenario as an example to illustrate the usefulness of goal-seeking. Mary and John Newlywed want to purchase a house. Their mortgage company is ready to give them an $80,000 loan at a 10.50% interest for 30 years. This works out to a monthly payment of $731.79 — but after the Newlyweds made out their budget, they decided they didn't want a mortgage payment in excess of $650.00. As their real-estate agent, you desperately want to help them get into a home (after all, you have bills to pay, too). You can use goal-seeking in Excel to change the financial scenario for your potential homebuyers. The Newlyweds want to know what they have to change to get that monthly payment. With this scenario in place, you can use Goal Seek by changing the principal on the loan, the interest rate, the term of loan, or whatever.

You perform the following steps to solve for a desired result by using the Goal Seek command:

1. Select the cell that contains the desired result that you want to see changed, as a result of your what-if analysis.

2. Choose Tools⇨Goal Seek to open the Goal Seek dialog box, as shown in Figure 21-1. In the Set Cell text box, you see the coordinates for the cell that you chose in Step 1.

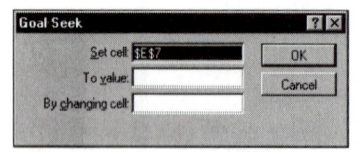

Figure 21-1: The Goal Seek dialog box.

3. In the To Value text box, enter the desired result that you are seeking.

4. In the By Changing Cell text box, enter the cell reference for the cell that Excel can modify to produce the end result that you want.

    For example, Figure 21-2 shows a loan worksheet for a mortgage payment. The Goal Seek dialog box is set to modify the monthly mortgage payment to $650 per month (cell E7) by changing the principal amount of the loan (cell E3). The interest rate and term of loan remain constant.

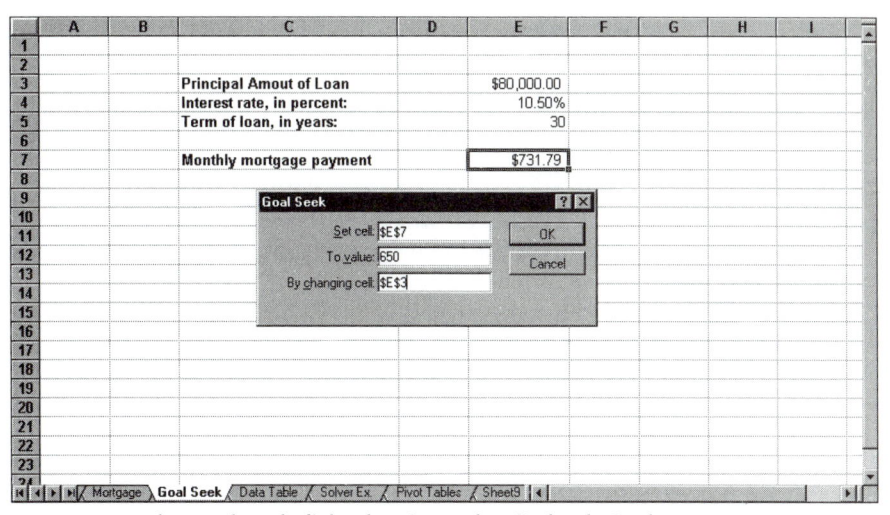

Figure 21-2: The Goal Seek dialog box is used to find a desired mortgage payment.

5. Click on the OK button. Excel's Goal Seek command begins experimenting with values, and it varies the input values until it comes up with a solution. If the process takes a while, Excel displays a status dialog box. In this dialog box, you can click on the Pause button to pause the process, or you can click on the Cancel button to stop the process. You can also click on the Step button to step through the process a single change at a time. To continue this process, click on the Continue button.

After Excel arrives at a solution, it displays the Goal Seek Status dialog box, as shown in Figure 21-3.

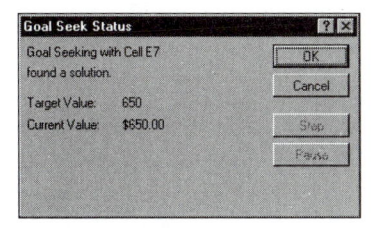

Figure 21-3: The Goal Seek Status dialog box.

If you're comfortable with the solution that Excel found, you can click on the OK button to insert the new values into the worksheet. If you'd rather leave things the way they were, you can click on the Cancel button to have the values in the worksheet revert back to their original values. Keep in mind that the entire purpose of what-if analysis is to see what works in different situations. You can try other values to see what the results would be.

> **Goal-seeking by dragging chart markers around**
>
> When you have two-dimensional bar, column, or line charts, and the markers are based on formulas (as opposed to fixed values), you can also perform goal-seeking by dragging the chart markers to a different location. If you drag a chart marker that's based on a formula to another location (for example, in a bar chart, clicking and dragging the top of the bar upwards or downwards to increase or decrease the value that it represents, or in a line chart, clicking and dragging a line marker up or down for the same reason), the Goal Seek dialog box and the worksheet appear. You can tell Excel which input value you need to change to produce the new value reflected by the new location of the chart's marker. For specifics on working with chart markers, refer to Chapter 17.

Before using the Goal Seek command, you need to keep the following points in mind:

- The cell that the Goal Seek command modifies to change your desired result can't contain a formula.

- The cell that the Goal Seek command modifies must contain a value on which the entry in the Set Cell text box in the Goal Seek dialog box depends (either directly or indirectly).

Using Solver

In complex what-if cases, you may need to find a desired result by manipulating a series of values, and you may have specific limitations to apply to the model. Suppose that you have a small mail-order firm that manufactures and sells directly to the public. You want to adjust advertising costs upward to increase revenues as much as possible but only within the limits of your advertising budget and the plant's manufacturing capacity. When what-if situations involve goal-seeking (as this example does), but they contain a number of variables and possible limitations, you can use Excel's Solver. Use Solver whenever you want to find the best value possible in a given cell by changing the values in several cells (as opposed to just one cell, which is the case with the Goal Seek command). You can also use Solver when you need to apply any sort of limitation to any of the values that you use in the worksheet's projections.

To use Solver, you specify the what-if question that you want answered by identifying a *target cell*, the *changing cells*, and any *constraints* (or limitations) that must be met. Solver then works with various iterations and manipulates the values that you've told it to work with until it finds a feasible solution. If Solver can find a solution, it then displays the new figures in the worksheet, along with a dialog box that gives you the opportunity to accept the new figures, reject them, or save the model as a new worksheet file. If Solver can't find a solution, it will tell you so, and the original figures are maintained in the worksheet.

In Figure 21-4, you see a worksheet typical of the type that Solver can deal with. The model shows the gross and net profits for a mail-order seed company. The monthly average figure reflects the fact that the business is highly seasonal — because it is a seed and garden supply company, the firm does much of its business in the spring of the year. And the amount of sales is based on a typical sales projection formula that factors in the effects of advertising on the number of sales.

	A	B	C	D	E	F
1						
2		30,000	Quarterly production run, seed kits			
3		59.95	Mail-order price per kit			
4		16.50	Production price per kit			
5						
6	Month	January	February	March	April	Total
7	Monthly average	9.00%	12.00%	8.50%	14%	
8	Seed kits sold	254	339	240	395	1228
9	Gross profit	$15,227	$20,323	$14,388	$23,680	$73,619
10						
11	Production costs per kit	$4,191	$5,594	$3,960	$6,518	$20,262
12	Advertising costs	$2,000	$2,000	$2,000	$2,000	$8,000
13	Overhead	$4,600	$4,600	$4,600	$4,600	$18,400
14	Net profit	$4,436	$8,130	$3,828	$10,563	$26,957

Figure 21-4: The sales worksheet for a small mail-order firm.

Solver is an *add-in*, which appears as an option on the Tools menu after you've added Solver to Excel. If you open the Tools menu and you see Solver as an option, it has already been installed, and you are ready to use it. If the option is not shown, choose the Add-ins command from the Tools menu to open the Add-Ins dialog box. If you see the Solver check box in the list of add-ins, turn it on and then click on the OK button in the dialog box. If the option is not included, you must run the Office Setup program to install Solver as one of the Excel options.

You can run Solver on a worksheet by performing the following steps:

1. Open the worksheet page that contains the model that you want to analyze.

2. Choose Tools⇨Solver. Excel loads the Solver add-in into memory (on machines with minimum memory, this process may take a while). After Solver is loaded, the Solver Parameters dialog box appears, as shown in Figure 21-5.

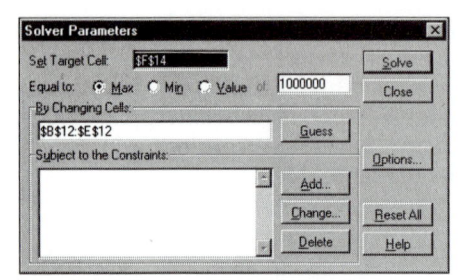

Figure 21-5: The Solver Parameters dialog box.

3. In the Set Target Cell text box, you enter the cell reference for the cell that you want to change (also known as the *target cell*). The target cell should contain a formula that is dependent on the cells that you specify next in the By Changing Cells box.

4. In the Equal To area of the dialog box, choose the Max option to maximize the target cell's value, the Min option to minimize the target cell's value, or the Value Of option to specify a certain value. If you choose Value Of, enter the desired value in the Value Of text box.

5. In the By Changing Cells text box, enter the cell or range of cells that you want Solver to modify to reach the desired results. If you want Solver to propose changes based on the target cell, click on the Guess button.

6. If you want to specify any constraints (or limitations) that Solver must follow as it adjusts the values, click on the Add button to display an Add Constraint dialog box. Here you can enter the cell that you want to constrain, followed by an operator and a value for the limitation. You can click on the Add button and then repeat this step to add more constraints, or you can click on the OK button if you're finished adding constraints.

When you are finished with the options in the Solver Parameters dialog box, click the Solve button. Solver proceeds to change the values that you've told it to work with until it finds a solution. If Solver can find a solution, it then displays the Solver Results dialog box (see Figure 21-6).

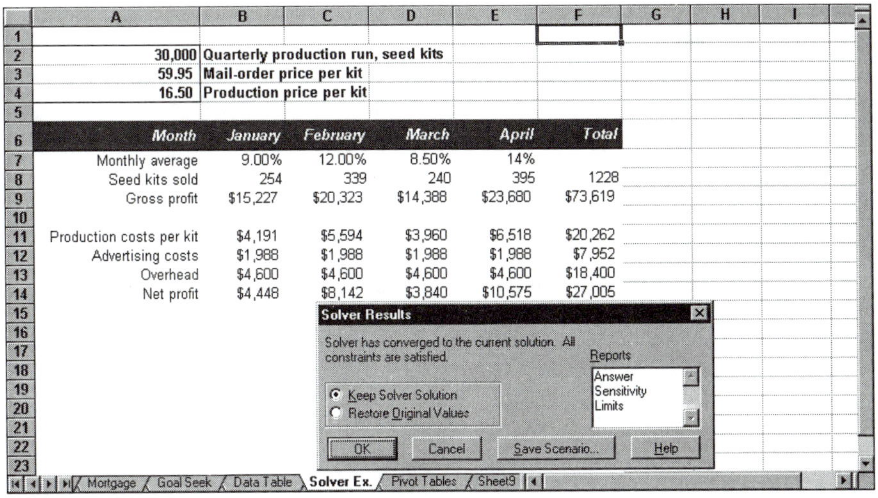

Figure 21-6: The Solver Results dialog box.

You can choose the Keep Solver Solution option and click on OK to accept the new figures and store them in the worksheet. Or you can choose the Restore Original Values option and click on OK to reject the changes suggested by Solver and return to the original worksheet values. If you click on the Save Scenario button, you are prompted for a name under which you can save the scenario suggested by Solver.

Note that if Solver can't find a solution, it will advise you so by displaying a dialog box warning that it could not find a solution. In such cases, the original figures are maintained in the worksheet.

Projecting Figures with Data Tables

Another way in which you can perform what-if analysis is to use *data tables*. With data tables, you can see how a change in certain values within your formulas affects the formulas' results. This may sound like goal seeking, but there is a difference. With goal-seeking, you are looking at varying one cell's end results at a time. Data tables, on the other hand, provide you with a *range* of cells that display the net results of substituting different values in your formulas. With a data table, you can examine the results of a group of what-if variations at one time. With goal-seeking, you would have to use the Tools⇨Goal Seek command a number of times to accomplish the same results.

In Excel, you can create two types of data tables: *one-input* data tables and *two-input* data tables. With one-input data tables, you enter multiple values for a single variable, and the resulting data table displays the effects of the what-if analysis on one or more formulas within your worksheet. With two-input data tables, you enter multiple values for two variables, and the resulting data tables display the effects of the what-if analysis for both variables on the formulas of your worksheet. The process of creating data tables is virtually the same, whether you want to create a one-input data table or a two-input data table. The only difference is that with a two-input data table, you fill in both input cell entries in a Table dialog box, rather than filling in just one entry. (This dialog box will be discussed shortly.)

You can use the Data⇨Table command to create a data table. Before using the command, you need the following:

- A cell that contains the value that you want to change (the input cell).
- A column or row that contains the values that you will apply to the input cell. When you use the Table command, these values will replace the values in the input cell one at a time, producing the result determined by your formulas.
- A row or column that contains the formulas that Excel uses to produce the values.

You can see how you can use a data table if you open a blank worksheet and build the structure for a table by entering the following data:

In cell	Enter
B2	**Monthly sales**
B4	**Increase rate**
B7	**Projected sales**
B8	**What-if rate**
C8	5%
C9	6%
C10	7%
C11	8%
C12	9%
C13	10%
D2	120000
D4	6%
D7	=D2+(D2*D4)

At this point, your worksheet should resemble the one shown in Figure 21-7. The simple formula in cell D7 projects a sales increase by multiplying current sales in cell D2 by a projected increase rate of six percent in cell D4 and adding the result to the current sales.

	A	B	C	D	E
1					
2		Monthly sales		120000	
3					
4		Increase rate		6%	
5					
6					
7		Projected sales		127200	
8		What-If rate	5%		
9			6%		
10			7%		
11			8%		
12			9%		
13			10%		
14					
15					

Figure 21-7: A sample worksheet containing the basis of a data table.

A table is a handy way of figuring different alternatives quickly. The alternative percentages entered in cells C8 through C13 are the input values for the table. To create this example (which in this case is a one-input table), follow these steps:

1. Choose the range of cells that contain the row or column of input values and the column or row of formulas that will be provided with the input values. In the example that you have created, select the range from cell C7 to D13. This range contains both the input values (in cells C8 to C13) and the formula (in cell D7).

2. Choose Data➪Table to open the Table dialog box, as shown in Figure 21-8.

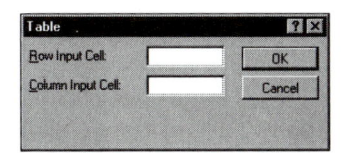

Figure 21-8: The Table dialog box.

3. If the input values occupy a row, enter the reference for the input cell in the Row Input Cell text box. If the input values occupy a column, enter the reference for the input cell in the Column Input Cell text box. (Note that you can have entries in both the Row Input Cell text box and the Column Input Cell text box; when you do so, the result is a two-input data table.)

   Because the input values in the example are arranged in a column, enter $D$4 in the Column Input Cell text box (or you can select the cell to put its address in the text box).

4. Click on the OK button or press Enter. The table is filled with the respective what-if values, as shown in Figure 21-9.

	A	B	C	D	E
1					
2		Monthly sales		120000	
3					
4		Increase rate		6%	
5					
6					
7		Projected sales		127200	
8		What-If rate	5%	126000	
9			6%	127200	
10			7%	128400	
11			8%	129600	
12			9%	130800	
13			10%	132000	
14					

Figure 21-9: The results of the Table command.

The range of values created by the Table command does not consist of separate values but rather numbers generated by a single formula. You cannot edit or clear an individual cell within a data table, and you cannot insert space, rows, or columns anywhere inside a data table. If you attempt any of these operations, Excel displays a `Can't change part of table` error message. You can, however, insert space in the top row or left column of a data table with the Insert menu commands. Doing so provides room for adding new comparison values or formulas. To delete or cut and paste a data table, you must select the entire table before using the Delete, Cut, or Copy commands from the Edit menu.

Working with PivotTables

You can use pivot tables to perform a different type of analysis that summarizes tabular data. You may often have worksheets that contain large amounts of data that you want to summarize. Such summaries are also known as *cross-tabulations* of data because they provide you with the capability to cross-tabulate data and examine the data from a summary perspective. Earlier versions of Excel helped you perform this kind of task by using a Crosstab Report Wizard. Since version 5.0 of Excel, this wizard has been updated to the PivotTable Wizard. With the PivotTable Wizard, you can create summaries of your worksheet data, and you can summarize the data in different ways. Pivot tables are an improvement over the crosstabs produced with the old Crosstab Report Wizard because pivot tables are *dynamic*, which means that you can rearrange them by dragging fields (text labels that categorize your data) to different locations on-screen.

To see an example of how you can use pivot tables, consider the worksheet page shown in Figure 21-10. This worksheet is typical of the kind of worksheet that lends itself to summary analysis. In this case, the worksheet lists sales of car models for each sales rep at a car dealership.

Chapter 21 ♦ Excel Analysis 473

	A	B	C	D	E	F	G	H
1			Ultima Motors of Northern California					
2								
3	Month	Sales Rep	Econobox 2000	Sunstar XL	Plethora Ultima	Speedster ZX90	Total	
4	January	A. Williams	$39,270	$52,800	$75,600	$67,890	$235,560	
5	January	S. Ray	$46,590	$58,350	$23,400	$45,800	$174,140	
6	January	N. Jones	$39,790	$55,320	$78,900	$72,300	$246,310	
7	February	A. Williams	$42,320	$45,650	$45,800	$45,210	$178,980	
8	February	S. Ray	$23,800	$72,100	$34,500	$69,800	$200,200	
9	February	N. Jones	$52,320	$41,200	$67,800	$94,560	$255,880	
10	March	A. Williams	$32,850	$61,900	$102,550	$89,120	$286,420	
11	March	S. Ray	$52,300	$45,300	$58,200	$57,800	$213,600	
12	March	N. Jones	$45,670	$67,800	$109,500	$101,200	$324,170	
13								

Figure 21-10: A worksheet containing car sales.

In its present form, the worksheet lists the data by month. But what if you want to see sales organized by sales rep or by car model? This is the kind of question that you can answer by using the PivotTable Wizard. For example, consider Figure 21-11. In this figure, the PivotTable Wizard has summarized the data from Figure 21-10 on the basis of the sales reps. To see each rep's sales information, you click on his or her name in the drop-down list box.

	A	B	C	D
1	Sales Rep	(All)		
2				
3	Month	Data	Total	
4	January	Sum of Econobox 2000	125650	
5		Sum of Sunstar XL	166470	
6		Sum of Plethora Ultima	177900	
7		Sum of Speedster ZX90	185990	
8	February	Sum of Econobox 2000	118440	
9		Sum of Sunstar XL	158950	
10		Sum of Plethora Ultima	148100	
11		Sum of Speedster ZX90	209570	
12	March	Sum of Econobox 2000	130820	
13		Sum of Sunstar XL	175000	
14		Sum of Plethora Ultima	270250	
15		Sum of Speedster ZX90	248120	
16	Total Sum of Econobox 2000		374910	
17	Total Sum of Sunstar XL		500420	
18	Total Sum of Plethora Ultima		596250	
19	Total Sum of Speedster ZX90		643680	
20				

Figure 21-11: The car sales summarized by sales reps.

After you have the worksheet data that you want to summarize, you can run the PivotTable Wizard by performing the following steps:

1. Choose Data⇒Pivot Table to open the first of four PivotTable Wizard dialog boxes, as shown in Figure 21-12.

Part III ✦ Excel

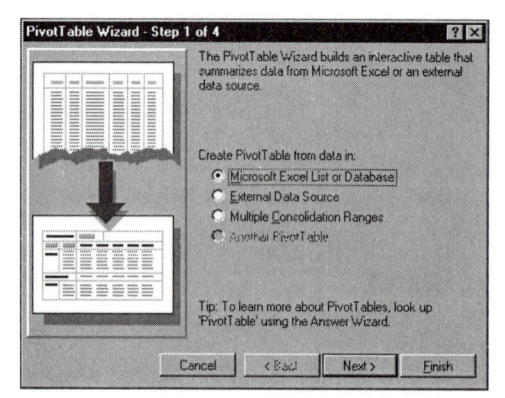

Figure 21-12: The first PivotTable Wizard dialog box.

2. Leave the default data source selected to tell Excel to use worksheet data (as opposed to data from an external source) and click on the Next button.

3. The second PivotTable Wizard dialog box appears, as shown in Figure 21-13. Here you tell Excel what range of cells should be used as the basis for the pivot table. Click and drag across the desired cells or enter the cell addresses that make up the desired range. (If the cursor is within a list of the data, Excel will makes its best guess as to the proper range, and you can accept Excel's guess or change it.)

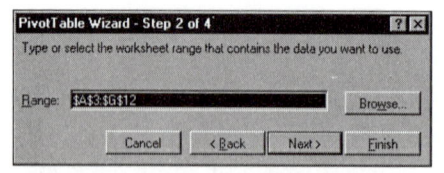

Figure 21-13: The second PivotTable Wizard dialog box.

4. Click on the Next button to display the third PivotTable Wizard dialog box, as shown in Figure 21-14. You can drag the various field buttons representing your worksheet's data to the appropriate areas of the dialog box to create the desired rows, columns, data, and optional pages. You should have in mind which data you want to use for each of the following areas of your pivot table:

   - **ROW** — To arrange any item in rows (with labels appearing along the left side), drag the field button here. A pivot table in Excel can contain up to eight rows.

- **COLUMN** — To arrange any item in columns (with labels appearing across the top), drag the field button here.
- **DATA** — These are the sums of values that you want to be added for every intersection of a column and row.
- **PAGE** — Use these to create a drop-down list for a desired row or column in the worksheet. The drop-down list enables you to quickly view a summary of the data for an item that you choose from the drop-down list. In effect, you can have a group of rows or a group of columns making up a page. For example, if you use Car Models as the Pages in the example shown, you can choose a different car model name in the drop-down list and see the appropriate data for that car model.

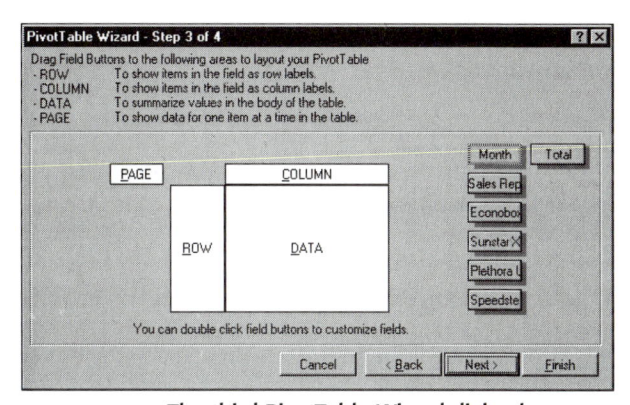

Figure 21-14: The third PivotTable Wizard dialog box.

5. Drag the field buttons at the right side of the dialog box to the desired locations for row headings and column headings.

6. If you want the summary data to be divided into pages, drag the desired field to the PAGE area in the dialog box. The field that you use for this option provides the choices in the drop-down list box that appears in the top row of the pivot table. In Figure 21-11, the Sales Rep is used category for a PAGE field, which permits the data to be summarized by sales rep name. All you have to do is click on the individual sales rep name in the drop-down list box to see the sales that belong to him or her.

7. Click on the Next button. The fourth PivotTable Wizard dialog box appears, as shown in Figure 21-15. This dialog box asks for a pivot table name and a starting cell location. You can also use the check boxes in the dialog box to indicate whether you want totals for columns and rows, whether data should be saved with the layout, and whether the pivot table should be formatted with Excel's AutoFormat capability.

Note: If you don't specify a location for the pivot table in Step 7, Excel automatically adds a new worksheet page in front of the current page and inserts the pivot table there.

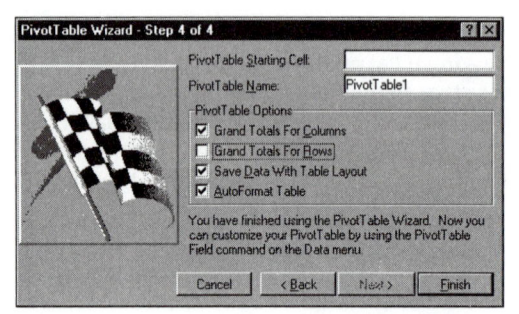

Figure 21-15: The fourth PivotTable Wizard dialog box.

8. Turn off any options that you don't want and then click on the Finish button. When you do so, the PivotTable Wizard creates the pivot table, which is based on your choices.

The data produced in a pivot table may look like worksheet data, but you can't modify it in any way. The pivot table is directly linked to the source of the data in the original worksheet. You can, however, apply any desired formatting changes to the data in the pivot table.

Hot Stuff If you create charts based on pivot tables that contain different PAGE areas, you can then select different choices from the drop-down list box of pages and generate different charts based on different summary data.

Pivot tables can be complex beasts to work with. If you create a pivot table, and you don't get the results that you expected, don't immediately rerun the PivotTable Wizard again. You may be able to get the results that you want by dragging the fields of the pivot table to different locations in the table.

After a pivot table exists, you can dynamically change how you view the data by dragging the different field tabs of the table to the desired areas. This is one of the most powerful features of pivot tables. For example, first refer back to Figure 21-11. In this figure, the data is shown with pages organized by sales rep name, and then the data is arranged by month and then by car model.

In Figure 21-16, the pivot table has been rearranged by dragging the Month tab up to the same level as the data tab. As a result, the data is now organized by car model and then by month.

	A	B	C	D
1	Sales Rep	(All)		
2				
3	Data	Month	Total	
4	Sum of Econobox 2000	January	125650	
5		February	118440	
6		March	130820	
7	Sum of Sunstar XL	January	166470	
8		February	158950	
9		March	175000	
10	Sum of Plethora Ultima	January	177900	
11		February	148100	
12		March	270250	
13	Sum of Speedster ZX90	January	185990	
14		February	209570	
15		March	248120	
16	Total Sum of Econobox 2000		374910	
17	Total Sum of Sunstar XL		500420	
18	Total Sum of Plethora Ultima		596250	
19	Total Sum of Speedster ZX90		643680	
20				

Figure 21-16: The pivot table with data arranged first by car model and then by month.

In Figure 21-17, the pivot table has been rearranged by dragging the Month tab directly below the Sales Rep tab. This produces separate pages for each month within the separate pages for each sales rep so that you can easily see data on car sales for any specific sales rep for any given month.

	A	B	C
1	Sales Rep	(All)	
2	Month	January	
3			
4	Data	Total	
5	Sum of Econobox 2000	125650	
6	Sum of Sunstar XL	166470	
7	Sum of Plethora Ultima	177900	
8	Sum of Speedster ZX90	185990	
9			

Figure 21-17: The pivot table with data arranged with separate pages for sales reps and for months.

Finally in Figure 21-18, the Sales Rep and Month tabs have been dragged to the same level as the Data tab, and to the right of it. This produces a pivot table with no pages, in this example arranged by sales reps, then by months.

	A	B	C	D	E
1					
2					
3					
4	Data	Sales Rep	Month	Total	
5	Sum of Econobox 2000	A. Williams	January	39270	
6			February	42320	
7			March	32850	
8		A. Williams Total		114440	
9		N. Jones	January	39790	
10			February	52320	
11			March	45670	
12		N. Jones Total		137780	
13		S. Ray	January	46590	
14			February	23800	
15			March	52300	
16		S. Ray Total		122690	
17	Sum of Sunstar XL	A. Williams	January	52800	
18			February	45650	
19			March	61900	
20		A. Williams Total		160350	
21		N. Jones	January	55320	
22			February	41200	
23			March	67800	
24		N. Jones Total		164330	

Figure 21-18: The pivot table with data arranged by sales rep and then by months.

Summary

This chapter has detailed the use of various analysis tools that you'll find helpful as you work with spreadsheet data. The chapter detailed the following points:

- You can use the Goal Seek command when you want to vary the value in a single input cell to achieve a desired result.
- You can use Solver when you want to vary the values in a series of input cells to achieve a desired result or when you want to apply limitations to any of the values used in a worksheet to achieve the desired results.
- You can use data tables to project how changes in a certain value will affect a series of formulas.
- You can use the PivotTable Wizard to create pivot tables, which enable you to summarize Excel data and dynamically change how the data is organized.

In the next chapter, you'll learn how you can use Visual Basic for Applications to extend the power of Excel macros.

Where to go next...

- With some business applications, large amounts of data involved in your analysis work may reside in a database. If this is the case, you'll find analysis to be an easier task if you can first filter the data to obtain a subset containing just the data you want to analyze. You can find out more about getting at specific data in a database by turning to Chapter 19.
- After you've used any of the analysis tools to your satisfaction, you may want to chart the data to visually demonstrate the results of your analysis. For specifics on charting data in Excel, see Chapter 17.

✦ ✦ ✦

CHAPTER 22

Using Visual Basic for Applications

In This Chapter

Using macros to learn Visual Basic for Applications

Understanding Visual Basic for Applications code

Using comments, cell selection techniques, and control statements

Displaying dialog boxes

Getting user input

Working in the Editor

This chapter details the use of Visual Basic for Applications (VBA), the programming language that is the basis for Excel macros. VBA is heavily based on Microsoft's Visual Basic programming language. Because Excel macros are based on VBA, you can use VBA to automate common tasks in Excel.

VBA can take you much further than simply duplicating keystrokes. VBA gives you full access to all of Excel's commands. You can modify Excel's own menus by adding your own commands and options; you can create custom dialog boxes to present messages and query users for information; you can even construct complete applications that users with a limited knowledge of Excel can work with. To accomplish these kinds of tasks, you need more than a familiarity with the recording and playing of macros — you need a basic understanding of VBA.

Using Macros to Learn Visual Basic for Applications

More Info Chapter 20 detailed the basics of using macros, which are sequences of instructions that cause Excel to perform a particular task. As that chapter demonstrates, macros can be very handy to use in your work because they greatly reduce the time that you spend performing routine, repetitive tasks. Macros are also an excellent starting point for understanding how VBA works and what you can do with the language. As Excel's Macro Recorder stores all the actions that you perform or the commands that you choose, it interprets these actions or commands into *statements*, or lines of code, by using VBA. These statements are automatically placed in a *procedure*, which is a block of VBA code. Procedures are stored in *modules*, which you can think of as containers for all VBA code.

Each module has its own page of a workbook. Each time that you create a macro, Excel adds a workbook page for a module at the end of your workbook and stores the Visual Basic code for the macro there. (By default, the pages are named Module1, Module2, Module3, and so on, as you create new macros.)

To get an idea of how all Excel macros use VBA, you should practice on an example. This chapter will familiarize you with Visual Basic code by examining the procedure that results when you record this sample macro. The following steps create the simple time sheet shown in Figure 22-1. Because time sheets typically are created weekly, it represents a typical task that can be automated by creating a macro.

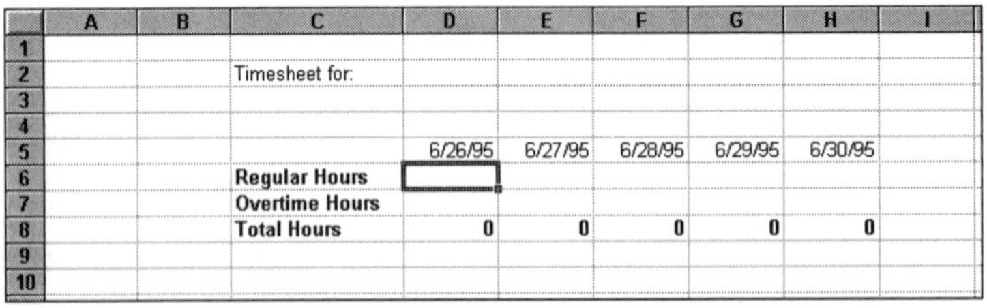

Figure 22-1: A time sheet that results from creating the sample macro.

Follow these steps to create the worksheet and the sample macro:

1. Open a new workbook.
2. Choose Tools⇨Record Macro⇨Record New Macro.
3. In the Record New Macro dialog box, enter the name **TimeEntry** and then click on the OK button. The Stop Macro button, which you can use to stop recording the macro, appears in the worksheet.
4. Click in cell C2 and enter **Timesheet for:** in the cell.
5. Click in cell D5 and enter =**Today()** in the cell.
6. Click and drag from cell D5 to H5 to select D5 and the next four cells to the right.
7. Choose Edit⇨Fill⇨Series.
8. In the Series dialog box, click on the OK button to accept the default options.
9. Click in cell C6 and enter **Regular Hours** in the cell.
10. Click in cell C7 and enter **Overtime Hours** in the cell.
11. Click in cell C8 and enter **Total Hours** in the cell.
12. Select the range of cells from C6 to C8 and press Ctrl+B to add bold formatting.

13. Click on the border between cells C and D and drag to widen column C until it is wide enough to display the longest text in the column.
14. Click in cell D8 and enter the formula **=D6+D7** in the cell.
15. Click and drag from cells D8 to H8 to select cell D8 and the four cells to the right of it.
16. Choose Edit⇨Fill⇨Right.
17. Press Ctrl+B to apply bold formatting to the selected cells.
18. Click in cell D6 (this repositions the cursor to prepare the worksheet for data entry).
19. Click on the Stop Macro button to stop the recording of the macro.

You can verify the effects of the macro by moving to a blank worksheet, choosing Tools⇨Macro, clicking on TimeEntry to select it, and clicking on the Run button. The time sheet is duplicated in the blank worksheet.

How similar is Visual Basic for Applications to Visual Basic?

If you've already worked with Microsoft's Visual Basic as a development language, you'll find Visual Basic for Applications to be a familiar friend; in fact, *sibling* is more accurate. Visual Basic for Applications is solidly based on Microsoft's Visual Basic programming language. The whole idea in developing Visual Basic for Applications was to replace the old macro-based languages, such as Excel 4.0's macro language and Access Basic, with a common development language so that developers who are familiar with applications development in Excel could easily develop applications in Access or in Word, and vice versa.

Microsoft uses Visual Basic as the base language, and it has added extensions to the language as implemented in Excel and in Access. At the time of this writing, Visual Basic for Applications is not implemented in Word for Windows. However, according to Microsoft, Word will eventually have Visual Basic for Applications implemented as its development language, as well. The commands, functions, methods, procedures, and program structures used in Visual Basic can all be used in Visual Basic for Applications for Excel and for Access. So if you are a Visual Basic programmer, you're on very familiar ground.

Understanding Visual Basic for Applications Code

Of course, the purpose of the exercise that you just completed is not to demonstrate how to create a macro but to show how Visual Basic for Applications code works as the basis of any macro. Using the scroll arrows at the lower-left corner of the worksheet, scroll the worksheet until you see the Module1 tab. Click on that tab to see the Visual Basic code that the Macro Recorder created as it recorded the macro. The code looks like this:

```
' TimeEntry Macro
' Macro recorded 6/20/95 by Derek Sutton
Sub TimeEntry()
    Range("C2").Select
    ActiveCell.FormulaR1C1 = "Timesheet for:"
    Range("D5").Select
    ActiveCell.FormulaR1C1 = "=TODAY()"
    Range("D5:H5").Select
    Selection.DataSeries Rowcol:=xlRows, Type:=xlChronological, Date _
        :=xlDay, Step:=1, Trend:=False
    Range("C6").Select
    ActiveCell.FormulaR1C1 = "Regular Hours"
    Range("C7").Select
    ActiveCell.FormulaR1C1 = "Overtime Hours"
    Range("C8").Select
    ActiveCell.FormulaR1C1 = "Total Hours"
    Range("C6:C8").Select
    Selection.Font.Bold = True
    Columns("C:C").ColumnWidth = 13.71
    Range("D8").Select
    ActiveCell.FormulaR1C1 = "=R[-2]C+R[-1]C"
    Range("D8:H8").Select
    Selection.FillRight
    Selection.Font.Bold = True
    Range("D6").Select
End Sub
```

Each of the steps that you took during the recording of this procedure resulted in the addition of one or more lines of Visual Basic code in the module. The code appears in color: comments are displayed in green; key words of the Visual Basic language appear in blue; and all other code appears in black. When you run this (or any) macro, you are in effect running the Visual Basic for Applications code that is contained in the module that was recorded by the Macro Recorder. As the module runs, each line of Visual Basic code is executed in turn, and Excel performs an appropriate action as a result.

About comments

You can include *comments* (lines that aren't acted upon by Excel when the code runs) by preceding the text with a single quotation mark. In the sample procedure, you can see that the first two lines are comments:

```
' TimeEntry Macro
' Macro recorded 6/20/95 by Derek Sutton
```

In this case, Excel added the comments based on the entries in the Macro Name and Description text boxes of the Record Macro dialog box. But you can place comments wherever you desire in your Visual Basic code by typing a single quote mark followed by the text of the comment. Comments can be quite helpful in your more complex procedures because they can help you remember what's going on at a specific point in the procedure. Comments can occupy an entire line, or you can put them at the end of a valid line of code by starting the comment with a single quotation mark. When the procedure runs, everything that follows the single quotation mark is ignored until Excel finds a new line of code.

About headers and footers

Following the comments, the next line of the procedure reads

```
Sub TimeEntry()
```

The matching last line reads

```
End sub
```

Think of these lines as the header and footer for the procedure. Every VBA procedure starts with a header that begins with `Sub` or `Function` and ends with a footer that says `End Sub` or `End Function`. VBA allows two types of procedures: *function procedures* and *sub procedures*. Function procedures are like Excel's built-in functions. They accept a value(s), act on the data, and return a value(s). Sub procedures do not return a value (although you can pass values from within a sub procedure through the use of statements inside the procedure). Any arguments used by a function procedure are placed inside the parentheses of the header. The footer tells Excel that it has reached the end of the procedure. When Excel reaches the footer in the module, it passes program control back to any other VBA procedure that called this one. If the procedure was not called by another procedure, Excel returns control from the procedure to Excel itself.

About selecting and entering data

Following the header statement are two lines of code that select cell C2 and insert a text entry into that cell. The Visual Basic code for these two lines is

```
Range("C2").Select
ActiveCell.FormulaR1C1 = "Timesheet for:"
```

The `Range` statement tells Excel to select a range. Because only one cell's address is given (cell C2), Excel selects only that cell. The next statement tells Excel to enter a text value (in this case, the words "`Timesheet for:`") in the active cell of the worksheet, which is now cell C2.

About control statements

Besides containing lines of code that cause cursor movement and data entry in the worksheet, various lines of code within the program control certain characteristics of the worksheet in Excel. For example, when you press Ctrl+B to apply bold formatting to a selection, the following code results:

```
Selection.Font.Bold = True
```

This line of code, when executed, takes the current selection and turns on bold character formatting. The following lines of code result from opening the Series dialog box (after choosing Edit⇨Fill⇨Series) and accepting the default options in the dialog box:

```
Selection.DataSeries Rowcol:=xlRows, Type:=xlChronological, Date _
    :=xlDay, Step:=1, Trend:=False
```

While examining this line, you should also notice the presence of the *continuation character* used in VBA. The underscore at the end of the first line is the continuation character, and it denotes that a line of program code is to be continued onto the line that follows. (Without this character, VBA considers any single line to be a complete program statement.)

As you grow accustomed to working in VBA, you'll find that you can accomplish a great deal of useful work by means of the various cell selection and control statements that can be used in the language.

About displaying dialog boxes

One of the reasons that you may actually want to do some Visual Basic programming yourself (rather than using only the Macro Recorder) is that you can do some custom programming — such as displaying dialog boxes — that you cannot do with recorded macros. To display a dialog box on-screen that contains a message with custom text, you can use VBA's MsgBox function. The syntax of the statement is simple — you add a line of code that reads `MsgBox("your custom text")`, where you put your desired text between the double quotation marks.

If you duplicated the example earlier in the chapter, go to the start of the last line of the procedure (the `End Sub` line) and press Enter to add a new, blank line. Move the insertion point into the blank line and enter the following:

MsgBox("Enter your week's time and save under a new name.")

Go to a blank worksheet page and choose Tools⇨Macro. In the Macro dialog box, select the TimeEntry macro and click on the Run button. When the macro completes this time, you see the dialog box shown in Figure 22-2. Dialog boxes such as this one can serve to inform users, providing needed guidance about tasks the user needs to perform.

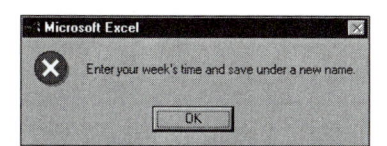

Figure 22-2: The dialog box presented by the MsgBox function.

About user input

Another useful task that you can handle by adding your own Visual Basic code is prompting users for information and acting on a user's response. The InputBox function acts in a manner similar to the MsgBox function, but with InputBox, a text box appears within the dialog box. The value that the user enters in the text box is returned by the function.

You can try using the InputBox function by getting back into the module that you created as part of this exercise. Find the following line:

```
ActiveCell.FormulaR1C1 = "Timesheet for:"
```

Place the cursor at the end of the line, and press Enter to add a new line underneath this one. Enter the following two lines as new code in the procedure:

Range("D2").Select

ActiveCell.FormulaR1C1 = InputBox("Employee Name:")

Move to a blank worksheet and run the macro again. (Choose Tools⇨Macro. In the Macro dialog box, select the TimeEntry macro and click on the Run button.) When the macro runs, a dialog box like the one shown in Figure 22-3 appears, asking for an employee name. After you enter a name, the macro will store that name in cell D2 of the worksheet.

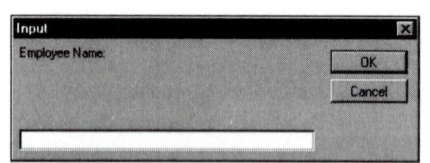

Figure 22-3: The dialog box presented by the InputBox function.

Learn by example

If you plan to get involved in VBA programming, one of the best ways to get familiar with what can be done with the language is to examine other tested, working applications and macros that range from the simple to the complex. If you installed the example worksheets when you installed the Excel portion of Office, you'll find some code samples in the Examples folder that is stored in the Excel folder. You will also find complete Excel applications (written in Visual Basic for Applications) supplied on the CD-ROM that's provided with this book.

Editing Visual Basic for Applications Code

When you click on a module tab, you can enter program code just like you type text in any word processor. You don't have to know the mechanics of entering text and correcting mistakes; suffice it to say that you can use the same text entry and editing techniques, including cutting and pasting, that you can use in any Windows word processor.

While a Visual Basic module is active, you can also insert text from another file into your existing program code. If you want to insert text into the program code, place the insertion point at the location in the module where you want to insert the code and choose Insert⇨File. In the File dialog box, select the file that contains the text that you want to insert and click on the OK button to read the text into the file.

Printing Visual Basic Code

You can print the code that is contained in your Visual Basic modules. To print the code, activate the module that contains the desired code by clicking on the module's tab. Then choose the Print command from the File menu or just click on the Print button on the Standard toolbar.

About the Visual Basic Toolbar

If you do much work in Visual Basic for Applications programming, you'll find the Visual Basic toolbar (Figure 22-4) to be useful. You can activate the Visual Basic toolbar by right-clicking on the toolbar area and choosing Visual Basic from the shortcut menu. Table 22-1 provides an explanation for the different buttons on the Visual Basic toolbar.

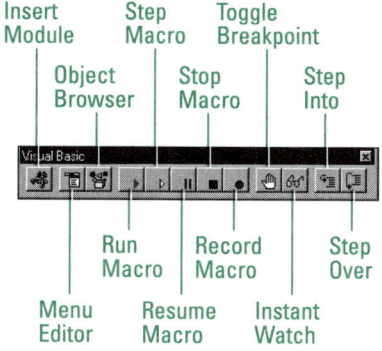

Figure 22-4: The Visual Basic toolbar.

Table 22-1
Buttons on the Visual Basic toolbar

Name	Function
Insert Module	Adds a new Visual Basic module to the workbook.
Menu Editor	Creates or customizes menus and menu bars.
Object Browser	Lists the procedures, properties, methods, and objects currently available.
Run Macro	Runs, deletes or modifies a selected macro.
Step Macro	Opens the Debug window to debug code.
Resume Macro	Resumes playing a macro that you have paused.
Stop Macro	Stops running or recording a macro.
Record Macro	Open the Record Macro dialog box, where you can fill in the desired options used to begin recording a macro.
Toggle Breakpoint	Removes or inserts a breakpoint in a line of code.
Instant Watch	Shows the value of the Visual Basic expression selected.
Step Into	Runs the next line of code that steps into any Visual Basic procedures.
Step Over	Continues running Visual Basic procedures without stepping into them.

Just A Beginning . . .

Make no mistake about it, using Visual Basic for Applications falls well into the realm of programming. (If you're completely new to programming, you should be congratulated for pressing this deeply into what, for many readers, is a subject of mystifying complexity.) You've not only learned how VBA lies at the heart of everything that you do with macros, but you've also learned how you can extend the power of your macros by adding your own Visual Basic code to provide items like dialog boxes and customized prompts. Still, you've only scratched the surface of what you can do with this language. VBA is a full-featured programming language that you can use to automate or customize virtually any conceivable task that can be done with Excel. If you're encouraged (dare we even say excited?) by the challenges of programming, you should look into additional resources for learning about Visual Basic programming. It's a subject about which entire books have been written. A good place to start is Wallace Wang's great book *Visual Basic 3 For Dummies* (IDG Books, 1994).

Summary

This chapter has provided an introduction to programming by using Visual Basic for Applications, the underlying language behind Excel macros. The chapter covered the following points:

- Every Excel macro exists as a series of Visual Basic program statements.

- The Visual Basic statements are stored in procedures, and one or more procedures are placed in modules. Each module occupies a module sheet in a workbook.

- Visual Basic procedures can be sub procedures or function procedures. Function procedures are like Excel's built-in functions because they accept a value(s), act on the data, and return a value(s). Sub procedures do not return a value (although you can pass values from within a sub procedure through the use of statements inside the procedure).

- You can modify the Visual Basic code that Excel's Macro Recorder creates to add special features like dialog boxes and custom prompts.

The next chapter will show how you can put Excel to work, by demonstrating how you can create and use worksheets for common business tasks.

Where to go next ...

- Because Visual Basic for Applications lies at the heart of macros that you create in Excel, you should also be intimately familiar with the use of macros before getting deeply involved with Visual Basic for Applications. See Chapter 20.

✦ ✦ ✦

Excel at Work

CHAPTER 23

◆ ◆ ◆ ◆

In This Chapter

Cash-flow management

Break-even analysis

IRA calculations

Mortgage loan calculation and amortization

◆ ◆ ◆ ◆

This chapter gets you started on your own applications by providing some examples and step-by-step instructions that you can use to build models of worksheets for various tasks.

Cash-Flow Management

Managing cash flow, or your accounts receivable and accounts payable, is a basic job that faces virtually every modern business. The following cash-flow worksheet is relatively simple to set up, yet it keeps a clear "picture" of available funds. The worksheet is patterned after the common single-entry debits and credits bookkeeping system. You enter a starting balance into cell H4. Use column A to record the dates of each transaction, whether a credit or a debit. Use columns B, C, and D to record credits by listing the creditor, the description, and the amount. Use columns E, F, and G to record debits by listing to whom the amount is paid, the description, and the amount. Column H contains the formulas that you use to keep a running total of the cash on hand. You compute the total by taking the preceding entry's running balance, adding the credits, and subtracting the debits. You can maintain this type of system by creating a separate worksheet for each month. At the end of the year, you can consolidate the totals into another worksheet to show yearly figures for cash flow. The worksheet is shown in Figure 23-1.

	A	B	C	D	E	F	G	H
1			**Cash Flow**					
2			**Little Springs Water Company, July 1995**					
3							**Starting**	
4							**Balance:**	$3,000.00
5		**CREDITS=**			**DEBITS=**			
6	**Date**	**rec'd from:**	**description**	**amount**	**paid to:**	**description**	**amount**	**balance**
7	7/3/97	J. Doe	June bill	$32.50				$3,032.50
8	7/3/97				Johnson Hardware	tubing & fittings	$48.70	$2,983.80
9	7/5/97	S. Smith	June bill	$29.75				$3,013.55
10	7/6/97	A. Anderson	May & June bills	$68.75				$3,082.30
11	7/6/97				Acme Automotive	truck repairs	$121.90	$2,960.40
12								$2,960.40
13								$2,960.40
14								$2,960.40
15								$2,960.40
16								$2,960.40
17								$2,960.40
18								$2,960.40
19								$2,960.40
20								$2,960.40
21								$2,960.40
22								$2,960.40

Cash Flow / Sheet2 / Sheet3 / Sheet4 / Sheet5 / Sheet6 / Sheet7 / She

Figure 23-1: A cash flow worksheet.

To build the worksheet, enter the following labels and formulas into the cells shown:

Cell	*Entry*
A6	Date
B5	CREDITS=
B6	rec'd from:
C1	Cash Flow
C6	description
D6	amount
E5	DEBITS=
E6	paid to:
F6	description
G3	Starting
G4	Balance:
G6	amount
H6	balance
H7	=H4+D7-G7
H8	=H7+D8-G8

In the area below cell C1, you may want to add the name of your company or organization. In the example, we used "Little Springs Water Company."

To copy the formula into successive cells in column H, select the range of cells from H8 to H40. Choose Edit⇨Fill⇨Down. To format the cells in Column H, select the range of cells from H4 to H40. Then choose Format⇨Cells to open the Format Cells dialog box, and then click on the Number tab. Click the Currency option in the list box, and then click OK. Using the same steps, choose the same currency format for the cells from D7 to D40 and from G7 to G40. To format a range of cells to display dates, select the range of cells from A7 to A40, and select the d-mmm-yy format on the Number tab of the Format Cells dialog box.

At this point, the worksheet is ready to use. Although you may want to use your own figures, Figure 23-1 shows part of the cash-flow worksheet that has been filled in with figures from a typical small business.

Break-Even Analysis

A common what-if scenario for almost any firm is the break-even analysis, which determines how many units of a given product must be sold before the producer shows a profit. A break-even analysis requires the juggling of two groups of figures: fixed costs and variable costs. *Fixed costs* do not directly increase with each unit sold. Such costs include the rental of the manufacturing plant, utilities to power the production line, and advertising expenses. Variable costs directly increase with each unit sold. Such costs include the cost of the materials to assemble each unit, labor costs per unit, packaging costs, and shipping costs.

A typical break-even analysis performs a one-time deduction of the fixed costs and then calculates the per-unit costs for each unit produced. These negative amounts are balanced against the net profits (the net sales cost times the number of units sold.) As the number of units sold increases, a break-even point is reached where the total profit equals the negative fixed and variable costs. An example of a break-even analysis worksheet illustrates the break-even point for a child's bicycle (see Figure 23-2).

496 Part III ◆ Excel

	A	B	C	D	E
1					
2					
3	Break-Even Analysis			Units Sold	Profit/Loss
4					
5	Name of Product:	Child's Bicycle		15	($2,479.00)
6	Sales Price:	$59.70		30	($2,158.00)
7				45	($1,837.00)
8	FIXED COSTS			60	($1,516.00)
9	Rent	$1,500.00		75	($1,195.00)
10	Telephone	$150.00		90	($874.00)
11	Utilities	$500.00		105	($553.00)
12	Advertising	$450.00		120	($232.00)
13	Miscellaneous	$200.00		135	$89.00
14	TOTAL Fixed Costs	$2,800.00		150	$410.00
15				165	$731.00
16	VARIABLE COSTS, PER UNIT			180	$1,052.00
17	Manufacturing	$22.08		195	$1,373.00
18	Labor	$8.07		210	$1,694.00
19	Packaging	$4.90		225	$2,015.00
20	Shipping	$3.25		240	$2,336.00
21	TOTAL Variable Costs	$38.30		255	$2,657.00
22				270	$2,978.00
23	QUANTITY INCREMENT	15		285	$3,299.00
				300	$3,620.00

Figure 23-2: A break-even analysis worksheet.

To build the model, open a new worksheet. Widen column A to roughly three times its default width and widen column B to roughly twice its default width. The other columns can remain at the default widths. Enter the following formulas into the cells shown:

Cell	Entry
A3	Break-Even Analysis
A5	Name of Product:
A6	Sales Price:
A8	FIXED COSTS
A9	Rent
A10	Telephone
A11	Utilities
A12	Advertising
A13	Miscellaneous
A14	TOTAL Fixed Costs
A16	VARIABLE COSTS, PER UNIT
A17	Manufacturing
A18	Labor
A19	Packaging

Cell	Entry
A20	Shipping
A21	TOTAL Variable Costs
A23	QUANTITY INCREMENT
B5	Child's Bicycle
B6	59.7
B9	1500
B10	150
B11	500
B12	450
B13	200
B14	=SUM(B9:B13)
B17	22.08
B18	8.07
B19	4.9
B20	3.25
B21	=SUM(B17:B20)
B23	15
D3	Units Sold
D5	=B23
D6	=D5+$B$23

You can create the remaining formulas in column D quickly by selecting the range from D6 to D41. Then choose Edit➪Fill➪Down.

Cell	Entry
D7	=D6+$B$23
D8	=D7+$B$23
D9	=D8+$B$23
D10	=D9+$B$23
D11	=D10+$B$23
D12	=D11+$B$23
D13	=D12+$B$23

(continued)

Cell	Entry
D14	=D13+$B$23
D15	=D14+$B$23
D16	=D15+$B$23
D17	=D16+$B$23
D18	=D17+$B$23
D19	=D18+$B$23
D20	=D19+$B$23
D21	=D20+$B$23
D22	=D21+$B$23
D23	=D22+$B$23
D24	=D23+$B$23
D25	=D24+$B$23
D26	=D25+$B$23
D27	=D26+$B$23
D28	=D27+$B$23
D29	=D28+$B$23
D30	=D29+$B$23
D31	=D30+$B$23
D32	=D31+$B$23
D33	=D32+$B$23
D34	=D33+$B$23
D35	=D34+$B$23
D36	=D35+$B$23
D37	=D36+$B$23
D38	=D37+$B$23
D39	=D38+$B$23
D40	=D39+$B$23
D41	=D40+$B$23

In column E, enter the following values and formulas:

Cell	Entry
E3	Profit/Loss
E5	=D5*$B$6-($B$14+($B$21*D5))

You can create the remaining formulas in column E quickly by selecting the range from E5 to E41. Then choose Edit➪Fill➪Down.

Cell	Entry
E6	=D6*$B$6-($B$14+($B$21*D6))
E7	=D7*$B$6-($B$14+($B$21*D7))
E8	=D8*$B$6-($B$14+($B$21*D8))
E9	=D9*$B$6-($B$14+($B$21*D9))
E10	=D10*$B$6-($B$14+($B$21*D10))
E11	=D11*$B$6-($B$14+($B$21*D11))
E12	=D12*$B$6-($B$14+($B$21*D12))
E13	=D13*$B$6-($B$14+($B$21*D13))
E14	=D14*$B$6-($B$14+($B$21*D14))
E15	=D15*$B$6-($B$14+($B$21*D15))
E16	=D16*$B$6-($B$14+($B$21*D16))
E17	=D17*$B$6-($B$14+($B$21*D17))
E18	=D18*$B$6-($B$14+($B$21*D18))
E19	=D19*$B$6-($B$14+($B$21*D19))
E20	=D20*$B$6-($B$14+($B$21*D20))
E21	=D21*$B$6-($B$14+($B$21*D21))
E22	=D22*$B$6-($B$14+($B$21*D22))
E23	=D23*$B$6-($B$14+($B$21*D23))
E24	=D24*$B$6-($B$14+($B$21*D24))
E25	=D25*$B$6-($B$14+($B$21*D25))
E26	=D26*$B$6-($B$14+($B$21*D26))
E27	=D27*$B$6-($B$14+($B$21*D27))
E28	=D28*$B$6-($B$14+($B$21*D28))

(continued)

Cell	Entry
E29	=D29*$B$6-($B$14+($B$21*D29))
E30	=D30*$B$6-($B$14+($B$21*D30))
E31	=D31*$B$6-($B$14+($B$21*D31))
E32	=D32*$B$6-($B$14+($B$21*D32))
E33	=D33*$B$6-($B$14+($B$21*D33))
E34	=D34*$B$6-($B$14+($B$21*D34))
E35	=D35*$B$6-($B$14+($B$21*D35))
E36	=D36*$B$6-($B$14+($B$21*D36))
E37	=D37*$B$6-($B$14+($B$21*D37))
E38	=D38*$B$6-($B$14+($B$21*D38))
E39	=D39*$B$6-($B$14+($B$21*D39))
E40	=D40*$B$6-($B$14+($B$21*D40))
E41	=D41*$B$6-($B$14+($B$21*D41))

Use Format⇨Cells to format the ranges from B6 to B21 and from E5 to E41 with the currency format (click the Number tab, choose Currency in the list box, and then click OK). To use the worksheet, enter your respective fixed and variable costs in the cells provided. In the quantity increment cell, enter the quantity that you want to use as a scale for the break-even analysis. For example, to see how many hundreds of units it will take to break even, enter 100 for a quantity increment. For a more detailed analysis, enter a smaller increment. You can extend the analysis to cover even more units by simply copying the respective formulas down the column past row 41. However, if you're not breaking even by row 41 of the worksheet, the analysis is trying to tell you that your pricing or manufacturing strategy has a serious flaw!

IRA Calculator

An IRA calculator is a straightforward financial tool that is designed to plot the increasing value of an IRA (Individual Retirement Account). Four columns within the worksheet contain a beginning balance in the account, a yearly contribution, an interest rate, and an ending balance. A less complex worksheet would assume a standard interest rate and yearly contribution, but in real life, your yearly contribution may vary, and it is virtually impossible to plan for a standard interest rate. Keeping separate columns for these values for each year gives you the ability to insert each year's interest rate and the amount of the IRA contribution.

In column C, you enter the beginning balance (starting with zero in the first row). Column D contains the yearly contribution, which for purposes of example, is $1,700 the first year, $1,850 the second, $1,900 the third, and assumed to be $2,000 per year afterwards. Column E contains the interest rate, assumed to be 14.5 percent the first year, 13.25 percent the second year, 10.8 percent the third year, and 13 percent per year afterwards. Column F contains the formula that calculates the effect of the accumulating interest and the added yearly investment. The formula calculates on the basis of simple interest by adding the current balance to the yearly contribution and adding the result multiplied by the yearly interest rate to provide the new balance. Each year's new balance is then carried to the successive balance column. The worksheet is shown in Figure 23-3.

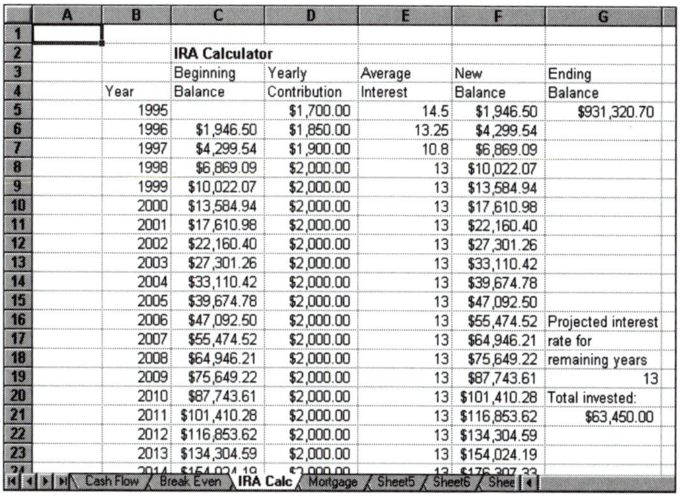

	A	B	C	D	E	F	G
1							
2			**IRA Calculator**				
3			Beginning	Yearly	Average	New	Ending
4		Year	Balance	Contribution	Interest	Balance	Balance
5		1995		$1,700.00	14.5	$1,946.50	$931,320.70
6		1996	$1,946.50	$1,850.00	13.25	$4,299.54	
7		1997	$4,299.54	$1,900.00	10.8	$6,869.09	
8		1998	$6,869.09	$2,000.00	13	$10,022.07	
9		1999	$10,022.07	$2,000.00	13	$13,584.94	
10		2000	$13,584.94	$2,000.00	13	$17,610.98	
11		2001	$17,610.98	$2,000.00	13	$22,160.40	
12		2002	$22,160.40	$2,000.00	13	$27,301.26	
13		2003	$27,301.26	$2,000.00	13	$33,110.42	
14		2004	$33,110.42	$2,000.00	13	$39,674.78	
15		2005	$39,674.78	$2,000.00	13	$47,092.50	
16		2006	$47,092.50	$2,000.00	13	$55,474.52	Projected interest
17		2007	$55,474.52	$2,000.00	13	$64,946.21	rate for
18		2008	$64,946.21	$2,000.00	13	$75,649.22	remaining years
19		2009	$75,649.22	$2,000.00	13	$87,743.61	13
20		2010	$87,743.61	$2,000.00	13	$101,410.28	Total invested:
21		2011	$101,410.28	$2,000.00	13	$116,853.62	$63,450.00
22		2012	$116,853.62	$2,000.00	13	$134,304.59	
23		2013	$134,304.59	$2,000.00	13	$154,024.19	
24		2014	$154,024.19	$2,000.00	13	$176,307.33	

Figure 23-3: An IRA calculator worksheet.

To build the worksheet, enter the following formulas into the cells shown:

Cell	*Entry*
B4	Year
B5	1995
B6	=B5+1

To create the following formulas, select the range from B6 to B37. Then choose Edit⇨Fill⇨Down.

Cell	Entry
B7	=B6+1
B8	=B7+1
B9	=B8+1
B10	=B9+1
B11	=B10+1
B12	=B11+1
B13	=B12+1
B14	=B13+1
B15	=B14+1
B16	=B15+1
B17	=B16+1
B18	=B17+1
B19	=B18+1
B20	=B19+1
B21	=B20+1
B22	=B21+1
B23	=B22+1
B24	=B23+1
B25	=B24+1
B26	=B25+1
B27	=B26+1
B28	=B27+1
B29	=B28+1
B30	=B29+1
B31	=B30+1
B32	=B31+1
B33	=B32+1
B34	=B33+1
B35	=B34+1
B36	=B35+1
B37	=B36+1

In column C of the worksheet, enter the following values and formulas:

Cell	Entry
C2	IRA Calculator
C3	Beginning
C4	Balance
C6	=F5

To create the following formulas, select the range from C6 to C37. Then choose Edit⇨Fill⇨Down.

Cell	Entry
C7	=F6
C8	=F7
C9	=F8
C10	=F9
C11	=F10
C12	=F11
C13	=F12
C14	=F13
C15	=F14
C16	=F15
C17	=F16
C18	=F17
C19	=F18
C20	=F19
C21	=F20
C22	=F21
C23	=F22
C24	=F23
C25	=F24
C26	=F25

(continued)

Cell	Entry
C27	=F26
C28	=F27
C29	=F28
C30	=F29
C31	=F30
C32	=F31
C33	=F32
C34	=F33
C35	=F34
C36	=F35
C37	=F36

In column D of the worksheet, enter the following values:

Cell	Entry
D3	Yearly
D4	Contribution
D5	1700
D6	1850
D7	1900
D8	2000

To create the following entries, select the range from D8 to D37. Then choose Edit⇨Fill⇨Down.

Cell	Entry
D9	2000
D10	2000
D11	2000
D12	2000
D13	2000
D14	2000
D15	2000

Cell	Entry
D16	2000
D17	2000
D18	2000
D19	2000
D20	2000
D21	2000
D22	2000
D23	2000
D24	2000
D25	2000
D26	2000
D27	2000
D28	2000
D29	2000
D30	2000
D31	2000
D32	2000
D33	2000
D34	2000
D35	2000
D36	2000
D37	2000

In column E of the worksheet, enter the following values and formulas:

Cell	Entry
E3	Average
E4	Interest
E5	14.5
E6	13.25
E7	10.8
E8	=$G$19

To create the following formulas, select the range from E8 to E37. Then choose Edit⇨Fill⇨Down.

Cell	Entry
E9	=$G$19
E10	=$G$19
E11	=$G$19
E12	=$G$19
E13	=$G$19
E14	=$G$19
E15	=$G$19
E16	=$G$19
E17	=$G$19
E18	=$G$19
E19	=$G$19
E20	=$G$19
E21	=$G$19
E22	=$G$19
E23	=$G$19
E24	=$G$19
E25	=$G$19
E26	=$G$19
E27	=$G$19
E28	=$G$19
E29	=$G$19
E30	=$G$19
E31	=$G$19
E32	=$G$19
E33	=$G$19
E34	=$G$19
E35	=$G$19
E36	=$G$19
E37	=$G$19

In column F of the worksheet, enter the following:

Cell	Entry
F3	New
F4	Balance
F5	=((C5+D5)*E5/100)+C5+D5

Select the range of cells from F5 to F37. Then choose Edit⇨Fill⇨Down to copy the formula into the successive cells.

In column G of the worksheet, enter the following values and formulas:

Cell	Entry
G3	Ending
G4	Balance
G5	=F37
G16	Projected interest
G17	rate for
G18	remaining years
G19	13
G20	Total invested:
G21	=SUM(D4:D36)

Using Format⇨Cells, format the ranges from C6 to C37, D5 to D37, and F5 to F37 in the dollars-and-cents format. Also format cells G5 and G21 for the same type of display.

After you have entered the formulas, the worksheet displays the interest accumulation and yearly balances, as shown in Figure 23-3. You can change the interest rates and investment amounts to correspond to your desired investment rates.

Mortgage Analysis and Amortization Schedule

The mortgage analysis worksheet has a straightforward design. It uses the PMT (payment) function to calculate the payments on a loan and displays an amortization schedule for the term of the loan. Figure 23-4 shows the worksheet.

	A	B	C	D	E	F
3		Mortgage Analysis				
4						
5		Principal amount of loan:		24000		
6		Interest rate, in percent:		10.50%		
7		Term of loan, in years:		30		
8						
9		Monthly mortgage payment		$219.54		
10						
11						
12						
13						
14						
15	YEAR	Starting Balance	Ending Balance	TOTAL PAID	PRINCIPAL	INTEREST
16						
17	1	24,000.00	23,879.88	2,634.45	120.12	2,514.33
18	2	23,879.88	23,746.52	2,634.45	133.36	2,501.09
19	3	23,746.52	23,598.47	2,634.45	148.06	2,486.39
20	4	23,598.47	23,434.09	2,634.45	164.37	2,470.08
21	5	23,434.09	23,251.61	2,634.45	182.49	2,451.96
22	6	23,251.61	23,049.01	2,634.45	202.60	2,431.85
23	7	23,049.01	22,824.09	2,634.45	224.92	2,409.53
24	8	22,824.09	22,574.38	2,634.45	249.71	2,384.74

Figure 23-4: A mortgage analysis worksheet.

Cells D5, D6, and D7 of the worksheet contain the principal loan amount, interest rate, and term of the loan in years. In cell D9, the following formula supplies the rate, number of periods, and present value:

=PMT((D6/12),(D7*12),-D5)

The rate and the number of periods are converted to months, and the present value is shown as a negative value, representing cash paid out.

Year one of the amortization schedule begins in row 17. The starting balance is derived from the amount entered in cell D5. To arrive at the ending balance in column C for the first year, use a formula containing the following variation of Excel's PV (Present Value) function:

=PV(($D$6/12),(12*($D$7-A17)),-$D$9)

It is now a simple matter to calculate the remaining forms in the row. The total paid (column D of the amortization schedule) is the monthly payment (cell D9) multiplied by 12 to compute a yearly amount. The principal in column E is calculated by subtracting column C of the schedule (the ending balance) from column B (the starting balance).

You calculate the interest (column F) by subtracting the difference between the starting and ending balance from the total paid. As the formulas are duplicated down the worksheet, relative references are adjusted upwards for each successive row location.

Choose Format⇨Column⇨Width to change the width of column A to 5 spaces and the width of columns B, C, D, E, and F to 15 spaces.

To build the worksheet, enter the following formulas in the cells shown:

Cell	Entry
A15	YEAR
A17	1

To enter the rest of the year numbers, select the range from A17 to A46. Then choose Edit⇨Fill⇨Series. Click on the OK button in the dialog box to fill the range. When you do so, cells A17 through A46 contain values from 1 through 30, representing 30 years of mortgage payments.

In column B of the worksheet, enter the following information:

Cell	Entry
B3	Mortgage Analysis
B5	Principal amount of loan:
B6	Interest rate, in percent:
B7	Term of loan, in years:
B9	Monthly mortgage payment
B15	Starting balance
B17	=D5
B18	=C17

In column C of the worksheet, enter the following information and formulas:

Cell	Entry
C15	Ending balance
C17	=PV(($D$6/12),(12*($D$7-A17)),-$D$9)
C18	=PV(($D$6/12),(12*($D$7-A18)),-$D$9)

In column D of the worksheet, enter the following values and formulas:

Cell	Entry
D5	24000
D6	10.5%
D7	30
D9	=PMT((D6/12),(D7*12),-D5)
D15	TOTAL PAID
D17	=$D$9*12
D18	=$D$9*12

In column E of the worksheet, enter the following information and formulas:

Cell	Entry
E15	PRINCIPAL
E17	=B17-C17
E18	=B18-C18

In column F of the worksheet, enter the following information and formulas:

Cell	Entry
F15	INTEREST
F17	=D17-(B17-C17)
F18	=D18-(B18-C18)

When you have entered these formulas, select the range of cells from B18 to F46. Choose Edit⇨Fill⇨Down to fill the successive formulas into the selected rows. To apply formatting to a range, select the range from B17 to F46. Choose Format⇨Cells and click on the Number tab in the Format Cells dialog box. Click Currency in the list box, and then click OK. At this point, your worksheet should resemble the example in Figure 23-4.

The range in this example assumes a 30-year loan. If you enter a period of 15 years but leave the formulas intact for 30 years, however, you will get the interesting benefit of a nest egg that has been calculated as an increasing negative balance when the mortgage ends and the amortization schedule shows mortgage payments still being added.

To avoid this situation, just adjust the range when you fill down as needed to match the number of years for the mortgage. If you want to get really fancy, you can record a macro that clears the range, gets the number of years from cell D7, selects a new range equivalent to that number of years, and performs a Fill Down command.

Summary

This chapter provided you with a step-by-step look at what is involved in creating various models that are typical of the types that you may find useful in Excel.

- ✦ You created a worksheet to handle mortgage loan calculation and amortization.
- ✦ You created a worksheet to handle break-even analysis.
- ✦ You created a worksheet to handle cash-flow management.
- ✦ You created a worksheet to handle IRA calculations.

The next chapter answers common questions that arise when you use Excel.

Where to go next...

As these examples demonstrate, much of the basic work behind creating and using spreadsheets involves routine data and formula entry and simple to moderately complex formatting. For many spreadsheet users, these tasks are 90% of what they do in Excel.

- ✦ You can find tips and techniques that help ease the tedium of basic data and formula entry in Chapter 14.
- ✦ For the complete scoop on how you can format your Excel worksheets, see Chapter 15.

✦ ✦ ✦

The Excel Top Ten

CHAPTER 24

In This Chapter

Specifying a default workbook to open on startup

Specifying a default working directory

Displaying more than one workbook at once

Bridging the gap between Excel 4.0 and Excel 95

Preventing numbers with slashes and hyphens from being interpreted as dates

Selecting cells and ranges with shortcuts

Formatting characters in cells

Combining the contents of two cells into one cell

Defining a print area of a worksheet

Making titles print on one page

As a whole, Excel users routinely find the same questions arising as they gain proficiency with the program. To save you time and effort, we've compiled the top ten Excel questions and their answers, based on inquiries to Microsoft Technical Support and the Microsoft forums on CompuServe.

Can I set up a workbook so that it opens each time I start Microsoft Excel?

You can open a workbook each time you start Excel by placing the workbook in the Xlstart folder. This folder is located in the same folder as the Excel program itself. All the workbooks placed in this directory will be opened at the start of Microsoft Excel. These workbooks can include worksheets, chart sheets, visual basic modules, dialog sheets, and Excel 4.0 macro sheets.

If a template is placed in the Xlstart folder, it appears as an option when you choose the New command from the File menu. The template also appears as an option in the Insert dialog box that appears when you choose the Insert command from the sheet tab shortcut menu. (This shortcut menu appears after you right-click on a sheet tab.)

How do I change the default working directory or the standard font in Microsoft Excel?

Changing the working directory and the standard font are simple tasks in Excel 5.0. To set these options for all workbooks, use the General tab of the Options dialog box, which appears after you choose Tools⇨Options. Follow these steps to change the default working directory:

1. Choose Tools⇨Options and click on the General tab in the Options dialog box.

2. In the Default File Location text box, enter the full path of the directory that you want to use for your Excel work directory.

   3. Click on the OK button.

To change the default font for all new workbooks, follow these steps:

   1. Choose Tools⇨Options and click on the General tab in the Options dialog box.

   2. In the Standard Font list box and in the Size list box, select the font and size that you want to use.

   3. Click on the OK button to make the changes.

How can I display more than one workbook at a time?

By default, each time that you open a workbook, it occupies the entire window. You can display multiple workbooks simultaneously with these steps:

   1. Use the File⇨Open command to open as many workbooks as you want to view.

   2. Choose Window⇨Arrange.

   3. In the Arrange Windows dialog box that appears, choose tiled, horizontal, vertical, or cascade as desired, and then click on OK to display the workbooks simultaneously.

I'm an accomplished Excel 4.0 user, and I'm having trouble getting used to the new menu structure of Excel 95. Does Excel 95 offer any help for Excel 4.0 users?

One option is to switch the program back to the menu structure of Excel 4.0. You can make this change by choosing Tools⇨Options and clicking on the General tab of the Options dialog box. Turn on the Microsoft Excel 4.0 Menus option and then click on the OK button.

It may be worth your while to learn the new menu structure. Many changes have been made to Excel since version 4.0 to make it easier to use and more consistent with other Microsoft applications. You will notice that many of the menus and commands have been reorganized. In Excel 95, many of the commands that execute similar actions are grouped together. For example, rather than seeing the Font, Pattern, and Borders commands on the Format menu, you now see the Cells command. You can use this single command to set options for your fonts, patterns, and borders.

How can I prevent a slash (/) or a hyphen (-) from being formatted as a date when it is entered?

Excel automatically applies built-in number formats to values entered in an unformatted cell. Normally the appearance of the value is not altered because the format is a general number format. However, if the entry contains a slash or a hyphen that separates values, Excel may have trouble interpreting the value because it may think it is a date. If the entry contains a colon, Excel may think that the value represents a time value (hours, minutes, seconds, and so on). If you want to display the value exactly as it was entered — with slashes, hyphens, or colons — and you don't want Excel to confuse the value with a date or time, then you must format the value as a text value. To create a text value, simply precede the entry with a single quotation mark (') or follow these steps:

1. Select the cells in which you want to enter data.
2. Choose Format⇨Cells and select the Number tab from the dialog box that appears.
3. In the Category list box, select the Text option.
4. Click on the OK button.

When you enter values in the selected cells, the values are displayed as you typed them. Remember that the cells must be formatted as text prior to entering your data.

What are some shortcuts for selecting cells and ranges?

Along with the normal clicking and dragging technique, you can use the Name list box on the left side of the formula bar to select cells and ranges on the active sheet and on other sheets within a workbook. The Name list box displays the cell reference or the cell name of the currently selected cell, and it provides a list of all the defined names in your workbook when you click on the arrow to the right of the list box. When you select a name or enter a cell reference in this list box, Excel selects the specified cell or range. You can also use the Name list box to define a name and insert the name into a formula. If you want to define a name for a cell or cell range so that you can select it later or use it in a formula, select the cell or range, click on the Name list box, enter a new name, and press the Enter key. Table 24-1 contains a list of shortcuts for selecting cells and ranges.

Table 24-1
Shortcuts for selecting cells and ranges

To select	Do the following
A named cell or range on the active sheet or on another worksheet	In the Name list box, type or select the name.
An unnamed cell	In the Name list box, enter the cell reference and press Enter.
An unnamed range	With your mouse, select the first cell in the range. If the last cell in your range is a named cell, hold down the Shift key and select the name from the Name list box or enter a cell reference and press Shift+Enter.
Nonadjacent named and unnamed cells	With your mouse, select the first cell or range. To make subsequent selections, hold down the Ctrl key while you select a name from the Name list box or enter a cell reference in the Name list box and press Crtl+Enter.

How do I format characters in a cell that I want to be superscript, subscript, or in a different font?

In Excel, you can add such character formatting as superscript, subscript, different fonts, styles, size, underlining, color, and so on to individual characters in a single cell. Table 24-2 contains a few examples of different kinds of formatting that you can add to the characters in a cell.

Table 24-2
Formatting that you can add to characters in a cell

Formatting	Example
Italics	*4th Quarter*
Superscript	2^3
Subscript	10_2
Different font	$\Phi(R-S)=\Phi-1(S)$

> **Note** The Φ character is a capital F in the Symbol font. (Use the Font list box in the toolbars to change to the Symbol font, then type **F**.) You can select individual text in a cell by clicking on the formula bar and then dragging to select the text. If you are using the in-cell editing feature, you must double-click in the cell and drag to select the text that you want to format. If you are in a text box, double-click in the text box and drag to make the selection that you want. When the text is highlighted, choose Format➪Cells and select the Font tab from the Format Cells dialog box. Then choose the options that you want. The multiple-character formatting applies only to text.

To enter superscript and subscript, you must enter the values as text by preceding the value with a single quotation mark ('). For example 2^3 and 10_2 would be displayed as 23 and 102 if they are not entered as text. A second option is to format the cell with the text number format before the value is entered.

How can I combine the contents of two cells into one cell?

If you have information in two separate cells that you want to combine into one cell, or if you want to combine text with a formula in a cell, use the CONCATENATE( ) function. This function takes up to 30 arguments, which can consist of cell references, text, and formulas. Note that the text arguments must be enclosed in quotation marks.

Say that someone's first name is stored in cell C1 and the last name is stored in cell D1. If you want to combine the text in those cells, enter the following formula in cell E1:

=CONCATENATE(C1, " ",D1)

The second argument in the formula is a space enclosed in quotation marks. If you wanted to combine the text *Amount Payable: $* with the sum of cells A1:B1, you could enter the following formula in cell E1:

=CONCATENATE("Amount Payable: $",SUM(A1:B1))

How can I define an area on my worksheet for printing?

To define a print area, choose File➪Page Setup and click on the Sheet tab of the Page Setup dialog box. Place the insertion point in the Print Area text box and, on your worksheet, select the range or ranges that you want to print. You can also enter references or names for the print area yourself. To make this task easy to do, you may want to add the Set Print Area button to a toolbar.

You also can simply select a range and print it. To do so, select the range or ranges that you want to print, choose File➪Print, and then choose the Selection option in the Print What area of the Print dialog box.

How can I make my titles print on each page?

If you want to print titles on each page, choose the Page Setup command from the File menu and click on the Sheet tab. Put your insertion point in the Rows to Repeat at Top box or the Columns to Repeat at Left box and then, on your worksheet, select the rows or columns that you want to print on each page. You may also enter references or names for the rows or columns in these boxes yourself.

Summary

This chapter covered the top ten Excel questions and their answers. The chapter also concludes the Excel section of this book. The section that follows describes Microsoft PowerPoint, the presentation graphics package provided with Office 95.

Where to go next...

- ✦ If you have questions regarding formatting that aren't covered here, you can find answers in Chapter 15.
- ✦ You can get help with your printing questions in Chapter 18.

✦ ✦ ✦

PowerPoint

PART IV

In This Part

Chapter 25
Working in PowerPoint

Chapter 26
Enhancing a Presentation

Chapter 27
Working with Charts in PowerPoint

Chapter 28
Producing Your Work

Chapter 29
PowerPoint for Windows at Work

Chapter 30
The PowerPoint Top Ten

Working in PowerPoint

CHAPTER 25

◆ ◆ ◆ ◆

In This Chapter

Understanding the presentation window

Working with shortcut menus and buttons

Using the toolbar

Using PowerPoint's default presentations

Opening and saving presentations

Working with text

Inserting, deleting, copying, rearranging, laying out, and moving between slides

Selecting, grouping, moving, copying, cropping, aligning, and stacking objects

Drawing, modifying, and manipulating shapes

◆ ◆ ◆ ◆

This chapter provides methods that you will find useful as you use PowerPoint. You will learn about the uses of the PowerPoint presentation window. You will learn how to move your toolbars, save presentations, and align objects. Objects become more important in PowerPoint as you experiment with different layouts. You will learn how to perform different tasks with the objects that you add to your presentation. You will also learn methods that you can use to rearrange a slide show and to make changes to the slide layout itself.

Learning About the Presentation Window

PowerPoint's *presentation window* is where you create slides and arrange them in your presentation — this is the bulk of the work you'll do in PowerPoint. Familiarizing yourself with the PowerPoint window (Figure 25-1) is very important in helping you function easily in PowerPoint.

At the lower-left corner of the presentation window, you will notice the view buttons, which enable you to switch among different views in the PowerPoint presentation window. The view buttons include the following: Slide view, Outline View, Slide Sorter View, Notes Pages View, and Slide Show. You can also change views by choosing the appropriate commands from the View menu.

Click on the Slide view button when you want only one slide to appear on-screen. Slide view enables you to do different maintenance on the slide, such as editing. Figure 25-1 shows Slide view.

Click on the Outline View button to show the slide in outline form so that you can move headings and other information by clicking and dragging (see Figure 25-2). Outline view enables you to see the title and body text of all your slides at the same time.

524 Part IV ✦ **PowerPoint**

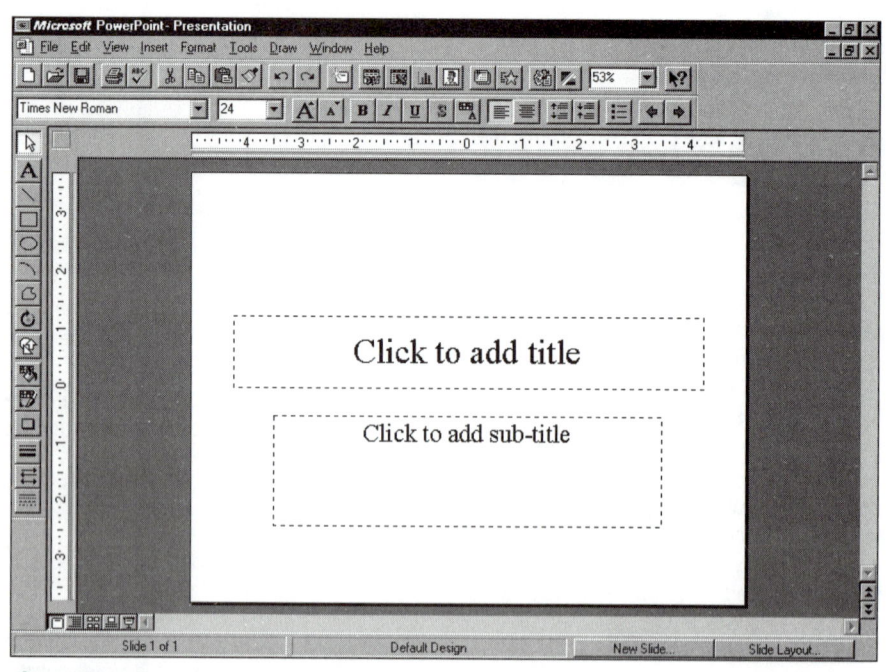

Figure 25-1: The PowerPoint window.

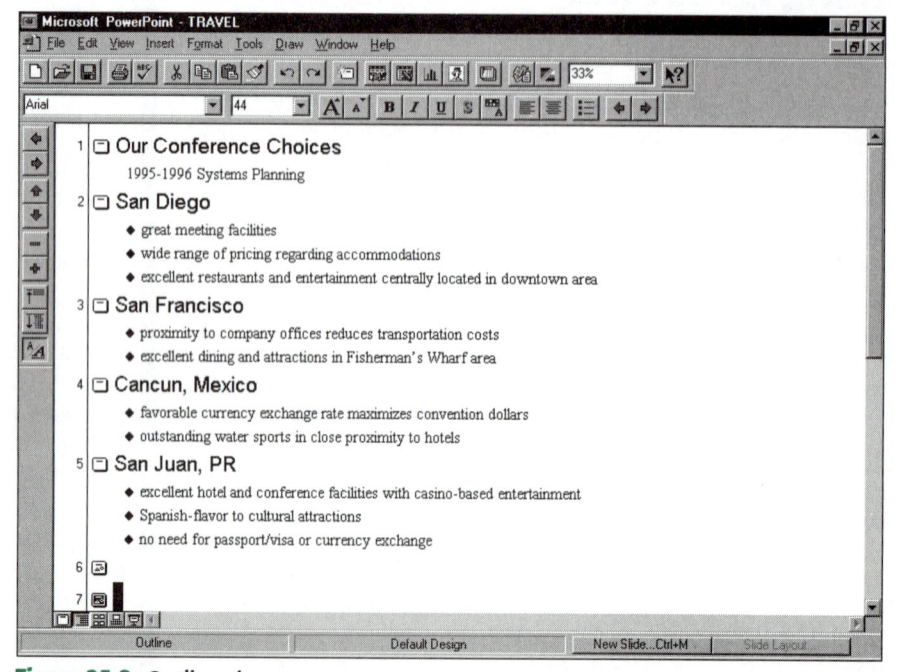

Figure 25-2: Outline view.

Click on the Slide Sorter View button to give you a view of all the slides in a presentation so that you can quickly see their layout and sequence (see Figure 25-3).

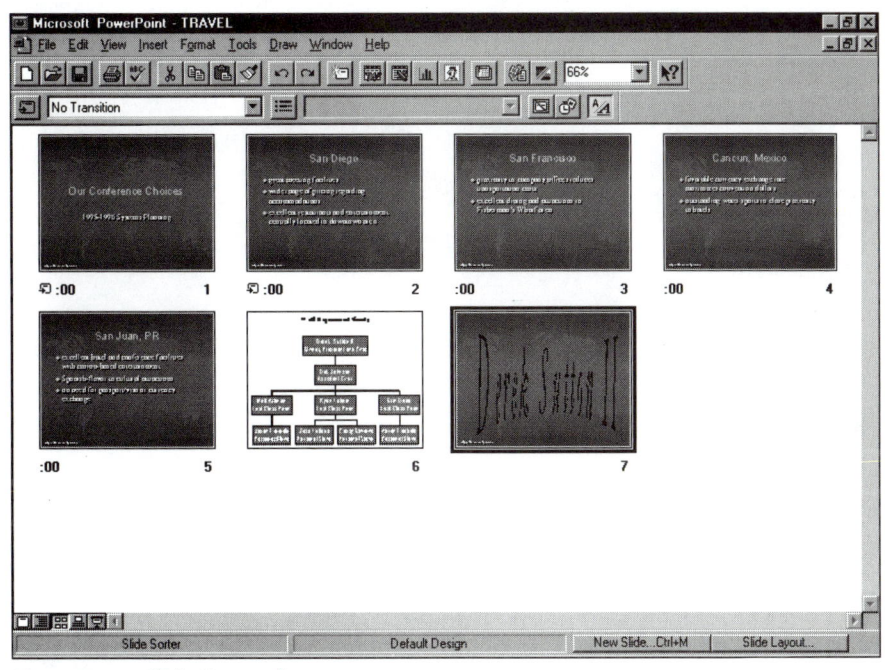

Figure 25-3: Slide Sorter view.

Click on the Notes Page View button to enter any notes that you may want to attach to the slide or to display any notes that you may have already written (see Figure 25-4).

Click on the Slide Show button to run the slide show after you have completed the slides. Notice how the slide now fills the screen (see Figure 25-5). You can also view your slides as a timed presentation.

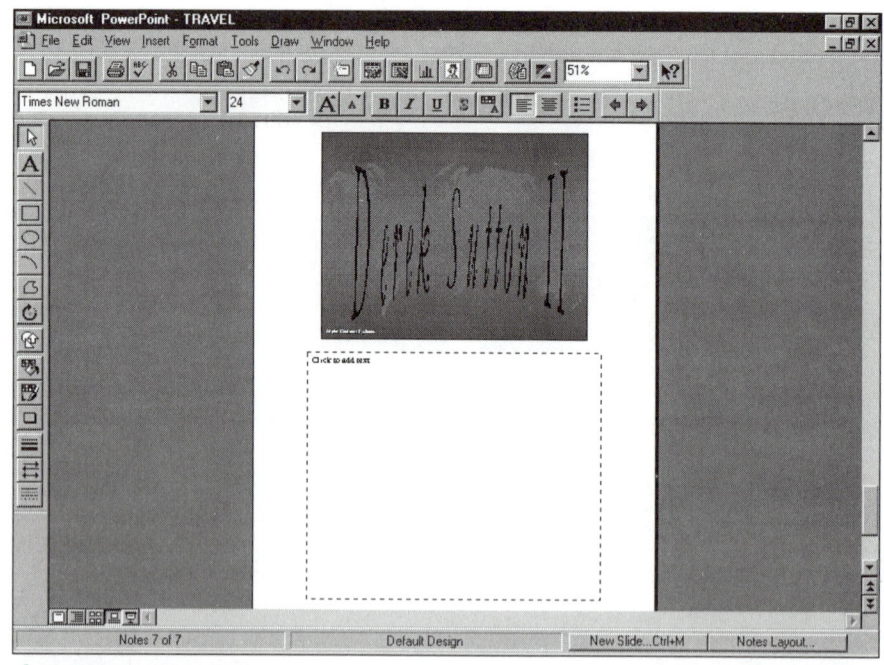

Figure 25-4: Notes Page view.

Figure 25-5: Slide Show view.

Working with Shortcuts and Toolbars

Just as with other Microsoft programs, PowerPoint offers shortcut menus, shortcut buttons, and toolbars to make it as easy as possible for you to create your presentations.

Using shortcut menus

PowerPoint provides shortcut menus so that you can perform different commands without having to use the pull-down menus. Shortcut menus can save lots of time. To activate any of the shortcut menus, move the pointer to the object that you want the command to act on and right-click with the mouse. Figure 25-6 shows a shortcut menu in PowerPoint.

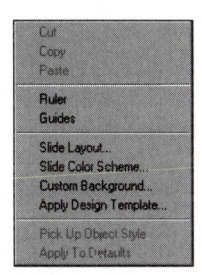

Figure 25-6: A shortcut menu in the PowerPoint window.

Using shortcut buttons

PowerPoint also offers three shortcut buttons that are located at the lower-right corner of the presentation window on the status bar. These buttons include the New Slide, Layout, and Template buttons. The New Slide button inserts a new slide into your presentation following the current one. The Slide Layout button displays the Slide Layout dialog box (see Figure 25-7). From here, you can choose a layout for the slide by clicking on the desired layout in the dialog box.

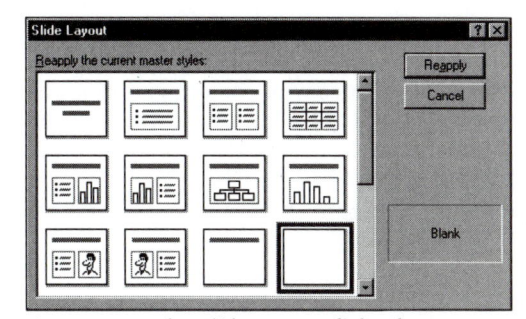

Figure 25-7: The Slide Layout dialog box.

Using the toolbars

When you open the PowerPoint window, you see three toolbars. Use the Standard toolbar to open presentations, to save, to print, or to insert objects and charts. Use the Formatting toolbar to perform tasks related to formatting, such as applying different fonts and styles and changing the indentation of the presentation. Use the Drawing toolbar, on the left side of the screen, to perform tasks related to controlling the appearance of shapes. You can draw shapes, rotate them, and control different aspects of their appearance on-screen. Use the Drawing+ toolbar to rotate shapes and group objects, or to change the order of your grouped objects.

You can activate the other toolbars that are available in PowerPoint by choosing the Toolbars command from the View menu and then selecting the toolbars from the list in the Toolbars dialog box (see Figure 25-8). Or you can right-click on the toolbar area of the screen and then select the toolbars that you want from the shortcut menu that appears.

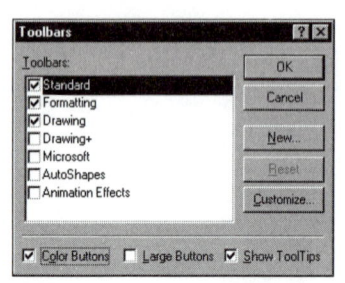

Figure 25-8: The Toolbars dialog box.

Use the AutoShapes toolbar to insert trapezoids, diamonds, or other shapes into your presentation and to size them. Use the Animation Effects toolbar to add different animation effects to your presentation. With the different effects, you can have words appear from left to right across a slide, or the words can appear as if they were being typed. You can also have words appear in a camera-like style.

Using PowerPoint's Default Presentations

By far, the easiest way to create a presentation in PowerPoint is to use one of the 44 default presentation formats that are provided with the software. The advantage of using a default format is that it already contains slides with content guidelines that you can follow to quickly build a presentation for a typical business need. PowerPoint provides one blank presentation, 23 presentation designs, and 20 complete presentations. The following list gives you an idea of the types of default presentations you will see in the New Presentation dialog box shown in Figure 25-9:

- Communicating Bad News creates a presentation for breaking bad news.
- Recommending a Strategy offers a slide layout that is useful for determining a strategy.
- Reporting Progress creates a presentation that gives a progress report.
- Selling a Product, Service, or Idea opens a presentation that you can use for a sales pitch.
- Training creates a slide layout that is useful for training.
- Azure, Color Boxes, and Tropical create slides with backgrounds that may be appropriate for a presentation you may want to give.
- General creates a blank presentation — you have to provide all of the formatting, layout, and content.

The last default presentation format is the Blank option, which enables you to create your own layout. You need to be an experienced PowerPoint user to feel comfortable using this option.

To create a presentation by using a default presentation format, follow these steps:

1. Start a new presentation by choosing New from the File menu. The New Presentation dialog box appears, as shown in Figure 25-9.

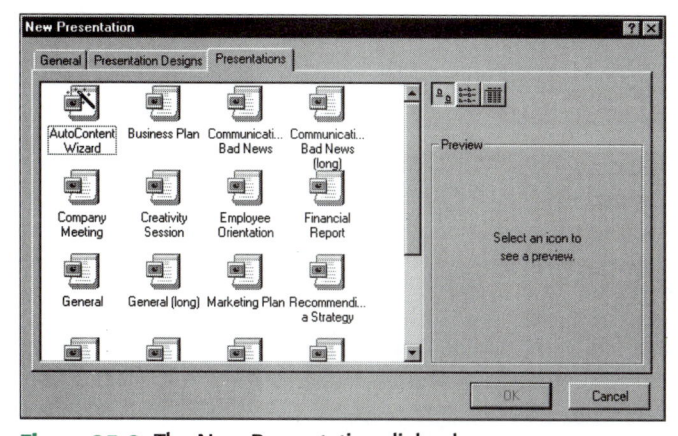

Figure 25-9: The New Presentation dialog box.

2. Click on the Presentations tab, if it is not already open, to show the default presentation formats.
3. Click on the desired presentation format and then click on the OK button (or double-click on the desired presentation format). PowerPoint loads the presentation format, and the first slide of the presentation appears. Figure 25-10 shows the first slide of the Reporting Progress presentation format.

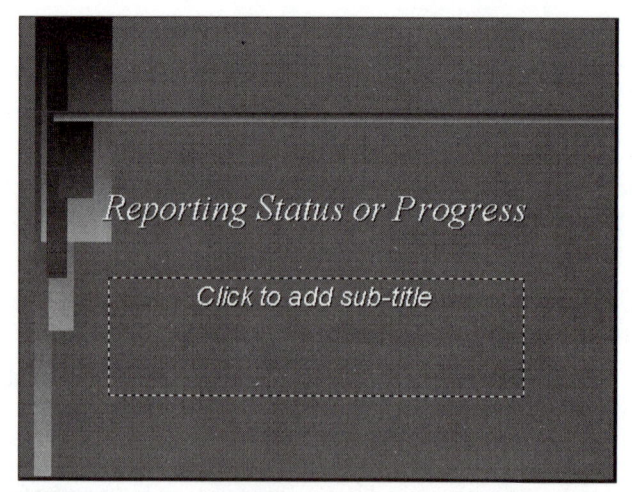

Figure 25-10: The first slide of the Reporting Progress presentation.

After you use these steps to create a presentation, you can modify the text in the slides by clicking on the text to select each item that you see (titles, subtitles, or text within the presentation) and typing your desired text. You can use the Page Up and Page Down keys or the Previous Slide and Next Slide buttons at the lower-right side of the window to move among the various slides of your presentation. Each slide contains text in the form of suggestions that you can modify. For example, Figure 25-11 shows the second of nine available slides in the Reporting Progress presentation. You can click on the existing text and edit it as desired while in Slide view.

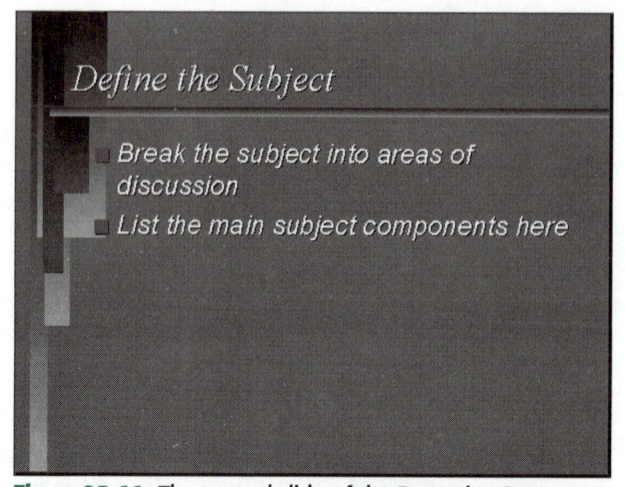

Figure 25-11: The second slide of the Reporting Progress presentation.

If you don't want one of the default slides in your presentation, just move to the unwanted slide and choose Edit➪Delete Slide. If you want to add a new slide to the presentation, move to the slide that you want the new slide to follow and choose Insert➪New Slide. The New Slide dialog box appears. Now choose the slide layout you want. Then you can click in the boxes and type the desired text for the slide. (You'll learn more about adding slides and about adding items to slides later in this chapter.)

After you've finished adding the needed text to the pages of your presentation, you can save it by choosing File➪Save. When you save a presentation for the first time, the File Save dialog box appears, as shown in Figure 25-12. Enter a name for the file in the File name text box and choose a different folder, if you want. Then click on the Save button to save the presentation.

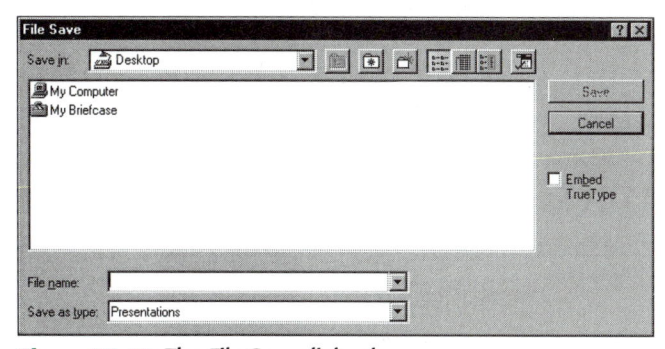

Figure 25-12: The File Save dialog box.

> **More Info** You can print your finished presentation by choosing File➪Print to open the Print dialog box. Choose All if you want to print all the slides in the presentation or choose Current Slide if you just want to print the slide that's currently visible in the PowerPoint window. After you make your selection, click on the OK button to begin printing. You can print information in PowerPoint in several ways. You'll find a full description of printing and of the other options in the Print dialog box in Chapter 28.

When you're finished with the presentation, choose File➪Close if you want to do other work in PowerPoint or choose File➪Exit to get completely out of PowerPoint.

Working with Presentations

The information that you have read so far can easily get you started with creating effective business presentations. However, you can do a lot more with PowerPoint, and the rest of this chapter will fill you in on the basics. For example, PowerPoint does not differ from other Microsoft applications in how you open and save a file — in this case, a presentation. Choosing File➪Open opens a presentation; choosing File➪Save saves the current presentation.

Opening a new presentation

When you want to open a new presentation, choose File➪New to open the New Presentation dialog box (see Figure 25-9, a few pages back). The dialog box contains three tabs: General, Presentation Designs, and Presentations. By default, the General tab is open, from which you can choose a default presentation format (see "Using PowerPoint's Default Presentations" earlier in the chapter).

The Presentation Designs tab contains a host of designs that you can use for your slide backgrounds (see Figure 25-13). Use the Preview window to view a design after you click on the icon of your choice.

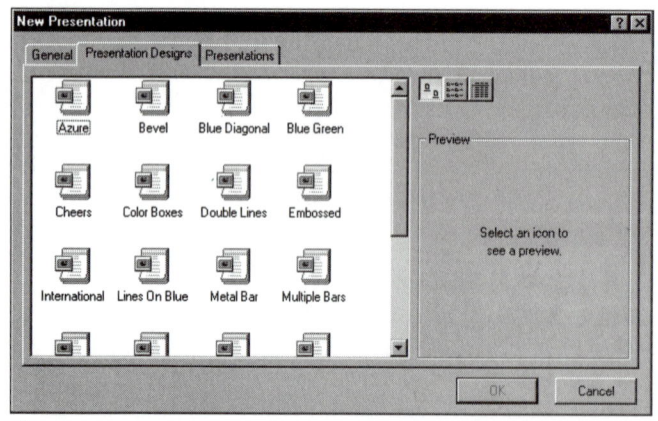

Figure 25-13: The Presentation Designs tab of the New Presentation dialog box.

After you click on the General tab, you will see the icon for a Blank Presentation (see Figure 25-14). Choose the Blank Presentation to create a default blank presentation.

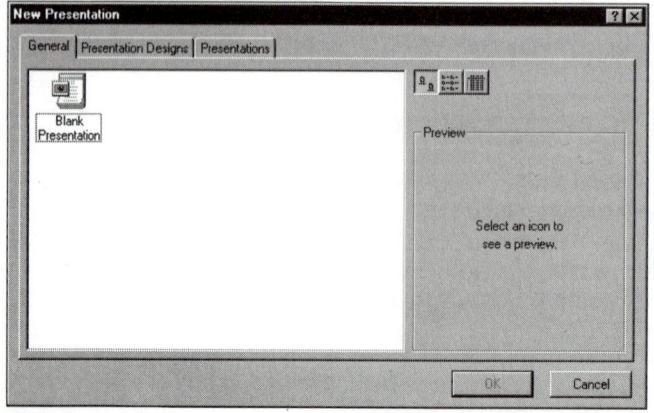

Figure 25-14: The General tab of the New Presentation dialog box.

After you have chosen the template that you want for your presentation, click on the OK button to begin filling out the template.

You can also create a presentation based on another presentation. Find the presentation you want to use as a base, and save it as a template (use File➪Save As and choose PowerPoint Templates in the Save as type area). Then choose Format➪Apply Design Template and choose the presentation you just saved as a template.

Several presentations can be opened at the same time in PowerPoint. Use File➪Open. Hold down the Ctrl key as you click on the presentations in the Open dialog box. The current presentation that you are working on appears on the top window. All the presentations that are open can be displayed using Ctrl+F6.

Saving a presentation

You save a presentation in PowerPoint the same way that you save a file in other Microsoft programs: you choose File➪Save. If you have not saved the presentation before, the Save As dialog box opens, where you are prompted to enter a name for the presentation. If you have already given the presentation a name, it is saved under that name.

You can also perform other tasks in the Save As dialog box. You can change the name of a presentation by entering a new name in the File name text box. You can save files as metafiles or outlines by selecting the new file type from the Save as type list box and then clicking on the OK button to save the file. Keep in mind that you can also save a presentation as a PowerPoint 4.0 file for use with PowerPoint 4.0.

When you have completed your work in PowerPoint and you want to exit, choose File➪Close.

Entering summary information

You can include summary information with the presentations that you save. You enter summary information — which includes a title, subject, and other key information to help you keep track of the presentations — in the Summary Information dialog box. To enter summary information for your presentation, perform the following steps:

1. Choose File➪Properties. The Properties dialog box appears, with the Summary tab open, as shown in Figure 25-15.

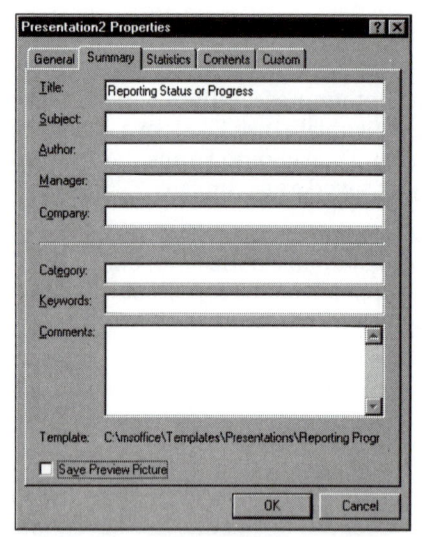

Figure 25-15: The Summary tab of the Properties dialog box.

2. Enter the information that you want in each of the following text boxes:

    - **Title** — Enter a name for the presentation.
    - **Subject** — Enter a brief description of the contents of the presentation.
    - **Author** — Enter the name of the author. The default name is the name that you entered when you installed Microsoft Office.
    - **Manager** — Enter a manager name, if you wish.
    - **Company** — Enter a company name, if you wish.
    - **Category** — Enter a category for the presentation if you wish to categorize it.
    - **Keywords** — Enter keywords that you associate with the presentation. These words can help you in a Find File search, if you need to use this command from the File menu. You can use the Copy and Paste commands from the Edit menu to insert the titles of your slides in the Keywords list box.
    - **Comments** — Enter any comments that you feel are needed.

3. When you have finished entering the information, click on the OK button to store the information.

4. The summary information can be viewed by choosing File⇨Properties. This displays the properties for the presentation. Then choose the Summary tab to display the summary info.

Working with Text

After you have opened a new presentation, it will not contain the text that you want to use, so you will have to add and edit your own text. The following section will teach you the basics of editing text in Outline and Slide views. Later in the chapter, you'll learn how to add objects to your presentation.

Editing in Outline view

Outline view is excellent for editing text, and it enables you to see the overall content of your presentation at the same time. You can switch to Outline view by choosing View⇨Outline or by clicking on the Outline View button in the status bar. After you are in Outline view, you can edit text by simply clicking on it and moving the cursor to the area that you want to change. Use the Delete key to remove characters to the right of the cursor and use the Backspace key to delete characters to the left of the cursor. Figure 25-16 shows a slide in Outline view ready for editing.

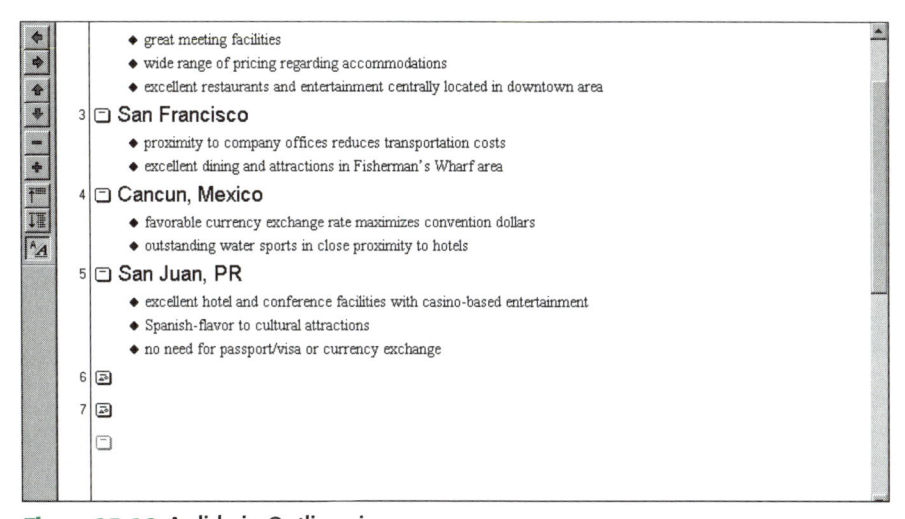

Figure 25-16: A slide in Outline view.

When you select text in PowerPoint, the program selects whole words. If you want to select individual characters, choose Tools⇨Options. In the Options dialog box, choose the Edit tab. Next, uncheck the Automatic Word Selection option and click on the OK button to turn it off.

Editing in Slide view

Slide view also provides an easy way to edit text, and you get a good opportunity to see the appearance of an individual slide. You can switch to Slide view by choosing View➪Slides or by clicking on the Slide view button in the status bar. As Figure 25-17 demonstrates, you can edit text or an object by clicking on the text or the object to select it and then clicking in the space where you want the cursor to appear and making the changes.

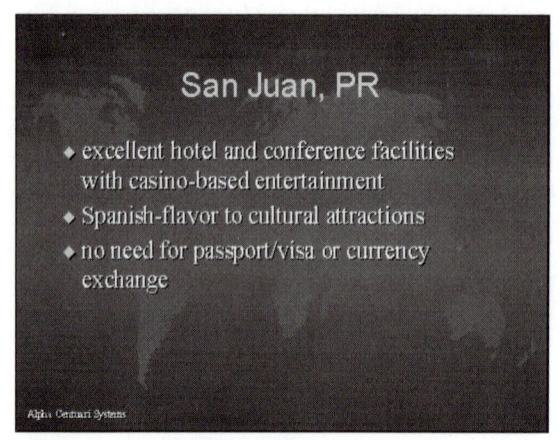

Figure 25-17: A slide in Slide view.

Working with Slides

You use slide view to do most of your work with slides. Slide view lets you see each slide pretty much as it will appear in your presentation. It also lets you move between the slides in your presentations, and it lets you click and drag to move the slide within your presentation.

Moving between slides

When you have more than one slide in a presentation, you must be able to move easily among the slides so that you can quickly work on all of them. (Remember that in all views except Slide Show you can perform edits by double-clicking on the slide.) How you move among the slides depends on the view that you are in at the time. Table 25-1 shows how you can move among slides in each of the views.

Table 25-1
Moving among slides in different views

View	How to move among slides
Outline	Use the scrollbar to move to the slide, click on the slide icon to the left of the slide's title, or click inside the text to perform the changes.
Slide Sorter	Click on the slide that you want to see. A border appears around the slide. If you then double-click on the slide, you are switched to Slide view where you can make changes to your slide.
Slide	Click on the Previous Slide or Next Slide button or drag the scrollbox until the slide that you want appears.
Notes Pages	Click on the Next Slide or Previous Slide button or drag the scrollbox until the slide that you want appears.

Inserting slides

As you build your presentations in PowerPoint, you naturally will need to make changes to the presentation by inserting, deleting, and copying slides. Follow these steps to add a slide to a presentation:

1. In any view, choose the slide after which you want the new slide to appear.
2. Choose Insert➪New Slide.
3. The New Slide dialog box appears. Choose the slide layout you want, then click the OK button to choose that slide layout.

If you want to change the new slide's layout (or create a slide layout), follow these steps:

1. Right-click on the slide and choose Slide Layout from the shortcut menu. The Slide Layout dialog box appears.
2. Choose the layout that you want and click on the Reapply button. (If you are creating a slide layout, the button is Apply.)

The layout is then applied to the slide.

Hot Stuff You can also add a new slide by clicking on the New Slide button located to the right-bottom of the status bar or by clicking on the Insert New Slide button on the Standard toolbar.

You can also add slides from a previous presentation to your current presentation. This shortcut is useful because it prevents you from taking the time to create an entirely new presentation when you already have slides that you can use from an old presentation. First, you must open the presentation to which you want to add the slide and choose the place where you want to insert the slide. The new slide will appear after the chosen slide. Then choose Insert➪Slides from File. The Insert File dialog box appears, as shown in Figure 25-18.

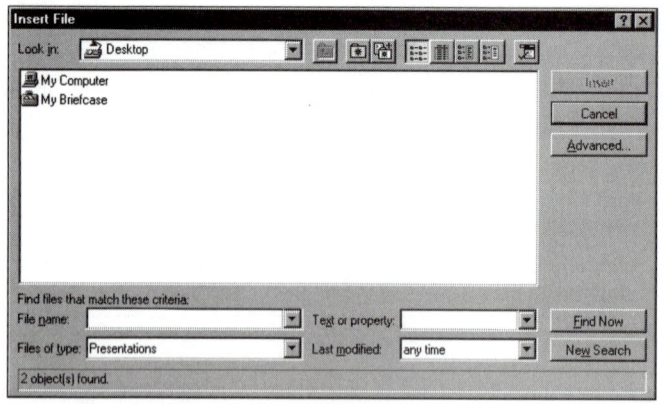

Figure 25-18: The Insert File dialog box.

Choose the drive and the folder that contain the presentation from which you want to insert the slides. To see the slides before you insert them, switch to Preview mode by clicking on the Preview button located at the top of the dialog box. Finally, double-click on the desired filename, and all the slides contained in that presentation will be inserted into the new presentation. Note that the inserted slides take on the look of the presentation in which they are inserted. This prevents you from having to make any changes to the look of the imported slides.

Deleting slides

Deleting a slide is relatively simple and can be performed in any view except Slide Show. Navigate to the slide, and choose Edit➪DeleteSlide to remove the slide. If you delete a slide by accident, choose Edit➪Undo or click on the Undo button on the Standard toolbar to bring back the slide.

Copying and moving slides

You copy slides in PowerPoint just like you copy items in other Windows programs by using the Copy and Paste commands from the Edit menu. You can copy a slide by performing the following steps:

1. Switch to Slide Sorter view.

2. Choose the slide(s) that you want to copy. To select more than one slide, hold down the Shift key while you select the slides.

3. Choose Edit➪Copy.
4. Move to the slide after which you want to place the copied slide.
5. Choose Edit➪Paste.

You use the same method to move a slide, except that you use the Cut command rather than the Copy command.

Rearranging slides

From time to time you will need to change the order in which the slides appear in your presentation. PowerPoint provides for this need in Slide Sorter or Outline views. In these views you can use the drag-and drop-technique to move slides around.

Follow these steps to rearrange the order of your slides in Outline view:

1. Click on the icon for the slide that you want to move.
2. Drag the icon up or down in the outline.

You can also select just one piece of information on a slide and move it to another slide by clicking and dragging it to the desired place.

In Slide Sorter view, perform the following steps to rearrange slides:

1. Select the slide that you want to move to a new location.
2. Drag the slide to its new location. As you drag the slide, a vertical line will mark the place where it will appear.
3. Release the mouse button to insert the slide in its new location.

Changing the slide layout

You can also change the slide layout after you have created a slide. To change a slide layout, follow these steps:

1. In Slide Sorter view, move to the side that you want to change.
2. Choose Format➪Slide Layout.
3. In the Slide Layout dialog box, choose the layout that you want to apply to the slide and click on the Reapply button (see Figure 25-19).

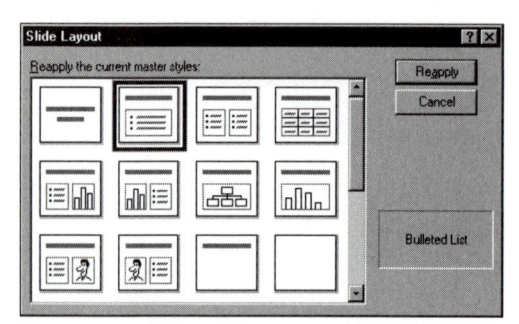

Figure 25-19: The Slide Layout dialog box.

Working with Objects

In PowerPoint, the basic component that you use to create a slide is an *object*. An object can be the box where you enter text, a picture brought in from another source, or the shape that you draw. You can have as many objects as you want on a slide.

Selecting and grouping objects

To select the object that you want to work with, click on it. Then you can add text to it and change its orientation, shape, color, or pattern. You can also select multiple objects by holding down the Shift key as you select the objects. To deselect an object, simply hold down the Shift key and click on the object again.

You can also group objects together, which is useful when you want to change the colors for a group of objects or align them horizontally. All the objects that you include in the group will act as one object. Therefore, if you perform an action on one of the objects, the action will affect all the objects in the group. When you group objects, you can flip, resize, or rotate them. If you want to change the grouping, you can do so by choosing Draw⇨Regroup after the objects have been grouped and ungrouped. Remember that the Regroup command will affect only the objects that were included in the original group.

You can also select and deselect noncontiguous objects in PowerPoint by clicking on the objects while you hold down the Shift key.

Moving and copying objects

As you work out a presentation, you may often have to move your objects around. PowerPoint provides for this need nicely with two options: the cut-and-copy method or the click-and-drag method.

To use the cut-and copy method to move objects, follow these steps:

1. Switch to Slide view and select the object(s) that you want to move or copy.
2. Choose Edit⇨Cut to move the object to a new location via the Clipboard; choose Edit⇨Copy to copy it.
3. Move to the slide on which you want to place the information.
4. Choose Edit⇨Paste to place the Clipboard information onto the slide.

Using the click-and-drag method to move objects is equally simple. To use this method, click on the object and hold down the mouse button. Then move to the area where you want to place the object. Release the mouse button to place the object.

Sometimes you may find that you need to remove an object from a slide. To remove an object, select it and press the Delete key or choose Edit⇨Clear.

Cropping objects

In your quest to give your presentation a refined look, you may find it necessary to crop the objects, both pictures and graphic insertions, that you add to your presentation. *Cropping* is the trimming of an object to remove elements that you don't want from the picture. Follow these steps to crop an object:

1. Select the object and then choose Tools⇨Crop Picture.
2. Place the mouse pointer over a selection handle. If you want to crop two sides at once, you will need to use a corner handle. If you want to crop only one side, use a top or bottom handle. Figure 25-20 shows a cropped image.

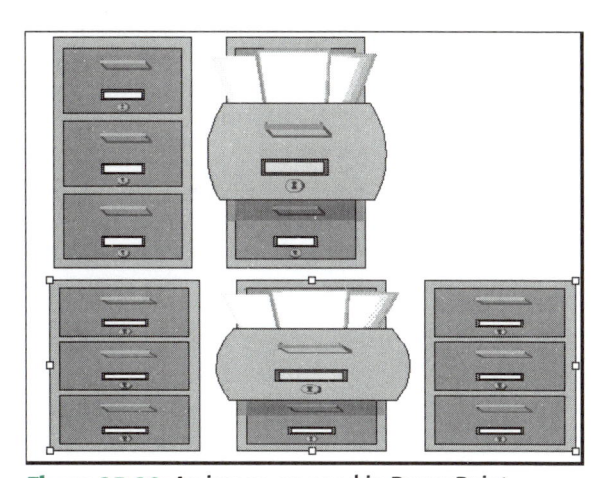

Figure 25-20: An image cropped in PowerPoint.

Aligning objects

When you create presentations, it is important that the objects have the same sort of alignment. Figure 25-21 shows a before and after shot of some objects on a slide in PowerPoint. As you can see, the slide with aligned objects has a better appearance than the one in which the objects are not aligned. Aligned objects make your objects appear more organized than those that aren't aligned.

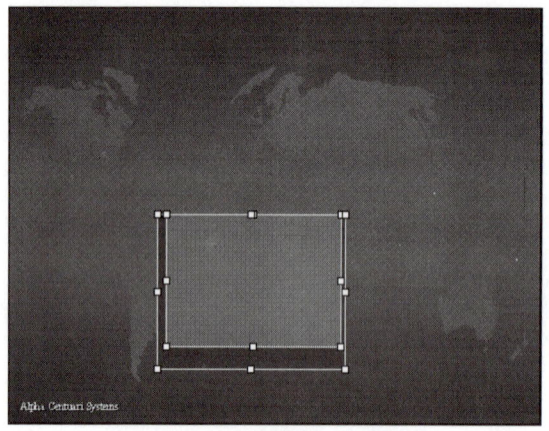

Figure 25-21: Objects aligned on a slide.

The Align command enables you to choose the method of alignment that you want to use. You can select objects and then align them, or you can use the rulers available in the PowerPoint window. PowerPoint is equipped with a reference system for aligning objects on slides. The system uses a grid and guides. The invisible grid covers the slide with twelve gridlines per inch and five lines per centimeter. When the objects are drawn, their corners align on the nearest intersection of the grid, which is how PowerPoint helps you to align objects.

The guides that PowerPoint provides are two rulers: one horizontal and one vertical. When the corners or center of an object (whichever is closer) is close to the guide, it snaps to the guide, which is how you align the object. You can even align a group of objects.

To align an object, follow these steps:

1. Select the object(s) that you want to align.
2. Choose Draw⇨Align, and then choose the alignment that you want from the submenu. You can choose from Lefts, Centers, Rights, Tops, Middles, or Bottoms.

If you want to automatically align your objects, choose Draw⇨Snap to Grid. If the grid is on, you will see a check mark beside the choice on the menu.

Hot Stuff You can use a number of toolbar buttons in the Customize dialog box that you'll find helpful in aligning objects. Choosing Tools⇨Customize opens the Customize dialog box with the Toolbars tab chosen. Choose the All commands category and you will see other toolbar buttons appear that you may find very useful in your work in PowerPoint. To add each of these buttons to your toolbar, click on the name of the button you wish to add from the Commands box. Next, drag the name up to the toolbar. You will notice the outline of a button appears. When you add the buttons to the top of the screen, you will notice that a toolbar is created for the button. Each of the alignment buttons that you wish to add will be added to that toolbar. If you are not sure of what each of the buttons do, the box at the bottom of the tab gives a description for each of the buttons as it is selected.

Stacking objects

When you are working with different objects, you will see that sometimes you have to overlap the objects to give them the correct effect. You may even want to change their order. You can also stack groups of objects in PowerPoint by moving a group of objects forward or backward. You can use the Tab key to navigate through the stacked objects.

Objects in a stack can be moved up or down one level at a time, or you can send an object all the way to the back or to the front at once. This feature prevents you from having to keep track of the objects as you draw them — in other words, you don't have to draw the bottom object first or the top object last and so on.

To bring an object to the front or to the back of a stack, select the object that you want to move and choose either Draw⇨Bring Forward or Draw⇨Send Backward. Remember that you can also use the drawing toolbar.

To bring an object forward one level or to send it back one level, use Draw⇨Bring Forward or Draw⇨Send Backward. Figure 25-22 shows the original positions of objects on a slide, and how Bring Forward can change their positions.

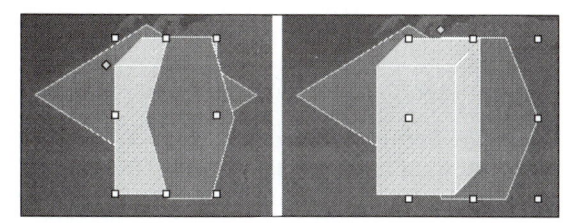

Figure 25-22: Left: The original positions of objects on a slide. Right: Changing the position of the objects with the Bring Forward command.

Working with Shapes

Sometimes when you work with PowerPoint, you will want to add your own shapes or art to the presentation. (Remember that these shapes are still considered objects by PowerPoint.) You can draw lines, arcs, rectangles, and ovals by using the Drawing toolbar. Figure 25-23 shows some examples of shapes that you can create in PowerPoint.

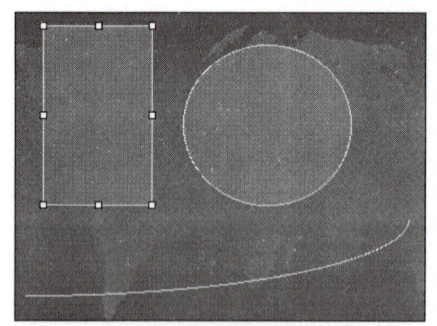

Figure 25-23: Examples of shapes that you can create in PowerPoint.

You can also add different attributes to the lines and shapes that you create. For example, you can insert dotted lines, color the lines, fill in the shapes, and add arrowheads to lines. Remember that you can't add text to your shapes except by grouping.

Drawing shapes

There are many tools you can use to perform your drawing tasks. On the Drawing toolbar you can use the Rectangle tool to draw rectangles, and the Line tool to draw lines. You can also use the Oval and Arc tools to create shapes.

Follow these steps to draw shapes in your slides:

1. Switch to Slide view, if you are not already there.
2. On the Drawing toolbar, click on the button for the object that you want to draw. Click on the Line Tool button if you want to draw a line; click on the Ellipse Tool button if you want to draw an oval or a circle; click on the Arc Tool button if you want to draw an arc; and so on.
3. Click on the place where you want the shape to begin and drag to the place where you want the shape to end.
4. Release the mouse button.

Constraint keys are used to create shapes that are difficult to create freehand. These constraint keys are available:

✦ Hold down the Shift key to draw a quarter of a circle.

✦ Hold down the Ctrl key to center the arc on the point of origin.

✦ Hold down Shift+Ctrl to draw a quarter of a circle centered on its starting point.

Drawing freeform shapes

You may want to add a freeform shape, such as a flower or an ice-cream cone, to a slide. You can create any kind of drawing that you want by clicking on the Freeform Tool button on the Drawing toolbar. Then you draw the shape that you want by clicking and holding down the mouse button as you draw. Double-click to stop drawing.

You can also use the Freeform tool to draw a *polygon*, a series of points joined by lines. After you click on the Freeform Tool button, you click on the point where you want the first vertex of the polygon to appear and release the mouse button. Then you click on the point where you want the second point to appear and release the mouse button. Continue to click on the desired points and release the mouse button until you create the polygon shape that you want.

Changing the color and style of shapes

You can change the color or style of the lines in a shape and you can apply a fill color to a shape, as well. To change the color or style of a line in a shape, follow these steps:

1. Select the shape that you want to change.

2. Choose Format⇨Colors and Lines to open the Colors and Lines dialog box, as shown in Figure 25-24. In the Line area, you can choose to change the color or style of the line in any shape. You also can add dashed lines and an arrowhead, if you want.

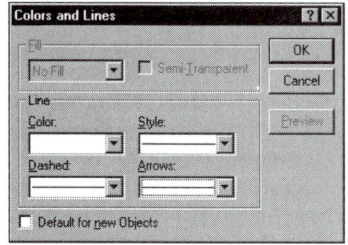

Figure 25-24: The Colors and Lines dialog box.

3. Clicking on the Preview button applies the selected options to the slide, so that you can see what they look like before making the changes. You may need to drag the dialog box out of the way to see the results, because the box appears on top of the slide.

You may also want to add a fill color to a shape. Simply select the shape that you want to fill in with color and then choose Format⇨Colors and Lines. In the Colors and Lines dialog box, select a color in the Fill list box and then click on the OK button.

Rotating and sizing shapes

Rotating and changing the size of a shape is also a simple matter with PowerPoint. To rotate a shape on its center point, first select the shape. Then click on the Free Rotate Tool button on the Drawing toolbar. Now drag a handle of the shape to rotate it. Figure 25-25 shows the difference with one arc rotated.

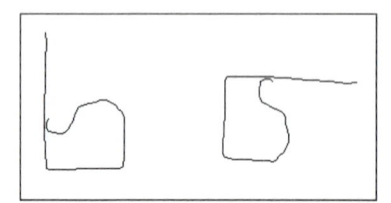

Figure 25-25: Left: A free-form object. Right: The same object, rotated.

To change the size of a shape, select the shape. You will see small black squares, called *handles*, appear around the shape. To resize the width of the shape, drag one of the side handles to the desired width. To change the height of the shape, drag a top or bottom handle. If you want to resize the shape proportionally, drag a corner handle. A shape can also be resized from its center by holding down the Ctrl key and dragging the handles.

Using AutoShapes and Clip Art

PowerPoint has many standard shapes and pieces of clip art available. To activate the AutoShapes toolbar, choose View⇨Toolbars and click on the AutoShapes check box. Or you can click on the AutoShapes button on the Drawing toolbar. Choose the shape that you want to add to your presentation and click on the corresponding button. Then move to the area of the presentation where you want to add the shape. Click to add the shape and then size it by using the resizing techniques. Remember that you can also add color to the shapes by choosing Format⇨Colors and Lines opening the Colors and Lines dialog box.

PowerPoint comes with a whole bunch of clip art — invaluable in creating your presentations. The clip art comes in many different categories. To access the ClipArt Gallery, perform the following steps:

1. Click on the Insert Clip Art button on the Standard toolbar.
2. The Microsoft ClipArt Gallery dialog box appears, as shown in Figure 25-26.

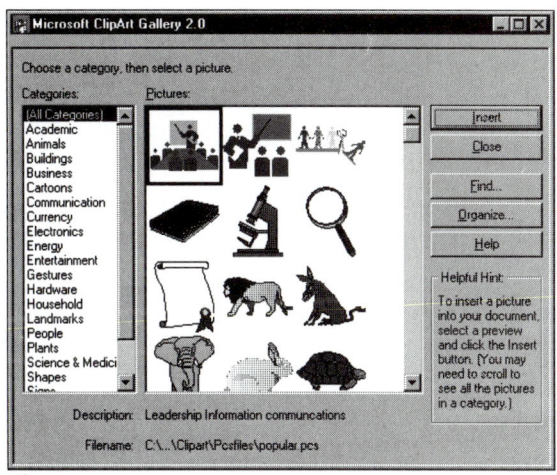

Figure 25-26: The Microsoft ClipArt Gallery dialog box.

3. Choose the category of clip art that you want.
4. Select the clip art that you want. PowerPoint inserts it at the insertion point.

Summary

This chapter described many techniques that you can use in the everyday use of PowerPoint. With these skills you can build presentations, enter the text that you want, and choose the correct slide layout. This chapter covered the following areas:

- ✦ You learned how to use the convenient shortcut menus. This makes life easy for you, providing you with quick access to the commands that you may need in Power Point.

- ✦ We also discussed different methods to lay out new slides and edit text. This ranged from slides with place holders for clip art and the other available slide layouts.

- ✦ You learned how to insert objects into your presentations and edit them. The use of the objects will help you make nicer presentations.

- ✦ You learned how to use the built-in templates and prefabricated presentations to make creating a presentation less time consuming.

- ✦ You learned how to save your presentations and how to enter summary information that will help you find the presentations if you tend to forget where they are. This is quite useful for those of you who create many presentations.

The next chapter covers ways that you can enhance the presentations you create in PowerPoint.

Where to go next...

- ✦ Now that you have the tools to begin your work in PowerPoint, you can begin refining the presentations that you create. Chapter 26 gets you started.

- ✦ Chapter 29 provides you with step-by-step details on how you can create some presentations you may need in the office.

- ✦ The obvious goal when you use PowerPoint is to produce a finished presentation from the slides you created with the software. Chapter 28 tells you how.

✦ ✦ ✦

Enhancing a Presentation

CHAPTER 26

In This Chapter

Using the Pick a Look Wizard

Using the AutoLayout feature

Using the Slide Master

Working with lists and columns

Working with fonts, styles, and colors

Creating special effects with WordArt

Adding Excel worksheets and Word tables

Adding sound to presentations

PowerPoint gives you lots of tools you can use to give your presentation a more professional look. To help you along, PowerPoint provides several wizards, most notably the Pick a Look Wizard, that provide simple ways to help you make your presentations look better. Creating columns and bulleted lists also helps because they help you set up the information in a way that gets the attention of your audience. Using different fonts and colors is another method that can help your presentation take on a different look. This chapter covers these methods and a few others that enhance the appearance of your presentation.

Using the AutoContent Wizard

PowerPoint includes the AutoContent Wizard to help you define your presentation's look — *and contents*. To use the AutoContent wizard, perform the following steps.

1. Choose AutoContent from the dialog box that appears after you activate PowerPoint. If you have already activated PowerPoint, choose File⇨New. From the New Presentation dialog box that appears, choose the Presentations tab. From the Presentations tab choose the AutoContent Wizard. This activates the AutoContent Wizard (Figure 26-1).

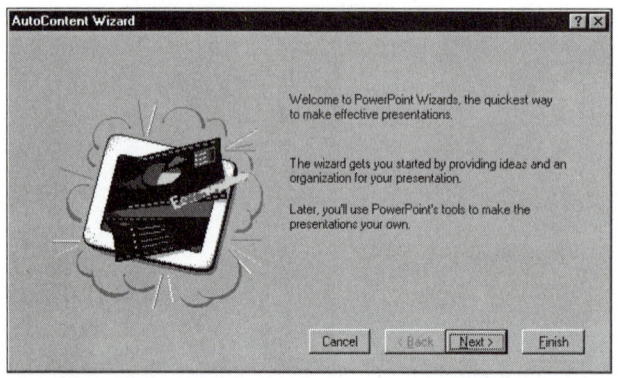

Figure 26-1: The first AutoContent Wizard dialog box.

2. Click on Next to see the second dialog box of the AutoContent Wizard (Figure 26-2). Use this dialog box to create your presentation's title slide. The title slide can include your name, subject, and so on.

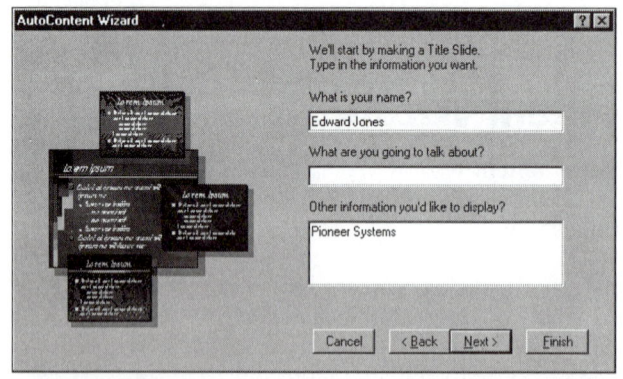

Figure 26-2: The second AutoContent Wizard dialog box.

3. Click on Next to move to the third AutoContent Wizard dialog box (Figure 26-3). This dialog box lets you choose the kind of presentation to create.

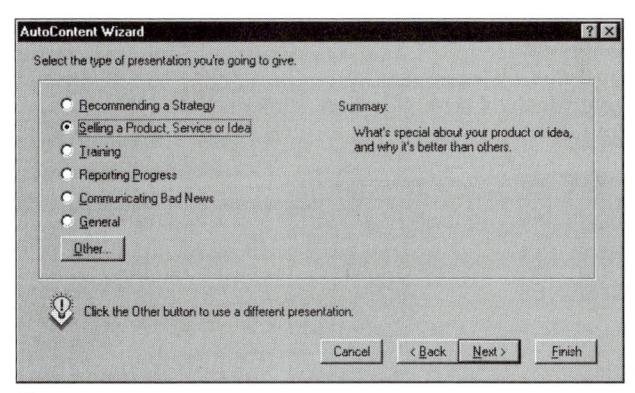

Figure 26-3: Third box of the Auto Content Wizard.

4. If you find that the listed presentations don't meet your needs, or if you want to use other saved templates, click on the Other button. The Select Presentation Template dialog box (Figure 26-4) opens. Select the template that you wish to use and click on the OK button.

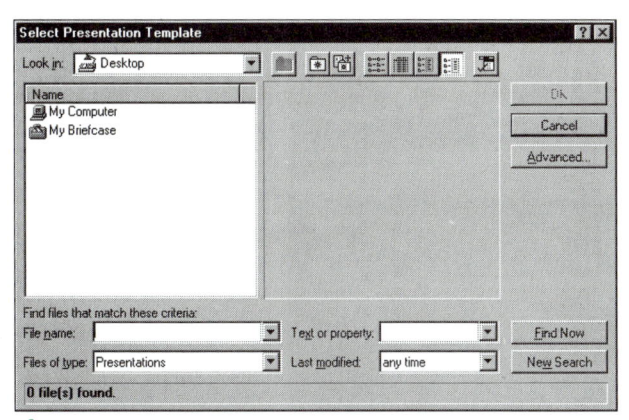

Figure 26-4: The Select Presentation Template dialog box.

5. Now the fourth AutoContent Wizard dialog box (Figure 26-5) appears. This box lets you select a time limit (30 minutes or less, More than 30 minutes, or Haven't decided) and a visual style (Professional, Contemporary, or Default) for your presentation. Make your desired selection, then click on Next.

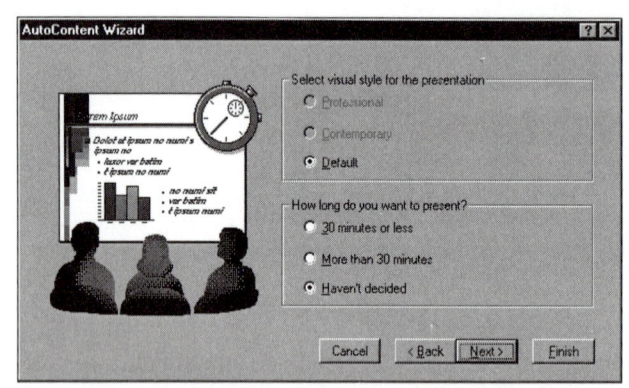

Figure 26-5: The fourth AutoContent Wizard dialog box.

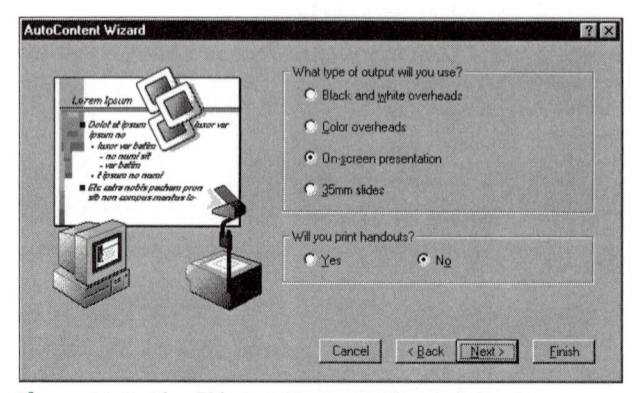

6. The fifth AutoContent Wizard dialog box (Figure 26-6) lets you choose the kind of output you wish for your presentation. You can choose Black and white overheads, Color overheads, On-screen presentations, and 35mm slides. You can also choose to print handouts with your presentation. Now click on the Next button to move to the final box of the AutoContent Wizard.

Figure 26-6: The fifth AutoContent Wizard dialog box.

7. In the final AutoContent Wizard dialog box, finalize the choices made in the wizard. If you want to change any of the choices that you made, click on the Back button to return to the box you used to make the choice and make the necessary changes.

8. After you have chosen all your settings, click on the Finish button. PowerPoint then creates the presentation using the settings you chose.

You can also change the look of your presentations by choosing the Apply Design Template command from the Format menu. This command is convenient if you know which template you want to use. You can choose it directly from the Apply Design Template dialog box.

Using the AutoLayout feature

The AutoLayout feature provides a series of slide layouts that you can use to speed up the process of laying out a slide. The layouts vary greatly. They may include the use of a graph, a piece of clip art, or just text. Figure 26-7 shows the Slide Layout dialog box.

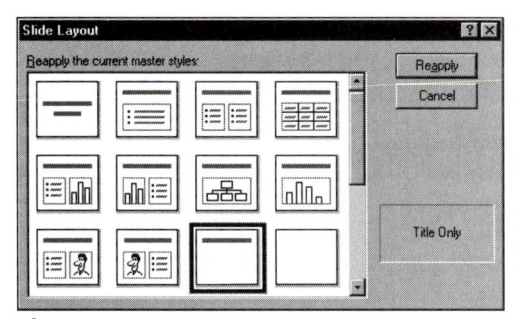

Figure 26-7: The Slide Layout dialog box.

To use the AutoLayout feature, follow these steps:

1. First switch to Slide view by clicking on the Slide View button at the lower-right corner of the PowerPoint window and move to the slide you wish to change.

2. Next choose Format⇨Slide Layout or click on the Slide Layout button at the lower-right corner of the PowerPoint window.

3. In the Slide Layout dialog box, select the layout that you want to use on the slide.

4. After selecting the layout, click on the Reapply button to apply the layout to the slide.

Using the Slide Master

You can use the Slide Master to control the overall appearance and layout of each slide in a presentation. Editing with the Slide Master is very useful because you can change all the slides in your presentation, not just one slide. You can even add graphics or other layouts to the Slide Master, and they will automatically show up in all the slides in that presentation. Make all the changes that you want on the Slide Master, and these new formats are applied to all the slides in your presentation.

The Slide Master contains two important elements: a title area and an object area. The formatting in the title area is specific to the title of each slide in your presentation. The title area tells PowerPoint the font size, style, and color to use for the text. The object area contains the formatting for the remaining text on the slide. The object area also sets up specifications for bulleted lists, which include the indents for each of the lists, the font styles, and size of the fonts. Figure 26-8 shows the Slide Master.

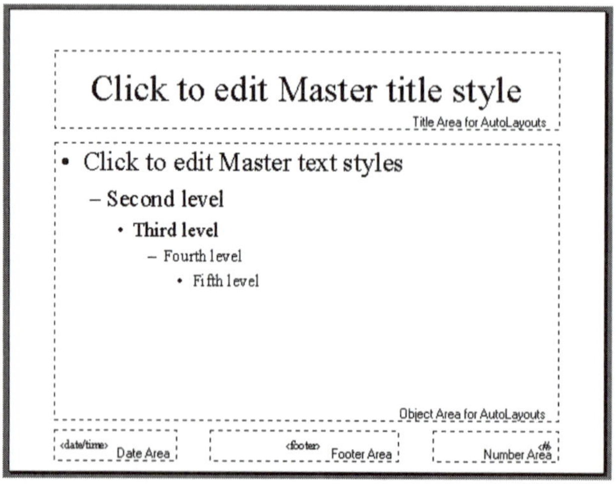

Figure 26-8: The Slide Master.

Along with the usual text formats and object setups, you can use the Slide Master to include borders, page numbers, logos, clip art, and many other elements on the slides of your presentation. Perform the following steps to view the Slide Master:

1. Choose View⇨Master⇨Slide Master. The Slide Master appears as shown in Figure 26-8.

Chapter 26 ✦ **Enhancing a Presentation** 555

2. You now can make any adjustment that you want to the Slide Master. To bring up a shortcut menu of available formatting options, right-click on the area beside the slide. You can change the Master Layout dialg box (Figure 26-9), the Custom Background dialog box (Figure 26-10), or the Color Scheme dialog box (Figure 26-11) options.

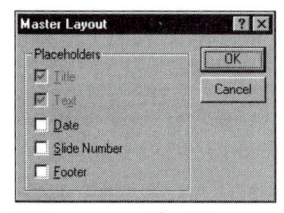

Figure 26-9: The Master Layout dialog box.

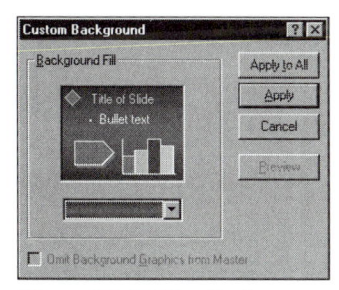

Figure 26-10: The Custom Background dialog box.

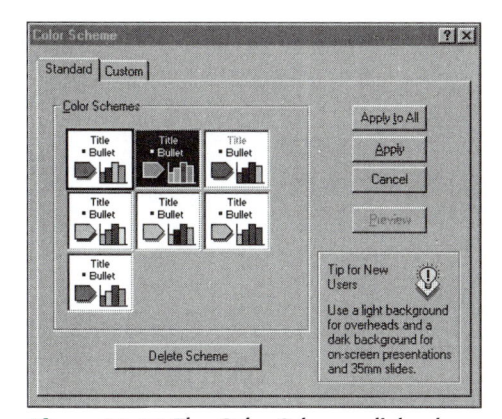

Figure 26-11: The Color Scheme dialog box.

3. When you have finished making the adjustments to Slide Master, you can get back to your regular slide by choosing the Slides command from the View menu or by clicking on the Slide View button at the lower-left corner of the PowerPoint window.

You can create a custom color scheme for your slides by clicking on the Custom tab in the Color Scheme dialog box (Figure 26-12). In the Scheme Colors area, click on the box whose color you want to change and then click on the Change Color button. A color dialog box appears appropriate to the box you selected. For example, if you selected a Fill box, the dialog box is titled Fill Color, while if you selected an Accent box, the dialog box is titled Accent Color, as shown in Figure 26-13. After creating the color scheme that you want, you can add it to the standard color schemes available by clicking the Add as Standard Scheme button.

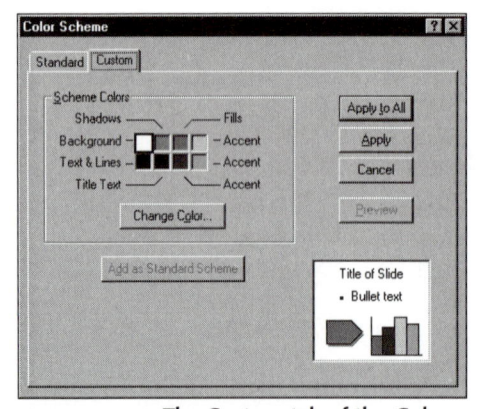

Figure 26-12: The Custom tab of the Color Scheme dialog box.

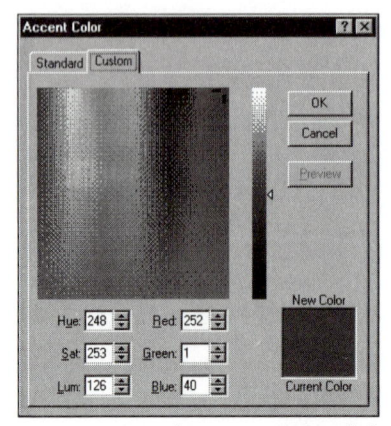

Figure 26-13: The Accent Color dialog box.

After you apply the editing in the Slide Master to all your slides, you can still edit and change individual slides in whatever way you want. You can even change the headings or the formatting that you have added with the Slide Master. If you don't like the editing that you have done to a slide, however, and you want to return it to its Slide Master state, you can simply reapply the Slide Master formatting. Follow these steps:

1. Move to the slide to which you want to reapply the Slide Master formatting.
2. Choose Format⇨Slide Layout. The Slide Layout dialog box appears with the current layout selected.
3. Click the Reapply button to reapply the format. The slide now contains the formatting of the Slide Master.

Working with Lists and Columns

When creating your presentations, columns and bulleted lists become important parts of your slides because you use them often. Putting columns and bulleted lists into your slides is easy with PowerPoint.

Creating bulleted lists

In PowerPoint, you use indents to create bulleted lists. You can use this technique for objects (shapes you can add) too. Figure 26-14 shows a bulleted list in PowerPoint.

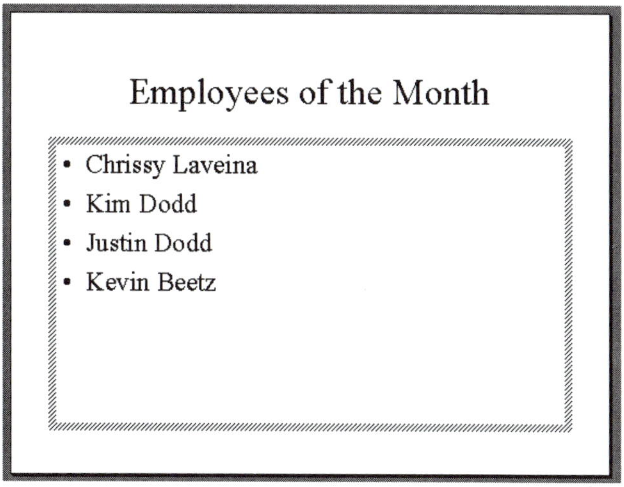

Employees of the Month
- Chrissy Laveina
- Kim Dodd
- Justin Dodd
- Kevin Beetz

Figure 26-14: A bulleted list of text in PowerPoint.

Perform the following steps to create a bulleted list:

1. Switch to Slide View and select the New Slide button from the bottom of the screen. Then select Slide Layout and choose the Bulleted List layout.
2. Choose View⇨Ruler so that the PowerPoint ruler is displayed on-screen.
3. Now enter the following names so you can get an idea of how the indent markers affect the text that you have entered on the bulleted list.

   Chrissy Laveina

   Kim Dodd

   Justin Dodd

   Kevin Beetz
4. Now drag the bottom indent marker to the right. You will notice that the bottom marker moves the text from the bullets, and the top marker moves the bullets. You can use this to set indentations.

In a text box, you can create up to five indent levels. To add an indent level, select the item to indent and click on the Demote (Indent more) button on the Formatting toolbar. You may find it easier to handle your indents in Outline View, in which you can create the headings by using the Demote and Promote buttons.

You can also change bullet characters. To do so, choose the paragraph with the bullet that you want to change. Then choose Format⇨Bullet to open the Bullet dialog box. Figure 26-15 shows the many different characters in PowerPoint that can be used as a bullet. From the list, select the character that you want to use as your bullet. If you want to change the color or size of the bullet, make the changes in the corresponding list boxes.

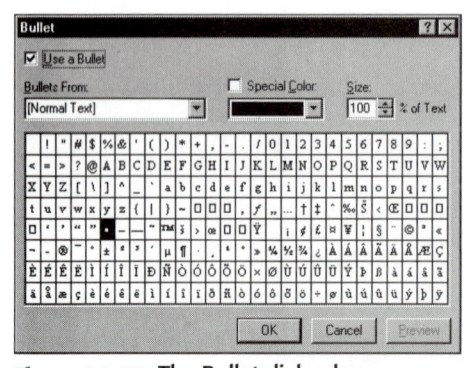

Figure 26-15: The Bullet dialog box.

In the Bullets From list box, choose the font from which you want to select the bullet; remember that each font has a set of bullet characters that go with it. Along with a bullet type you can select a color and size for the bullet also by making your choices from the desired boxes.

Creating columns

Columns are also a useful thing you can create in PowerPoint. (See Figure 26-16.) Most people have an easier time reading long lines of text, and columns are a good way to make them narrower. This is why newspapers contain multiple columns. If you have a large amount of textual information to get across in your presentation, you can take advantage of columns to make the information easier to comprehend.

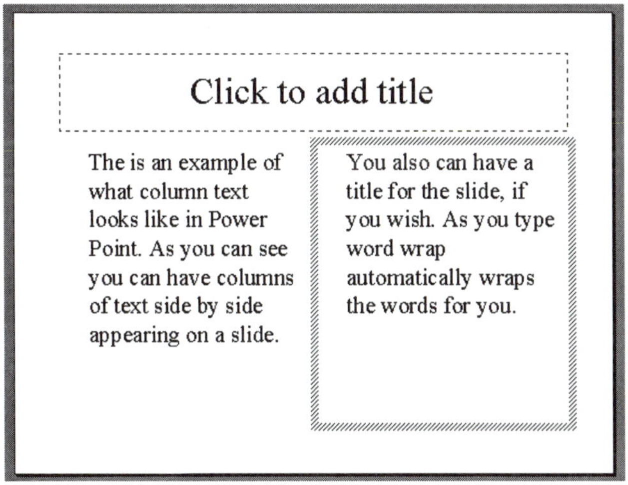

Figure 26-16: Columns displayed on a PowerPoint slide.

To add columns to a slide, perform the following steps:

1. Select the text in which you want to set the tabs.
2. Choose View➪Ruler.
3. Click on the Tab button in the upper-left corner of the presentation window (to the left of the ruler). Keep clicking on the button until you get the type of tab that you want.
4. Click on the place on the ruler that you want that particular tab type. Do this for each of the tab stops that you want.
5. If you want to change the position of a tab, click on it and drag it to the desired position. To remove a tab, click on it and drag it off the ruler.

So you can see that columns can be set up the old-fashioned way, by setting the tabs the way you want and then enter the text you wish and tab to create your text columns. This method is still useful if you have a specific columnar layout in mind. If you wish to use a preset column, you can perform the following steps.

1. Before entering the text, choose the Slide Layout button and select 2 Column Text as the layout for the slide.
2. Next, right click on the bullet in the column text box. From the shortcut menu that appears, choose Bullet.
3. When the Bullet dialog box appears, choose the box at the upper left, which contains nothing. This removes the bullet and lets you enter columnar text.

If you want to create columns of bulleted lists, however, you can use one of the slide layouts from the Slide Layout dialog box. To apply it, choose the Slide Layout button, then select the 2 Column Text choice. By default, this is a bulleted list. Enter the text you want, and press Enter at the end of the lines to move to the next bullet.

Remember that these changes can be performed on the Slide Master if you want them to apply to all your slides.

Working with Fonts, Styles, and Colors

Fonts, styles, and colors also contribute to the look of a presentation. Just as with most Windows applications, the Formatting toolbar in PowerPoint makes it easy to change the font or apply styles to the text in your presentation. Select the text that you want to change and click on a button on the Formatting toolbar to change the font, the point size, or to apply bold, italic, underlining, shadow, or color. The two font-sizing buttons enable you to change the font of the selected text painlessly by just clicking on them. If you click on a formatting button before you begin to type, the formatting is applied to all the text that you type until you click on the button again.

Applying shadowing and embossing

Shadowing and embossing are techniques that you can use to add emphasis to text in a presentation. These techniques are extremely effective in making certain words or phrases stand out. They also add a more refined look to a presentation when you use them correctly.

Shadowing adds a drop shadow behind your text to emphasize it. This effect is useful in headings. To add shadowing to your presentation, select the text and click on the Text Shadow button on the Formatting toolbar.

Embossing is similar to shadowing, but it adds a highlight rather than a shadow to words. This effect gives the text the appearance of being slightly raised. To add embossing to your presentation, select the text and choose Format➪Font. In the Font dialog box, click on the Emboss check box in the Effects area (see Figure 26-17) and click on OK.

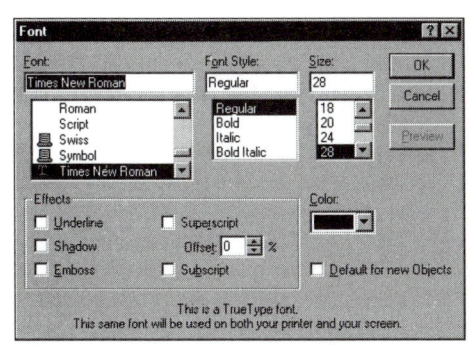

Figure 26-17: The Font dialog box.

Applying superscript and subscript

You can also apply superscript and subscript to text in your slides. Choose Format➪Font. In the Effects area of the font dialog box, you will see the two check boxes for these options. After you click on one of the options, enter a percentage by which to offset the text in the Offset box and click on OK. Superscript looks like ^this^; subscript looks like ~this~.

Creating Special Effects with WordArt

You can also enhance a presentation by using WordArt, a program in Office that lets you make text take on a variety of shapes. You can access WordArt through Insert➪Object. Scroll down the Object Type list in the Insert Object dialog box until you come to the Microsoft WordArt 2.0 choice. Microsoft WordArt produces the dialog box and toolbar shown in Figure 26-18.

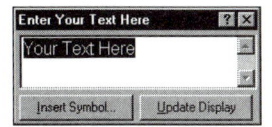

Figure 26-18: The WordArt dialog box and toolbar.

If you use WordArt a lot, you can put its button on the Standard toolbar by choosing Tools⇨Customize. In the Categories list, select Insert. You will now see the Insert WordArt button in the Buttons area. Drag the button to the place where you want it to go on the Standard toolbar. Now when you are in Slide view, you can click on the button to bring up the WordArt dialog box.

After you have entered the text that you want in the Enter Your Text Here box, you can use the different buttons and menus in the WordArt toolbar to create the effects that you want. The Layout list box, the leftmost list box on the toolbar, shows some of the changes that you can make to the text. See Figure 26-19.

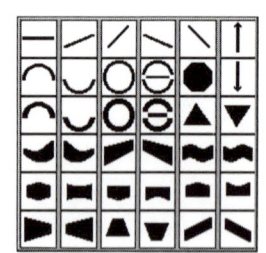

Figure 26-19: The WordArt Layout options list

Table 26-1 explains the menu options available on the WordArt Format menu.

Table 26-1
WordArt Format menu options

Option	Explanation
Spacing Between Characters	Opens the Spacing Between Characters dialog box shown in Figure 26-20, which lets you adjust the spacing between the characters.
Border	Opens the Border dialog box, where you can select a line thickness for the border.
Shading	Opens the Shading dialog box shown in Figure 26-21, which lets you choose foreground and background coloring.
Shadow	Opens the Shadow dialog box, where you can select the type of shadow you want and its color.
Stretch To Frame	Stretches the text vertically to the frame.
Rotation And Effects	Opens the Special Effects dialog box, where you can enter values in the Rotation and Slider boxes to change the shape of the WordArt special effect.

Chapter 26 ✦ **Enhancing a Presentation**   563

If you want to change the WordArt text after you have inserted it into the slide, double-click on the text to activate the text box and to make changes to it. Figure 26-22 shows an example of text that has been formatted with WordArt.

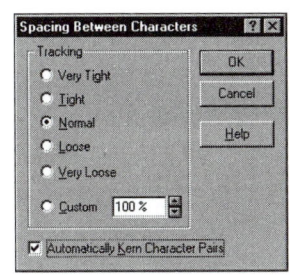

Figure 26-20: The Spacing Between Characters dialog box.

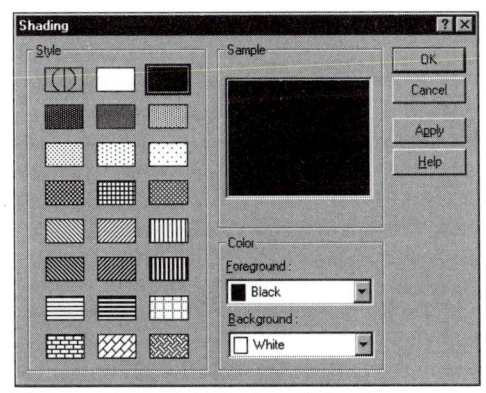

Figure 26-21: The Shading dialog box.

Figure 26-22: Examples of what can be done with WordArt.

Adding Excel Worksheets and Word Tables

Working Together

Another strong feature of PowerPoint is that it lets you embed Excel worksheets and Word tables in the slides. This feature saves a lot of time because you don't have to retype the information. You can use the information that already exists.

It is important to explain the difference between the two methods that can be used to insert information into PowerPoint. One method uses Edit⇨Copy and Edit⇨Paste. The other method uses Insert⇨Object. Although the two methods accomplish the same goal, they do work differently. If you want to insert a workbook, you will need to use Insert⇨Object. If you wish to insert more than one worksheet, you will need to use copy and paste. (To select the worksheets, shift-click on the worksheets you wish to insert. Then use File⇨Copy to copy the worksheets, move to where you want to paste the worksheets, and choose File⇨Paste to place them there.)

More Info

You may find that you may not want to insert an entire worksheet, because it may be too hard to see on a slide. It is often better to just paste in the table that you created in Excel. See Chapter 13 for information.

Double-clicking on the sheet after it is inserted activates the Excel menus. Now you can also perform maintenance on the workbook or worksheet. These tasks would normally have to be performed in Excel. Remember that the embedding principles that are explained here apply to all applications that support OLE2.

Inserting Excel worksheets into PowerPoint

Follow these steps to insert an Excel worksheet into a PowerPoint slide by using Edit➪Copy and Edit➪Paste:

1. From Excel, choose the worksheet that you want to insert into your presentation.
2. Select the information by using the standard selection methods. Remember that you need to select just the area of the worksheet you wish to paste on the slide. This will let you size your insertion to fit the slide. If you don't do this, the worksheet will appear to flow off the slide.
3. Click on the Copy button on the Standard toolbar or choose Edit➪Copy.
4. Switch to PowerPoint and the slide in which you want to place the information.
5. Click on the Paste button on the Standard toolbar or choose Edit➪Paste.
6. Size the worksheet as you please.

Figure 26-23 shows an Excel worksheet on a PowerPoint slide.

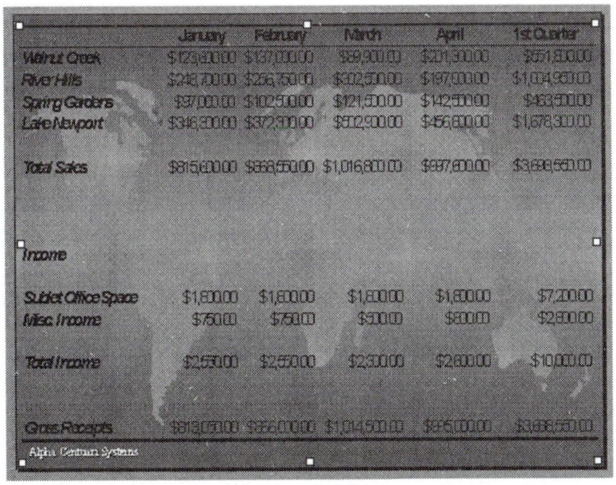

Figure 26-23: A PowerPoint slide with an Excel worksheet.

To add an Excel worksheet to a PowerPoint presentation with Insert➪Object, follow these steps:

1. From PowerPoint choose Insert➪Object to bring up the Insert Object dialog box shown in Figure 26-24.

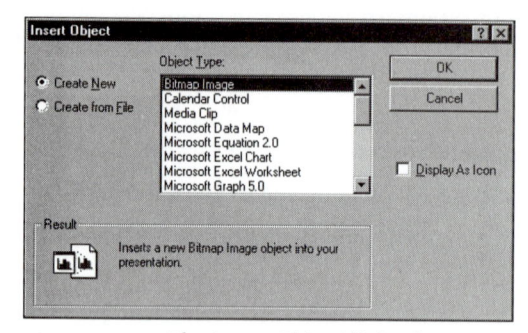

Figure 26-24: The Insert Object dialog box.

2. Now choose the Microsoft Excel Worksheet. An Excel worksheet is then inserted onto the slide. The default addition to PowerPoint is a workbook that contains one sheet. To add a sheet, select the workbook and choose Microsoft Excel Worksheet from the Insert menu.

3. After inserting the worksheet onto the slide, you may want to insert an object or create a new object from another application to insert into the Excel worksheet. To do this, choose Insert➪Object again, click on the Create New tab to create a new object, and select the application you wish to use. If you want to create an object from an existing file, click the Create from File tab. Click on the browse button to help you find the file that you want to insert. Click on OK.

Inserting Word tables into PowerPoint

Working Together Word tables can also be inserted into PowerPoint slides. Because Word tables are the easiest way to insert tabular information into a PowerPoint slide, this is an important feature. To insert a Word table, perform the following steps.

1. Choose Insert➪Microsoft Word Table to bring up the Insert Word Table dialog box (see Figure 26-25).

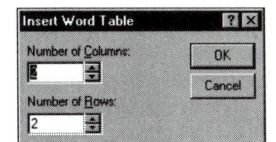

Figure 26-25: The Insert Word Table dialog box.

2. Enter the number of columns and rows that you want for the table. A Word table is then inserted onto the slide (see Figure 26-26). If you open the Insert menu you will notice that the Word menu options are now active.

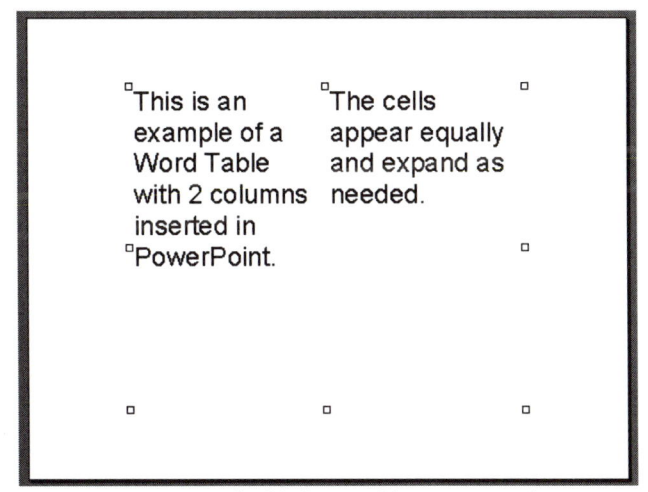

Figure 26-26: A Word table inserted into PowerPoint.

Adding Sound to Presentations

When it comes to enhancing a presentation, sound can also be an effective tool. If you have sound files (.WAV or .MID files) stored on your computer, you can place sound in your presentation. Remember that you will need a sound card in order to play the sound files. To add sound to your presentation, perform these steps:

1. Move to the slide to which you want to add sound.
2. Choose Insert⇨Sound to produce the Insert Sound dialog box, shown in Figure 26-27.

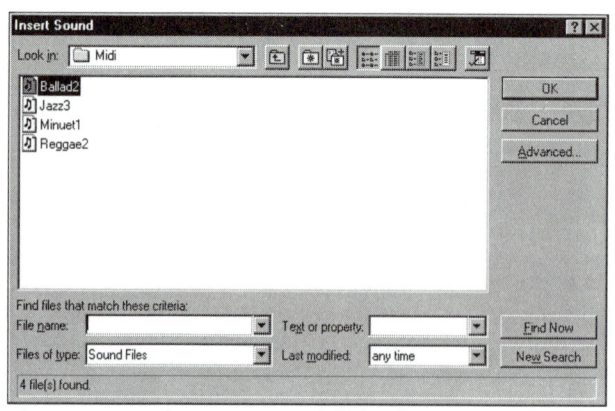

Figure 26-27: The Insert Sound dialog box.

3. After finding the desired sound file, click on OK. A small icon then appears in the center of the slide.

You can use the usual selection techniques to drag the icon to a desired location on the slide. When you run the presentation, clicking on the icon plays the sound.

Summary

This chapter covered the techniques that you can use to enhance the appearance of a presentation. This included the following topics:

- ◆ The different methods of formatting text
- ◆ How WordArt can be used to enhance text entries
- ◆ How the Slide Master can be used to apply universal options to your presentation
- ◆ How you can use the AutoContent Wizard to create a presentation

Where to go next . . .

- ◆ Now that you have learned steps to enhance a presentation, you will want to produce your work. Chapter 28 tells you how.
- ◆ Charts are another thing you may find useful in your efforts to enhance your presentation. See Chapter 27 for the whole scoop.

◆ ◆ ◆

CHAPTER 27

Working with Charts in PowerPoint

In This Chapter

Inserting and editing charts

Using the Datasheet window

Changing chart types

Using AutoFormat for a predefined appearance

Changing fonts and colors

Adding titles

Working with axes

Inserting and creating general and organizational charts

Among PowerPoint's strong features is its ability to create charts that can be included in your business presentations. Charts in PowerPoint are based on numeric data that you enter into a spreadsheet-like window called a *datasheet*. The charts are generated by Microsoft Graph, a Windows mini-application included with many Microsoft applications (including Word and Access).

One improvement in PowerPoint 95 over previous versions is that both the program and Microsoft Graph support OLE2. In a nutshell, this means that when you work with a chart, you no longer temporarily leave PowerPoint and go to what was a separate application (Microsoft Graph). You now remain within PowerPoint as you work with a chart, and the menus and toolbars change to reflect choices appropriate to working with charts.

Figure 27-1 shows an example of a typical chart in a PowerPoint presentation. (Note that charts are sometimes referred to as *graphs*; in fact, Microsoft uses the terms interchangeably.) Each chart is made up of a series of *markers*, which represent the data that you enter in the datasheet. The appearance of the markers varies according to what type of chart you decide to insert in your presentation. In a bar chart, the markers appear as a series of horizontal bars. In a column chart, they look like a series of vertical columns. Line charts use markers that look like a series of thin lines. In pie charts, the markers are the wedges of the pie, and doughnut charts use markers that appear as slices of the doughnut.

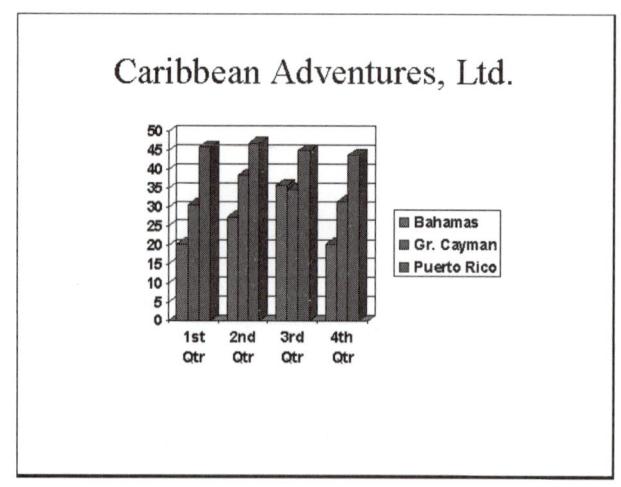

Figure 27-1: A typical chart.

With the exceptions of pie charts and doughnut charts, all charts use at least two axes: a horizontal axis (also known as the *category axis*) and a vertical axis (also known as the *value axis*). With three-dimensional charts, you also have a third axis, called the *series axis*.

In addition to the markers aligned along the axes, charts can also contain titles and *legends* (which serve to identify the categories indicated by the various markers). Microsoft Graph, running from within PowerPoint, lets you customize any of these items in your charts.

Charts in Excel or in PowerPoint?

You can create charts in PowerPoint using Microsoft Graph and the techniques detailed in this chapter, or you can create charts in Excel using the techniques detailed in Chapter 17. Because Excel charts can be selected, copied, and pasted into a PowerPoint presentation, you have *two* ways of creating charts in PowerPoint. So, where should you create your charts?

If you don't mind the added complexities of a spreadsheet (maybe you're already an accomplished Excel user), you're probably better off creating your charts in Excel and then pasting them into PowerPoint. Why? Because Excel's charting capabilities exceed those of Microsoft Graph, and Excel has Chart Wizards that help you quickly design the precise kind of chart that you need. Also, you can take advantage of Excel's ability to perform calculations on the data that's used as the basis of the chart. In contrast, the Microsoft Graph Datasheet window won't let you add two and two, much less perform any complex calculations.

On the other hand, if you're not an Excel user and have no desire to become one, stick with Microsoft Graph within PowerPoint for producing your charts.

Chart Types

Microsoft Graph, the program used to insert charts in PowerPoint, provides area, bar, column, line, pie, doughnut, radar, and scatter charts. Each chart type has optional subtypes that can also be chosen. The following descriptions identify the various chart types.

- **Area charts** show the significance of change during a given time period. The top line of the chart totals the individual series, so area charts make it visually apparent how each individual series contributes to the overall picture. Area charts emphasize the magnitude of change as opposed to the rate of change. (If you want to emphasize the rate of change, use line charts instead.)

- **Bar charts** use horizontal bars to show distinct figures at a specified time. Each horizontal bar in the chart shows a specific amount of change from the base value used in the chart. Bar charts visually emphasize different values, arranged vertically.

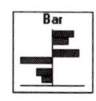

- **Column charts** are very much like bar charts, using columns to show distinct figures over a time period. The difference is that column charts are oriented *horizontally*, with the columns running up or down from a base value used in the chart. When you want to show numeric values across a passage of time in the chart, column charts usually work well.

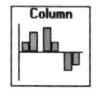

- **Line charts** are perfect for showing trends in data over a period of time. Like area charts, line charts show the significance of change, but line charts emphasize the rate, instead of the magnitude of change.

- **Pie charts** show relationships between the pieces of a picture. They also can be used to show a relationship between a piece of the picture and the entire picture. A pie chart can be used to display only one series of data at a time, because each piece of a pie chart represents part of a total series. If you have a large number of series to plot, however, you are probably better off with a column chart, because a pie crowded with slices is hard to interpret.

- **Doughnut charts** show relationships between pieces of a picture, as are pie charts. The difference is that the doughnut chart has a hollow center.

- **Radar charts** show the changes or frequencies of a data series in relation to a central point and to each other. (Every category has an axis value that radiates from a center point. Lines connect all data in the same series.) Radar charts can be difficult to interpret, unless you're accustomed to working with them.

- **XY Scatter charts** show relationships between different points of data, to compare trends across uneven time periods, or to show patterns as a set of *x* and *y* coordinates. These charts are commonly used to plot scientific data.

Inserting Charts

PowerPoint includes a mini-application, Microsoft Graph, that helps you create charts. Microsoft Graph displays a Datasheet window, where you can enter the numeric data that will serve as the chart's basis. After you enter your data, Microsoft Graph translates it into professional-looking charts.

The nice thing about Microsoft Graph is that, thanks to OLE2, it now lets you create your chart right in PowerPoint. Here's how to insert a chart on a PowerPoint slide:

1. Choose Insert⇨Microsoft Graph or click on the Insert Graph button on the Standard toolbar. A bar chart appears in your presentation (this is the default type, but you can easily change it), and a Datasheet window appears atop the chart, as shown in Figure 27-2. Also, note that the menus and toolbar change to reflect the fact that Microsoft Graph is active within PowerPoint.

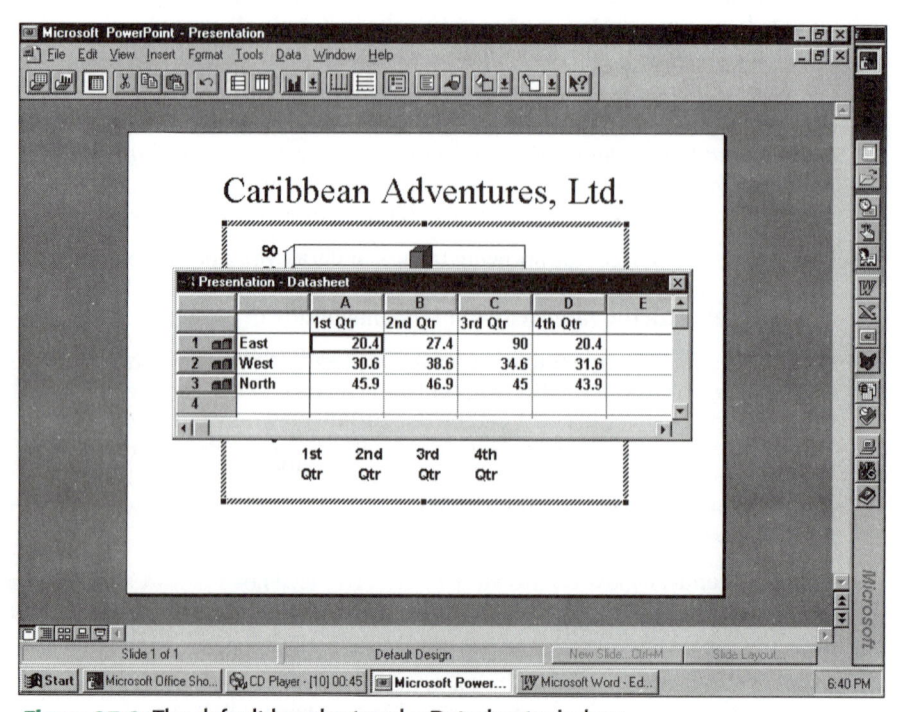

Figure 27-2: The default bar chart and a Datasheet window.

2. Enter your data directly into the Datasheet window. (You'll find more details on this in "Entering and editing data in the Datasheet window" later in this chapter.)

3. Choose Format⇨Chart Type to select the type of chart that you want. After selecting the chart type you want, click on OK.

4. Open the Insert menu and use its various options to add titles, legends, gridlines, or other items to the chart. The following are the options available on the Insert menu.

   Titles — This option displays the Titles dialog box, which can be used to add titles to the chart or its axes.

   Data Labels — This option displays the Data Labels box, which can be used to add data labels to a data series, or to all data points in the chart.

   Legend — This option adds a legend to the chart.

   Axes — This option displays a dialog box that you can use to show or hide axes in the chart.

   Gridlines — This option displays a dialog box that you can use to show or hide major and minor gridlines along any of the chart axes.

   Trendline — This option adds trendlines to area, bar, column, line and scatter charts.

   Error Bars — This option adds error bars to area, bar, column, line and scatter charts.

5. When done refining the chart, click anywhere outside it. The chart will appear inside your presentation, and the menus and toolbars will revert back to those of PowerPoint.

If you later want to make more changes to the chart's design, you can double-click on the chart to switch back to the Microsoft Graph menus and toolbar.

> **Hot Stuff** You can move and size your completed chart as you would any other object in a presentation — either by dragging it to the desired location or by dragging its size handles.

Entering and editing data in the Datasheet window

To enter data in the Datasheet window, just move to the desired cell and type the data. You'll also want to enter the names for each data series into the leftmost column, and the labels for each category into the top row. (The default data that appears in the Datasheet window gives you a model that you can follow when you enter your own data.) When you enter text in the top row and the leftmost column, Microsoft Graph assigns that text as category names and legend names in the resulting chart.

For example, with the default data provided in the Datasheet window in Figure 27-3, the text labels in the leftmost column of the datasheet — Bahamas, Grand Caymans, and Puerto Rico — are automatically used for the legend that accompanies the chart. The headings that are entered in the top row of the datasheet — 1st, 2nd, 3rd, and 4th Qtr — appear as labels for the markers in the chart.

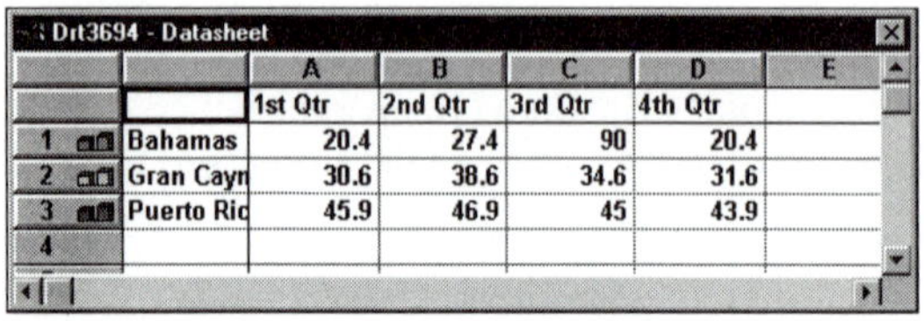

		A 1st Qtr	B 2nd Qtr	C 3rd Qtr	D 4th Qtr	E
1	Bahamas	20.4	27.4	90	20.4	
2	Gran Cayn	30.6	38.6	34.6	31.6	
3	Puerto Ric	45.9	46.9	45	43.9	
4						

Figure 27-3: The Datasheet window.

Navigate within the Datasheet window with either the mouse or the arrow keys. You can widen the columns if they're too narrow to display the numbers that you enter. Do this either by dragging the column's right edge with the mouse or by clicking in any cell in the column that you want to widen, choosing Format⇔Column Width, and then entering a width for the column.

When typing numeric data into cells, you can include dollar signs in front of the numbers to cause them to appear as currency values. When you do this, Microsoft Graph automatically includes the dollar sign with the values in the value axis in the chart. To apply a specific format by selecting a cell or group of cells in the datasheet, open the Format menu and choose Number. In the Number Format dialog box that appears, choose a desired number format and then click on OK.

After the chart exists on a slide, you can bring up the Datasheet window at any time by double-clicking on the chart to make it active, and choosing View⇔Datasheet.

Editing Charts

Changing circumstances may require the figures used to create a chart to change. When this happens, you'll need to make adjustments to the chart's datasheet. At times you many also want to edit a chart for the sake of altering a presentation.

If you wish to update figures used when you created a chart, choose View⇔Datasheet and then make the necessary changes in the datasheet (using the customary methods of editing).

Excel users may prefer Excel charts

If you're familiar with Excel, you may prefer using Excel's worksheet and charting techniques for producing charts to use in your PowerPoint presentations.

To add an existing Excel chart to a PowerPoint presentation, go into Excel, select the chart, and choose Edit⇨Copy. Switch to PowerPoint, move to the slide where you want to insert the chart, and choose Edit⇨Paste. The Excel chart appears in the slide, and you can move and size it to your liking using the usual Windows moving and sizing techniques.

To add a new Excel chart to a PowerPoint presentation, go into PowerPoint and move to the slide where you want to place the chart. Next, choose Insert⇨Object, and then choose Microsoft Excel Chart from the list of objects to insert. PowerPoint then inserts a default Excel chart on the PowerPoint slide, and Excel menus become active within PowerPoint. You can then use Excel techniques (detailed in the Excel section of this book) to manipulate the data that produces the chart and to change the chart's appearance.

Changing the data series

In some cases, you may want to swap the data series for a chart. For example, you'd want to do this is if you had set up a chart to show the total of sales over four years for divisions of a company, and you wanted the columns to symbolize each division — but instead, the columns represent years. Swapping the data series would fix that.

You do this by choosing either Data⇨Series in Rows or Data⇨Series in Columns. Alternatively, you can click on the By Row or By Column buttons in the Standard toolbar while the datasheet is active. To see an example of the effects of the selection of data series, take a look at Figure 27-4, which shows a data series arranged by rows.

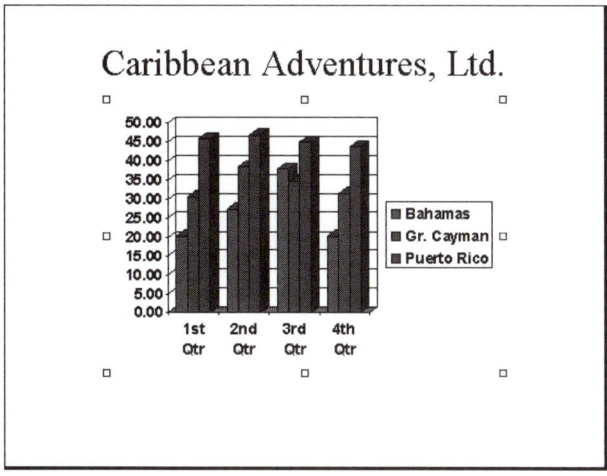

Figure 27-4: A data series arranged by rows.

In contrast, note the same data shown in Figure 27-5. Here the data in the datasheet is arranged by columns in the resulting graph.

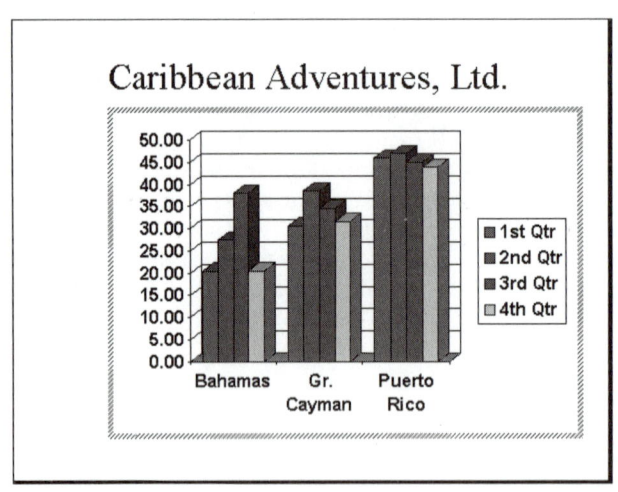

Figure 27-5: A data series arranged by columns.

You can also change the actual display of the information. Do this using the shortcut menu that appears when you right-click on the bars, columns, lines, or pie slices of the chart. This shortcut menu contains commands related to changes in the display of the chart information. The shortcut menu is shown in Figure 27-6 and includes the following commands.

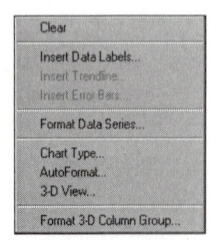

Figure 27-6: The shortcut menu for a data series.

- ◆ **Clear** — This command removes a data series, the actual markers related to that series of numbers.
- ◆ **Insert Data Labels** — This command adds number labels, or labels the markers in relation to what they represent.

✦ **Format Data Series** — This command lets you add labels or change the color of the data series. When you choose this option, the Format Data Point dialog box appears (Figure 27-7) with the Patterns tab visible. Using the Patterns tab, you can add a border to the data series by setting the options in the Borders portion of the dialog box. You can vary the border's style, color, and thickness, by selecting what you want in the Style, Color, and Thickness list boxes.

In the Area portion of the dialog box, you can change the color of the data series to your liking. You can select a color, or you can turn on the Automatic option, which applies the Windows default. Choosing None makes the marker invisible. Turning on the Invert If Negative option in the dialog box reverses the foreground and background colors for a marker if the value is negative.

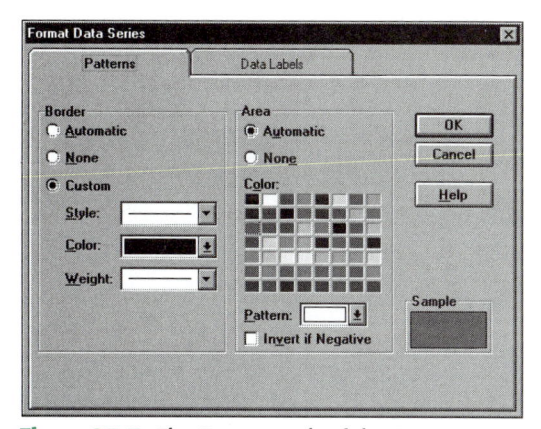

Figure 27-7: The Patterns tab of the Format Data Series dialog box.

The Data Labels tab (Figure 27-8) of this dialog box lets you determine whether labels appear beside the markers to the data series. You can also have a legend appear next to the label; do this by turning on the corresponding check box.

✦ **Chart Type** — This command lets you change the chart type. When you choose this option from the shortcut menu, the Chart Type dialog box (Figure 27-9) appears. The options for this dialog box are discussed in the next section.

✦ **AutoFormat** — This command lets you apply a built-in format or a custom format; this is discussed in the "Using AutoFormat" section, later in this chapter.

Changing the chart type

After creating a chart, you can experiment to be sure you've selected the type that best represents your data. Microsoft Graph provides a range of chart types that can be viewed with a few mouse clicks; Table 27-1 lists them.

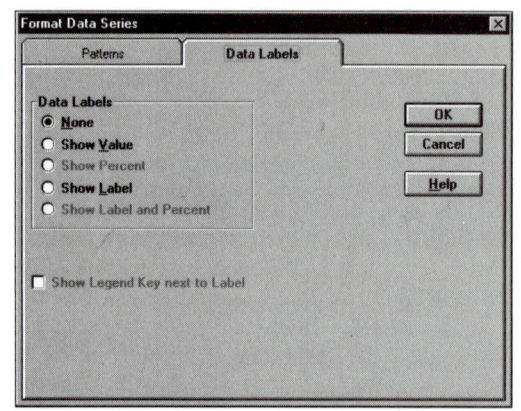

Figure 27-8: The Data Labels tab of the Format Data Series dialog box.

Table 27-1
PowerPoint's chart types

Two-dimensional charts	Three-dimensional charts
Area	3-D Area
Bar	3-D Bar
Column	3-D Column
Line	3-D Line
Pie	3-D Pie
Doughnut	3-D Surface
Radar	
XY Scatter	

You can select chart types using different methods. One way is to select the chart and then choose Format⇨Chart Type. The Chart Type window then appears, as shown in Figure 27-9.

When you select a chart type, you can also click on the Options button in the dialog box. This open a window that displays subtypes available for the chart that you selected. Click on the chart type that you want (and the subtype, if you use the Options button) and then click on OK.

You can also change the chart type by using the Chart Type button in the Standard toolbar. Click on the down arrow to the right of the Chart Type button on the Standard toolbar; a list box appears showing the available chart types, as shown in Figure 27-10. Just select one of the chart types from the list box.

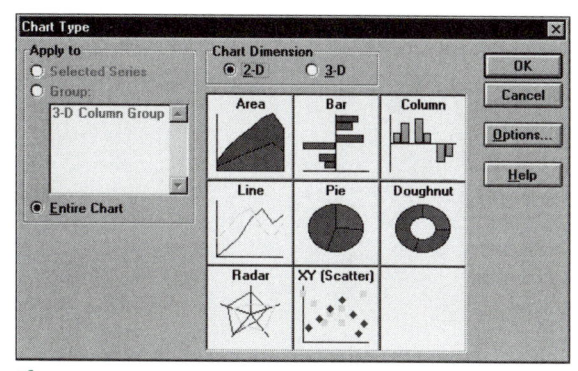

Figure 27-9: The Chart Type window.

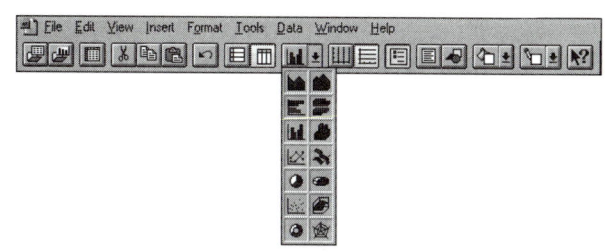

Figure 27-10: Chart types available from the Chart Type button on the Standard toolbar.

Using AutoFormat to select a chart design

You've seen that you have a great deal of flexibility in formatting a chart's individual elements. Often, however, it's the designing of these elements that can be time-consuming. But there's a way around that.

Instead of selecting and formatting individual elements to a chart's design one at a time, you can apply an AutoFormat to the chart. If you've worked with templates or styles in Word for Windows, think of AutoFormat as the same concept applied to charts. You can apply an AutoFormat to any active chart; AutoFormat changes the chart's appearance without changing the underlying data.

Apply an AutoFormat to a chart this way:

1. Double-click on the chart to make it active.
2. Choose Format⇨AutoFormat. The AutoFormat dialog box appears, as shown in Figure 27-11.
3. In the Galleries list box, choose a chart type. You'll then see a list of the formats available for that chart type.

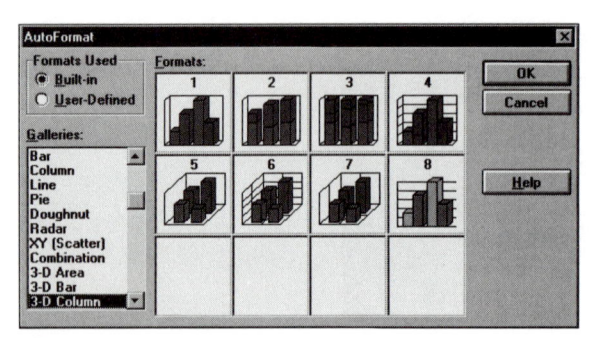

Figure 27-11: The AutoFormat dialog box.

4. Choose the format you want from the Formats box.
5. Click on OK. The chart is automatically reformatted to match the appearance of the AutoFormat options that you chose.

Enhancing a Chart's Appearance

You can do several things to enhance the appearance of a chart. A few are simple, such as changes to fonts and colors. Others, however, are a little more involved, such as adding text boxes. All can make a difference in the appearance of the presentation.

Changing fonts

You can easily change the fonts used for text anywhere in your chart. This includes fonts used for titles, legends, or axes.

To change the fonts, right-click on the text for what you want to change. For example, if you want to change the fonts used for a legend, right-click on the legend. From the shortcut menu that appears, choose the Format option. (If you right-click on a legend, the menu choice is Format Legend; if you right-click on a title, the menu choice is Format Title; and if you right-click on an axis, the menu choice is Format Axis.) In the dialog box that opens, click on the Font tab, which looks like Figure 27-12.

Under the Font tab, you'll see your options for setting the fonts used by the selected item. Choose a font, font style, and font size using the options displayed. You can also select underlining, color, and background, and you can turn on special effects such as strikethrough, superscript, and subscript. When done making selections, click on OK to put them into effect.

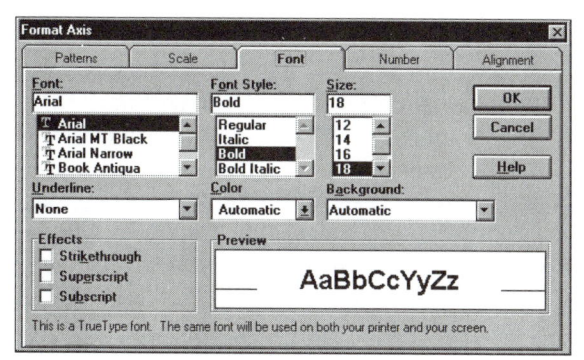

Figure 27-12: The Font tab in the Format Axis dialog box.

Changing chart colors

Creating and changing color schemes is another effective way to improve your chart's appearance. Color schemes are sets of colors that are designed to be used as main colors for presentations and to ensure that the presentations have a professional look.

Each presentation that you open in PowerPoint has a default color scheme, but as you work with the program more and more, you'll want to create your own schemes. Chapter 25 discusses in detail what's involved in doing this for an entire presentation. This section focuses on changing chart colors.

Looks aren't everything, but...

As you work with fonts, colors, and other appearance-related aspects of a chart, remember the principles of good design by using fonts and colors wisely. It's easy to get carried away with fonts and colors and produce a chart that is so visually "busy" that it distracts the reader. You should rarely need more than two and never more than three fonts in the same chart. You'll probably need more colors, because each set of markers typically uses its own color — but again, be judicious. Stick with complementary colors. PowerPoint does this automatically — but if you customize the colors, avoid clashing combinations like bright pink against lime green. (Some designers argue strongly against using these two colors anywhere, any time!) Keep colors elsewhere in the chart to a minimum. Before committing the chart to your presentation, step back and give it a critical, overall review for visual clarity and organization. Better charts in your presentations make for better overall presentations.

Changing the colors of your chart is relatively simple, thanks to shortcut menus:

1. After choosing a chart and setting it up on your slide, double-click on the chart to make it active for edits and then right-click on the bar or section of the chart that you want to change. This opens the shortcut menu shown earlier in Figure 27-6.

2. From the shortcut menu, choose Format Data Series. The Format Data Series dialog box is then opened with the Patterns Tab visible, as shown earlier in Figure 27-7. This dialog box lets you change the Border Settings, selecting from a range of line styles.

3. To change the color of the particular section of the chart that you want to change, move to the Area portion of the Patterns tab and then click on the color that you want. You can also add patterns if you wish by clicking on the Patterns list box and then choosing a pattern from the list. When done, click on OK to accept the changes.

Adding titles

You might find it useful to add titles to your charts. For one thing, titles help an audience understand what a chart means. And they help you quickly find values that you want to point out when giving your presentation.

To add titles to a chart area, right-click on the area to open the shortcut menu. Next, choose Insert Titles; this opens the Titles dialog box, shown in Figure 27-13.

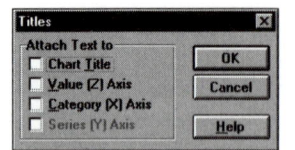

Figure 27-13: The Titles dialog box.

The Titles dialog box lets you add a title either to your entire chart or to just one of the available axes. Turn on the option that you want and then click on OK; the cursor appears in a text box where you insert the title. If you choose more than one area to receive a title, use the mouse and click on the text boxes for each of the titles. To enter the titles, click in the text boxes and type the titles that you want.

You can also format the text on a chart after the text has been entered. To do this, double-click on the text and choose the formats that you want from the Format dialog box.

Changing axes

You can modify the axes used by your charts in order to emphasize the points that you're trying to get across. You can change the line style, the font of the axes' text, the scale used by the numbers, and the alignment.

To change any of these formats, select one of the axes by clicking on it. Next, either choose Format➪Selected Axis, right-click on the axis and choose Format Axis, or double-click on the selected axis. This opens the Format Axis dialog box, as shown in Figure 27-14. You can now select the options that you want from the various tabs. Table 27-2 tells what you can accomplish with each of these tabs.

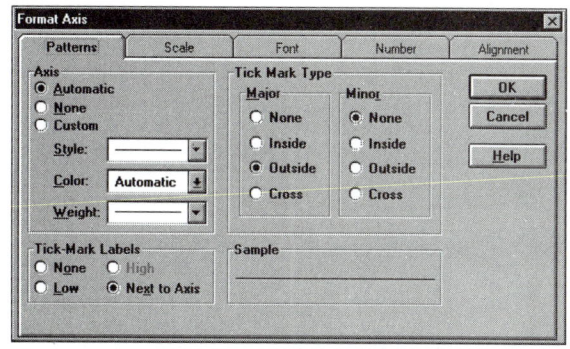

Figure 27-14: The Format Axis dialog box.

Table 27-2
Tabs of the Format Axis dialog box

Tab	Purpose
Patterns	Change axis formatting or to choose tick mark types, both major and minor.
Scale	Control the scale settings for axis values. Logarithmic scales can also be set, along with reversing the order of the values and setting the `Floor XY Plane` (the floor of the chart) at a value other than zero.
Font	Change font settings for the axis.
Number	Control the number formats for the numbers used for the axis.
Alignment	Control the alignment of text used in the axis.

Changing borders

You can also change a chart by changing its borders. To do this, click outside the chart's area and choose Format➪Selected Chart Area. The Format Chart Area dialog box appears, as shown in Figure 27-15. This dialog box has two tabs, Patterns and Font. Make the changes that you want and then click on OK.

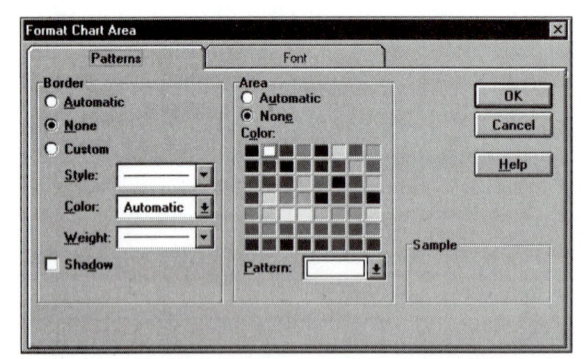

Figure 27-15: The Format Chart Area dialog box with the Patterns tab displayed.

Changing the Appearance of 3-D Charts

Three-dimensional (3-D) charts are a popular variation of basic charts. Creating 3-D charts is simple in PowerPoint: when you choose Format➪Chart Type, the Chart Type dialog box that appears (shown earlier in Figure 27-9) gives you the option of selecting a 2-D or a 3-D chart.

If you use 3-D charts often, it's good to know about the flexibility that Microsoft Graph offers for changing various aspects of appearance of 3-D charts. You can change the elevation, the rotation, and the perspective used for the chart with the following steps:

1. Double-click on the 3-D chart to activate it, and choose Format➪3-D View. (Alternatively, you can right-click on the chart and select 3-D View from the shortcut menu that appears.) The Format 3-D View dialog box (Figure 27-16) appears. As you change the settings in this dialog box, the picture of a chart near the center of the dialog box reflects your changes.

2. To change the chart's elevation, either click on the Up Arrow or Down Arrow buttons above Elevation or enter a value in the Elevation text box.

3. To change the chart's rotation, either click on the Left or Right Rotation buttons or enter a value in the Rotation text box.

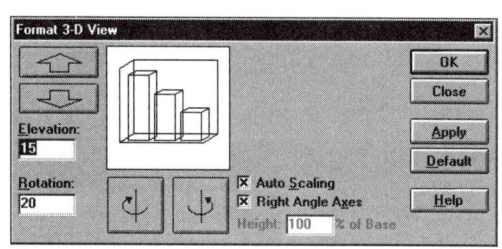

Figure 27-16: The Format 3-D View dialog box.

4. To change the chart's perspective, if Right Angle Axes is not turned on, either click on the Up Arrow or Down Arrow buttons above Perspective or enter a value in the Perspective text box. The Format 3-D View dialog box also contains options for AutoScaling, Right Angle Axes, and Height % of Base.

- Right Angle Axes — This option, when turned on, sets the chart's axes at right angles independent of what you set the rotation or elevation to. (If you want to see the axes in perspective, you must turn off this option.)

- Auto Scaling — If Right Angle Axes is turned on, then this option is enabled. The AutoScaling option scales 3-D charts so that they are closer in size to 2-D charts.

- Height % of Base — This option controls the height of the value axis and walls of the chart, relative to the length of the category axis (the base of the chart). For example, if you enter **300%** in this box, the chart's height becomes three times the length of the base.

You can see how your changes will affect your chart in PowerPoint while leaving the dialog box open; do this by clicking on the Apply button. When done with your changes, click on the OK button. You can use the Default button to undo your changes and return the settings to their defaults.

3-D Charts can lie (or at least, greatly mislead . . .)

With 3-D charts, it's easy to get carried away with changing the various viewing angles by modifying the chart's elevation and perspective. Get *too* carried away, and you can wind up with a chart that's so hard to interpret, it becomes meaningless. Get even slightly carried away, and you can produce charts that distort the meaning of the underlying numbers.

For example, changing the elevation so that a chart is viewed from a high angle tends to overemphasize growth; presenting the chart as viewed from a low angle tends to minimize growth. (Could that be why many advertisements in business and financial magazines use 3-D charts viewed at high angles?) As an example, the figure below shows a 3-D chart with an elevation of 90, which severely distorts the visual growth represented by the chart.

(continued)

(continued)

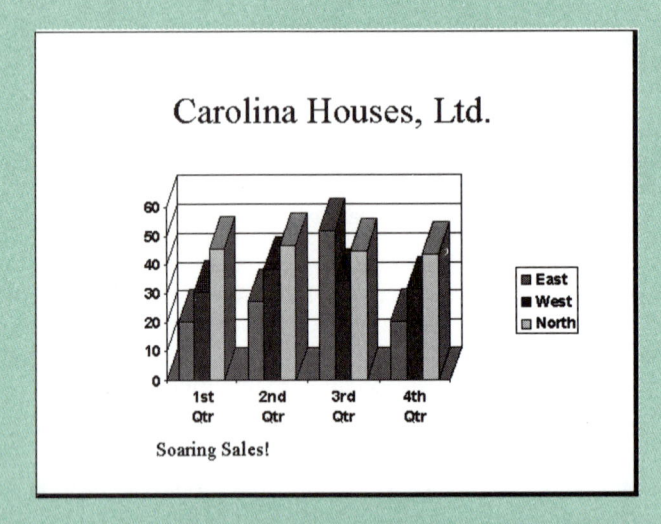

By comparison, this next figure shows the same 3-D chart with a moderate elevation of 10, which avoids the visual distortion produced by the earlier chart.

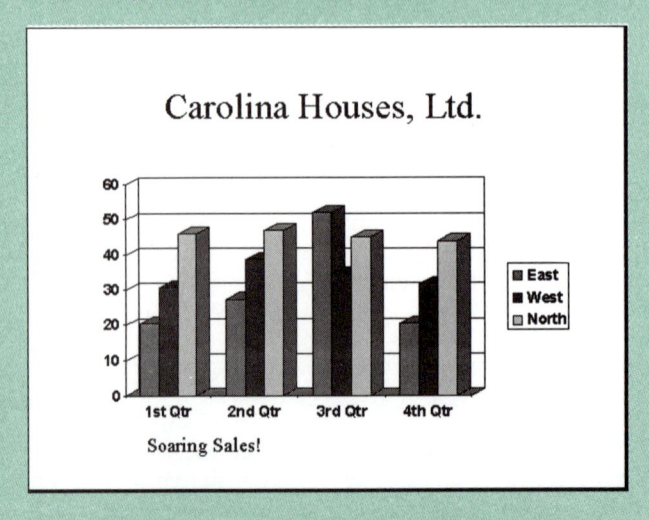

Be aware of the effects that such changes can have on your charts and use them only when you intend to obtain such distorted results.

Creating Organizational Charts

Organizational charts are useful in a presentation for showing the hierarchy of an organization. You can create this type of chart from scratch, but PowerPoint provides an application called Microsoft Organizational Chart that greatly simplifies the process.

The following steps tell you how to create a simple organizational chart. (See Chapter 28, "PowerPoint at Work," for an example of creating a more complex organizational chart.)

1. Choose Insert⇨Object and then select MS Organizational Chart 2.0 from the Insert Object dialog box. (Or you can click on the MS Organizational Chart button in the Standard toolbar.)

    Keep in mind that you should select a slide layout with the organizational chart placeholder on it. Also remember that the chart you create will be significantly smaller when placed in the placeholder area; if you have a large chart, you may want to use a blank slide.

2. The window then opens with a simple chart layout. You can proceed with this default layout if you wish, adding boxes to the chart as needed. On the toolbar, you'll see buttons for adding boxes for the different levels of an organization. Each of the buttons lets you add boxes for the respective level of the chart. Choose the button that corresponds to the level of organization you want and then click next to the box that you want to add the selection under or next to; the box is then added to the chart.

3. After creating your chart, you may want to edit it. To do that, first click on the box containing the name or entry that you want to change; you can then make the changes. Afterward, be sure to update the presentation within PowerPoint by choosing File⇨Update Presentation. Then if you want to save the changes to the presentation, choose File⇨Save.

4. If you prefer, you can create an organizational chart from scratch. Choosing Style from the menu bar gives you a selection of organizational chart types. As Figure 27-17 shows, there are several ways that these charts can be laid out.

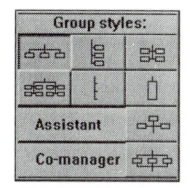

Figure 27-17: The Organizational Chart Style box.

After choosing a chart style, you can add boxes to it using the toolbar. Choose the level of the chart to which you want to add boxes and then click on the box that you want connected.

Once the chart is placed in PowerPoint, you can size it to your liking by selecting the object and clicking on the handles.

Summary

This chapter showed you the different options for using charts in your PowerPoint presentations. The following topics were covered:

- ✦ You can add a chart to any slide of a presentation either by choosing Insert⇨Chart or by clicking on the Insert Chart button on the Standard toolbar.
- ✦ When you add a chart, a Datasheet window appears where you can enter the numeric information that serves as the chart's basis.
- ✦ After adding a chart to a presentation, you can double-click on the chart and then choose Format⇨Chart Type to change the chart's type.
- ✦ You can use the AutoFormat feature to give a coordinated look to all aspects of your chart.
- ✦ You can right-click on any object in a chart and then choose Format from the shortcut menu that appears in order to display a dialog box that lets you change the appearance of the selected object.
- ✦ In addition to conventional charts, you can create organizational charts in PowerPoint.

Where to go next...

- ✦ Now that you have completed charts in PowerPoint, you will want to produce your work. Chapter 28 has the story.
- ✦ If you want to produce more elaborate charts, use Excel's chart making feature. Head straight for Chapter 17.

✦ ✦ ✦

Producing Your Work

CHAPTER 28

In This Chapter

Printing slides

Printing notes pages, handouts, and outlines

Producing on-screen slide shows

Producing slide shows

Transitioning between slides

Adding speaker's notes and audience handouts

Using the PowerPoint Viewer

Using Pack & Go to package presentations for use elsewhere

After you have created all the slides, you will want to prepare your work for presentation. This chapter covers the methods that you can use to produce your work, including printing presentations, creating slide shows, and creating speaker's notes and audience handouts.

Printing Presentations

PowerPoint lets you print slides, outlines, speaker's notes, and audience handouts. These items all can be printed on overhead transparencies or on paper. Slides can also be saved to a file or shipped to an outside graphics shop to create them. The printing process is pretty much the same, regardless of whether you are printing outlines, notes, or handouts: you open the presentation, identify what you want printed, specify the range of slides to be printed, and choose the number of copies.

Setting up your slides for printing

Before you print your presentation, you need to open it and set it up for printing. Follow these steps:

1. Choose File⇨Slide Setup. The Slide Setup dialog box appears, as shown in Figure 28-1.

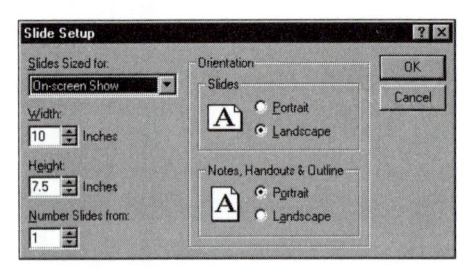

Figure 28-1: The Slide Setup dialog box.

2. In this dialog box, select the desired size for the slides. Keep in mind that, by default, PowerPoint is set up to create and print slides in Landscape orientation. Also remember that, by default, the slides are set up to print 10 inches wide by 7.5 inches tall. The Slides Sized for list box is set at Custom, which lets you change these settings to the following:

   - **On-screen Show** — This option sets the width at 10 inches and the height at 7.5 inches with Landscape orientation.

   - **Letter Paper (8.5 x 11 inches)** — This option sets the width at 10 inches and the height at 7.5 inches with Landscape orientation. These measurements cause the slides to fill the page. Choose this option when you want to print on paper and fill the entire page.

   - **A4 Paper (210 x 297 mm)** — This option sets the width at 10.83 inches and the height at 7.5 inches with Landscape orientation. The slides then fill A4 (European size) paper.

   - **35mm Slides** — This option sets the width at 11.25 inches and the height at 7.5 inches. These measurements allow the contents to fill the slide area in Landscape orientation, ideal for reduction to a 35mm slide.

   - **Overhead** — Use this option when you want to create transparencies. It makes slides fill the transparencies, making them easier to see when they are placed on an overhead projector.

   - **Custom** — This option lets you set dimensions of your own choosing, either by entering values in the Width and Height boxes or by clicking on the up and down arrows to enter the desired value.

3. In the Orientation portion of the dialog box, choose the desired orientation (Portrait or Landscape). Keep in mind that you can separately set the orientation for your speaker's notes, handouts, and outlines.

4. If you want to use a starting number other than 1 for your slides, enter a desired number in the Number Slides from list box.

5. Click on OK.

Printing parts of your presentation

After your printing dimensions have been set by means of the Slide Setup dialog box options, you can choose File➪Print to reveal the Print dialog box (see Figure 28-2).

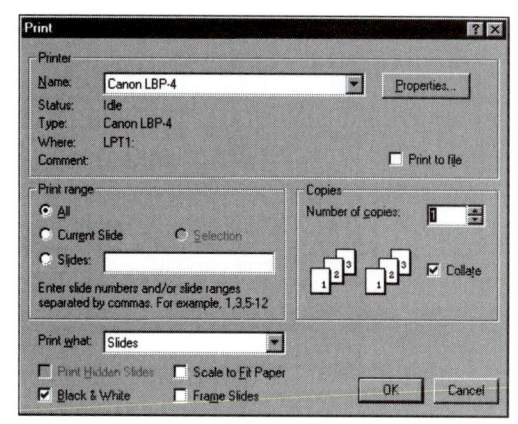

Figure 28-2: The Print dialog box.

In this dialog box, you can choose what parts of the presentation you want to print. In the Print range area, choose All to print all slides, or choose Current Slide to print just the slide that is currently visible. In the Number of copies box, you can enter the number of copies that you want, and you can turn on the Collate option if you want multiple copies to come out in collated order.

Use the Print what list box to tell PowerPoint exactly which parts of your presentation you want to print. The choices that you have from the Print what list box include the following:

✦ **Slides** — This option prints your slides on paper or on overhead transparencies.

✦ **Notes Pages** — This option prints the speaker's notes pages that correspond to the slides that you decide to print.

✦ **Handouts** — You can print audience handouts that contain two, three, or six slides per page. Two slides per page is a good choice for a large image with great detail. Use three slides per page if you want to leave space for the audience to write notes. If you want to provide a presentation outline with the most information on each page of the audience handout, use six slides per page.

✦ **Outline View** — This option prints the outline that appears on-screen in Outline view.

In the dialog box you can also specify the number of copies that you want to print, along with the range of slides or notes. If any slides in the presentation have been hidden (by choosing Tools⇨Hide Slide), the Print Hidden Slides check box becomes available in the Print dialog box. (choose File⇨Print), and you can click on it to tell PowerPoint to include hidden slides in the printout. The Black & White option tells PowerPoint to print the presentation in black and white. (This option is useful only if you have a color printer and, for some reason, you don't want the presentation in color.)

The Frame Slides option frames the printouts so that they best fit transparencies when they are reduced, and the Scale to Fit Paper option scales the printout to the paper that you have loaded in the printer. Choose your desired printing options in the dialog box and then click on OK.

Note If you turn on the Print to file check box after you choose the other desired options and click on OK, a Print to File dialog box appears, where you can enter a filename. When you enter a name and click on OK, PowerPoint writes the file as an encapsulated print file that can be used at a later time (you can select the file in Explorer or in My Computer and print it).

Producing On-Screen Slide Shows

Slide shows are another strength of PowerPoint because you can create professional-looking slide shows without a great deal of hassle. You can create a slide show by accepting PowerPoint's defaults and then choosing the Slide Show command from the View menu. The Slide Show dialog box appears, as shown in Figure 28-3.

Figure 28-3: The Slide Show dialog box.

In the Slides area of the dialog box, click on All to show all the slides or click on From and enter starting and ending values in the From and To boxes to show a range of slides.

> ### Getting the results you want
>
> Don't be in a rush to print by clicking on the Print button on the Standard toolbar or by immediately clicking on the OK button in the Print dialog box to accept the defaults, which you do in many Windows applications. Because PowerPoint has so many options for what you can print and how you can print it, you may not get what you want by fast clicking. Think of the Print dialog box and the Slide Setup dialog box as working in combination to give you exactly what you want. Be sure that you set the options correctly before you start printing.

In the Advance area of the dialog box, choose Manual Advance if you want to move from slide to slide manually during the show, or choose Use Slide Timings if you want the slides to advance automatically at timed intervals. (You'll learn how to change the intervals later.)

The Loop Continuously Until 'Esc' check box can be turned on if you want slides that are set for timed intervals to run continuously until the Escape key is pressed (a great option for unattended displays, like those you see running in computer stores).

When you are finished choosing the various options in the dialog box, click on Show to run the presentation.

If you want to set your own timings for the slide show, choose the Rehearse New Timings option, which lets you advance the slides by using the Page Down button or clicking on the mouse. PowerPoint then keeps track of the time that you take to advance from one slide to another. If you forget the timings that you set from one slide to another, switch to Slide Sorter view. Underneath each slide you will see the time that you have allotted for the slide.

Creating build slides

Have you ever seen a presentation that included a slide that was nearly blank at first, but as the speaker talked, points seemed to magically appear on it? That savvy speaker used *build slides* to create that effect. Build slides let your audience see your presentation develop and help them remember the last point that you made. A build slide is also called a *progressive disclosure slide* because you progressively reveal the points of your presentation. You can create a build slide by performing the following steps:

1. Switch to Slide view and choose the text or the text object that you want to build.
2. Choose Tools⇨Animation Settings to reveal the Animation Settings dialog box shown in Figure 28-4.

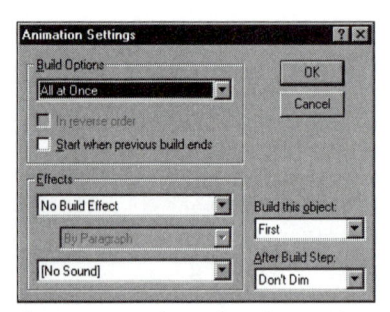

Figure 28-4: The Animation Settings dialog box.

3. In the Build Options list box, select the type of build that you want for the selected text or text object. After you select a build option, the various special effects options become available in the Effects area of the dialog box.

4. Select the desired options and then click on OK.

> **Hot Stuff** You can quickly create a default build slide by selecting the text and choosing Tools⇨Build Slide Text. When you run the slide show, the text flies in from the left.

Giving slide shows with polish

Giving a good presentation isn't entirely a matter of mastering PowerPoint technique. Most of what creates a presentation that captivates (rather than enslaves) your audience falls under the more general heading of "tips for better presentations."

Always, always, always, *always* (did we say that enough?) test your presentation on the hardware that you plan to use *before* the audience starts taking their seats. No matter how well things worked back in the home office and at the last 27 on-site presentations you've given, there's no guarantee that the hardware you're using at the 28th site is correctly set up or will behave as well as the rest.

Try not to spend too much time on a single slide. If a slide stays on-screen for five minutes or more, rethink your content. Believe it or not, five minutes is a long time when a speaker drones — this has put many an audience to sleep. The audience stays with you if you break up big chunks of information into two or three separate slides.

Add a blank slide (or a slide with nothing more than an attractive background) as the last slide in your presentation. Then when you finish, the audience has an attractive slide to look at, as opposed to being dumped back in Slide view of PowerPoint.

As you verbally emphasize points, you can use the mouse pointer as an on-screen pointer. (A commercial laser pointer is nicer but also costs a lot more than the mouse that's already installed on your computer.)

Hiding and unhiding slides

The capability to hide or unhide slides is another useful PowerPoint feature. You may want to give similar presentations to different groups, but modify the content to fit each group. For example, you might want to present revenue data to each department in a company. It might make sense to show detailed financial data to, say, Sales, but more general numbers to production workers. PowerPoint lets you use one presentation for both groups — but you hide slides so that they do not appear for one group, and then unhide the slides so that they do appear for the other group. To hide a slide, perform the following steps:

1. Display the slide that you want to hide. In Slide Sorter view, you can select more than one slide by holding down the Shift key while you click on each slide that you want to hide. When you do this, the slide's number is marked with a line through it.

2. Choose Tools⇨Hide Slide. (If you are in Slide Sorter view, you can also click on the Hide Slide button in the Slide Sorter toolbar.) During the slide show, the slide will not appear, but you will know that you have a hidden slide because a hidden slide icon appears in the lower-right corner of the preceding slide.

   The menu option is a toggle, so you can unhide a hidden slide by selecting it in Slide Sorter view and choosing Tools⇨Hide Slide. Or you can simply click on the Hide Slide button again.

During a slide show, you can display a hidden slide. Simply click on the hidden slide icon that appears on the preceding slide in the lower-right corner of the screen.

You can also "unhide" slides before you give a presentation. To do this, right-click on the slide in Slide Sorter view and choose Hide Slide from the shortcut menu.

Adding Speaker's Notes and Audience Handouts to a Presentation

In PowerPoint, you can add two items to your presentation that help improve the presentation: speaker's notes and audience handouts. Each of the slides has a companion notes page that includes a small version of the slide and room for typed notes. You can print the notes and use them to recall the points that you want to make for each slide. You can also print audience handouts. Audience handouts make it easy for the audience to follow your presentation and give the audience members something to take with them after the presentation is over. The handouts can contain two, three, or six slides per page.

To create speaker's notes for a presentation, perform the following steps:

1. Select the slide to which you want to add a notes page. Choose View⇨Notes Pages. The notes page appears, as shown in Figure 28-5.

Figure 28-5: A typical notes page.

2. At this size, you will have difficulty reading the notes that you add to the notes page. Use the Zoom Control on the Standard toolbar to increase the size of the notes page to 75 percent (see Figure 28-6).

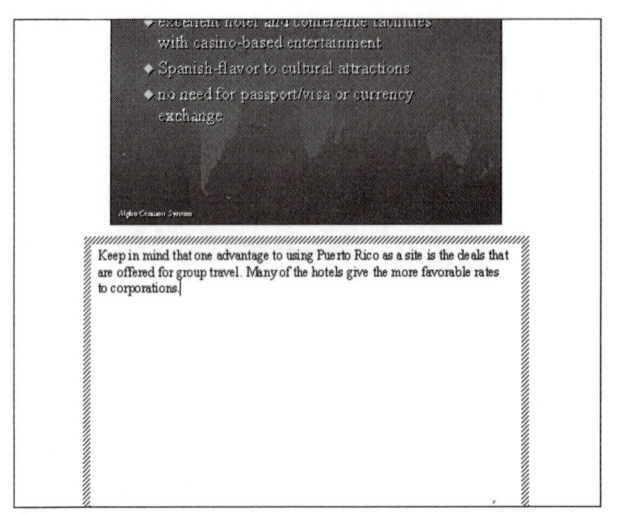

Figure 28-6: The notes page magnified by 75 percent.

3. To enter the notes, click on the box provided for notes and type your entry. After you have added speaker's notes to a presentation, you can print the notes by using the steps outlined under "Printing parts of your presentation" earlier in this chapter.

Chapter 28 ✦ Producing Your Work 601

> **Hot Stuff**: It's generally easier to see the text that you type in the notes box if you change the default magnification. From the Zoom Control list box on the Standard toolbar, choose a magnification of 75 percent or larger.

You can create audience handouts by performing the following steps:

1. Choose View⇨Master⇨Handout Master. Your screen takes on the appearance shown in Figure 28-7. In the figure, the areas outlined by means of dotted lines represent where your slides will appear, depending on whether you've selected two, three, or six slides per page. Two slides appear in the two large dotted-line boxes; three slides appear in the three smaller boxes at the left side of the page; and six slides appear in the six smaller boxes that occupy the full page. To select the number of slides you want to appear per page, choose File⇨Print and specify the number in the Print what list box of the Print dialog box.

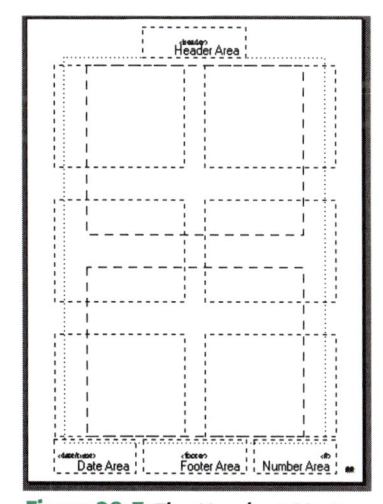

Figure 28-7: The Handout Master screen.

2. Be sure that the Drawing toolbar is displayed. If not, turn it on by choosing the Toolbars command in the View menu and clicking on the Drawing check box in the Toolbars dialog box.

3. Click on the Text tool on the Drawing toolbar, click anywhere outside the dotted lines of the layout that you want to use, and type the desired text (see Figure 28-8). The figure shows the text entered in the Handout Master. The Handout Master controls the layout for all of the handout pages.

> **Note**: You can use cut-and-paste to insert text from each slide on the Handout Master.

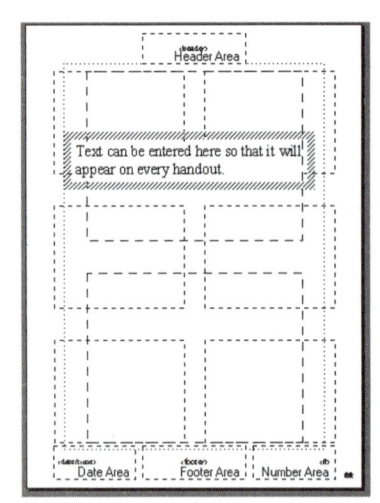

Figure 28-8: Adding a text box and text to the Handout Master.

> You can add the date and time or page numbers to text boxes in your handouts. To do so, place the insertion point where you want the text inside the text box, open the Insert menu, and choose the Date and Time or Page Number command. Then select the format that you want in the dialog box that appears.

Using the PowerPoint Viewer

Your Microsoft Office package includes the PowerPoint Viewer, a separate program that is useful when you want to view a presentation with another computer that does not have PowerPoint installed. The PowerPoint Viewer provides the software needed to load and view any presentation created in PowerPoint. You can also use the Pack & Go Wizard in PowerPoint to package any presentation onto one or more floppy disks (see the next section). Then all you need to give your presentation at a site lacking PowerPoint is the PowerPoint Viewer disk and the disks containing your presentation.

Notes and handout pages have masters, too

In PowerPoint, both notes pages and handout pages have masters, so you can use them the way you use the Slide Master. When you change the appearance of something in Notes Master, for example, the change is reflected in every notes page of the presentation. Likewise, any change in the Handout Master is reflected in every handout page of a presentation. You can take advantage of this design trait by placing information on the masters that should appear on every notes page or handout page.

According to the label on the PowerPoint Viewer disk, Microsoft freely gives permission for this disk to be copied and installed on other systems. The Viewer disk does not provide an operational copy of PowerPoint. Let's get real — to do that would be a *major* violation of your software license agreement! The Viewer only lets you view presentations.

To install the PowerPoint Viewer, perform these steps:

1. Insert the PowerPoint Viewer disk (it's provided with your software) into the computer's floppy drive.
2. Choose Run from the Start menu.
3. In the Run dialog box, enter **A:\SETUP** (if the disk is in drive A) or **B:\SETUP** (if the disk is in drive B) and then click on OK.

The installation program runs, and a dialog box appears that asks for a folder name, which is where the program should be installed. After the installation is complete, you can run the PowerPoint Viewer on that computer by opening the Start menu, choosing Programs, and then choosing PowerPoint Viewer. The Viewer displays an Open dialog box that asks for the name of the PowerPoint presentation that you want to view. Find the desired presentation in the folder it is stored in, select it, and click on Open to view the presentation.

Using the Pack & Go Wizard

You can use the Pack & Go command from the File menu to create a packaged presentation on one or more disks. This menu command launches the Pack & Go Wizard, which then steps you through the process of packaging a presentation and saving it to as many floppy disks as are needed. You can then carry the disks from site to site and give the presentation on any computer that has either PowerPoint or the PowerPoint Viewer installed. To package a presentation for use elsewhere, perform the following steps:

1. Choose File⇨Pack & Go to display the first Pack & Go Wizard dialog box. This dialog box explains the purpose of the wizard but in other respects is pretty useless. Click on the Next button.
2. In the next dialog box presented by the wizard, you can choose to package the presentation that is currently open, or you can click on the Other Presentations button and choose another presentation from the dialog box that appears. Make your desired selections and then click on the Next button.
3. The next dialog box asks which floppy disk drive you want to use to store the presentation. (If you have only one floppy drive, you obviously won't be able to choose anything but the default.) Select the desired drive, if necessary, and then click on the Next button.

4. The next dialog box asks whether you want to include any linked files (such as an Excel worksheet that may be pasted into your presentation) and any embedded fonts that may be in your presentation. Turn on any desired options and then click on the Next button.

5. The last dialog box (about as useful as the first) asks you to click on the Finish button. Make sure that there is a blank floppy disk in the drive that you selected earlier. If any additional disks are needed, PowerPoint asks you to insert them when it needs one. When the process is complete, you are returned to whatever view of PowerPoint you were in when you started the wizard.

To install the presentation on another machine, insert the first floppy disk created by the wizard into the drive and choose the Run command from the Windows 95 Start menu. In the Run dialog box that appears, browse the floppy drive, find and select the program called PNG Setup, and click on Open to run that program. When you run the program, it displays a Pack & Go Wizard setup dialog box like the one shown in Figure 28-9, which asks you for a destination folder in which to store the presentation. Enter a folder name and then click on OK. (If you enter a new folder name, the program asks you for confirmation before creating the folder.)

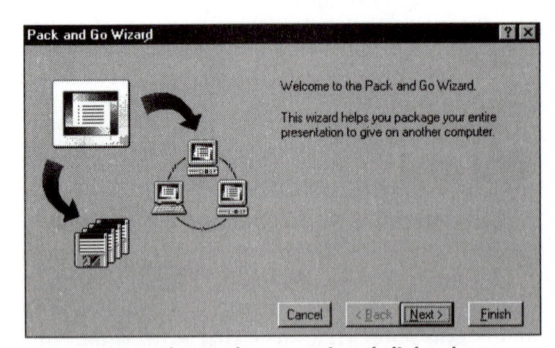

Figure 28-9: The Pack & Go Wizard dialog box.

If the program created more than one disk, the program asks for the additional disks as it needs them. When the installation is complete, you can view the presentation by opening it in PowerPoint or by using the PowerPoint Viewer (described in the preceding section).

> **All this wizard stuff! Why can't I just copy the presentation file to the other computer?**
>
> Actually, you probably can. The Pack & Go Wizard makes life easier if you're not comfortable with moving files around to package a presentation and install it on another system. If you're perfectly comfortable with using Explorer, My Computer, or (horrors!) MS-DOS commands to copy files from place to place, you can always just copy the presentation file onto the other system and open it in PowerPoint or in the PowerPoint Viewer. Keep in mind that if your presentation has any OLE objects in it (such as parts of Word documents or Excel worksheets), it's probably a wise idea to use the Pack & Go Wizard, because it includes any linked files. You, on the other hand, may very well leave them in New York and discover that they are missing when you are in Omaha. Using Pack & Go, however, prevents you from forgetting those needed files for your big presentation.

Using the Send Command

One other common option that you have for "producing" your presentation (in a manner of speaking) is the Send command from the File menu. With this command, you can send the presentation to another person on a network. This command uses Microsoft Exchange, which is provided with Windows 95. (The complete use of Microsoft Exchange is a subject beyond the scope of this book, but you can find details about it in your Windows documentation or in Alan Simpson's *Windows 95 Uncut,* another fine book from IDG Books Worldwide.) To send a presentation by using Microsoft Exchange, choose File⇨Send. PowerPoint saves the presentation to a temporary file, launches Microsoft Exchange, and transfers the temporary file containing the presentation to the New Message window of Microsoft Exchange, as shown in Figure 28-10.

Figure 28-10: The New Message window of Microsoft Exchange.

From here, you can use the techniques that apply to Microsoft Exchange to send the presentation to the desired recipient.

Summary

As demonstrated in this chapter, producing your work in PowerPoint is not an incredibly involved process. This chapter showed you how you can print presentations and how you can use different methods to improve your slide presentations. The chapter covered the following points:

- ◆ You can print presentation slides by choosing File⇨Print, but you should first set up your presentation for the type of printing that you want. First choose File⇨Slide Setup and then select the desired options in the Slide Setup dialog box.

- ◆ You can produce on-screen slide shows by choosing View⇨Slide Show and selecting the desired options from the Slide Show dialog box.

- ◆ You can add transitions or builds to each slide to enhance the effects of an on-screen presentation.

- ◆ You can add speaker's notes or audience handouts to presentations. You can print these items separately for distribution to the speaker or the audience.

- ◆ You can use File⇨Pack & Go to launch a wizard that lets you package a presentation to run on any computer.

The next chapter will demonstrate how you can put PowerPoint to work in real-world applications.

Where to go next . . .

- ◆ PowerPoint offers lots of ways to enhance your presentation. It's never too late to make a better presentation! See Chapter 26 for details.

- ◆ PowerPoint presentations can be used as part of complex documents in Word. Chapter 33 has the scoop on using linking and embedding to share data between applications.

◆ ◆ ◆

CHAPTER 29

PowerPoint for Windows at Work

In This Chapter

Creating an organization chart

Creating a travel presentation

Adding bulleted lists to the travel presentation

Applying templates to a presentation

This chapter shows you a pretty nifty trick: You can create organization charts in PowerPoint. Executive secretaries throughout the corporate world rejoice in this feature, because so many companies regularly play Musical Vice-Presidents in these days of downsizing.

This chapter also walks you step-by-step through creating a presentation about choosing a site for a convention. In this case, the presentation's contents are less important than the general ideas you'll learn — you can use them to create *any* kind of presentation.

Creating an Organization Chart

PowerPoint's organization chart feature lets you create company hierarchy diagrams in a hurry. By way of example, here's how to create a chart for the fictitious Johnson Shoe Corporation (see Figure 29-1).

To create this organization chart, perform the following steps:

1. Create a new presentation in PowerPoint by choosing the Template option from the opening PowerPoint window. You then see the New Presentation dialog box, as shown in Figure 29-2.

    The New Presentation dialog box contains three tabs: General, which has a template for a blank presentation; Presentation Designs, which has templates that can be used to create new presentations; and Presentations, which contains templates for presenting presentations for different occasions. These templates are useful in cases when time is an important factor because they simplify the creation of your presentation. The templates also have placeholders that make suggestions on what you can include in the presentation.

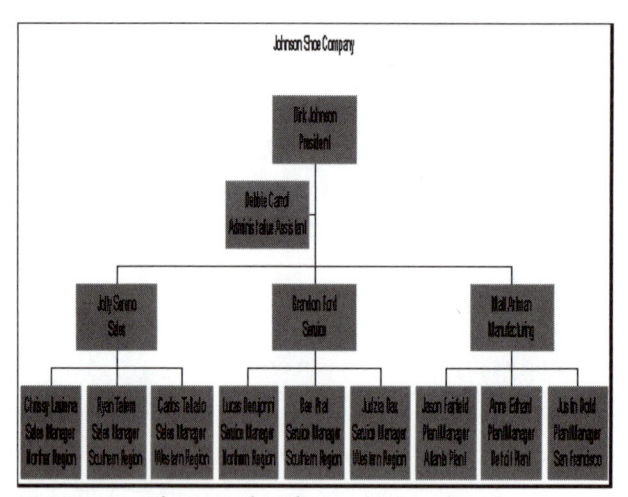

Figure 29-1: The completed organization chart in PowerPoint for the Johnson Shoe Company.

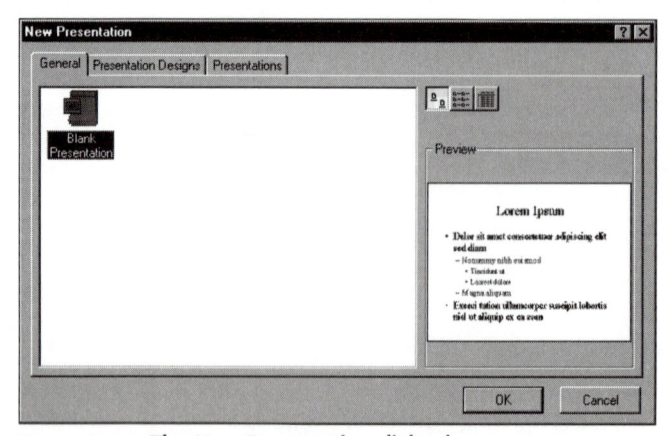

Figure 29-2: The New Presentation dialog box.

2. From the General tab of the New Presentation dialog box, choose Blank Presentation and click on OK.

3. The New Slide dialog box appears. Choose the Organization Chart layout (see Figure 29-3).

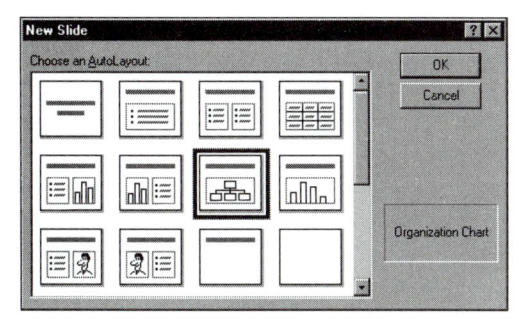

Figure 29-3: Choosing the Organization Chart layout in the New Slide dialog box.

4. Next double-click on the Organization Chart placeholder to activate the Microsoft Organization Chart application and to display a default chart. Organization Chart opens with the default chart shown in Figure 29-4.

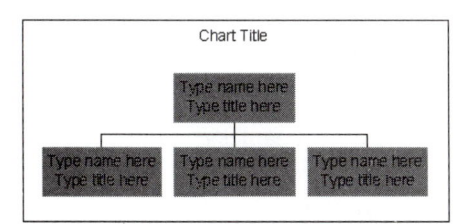

Figure 29-4: The default organization chart.

5. Click in the first box of the chart. In the box, type **Dirk Johnson** for the name and **President** for the title (or enter a name and title of your own choosing).

6. Next you add the administrative assistant.

7. Click on the Assistant button on the toolbar and move the pointer and click in the the President's box. Enter **Debbie Carroll** for the name and **Administrative Assistant** for the title (or enter a name and title of your own choosing).

8. Enter the following names and titles for the division managers, (or names and titles of your own choosing), from left to right in the next level of boxes that appear below Administrative Assistant.

    Jolly Sereno, Sales

    Brandon Ford, Service

    Matt Artman, Manufacturing

9. Click on the Styles menu to drop down its Groups styles options. Click the upper left icon shown in Figure 29-5. This creates subordinate levels in the chart levels.

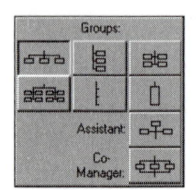

Figure 29-5: The Groups styles menu.

10. Click on the Subordinate button on the Organization Chart toolbar and then click on Jolly Sereno's box. Then enter the following names and titles (or use names and titles of your own choosing). Remember that you will need to click on the Subordinate button for each of the subordinate entries that you make:

    Chrissy Laviena, Sales Manager, Northern Region

    Ryan Tatiem, Sales Manager, Southern Region

    Carlos Tellado, Sales Manager, Western Region

11. Using the procedure in Step 10, enter the following names and titles (or use names and titles of your own choosing) underneath Brandon Ford's box:

    Lucas Derujonni, Service Manager, Northern Region

    Bee Prat, Service Manager, Southern Region

    Judzia Dax, Service Manager, Western Region

12. Using the procedure in Step 10, enter the following names and titles (or use names and titles of your own choosing) underneath Matt Artman's box:

    Anne Edhard, Plant Manager, Detroit Plant

    Jason Farifield, Plant Manager, Atlanta Plant

    Justin Dodd, Plant Manager, San Francisco Plant

13. Now choose File⇨Update Presentation to update your presentation and to place the chart on the blank slide.

14. Return to PowerPoint to see the chart.

15. Choose File⇨Save to save the presentation. Save your presentation as Chart. Your finished chart should look like the one shown in Figure 29-1.

Creating a Travel Presentation

You head the committee to choose the site for your company's annual convention this year. Your first meeting with the committee is right around the corner. It's PowerPoint to the rescue.

Applying a template to the presentation

This example applies a template to the presentation. This gives the presentation's slides a consistent look to them. PowerPoint comes with many different templates that you can apply to your presentation — choose the one that works best for you.

Perform the following steps to duplicate this example:

1. Choose File⇨New. Click on the Blank Presentation option in the New Presentation dialog box.
2. Choose the Blank slide option from the New Slide dialog box. A slide appears without any formatting.
3. Right-click on the slide and choose Slide Layout from the shortcut menu. You will then see the Slide Layout dialog box. From the Slide Layout dialog box, choose Title Slide as the slide layout and then click on the Apply button.
4. Enter the title **Convention Site Option for 1993**.
5. Right-click on the PowerPoint window. From the shortcut menu that appears, choose Apply Design Template to open the Apply Design Template dialog box, as shown in Figure 29-6. Choose a template design that is to your liking and click on the Apply button.

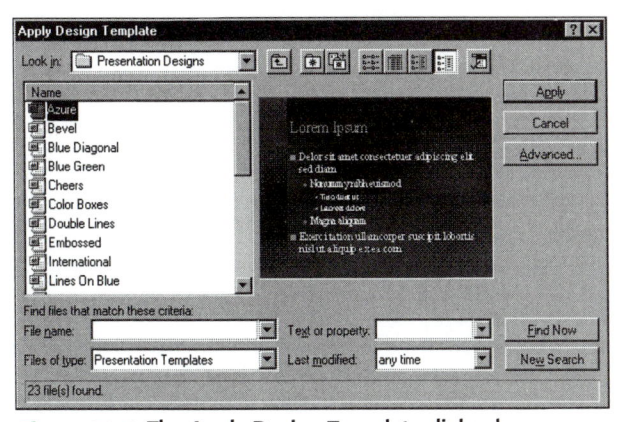

Figure 29-6: The Apply Design Template dialog box.

6. Click on the Insert New Slide button on the Standard toolbar and select Bulleted List as the slide layout. Enter **San Diego** as the title, and in the bulleted list, enter the following:

   Wide range of pricing regarding accommodations

   Excellent restaurants and entertainment

   Close to Mexico

   Beautiful scenery

7. Click on the Insert New Slide button on the Standard toolbar and select Bulleted List as the slide layout. Enter **San Francisco** as the title, and in the bulleted list, enter the following:

   Excellent dining and attractions in Fisherman's Wharf area

   Proximity to sites of interest reduces transportation costs

8. Click on the Insert New Slide button on the Standard toolbar and select Bulleted List as the slide layout. Enter **Cancun, Mexico** as the title, and in the bulleted list, enter the following:

   Favorable currency exchange rate maximizes dollar usage

   Outstanding water sports in close proximity to hotels

9. Click on the Insert New Slide button on the Standard toolbar and select Bulleted List as the slide layout. Enter **San Juan, PR** as the title, and in the bulleted list, enter the following:

   Excellent hotel and conference facilities with casino-based entertainment

   Spanish flavor to cultural attractions

   No need for passport/visa or currency exchange

Applying a background to the slides

Now that you have applied the template to the presentation and entered the text, apply a background to all the slides in the presentation by performing the following steps:

1. Switch to Slide Master view by choosing View⇨Master⇨Slide Master.

2. Choose Format⇨Custom Background to open the Custom Background dialog box (see Figure 29-7).

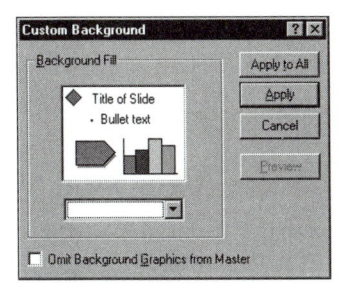

Figure 29-7: The Custom Background dialog box.

3. Choose gray as the background color and click on the Apply to All button.

Adding notes and handouts to the presentation

After you have created the presentation and applied a template to it, you can create a set of speaker's notes. Perform the following steps to create these items:

1. The notes page that appears on-screen corresponds to the slide that you are currently working on. Therefore, switch to Slide view and move to the San Diego slide.

2. Choose View➪Notes Pages.

3. Click inside the notes box to make it active. Note that you may need to use the Zoom Control so that you can see the text better. Click on the Zoom Control button on the Standard toolbar and choose a larger percentage to increase the size of the box.

4. Enter the following notes:

    To Garfinkles/$75 and up a meal/two persons

    Broadway shows at San Diego Theater

    Venture to Tijuana to purchase authentic Mexican arts and crafts

    Genuine Mexican food available (not those so-called imitations)

5. Move to the San Francisco slide and create a notes page by entering the following notes:

    From Hilton/double occupancy/$200 per night

    To La Quinta/double occupancy/$75 per night

    From Fisherman's Wharf/$20-$75 a meal/two persons

    Down by the Sea Restaurant rated best in San Francisco, widest selection of seafood

    12 other wharf restaurants to choose from

    5 different options of transportation with low costs as opposed to cabs

6. Move to the Cancun, Mexico slide and create a notes page by entering the following notes:

   5 pesos to a dollar

   Outstanding snorkeling and scuba diving

   Most hotels offer snorkeling gear on-site and are located on the beach

7. Move to the San Juan, PR slide and create a notes page by entering the following notes:

   ESJ Hotel facilities perfect for working vacation

   Many Puerto Rican art museums

   Puerto Rico is a commonwealth of the United States, so you need no special paperwork to visit there.

Adding headers and footers to your presentation

After creating the notes pages, you can add page numbers by choosing View⇨Header and Footer. The Header and Footer dialog box appears, as shown in Figure 29-8.

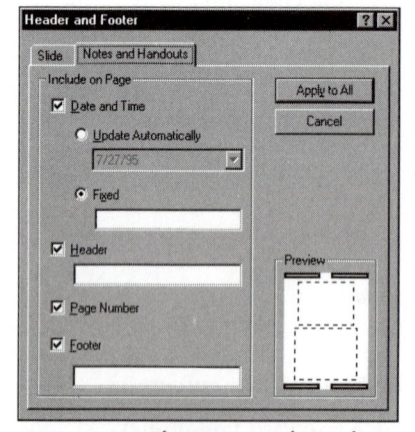

Figure 29-8: The Notes and Handouts tab of the Header and Footer dialog box.

You can use this dialog box to include headers and footers on the slides and slide notes. (You can do this only from the Slide Master.) If you click on the Slide tab, you can add the date, time, and slide numbers to your slides. While you're at it, you can exclude the title slide from getting these additions. You apply these items by clicking the corresponding check boxes on the Slide tab.

You use the Notes and Handouts tab to apply these same elements to the notes pages and handouts that may be included with a presentation. The one additional option you have here is the addition of headers. You may need to add headers to identify your handouts or notes. You can click on the Page Number box to add page numbers to your speaker's notes. The Preview box shows you where the page numbers will appear.

Printing your notes pages

You can print your notes pages by performing these steps:

1. Be sure that your printer is ready (check to see if it is on-line).
2. Choose File⇨Print.
3. In the Print what list box of the Print dialog box, choose Notes Pages.
4. Click on OK.

Adding transitions to your presentation

Transitions are another feature that you can add to the presentation. Transitions are visual changes between the slides. For example, one kind of transition makes one slide appear to dissolve into another. Transitions can make a presentation more appealing to an audience and can be a good special effect to add to a presentation. Perform the following steps to create a transition between two slides. You must perform these steps for each slide transition.

1. Switch to Slide Sorter view by clicking on its button on the left side of the status bar.
2. Choose Tools⇨Slide Transition to open the Slide Transition dialog box (see Figure 29-9).

Figure 29-9: The Slide Transition dialog box.

3. In the Effect list box, choose Box Out for the transition. You can see the effect of this transition in the Preview box.

4. In the Speed area, choose Slow.

5. Click on OK.

You can also insert transitions by using the Transition Effects list box on the Slide Sorter toolbar at the top of your screen. Use the arrow keys to move to the slide that you want to set a transition for. Then click the arrow of the list box and choose the effect that you want to apply to the slide.

The benefit of using the dialog box is that you have a chance to preview the transition before it is applied. However, you can click on the Transition button on the Slide Sorter toolbar to open the Transitions dialog box. Here you can preview the transition by selecting it from the list of transitions.

Finally, save the completed presentation by choosing the Save command from the File menu. When asked for a name, you can call the presentation **Travel 1**. Run the presentation by clicking on the Slide Show button on the left side of the status bar.

Summary

This chapter provided you with a step-by-step look at what is involved in creating an organization chart, and walked you through creating a presentation.

+ You can use the Organization Chart layout in the New Slide dialog box to create organization charts.

+ To apply a design to a presentation, you right-click on any blank part of the PowerPoint window and choose Apply Design Template from the shortcut menu.

+ While in Slide View, you can create notes pages that provide speaker's notes to work from while giving your presentation.

+ While in Slide Sorter view, you can use Tools⇨Slide Transition to add transitions to your slides.

The next chapter answers common questions PowerPoint users have.

Where to go next...

+ Now that you have created a presentation in PowerPoint, you may want to take some time to make it more visually appealing. Chapter 26 tells you how.

+ You also may want to produce the presentation that you may have created with this chapter. See Chapter 28.

✦ ✦ ✦

The PowerPoint Top Ten

CHAPTER 30

In This Chapter

Formatting entire presentations

Grouping and editing objects

Copying formatting among objects

Reusing a presentation as a template

Changing slide layouts

Previewing transitions between slides

Looking at a presentation without using PowerPoint

Putting slides in reverse order

Adding and erasing annotations

Viewing presentations without PowerPoint installed

In this chapter you'll find questions and answers detailing the most common problems encountered by users of PowerPoint. As usual, the answers are based on information we picked up from the Microsoft Technical Support and the Microsoft forums on CompuServe.

How can I format the title and text for an entire presentation?

Sometimes you will need to make formatting changes to an entire presentation, whether those changes are for the text or for the layout of your slides. Choose View⇨Master⇨Slide Master. When you make the changes in the Slide Master, they are applied to the entire presentation.

How can I group and edit objects as one?

To group objects, select them and choose Draw⇨Group. This action groups the selected objects as one. If you want to edit the objects, use the editing techniques that you learned in the PowerPoint section of this book.

How can I copy the formatting of one object to another?

First, highlight the object that contains the formatting you want to copy. Next, double-click on the Format Painter button on the Standard toolbar. Finally, select the object(s) to which you want to apply the formatting, and the formatting is automatically applied.

How can I apply a PowerPoint presentation as a template?

Applying a PowerPoint presentation as a template is, in essence, creating a new template. First, create the presentation exactly the way you want it with all the formatting and objects. Next, choose File➪Save As Presentation Template. In the Save As dialog box, choose Save As type. In the File Type box, choose Design Template. The file is then saved as a template file that you can later use to create new presentations.

How can I change the layout of my slide without losing my existing work?

If you decide to change the layout of your slide while you are working on it, first click on the Layout button on right side of the status bar to open the Slide Layout dialog box. From this dialog box, choose the desired slide layout. After you click on OK, the layout is applied to the slide.

How can I preview all my slide transitions?

To preview all your slide transitions, switch to the Slide Sorter view by clicking on its button on the left of the status bar. After switching to Slide Sorter view, click on the transition icon underneath each slide to see the transition.

How can I view my presentations on a business trip without installing PowerPoint?

PowerPoint comes with the PowerPoint Viewer, which lets you view PowerPoint presentations on a computer that does not have PowerPoint installed on it. Install the PowerPoint Viewer on the other computer, open a copy of the presentation in PowerPoint Viewer, and run it. Remember that you must save the presentation on a separate disk. (Choose File➪Pack & Go to launch a wizard that helps you put a presentation on a floppy disk.). You can also give the presentation and the PowerPoint Viewer to others so that they can view the presentation that you have created — without pressure from you. Microsoft lets you freely copy and distribute the PowerPoint Viewer disk.

How can I print slides in reverse order?

To print slides in reverse order, choose File➪Print to open the Print dialog box. In the Slides text box under the Print Range portion of the dialog box, enter the order of the slides as you want them to print and remember to enter a comma after each slide number. For example, to print slide 3, then slide 2, then slide 1, enter **3,2,1** in the Slides text box.

How can I add and erase on-screen annotations in a slide show?

Annotations are useful in a slide show to make different points in your presentation. To add annotations, switch to the Slide Show view and then right-click on any portion of the screen. In the shortcut menu that appears, choose Pen. The pointer then becomes a pen allowing you to make the needed annotations to your slide show. You can also change the color of the marks by using the same shortcut menu. Choose Pointer Options and then Pen Color. From the next menu that appears, choose the color of your choice.

Hot Stuff: If you want to draw a straight line with the pen cursor in Slide Show view, hold down the Shift key while you draw the line.

After you have made the marks that you need, you can press the E key to remove them. Remember that all annotation marks are temporary. When you advance to the next slide, the marks are automatically erased.

How can I create new slides without using the New Slide dialog box?

If you want to create new slides without using the New Slide dialog box, you need to make an adjustment in the Options dialog box. To do so, choose Tools⇨Options to open the Options dialog box. Here, turn off the Show New Slide Dialog check box. With this option turned off, you can add new slides without using the New Slide dialog box each time. PowerPoint adds a slide with a title box and text area each time you ask for a new slide.

Summary

This chapter has covered the top ten PowerPoint questions and their answers. The chapter also concludes the PowerPoint section of this book.

Where to go next...

✦ Many of the common PowerPoint questions have to do with working with presentation formats and layouts. Chapter 26 gives you specifics that will help you change your presentation's appearance.

✦ Producing finished presentations generates a disproportionate number of questions, too. Chapter 28 takes you by the hand and leads you through it.

✦ ✦ ✦

Office Works Together

PART V

In This Part

Chapter 31
Working with Schedule+

Chapter 32
Using the Binder

Chapter 33
Sharing Data between Applications with OLE

Using Schedule+

CHAPTER 31

In This Chapter

Starting Schedule+

Understanding the Schedule+ window

Making appointments

Using the To Do list

Adding, editing, and deleting contacts

Sending and receiving meeting requests

Printing in Schedule+

Using the Timex DataLink Watch Wizard

Schedule+ is a user-friendly time management tool that you can use alone or as part of a group. Schedule+ can facilitate the organization of your life because it has the capability to track your appointments, meetings, tasks, contacts, and events. Schedule+ can literally be your planning assistant. It can help you keep track of your various tasks and projects. Schedule+ has a To Do list, which you can see from most of its different calendar views, where you can group your various tasks by category — by project, by priority, or by due date. By looking at an appropriate tab, you can see whether you should be working on a particular project on a given day, or what your upcoming work week looks like.

In addition to organizing your to do list, Schedule+ also provides a contacts list to let you maintain information about your personal and business contacts, including notes about phone conversations, and action items. For those of you who are connected to a mail server on a network, you will be able to organize meetings, send requests, and track the replies by using Schedule+. You will also be able to make your schedule available to others while maintaining privacy where needed.

Starting Schedule+

You can start Schedule+ by opening the Windows 95 Start menu, choosing Programs, choosing Microsoft Office, and then choosing Microsoft Schedule+. When you do so, you will see the Schedule Logon dialog box (Figure 31-1), asking for an appropriate logon name for the schedule that you want to work with. In this dialog box, you type a user name for the desired schedule, then click on OK.

If you're starting Schedule+ for the first time and you're not working with others on a local-area network, the appearance of this dialog box can be rather confusing. The obvious question is, "What am I supposed to enter in here?" On a system that's not connected to a network, it actually doesn't matter what you enter in this dialog box, as long as you remember the name you enter so that you can "log on" to that same schedule in the future. The dialog box appears by default because Schedule+ is the kind of application that's designed to help groups of people working together on a network. If you're what's known as a "stand-alone" user, you shouldn't feel left out just because you don't have a massive network in that office (or home) of yours; you can get a lot of use out of Schedule+ whether you are working with others or not. If you are on a network, someone (likely your network administrator) should coordinate the assigning of logon names, simply so that all users in your workgroup know other users' names, and everyone can look at the schedules of others.

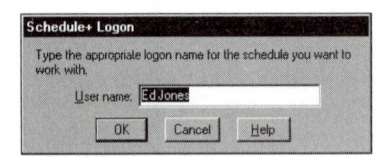

Figure 31-1: The Schedule+ Logon dialog box.

Once you enter a logon name and click on OK, Schedule+ appears in its own window, as shown in Figure 31-2.

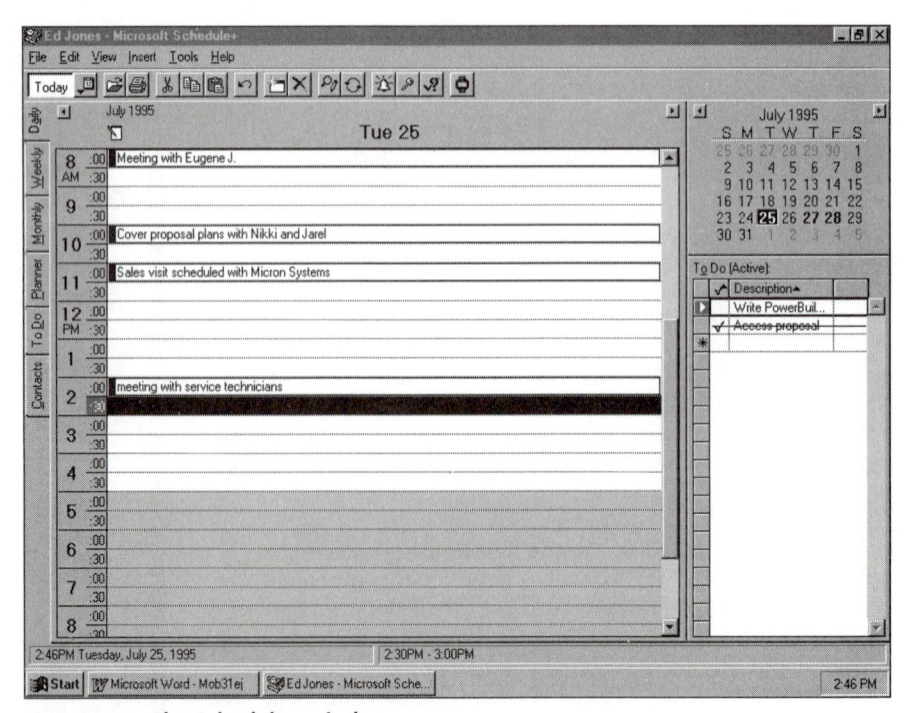

Figure 31-2: The Schedule+ window.

More Info Note that you can also start Schedule+ from the Office Shortcut Bar if it is running (see Chapter 1 for specifics on using the Office Shortcut Bar). By default, the Office Shortcut Bar contains three buttons labeled Make an Appointment, Add a Task, and Add a Contact. Clicking on any of these buttons starts Schedule+, with a new appointment, task, or contact visible.

Understanding the Schedule+ Window

The Schedule+ window contains a menu bar at the top and a status bar at the bottom, like all Windows applications. There's also a toolbar, located directly below the menu bar. In addition to these items, in the main part of the window, Schedule+ displays one of several possible *views* of your schedule. Each view is clearly indicated by a tab at the left side of the window. The views, as marked by the tabs, are Daily, Weekly, Monthly, Planner, To Do, and Contacts.

✦ **Daily, Weekly, and Monthly** — The Daily tab lists your appointments one day at a time. The Weekly tab displays your appointments in a weekly fashion. The Monthly tab displays your appointments in a monthly fashion. You can move between days, months, or years by clicking on the left or right arrow buttons that appear directly below the toolbar.

✦ **Planner** — Use the Planner tab to set plans with other users. This tab is especially useful if you need to set appointments that involve more than two people. On a network, you can view this tab to tell whether others are available when you schedule an event.

✦ **To Do** — The To Do tab brings up a to do list (also known as a "projects" list), which includes all the tasks that you have scheduled to accomplish. You mark the tasks as done by clicking on the Completed column of the To Do tab.

✦ **Contacts** — The Contacts tab lets you move through your contacts list. This tab is useful for finding the name, address, and other entered information on a contact that you may have on the phone. You can use much of the information found in these tabs to make you more effective in the tasks that you need to accomplish.

Like all Windows applications written by Microsoft, Schedule+ also includes a toolbar that provides you with fast access to common tasks. See Figure 31-3. The buttons on the toolbar can be used to perform the tasks indicated in Table 31-1.

Note If you're on a network, you'll see two extra buttons on this toolbar: Meeting Wizard and View Mail. The table describes these buttons, and lists them where they appear on the toolbar.

Part V ✦ Office Works Together

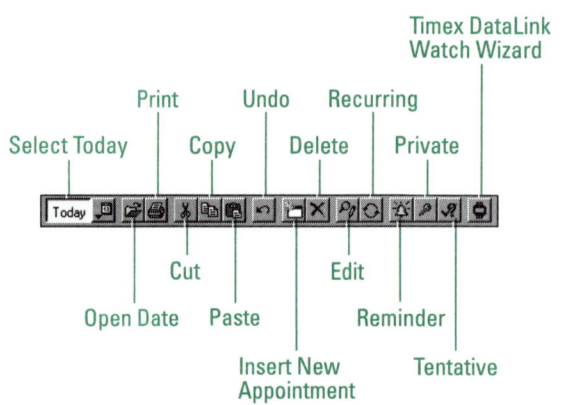

Figure 31-3: The Schedule+ toolbar.

(Toolbar labels: Select Today, Print, Undo, Recurring, Timex DataLink Watch Wizard, Copy, Delete, Private, Open Date, Cut, Paste, Edit, Reminder, Insert New Appointment, Tentative)

Table 31-1
Schedule+ toolbar buttons

Name	Function
Select Today	Selects the current day for display
Go To Date	Takes you to a specific date on the calendar
Open	Opens an archived file, another user's appointment book, or a project schedule
Print	Prints your schedule
Cut	Removes the selected item and places it on the Clipboard
Copy	Copies the selected information onto the Clipboard
Paste	Places the Clipboard information at the cursor
Undo	Undoes the last action
Insert New Appointment	Opens a new appointment box, where you can enter a new appointment
Delete	Deletes a selected appointment
Edit	Edits an appointment
Recurring	Sets an appointment as recurring
Reminder	Sets a reminder

Name	Function
Private	Sets an appointment as private so that other Schedule+ users can't read it
Tentative	Sets an appointment as tentative and enables others to schedule something in that time slot
Meeting Wizard	If you are using Schedule+ on a network, you will see this button. You can use it to start the Meeting Wizard, which helps you schedule meetings among members of your workgroup.
Timex Watch Wizard	Send data to your Timex DataLink watch
View Mail	If you are using Schedule+ on a network, you will see this button. It displays your mail inbox, so you can read your meeting messages.

Now that you have read a quick overview of the Schedule+ window, you may want to consider each of the tabs in more detail.

The Daily tab

The Daily tab shows your day's plans (see Figure 31-2, shown earlier). At the right of the Daily tab is a To Do list that contains a list of tasks. You can look at the tasks by clicking on them and scrolling. The Daily tab also displays the current month's calendar so that you can find a date in that month at a glance. If you need to move forward to another month or backward to a previous month, just click on the left- or right-pointing arrow buttons above the calendar.

The Weekly tab

The Weekly tab (Figure 31-4) displays the appointments and plans for the week. This tab let you see your schedule for the week at a glance. The tab displays all the appointments that you have for that week, and it lets you enter or make changes to the appointments by double-clicking any entry within the calendar. (For more about the process of entering appointments, see "Making Appointments," later in this chapter.)

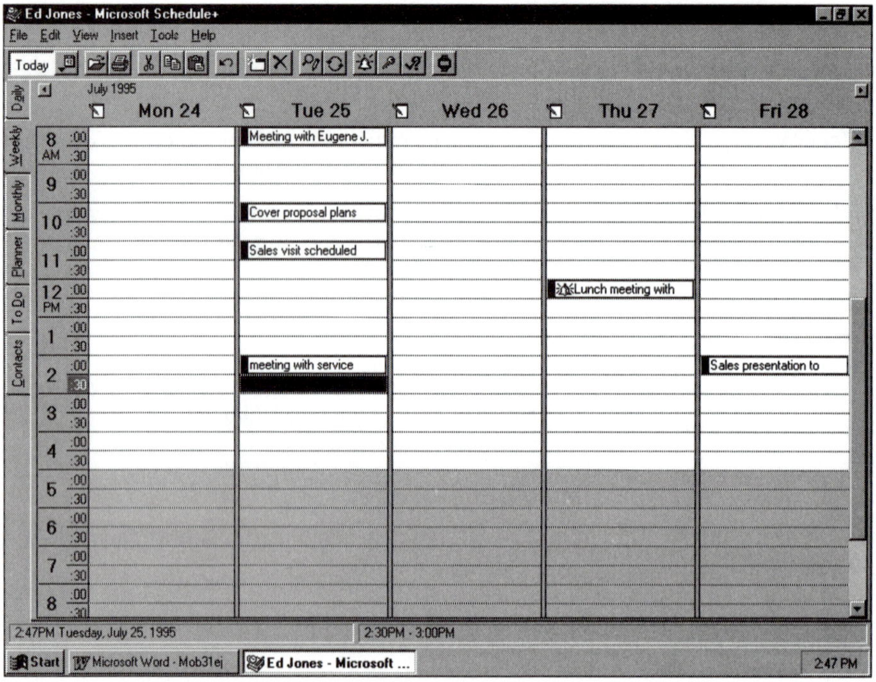

Figure 31-4: The Weekly tab.

To see more than just the days listed, you can click on the left or right arrows directly beneath the toolbar. Clicking on these arrows lets you view the schedule for the next week or the preceding week. This feature is especially useful when you need to recall meetings from the previous week or look into the future to see what next week holds.

You can use the Weekly tab to set event reminders right below the date. This feature helps remind you of an important event. You can set a reminder by right- or left-clicking on the check box to the left of the day of the event. If you left-click on the check box, your choices in the shortcut menu are Insert event and Insert annual event. If you right-click on the check box, your choices in the shortcut menu are New event and New annual event. Using the shortcut menu, choose New event or Insert event, depending on which clicking method you used. If the event is annual, choose New annual event or Insert annual event. Depending on which option you choose, you will see an Event dialog box, similar to the one shown in Figure 31-5. In this dialog box, enter the event that you want to remember. Enter the start and finish day for the event. You also can set an audible reminder, and you can use the list boxes at the bottom of the dialog box to determine how many minutes before the event the audible reminder should sound. When you have entered an event, the event appears below that day and date on each of the tabs.

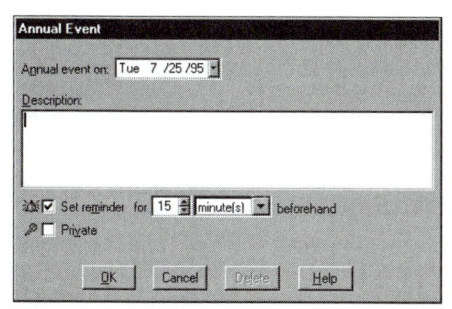

Figure 31-5: The Annual Event dialog box.

The Monthly tab

The Monthly tab (Figure 31-6) functions in much the same way as the Daily and Weekly tabs; you can click the tab and view your appointments in the window. The Monthly tab is most useful for getting a broad view of your working schedule for any given month. While using this tab, the left and right arrows directly below the toolbar will move you forward and backwards a month at a time. Given that the window has to display an entire month, you can't see very much detail about any specific appointment; just a few characters of text will appear, as demonstrated by the figure. However, you can double-click on any appointment, to open an Appointment window that provides full details about the appointment. (For more specifics about the Appointment window, see "Making Appointments," later in this chapter.)

Hot Stuff The Monthly tab can provide a useful way to navigate within your appointment schedule. You can click on the Monthly tab and then click on the day of the month that you want to view, then click on the Daily tab to see the appointments for that day. This is just an alternative method to using the calendar at the upper right of the Daily tab to navigate within the schedule; some people like to use the Monthly tab for navigation, because it shows you portions of your appointments within the days of the months.

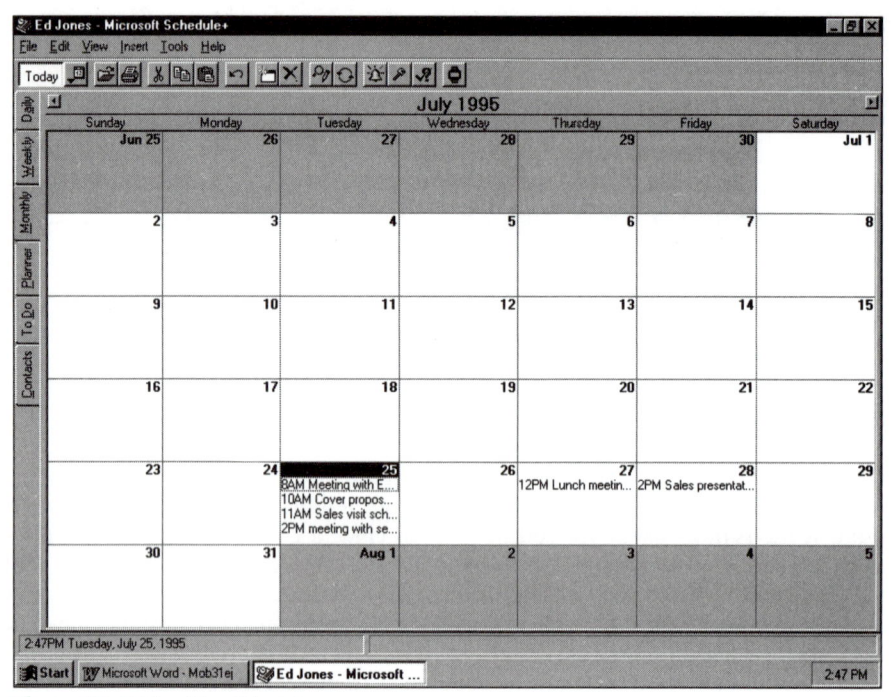

Figure 31-6: The Monthly tab.

The Planner tab

The Planner tab (Figure 31-7) is useful when you have to schedule events with multiple users. This tab lets you schedule appointments with others on the network without talking to the people directly about their schedules. The Planner tab can save you a lot of wasted time on the telephone.

While viewing the Planner tab, you can set appointments with others on the network by performing the following steps:

1. Select the day for the appointment.
2. Right-click on the square of the day for the appointment.
3. From the shortcut menu, choose New Appointment. The appointment window is then opened, as shown in Figure 31-8.
4. Enter the desired information in the General tab to set the appointment.
5. After entering your desired notes, click on the Planner tab.
6. If you are on a network, you can automatically set the meeting for a time when all can attend. The calendar shows the busy times for each of the attendees. Clicking on the AutoPick button automatically chooses a time for the meeting when all attendees are available.

Chapter 31 ✦ **Using Schedule+**   633

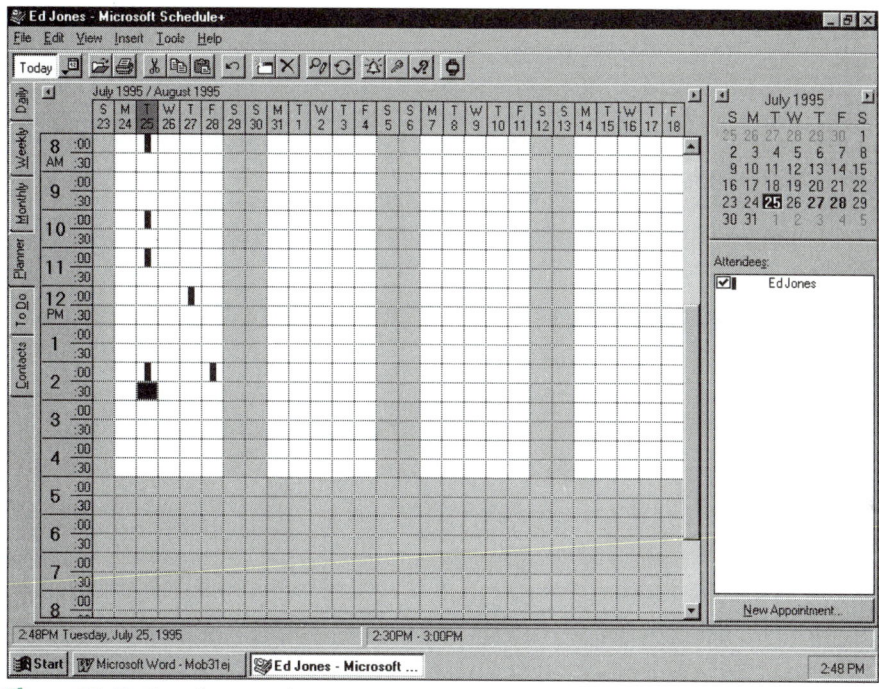

Figure 31-7: The Planner tab.

Figure 31-8: The Appointment window.

The To Do tab

To enter and manage activities associated with a specific date, you need to use the To Do tab (Figure 31-9). This tab displays all the tasks that you have to do. The tab gives a description of the tasks, lists them in priority, and also lists duration and completion time. You can easily add items to your to-do list by just clicking in the first blank line and typing a desired entry. If a task has been performed, you can click on the check box to the left of the task, thus showing that it has been completed.

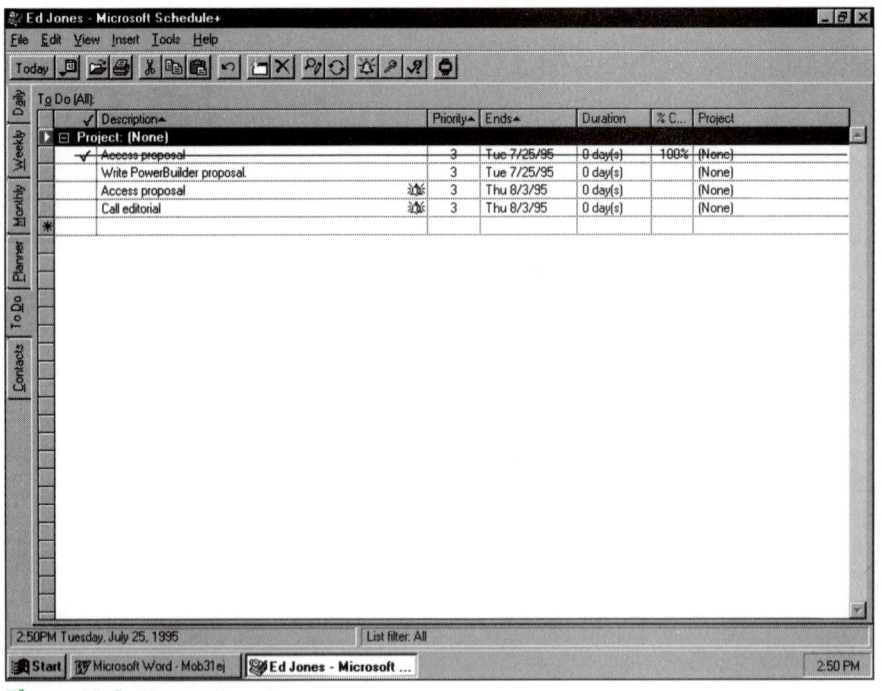

Figure 31-9: The To Do tab.

Note that the same to-do list appears, in condensed form, at the right side of the Daily tab. You can enter tasks in your to-do list from the Daily tab, as well as from the To Do tab, and you can mark them as being completed from either tab.

From time to time, you will need to perform maintenance on your To Do list. To do so, double-click on the section of the entry that you want to change. You then can then enter the desired changes.

The Contacts tab

The Contacts tab (Figure 31-10) is the last tab that you see on the Schedule+ window. This tab's function is simple: you use it to display and enter your business or personal contacts. The last and first names of all your contacts are displayed in the left portion of the Schedule+ window. If you want to make amendments to a phone number, name, and so on, simply click on the entry and make the desired changes in the right portion of the window.

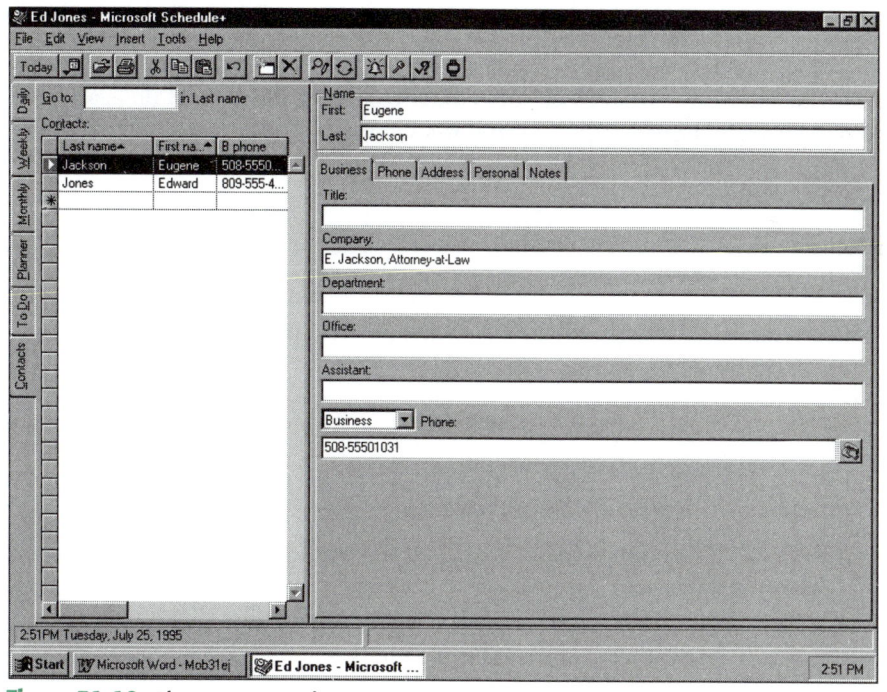

Figure 31-10: The Contacts tab.

In the right portion of the window, you see the various fields that you use to enter your contact information. This form has numerous fields for contact information (such as Title, Company, Home and Fax Phone, Address, and so on), divided across five tabs titled Business, Phone, Address, Personal, and Notes. You don't have to fill in all the fields, but the more information you have about each contact, the better.

Now that you have been given the grand tour of the overall layout of Schedule+, you can consider how to work with the program's various features to better organize your business life.

Making Appointments

You can use the Appointment dialog box, available from various places within Schedule+, to view the appointments that you have planned for the day, week, month, or year. Schedule+ lets you set appointments so that you can keep track of all the engagements that you tend to forget. You can set reminders that will tell you when you need to prepare for your meeting.

To make an appointment, begin by clicking on the Daily, Weekly, or Monthly tab to display your schedule in the form you desire. (You may find it easier to use the Daily tab or the Weekly tab, because you can click on a desired time of the day in either of these tabs. Because you can't choose a time of day from the Monthly tab, any appointment you enter there will default to the hour closest to the current time, and you'll have to change it to whatever time you want in the Appointment dialog box.) Once you are in the view you want and at the time that you want, choose Insert⇨Appointment to display the Appointment dialog box.

Hot Stuff If you are using the Daily tab or the Weekly tab, you can also double-click on any time slot to open the Appointment dialog box for that particular time.

At the bottom of the Appointment dialog box are five buttons. These buttons perform the following tasks:

- ✦ **OK** — This button accepts the changes to the calendar that you are working on.
- ✦ **Cancel** — This button cancels the last entry.
- ✦ **Delete** — This button deletes a selected appointment.
- ✦ **Help** — This button displays a Help file that explains the various options in the Appointment dialog box.
- ✦ **Make Recurring** — This button makes an appointment recurring. This feature makes it easy to schedule regular meetings, such as those that occur weekly or monthly.

The Appointment window also has four tabs: General, Attendees, Notes, and Planner. These tabs are the key to the Appointment window's power.

The General tab

Use the General tab (Figure 31-11) to set the time for an appointment. In the When portion of the dialog box, use the arrows in the Start and End list boxes to set the time and the date of your appointment. If the appointment is an all-day offering, click on the All day check box.

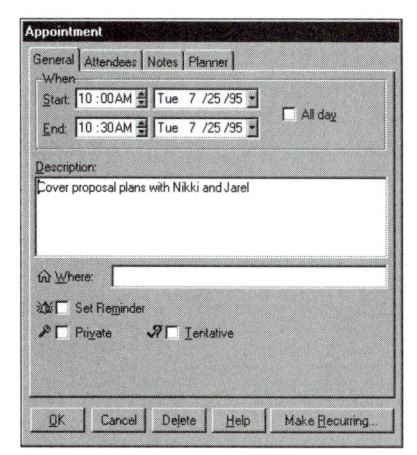

Figure 31-11: The General tab of the Appointment window.

The Description text box lets you enter a description for the appointment, a key to Schedule+'s effectiveness. The description helps you remember exactly what your appointment is about, and it provides other details that you need to be effective. Remember, since your descriptions are what you see in your Daily and Weekly tabs, you'll want to be clear enough with your descriptions so that you recognize them when you view them days or weeks later. In the Where text box, located below the Description text box, you can enter the location of your appointment.

Hot Stuff If you can provide an accurate description of your appointments using the first ten characters of the entry in the Description text box, you'll be able to recognize all your appointments at a glance in the Monthly tab. (You can also then print out the Monthly view of the schedule and pin the resulting calendar to your wall, as an annoying reminder of how many things you still have to do this month!)

Next, you can use the check boxes and list boxes at the bottom of the dialog box to set various options for the appointments. For example, you can set a reminder for the appointment; you can designate the appointment as private; and you can indicate that the appointment is only tentative. If you want to set a reminder, click on the Set Reminder check box and then use the list boxes to the right of the check box to set the minutes, hours, weeks, or months before which you want to be reminded. Click on the Private check box so that others cannot have access to your schedule on a network. If you activate the Tentative check box, the appointment will not appear as busy time on you calendar, so others on a network can schedule events in that time if they care to. If the meeting you have is an important one, you will want to set it as a priority meeting.

The Attendees tab

Use the Attendees tab (Figure 31-12) to show the status of the people attending a meeting that you have scheduled. If a person has accepted your invitation, declined, or tentatively accepted, and if the person included a response, you will see it on-screen.

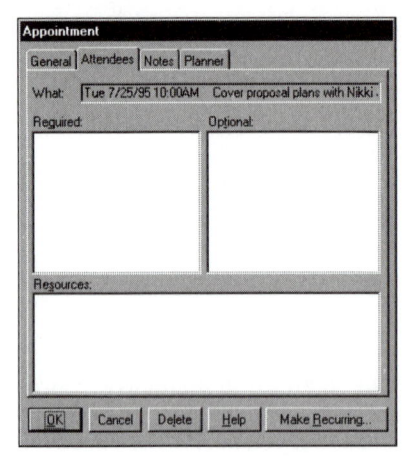

Figure 31-12: The Attendees tab of the Appointment window.

This tab displays the date and time for the meeting in the What box. It also has boxes that display required and optional attendees along with resources for the meeting. If you are on a stand-alone system, don't be surprised by the fact that you can't make any entries in this tab; in Schedule+, you must be on a network to actually schedule meetings.

The Notes tab

Use the Notes tab (Figure 31-13) to enter notes on the appointment that you have scheduled. These notes can help you keep track of any special information that you may need in the meeting to help you be prepared. This information in this tab also helps if you want to set an appointment because you can enter information about the attendees that may be very useful.

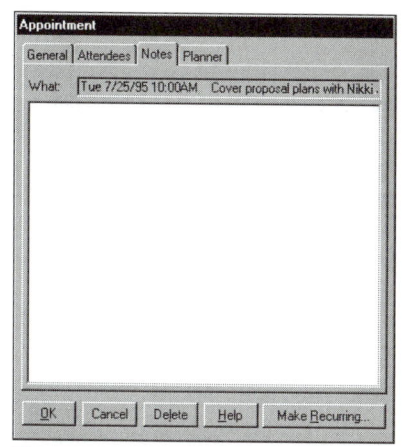

Figure 31-13: The Notes tab of the Appointment window.

The Planner tab

The Planner tab (Figure 31-14) displays the free and busy times for all the attendees of your meeting. With this information, you can schedule a meeting time when all the people can attend. This tab also includes the AutoPick button. This button automatically selects a time when all your selected attendees are available to attend. This feature saves lots of scheduling time.

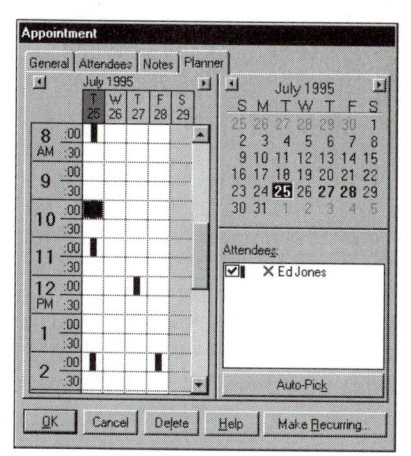

Figure 31-14: The Planner tab of the Appointment window.

Recurring meetings

You can schedule meetings that occur at the same time daily, weekly, or monthly by clicking on the Make Recurring button in the Appointment dialog box. After you click on this button, the Appointment Series dialog box opens, as shown in Figure 31-15. This dialog box appears similar to the Appointments dialog box, except that the Planner tab has been replaced with the When tab, as shown in the figure. The When tab is active when you open the Appointment Series dialog box.

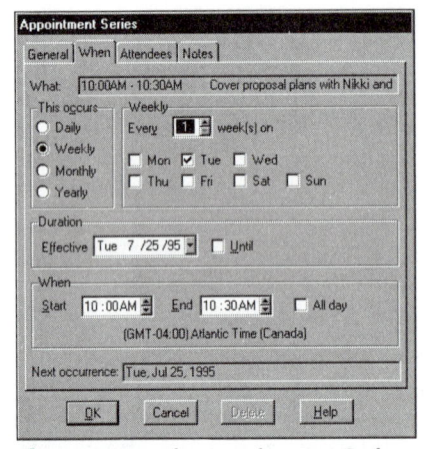

Figure 31-15: The Appointment Series dialog box.

The What box displays the time for your appointment. In the This occurs area, you can set the appointment to occur on a daily, weekly, monthly, or yearly basis. The default option is Weekly. As you select one of the choices, the box to the right changes so that you are able to specify the day or month of the appointment. In Figure 31-15, the appointment time is set for every Tuesday from 10:00 a.m. to 10:30 a.m.

Changing and deleting appointments

To change an existing appointment, just find the desired appointment in any of the views (daily, weekly, or monthly), and double-click on it. When you do so, the Appointment dialog box appears. You can proceed to make the desired changes to the appointment using the tabs of the dialog box, as discussed earlier in this section. When done making your changes, click on OK to put away the dialog box.

To delete an existing appointment, select the desired appointment in any of the views. Then, click on the Delete button on the toolbar, or choose Edit⇨Delete.

Using the To Do List

You can add projects to your To Do list in a number of ways. You can click on the To Do tab to display your To Do list, and you can then click in the first blank row, and type your entry directly into the list. Figure 31-16 shows an entry being edited in the To Do tab.

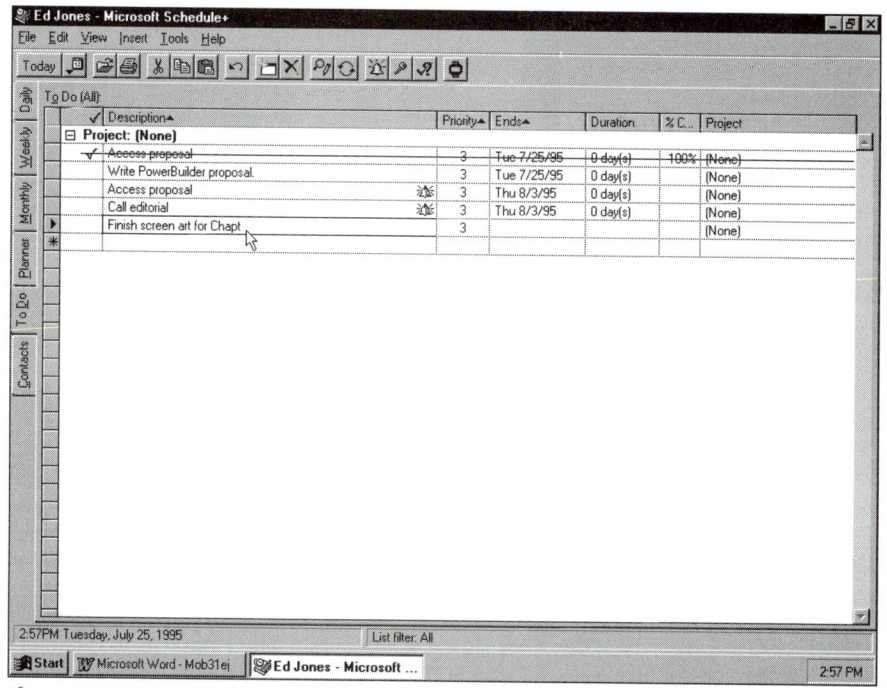

Figure 31-16: The To Do tab of Schedule+, with an entry being edited.

Alternately, you can click on the To Do tab, and then click on the Insert New Task button in the toolbar, or choose Insert➪Task. With either method, a Task dialog box appears and you can enter a description, a priority, and a status in the dialog box, and click on OK. This information then appears in the To Do tab of Schedule+.

To delete a contact, click in the column at the left edge of the contact name to select the row containing the contact. Then, click on the Delete button in the toolbar, or choose Edit➪Delete Item.

Adding, Editing, and Deleting Contacts

To add a contact, click on the Contacts tab. This displays your contacts. Then, click on the Insert New Contact button in the toolbar (it's the one that looks like a file folder with a star in the left corner), or choose Insert⇨Contact. With either method, a Contact dialog box appears, as shown in Figure 31-17.

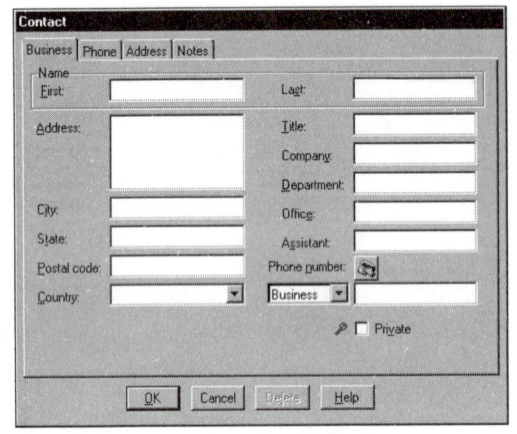

Figure 31-17: The Contacts dialog box.

The fields and tabs of this dialog box are identical to those that appear in the Contacts tab of Schedule+. You can enter the desired data, and click on OK to store the new contact.

To edit an existing contact, click on the desired contact at the left side of the Contacts tab in Schedule+. You can then directly edit the fields at the right. Or, you can click on the Edit button in the toolbar (the one with the magnifying glass) or choose Edit⇨Edit Item, to bring up the existing contact in the same dialog box shown in Figure 31-16. When you're done editing in this dialog box, click on OK.

To delete a contact, click in the column at the left edge of the contact name, to select the row containing the contact. Then, click on the Delete button in the toolbar, or choose Edit⇨Delete Item.

Sending and Receiving Meeting Requests

If you are using Schedule+ on a network with a mail server, you can schedule and receive meeting requests. You use the Meeting Request form in Schedule+ to send meeting request messages to others on your network. (Keep in mind that for all of this to work, your PC must be connected to a mail server, and the meeting attendees must also have Microsoft Exchange, a feature of Windows 95, installed on their systems.)

While you can schedule meetings by clicking on the Request Meeting button in the Planner tab, the easiest way to schedule your meetings is to let the Meeting Wizard help you through the process. When you are running Schedule+ on a network, the Meeting Wizard button will be visible in the right-hand portion of the toolbar. Click on this button to display the first Meeting Wizard dialog box. You can then proceed to answer the questions presented by the wizard, to schedule your meeting.

Alternatively, you can also schedule a meeting by performing the following steps:

1. On the Planner tab, click on the Request Meeting button located at the lower-right corner of the dialog box. This causes a Meeting Request form to appear.

2. Enter a description of the meeting in the Subject box of the Meeting Request form. This description will appear in your appointment book.

   If you are turning an appointment into a meeting, and the appointment already has a description, the description automatically appears in the Subject box.

3. You can add recipients and message text, or you can attach files just as you do with your e-mail.

4. Click on the Send button on the toolbar to send the message.

The meeting is automatically marked in your Planner and the meeting is placed in your list of appointments.

Printing in Schedule+

Schedule+ lets you print your appointments by choosing File⇨Print or by clicking on the Print button in the toolbar. In addition to your appointments, you can also print your To Do list or Contacts list for use away from the office. Schedule+ provides you with a variety of layout choices and paper formats so that you can print only the information that you need in the format that's most convenient for you.

Schedule+ prints the appointments in a way that allows you to identify the different appointment types that you have. When you print your appointments, the tentative appointments print in italic. Overflow appointments that do not fit in the selected layout print in the area of the printout labeled Other Appointments. In Schedule+, printing is more or less "what you see is what you get."

If you don't want to waste paper, try Print Preview. It lets you see the results before they are produced so that you can make changes if you need to. You can use Print Preview to double-check that your print settings are the way that you want them before you print.

To print your appointments, perform the following steps.

1. Choose File⇨Print or click on the Print button on the Schedule+ toolbar. With either method, the Print dialog box appears, as shown in Figure 31-18.

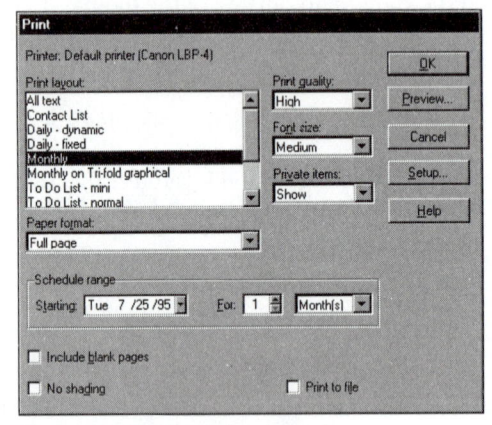

Figure 31-18: The Print dialog box.

2. In the Print layout portion of the dialog box, select the layout that you want to print.

3. Using the Paper format list box, choose the settings that you want for paper size.

4. In the Schedule range box, select the range of dates that you want to include in the printout by first selecting a starting date and then selecting the number of days, weeks, or months to print from that date.

Note: This date range is used only for the To Do list if no view of the To Do list is currently displayed.

5. You can choose from one or more of the following options, as appropriate:
   - Include blank pages — Choose this option for days with no appointments.
   - No shading — This option prevents shading for appointments in graphic layouts.
   - Print to file — Choose this option if you want to print to a file as opposed to the printer.

6. Click on the Preview button in the dialog box if you want to see a preview of the printout.

7. If you need to customize the margins, paper orientation, or printer, click on the Setup button and make the desired changes in the Print Setup dialog box that appears.

8. When done choosing your options, click on the OK button to print the selection.

This procedure will give you a hard copy of your appointments, your to-do list, or your contacts list. This information can prove quite valuable to you when you are away from the office. (Of course, you can also choose to wear much of this information on your wrist, which brings up our next topic.)

Using the Timex Data Link Watch Wizard

Believe it or not, Schedule+ can export its data to a Timex DataLink watch. The Timex DataLink watch is a wristwatch that works with Windows software to store phone numbers, a to-do list, appointments, and multiple alarms. The watch receives data from Windows through an infrared sensor built into the watch. The watch reads data sent off the screen through software that comes with the watch or through Schedule+. With this watch, you can carry much of your appointment data, phone numbers, and to-do list information with you.

To export data to a Timex DataLink watch, follow these steps:

1. From the Schedule+ window, choose File⇨Export⇨Timex Data Link Watch (or click on the Timex Watch Wizard button in the toolbar) to open the first Timex Watch Wizard dialog box, as shown in Figure 31-19.

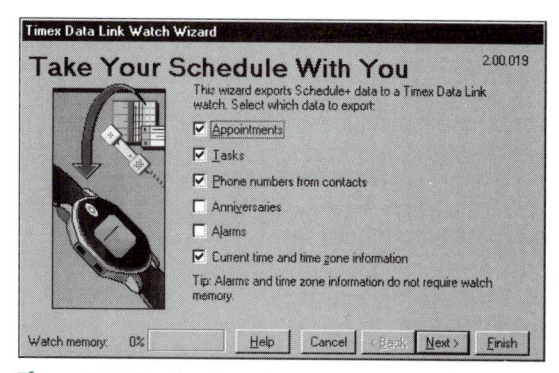

Figure 31-19: The first Timex Watch Wizard dialog box.

2. Turn on the desired options for the data that you want to export. You can choose whether you want to export appointments, tasks, phone numbers from contacts, anniversaries, alarms, or time zone information. After activating your choices, click on the Next button to reveal the second Timex Watch Wizard dialog box, as shown in Figure 31-20.

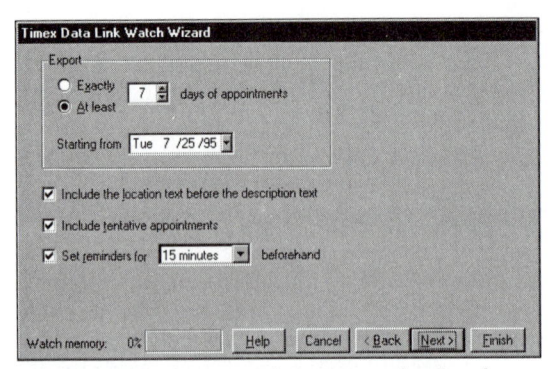

Figure 31-20: The second Timex Watch Wizard dialog box.

3. In the second dialog box, choose how many days of appointments you want to send, whether descriptive text of the appointment should be included, and whether reminder alarms for the appointments should be set. (If you turned off the Appointments option at the first dialog box, you won't see this dialog box.) When you are finished setting the options, click on the Next button to reveal the third Timex Watch Wizard dialog box, as shown in Figure 31-21.

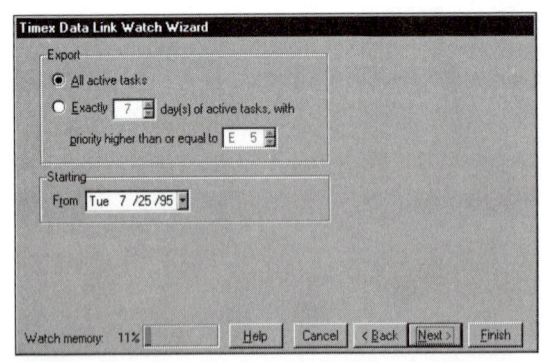

Figure 31-21: The third dialog box for the Timex Watch Wizard.

4. In the third dialog box, choose how many days of tasks to export to the watch and a starting date for the tasks that you want to export. Exported tasks appear in the To Do list of the watch. (If you turned off the Tasks option in the first dialog box, you won't see this dialog box.) When you are finished setting the options, click on the Next button to reveal the fourth Timex Watch Wizard dialog box, as shown in Figure 31-22.

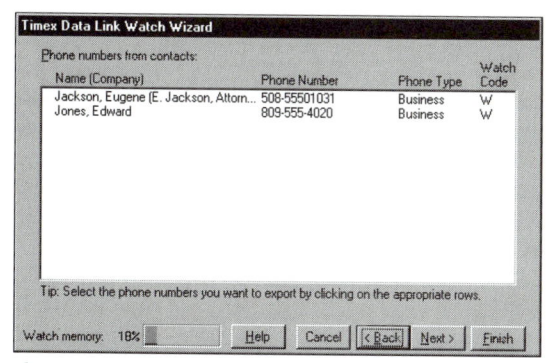

Figure 31-22: The fourth Timex Watch Wizard dialog box.

5. In the fourth dialog box, select the phone numbers that you want to export by clicking on the appropriate rows in the dialog box. If you've used the Timex software supplied with the watch, you should be aware of a difference between the way that software works and the way the Timex Watch Wizard works in Schedule+. The Timex software sends all phone numbers to the watch by default. By comparison, in this dialog box, you must choose the phone numbers that you want to send each time you export. (If you turned off the Phone Numbers option in the first dialog box, you won't see this dialog box.) When you are finished setting the options, click on the Next button to reveal the fifth dialog box for the Timex Watch Wizard, as shown in Figure 31-23.

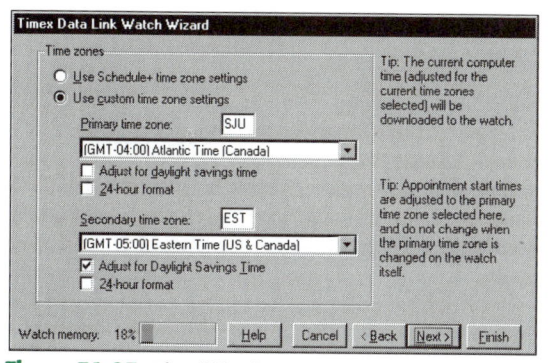

Figure 31-23: The fifth Timex Watch Wizard dialog box.

6. In the fifth dialog box, choose your desired time zone settings. You can use those already used by Schedule+, or you can turn on the Use Custom Time Zone Settings option and then choose your desired time zones from the list boxes shown in the dialog box. When you are finished selecting the options, click on the Next button. A dialog box appears that tells you to put the watch into its Comm Ready Mode.

7. Put the Timex DataLink watch into Comm Mode by pressing the Mode button until *Comm Mode* and then *Comm Ready* appear on the face of the watch.

8. Hold the watch so that it's facing the screen about a foot away and click on the OK button. Schedule+ proceeds to download the data into the watch. When the process is over, you can click on the yes button in the dialog box that appears to return to Schedule+. If for some reason the watch did not successfully receive all of the data (for example, you moved it wildly during the transmission), you can click on No in the dialog box to resend the data.

Summary

This chapter covered Schedule+, an electronic daily organizer, and the use of the Timex DataLink watch. The following topics were covered in relation to these two items:

✦ You can start Schedule+ by opening the Windows 95 Start menu and choosing Programs➪Microsoft Office➪Microsoft Schedule+. Once Schedule+ opens in its window, you can click on any of the tabs visible at the left edge to view your schedule in different ways, or to view the Planner, the To Do list, or the Contacts list.

✦ To make an appointment, click on the desired time in the Daily or Weekly tab (or the desired day in the Monthly tab), and choose Insert➪Appointment, or double-click on a desired time slot in the Daily or Weekly tab. When the Appointment dialog box opens, you can fill in the needed data for the appointment.

✦ To add to the To Do list, click on the To Do tab to display the list, then click in the first blank row and type the entry, or choose Insert➪Task and enter the desired information in the dialog box which appears.

✦ To add to the Contacts list, click on the Contacts tab. Then, use the Insert New Contact button on the toolbar to add a new contact. Or, select an existing contact that you want to edit, and click on the Edit button on the toolbar.

✦ To plan a meeting, click on the Meeting Wizard button in the toolbar. Then follow the instructions presented by the wizard dialog boxes.

✦ To print any of the information stored in Schedule+, choose File➪Print, or click on the Print button in the toolbar. In the Print dialog box which opens, select the desired options, then click on OK.

The next chapter will cover the Binder, a useful utility that you can use to organize a group of different Microsoft Office documents into a single project.

✦   ✦   ✦

Using the Binder

CHAPTER 32

♦ ♦ ♦ ♦

In This Chapter

Starting the Binder

Adding existing documents to the Binder

Adding new documents to the Binder

Moving and copying documents within the Binder

Deleting documents within the Binder

Printing the entire Binder

Printing documents within the Binder

♦ ♦ ♦ ♦

The Binder is a utility provided with Microsoft Office that you can use to organize different types of documents into a single container. The Binder gives you easy access to all of your documents for editing or printing.

What Is the Binder?

The Binder lets you combine documents that are created with Microsoft Office applications. You combine documents into units that are also called *binders*; and you can drag Word, Excel, and PowerPoint documents into the binder. You can also create new documents from within the binder. When you've stored documents in a binder, you can edit and print them as though you were working with a single file. You can create as many binders as you want: each binder is saved under its own filename.

Note Don't be confused by Binder and binder. When we write uppercase-B *Binder*, we mean the program. When we write lowercase-b *binder*, we mean one of the document containers that the Binder program creates.

You can store any combination of Microsoft Office documents inside a binder. For example, a single binder may contain two Word documents, three Excel workbooks, and a PowerPoint presentation. Figure 32-1 shows an example of a binder document that contains documents from Word, Excel, and PowerPoint.

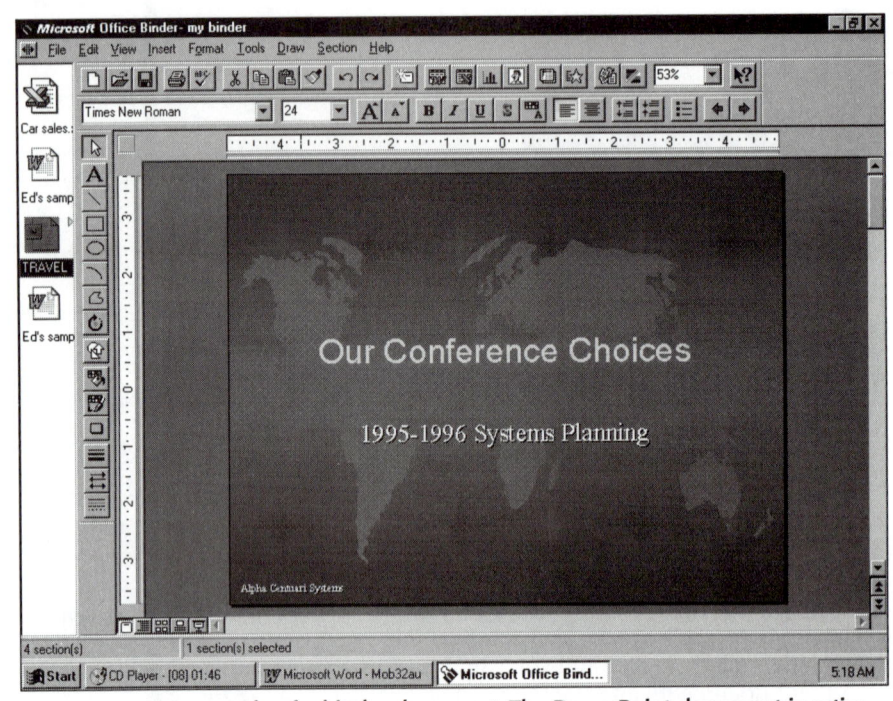

Figure 32-1: An example of a binder document. The PowerPoint document is active.

The Binder gives you a central location where you can get quick access to all the documents that you have created within Office without having to launch each of the applications separately. In Binder, all you do is click on an icon representing a document, and its source application launches automatically. Binder is also quite useful for printing a project composed of different types of Microsoft Office documents; you can print the entire contents of the project with a single command.

Using the Binder

You can start the Binder from the Windows 95 menus or from the Microsoft Office Manager toolbar. If you use the menus, choose the Programs command from the Start menu. From the first submenu, choose Microsoft Office and from the next submenu, choose Microsoft Binder. Or if the Office Shortcut Bar is visible, just click on the Binder button in the toolbar. With either method, a blank binder page appears, like the one shown in Figure 32-2.

Figure 32-2: A blank binder page.

Adding existing documents to a binder

You can add existing documents to a binder in either of two ways. You can use drag-and-drop, or you can choose the Add from File command from the Binder's Section menu. To use the drag-and-drop technique, open My Computer or Explorer under Windows 95 and find the desired document. Then click and drag the document into the left pane of the Binder window.

To add an existing document by using the menus, choose Section➪Add from File. In the Add from File dialog box that appears (Figure 32-3), click on the drive and folder that contain the file that you want to add. Then click on the desired file to select it and click on the OK button.

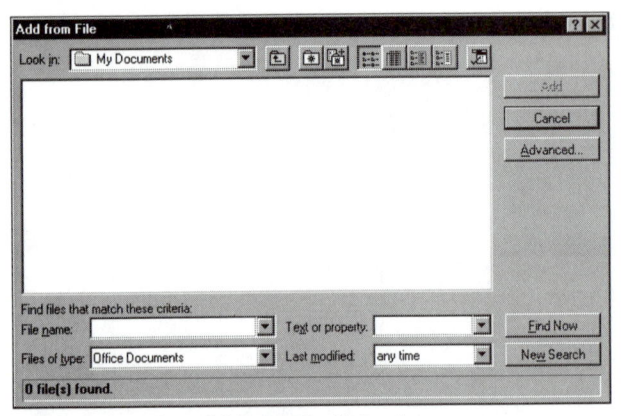

Figure 32-3: The Add from File dialog box.

Adding new documents to a binder

To add a new document to a binder, choose Section➪Add. In the Add Section dialog box that appears (Figure 32-4), click on the type of document that you want to add, then click OK.

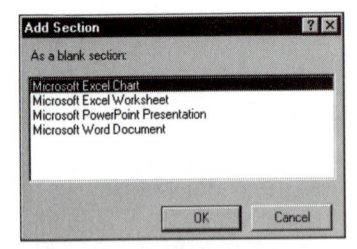

Figure 32-4: The Add Section dialog box.

A new, blank document of the chosen type appears in the binder, similar to the example shown in Figure 32-5. In this example, a new PowerPoint document has been added to the binder. You can click on the document's icon at the left side of the binder to change to the menus of the source application so that you can edit the document as desired.

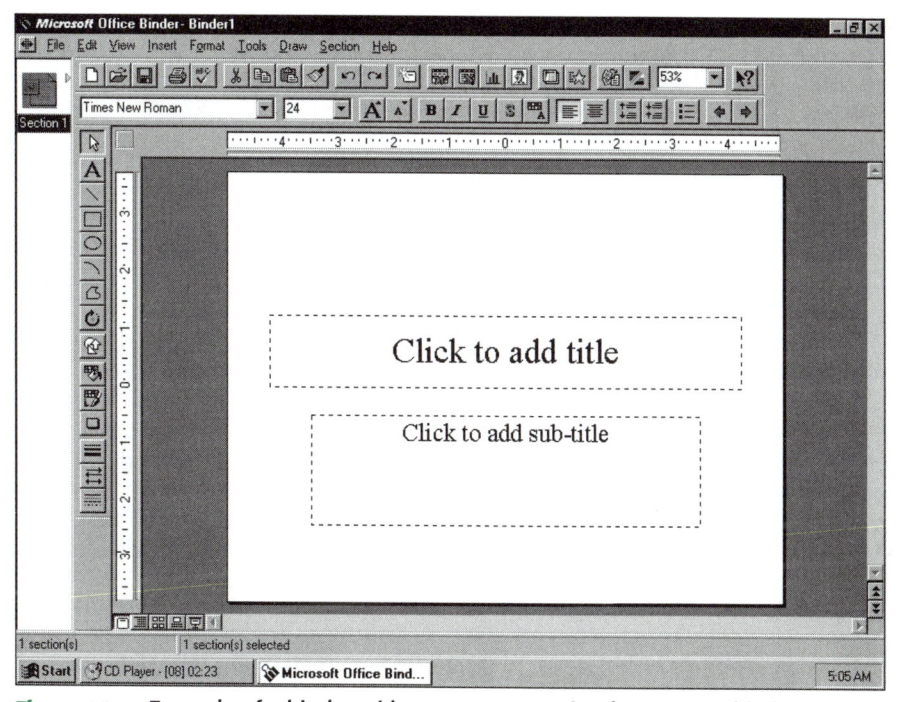

Figure 32-5: Example of a binder with a new PowerPoint document added.

Saving a binder

To save a binder, choose File⇨Save Binder. If you're saving the binder for the first time, you'll be prompted for a filename for the binder. Enter a filename in the Save Binder As dialog box (Figure 32-6) and click on the Save button.

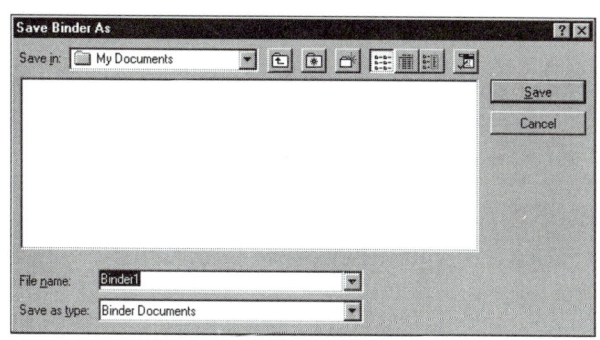

Figure 32-6: The Save Binder As dialog box.

To save a binder under a new name, choose File⇨Save Binder As. In the Save Binder As dialog box that appears, enter the desired filename for the binder and click on the Save button.

Opening an existing binder

To open an existing binder, choose File⇨Open Binder. In the Look In list box inside the Open Binder dialog box, click on the drive and folder that contain the desired binder and double-click on the desired binder name to open the binder.

Working with Documents in the Binder

After you've added a document to a binder, you can use the binder as a central point for editing your documents. In the column at the far left side of the Binder window, you can see icons representing the documents that you've added to the binder. After you click on any of the icons, the appropriate document appears in the binder window. You can then use the techniques appropriate to the application to edit the document as desired.

Moving and copying documents within a binder

After you've added documents to a binder, you can reorganize the binder's contents by moving around the documents as needed. Click and drag the icons representing your documents in the left pane of the Binder window to move them to the desired location. Note that you can also drag documents between the left pane of the Binder window and windows of Explorer or My Computer. (If the Binder doesn't have separate left and right panes, click on the button to the left of the File menu.)

To make a copy of an existing document, right-click on the icon of the document, hold down the mouse button, and drag the document to where you want the copy to appear. From the shortcut menu that appears, choose the Copy Here option.

Renaming documents

To rename a document within the binder, double-click on the name of the desired document in the left pane of the Binder window. When you do so, the insertion pointer appears within the name. You can then edit the name and then press Enter to finish renaming the document.

Deleting documents

To delete a document from a binder, right-click on the desired document in the left pane of the Binder window. From the shortcut menu that appears, choose Delete.

Printing binder documents

You can print the entire contents of a binder, you can print selected documents, or you can print a single document. To print the entire contents of a binder, choose File⇨Print Binder to open the Print Binder dialog box, as shown in Figure 32-7. In the Print What area of the dialog box, choose the All Sections option. Make any desired changes to the Number of Copies option and turn on the Collate option, if you want. Then click on the OK button to begin printing.

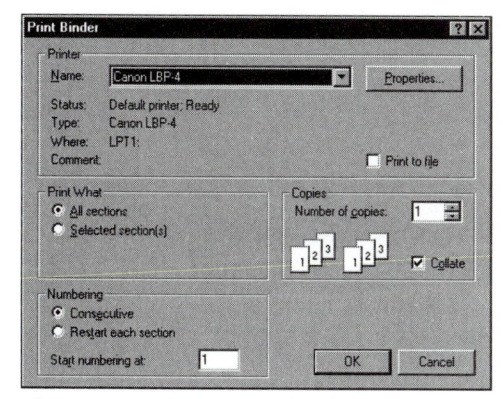

Figure 32-7: The Print Binder dialog box.

To print multiple documents in a binder, first select the desired documents in the left pane of the Binder window by holding down Ctrl as you click on each document that you want to print. Then choose File⇨Print Binder. In the Print Binder dialog box, turn on the Selected Section(s) option and then click on the OK button.

To print a single document, first select the desired document in the left pane of the Binder window. Then choose Section⇨Print. In the Print dialog box, specify the desired range of pages, make any changes to the Number of Copies option, and turn on the Collate option, if desired. Then click on the OK button to begin printing.

Summary

This chapter has detailed the use of the Binder. If you work with projects that use different types of Office documents, you'll find the Binder to be a useful organizational tool. The chapter has detailed the following points:

- Using the Binder, you can combine documents that you created in different applications of Microsoft Office into a single unit.
- To start the Binder, click on the Binder button in the Microsoft Office toolbar. Alternatively, choose the Programs command from the Start menu. From the first submenu, choose Microsoft Office and from the next submenu, choose Microsoft Binder.
- You can add existing documents to a binder by dragging them from My Computer or from Explorer or by choosing Section➪Add from File.
- You can create new documents in a binder with Section➪Add.
- You can move documents in a binder to different locations, and you can copy, rename, or delete documents in a binder.
- You can print all of a binder's contents or just selected documents in a binder by using File➪Print Binder.
- You can print a single document in a binder by using Section➪Print.

In the next chapter, you'll learn how you can use Object Linking and Embedding (OLE) to share information between applications.

Where to go next...

- The Binder is a tool that, by nature, helps you manage large and complex projects in Office. Projects of this nature are often made up of complex documents (meaning binder documents that contain documents from different Office applications), and of compound documents (or documents that make use of OLE objects). See Chapter 33 for more information.
- If you need to create complex documents and you are unfamiliar with any of the major Office applications, see Appendix B for an introduction to Word, Appendix C for basic Excel information, and Appendix D to get you started in PowerPoint.

♦ ♦ ♦

Sharing Data between Applications with OLE

CHAPTER 33

♦ ♦ ♦ ♦

In This Chapter

Defining OLE

Linking versus embedding

Linking with Paste Special

Linking with Insert Object

Embedding with Paste Special

Embedding with Insert Object

Editing embedded objects

♦ ♦ ♦ ♦

Working Together

This chapter explains *object linking and embedding* (OLE) and shows how you can put OLE to work with the different applications of Microsoft Office and with other Windows applications that support OLE.

Defining OLE

If you've ever pasted a picture from Windows Paint into a Word document, if you've ever inserted charts into a Word document or into a PowerPoint presentation, or if you've ever used sound or video with any of the Office applications, you've used OLE. OLE is a *protocol* (an established set of communications rules) under Windows. This protocol enables objects that are created by one Windows application to be stored by means of *linking* or *embedding* in the documents of another Windows application.

Figure 33-1 shows an example of OLE at work. In the figure, a Word document contains an Excel worksheet and a Windows Paint drawing. Both items have been inserted into the document as OLE objects. In OLE terminology, *objects* are selections of data that you insert into your documents. An object may be a part of a Word document, an organizational chart from PowerPoint, a portion of an Excel worksheet, Windows data from another program like CorelDRAW! or Microsoft Visual FoxPro, or a sound or video clip.

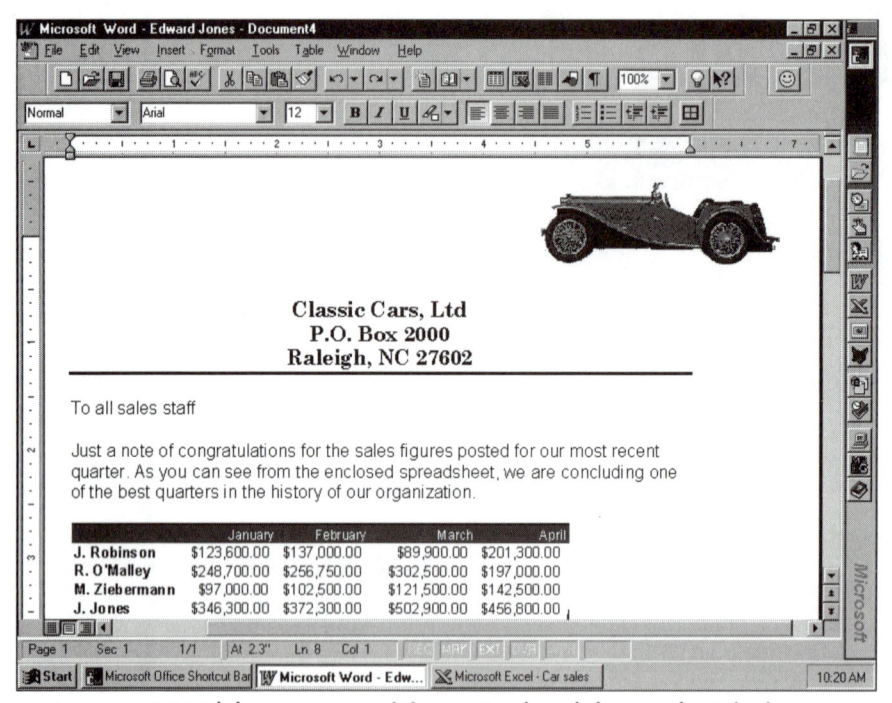

Figure 33-1: A Word document containing an Excel worksheet and a Paint image.

The only common requirement for using OLE is that the Windows software that you are using must support it. All of the Office applications support OLE. Windows applications can be OLE servers, OLE clients, or both.

- Some Windows packages (including Windows Paint) are OLE *servers* (also called *server applications*). An OLE server can provide data to other Windows software, but it can't accept data from other packages.

- Some Windows packages are OLE *clients* (also called *client applications*). An OLE client can accept OLE data from other Windows software, but it cannot supply OLE data to other software. When you work with OLE, the client application is the application where you are inserting the OLE data, and the server application is the application that is providing the data.

- Some Windows packages (including all that are provided with Microsoft Office) can act as both OLE clients and as OLE servers.

If you work with OLE, you'll also hear the terms *source document, destination document,* and *compound document.*

- Compound documents contain the OLE objects that you insert. For example, a Word document that contains an embedded Excel worksheet is a compound document. And a PowerPoint presentation that contains rows of data inserted from an Access table is a compound document.

- ◆ A source document is the document that contains the object that you want to link or embed in the document that you are working on.

- ◆ The destination document is the document where you are inserting your OLE objects.

You may also hear the term *OLE2*, which refers to Microsoft's newer standard for object linking and embedding. Both OLE and OLE2 let you move data among applications. Windows applications that support OLE2 make using OLE easier by allowing you to work with OLE data while remaining inside the current application. For example, with previous versions of Word and Excel that supported OLE, if you put an Excel worksheet inside a Word document as an OLE object and then double-clicked in the worksheet to change the worksheet data, a copy of Excel was automatically loaded, and you made the desired changes within Excel. With OLE2, if you double-click an Excel worksheet that's been inserted into a Word document, you remain in Word for Windows, but the menu choices and toolbar options change to reflect the choices appropriate to Excel.

You may have noticed this OLE2 behavior if you ever created a graph in Access, Word, or PowerPoint. If you double-click the graph, the toolbars and menu options change to those of Microsoft Graph, while you remain in the program you were working in. Figure 33-2 shows a graph that's active in a Word document with the toolbar and the menu options for Microsoft Graph visible. You don't do anything to make this change take place — it happens automatically, thanks to OLE2.

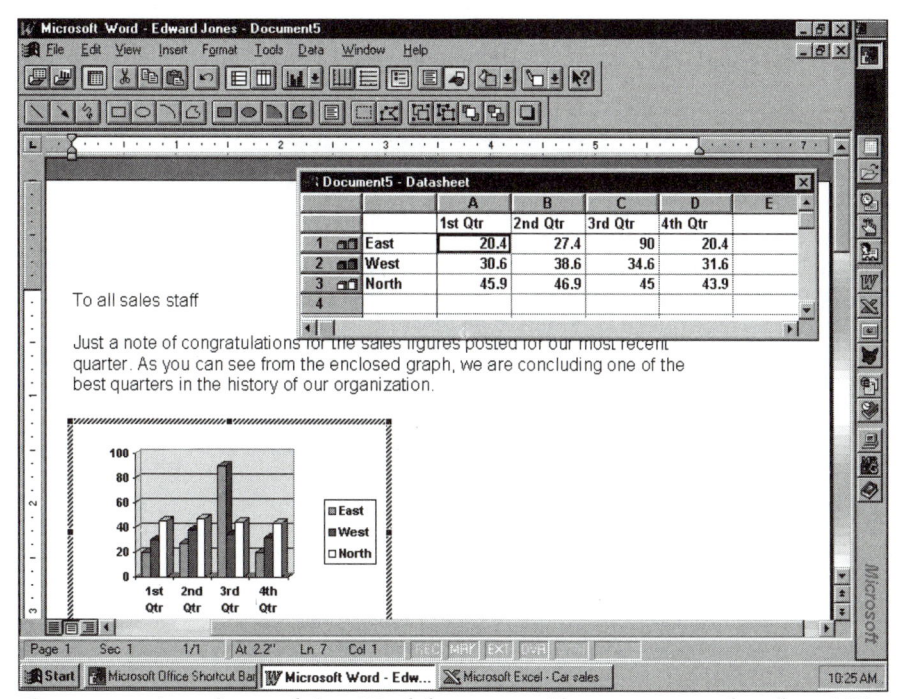

Figure 33-2: An active graph in a Word document with new menu and toolbar visible.

Previous versions of Windows (versions 3.11, 3.1, and 3.0) usually support OLE, but they rarely make use of OLE2. Windows applications written for Windows 95 generally support OLE2. (Note that Windows Paint, supplied with Windows 95, is an exception because it supports OLE, but not OLE2.)

Linking Versus Embedding

Before you get deeply involved with using OLE, you should be familiar with the differences between linking and embedding. The two are often confused by new users of OLE, and they don't mean the same thing. Each offers advantages and disadvantages over the other. As their very names imply, one method involves establishing a *link* to the existing data, while the other involves *embedding* or inserting a copy of the existing data that maintains a link to the source application.

Linking

When you insert an OLE object in a document that is *linked* to existing data in another Windows application, the data remains stored elsewhere, and the current document (where you put the linked object) will be automatically updated whenever you make any changes to the data in the source document. For example, if you create and save a drawing in Windows Paint, and you later add it as a linked object in a Word for Windows document, the drawing exists only in the folder where you originally saved it by using Windows Paint. If you open the document containing the drawing in Word and double-click on the drawing, the file that opens through Windows Paint's use of OLE is the original file, and any changes that you make to that drawing will be saved to the original file and reflected in the Word document.

Embedding

With embedding, on the other hand, an OLE object that you add to the document in your current application becomes a part of that document; it is, in effect, *embedded* within the document. The most important thing to realize about embedding compared to linking is that with embedding, you can't expect changes made in the source document to appear in the embedded copy because they won't. Again, take Word for Windows as an example. If you embed an existing Excel worksheet into a Word document, the Excel worksheet becomes a part of the Word document. There is no link of any sort between the worksheet in the Word document and any worksheet it may have been based on back in Excel. So if you double-click on the embedded worksheet while you are in the Word document and then make changes to the worksheet, those changes are stored with the Word document, but they don't appear in any original Excel worksheet.

When to use linking and when to use embedding

Linking is the only method to use when, for any reason, you need to maintain a link to the original data, and you want the OLE object in the destination document automatically updated when changes are made to the data in the source document. A good example of linking may be a newsletter produced in Word that contains an Excel worksheet showing monthly sales. You would want the worksheet to update each month based on the new sales, so you would add the worksheet as a linked object. Linking also takes up considerably less disk space than embedding because your document with the link doesn't have to store a complete copy of the data. This point is particularly important with sound or video, which consumes large amounts of disk space.

Embedding is generally advantageous when it's not important to keep the destination data updated based on the source document, and you need *portability* (the capability to move your documents from PC to PC). Because linking depends on your software knowing where to find the source of the data, to move documents containing linked OLE objects to other PCs can be very troublesome because the other PCs probably don't have the same objects stored in the same folders.

Why can't I just use the Copy and Paste commands to add OLE objects?

If you've tried using the Copy and Paste commands from the Edit menu to move data from one Windows application to another, you may have noticed that the data generally is *not* automatically updated if you go back and change the source data. (Some older Windows applications will insert "live" data with these commands, but they usually do so by using an older Windows technology known as DDE, for Dynamic Data Exchange.)

Using the Copy and Paste commands in Windows applications generally results in the transfer of "static" data that is converted into the format of the destination document.

For example, if you select a range in Excel and choose the Copy command, and then you switch to Word and choose the Paste command, what you get is a Word table containing a copy of the Excel data, because a Word table is how Word best understands the layout of the incoming data. To be assured of getting an OLE object of the type that you want, don't use the regular Paste command to insert the data in the destination document. Use the Paste Special command from the Edit menu or the Object command from the Insert menu.

Establishing Links in Your Documents

After you decide to use links to include data (as opposed to embedding data), you can proceed in either of two ways: you can use the Edit➪Paste Special command, or you can use the Insert➪Object command. And after you've established a link, you can change its update settings, and you can break and later restore the link.

Linking with the Paste Special command

When you need to add a selection of data (as opposed to an entire file), and you want to have it automatically updated when the source data changes, you want to use linking with the Paste Special command. Follow these steps to create a link with the Paste Special command:

1. Start the server application and open (or create) the document that will provide the data to which you want to establish the link. If you create a new document, you need to save it before you can link to the data from the other application.

2. Select the object that you want to place in the other application's document.

3. Choose Edit➪Copy.

4. Start the other application, if it isn't already running.

5. Open the destination document (the document where you want to insert the OLE link).

6. Place the cursor where the linked object should appear.

7. Choose Edit➪Paste Special to open the Paste Special dialog box, as shown in Figure 33-3. In the As list box, you'll see the different data formats that you can use to paste the data.

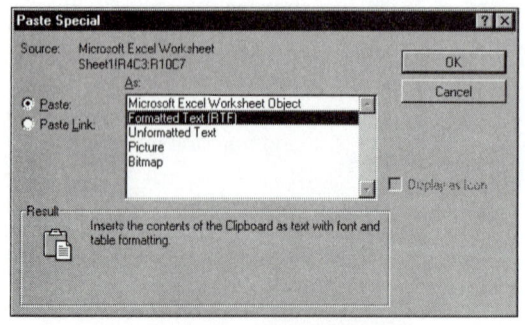

Figure 33-3: The Paste Special dialog box.

8. Choose the desired format. (Typically, you'll want to use a choice that is an object of some type. The types will vary, depending on what software packages are installed on your system).

> ### I don't see any Paste Special command!
>
> Before trying to establish any OLE links, note that the menu options used by some Windows applications may differ from those that are described in this chapter. The steps outlined in this chapter will work for all the Microsoft Office applications, but some other Windows applications (especially older ones) may use a Paste Links command rather than a Paste Special command. If you can't find a Paste Links command or a Paste Special command anywhere on the menus, the Windows application that you are using probably doesn't support OLE. If in doubt, check the documentation or the online help for the package that you are using to see how (and if) you can use OLE.

9. Turn on the Paste Link option in the dialog box.

10. Click on the OK button to paste the linked object into your document. The object appears at the cursor location, and any changes you later make to the data in the source document are automatically reflected in the destination document.

Linking with the Object command

When you want to add an entire file (as opposed to just a selection of data), and you want to keep the destination document updated from any changes in the source document, you can use Insert⇨Object. Follow these steps to create an OLE link by using the Object command:

1. Start the client application (if it isn't already running) and create or open the destination document.

2. Place the cursor where the inserted object should appear.

3. Choose Insert⇨Object to open the Object dialog box, as shown in Figure 33-4.

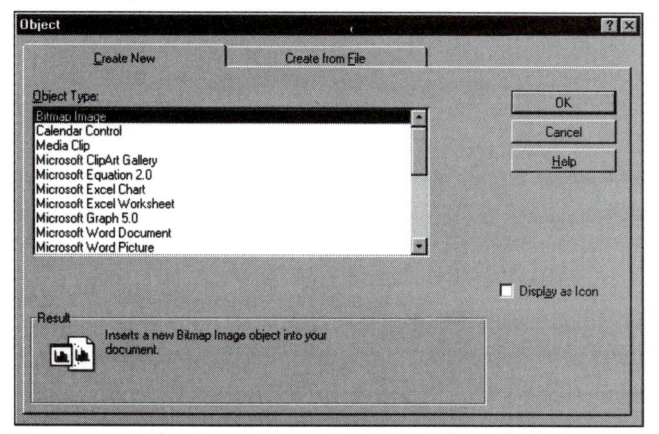

Figure 33-4: The Create New tab of the Object dialog box.

4. Click on the Create From File tab. When you do so, you see the options shown in Figure 33-5.

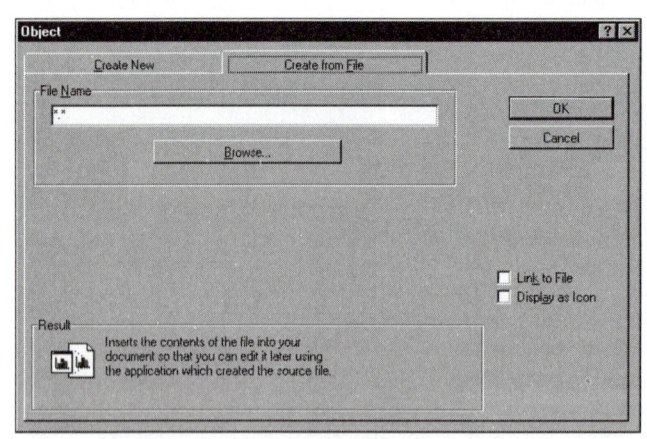

Figure 33-5: The Create from File tab of the Object dialog box.

5. Click on the Browse button to display the Browse dialog box (see Figure 33-6).

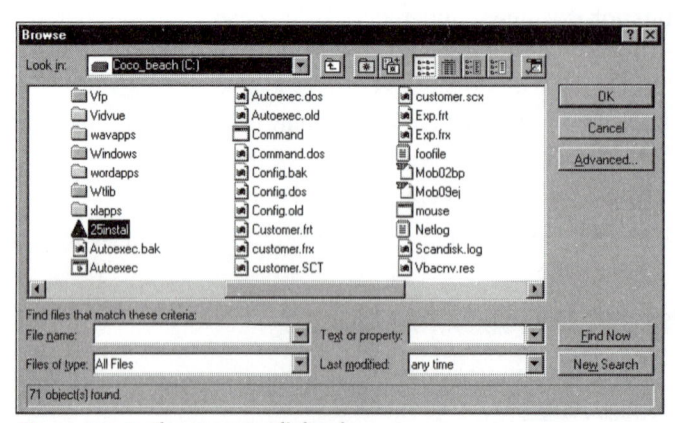

Figure 33-6: The Browse dialog box.

6. Use the Look In list box and click on the Up One Level button to navigate to the folder that contains the file to which you want to link. Then select the file in the File Name list box and click on the OK button to close the Browse dialog box.

7. Turn on the Link to File option in the Create from File tab of the Object dialog box.

8. Click on the OK button to close the dialog box and to insert the linked file into the destination document.

Changing a link's update settings

By default, linked OLE objects that you insert in the destination document are automatically updated when you make changes to the data in the source document. You can change this situation so that the data is updated only upon your command. Use the following steps to change the update settings for the links to your OLE object:

1. Open the destination document that contains the OLE object whose link you want to change.

2. Choose Edit⇨Links. (In some Windows applications, this choice is called Link Options.) The Links dialog box appears, as shown in Figure 33-7. In the Source File list box, you see the name for all linked objects in the document along with the path of the source data.

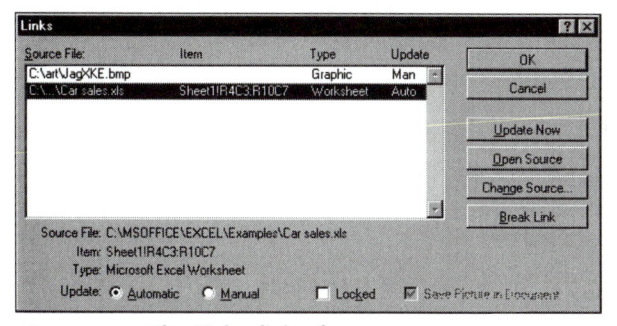

Figure 33-7: The Links dialog box.

3. Select the link that you want to update.
4. Change the Update setting to Manual.
5. To update the link with the latest data from the source document, click on the Update Now button.
6. Click on the OK button to close the dialog box.
7. Save the document in the usual manner.

After you have changed a link's update status from Automatic to Manual, you will need to open the Links dialog box (by choosing the Links command from the Edit menu) and click on the Update Now button every time that you want to update the OLE object with the latest data.

Breaking and restoring links

At times, you may want to break a link intentionally between an OLE object and the source data. For example, when you are sure that you will never need updates in the linked object, you can break the link so that the data becomes a "static" or unchanging copy of the original data. You can break an existing link by performing the following steps:

1. Open the destination document that contains the OLE object whose link you want to change.
2. Choose Edit⇨Links. (In some Windows applications, this choice is called Link Options.) The Links dialog box appears.
3. Select the link that you want to break.
4. Click on the Break Link button. (In some Windows applications, this button may be named Delete Link.) In the confirmation dialog box that appears, click on the Yes or the OK button to break the link.

If you accidentally break a link (which usually happens when you move a document containing a linked object to another PC), you can re-create the broken link by telling Windows where it can find the source of the data. You perform the following steps to recreate a link that has been broken:

1. Open the destination document that contains the OLE object whose link is broken.
2. Choose Edit⇨Links. (In some Windows applications, this choice is called Link Options.) The Links dialog box appears.
3. In the dialog box, select the broken link.
4. Click on the Change Source button to open the Change Source dialog box, as shown in Figure 33-8.

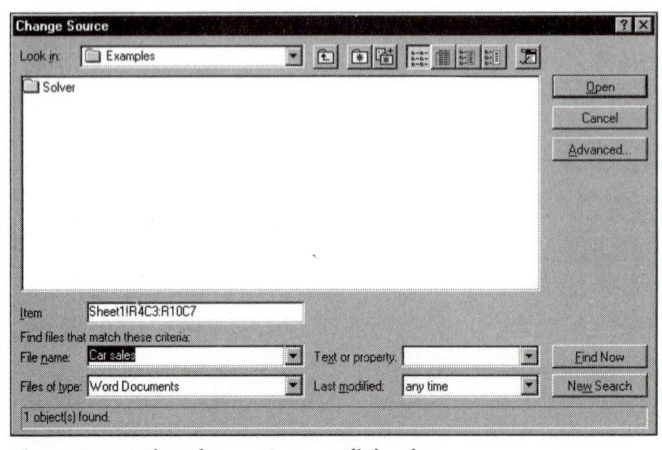

Figure 33-8: The Change Source dialog box.

5. Use the Look In list box and click on the Up One Level button to navigate to the folder that contains the file to which you want to reestablish the link. Then select the file in the File Name list box.

6. Click on the OK button to close the Links dialog box and to re-create the link to the destination document.

Embedding Objects in Your Documents

When you decide to embed OLE data (as opposed to establishing links to it), you can use the Edit⇨Paste Special command (with the Paste Link option turned off), or you can use the Insert⇨Object command to embed the data.

Embedding with the Paste Special command

You want to use embedding rather than linking when you don't need a connection to the source data, but you want to be able to edit the inserted object. When you want to embed a selection of data (as opposed to an entire file), you use the Paste Special command in most Windows applications, *but leave the Paste Link option turned off*. Follow these steps to embed data by using the Paste Special command:

1. Start the server application and open (or create) the document that will provide the data that you want to embed in the destination document.

2. Select the object that you want to place in the other application's document.

3. Choose Edit⇨Copy.

4. Start the other application, if it isn't already running.

5. Open the destination document (the document where you want to embed the data).

6. Place the cursor where the embedded object should appear.

7. Choose Edit⇨Paste Special to open the Paste Special dialog box. In the As list box, you'll see the different data formats that you can use to paste the data.

8. Choose the desired format (typically, you'll want to use a choice that is an object of some type). The types will vary, depending on what software packages are installed on your system.

9. If there is a Paste Link option in the dialog box, make sure that it is turned off.

10. Click on the OK button to embed the object in your document. The object appears at the cursor location. You can later edit the object by double-clicking to bring up the original application (if it supports OLE) or to change to the toolbars and menus of the application (if it supports OLE2).

Embedding with the Object command

When you want to embed an entire file (as opposed to just a selection of data), or if you haven't yet created the object that you want to embed, you can use Insert➪Object to embed an object in your destination document. Follow these steps to embed an object by using the Object command:

1. Start the client application (if it isn't already running) and create or open the destination document.
2. Place the cursor where the inserted object should appear.
3. Choose Insert➪Object to open the Object dialog box.
4. If you are embedding an object that you haven't yet created, click on the Create New tab, choose the desired object type in the list box, and click on the OK button. (If you want to create the object based on an existing file, skip to Step 8.)
5. After you've clicked on the OK button in the dialog box, a window appears in your destination document that contains a new version of the desired object, and (depending on what software you are using) the other program is launched or the menus and toolbars change to reflect the appropriate choices of the other program. You can now use the usual techniques of the other program to create the desired object.
6. When you are finished creating the object, click on any part of the destination document's window to change back to the destination application. (If you are using a very old Windows application, you may have to choose File➪Save Changes and then choose File➪Exit to get back to the destination application.)
7. Save the destination document.
8. If you are embedding an object based on an existing file, click on the Create from File tab in the Object dialog box.
9. Click on the Browse button to open the Browse dialog box.
10. Use the Look In list box and click on the Up One Level button to navigate to the folder that contains the file that you want to embed. Then select the file in the File Name list box and click on the OK button to close the Browse dialog box.
11. Turn off the Link to File option in the Object dialog box.
12. Click on the OK button to close the dialog box and to embed the file as an OLE object into the destination document.

> ### Why can't I find the object I want in the Object dialog box?
>
> In a few (fortunately rare) cases, you won't be able to find the type of object that you want to insert in the list box in the Object dialog box. This missing object type is not a sign that you've done something wrong (unless you're the type to go around randomly deleting important files that Windows needs.) The missing object type is a sign that the *Registry*, a bit of hocus-pocus that Windows 95 uses, has somehow become incomplete or corrupted.
>
> Each time that you install software that supports OLE, that software's own installation routine updates the Registry. When you choose Insert➪Object in any Windows program, the list of possible object types in the Object dialog box is based on what Windows knows from the registry database. If you have installed a program that you know supports OLE, and the program doesn't appear as a valid type in the dialog box, the only easy way to correct the problem is to re-install the program so that the registry database is updated. (From a technical standpoint, there are *harder* ways to fix an incorrect Registry, but they get so into the realm of the technical that we're not about to delve into them here.)
>
> Brian Livingston's *Windows 95 SECRETS* (IDG Books, 1995) tells you all about the Registry.

Editing embedded OLE objects

To edit embedded OLE objects, just double-click on the object. Depending on whether the applications that you are using support OLE or OLE2, one of two things will happen:

- ✦ If you're using OLE2, the object will become active in a window, and the menus and toolbars will change to reflect choices available in the source application.

- ✦ If you're using OLE, a copy of the source application will be launched containing the object.

In either case, you can make the desired changes to the object. When you are finished editing the object, click on any part of the destination document's window to change back to the destination application. (If you are using an older Windows application, choose File➪Save Changes and then choose File➪Exit to get back to the destination application.)

If your OLE object is a link to existing data in another document, you can also launch the source application, open the document containing the data, and edit the document from within the source application. When you save the changes, however, the data will be automatically updated in the destination document.

Converting file formats of embedded objects

One problem occasionally arises when you move documents containing embedded objects from PC to PC: what if you want to edit the embedded object, but you don't have the source application installed on your PC? Suppose that a co-worker or a client sends you a disk with a Word document that contains an embedded spreadsheet created in Novell's Quattro Pro for Windows. You want to edit the spreadsheet data, but you don't have Quattro Pro for Windows; instead, you're using Excel as your preferred spreadsheet. With all the Microsoft Office applications, you can use a Convert option that is available through the Edit menu to convert the embedded object to a format that your Microsoft Office application can work with.

Follow these steps to convert an embedded object to another file format:

1. Open the document that contains the embedded object and select the object.

2. From the Edit menu, choose the last command shown on the menu. (The name of this command will vary, depending on what type of object you've selected.)

3. From the submenu that appears, choose Convert to open the Convert dialog box, as shown in Figure 33-9.

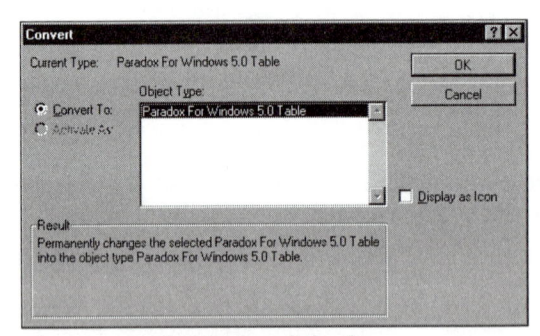

Figure 33-9: The Convert dialog box.

4. Turn on the Convert To option in the dialog box. (The other option, Activate As, enables you to activate temporarily an object that uses a different file format.)

5. In the Object Type list box, choose the type of file format to which you want to convert the object.

6. Click on the OK button to perform the conversion. After you've converted the object, you can double-click on it in the document to edit it.

Adding Sound and Video to Office Documents

You can insert sound and video clips into the various documents that you create in the different Microsoft Office applications by using Insert⇨Object, just like you do to insert other types of OLE objects. If your machine doesn't have Windows sound or video drivers already installed, you won't be able to use sound or video on your system. Sound drivers are usually installed when you add a sound card to your system, and video drivers are usually installed by programs that use video, such as many of the CD-ROM encyclopedias on the market.

To add sound or video to a document, start the destination application, open the destination document, and place the cursor where the sound clip or video clip should appear. Then choose Edit⇨Object. In the Object dialog box, choose Video Clip or Wave Sound if you want to add the clip by using the toolbar and menu options of Windows Media Player. Or you can click on the Create from File tab in the Object dialog box if you want to insert the object based on an existing sound (.WAV) or video (.AVI) file. If you choose the Create from File tab, you can enter the filename in the text box or you can click on the Browse button to open a Browse dialog box, where you can find the desired sound or video file. Then you click on the OK button to insert the sound or video.

You can play the sound or video by selecting the object, choosing the last menu option on the Edit menu, and then choosing Play from the submenu that appears.

Creating an OLE Example

The best way to get an idea of the usefulness of OLE is to try creating and working with compound documents. Assuming that you have at least the Word and Excel components of Microsoft Office installed on your system, you can duplicate the following example to demonstrate how you can use OLE to add an Excel worksheet to a Word for Windows document.

Working Together

To create an OLE link in an example, follow these steps:

1. Start both Word and Excel in the usual manner.
2. In Word, open any document containing two or more paragraphs of text.
3. Switch to Excel (click its icon in the taskbar or use Alt+Tab to switch to it) and open an existing worksheet containing data.
4. Select a range of the worksheet that you want to insert into the Word document (click and drag from the upper-left corner to the lower-right corner of the desired range). Then choose Edit⇨Copy.

5. Switch back to Word (with the taskbar or Alt+Tab) and place the insertion point on a blank line between two existing paragraphs.

6. Choose Edit⇨Paste Special.

7. In the Paste Special dialog box, click on Excel Worksheet Object to select it.

8. Turn on the Paste Link option and then click on the OK button.

In a moment, the worksheet appears in the Word document. It should look something like the example shown in Figure 33-10.

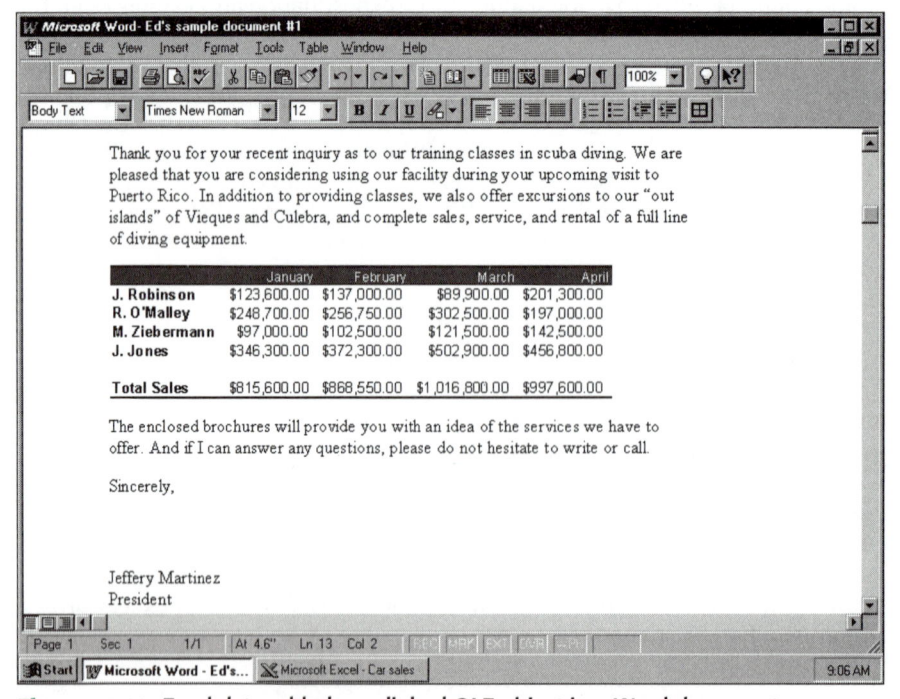

Figure 33-10: Excel data added as a linked OLE object in a Word document.

You can try switching back to Excel and changing the worksheet data in the range that you originally selected. When you switch back to Word, you will see that the Excel data in the Word document changes accordingly.

Summary

This chapter has covered the use of object linking and embedding, and it has provided details concerning how you can put OLE to work with the different applications of Microsoft Office and with other Windows applications. The chapter covered the following points:

- Linking involves inserting an OLE object in a destination document that maintains a link to the source data.

- Embedding involves inserting an OLE object that does not maintain a link to any source data, but it exists independently in the destination document.

- In most Windows applications, you can use the Paste Special command to insert OLE objects containing portions of data from other Windows applications.

- In most Windows applications, you can use Insert⇨Object to insert OLE objects as entire files or to add new OLE objects to a destination document.

- You can edit OLE objects by double-clicking on the object in the destination document.

- You can change the update settings for linked objects, and you can break and restore links to objects by using Edit⇨Links.

Where to go next...

Much OLE work is visual in nature: Often, you're adding Excel graphics to a Word document, or perhaps you are putting Word or Excel data into a PowerPoint presentation.

- For thoughts on integrating visual elements into a Word document, see Chapter 10.

- If you're working in Excel, Chapter 16 gives useful tips on working visual elements into Excel worksheets.

- You can also add Excel worksheets and Word tables to PowerPoint presentations; Chapter 26 has the details.

✦ ✦ ✦

Appendixes

✦ ✦ ✦ ✦

In This Part

Appendix A
Installing Office

Appendix B
Word Basics

Appendix C
Excel Basics

Appendix D
PowerPoint Basics

Appendix E
On the CD-ROM

✦ ✦ ✦ ✦

Installing Microsoft Office

APPENDIX A

◆ ◆ ◆ ◆

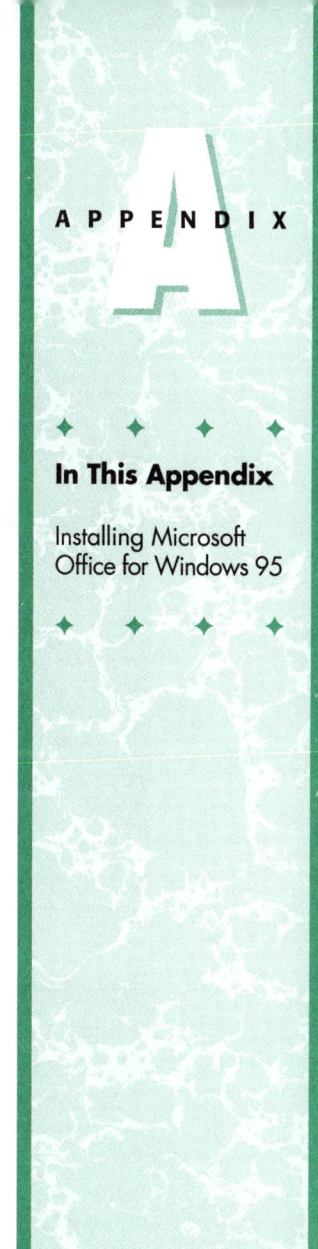

In This Appendix

Installing Microsoft Office for Windows 95

◆ ◆ ◆ ◆

Microsoft Office 95 comes either in the form of a CD-ROM or as a (rather large) collection of floppy disks. As far as hardware requirements are concerned, any system that will run Windows 95 will run Microsoft Office 95.

Beginning the Installation

You can perform the following steps to install Microsoft Office 95 on your hard disk:

1. Put the Office CD-ROM into the CD-ROM drive and close the door. Windows 95 starts the installer.

2. Select Install Microsoft Office from the window that appears. A welcome screen appears, as shown in Figure A-1. Click Continue to proceed.

3. The Name and Organization Information dialog box (Figure A-2) appears next. It asks for your name and the name of your organization. Enter the data and then click on the OK button. You will then see another screen asking you to confirm your name and organization name; again, click OK to proceed.

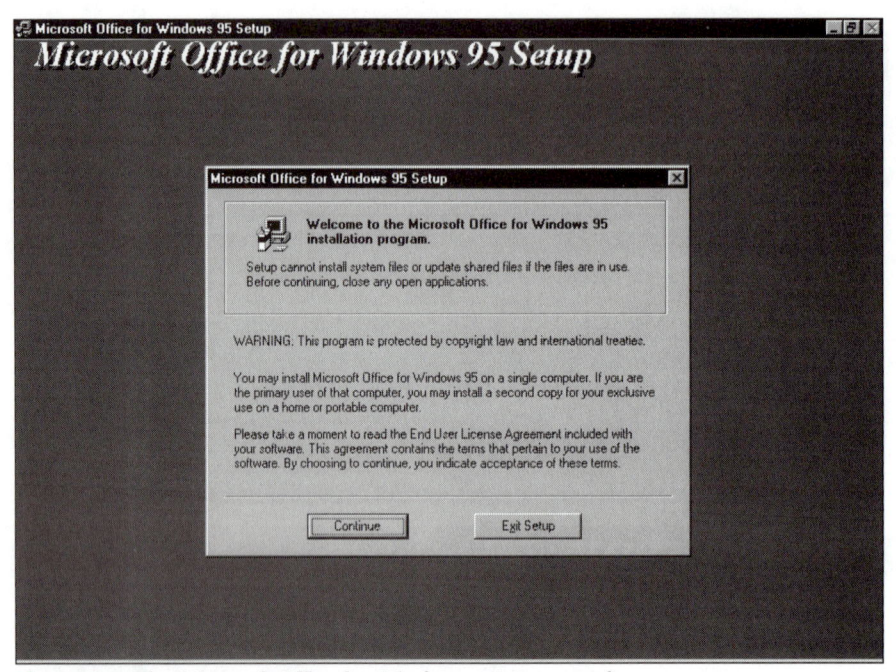

Figure A-1: The Microsoft Office for Windows 95 Setup welcome screen.

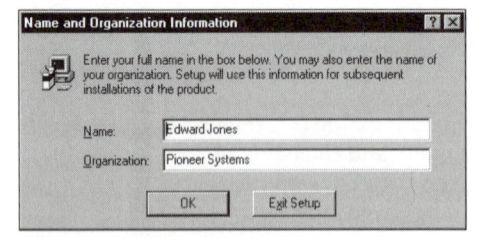

Figure A-2: The Name and Organization Information dialog box.

4. The next dialog box to appear shows the product ID number for your version of Microsoft Office. You may want to make a note of this number because it may come in handy if you ever need to contact Microsoft Customer Support for any reason. When you are finished, click on the OK button to proceed.

Appendix A ✦ **Installing Microsoft Office** 681

5. The first Microsoft Office for Windows 95 Setup dialog box (Figure A-3) appears next. It asks you to choose the folder in which Microsoft Office should be installed. By default, the program is installed in C:\MSOffice. If the default location suits you, click on the OK button to proceed. If you want to install Office into a different directory, click on the Change Folder button to display the Change Folder dialog box, shown in Figure A-4. Choose the desired folder, and click on the OK button.

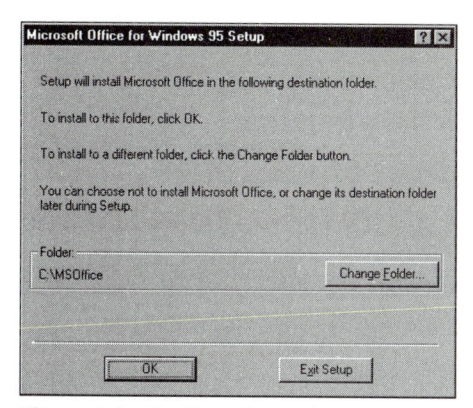

Figure A-3: The first Microsoft Office 95 Setup dialog box.

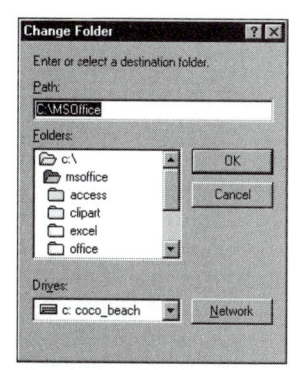

Figure A-4: The Change Folder dialog box.

Danger Zone: If you have an older version of Microsoft Office, and you want to keep using the older applications along with the current version, you will need to choose a different folder for storing Microsoft Office. If you accept the default, you will overwrite any earlier version of Microsoft Office that is installed on your system.

6. After a brief period of time (during which the Setup program scans your hard disk), you'll see the second Microsoft Office 95 Setup dialog box. It displays options of Typical, Compact, and Custom options, as shown in Figure A-5.

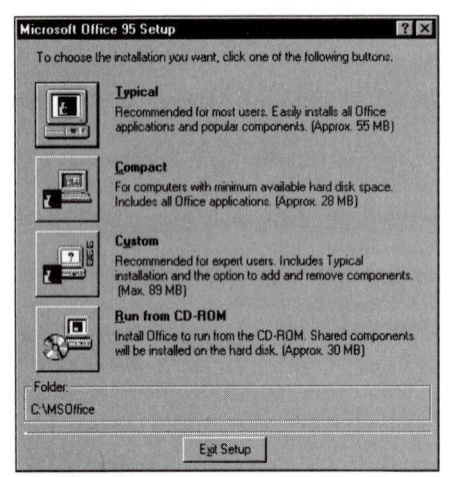

Figure A-5: The second Microsoft Office 95 Setup dialog box.

7. Choose the Typical, Compact, Custom, or Run from CD-ROM option from the dialog box, as desired. The Typical option results in what Microsoft calls a "typical" installation, with the options used by most users of Office added to your hard disk (this option takes 55 MB of disk space). The Compact option results in a "space-saving" installation, with minimal options but with less hard disk space used (taking 28 MB of disk space). The Custom option enables you to specify which applications will be added, as detailed in the next section. If you choose the Custom option and install all the features of Microsoft Office, you will need 89 MB of disk space. If you choose the Typical or the Compact option, the installation process will begin.

When the installation process is complete, Setup displays a dialog box that says so. Click on the OK button to return to Windows 95.

About the Custom Installation Options

When you choose the Custom installation, the dialog box in Figure A-6 appears. It lists seven different groups of components for Microsoft Office:

- ✦ The Office Binder and Shortcut Bar
- ✦ Microsoft Excel
- ✦ Microsoft Word
- ✦ Microsoft PowerPoint
- ✦ Microsoft Schedule+
- ✦ Office Tools
- ✦ Converters, Filters, and Data Access

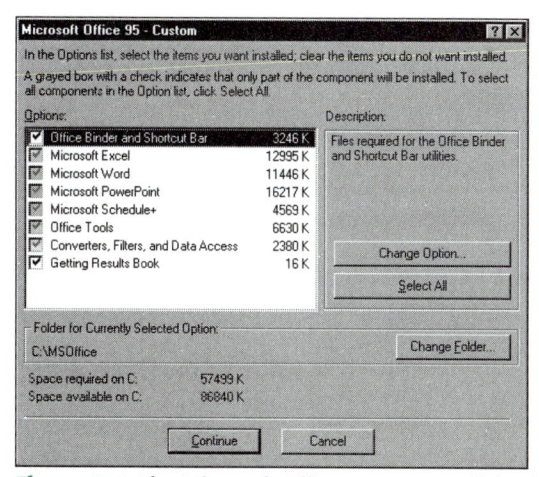

Figure A-6: The Microsoft Office 95 Custom dialog box.

By default, check boxes are turned on for all these applications. You can turn off a check box for any application that you don't want to install. Also, while a particular option is highlighted, you can click on the Change Option button in the dialog box to reveal individual features for that option that you can turn on and off. Selecting an option means it will be installed. If an item is turned off, it won't be installed. These options are further noted in the paragraphs which follow.

What should I install?

When you use the Customize options as part of the installation process, a natural question that arises in every case is which Office options you should consider installing, and which ones you can omit. The answer is going to vary for every individual — after all, what you should install depends on your needs. One point to keep in mind is that it may be worth your time to use the Change Option button in the Custom dialog box to examine each of the options. You may find that some of the ones that are enabled by default aren't really needed in your case, while others that aren't turned on by default will make your life easier if you have them.

Office Binder and Shortcut Bar options

If you select the Office Binder and Shortcut Bar option in the Custom dialog box and then click Change Option, you see the Office Binder and Shortcut Bar dialog box, as shown in Figure A-7.

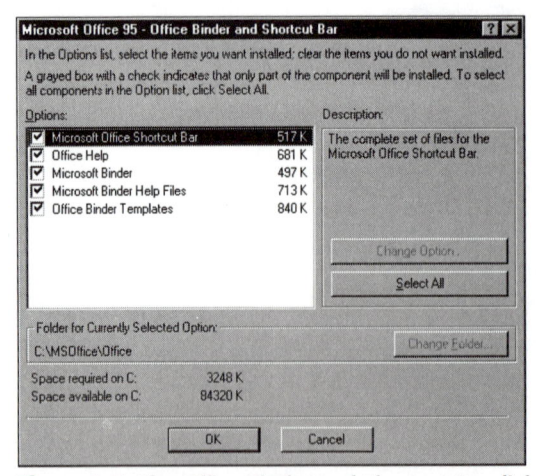

Figure A-7: The Office Binder and Shortcut Bar dialog box.

In the dialog box, you can turn on or off any of the desired components: the Microsoft Office Shortcut Bar, Microsoft Binder, Office Help, Microsoft Binder, Microsoft Binder Help Files, and the Office Binder Templates. When done choosing the desired options, click OK to return to the Custom dialog box.

Excel options

If you select the Microsoft Excel option in the Custom dialog box and then click Change Option, you see the Microsoft Excel dialog box, as shown in Figure A-8.

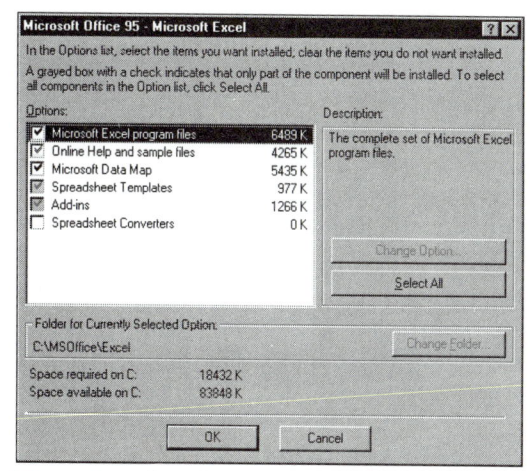

Figure A-8: The Microsoft Excel dialog box.

In the dialog box, you can turn on or off any of the desired components: Microsoft Excel program files, Online Help and sample files, Microsoft Data Map, Spreadsheet Templates, Add-ins, and Spreadsheet Converters. When done choosing the desired options, click OK to return to the Custom dialog box.

Word options

If you select the Microsoft Word option in the Custom dialog box and then click Change Option, you see the Microsoft Word dialog box, as shown in Figure A-9.

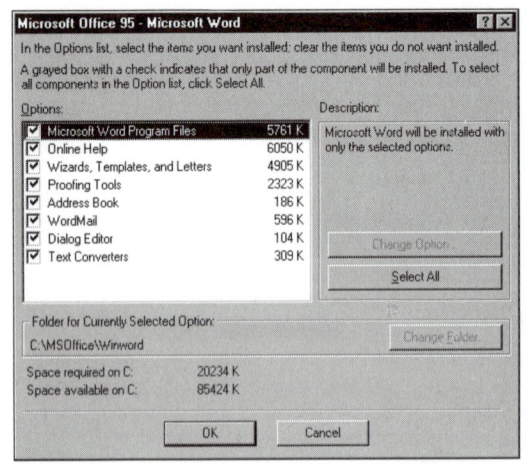

Figure A-9: The Microsoft Word dialog box.

In the dialog box, you can turn on or off any of the desired components: Microsoft Word Program Files; Online Help; Wizards, Templates, and Letters; Proofing Tools; Address Book; WordMail; Dialog Editor; and Text Converters. When done choosing the desired options, click OK to return to the Custom dialog box.

PowerPoint options

If you select the Microsoft PowerPoint option in the Custom dialog box and then click Change Option, you see the Microsoft PowerPoint dialog box, shown in Figure A-10.

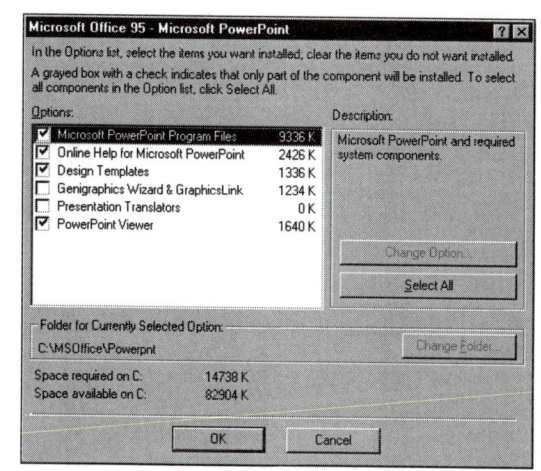

Figure A-10: The Microsoft PowerPoint dialog box.

In the dialog box, you can turn on or off any of the desired components: Microsoft PowerPoint Program Files, Online Help, Design Templates, Genigraphics Wizard & GraphicsLink, Presentation Translators, and PowerPoint Viewer. When done choosing the desired options, click OK to return to the Custom dialog box.

Schedule+ options

If you select the Microsoft Schedule+ option in the Custom dialog box and then click Change Option, you see the Microsoft Schedule+ dialog box, as shown in Figure A-11.

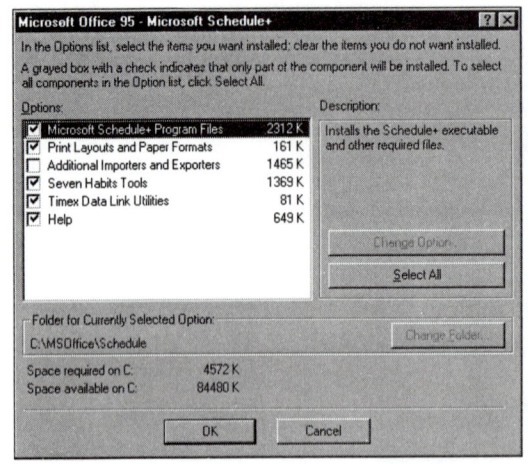

Figure A-11: The Microsoft Schedule+ dialog box.

In the dialog box, you can turn on or off any of the desired components: Microsoft Schedule+ Program Files, Print Layouts and Paper Formats, Additional Importers and Exporters, Seven Habits Tools, Timex Data Link Utilities, and Help. When done choosing the desired options, click OK to return to the Custom dialog box.

Office Tools options

If you select the Office Tools option in the Custom dialog box and then click Change Option, you see the Office Tools dialog box, as shown in Figure A-12.

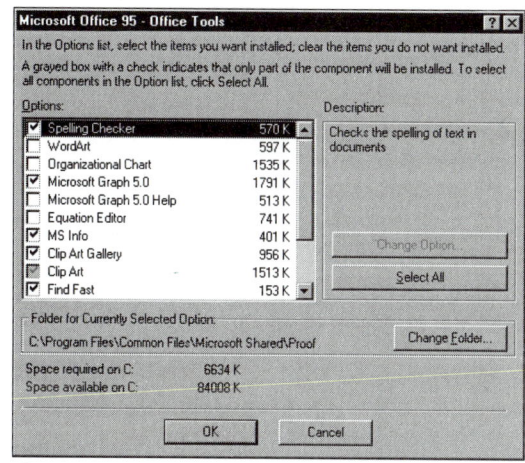

Figure A-12: The Office Tools dialog box.

In the dialog box, you can turn on or off any of the desired components, including Spelling Checker, WordArt, Organizational Chart, Microsoft Graph 5.0, Microsoft Graph 5.0 Help, Equation Editor, MS Info, Clip Art Gallery, Clip Art, and Find Fast. When done choosing the desired options, click OK to return to the Custom dialog box.

Converters, Filters, and Data Access options

If you select the Converters, Filters, and Data Access option in the Custom dialog box and then click Change Option, you see the Converters, Filters, and Data Access dialog box, as shown in Figure A-13.

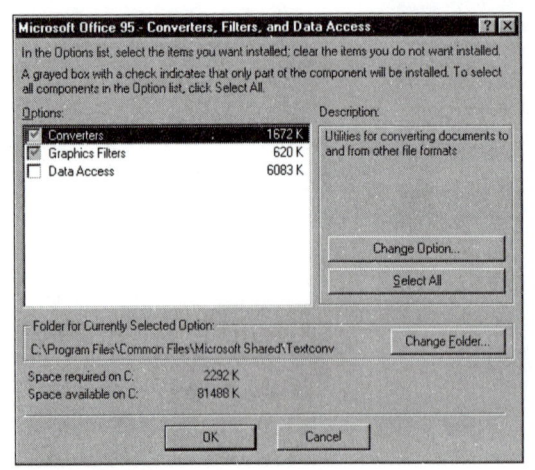

Figure A-13: The Converters, Filters, and Data Access dialog box.

In the dialog box, you can turn on or off any of the desired components: Converters, Graphics Filters, and Data Access. When done choosing the desired options, click OK to return to the Custom dialog box.

Completing the installation process

When you are finished choosing your desired options, click on the Continue button to proceed. The Setup program checks your system for the necessary disk space, and then begins installing the options you selected. If you are installing from floppy disks, the system will ask you to insert the next disk, as needed. When the installation process is finished, Setup displays a dialog box that says so. Click on the OK button to return to Windows 95.

✦ ✦ ✦

Word Basics

APPENDIX B

This appendix provides a fast-paced overview of Word for Windows basics. If you've never used Word, start here.

Starting Word

You can start Word in two ways. The simple way is to click on the icon that looks like a *W* in the Microsoft Office Manager. You can use the Start menu: choose Programs, then Microsoft Office, and then Microsoft Word. If you like to stick to the keyboard: First press Alt+S to open the Windows Start menu. Then use the arrow keys to navigate to the Word item, and press Return to start it.

About the Screen

More Info When Word starts, you're placed in a blank document where you can begin to enter text. Figure B-1 shows the different parts of the screen. Title bars, menu bars, toolbars, and scroll bars are common to all Windows applications. The Ruler lets you use the mouse to change paragraph indents, adjust page margins, change the width of columns, and set tab stops. See Chapters 2, 3, and 5 for more information. When you're working with a document, the document area contains the document. When you're not working with a document, the document area contains nothing but a gray background. The status bar gives you information about your document. These elements are discussed in more detail throughout this appendix.

More Info Figure B-2 shows the toolbars that, by default, appear when you start Word: the Standard and Formatting toolbars. Table B-1 describes the Standard toolbar's buttons. Table B-2 briefly describes the Formatting toolbar's buttons; for detailed information, see Chapter 3.

In This Appendix

Starting Word

Understanding Word's screen

Opening new and existing documents

Navigating documents

Editing documents

Saving documents

Using File⇨Save All

Printing documents

Appendixes

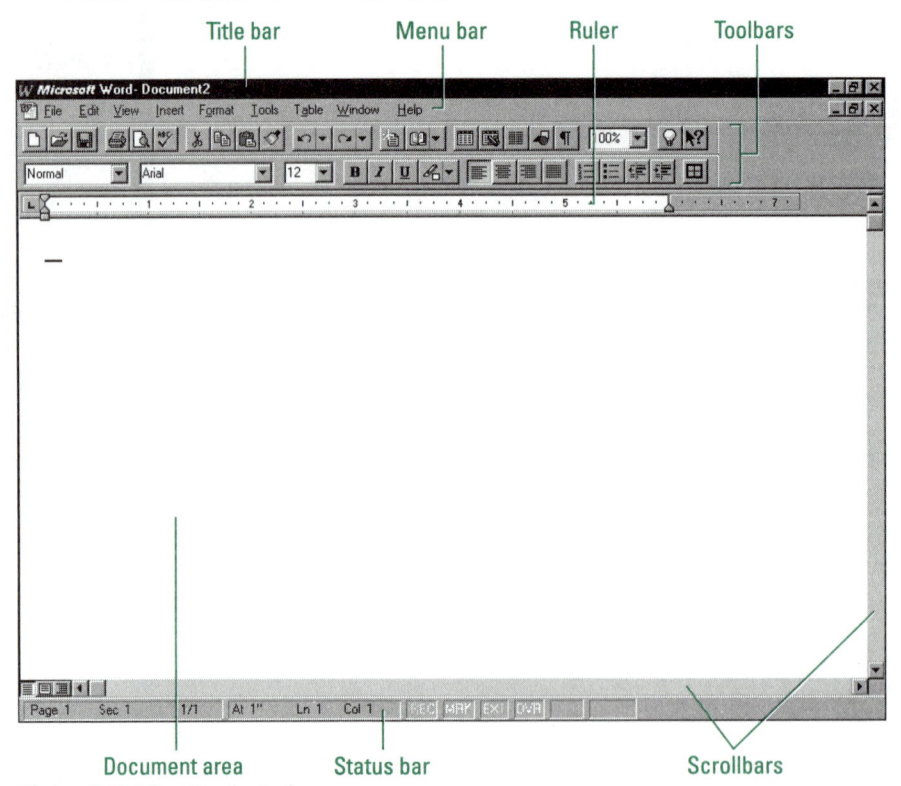

Figure B-1: The Word window.

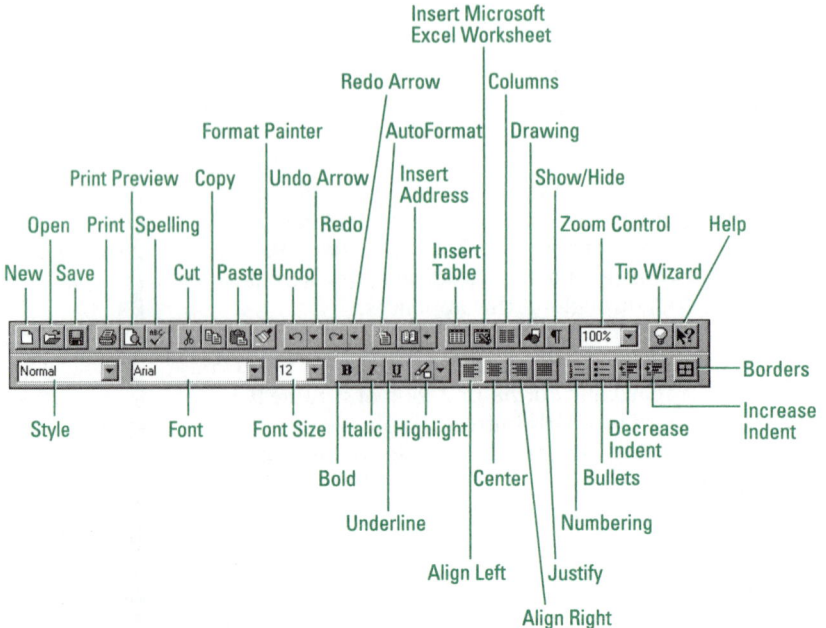

Labels: Title bar, Menu bar, Ruler, Toolbars, Document area, Status bar, Scrollbars.

Figure B-2: The Standard and Formatting toolbars.

Labels: New, Open, Save, Print, Print Preview, Spelling, Cut, Copy, Paste, Format Painter, Undo, Undo Arrow, Redo, Redo Arrow, AutoFormat, Insert Address, Insert Table, Insert Microsoft Excel Worksheet, Columns, Drawing, Show/Hide, Zoom Control, Tip Wizard, Help, Style, Font, Font Size, Bold, Italic, Underline, Highlight, Align Left, Center, Align Right, Justify, Numbering, Bullets, Decrease Indent, Increase Indent, Borders.

Table B-1
Standard toolbar buttons

Name	Description
New	Opens a new document using the default page settings.
Open	Opens an existing document.
Save	Saves the current document under its present name; if no name exists, the Save As dialog box appears so you can provide one.
Print	Prints one copy of all pages in the current document.
Print Preview	Lets you see what your current document will look like when printed and to make layout changes.
Spelling	Checks the spelling of the current section (see Chapter 3 for an explanation), or of the entire document if no section exists.
Cut	Removes a section of highlighted text and places it into the Clipboard.
Copy	Makes a copy of the current section of text and places it into the Clipboard.
Paste	Pastes the contents of the Clipboard into the document at the insertion pointer.
Format Painter	Copies formatting characteristics from one selection of text to another.
Undo	Reverses the last action.
Undo Arrow	Lets you choose the action that you wish to undo.
Redo	Redoes the last action that was undone.
Redo Arrow	Lets you choose the undone action that you wish to redo.
AutoFormat	Automatically formats a document from a preset group of formats after analyzing the document. (Chapter 10 describes AutoFormat in detail.)
Insert Address	This button is used to insert an address from your personal address book in Schedule+. (For more information on Schedule+, see Chapter 31.)
Insert Table	Inserts a table in your document. (Chapter 5 tells you all about tables.)
Insert Microsoft Excel Worksheet	Inserts a Microsoft Excel Worksheet in Word for Windows.
Columns	Formats the current section into columns.
Drawing	Shows or hides the drawing toolbar.

(continued)

Table B-1 *(continued)*

Name	Description
Show/Hide	Shows or hides all nonprinting characters.
Zoom Control	Lets you scale the editing view. This lets you get a closer or less close look at the screen. If text is particularly small, use this button to make it appear larger. If text is particularly large, use this button to make it appear smaller. This doesn't affect the *actual* characteristic of the text — only its appearance on the screen. 8-point Arial, zoomed so it's larger, is still 8-point Arial.
Tip Wizard	This button hides or displays the Tool Tip Wizard. This wizard provides you with more efficient ways to accomplish tasks you may find yourself doing each time you use Word.
Help	Gives help on a command, a screen region, lets you examine text properties. To activate general help, double-click on the Help button. To get help on a specific area of the screen or some text properties, click on the Help button once to make a question mark appear. Then move it to the region of the screen and click on again. If help is associated with that area, it appears.

Table B-2
Formatting toolbar buttons

Name	Description
Style	Lets you choose a style for your text.
Font	Lets you choose a font for your text.
Font Size	Lets you choose a size for your text's font.
Bold	Applies or removes boldfacing from text.
Italic	Applies or removes italics from text.
Underline	Applies or removes underlining from text.
Highlight	Applies or removes highlighting from text.
Align Left	Aligns text to the left margin.
Center	Centers text.
Align Right	Aligns text to the right margin.
Justify	Aligns text to both the left and the right margins.

Name	Description
Numbering	Creates a numbered list from a selected set of items.
Bullets	Creates a bulleted list from a selected set of items.
Decrease Indent	Indents a paragraph to the previous tab stop.
Increase Indent	Indents a paragraph to the next tab stop.
Borders	Lets you apply borders and shading to your text.

Starting from the left side of the Formatting toolbar, you'll first see the Style list box. This lets you apply any of Word's styles to a section (a paragraph where the insertion point is placed). Next comes the Font list box, which lets you change the appearance of characters by choosing different typefaces. Near the center of the Formatting toolbar, you'll find the Font Size list box; this lets you change the size of a document's characters. Next are the three character-formatting buttons: **Bold,** *Italic,* and Underline. Next, you'll see the Highlight button, which lets you highlight text in a color.

The four alignment buttons come next — Align Left, Center, Align Right, and Justify. Following those are the Numbering, Bullets, Decrease Indent, and Increase Indent buttons. Finally, you'll find the Borders button, which lets you place various types of borders and shading on sections of a document.

Each component of the Formatting toolbar is discussed in detail in the corresponding section.

Opening New or Existing Documents

You can create new documents from a blank document screen in either of two ways. You can start Word in the usual manner by clicking on the Word icon, or by choosing Programs from the Start menu and then using the arrow keys to select Word from the list of programs. Or, from within Word, you can choose File⇨New. If you don't use a template when creating a document, the document screen appears resembling a blank sheet of paper, and formatting takes on a standard appearance, with default margins and text style controlled by the default template, `Normal.dot`.

You insert text into a document either by typing it or by pasting it from the Clipboard. If you're completely new to Word for Windows, practice by typing the following text. Humor me on this — I'll use this example again later, and it'll help if you've already typed it in.

Chess

Chess is a very old game of strategy in which players try to capture, or checkmate, their opponent's King. Players alternate turns, making one move at a time. Each player has 16 playing pieces.

The Pawn usually moves first. Normally, it can move only forward, one square at a time. The exceptions are during its first move (when it can go one or two squares) or when it is capturing (when it advances diagonally one square). The Rook can move in a straight line forward, backward, or to either side. The Bishop moves and captures diagonally. The Queen can move in a straight line any number of spaces or diagonally any number of spaces. The King can move in any direction, but only one space at a time.

> **Note** To open an existing document, choose File➪Open and enter the filename in the File name field that appears.

Basic Navigation

Now that you have some text in your new document, you can practice some basic navigation skills. Table B-3 lists keystrokes that move you around your documents.

Table B-3
Navigation keystrokes

Keystroke	Function
Arrow keys	Move around in your document.
Ctrl+Up Arrow	Move up one paragraph.
Ctrl+Down Arrow	Move down one paragraph.
Alt+Left Arrow	Move the cursor one word to the left.
Alt+Right Arrow	Move the cursor one word to the right.
Page Up	Move up one screenful.
Page Down	Move down one screenful.
Home	Move the cursor to the beginning of the current line.
Ctrl+Home	Move the cursor to the beginning of the document.
End	Move the cursor to the end of the current line.
Ctrl+End	Move the cursor to the end of the document.

The scroll bars will move you through a document, too. There are four ways to scroll with the scroll bar: click on the arrows incrementally, hold down the mouse button on the scroll arrow, drag the scroll bar box, or click on the scroll bar.

Basic Text Editing

Text editing is also relatively simple in Word. You can do it in several ways.

Return to the second line of the "Chess" document that you typed earlier and now type the letter **R**. As you can see, the letter is added to the line of text. But if you press the Insert key and then type something, what you type replaces the text that was there. You can delete letters by using the Delete key: Place the cursor at the beginning of your second line in front of your *R* and then press Delete. Presto, the *R* is removed. The Insert key is a toggle key — the first time you press it, text you type replaces existing text (Overtype mode); the second time you press it, text you type is inserted into the existing text (Insert mode). The status bar at the bottom of the Word window tells you which mode you're using. Look for the REC, MRK, EXT, OVR, and WPH boxes. If OVR appears in black letters, then you're in Overtype mode. Otherwise, you're in Insert mode.

If you want to replace a paragraph or a large section of text, there are two methods that you can use. One is to press the Insert key until you are in Overtype mode and to then begin typing. This replaces all text until you stop typing, so be careful not to overwrite what you want to keep. If you happen to find something that you do want to keep, press the Insert button again and Overtype is turned off.

The second method is to highlight a word, sentence, or paragraph and then press Delete to remove it from your document. Make sure that Overtype is off if you replace an area of text; otherwise, when you begin to type again, you'll overwrite the text that was moved as a result of the deletion.

Saving

Saving documents is a basic but important operation that you can do with any word processor. Word provides a variety of options. You can save a file either under a new name or an existing one. You can save files in Word's own file format, or you can do it in the formats of other popular word processors. And you can save all open files with a single command.

Saving a document

To save a file, either choose the Save icon from the Standard toolbar or File➪Save. If the file has been saved previously, Word saves the file without prompting you for any information; the document remains on the screen. If you want to leave Word, you must also use the File➪Exit command, or its equivalent, Alt+F4.

If you use the File➪Save command to save a document that has never been saved, Word displays the Save As dialog box (Figure B-3) asking for the name for the file. Enter the filename that you want. Word ordinarily assigns an extension of .DOC to all files saved in its normal file format. Since Word assumes that files have this .DOC extension, you need not include it when entering names for saving and loading files. You can assign your own extension by typing the period and the extension that you want along with the filename; however, if you do this, you'll have to type the extension whenever you later open the file with the File➪Open command.

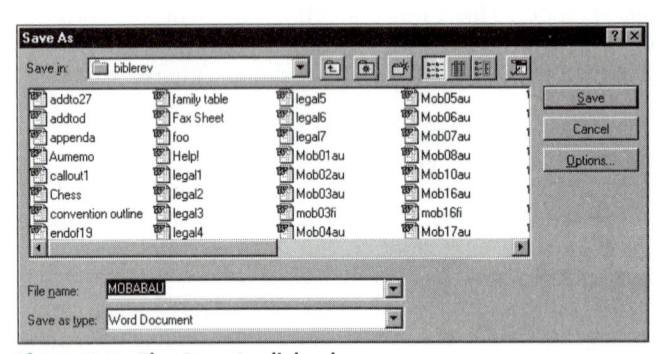

Figure B-3: The Save As dialog box.

If you created the example document "Chess," save it now by performing these steps:

1. Choose File➪Save. Because you have never saved this file, the Save As dialog box appears.
2. In the File name field, type **Chess**.
3. Click on OK. Word saves the document under the name `Chess.doc`.

Word also provides an easy way to save files to other directories or to floppy disks, with the File➪Save As command (see the following section, "Using File➪Save As").

Note If you want to save a document and exit from Word, the Alt+F4 (File➪Exit) hot key is useful. When you press Alt+F4 to exit, Word automatically prompts you to save any changes made to the document. Click on Yes, and your changes are saved. If the document has not been saved before, you are prompted to supply a filename in the Save As dialog box. Enter a file name, click on OK, and the document is saved.

Using File➪Save As

You can use the File➪Save As command to save files to other directories or to a floppy disk. You can also use this command to save a copy of your file in the format of another word processor or as ASCII text. When you choose File➪Save As, the same dialog box appears as the one shown earlier in Figure B-3.

The name of the file appears in the File name field (if the document has ever been saved). If you want to save the file under a different name, you can type a new name, and that name will replace the existing one. If the document has never been saved, this field is blank; you can type in an original filename for the file.

To save the file to a different directory or drive, tab to or click on the list box beside the Save in field and select the drive or directory that you want. You can navigate up and down within subdirectories by using the list box. To move to a subdirectory, select it by name.

You can also use the File➪Save As command to save a document in the format of another word processor. To do this, choose File➪Save As and then click on the arrow of the Save as type list box. When you do this, the dialog box expands to show additional formats that you can save your document in (as shown in Figure B-4).

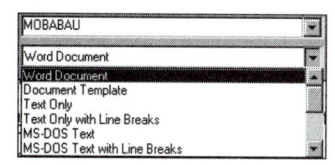

Figure B-4: The Save as type list box.

Tab to or click on the Save as type list box to choose a desired file format other than the standard Microsoft Word format. The text choice that you see in the list box can be used to save a document as ASCII text. Keep in mind that the other available formats you'll see will depend on what formats were installed along with Word. If you need a popular file format and you don't see it in the list box, it may not have been added during the installation process.

To look at the options for saving a file, open the Save As dialog box and choose Options. A list of options will appear: Always Create Backup Copy, Allow Fast Saves, Prompt for Document Properties, Prompt to Save Normal Template, Save Native Picture Formats Only, Embed True Type Fonts, Save Data Only for Forms, and Automatic Save Every x Minutes. The following sections cover the most basic options for saving files.

> **Note** When the Always Create Backup Copy option is on, Word will create a backup file every time you save. The backup file will have the .BAK extension.

Allow Fast Saves

Some of Word's behavior when saving files depends on how much editing you've done to the file since it was saved last.

Word saves files using either of two methods: a *fast save* or a *full save*. When you choose File⇨Save, Word saves your file using the method indicated by the circumstances.

Normally, Word performs a fast save, where your changes are appended onto the end of an existing file. With a full save, Word saves the entire document, including unchanged parts, as if you were saving the file for the first time.

The first time a document is saved, Word performs a full save. After that, Word usually performs a fast save whenever you save updates to your document. (If you make massive changes, Word may perform a full save automatically.)

Operationally, you'll see no difference between the two methods other than in speed. Full saves take somewhat longer than fast saves; exactly how much longer varies greatly depending on the speed of your hardware. To turn fast saves on or off, go to the Save Options list box in the Options dialog box by choosing File⇨Save As, click on Options, and turn off the Allow Fast Saves check box by either clicking on it or pressing Alt+F.

Prompt for Document Properties

The Prompt for Document Properties option will show the Summary tab of the Properties dialog box. This tab lets you store general information about the document, such as title, subject, author, and so on.

Automatic Save Every *x* Minutes

You can set the Automatic Save option for whatever time period you want, depending on your preference and work speed.

Using File⇨Save All

You can use the File⇨Save All command to save all open documents. Choose File⇨Save All, and Word will then display a dialog box for each document and ask if the document should be saved. Choose Yes from the dialog box, and a similar dialog box for the next document will appear. To save all documents, continue choosing Yes. If any of the documents were not saved previously, Word will prompt you for filenames as necessary.

> **Note** In addition to saving all open documents, File➪Save All will save any open global macros, templates, or glossaries.

Printing

You'll want to print most of the documents that you create. Printing is covered in detail in Chapter 4; this section shows how to print one copy of a document.

To print a document, choose File➪Print (or press Ctrl+P). The Print dialog box appears, as shown in Figure B-5.

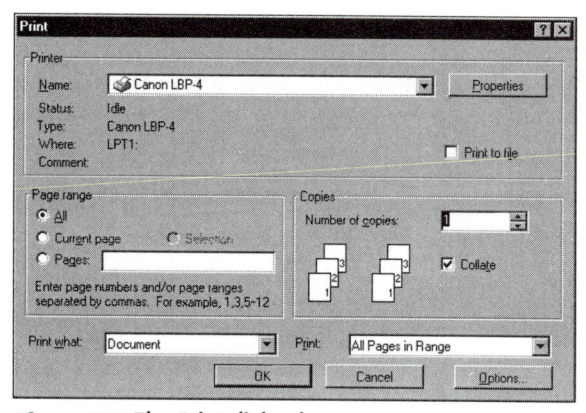

Figure B-5: The Print dialog box.

Assuming that the printer name that appears at the top of the dialog box matches the printer connected to your PC, you're ready to print. The default options in the dialog box assume that you want one copy of the document and that you want all pages in the document printed. You can change the defaults by changing the number of copies in the Number of copies field or by changing the beginning and the ending page numbers in the Pages field.

After selecting the options that you want, choose OK to begin printing your document. If you have difficulty printing — or if the printer name in the Print dialog box doesn't match the printer that's actually connected to your PC — the problem may lie with how Windows is set up on your system. If you can't print from any Windows application (for example, Cardfile or Notepad), you won't be able to print from Word, either. Make sure that the correct printer chosen is on the Printer name field. See Chapter 4 for more information on Print Setup.

Printing part of a document

Keep in mind that you can quickly print specific pages of a document by entering beginning and ending page numbers in the Print dialog box. Just enter the starting and ending page numbers in the Pages field of the Page range area of the dialog box.

To print a selected portion of a document, first highlight the selection and then choose File⇨Print. In the Print dialog box, choose Selection (Alt+S). After you click on OK, only the selected text is printed.

Opening Existing Documents

To open a document, either click on the Open icon on the toolbar, choose File⇨Open or press Ctrl+O. The Open dialog box appears. From there, either choose the name of the document that you want to open by scrolling to its name or type the name of the document in the File name field and then press Enter. If the document is on another drive, change the drive in the Look in list box.

This appendix provides just an overview of the workings of Word. Each of the topics touched on here is covered in detail in the Word section of this book.

Summary

This appendix covered topics related to the basics of Word. All of these topics are covered in more depth in their respective chapters. Here are some of the topics that we covered.

- ✦ You start Word by clicking on the *W* icon in the Microsoft Office Manager, or by using the Start menu in the taskbar.
- ✦ You can use Word's Standard and Formatting toolbars to open, close, print, and save documents; to cut and paste text; to insert objects such as graphics and Excel worksheets; to get help; and to apply formatting to text.
- ✦ You can create a new document by starting Word — a blank document automatically appears. If you're already in Word, create a new document with File➪New. Then insert text by typing.
- ✦ Several keystrokes and commands are available for navigating your document.
- ✦ You can use Overtype mode (press the Insert key until OVR appears in the status bar) to replace text. Click on where you want to replace text, turn on Overtype mode, and type. Alternatively, you can select text you want to replace, press Delete, make sure you're in Insert mode (press the Insert key until OVR does *not* appear in the status bar), and type the new text.
- ✦ You save a document with File➪Save. To save a document under a new name, use File➪Save As.
- ✦ Print your document with File➪Print.

Where to go next...

- ✦ Part II describes all of Word's features. Start in Chapter 2.

✦ ✦ ✦

Excel Basics

APPENDIX C

After you installed Excel, you were returned to the Windows A95 desktop. To start Excel, choose Programs from the Windows 95 Start menu, choose Microsoft Office, and then choose Microsoft Excel.

Understanding Spreadsheets

A spreadsheet is an electronic version of old bookkeeping tools: the ledger pad, pencil, and calculator. Excel spreadsheets, called *worksheets* in Microsoft terminology, can be likened to huge sheets of ledger paper. Each worksheet measures 16,384 rows by 256 columns — realistically, more size than you should ever need on a single page. Each intersection of a row and column comprises a cell, and cells are identified by their row and column coordinates. A1 is the cell in the upper-left corner of the worksheet.

Data that you enter in a worksheet can take the form of *constant values* or of *variables* that are based on formulas. Constant values, such as a number (81.5) or a name (Eugene Jackson), do not change. Values derived from formulas often refer to other cells in the worksheet. For example, a cell might contain the formula C5+C6, which adds the contents of two other cells in the worksheet, C5 and C6.

Excel's worksheets can display data in a wide variety of formats. You can display numeric values with or without decimals, currency amounts, or exponential values. You can also enter text, such as the name of a month or a product model name. And you can store and display date and time-of-day data in worksheet cells.

Besides storing your data, in most cases you will want to perform calculations on that data — after all, calculations are what nearly all spreadsheet models are about. Excel helps you in this regard by providing a rich assortment of *functions*, which are special built-in formulas that provide a variety of calculations

In This Appendix

Opening workbooks

Understanding the Excel screen

Understanding the workbook concept

Navigating workbooks and worksheets

Entering and editing data

Building formulas

Printing worksheets

Saving worksheets

(the average of a series of values, for example, or the square root of a number). Excel provides functions for mathematical, statistical, financial, logical, date and time, text, and special-purpose operations.

As a product, Excel appeals to numbers-oriented PC users who must manage numbers on a day-to-day basis. Thanks to its extensive built-in graphics support, Excel also works well for those who need to highlight numeric data with presentation graphics.

Understanding the Excel Screen

When you look at the Excel screen, you'll see some buttons that may be unfamiliar to you although you may be a regular user of Microsoft products. This section describes Excel's toolbars.

Figure C-1 shows what Excel looks like when first opened; you'll see a new workbook with the title Book1.

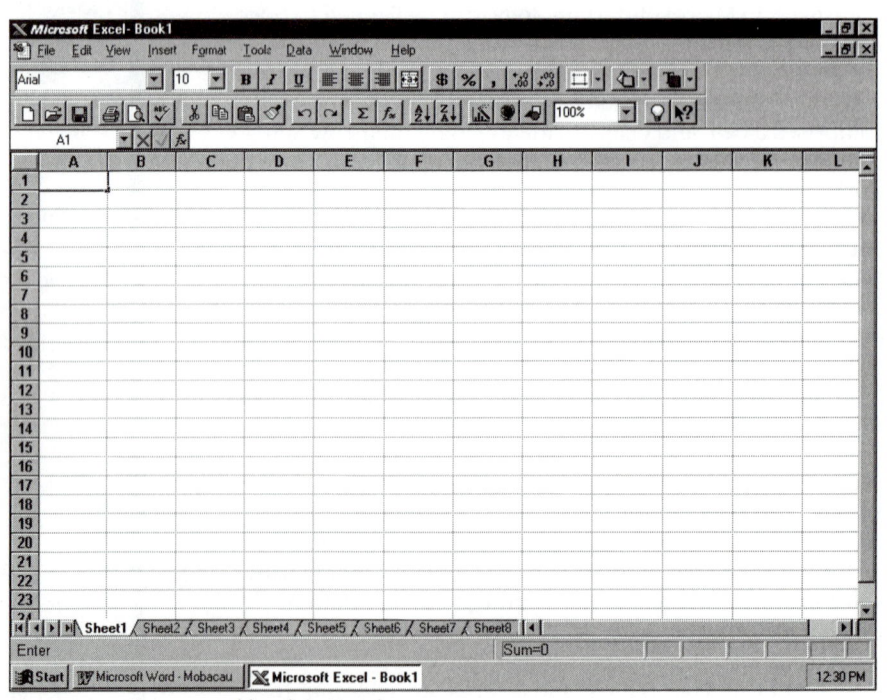

Figure C-1: A new workbook in Excel.

Figure C-2 shows Excel's Standard toolbar. Table C-1 shows its buttons.

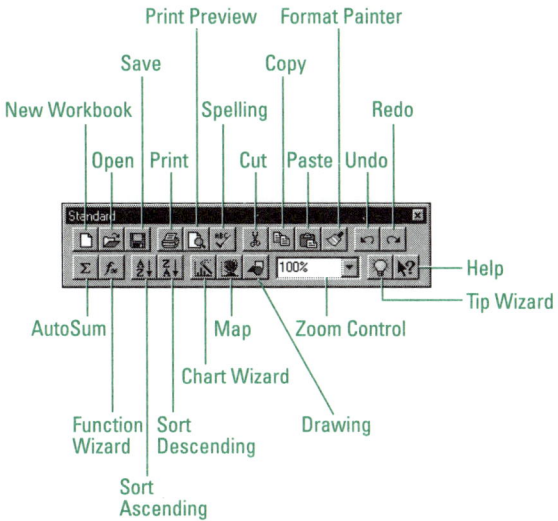

Figure C-2: The Standard toolbar.

Table C-1
Toolbar buttons

Name	Function
New Workbook	Opens a new workbook.
Open	Opens a workbook file.
Save	Saves a current workbook; if it has not been saved before, you are prompted to enter a name for the workbook.
Print	Opens the Print dialog box for printing.
Print Preview	Shows you what the workbook will look like when printed.
Spelling	Checks the spelling for the current sheet or the selected section.
Cut	Cuts the selected information and places it on the clipboard.
Copy	Copies selected text and places it on a clipboard.
Paste	Pastes selected text in the document at the insertion pointer.
Format Painter	Copies text formatting from one area to another.
Undo	Reverses last action.

(continued)

Table C-1 (continued)

Name	Function
Redo	Redoes last action.
AutoSum	Invokes the sum function, which adds a column of numbers.
FunctionWizard	Activates the Function Wizard, which quickly locates a desired function for use in a formula.
Sort Ascending	Sorts list information in ascending order.
Sort Descending	Sorts list information in descending order.
ChartWizard	Activates the Chart Wizard, which creates a chart based on worksheet data.
Map	Activates the Map Wizard, which inserts a map into a worksheet.
Drawing	Displays the Drawing toolbar, which contains various tools which can be used to draw graphic shapes in a worksheet.
Zoom Control	Controls the size of a document's appearance on-screen.
TipWizard	Displays or hides the Tip Wizard toolbar, which provides tips about how to do your work more efficiently.
Help	Activates Help.

Figure C-3 shows Excel's Formatting toolbar. Table C-2 explains its butons.

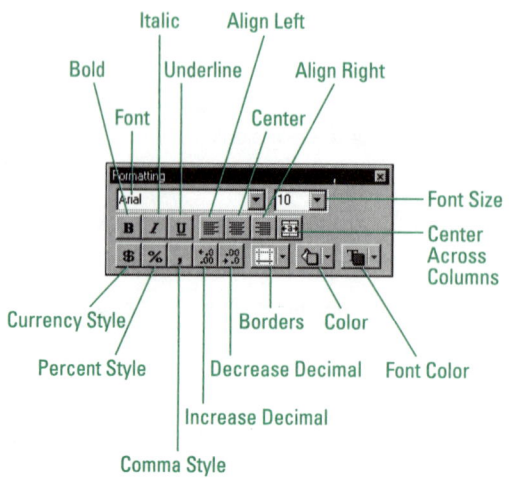

Figure C-3: The Formatting toolbar.

Table C-2
Formatting toolbar

Name	Function
Font	Displays list of fonts.
Font Size	Displays available font sizes.
Bold	Changes the selected text to boldface.
Italic	Changes the selected text to italics.
Underline	Underlines the selected text.
Align Left	Left-aligns cell entries.
Center	Centers cell entries.
Align Right	Right-aligns cell entries.
Center Across Columns	Centers cell entries across the columns.
Currency Style	Applies currency formatting to the current selection.
Percent Style	Applies percent formatting to the current selection.
Comma Style	Applies comma formatting to the current selection.
Increase Decimal	Increases the number of digits shown after the decimal point in the selection.
Decrease Decimal	Decreases the number of digits shown after the decimal point in the selection.
Borders	Displays a Borders palette, which can be used to apply a border to the current selection.
Color	Displays a Color palette, which can be used to apply a color choice to the current selection.
Font Color	Displays a Font Color palette, which can be used to apply a font color choice to the current selection.

Understanding the Workbook Concept

The concept of workbooks may be new to Excel users who haven't upgraded since the dark ages (specifically, before version 5.0). In a nutshell, a *workbook* is a collection of worksheets. Each of the worksheets consists of columns and rows that form cells. There are tabs at the bottom of each of the sheets; you can click on each of these tabs if you want to change to a different sheet.

The advantage of using workbooks is that you can keep more than one spreadsheet in a file. This is especially useful when you have a series of worksheets that track time-related data, such as sales or expenses for a series of months. Instead of having to open several files, you can place all the worksheets in the same workbook and look at each of them with a click of your mouse.

Opening an Existing Workbook

To open a previously saved workbook, choose File➪Open. In the Open dialog box that appears (see Figure C-4), you can choose the file that you want.

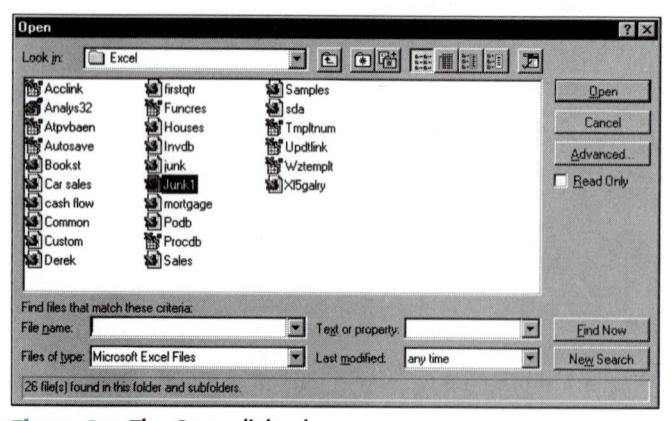

Figure C-4: The Open dialog box.

If the file is in a folder, you can double-click on the folder to open it. You may need to navigate within the folders to find your file; you can click on the Up One Level button in the dialog box to see higher-level files and folders.

Workbook and Worksheet Navigation

This section teaches the basics of navigation in a worksheet and a workbook. As always, you can use either the mouse or the keyboard, depending on preference.

Navigating in the workbook window

When Excel starts, you see a workbook with the current worksheet in front. All workbooks consist of 16 worksheets by default, so you need a quick, convenient way to move from worksheet to worksheet.

Keyboard users can do this by pressing Ctrl+PgDn to move to the next sheet or Ctrl+PgUp to move to the preceding sheet. If you prefer the mouse, click on the desired worksheet's tab at the bottom of the window. Figure C-5 shows the worksheet tabs in an Excel workbook. (If you can't see the needed tab, use the scroll buttons at the lower left to move it into view.)

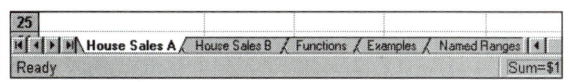

Figure C-5: The tabs of an Excel workbook.

Navigating in a worksheet

After selecting the worksheet that you want, you need to be able to move about in it. Keep in mind that the part of the spreadsheet you see on-screen is but a small section of the entire worksheet. Table C-3 shows the key combinations that move you around in an Excel worksheet. (The key combinations are especially beneficial for those who customarily keep their hands on the keys for quick text entry.)

Table C-3
Keys and key combinations for navigating in a worksheet

Keys	Function
Arrow keys	Move the insertion point in the direction of the arrow.
Ctrl+↑ or Ctrl+↓	Moves to the top or bottom of a region of data.
Ctrl+← or Ctrl+→	Moves the insertion point to the left-most or right-most region of data.
PgUp or PgDn	Moves up or down one screen.
Home	Moves to the first cell in a row.
Ctrl+Home	Moves the insertion point to the top left corner of the worksheet.
End	Moves to the last cell in a row.
Ctrl+End	Moves to the first cell of the last row in a worksheet.
End+← or End+→	Moves the pointer to the next blank cell in the direction of the arrow when the active cell is blank.
End+Enter	Moves the pointer to the last column in a row.

If you like using the mouse, it's also easy to navigate in a worksheet that way. You can use the scroll bars to move to the screen area containing the cell that you want to work with and then click in any cell to make it active. There are four ways to scroll with the scroll bar: click on the arrows incrementally, hold down the mouse button of the scroll arrow, drag the scroll bar box, or click on the scroll bar.

A third option for moving about in Excel is with the Go To command. If you want to move to a specific cell on a worksheet, either choose Edit⇨Go To or press F5. This opens the Go To dialog box, as shown in Figure C-6. Here you can enter the cell address that you want to see and then click on OK to go directly to that cell.

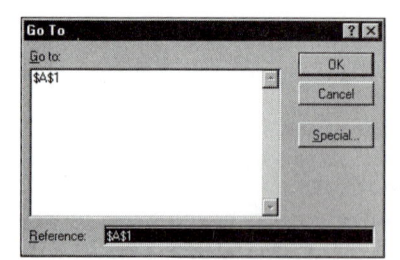

Figure C-6: The Excel GoTo dialog box.

Entering and Editing Data

You can enter combinations of numbers and letters. Just move to any cell and start typing. When done with your entry, press Enter to store it in the cell.

As you enter text, you'll sometimes want to edit it. You can use the following steps to edit existing data in worksheet cells:

1. Move the cursor to the cell containing the data that you want to edit.
2. Move the mouse pointer over the Formula bar. (As you do so, the mouse pointer takes on the shape of an I-beam.)
3. Place the mouse pointer at the location where you want to start editing, and click. A flashing insertion point in the Formula bar indicates where your editing will occur, and you can proceed to make the necessary edits. You can press Enter when done.

If you haven't completed your entry and decide that you want to change it, click on the Cancel button in the Formula bar (the button with the red X in it, as shown in Figure C-7) or press Esc. If you've already entered the text by pressing Enter, you can erase the entry by clicking on the Undo button on the Standard toolbar.

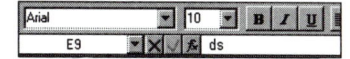

Figure C-7: The Cancel button of the Formula bar.

Two kinds of data can be entered into a worksheet: *values* and *formulas*.

- Values are data such as dates, time, percents, scientific notation, or text; values don't change unless the cell is edited.

- Formulas are sequences of cell references, names, functions, or operators that will produce a new value based on existing values in other cells of the worksheet.

Figure C-8 shows a typical worksheet containing both values and formulas.

Figure C-8: A typical worksheet with values and formulas stored in cells.

Numbers

When you begin a new worksheet in Excel, the cells are formatted with the General Number format. This causes Excel to display numbers as accurately as possible using the integer, decimal fraction, and — if the number is longer than the cell — scientific notation.

In most cases, Excel automatically assigns the correct format for your number as you enter it. If you enter a percent sign before your number, the number is assigned the percent format; if you enter a dollar sign before the number, the number is assigned a currency format. In cases where the number is too large to fit in the column, Excel displays a series of # symbols. To see the entire number, simply widen the column by double-clicking on its right border.

Entering numbers as text in Excel can be useful at times; for example, when you want to enter zip codes or other numbers that should appear as text. To do this, you must tell Excel by entering a single quotation mark (') before the number. This tells Excel to format the numbers as text and left-align them.

You can enter numbers in your worksheet using any of the numeric characters along with any of the following special characters:

```
+ - ( ) , / $ % . E e
```

Times and dates

You may often want to enter times and dates in your worksheets. While Table C-4 shows Excel's standard date and time formats, you can create custom formats of your own, as well. (Chapter 14 tells you how.) You can use any of Table C-4's formats to enter dates and times.

Table C-4
Date and Time Formats

Format	Example
D/M	3/5
D/M/YY	3/5/95
DD/MM/YY	03/04/95
D-MON	3-Apr
D-MON-YY	3-Apr-95
DD-MON-YY	03-Apr-95
MON-YY	Apr 95

Format	Example
MONTH-YY	April 95
MONTH-D-YYYY	April-5-1995
HH:MM	10:30
HH:MM AM/PM	02:30 PM
HH:MM:SS	10:30:55
HH:MM:SS AM/PM	02:30:55 PM
HH:MM.n (with tenths)	02:30.7
HH:MM:SS (24-hour)	14:30:55
D/M/YY H:MM	3/4/95 2:30
D/M/YY H:MM AM/PM	3/4/95 2:30 PM

To enter a date or time, simply enter it in one of the acceptable formats and press Enter.

Text entry

To enter text in Excel, type the text in the cell where you want it. You can type no more than 255 characters into a cell. Entries can include text and numbers and, as mentioned earlier, numbers can also be entered as text.

You may want to format large amounts of text in a way that presents an attractive display. To do this, choose Format⇨Cells; you'll see the Format Cells dialog box shown in Figure C-9.

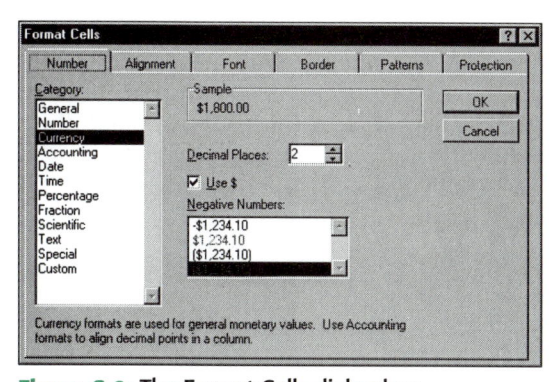

Figure C-9: The Format Cells dialog box.

If you'll be entering a long display of text, you can activate the Wrap Text option in the Wrap Text dialog box; this prevents long strips of text from overflowing into other cells. First, though, be sure that your columns are the width that you want them.

To activate text wrap, click on the Alignment tab in the dialog box and turn on the Wrap Text check box. This lets you have multiple lines of text in your cells.

Building Formulas

The whole point of spreadsheets is to manipulate the numbers. Add them. Multiply them. Calculate their cosines, if you're trigonometrically inclined. You use *formulas* to do this. You build a formula by indicating which values should be used and which calculations should apply to these values. Formulas always start with an equal sign.

For example, if you wanted to add the values in cells B1 and B2 and then display the results of that calculation in cell B5, you could place the cursor in cell B5 and enter the simple formula **=B1+B2**.

A formula calculates a value based on a combination of other values. These other values can be numbers, cell references, operators (+, -, *, and /), or other formulas. Formulas can also include the names of other areas in the worksheet, as well as cell references in other worksheets.

> **More Info** Math operators produce numeric results. Besides addition (+), subtraction (-), multiplication (*), and division (/) symbols, Excel accepts as math operators the exponentiation (^) and percentage (%) symbols. A number of other types of characters can be used in formulas for manipulating text and numbers; Chapter 14 covers them in detail.

Printing the Worksheet

To print an Excel worksheet, choose File⇨Print. A Print dialog box appears, as shown in Figure C-10. You can press Enter or click on OK to begin printing; this selects the default values for the options shown. If you want an option other than the default options, click on the option you want and then click on OK to start printing. If you want to print one copy of all the data that is in the currently selected worksheet, just click on the Print button on the Standard toolbar.

> **More Info** Chapter 18 covers printing options in detail.

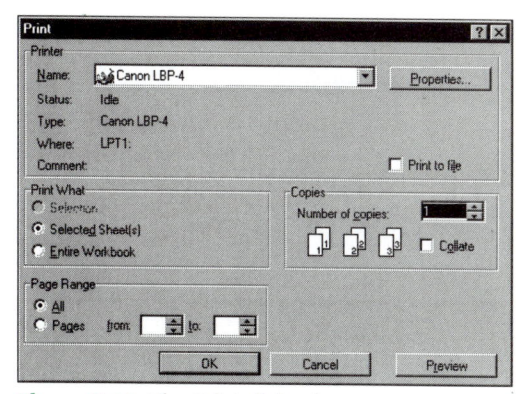

Figure C-10: The Print dialog box.

Saving the Worksheet

It's a good practice to save your worksheet on disk periodically, even if you plan to continue working on the worksheet later. Doing so reduces the possibility of losing large amounts of information because of a power failure or system crash. The commands used for saving worksheets — Save, Save As, and Save Workspace — are found in the File menu.

The Save and Save As commands save worksheets to disk. Save As prompts you for a new filename; Save saves the worksheet under the existing name (after it has been saved once).

Save As saves files in different formats from Excel's normal one. Worksheet data can be saved as ASCII text (a format that virtually all word processors can read), in Excel for Windows 95 format, in the formats of older versions of Excel, in Lotus 1-2-3 format, and in many other database and spreadsheet file formats.

To save your worksheet, choose File⇨Save. When you do this the first time, the dialog box shown in Figure C-11 appears.

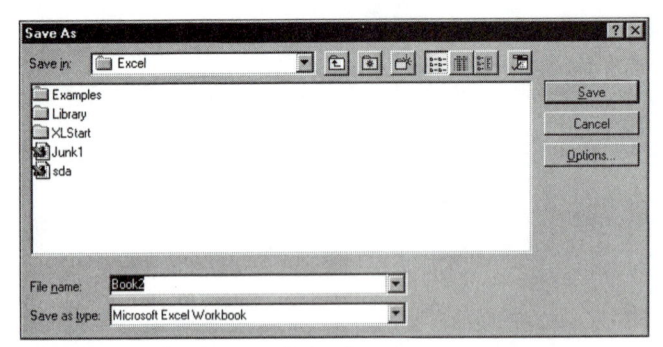

Figure C-11: The Save As dialog box.

Here you can enter a title for the worksheet in the File name text box. When you press Enter, the worksheet is saved on disk.

Summary

This appendix provided an overview of Excel basics for those who have never worked with the program. This appendix covered these points:

- ✦ Excel stores information in worksheets.
- ✦ Excel provides several toolbars to help you enter and format worksheet entries.
- ✦ Excel lets you store related worksheets in a workbook.
- ✦ You can use either the keyboard or the mouse to navigate a worksheet and a workbook.
- ✦ You enter data just by clicking in a cell and typing away; and you edit data by clicking in a cell and retyping the value, or by modifying the value in the Formula bars.
- ✦ You can format entries as numbers (the default), as times and dates, and as straight text.
- ✦ Excel lets you create formulas to manipulate the data you enter into a worksheet.
- ✦ You can save and print your worksheets and workbooks.

Where to go next...

Part Three tells you the whole Excel story. Start with Chapter 13.

✦ ✦ ✦

PowerPoint Basics

APPENDIX D

This introduction to PowerPoint provides details regarding basic PowerPoint skills. It is designed to familiarize readers who have never worked with PowerPoint before with the basics of the package. In this introduction, you'll learn how to create presentations with and without the aid of the wizards, how to enter and edit text, how to add clip art to slides, and how to print your slides. You'll also learn some basic terminology that applies to using PowerPoint. When you feel familiar with the basics, you'll find the more advanced details of PowerPoint in Chapters 25 through 30.

Understanding PowerPoint Terminology

As you work with PowerPoint, you'll often encounter some common terms. Being familiar with these terms will maximize your effectiveness in using PowerPoint. Check over the following list to familiarize yourself with these common PowerPoint terms:

- **Presentation** — In PowerPoint, a *presentation* is the container holding all the individual slides, text, graphics, drawings, and other objects that make up your presentation in its entirety. PowerPoint stores each presentation in a separate file on your hard disk.

- **Template** — A *template* is a kind of "formatting model" in PowerPoint. You use templates to apply a chosen group of styles, colors, and fonts to the slides that you are working with. PowerPoint comes with over 150 different templates; you can see examples of the style and layout of each of these by referring to Appendix F of the *PowerPoint User's Guide*.

- **Slides** — *Slides* are the individual screens or pages that you see within your presentation.

In This Appendix

Understanding PowerPoint terminology

Creating presentations

Working with existing presentations

Understanding views

Moving among slides

Editing slides

Adding clip art to a presentation

Printing presentations

- **Slide masters** — *Slide masters* are master documents that control the appearance and the layout of the slides that you create. If you make a design change to a slide master, the same change is reflected in all the new slides that you create based on that master.
- **Layout** — The term *layout* refers to the overall appearance of a single slide. You can change the layout for any slide on an individual basis without affecting other slides in the presentation.

Creating Presentations

To create a new presentation, choose File➪New to open the New Presentation dialog box shown in Figure D-1. When the New Presentation dialog box opens, the General tab is displayed along with the Blank Presentation icon. Choose from among these options:

- **General** — This tab contains the Blank Presentation icon. Use it to create a presentation that contains no preformatted slides. Next you will see the New Slide dialog box. Choose the layout for the first slide of your presentation.
- **Presentation designs** — This tab contains templates that you can use for the presentations that you create. PowerPoint contains 27 template designs that you can use to design your presentations.
- **Presentations** — This tab contains 20 different presentations that you can use for different subjects. You will also see the AutoContent Wizard that will help you create a presentation if those listed do not meet your needs. The AutoContent Wizard produces six styles of presentations, including strategy, sales, training, progress report, and bad news.

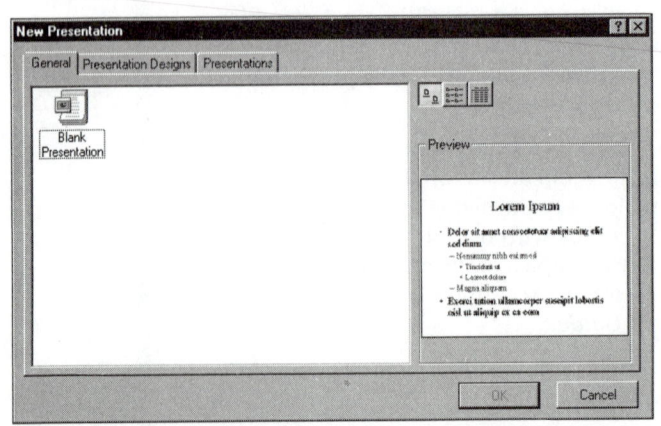

Figure D-1: The General tab of the New Presentation dialog box.

After you choose the way in which you want to create the new presentation, click on the OK button. If you chose a Wizard, you may be asked additional questions to help determine the layout and content of your presentation. When you are finished answering the questions, the basis of your presentation appears on-screen, and you can edit it as you see fit.

Using the AutoContent Wizard

When you start a new presentation with the AutoContent Wizard option, the first AutoContent Wizard dialog box appears explaining the purpose of the wizard. After you click on the Next button, the second AutoContent Wizard dialog box appears, as shown in Figure D-2.

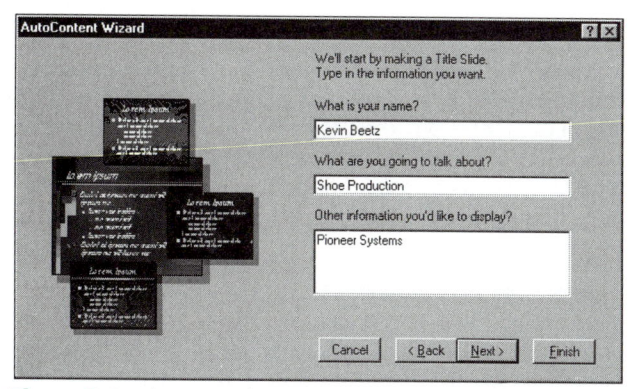

Figure D-2: The second AutoContent Wizard dialog box.

In the first text box, you can enter a title for the first slide of your presentation. The second text box asks for your name, but you don't have to include a name in this text box. In fact, whatever you enter in this text box appears as a subtitle on the first slide of the presentation, so if you want a subtitle other than your name, you can enter it here. After you fill in the entries and click on the Next button, you see the third AutoContent Wizard dialog box, as shown in Figure D-3.

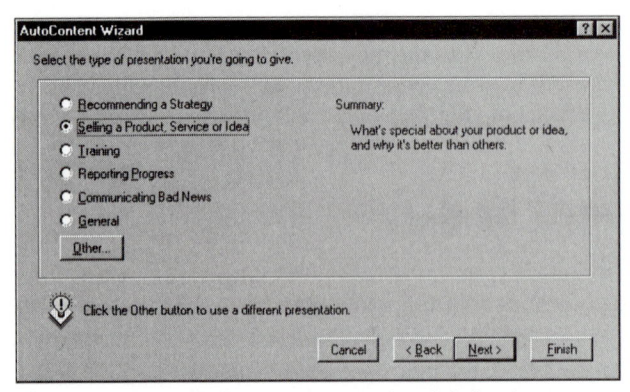

Figure D-3: The third AutoContent Wizard dialog box.

In this dialog box, you can choose the type of presentation that you want to give. In the preview area to the left of the dialog box, PowerPoint provides an outline of the common points for that type of presentation. Your options here are Recommending a Strategy; Selling a Product, Service, or Idea; Training; Reporting Progress; Communicating Bad News; and General. After you choose an option, click on the Next Buttons to show the Fourth dialog box (Figure D-4).

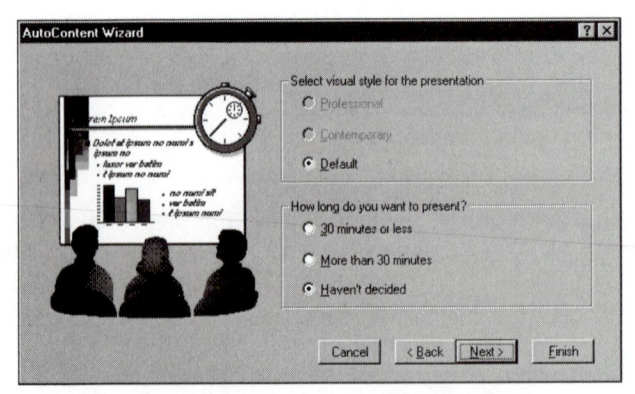

Figure D-4: The fourth AutoContent Wizard dialog box.

With the presentation completed, click the Next button to move to the final window of the AutoContent Wizard. Click the finish button to create the presentation. You can switch to Slide view or Outline view and modify the contents of the presentation.

Using a template

To use a template, choose File⇨New, and then select the Presentations tab. Now choose the template on which you want to base your presentation. Choose the desired template and click on the OK button. Next, you see the New Slide dialog box, as shown in Figure D-5.

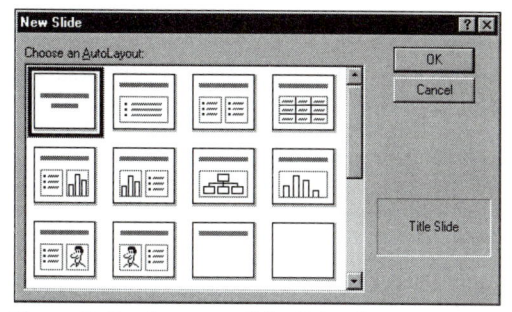

Figure D-5: The New Slide dialog box.

After you choose one of the layouts shown in the dialog box, click on the OK button. PowerPoint creates a presentation containing a single slide that uses the style and layout that you have specified. You can then add text and graphics to the slide and insert additional slides into the presentation.

Starting a blank presentation

The Blank Presentation option is suited to PowerPoint users who are familiar with the package. This option assumes that you want to handle all the design and content decisions on your own. After you choose the Blank Presentation option from the General tab of the New Presentation dialog box, the New Slide dialog box appears. After you select the layout that you want, click on the OK button. The result is a blank presentation containing a single slide, like the one shown in Figure D-6. You can add text and add slides as desired.

Figure D-6: The result of selecting the Blank Presentation option. Yes, this is supposed to be blank.

Opening a Presentation

You can open an existing presentation by choosing File➪Open or by clicking on the Open button on the Standard toolbar. Either method results in the appearance of the Open dialog box. Choose the presentation that you want and click on the OK button. You can open and work with multiple presentations simultaneously. As you open each presentation, its name is added to the bottom of the Window menu. You can switch among presentations by clicking on the presentation name from the Window menu or by pressing Ctrl+F6.

Saving and Closing a Presentation

PowerPoint uses the standard Windows methods to save files. When you choose File➪Save or click on the Save button on the Standard toolbar, PowerPoint saves the presentation to a file. If you are saving the presentation for the first time, a Save As dialog box appears, where you provide a filename for the presentation. You can save an existing presentation under a different filename by choosing File➪Save As and entering the new name for the presentation.

To close a presentation that you are finished working with, choose File➪Close or double-click on the close box in the presentation's window.

Understanding PowerPoint's Views

As you work with your presentations, you can switch between any one of five different views: Slide, Outline, Slide Sorter, Notes Pages, and Slide Show. Each of these views provides you with a different way of looking at the same presentation. To switch between the available views, you can click on the appropriate View button at the lower-left corner of your screen. You can also choose the corresponding view from the View menu. For example, choosing View⇨Outline switches you to Outline view.

Slide view fills the window with a view of the current slide. In this view, you can add and edit text and graphics or change the layout of the slide. Figure D-7 shows an example of a presentation in Slide view.

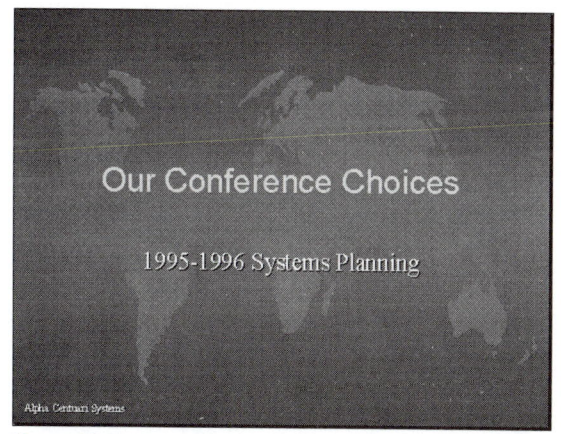

Figure D-7: An example of a presentation in Slide view.

Outline view provides a view of the overall organization of the text in your presentation. In this view, it's easier to see a large portion of your presentation's contents. Although you can't change the slide layouts or modify graphics in this view, you can add and edit the slide titles and the main text. Figure D-8 shows an example of a presentation in Outline view.

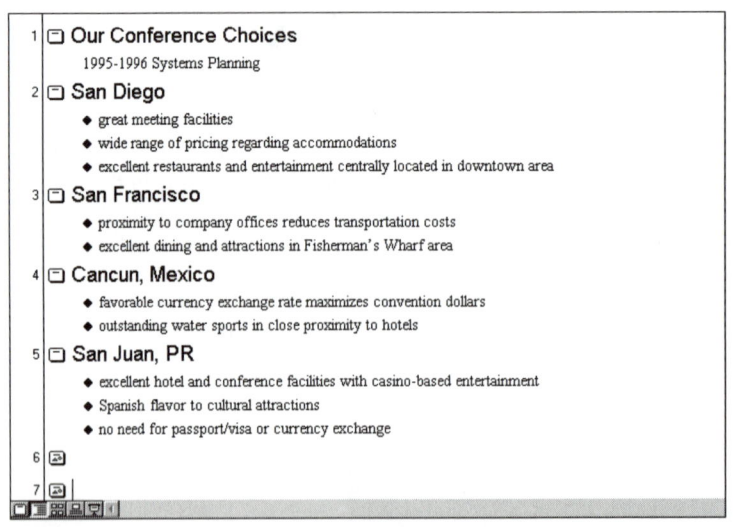

```
1 □ Our Conference Choices
     1995-1996 Systems Planning
2 □ San Diego
     ◆ great meeting facilities
     ◆ wide range of pricing regarding accommodations
     ◆ excellent restaurants and entertainment centrally located in downtown area
3 □ San Francisco
     ◆ proximity to company offices reduces transportation costs
     ◆ excellent dining and attractions in Fisherman's Wharf area
4 □ Cancun, Mexico
     ◆ favorable currency exchange rate maximizes convention dollars
     ◆ outstanding water sports in close proximity to hotels
5 □ San Juan, PR
     ◆ excellent hotel and conference facilities with casino-based entertainment
     ◆ Spanish flavor to cultural attractions
     ◆ no need for passport/visa or currency exchange
6 □
7 □
```

Figure D-8: An example of a presentation in Outline view.

More Info — Slide Sorter view provides a window containing up to 12 slides, each in reduced form. This view is best when you want an overall view of your presentation or when you want to see the overall appearance of the text and the graphics. You can't edit text or graphics in this view, but you can reorder the slides. When you are working with electronic slide shows, you can also add transitions between slides and set the timing in this view (see Chapter 28). Figure D-9 shows an example of Slide Sorter view.

Notes Pages view provides a view where a single slide is placed in the top half of a page, and the bottom half of the page is reserved for the typing of notes. This view is useful when you want to add speaker's notes that you can refer to during your presentation. PowerPoint lets you print the notes pages separately from the slides or overheads that you produce for your presentation. Figure D-10 shows an example of Notes Pages view.

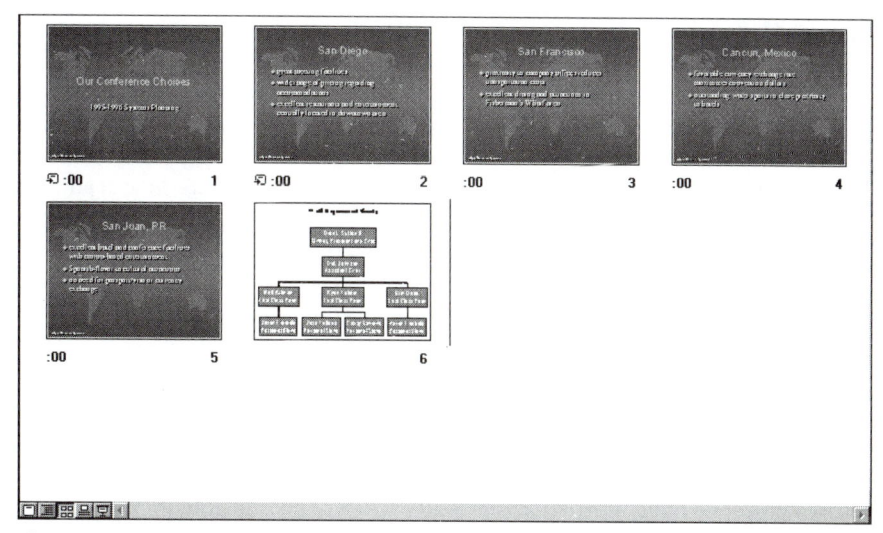

Figure D-9: An example of a presentation in Slide Sorter view.

Figure D-10: An example of a presentation in Notes Pages view.

Slide Show view fills the screen with a view of one slide at a time. In this view, you also see the effects of any transitions and timing that you have added to the presentation.

Adding Slides

If you use PowerPoint much, you'll often find yourself adding slides to presentations. To add a slide to your presentation, perform the following steps.

1. In any view, choose Insert⇨New Slide. (You can also use Ctrl+M as a shortcut.) The New Slide box appears.
2. Choose the layout you want for the new slide and click on OK.

The slide is then added to the end of your presentation. It has the same design as the other slides in your presentation.

Moving Among Slides

Most presentations have more than one slide, so you must be able to move among slides to work on your whole presentation. How you move among slides depends on which view you're in. Table D-1 shows the different methods for moving around within the different slide views.

Table D-1: Methods of moving among slides

View	How to move among slides
Outline view	Drag the scroll box to display the desired slide. Click on the slide icon to the left of the slide's title to select the slide. Click anywhere within the slide's text to edit it.
Slide view	Drag the scroll box until you reach the desired slide number or click on the Previous Slide or Next Slide button at the bottom of the vertical scrollbar.
Slide Sorter view	Click on the desired slide.
Notes Pages view	Drag the scroll box until you reach the desired slide number or click on the Previous Slide or Next Slide button at the bottom of the vertical scrollbar.

Editing a Slide's Contents

If you've created a presentation based on a blank slide, you must enter all the required text. If you used an AutoContent Wizard, you've got a fair amount of text in your presentation already, but it's probably not precisely what you want. In either case, you need to add or edit the text that you want in your presentation. This section details how you can add or edit text in Slide view or in Outline view.

Editing text in Slide view

In Slide view, you see your text along with any graphics that you have added to the slide, and you can edit any object in the slide by clicking on the object. To add text, click in the placeholder labeled *Click to add title* and type the text, as shown in Figure D-11. To edit existing text, click on the text to select it and then edit it as you normally would. If you're working with a bulleted list of topics, you can add a new topic by placing the insertion point at the end of an existing topic and pressing Enter.

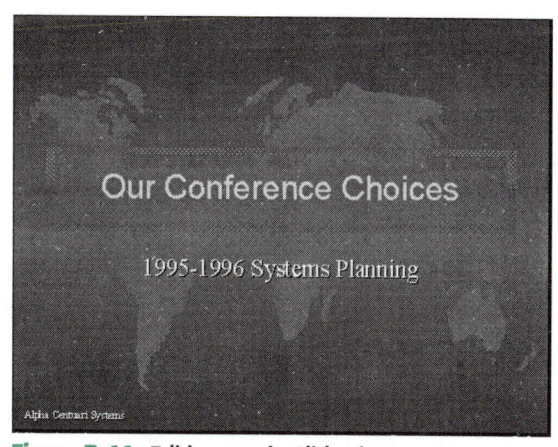

Figure D-11: Editing text in Slide view.

Editing text in Outline view

Outline view provides an easy way to edit text because you can view a lot of your presentation at one time. To edit text, just click to place the insertion point where you want it and type the desired text, as shown in Figure D-12. You can use the Delete or Backspace keys to remove unwanted text.

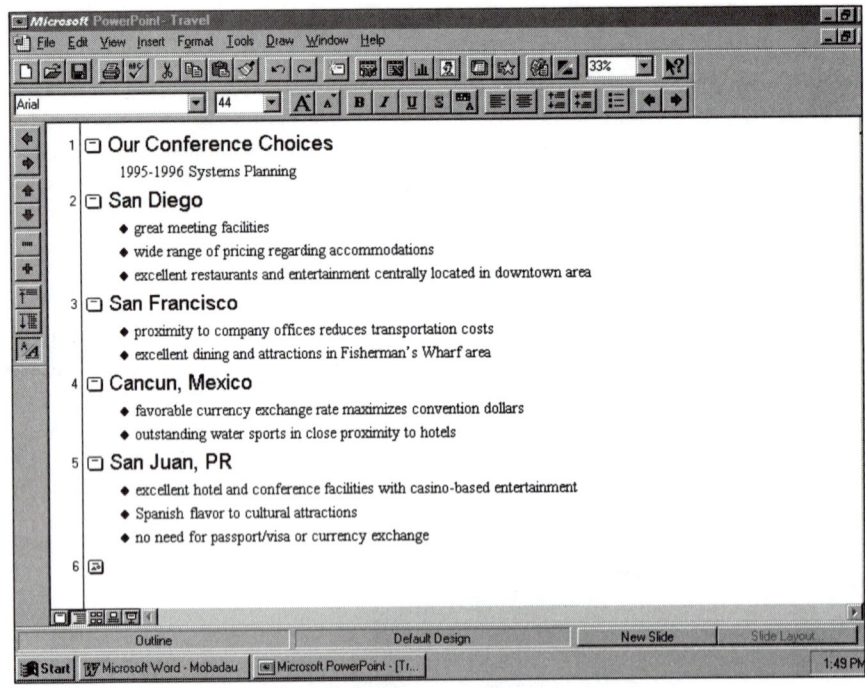

Figure D-12: Editing text in Outline view.

As you work with text in Outline view, keep in mind that you can use the Promote, Demote, Move Up, and Move Down buttons on the Outlining toolbar to the left of the screen to change the levels or the locations of the items that you are working with. Simply place the insertion point anywhere inside the desired entry and then click on the appropriate button. The Outlining buttons perform the following tasks:

- **Promote (Indent less)** — Click on this button to remove an indent and to move the entry one level higher (in importance) within the list. The item moves to the left, and in most cases, the font size increases.

- **Demote (Indent more)** — Click on this button to add an indent and to move the entry one level lower (in importance) within the list. The item moves to the right, and in most cases, the font size decreases.

- **Move Up** — Click on this button to move the entry up in the list by one line.

- **Move Down** — Click on this button to move the entry down in the list by one line.

Adding Clip Art to a Presentation

PowerPoint comes with hundreds of clip art images that you can easily add to your presentations to add pizzazz to your slides. Note that before you can insert clip art, you must have installed the ClipArt Gallery along with PowerPoint. You can add clip art by performing the following steps:

1. Switch to Slide view and display the slide where you want to add the clip art.
2. Choose Insert⇨Clip Art or click on the Insert Clip Art button on the Standard toolbar to open the ClipArt Gallery dialog box, as shown in Figure D-13.

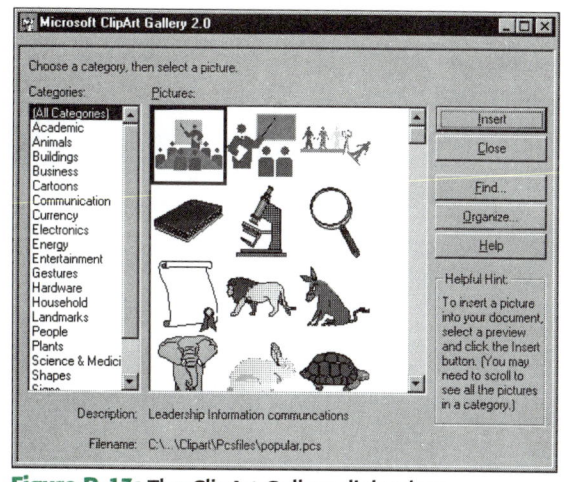

Figure D-13: The ClipArt Gallery dialog box.

Note

If you're inserting clip art for the first time, you'll see a dialog box warning you that the process may take some time because PowerPoint has to organize the files first.

3. In the Categories list box at the top of the dialog box, click on the desired category.
4. In the right half of the dialog box, click on the desired image. You can use the scrollbar at the right side of the dialog box to see additional images.
5. Click on the OK button to place the clip art in the slide.

After the clip art appears in the slide, you can click on it to select it. Then hold down the mouse button while you drag it to the location that you want. You can resize the clip art by clicking on one of the sizing handles (the small rectangles that surround the clip art when you select it) and dragging it until the clip art reaches the desired size.

Hot Stuff: You may often want to add clip art to the same area as existing text, but by default, any clip art that you add covers the existing text. To solve this problem, go into Slide view and select the clip art by clicking on it. Then choose the Send to Back command from the Draw menu to place the clip art underneath the text, which makes the text visible.

Printing Your Presentation

You can print various parts of your presentation or all of your presentation. To print your presentation, choose File⇨Print or click on the Print button on the Standard toolbar. The Print dialog box appears, as shown in Figure D-14.

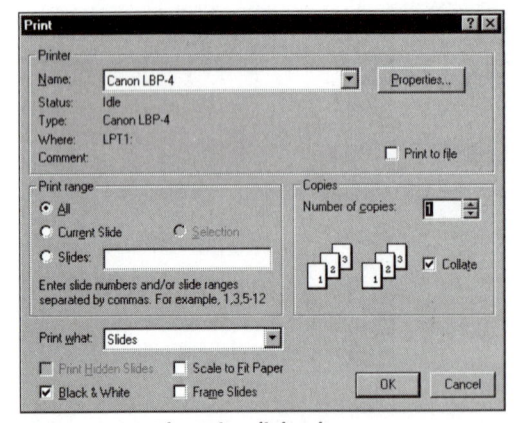

Figure D-14: The Print dialog box.

More Info: You will learn more about the Print dialog box in Chapter 28, but for now, the most important point is to remember to select exactly what you want to print. In the Print What list box, you can choose Slides, Note Pages, Handouts, or Outline View. Then choose a range of slides by selecting the desired options in the Slide Range area of the dialog box (the default option is All). Select any other desired options in the dialog box and click on the OK button to begin printing.

This appendix has provided an introduction to the basics of PowerPoint with the goal of getting you up and running quickly. The PowerPoint section of this book provides you with much more detail about what you can accomplish with all the features of PowerPoint.

Summary

This appendix covered topics relevant to quickly getting started in PowerPoint. All of the topics that were considered are considered in more depth in their respective chapters. These are some of the topics we covered.

- ✦ To work effectively with PowerPoint, you must understand these terms: Presentation, Template, Slide, Slide Master, and Layout. (They're explained at the beginning of the chapter.)
- ✦ Use File➪New and the New Presentation dialog box to create a presentation. This dialog box gives you several options. You can use the AutoContent wizard to customize one of several presentations. You can use a template to start with a basic structure for your presentation. Or, you can start with a blank presentation, and design it from the ground up.
- ✦ PowerPoint has five *views* in which you can create and edit your presentation: Slide, Outline, Slide Sorter, Notes Pages, and Slide Show.
- ✦ Use Insert➪Slide to insert a slide into a presentation. This command works from any view.
- ✦ You can edit slide text in either Slide view or Outline view.
- ✦ Use Insert➪Clip Art to insert clip art into a presentation.
- ✦ Use File➪Print to print your presentation.

Where to go next..

Part IV describes PowerPoint in detail. Start with Chapter 25.

✦ ✦ ✦

On the CD-ROM

APPENDIX E

In our travels, we've found a few nifty bits of shareware that we've enjoyed. We thought we ought to share some of it with you; hence, the CD-ROM stuck to the back cover of this book.

The book and this CD-ROM each stand on their own — you don't have to have one to use the other. You don't need the book to use the CD-ROM, because it has a front-end program that either installs, or tells you how to install, everything the disc contains. The CD-ROM also includes all the documentation that comes with each shareware package, so you can get help at any time.

We've also included the original files we created for all of the examples you've seen throughout the book. We hope you pick up a few tricks and techniques just from opening our example files and seeing how we created them.

The rest of this appendix contains excerpts from the README files for the shareware programs on the CD-ROM. We submitted these files as we found them so you can read about these programs in the authors' own words. (Our editor, however, did trim and tighten the instructions a bit for space considerations.)

Using the CD-ROM

The CD-ROM comes with a Windows Help file that gives you information about each item on the CD-ROM, including installation instructions. Some programs on the CD-ROM come with their own installation utilities. The Windows Help file lets you execute those installation utilities with a mouse click.

Here's how to get to the Windows Help file on the CD-ROM:

1. Place the CD-ROM into your CD-ROM drive and close the door.

2. Double-click on the My Computer icon on the desktop. When the My Computer window opens, double-click on the CD-ROM icon it contains. A window appears (Figure E-1) that shows the CD-ROM's contents.

In This Appendix

Word templates and utilities

Excel templates and utilities

Fonts

General utilities to help you get more from your system and from Office

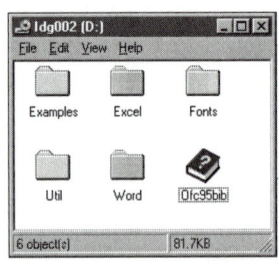

Figure E-1: The CD-ROM's contents.

3. Double-click on the Ofc95bib icon. The Windows Help file opens, as shown in Figure E-2.

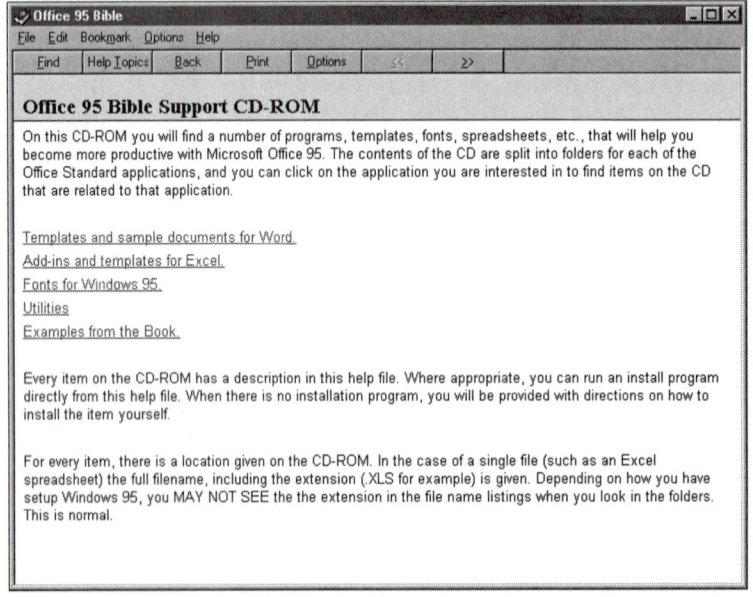

Figure E-2: The Windows Help file that describes the CD-ROM's contents and tells you how to install each item from the CD-ROM.

Navigate the Windows Help file to learn more about each item on the CD-ROM.

About Shareware

Shareware is a way for you to try software before you buy it. If you use a shareware program for a while and like it, you register the program with its author. This usually means you send the author some quantity of money — $30 seems to be the norm, but many of the shareware packages on this CD-ROM cost $6 to $10 to register.

Shareware is usually produced by talented programmers who don't have the resources to shrink-wrap and aggressively market their product. They let people use their software on the honor system. The registration funds they receive encourage them to write more shareware, and to support the shareware they've written.

The caveat about shareware is that the authors don't promise perfection. The authors don't have the resources to perform large-scale beta testing of their software. If you find a bug, send a note to the author. He or she will probably fix the problem in a future release of the software.

While our publisher would love it if you thought that the only way to get shareware is to buy more books with CD-ROMs, there's another way. The Internet, online services such as CompuServe and America Online, and independent bulletin board systems (BBSs) are hotbeds of shareware distribution. If you have an account on CompuServe, America Online, or a local BBS, look for their shareware directories. It's a little trickier to find shareware on the Internet, but it's out there.

Excel

We've included three Excel utilities and templates. The first is John Walkenbach's great Power Utility Pak, which gives you all sorts of cool features you'll like having around. You'll also find the amort.xlm template that calculates an amortization table, and the deprec8.xlm template, which calculates a depreciation schedule.

The Power Utility Pak

The Power Utility Pak was developed by John Walkenbach, author of *Excel for Windows 95 Bible, Excel for Windows 95 Power Programming Techniques, 2nd Edition* (available in early 1996), and many other IDG books. The shareware version of the Power Utility Pak contains most (but not all) of the functionality of the full registered version. The version on the CD-ROM is a special 32-bit version (2.0a) for Excel for Windows 95, and will not work with Excel 5. (A separate version for Excel 5 is also available.)

Appendixes

Description

The Power Utility Pak is a comprehensive package that adds new features to Excel and can make you more productive. The package includes

- 21 general-purpose spreadsheet utilities
- 22 new worksheet functions
- Enhanced shortcut menus
- A new Utilities menu to access the utilities
- A custom toolbar to access the utilities (optional)
- Detailed, context-sensitive, online help for the utilities and functions

Note The complete source code for the Power Utility Pak also is available. This well-documented VBA code contains a wealth of information and dozens of useful techniques that will help users master Visual Basic for Applications. The complete source files are available to registered users for an additional $20.

These utilities add new features to Excel and can improve productivity by performing multiple operations with a single command — or by doing things that are otherwise impossible in Excel. Following is a brief description of the utilities included with the Power Utility Pak.

Text Tools: Manipulates text in cells in a number of ways. Text can be changed to uppercase, lowercase, or proper case. This utility can also add specific text to the beginning or end of each cell — or delete a fixed number of characters from each cell. The Stats button displays the number of words and characters in the selected text. This utility also works with cells that contain values.

Select by Value: Selects a group of cells based on its value or text content. For example, this utility can be used to flag all cells in a range that have a negative value. The Select by Value utility selects these cells automatically, and you can then apply formatting to make the values stand out. This utility also works with dates and text.

Interactive Zooming: Magnifies or reduces a worksheet or chart interactively. A handy scroller and preview button lets you see the results that you commit to it.

Reminder Note: Adds a reminder note to a worksheet, chart, or dialog sheet. You can choose the color and text style and determine whether it will print. Other options hide, display, or delete all reminder notes.

Object Align, Size and Space: A fast, easy, and reliable way to align and resize drawn objects on a worksheet, chart, or in a custom dialog box. Another option adjusts the objects so that they are evenly spaced.

Calculator: Displays a handy mousable calculator (which also accepts input from the keyboard). The result of the calculation can be pasted into a cell.

3D Cell Shading: Adds an attractive three-dimensional background to a cell or range. You can choose either a raised look or a depressed look, choose the color, and specify the line thickness.

Insert 3D Text: Converts the text in a cell or range to an attractive graphic object with a 3-D look.

Date and Time: Runs the Windows 95 Date/Time utility, which displays the current date, time, and day of the week. You also can adjust the system time and date.

Insert-a-Date: Inserts a formatted date into a cell. You choose the date from a calendar display and can select from a variety of date formats. As an option, the column width can be automatically adjusted to accommodate the pasted date.

Perpetual Calendar: Displays a handy and attractive pop-up calendar for any month in years between 1900 and 2078. The calendar picture can even be pasted into a worksheet or chart. Another option creates a new workbook nicely formatted as a calendar — perfect for scheduling.

Reminder Alarm: Displays a reminder message at a specified time. After setting the alarm, Excel's title bar displays the time that the alarm is set for. The reminder message is accompanied by three beeps, so the reminder will be effective even if you're not working in Excel.

Time Tracker: Keeps track of the amount of time spent working on various projects (and the projects need not be Excel projects). You can track time spent on up to four projects and customize the project or client names used.

Object Properties: Displays the dimensions and position of graphic objects. You can enter new dimensions or reposition the object by specifying coordinates, or use the "nudge" buttons to move or resize in 1-pixel increments. This utility also lets you hide and unhide objects (something that normally requires a macro).

Super Go To: Allows easy navigation through multiple workbooks and worksheets. You can select the workbook, sheet, or range to activate. A handy preview mode displays the selection (even if it's in a hidden or minimized workbook). The dialog box can be used in two sizes (smaller, if range names aren't used).

Workbook Table of Contents: Displays a handy table of contents that lists all sheets in the active workbook. It also displays the type of sheet (worksheet, macro sheet, chart, and so on), and you can filter the display to show only sheets of a certain type. Double-clicking quickly activates the selected sheet.

Save With Backup: Saves the active workbook with a backup copy. Normally, saving a workbook to a floppy disk to make a backup is a cumbersome procedure, because Excel "remembers" the floppy drive as the workbook's location. When the file is saved again, it will be saved to the floppy disk — unless you remember to use the File⇨Save As command to redirect the save back to the hard drive. This utility saves a workbook to the selected floppy disk (or another directory) and then saves it back to the hard drive — all in one step.

Batch Printing: Prints a group of workbooks unattended. The user can choose any number of files to print. The user can choose exactly what gets printed — worksheets, chart sheets, VBA modules, or dialog sheets.

Auditing Tools: Creates a new workbook with information about the active worksheet, a graphical map, and a list of formulas.

Bubble Chart Wizard: Converts an X-Y chart into an attractive bubble chart — a chart type that Excel does not directly support.

Toolbar Tools: Lets the user change the Tooltips associated with any toolbar button. Also supports copying and renaming toolbars (operations that most users would say are impossible).

The Power Utility Pak also includes 22 functions that can be used in worksheets. These functions work exactly like Excel's built-in functions and even appear in the Function Wizard. The functions are described next.

Contains(text1,text2,casesensitive): Returns TRUE if text1 is contained in text2.

CountAVisible(value1,value2...): Similar to Excel's COUNTA function, but it returns the count of just the visible cells — perfect for use with Excel's autofilter and outline features.

DaysinMonth(date): Returns the number of days in the month for a date.

ExcelDir(): Displays the full path for the folder in which Excel is installed.

FileExists(Filename): Returns TRUE if a specified file exists.

FileName(): Displays the full path and filename of the workbook.

GetINISetting(INIfile,Section,Entry): Returns the setting for a particular entry in an .INI file.

InsertString(instring,origstring,pos): Inserts a string at a specified position in another string.

IsLike(text,pattern): Returns TRUE if text is "like" pattern. Pattern is a string that uses * and ? wildcard characters. For example, =IsLike("Johnson","John*") returns TRUE.

MonthWeek(date): Returns the calendar week in the month for any date. Perfect for applications such as payroll.

NoExtremesAvg(range): Returns the average of a range of values, but excludes the highest and lowest values — a common procedure to eliminate the effects of extreme values or outliers.

ParseName(string,name): Splits a name into its component parts: first name, last name, middle name. It even handles common titles (Mr., Ms., Dr.) and knows what to do when a name is followed by "Jr."

ReadRegistry(key,valuename): Returns an entry from the Windows 95 Registry database.

RemoveSpaces(text): Removes all of the spaces from a string.

Scramble(text,recalc): Accepts text or a value and returns it — scrambled randomly.

SelectOne(range,recalc): Returns a single value chosen at random from a range.

StaticRand(): Returns a random number that doesn't change when the worksheet is recalculated.

SumVisible(number1,number2...): Similar to Excel's SUM function, but it returns the sum of just the visible cells — perfect for use with Excel's autofilter and outline features.

User(): Returns the name of the current user.

WhichDay(weekdaynum,DOW,themonth,theyear): Returns a date that corresponds to a request such as "the first Friday in November," or the "last Monday in June."

WindowsDir(): Displays the full path of the Windows folder.

WindowsVersion(): Returns the version number of the version of Windows that is currently running.

Installation instructions

Note Running the Power Utility Pak directly from the CD-ROM is not recommended.

To install the Power Utility Pak, follow these instructions:

1. Create a new folder on your hard drive. I recommend that you create a folder named Power inside your `Excel\Library` folder.
2. Copy all of the Power Utility Pak files to this new folder.
3. Start Excel.
4. Select the <u>T</u>ools⇨Add-<u>I</u>ns command. Excel will display its Add-Ins dialog box.
5. Click on the Browse button in the Add-Ins dialog box.
6. Locate the folder where you copied the files, and select the `Power.xla` file.
7. Close the Add-Ins dialog box.
8. The Power Utility Pak add-in will be installed. You will also get a new custom toolbar, plus a new menu command: <u>U</u>tilities.

Complete online help is provided for all of the utilities and worksheet functions.

How to register

As a special offer for readers of this book, you can register the Power Utility Pak for only $9.95 (a savings of $30). To do so, you must use the coupon located in the back of this book. You can contact John Walkenbach at the following address:

JWalk and Associates
P.O. Box 12861
La Jolla, CA 92039-2861

e-mail: 70363.3014@compuserve.com

Amort.xlm version v.4.1

This Microsoft Excel macro application generates fixed rate and variable rate loan schedules. It allows for variable interest rates and extra principal payments. For variable rate loans, it can project a worst-case interest rate change based on the loan's maximum rate and maximum increase per adjustment period. It lets you change any component of the monthly payment (insurance, taxes, and so on) at any point in the loan. The amortization schedules show annual totals for interest and principal paid. Generated spreadsheets are complete and functional, but not customizable without the password you get when you register for $10.

Installation

Copy this file into your Excel directory. This is `\MS Office\Excel` on most computers.

Usage

The macro runs automatically when opened. It asks you to supply information about the loan (length, rate, and so on). You cannot enter any data into the variable rate-related fields unless you select the variable rate option. When you complete all the fields and click on OK, the macro generates a loan schedule based on the information provided.

Registration

When you register this product, we'll send you the password to unprotect the generated spreadsheets. The unprotected spreadsheets can be customized in any manner you wish, to change fonts, colors, column widths, and so on. You will be able to see and adjust all formulas, and customize the text to fit your needs.

Registration costs $10; send your check with a copy of the following form. For faster service, mail the check to the address shown in the form, and send us an e-mail message saying, "The check is in the mail for Amort.xlm 4.1." We will then reply to your e-mail with the password and instructions to unprotect the generated schedules. You can reach us on CompuServe at 70412,2455. From the Internet, that's 70412.2455@compuserve.com

> **Order form: Amort.xlm v. 4.1**
> Yes, I want to register Amort.xlm v. 4.1.
>
> Name: _____
>
> Address: _____
>
> City, State, Zip: _____
>
> Send this form and a check for $10.00 to:
>
> Ohio Star Software
> Amort.xlm 4.1 Registration
> 8919 Deep Forest Ln.
> Centerville, OH 45458

Deprec8.xlm version 1.0

Deprec8.xlm is a Microsoft Excel macro application that generates depreciation schedules for tax and book purposes. For tax purposes, it uses the IRS-defined Modified Accelerated Cost Recovery System (MACRS) to calculate annual depreciation amounts. For tax purposes, most tangible depreciable property placed in service after 1986 must be depreciated under MACRS. Deprec8.xlm gives you the option of using the MACRS half-year or midquarter convention for property being depreciated over 3, 5, 7, 10, 15, or 20 years. Schedules for 27.5 and 39 years use the IRS-defined MACRS midmonth convention. For book purposes, Deprec8.xlm generates schedules of any duration with either straight line, double declining balance or the sum of the years digits method. Deprec8.xlm handles fiscal years that do not follow the calendar year, and salvage values for book purposes.

Deprec8.xlm cannot eliminate the need for consulting advice from an accountant. Ohio Star Software is not responsible for any problems caused by the improper use of this software, the improper application of accounting principles, or the violation of tax laws.

Installation
Copy this file into your Excel directory. This is `\MSOffice\Excel` on most computers.

Usage
Running Deprec8.xlm is easy. Deprec8.xlm is a Microsoft Excel macro that runs automatically when opened by Excel. Deprec8.xlm can also be restarted during the same Excel session by pressing Ctrl+Shift+A (for the input screen) or Ctrl+Shift+Z (for the introductory screen).

When you load Deprec8.xlm, you will see an introductory screen. Select "Generate a Depreciation Schedule" to go on to the input screen. The input screen is used to provide basic information about the asset (value, description, and so on). When you have completed all fields, click on OK. The macro generates a depreciation schedule based on the information provided.

Registration

Deprec8.xlm is not completely functional in its distributed shareware form. For tax purposes, it will only generate a 10-year schedule. For book purposes, it will only generate straight-line depreciation schedules. If you would like to have the tool generate other lengths of tax-purpose schedules or a double-declining balance schedule, you will need to register the product.

- **Level 1: $10.00** — You will receive the Full Function Password required to generate all of the possible schedule lengths and types. If you only have a couple of assets to account for, then this is the best way to go.

- **Level 2: $25.00** — You will receive the commercial (nonshareware) version of this product without password protection on the macro itself. This will give you complete control over how the schedules are generated. You won't have to enter a password to generate a schedule. You will be able to modify the macro source code to customize the generated schedules for your business. If you need to generate a lot of schedules and you need them customized for your business, this is the best way to go.

For faster service with level 1 registrations, mail the $10 check to the address shown in the coupon below and send us an e-mail message saying, "The check is in the mail for Deprec8 ver 1.0." We will reply to your e-mail with the Full Function Password and wait for your check to arrive. You can reach us on CompuServe at 70412,2455. From the Internet, reach us at 70412.2455@compuserve.com.

Order form: Deprec8.xlm v. 1.0

Yes, I want to register Deprec8.xlm v. 1.0.

Name: _____

Address: _____

City, State, Zip: _____

Check one: ___ Level 1 Registration ($10.00) ___ Level 2 Registration ($25.00)

Send this form and your check to:

Ohio Star Software
Deprec8.xlm 1.0 Registration
8919 Deep Forest Ln.
Centerville, OH 45458

Fonts

We found a great set of fonts you can use to grab attention in your presentations and documents. The designer of these fonts graciously let us include a few of them on our CD-ROM. When you register, he'll send you the whole package.

Fonts from the 35HEADS collection

The fonts in this directory are from the 35HEADS font set, a collection of headline and decorative fonts. This directory includes six of the 35HEADS fonts: Akenaten, BeesWax, CindyBob, Coliseum, Comaro, and HolyMoly. It also includes the file SEE35HDS.EXE, a Windows CardFile file that shows you all the fonts in the package. If you didn't delete CardFile after installing Windows 95, you can see examples of all the 35HEADS fonts by copying that file to some temporary directory that has about 450,000 bytes available and running it. You'll also find some additional technical information and details not included here.

Installation

Drag the fonts from the CD into the \Windows\Fonts directory.

Your rights and obligations

These free fonts are provided as shareware. However, you have already fulfilled your obligation by receiving the complete archived file, which includes the font and the promotional information about other fonts that you may purchase. For having received and read these files, you may use the free fonts for as long as you wish.

You have unlimited rights to use these fonts in any form that your software can use them, except to re-create font files. You may not do anything with the complete font file itself except install it, make backup copies, and let your software use it to format and create characters. You may not convert the fonts to another format and redistribute it.

Your installation and use of the free fonts signifies your acceptance of these terms.

My rights and obligations

These fonts are distributed in the belief that they will be useful, but without any express warranty including even the implied warranty of merchantability or fitness for a particular purpose.

I retain ownership of the creation of these font files and rights of distribution of these fonts in any form.

Registration

If you enjoy these fonts, you can order the entire 35HEADS package for $10. You'll get all of the fonts in TrueType or PostScript, Type 1, format. (I'll send you both formats for $12.50.) You have the right to use the fonts for anything for which you would use any other purchased font. Of course, you can't resell or pass on copies of the font files themselves. You may not give copies to friends. You may not load the purchased fonts onto any bulletin board. You have a full money-back guarantee if you're not happy with these fonts.

> **Note** If you're a registered previous purchaser of 15FONTS or 25FONTS, send only $5 and you'll get a complete new set in the format and disk type of your choice.

To order, photocopy the order form below and then fill it out. Or write it out on a separate piece of paper. Or, if you're really frugal, forget the order form and just mark the options (format/disk size) on the "notes" line of your check. Send your check to the address shown in the order form below. I'll send you your fonts on the business day after I receive your order.

You can reach me online. On CompuServe, I'm 72327,1702. On America Online, I'm ThomasH53.

Order form: 35HEADS

Hey Tom! I've taken a look at your free fonts and I want the whole thing! Please send me the complete 35HEADS font package!

Your name: _____

Address: _____

City/State/Zip/(Country): _____

Please mark one disk size: ___ 3 $1/2$" HD or ___ 5 $1/4$" HD

Please check one box only:

___ TrueType only ($10.00)

___ PostScript only ($10.00)

___ TrueType and PostScript ($12.50)

Write your check or money order to Thomas E. Harvey, and send it and this form to:

Thomas E. Harvey
420 N. Bayshore Blvd., #206
Clearwater, FL 34619

Utilities

Because Office applications can use graphics and sounds, it's useful to have a few utilities lying around that help you manipulate and keep track of your graphics and sound files. We've provided Jasc Media Center, which helps you keep track of such files, and Jasc Paint Shop Pro, which lets you paint images, retouch existing images, convert images to other formats, and capture your computer's screen as an image. NoteWorthy Composer lets you compose music that you can use as sounds in your applications. Finally, we've included WinZip95, which decompresses archived files. If you spend any time on online services or the Internet, you'll come across archived files — and you'll need WinZip.

Jasc Media Center

Jasc Media Center is designed to be your command center for multimedia file management and manipulation. It consists of all the necessary commands to manage your multimedia files. You can organize your multimedia files into albums via thumbnails. You can arrange the album using drag and drop or one of many sort options. You can catalog your multimedia files using keywords and comments for future searches. You can scan for all the multimedia files on your system to hunt down those unneeded, space-wasting files.

Jasc Media Center lets you view your images full screen or in a configurable slide show. You can also play your .WAVs, .MIDs, .AVIs and .FLC/.FLIs individually or with the configurable slide show. You may also associate a .WAV with images in the slide show, or play an audio CD in the background.

You can configure Jasc Media Center to summon your favorite media file editors, even one for each file extension. You can also print your entire album as a catalog or individual images. You can convert, move, copy, delete, or rename your original multimedia files.

Jasc Media Center supports over 35 different file formats.

Multimedia files of an album may come from different directories and different drives. Special support for removable disks and CD-ROMs lets you track your files and have Jasc Media Center tell you which disk you need.

Installation

Before you can use Jasc Media Center, you have to run the Jasc Media Center setup program from Windows so it will work properly on your computer. You cannot just copy the files from the Jasc Media Center disk to your hard disk. The files on the distribution disk are packed in a special way to save space. The setup program unpacks those files and builds them on your working disk.

You can run the Setup program from the CD-ROM's Windows Help file. See "Using the CD-ROM" at the beginning of this Appendix for details.

Usage

You will find that documentation of all menu items and associated dialog boxes, along with general information, is provided online using the program's HELP-INDEX menu option.

When you purchase the licensed version of Jasc Media Center, you will receive a fully illustrated, bound User's Guide.

Registration

You may use the shareware version of Jasc Media Center for a 30-day trial period. If you would like to continue to use Jasc Media Center after the 30-day trial period, you are required to purchase the licensed version of Jasc Media Center. When you purchase the licensed version of Jasc Media Center, you will receive a disk with the licensed version and the printed User's Guide.

Jasc Media Center may be purchased from a number of sources. You are free to purchase your copy from wherever you desire.

To obtain the listing of vendors, and print an order form

1. Start Jasc Media Center.
2. At the Shareware Dialog Box, click on the Help button.
3. Click the left mouse button on the vendor of your choice.
4. Click on the Print button in the Help System.

Paint Shop Pro

Paint Shop Pro is the only photo retouching, painting, image format conversion, and screen capturing program you will need. Its features include

- **Painting** — Paint Shop Pro supports eight different brushes — pen, pencil, marker, crayon, chalk, charcoal, airbrush, and paintbrush — to edit an existing image, or create a new image. A user-defined brush lets you combine elements of any of the other brushes to create a unique effect, while the fill tool lets you easily fill large areas. You don't need to worry about errors — the undo brush lets you correct mistakes easily.

- **Photo Retouching** — Work on existing images with the clone brush for easy duplication of image areas, or with the magic wand for quick selection of similar areas for manipulation. Also provided are a push brush for easy touch-up, a sharpen brush to enhance detail in small areas, and a smooth brush for easy blending. You can also use the eyedropper to pick up and analyze a color from an image.

- **Image Enhancement and Editing** — Paint Shop Pro lets you perform flip, mirror, rotate, and crop operations. It also lets you add borders and frames, as well as resize and resample your image. Paint Shop Pro ships with 20 standard image filters. You can also create your own filters. Also included are 12 image deformations, including skew and circle. Filter and deformation browsers are also provided. Paint Shop Pro supports Adobe-compatible plug-in filters.

- **Color Enhancement** — With Paint Shop Pro, you can alter hue, saturation, lightness, and RGB levels. You can also adjust brightness and contrast, and change highlight, shadow, and midtone. Palette editing and direct palette mapping let you globally change multiple images. Gamma correction and color reduction are also provided.

- **Image Browser** — The browser, using thumbnails, lets you visually search directories for those easy-to-lose images. The thumbnails may optionally be saved for super-quick access. You can also select multiple images to be loaded directly into Paint Shop Pro for editing. Complete file management functions allow you to easily keep track of images.

- **Batch Conversion** — When it comes to converting a large number of images from one format to another, Paint Shop Pro has made it as easy as possible. All messages during the conversion are sent to the log window for unattended operation, and the log may be saved to a file for later inspection.

Paint Shop Pro also provides image viewing and printing functions to give you complete control over how your images appear. Support for TWAIN-compliant scanners is also included.

Installation

Before you can use Paint Shop Pro, you have to run the Paint Shop Pro setup program from Windows so it will work properly on your computer. You cannot just copy the files from the Paint Shop Pro disk to your hard disk. The files on the distribution disk are packed in a special way to save space. The setup program unpacks those files and builds them on your working disk.

You can run the Setup program from the CD-ROM's Windows Help file. See "Using the CD-ROM" earlier in this Appendix for details.

Usage

In order to keep the size of the Shareware version of Paint Shop Pro reasonable, no user's manual is provided. You will find that documentation for all menu items and associated dialog boxes, along with general information, is provided online using the HELP-CONTENTS menu option of the program.

When you purchase the licensed version of Paint Shop Pro, you will receive a fully illustrated, bound User's Guide.

Registration

You may use the shareware version of Paint Shop Pro for a 30-day trial period. If you would like to continue to use Paint Shop Pro after the 30-day trial period, you are required to purchase the licensed version of Paint Shop Pro.

When you purchase the licensed version of Paint Shop Pro, you will receive disk(s) with the licensed version and the printed User's Guide.

Paint Shop Pro may be purchased from a number of sources. You are free to purchase your copy from wherever you desire.

To obtain the listing of vendors and print an order form:

1. Start Paint Shop Pro.
2. At the Shareware Dialog Box, click on the Help button.
3. Click the left mouse button on the vendor of your choice.
4. Click on the Print button in the Help System.

NoteWorthy Composer

NoteWorthy Composer is a shareware music composition and notation processor for Windows, providing for the creation, playback, and printing of your own musical scores. You can

- ◆ Print your whole score (for a conductor's view), or just the staves you select, in several font sizes.
- ◆ Import and export standard MIDI files.
- ◆ Use the keyboard or the mouse for notation editing.
- ◆ Selectively add or remove slurs, staccato, accents, beams, triplets, and accidentals through toolbar buttons.
- ◆ Use the included tools to automatically transpose, beam, and arrange accidentals in your score staves to make them look professional.
- ◆ Create up to four lyric lines per staff.
- ◆ Add various performance expressions, such as crescendos, fermatas, breath marks, and accelerandos that are recognized and performed during playback.

You'll be composing, arranging, and printing in no time!

Installation

To install NoteWorthy Composer, run the Setup program. You can run the Setup program from the CD-ROM's Windows Help file. See "Using the CD-ROM" earlier in this Appendix for details.

Danger Zone: This program's installation utility may not exit on some systems. If the installer does not seem to exit on your system, do the following: Press Ctrl+Alt+Del to bring up the Close Program window; select "NoteWorthy ArtWare Setup" and click on the End Task button. Then, press Ctrl+Alt+Del again; select "Setup (Not Responding)" and click on the End Task button. The installer will exit, and you will be able to run NoteWorthy Composer.

Support and Feedback

You can reach NoteWorthy ArtWare at one of the following addresses:

Internet E-Mail: NtWorthy@aol.com
America Online: NtWorthy
Compuserve: 73561,1021
Prodigy: KBHV62B

If you do not have access to online e-mail to one of the above addresses, you may write to us at the following postal address:

NoteWorthy ArtWare
9432 Jenmar Drive
Fuquay-Varina, NC 27526-9647
USA

Note to registered users: For best service, be sure to indicate that you are a registered user on any correspondence with NoteWorthy ArtWare. Response time for e-mail queries from registered users will typically be within 48 hours.

Registration

Upgrading to the registered version is still priced at $39. See online help and associated order forms for details on how to order.

If you wish to purchase a site license for NoteWorthy Composer, please contact us directly for a quote. We will need to know the number of stations that you are interested in licensing.

Order form: NoteWorthy Composer

Please send me a licensed copy of NoteWorthy Composer Version 1.

Name: _____

Address: _____

Daytime phone: _____

Evening phone: _____

Fax: _____

E-mail: _____

Diskette Size (circle): $3^1/_2$" or $5^1/_4$"   (high density diskettes are provided)

I have enclosed a check or money order drawn from a U.S. bank or institution made payable to NoteWorthy ArtWare for the amount totaled below:

NoteWorthy Composer Price	=	$	39.00
Shipping and Handling (Free!)	+	$	0.00
North Carolina Residents, add 6% sales tax (add $2.34)	+	$	_____
Total Enclosed Payment:	=	$	_____

Current price guaranteed through 31 December 1995. Customers outside of the U.S. must use an international money order. U.S. and Canadian customers, please allow 2 to 4 weeks for delivery. Customers outside of the U.S. and Canada, please allow 4 to 8 weeks for delivery.

Send your check and this form to:

NoteWorthy ArtWare
9432 Jenmar Drive
Fuquay-Varina, NC 27526-9647
USA

WinZip95

Have you ever used the Internet or CompuServe? If so, you've probably encountered .ZIP files. Are you a Windows user? If so, WinZip is *the* way to handle these archived files.

This is the prerelease (beta test) version of WinZip, with specific features for Windows 95. See Help in the program for more information.

WinZip brings the convenience of Windows to the use of .ZIP files without requiring PKZIP and PKUNZIP. It features an intuitive point-and-click, drag-and-drop interface for viewing, running, extracting, adding, deleting, and testing files in archives. .ARJ, .LZH, and .ARC files are supported via external programs. WinZip interfaces to most virus scanners.

WinZip Windows 95-specific features include

- Extract an archive to any directory via drag and drop without leaving the Explorer. Use the right mouse button to drag and drop a .ZIP from an Explorer window to any directory, and then choose Extract to from the context menu. Remember to use the *right* mouse button while dragging.

- Add selected file(s) to a .ZIP directly from the Explorer. Right-click on any file (or selected group of files) in the Explorer and choose Add To Zip from the context menu. This provides a function similar to the Add entry in the WinZip File Manager Extension.

- Explorer-style Add dialog box.

- The Delete Archive operation moves archives to the Recycle Bin rather than permanently deleting the archive.

- The Rename, Copy, and Move operations use the Windows 95 "overwrite" user interface.

- .ZIPs opened with WinZip are properly added to the Documents menu in the Start menu.

- Explorer-style New and Open dialog boxes.

- Extract files from a .ZIP in the Explorer by right-clicking on the .ZIP and choosing "Extract To" from the context menu.

- Create archives on the desktop by right-clicking on the desktop and choose WinZip File from the New context menu entry.

- Uninstall WinZip using Add/Remove Applications in the Control Panel.

- WinZip uses the correct colors if you change color schemes.

- The WinZip toolbar buttons and status line colors will match the rest of your desktop.
- The WinZip Options/Explorer Configuration dialog box lets you add WinZip to the Start menu.
- Long filename support and Universal Naming Convention support.

Additional Windows 95 features are under development. Stay tuned!

Registration

This is not free software. You are hereby licensed to use this software for evaluation purposes without charge for a period of 21-days. If you use this software after the 21-day evaluation period, a registration fee of $29 is required. When payment is received you will be sent a registered copy of the latest version of WinZip.

Unregistered use of WinZip after the 21-day evaluation period is in violation of U.S. and international copyright laws.

WinZip 5.6a has not yet been released. If you order WinZip now you will receive WinZip 5.6 and will be able to upgrade to WinZip 5.6a for free when it is released.

Ordering by check: To order by check, send the following order form and a check to Nico Mak Computing, Inc., P.O. Box 919, Bristol, CT 06011. Payments must be in U.S. dollars drawn on a U.S. bank, or you can send international postal money orders in U.S. dollars.

CompuServe Registration: To have the registration fee added to your CompuServe bill, type GO SWREG at the ! prompt and follow the menus. WinZip's registration ID is 402.

For information about ordering by credit card, about site licenses, and about ordering outside the USA and Canada, see the file `Order.txt` on the CD-ROM.

Any questions about the status of the shipment of an order, refunds, registration options, product details, technical support, volume discounts, dealer pricing, site licenses, etc., must be directed to Nico Mak Computing, Inc., P.O. Box 919, Bristol, CT 06011, USA; or by CompuServe mail to 70056,241; or by Internet mail to 70056.241@compuserve.com

Order form: WinZip 5.6
WinZip Single Copy

____ copies at $29 each   = _____

Connecticut residents add 6% sales tax   + _____

Total payment   _____

Prices guaranteed through August 1995. WinZip is shipped on 3.5" disks only.

Name: _____

Company: _____

Address: _____

City, State, Zip: _____

Country: _____

Phone (day and evening): _____

Electronic mail address: _____

How did you hear about WinZip? _____

Comments: _____

Word

We found three Word utilities and templates we think you'll find useful. APAswen.dot is a series of templates that let you easily create documents that use American Psychological Association formatting guidelines. (Many organizations expect you to submit articles and reports using APA formatting rules.) Carrier Pigeon lets you share your macros with other Word users — you collect them in a Carrier Pigeon document and give them to another user, who clicks on a button to install them on his or her machine. Finally, if you're like us, you probably forget what most of the fonts on your system look like. Type Rodent creates an *incredibly* useful list that shows all the fonts on your system and what they look like. Tape it to the wall next to your computer and you'll never have to play font guessing games again.

TypeRodent

TypeRodent is a Word for Windows font utility. Using TypeRodent, you can generate a document containing a complete list of the installed fonts on your system along with a formatted sample of your choice.

TypeRodent will also print out a two-page document that will put a selected typeface through its paces. This two-page printout is suitable for use in a typeface sample collection. It includes a one-page chart showing the ANSI character value for each character any typeface produces. The second page also includes a handy keyboard reference showing the character each key can produce using any particular typeface.

Save this file to your hard drive. Double-click on its icon to open it. Follow the dialog boxes.

Installation

Copy the file Typerat.doc to your Word template directory. On most computers, this is `\MSOffice\Winword\Template`.

Registration

TypeRodent is freeware. Send comments, gripes, etc. to Rich Tatum at rtatum@ozarks.sgcl.lib.mo.us.

APA Style Templates

These templates set up margins, headers, page numbers, and headings for documents conforming to the style developed by the American Psychological Association (APA). They are designed to reduce the mechanical formatting time spent by anyone writing in the APA style. Psychology, some other social sciences, and some business programs require papers to conform to APA style.

These templates are written in Word Basic. They are saved in Word 2.0 and 6.0 formats, but will work with Word for Windows 95.

Template	Purpose
Apa4sw2p.dot	Template saved as a Word 2.0 file, "pretty" formatting
Apa4sw2s.dot	Template saved as a Word 2.0 file, "strict" formatting
Apa4sw6p.dot	Template saved as a Word 6.0 file, "pretty" formatting
Apa4sw6s.dot	Template saved as a Word 6.0 file, "strict" formatting

The CD-ROM also contains Apaman95.doc, which is a manual describing these templates in detail; and Apaguide.doc, which is a short guide to APA style and paper writing in general.

Installation

Copy the templates to Word's template subdirectory, usually \MSOffice\Winword\Templates.

Usage

Open Word in the usual way. Select File⇨New and you will be presented with a dialog box. Scroll to the top of that box and you will see the APA templates. Click on the template you want to use. A welcome screen appears; click on OK. A dialog box appears, asking if you want to set up an APA-style paper. If you click on No, the template remains with its APA-style margins and page numbers, and you can start typing. If you click on Yes, more dialog boxes will appear, asking what the title is, who the author of the paper is, your affiliation (normally the name of your college or university), if you want the date on your cover sheet, and what keywords you want in the header at the top of each page. The program puts all that information in the right places and nicely formats it. Then it asks if you are writing an experimental psychology paper. These papers have various headings, and if you click on Yes, the program sets them up for you. Because headings for the Methods section of experimental papers are not always standard, the program asks if you want to consider alternative headings. If you click on Yes, it provides some for you.

Registration

Please register to receive notices of updates and support. If you ask, I will also send you a copy of the program that doesn't nag you to register. The recommended license fee is only $6. At this price, I cannot provide telephone support, but I will provide support via electronic mail. If you're on America Online, reach me at Otterguy. From the Internet, reach me at otterguy@aol.com or lswenson@lmumail.lmu.edu.

760 Appendixes

Order form: APAswen.dot

Your name: _____

E-mail address: _____

Street address: _____

Other address: _____

City, State, Zip: _____

Version of Word used: _____

Your occupation (optional): _____

Comments: _____

Send this form with your check for $6.00 and any questions to:

MindArts c/o Leland C. Swenson,
12615 Woodgreen St.
Los Angeles, CA 90066-2725

Thank you for registering.

Carrier Pigeon

Carrier Pigeon is a document that lets you share your macros with others. You select the macros you want to share with others; Carrier Pigeon creates a copy of itself that includes a button that will install the selected macros as global. You can then transport the document to any other machine running Word, and with the document, install your macros globally in that machine's copy of Word.

Installation

Copy the templates to your Word directory, which is `\MS Office\Winword` on most computers.

Registration

This software may be used for evaluation purposes for up to 30 days without payment. If you wish to continue to use the software, you are required to purchase one license for each computer on which it will be used. Registration costs $20 (U.S.) for a registered copy on 3.5-inch disk (use the order form below); $15 (U.S.) for file transfer in the CompuServe Software Registration Database (GO SWREG). You can reach me on CompuServe at 71750,1036.

> **Order form: Carrier Pigeon**
>
> Name: _____
>
> Address: _____
>
> City, State, Zip: _____
>
> Send this order form with a check or money order for $20.00 (U.S. funds) to:
>
> Edward Guy
> 1752 Duchess Ave.
> West Vancouver, BC
> V7V 1P9
> CANADA

Book Examples

The CD-ROM includes all of the examples used in the book.

Part II used these Word documents:

- Chess.doc, the Chess document.
- Sample1.doc, the Fajardo Sailing School letter that appears in several figures.
- Sample2.doc, the Dive Virgin Islands letter that appears in several figures.
- Sample3.doc, the Caribbean Divers letter that appears in several figures.

Part III used these Excel worksheets:

- `Car Sales.xls`, the Classic Car Sales worksheet (it looks great in color).
- `Cash Flow.xls`, which shows cash flow for the Little Springs Water Company.
- `Houses.xls`, which shows house sales data with some charts and graphs.
- `Invoice.xls`, which lets you create invoices in Excel.
- `Loan Manager.xls`, which lets you create tables for loan information.
- `Mortgage.xls`, which shows a mortgage analysis.
- `Purchase Order.xls`, which lets you create purchase orders.

We've also included `Travel.ppt`, the PowerPoint presentation we used throughout Part IV.

Index

Symbols

3-D charts
    appearance enhancements, 586–588
    avoiding distortions, 587–588

A

absolute cell references, 328
    versus relative cell references, 459
Accent Color dialog box, 556
Access, linking to Word documents, 160–163
Active Cell (Ctrl+Backspace) key
        combination, 278
Add Custom Dictionary dialog box, 52
Add from File command, 653
Add from File dialog box, 653–654
Add Section dialog box, 654
add-in, Solver, 466–469
Add-Ins command, 467
Add-Ins dialog box, 290–291
adjacent worksheets, 280–281
Advanced Find dialog box, 65, 298
Agenda Wizard, 28–29
Align command, 542
aligning
    objects, 542–543
    paragraphs, 80–81
    worksheets, 346–347
Amort.xlm v4.1, 744–745
amortization schedule, mortgage analysis
        worksheet, 507–511
Animation Settings dialog box, 597–598
Annotation (Alt+I+A) key combination, 60
Annotation command, 60
annotations, 60–62
    add/erase on-screen, 621
    creating, 60–61
    deleting, 62
    finding, 62
    locking documents, 62
    printing, 62, 105
    viewing, 62
Annotations window, 61
Annual Event dialog box, 631
Answer Wizard, 13
Answer Wizard dialog box, 13–14
APA Style Templates, 758–760
applications code, VBA (Visual Basic for
        Applications), 484–488
applications
    See also programs
    adding/removing, 19–20
    effects on system resources, 13
    sharing data, 659–676
Apply Design Template command, 553
Apply Design Template dialog box, 611
Appointment command, 636
Appointment dialog box, 636
Appointment Series dialog box, When tab, 640
Appointment window, 633
    Attendees tab, 638
    changing/deleting appointments, 640
    General tab, 636–637
    Notes tab, 638–639
    Planner tab, 639
appointments
    changing/deleting, 640
    printing, 644–645
arcs, drawing, 371
area charts, 402, 573
arithmetic operators, 325
.ASD file extension, 267
Assign Macro dialog box, 382, 454
attributes, database, 446
AutoContent Wizard, 549–553, 723–726
    templates, 725
AutoContent Wizard dialog boxes,
        550–552, 723–724
AutoFill
    copying cell data, 314–316
    data series, 316–318

AutoFilter command, 435, 440–442
    complex criteria, 442–443
    printing database report based on specific data, 442
    turning off effects, 443–444
AutoFit Selection command, 344
AutoFormat command, 223–225, 339–343, 405–406
    database uses, 436–440
    sorting a database, 436–440
    selecting chart design, 581–582
AutoFormat dialog box, 339–342, 405, 581–582
AutoLayout feature, 553
automatic hyphenation, 56–57
Automatic Save option, 700
automatic spell checking, 52
AutoSave, 290–293, 700
    saving all changes to a document, 267–268
AutoShapes, Clip Art, 546–548
AutoSum, 330–331
AutoText, 57–60
    assigning to toolbar, 58–59
    changing entries, 60
    deleting entries, 60
    printing entries, 105
AutoText dialog box, 57–58
Average function, 329–330
Avery labels, printing, 157–158
Award Wizard, 29–30
axes
    chart, 385, 572, 585
    formatting charts, 400

B

Backspace key, 34, 535
.BAK file extension, 293
bar charts, 402, 573
Bar tabs, 42
Binder, 651–658
    add new documents, 654–655
    adding existing documents, 653–654
    deleting documents, 656
    description, 651–652
    moving/copying documents, 656
    open existing binder, 656
    printing documents, 657
    renaming documents, 656
    saving binders, 655–656
    using, 652–656
    working with documents, 656–658
binder documents, printing, 657
binders
    open existing, 656
    printing documents, 656
    saving, 655–656
bitmapped images, 227–228
blank presentations, 725
.BMP file extension, 228
body text, outlines, 131
boilerplate text, 27
book
    CD-ROM, 2
    conventions used, 7
    how to use, 8
    icons, 7–8
    organizations of, 2–7
    sidebars, 8
Border dialog box, 381
Borders and Shading command, 265
Borders toolbar, 82
borders
    adding to graphic images, 234
    charts, 586
    graphic objects, 374–375
    paragraph, 82–83
    worksheets, 351–353
break-even analysis worksheet, 495–500
breaking links, 668–669
Browse dialog box, 666
building formulas in Excel, 716
Bullet dialog box, 558, 560
bulleted lists, 557–559
    creating, 268
bullets, 57
Button Editor dialog box, 59
buttons, assigning Excel macros to, 454–456

C

Calendar Wizard, 30
callouts
   graphic images, 234
   tables of figures, 172–173
Carrier Pigeon utility, 760–761
cash-flow management worksheet, 493–495
category axis, charts, 385, 572
CD-ROM, 737–762
   book examples, 761
   Excel, 739–746
   fonts, 747–748
   shareware, 739
   utilities, 749–760
   Windows Help file, 737–738
   Word utilities, 757–760
Cell Borders and Shading dialog box, 127
Cell Height and Width dialog box, 124–125
   Column tab, 126
Cell Note dialog box, 308
cell ranges, worksheet, 281–283
cells
   absolute references, 328
   adding notes to, 308–310
   adding sound notes, 309
   automatic formatting, 304
   clearing data from, 311
   combining contents, 517
   copying, 312–319
   copying data with AutoFill, 314–316
   copying data with Cut/Copy/Paste, 312–313
   copying data with drag-and-drop, 313–314
   copying data with Fill command, 314–316
   data editing, 310–311
   deleting tables, 120–122
   deleting worksheet, 320–321
   format protection, 361–362
   formatting, 516
   in-cell editing, 311
   inserting in tables, 120–122
   inserting worksheet, 319–320
   merging tables, 123
   moving, 312–319
   moving data with Cut/Copy/Paste, 312–313
   moving data with drag-and-drop, 313–314
   named ranges, 321–322
   pasting with Paste Special command, 318–319
   relative references, 328
   selecting in tables, 119
   selection shortcuts, 516
   table text, 118
   tables, 113–114
   text entry limitations, 305
Centered tabs, 42
Change Folder dialog box, 681
Change Source dialog box, 668
changing cells, Solver, 466
character formatting, 67–75
   changing fonts, 73–74
   changing point sizes, 73–74
   copying, 75
   kerning, 71–72, 75
   options, 69–72
   shortcuts, 72–73
   spacing between, 71–72
   subscript, 74
   superscript, 74
character spacing, 71–72
character styles, 182–183
characters
   field, 146
   special, 47–48
chart sheets, 387–391
Chart toolbar, 397–398
Chart Type dialog box, 403
Chart Type window, 580–581
Chart Wizard, 386–391
Chart Wizard dialog box, 389–391
charts, 385–410
   3-D appearance enhancements, 586–588
   adding gridlines, 401
   adding legends, 400
   adding titles, 398
   adding unattached text, 399
   appearance enhancements, 582–586
   AutoFormat, 405–406
   axes, 385, 572, 585
   borders, 586

(continued)

charts *(continued)*
  category axis, 385
  changing data series, 577–579
  changing type, 579–581
  colors, 583–584
  components, 393–396
  converting old formats, 396
  creating, 391–392
  creating chart sheet, 388
  creating embedded chart, 388
  customizing area, 401–402
  data series shortcut menu, 578–579
  datasheet, 573
  default format, 405
  editing, 576–582
  embedded, 387–391
  Excel versus PowerPoint, 572, 577
  fonts, 582–583
  formatting axes, 400
  gridlines, 386
  inserting into presentations, 574–576
  legends, 572
  markers, 573
  MS Organizational Chart, 589–590
  organizational, 589–590, 607–610
  plotting, 406–409
  PowerPoint, 573–591
  printing, 393
  saving, 393
  selecting in AutoFormat, 581–582
  selecting parts of, 396–397
  series axis, 385
  titles, 584
  types, 402–405, 573
  value axis, 385
circles, drawing, 371
client applications, 660
clients, 660
clip art, 36, 227–228
  See also pictures
  adding to presentations, 733–734
  AutoShapes, 546–548
Clip Art command, 733
ClipArt Gallery dialog box, 733
Clipboard
  copying graphs into Word documents, 236
  copying/moving text, 45–46
  inserting graphics into documents, 35–36
  inserting pictures into documents, 232
  inserting text into documents, 35
  text search, 47
closing/saving presentations, 726
codes
  field, 148
  TOC, 167
Color Scheme dialog box, Custom tab, 556
Colors and Lines dialog box, 545–546
colors
  chart, 583–584
  shapes, 545–546
  worksheets, 351–353
column charts, 402, 573
columns, 559–560
  adjusting worksheet widths, 343–344
  deleting worksheet, 320–321
  desktop publishing, 221–223
  hiding worksheet, 345
  inserting worksheet, 319–320
  Page Layout view, 223
  table column widths, 124–125
  table spacing between, 125–126
  tables, 116–117
  viewing, 223
Columns dialog box, 221–223
comma-delimited files, 159
command macros (Excel), 450
commands
  Add-Ins, 467
  Align, 542
  Annotation, 60
  Apply Design Template, 553
  Appointment, 636
  AutoFilter, 435, 440–442
  AutoFit Selection, 344
  AutoFormat, 223–225, 339–343, 405–406
  Borders and Shading, 265
  Clip Art, 733
  Copy, 664
  Data⇨Filter, 440
  Data⇨Filter⇨AutoFilter, 441
  Data⇨Form, 433–434
  Data⇨Pivot Table, 473–474

Data⇨Series in Columns, 577
Data⇨Series in Rows, 577
Data⇨Sort, 437
Data⇨Table, 470–471
Database, 160
Draw⇨Align, 542
Draw⇨Bring Forward, 543
Draw⇨Regroup, 540
Draw⇨Send Backward, 543
Draw⇨Snap to Grid, 542
Edit⇨Clear, 311, 321
Edit⇨Copy, 35, 45, 312, 541, 565, 664
Edit⇨Cut, 35, 313, 541
Edit⇨Delete, 311, 321, 432
Edit⇨Delete Item, 641
Edit⇨Delete Slide, 531
Edit⇨Fill, 314
Edit⇨Fill⇨Series, 316
Edit⇨Find, 46, 332
Edit⇨Go To, 62
Edit⇨Links, 667–668
Edit⇨Paste, 35, 45, 312, 541, 565
Edit⇨Paste Special, 664–665, 669
Edit⇨Replace, 46, 48, 332
Edit⇨Undo, 306
Edit⇨Undo Style, 184
File⇨Close, 294
File⇨Exit, 294, 531, 671
File⇨Export⇨Timex Data Link Watch, 645
File⇨Macro, 210
File⇨New, 275, 549, 695, 725
File⇨Open, 34, 275, 295, 531, 696, 698
File⇨Pack & Go, 603
File⇨Page Setup, 40, 86, 413
File⇨Print, 101, 106, 393, 411, 423, 531, 595, 643, 701, 734
File⇨Print Binder, 657
File⇨Print Preview, 417
File⇨Properties, 63, 289, 533
File⇨Save All, 700–701
File⇨Save As, 288, 698–699
File⇨Save Binder As, 656
File⇨Save Changes, 671
File⇨Save, 393, 531, 589, 717
File⇨Save Workspace, 293–294
File⇨Send, 426, 605
File⇨Slide Setup, 593
File⇨Update Presentation, 589
Fill Series, 316–318
Format Object, 374
Format⇨3-D View, 586
Format⇨Apply Design Template, 533
Format⇨AutoFormat, 223, 339, 405, 436, 581
Format⇨AutoFormat⇨Options, 224
Format⇨Borders and Shading, 127, 234
Format⇨Bullet, 558
Format⇨Bullets and Numbering, 57, 136
Format⇨Cells, 346, 352
Format⇨Chart Type, 403, 580, 586
Format⇨Colors and Lines, 545–546
Format⇨Column, 343
Format⇨Column⇨Hide, 345
Format⇨Column⇨Unhide, 345
Format⇨Columns, 221
Format⇨Custom Background, 612
Format⇨Font, 70, 268, 561
Format⇨Paragraph, 43, 76
Format⇨Row, 344
Format⇨Selected Axis, 585
Format⇨Selected Chart Area, 586
Format⇨Slide Layout, 539, 557
Format⇨Style, 185–187, 360
Format⇨Style Gallery, 192
Format⇨Tabs, 40–43
Go To, 62, 712
Goal Seek, 464–466
Grammar, 53
Gridlines, 401
Hyphenation, 56
Insert⇨Appointment, 636
Insert⇨Caption, 172
Insert⇨Cells, 319
Insert⇨Chart⇨As New Sheet, 388
Insert⇨Chart⇨On This Sheet, 388
Insert⇨Clip Art, 733
Insert⇨Contact, 642
Insert⇨Field, 146
Insert⇨Footnote, 91
Insert⇨Frame, 238

(continued)

commands *(continued)*
  Insert⇨Function, 331
  Insert⇨Index and Tables, 141, 166, 173
  Insert⇨Legend, 400
  Insert⇨Microsoft Graph, 576
  Insert⇨Microsoft Word Table, 566
  Insert⇨Name⇨Define, 321
  Insert⇨New Slide, 531, 537
  Insert⇨Note, 308–309
  Insert⇨Object, 564, 589, 664–666, 670
  Insert⇨Page Break, 420
  Insert⇨Page Numbers, 90
  Insert⇨Picture, 230, 366
  Insert⇨Sound, 567–568
  Insert⇨Task, 641
  Insert⇨Titles, 398
  Language, 200
  Links, 667
  New, 26
  Object, 670–671
  Options, 39
  Paste, 664
  Paste Links, 664
  Paste Special, 318–319, 664–665
  Picture, 36, 366
  Print Binder, 657
  Print, 734
  Print Preview, 98
  Ruler, 40
  Save As, 717
  Save, 717
  Section⇨Print, 657
  Send, 605
  Slide Show, 596
  Sort, 129–130
  Spelling, 50
  Table Borders and Shading, 265
  Table⇨Cell Height and Width, 124–125
  Table⇨Convert Text to Table, 128
  Table⇨Delete Cells, 120
  Table⇨Gridlines, 114
  Table⇨Insert Cells, 120
  Table⇨Insert Table, 114, 234
  Table⇨Merge Cells, 123
  Table⇨Sort, 130
  Table⇨Split Table, 123
  Table⇨Table AutoFormat, 124, 264
  Tabs, 40–43
  Thesaurus, 53
  Tools⇨Mail Merge, 153
  Tools⇨Add-Ins, 290, 467
  Tools⇨Animation Settings, 597
  Tools⇨Assign Macro, 383, 456
  Tools⇨AutoSave, 290
  Tools⇨Build Slide Text, 598
  Tools⇨Crop⇨Picture, 541
  Tools⇨Customize, 543, 562
  Tools⇨Envelopes and Labels, 110, 263
  Tools⇨Goal Seek, 464–466
  Tools⇨Grammar, 53
  Tools⇨Hide Slide, 599
  Tools⇨Macro, 209–210, 214, 382, 457–458
  Tools⇨Options, 52, 315, 376, 535
  Tools⇨Protection, 361–362
  Tools⇨Protection⇨Protect Workbook, 362
  Tools⇨Record Macro⇨Record at Mark, 452
  Tools⇨Record Macro⇨Record New Macro, 451, 459
  Tools⇨Slide Transition, 615
  Tools⇨Solver, 467
  Tools⇨Spelling, 50, 334
  Tools⇨Thesaurus, 53
  Undo AutoFormat, 436
  View⇨Datasheet, 576
  View⇨Header and Footer, 88, 614
  View⇨Master⇨Handout Master, 602
  View⇨Master⇨Slide Master, 554, 612
  View⇨Notes Pages, 599, 613
  View⇨Outline, 38, 132, 535, 727
  View⇨Ruler, 100, 558–559
  View⇨Slide Show, 596
  View⇨Toolbars, 183, 207, 286, 368, 397, 546
  Window⇨Freeze Panes, 286
  Window⇨Remove Split, 286
  Window⇨Split, 285
Commands and Settings menu, 297
comparison operators, 325
  database criteria searches, 434
compound documents, 660
computed criteria, 434
constraint keys, 545
constraints, Solver, 466

Index ✦ C-D

Contacts dialog box, 642
conventions used, 7
Converters, Filters, And Data Access dialog box, 690
Copy (Ctrl+C) key combination, 35
Copy command, 664
copy/move slides, 538–539
cover sheet, fax, 251–254
Create Data Source dialog box, 154
Create Labels dialog box, 158
criteria range, database, 432
criteria searches
  and-based criteria, 435
  comparison operators, 434
  computed criteria, 434
  database records, 434–436
  or-based criteria, 436
  wildcards, 435
cropping, 232
  objects, 541
cross-tabulations, 472
curly braces {}, with Word fields, 146
Custom AutoFilter dialog box, 442
Custom Background dialog box, 555, 612–613
Custom Button dialog box, 59, 212
Custom dialog box, Menus tab, 213
Custom Dictionaries dialog box, 51
custom dictionary, 335–336
  adding words to, 50–51
custom installation
  completing the process, 690
  Converters, Filters and Data Access options, 690
  Excel options, 685
  Office Binder and Shortcut Bar options, 684
  Office Tools options, 689
  PowerPoint options, 687
  Schedule+ options, 688
  what to install, 684
  Word options 686
Custom Installation Options, 683–690
custom number formats, worksheets, 356–359
custom tabs, 40–41
Custom.dic dictionary, 50
Customize dialog box, 189, 543
  Buttons tab, 14–15
  Keyboard tab, 213
  Settings tab, 18–19
  Toolbars tab, 17–18, 58, 212
  View tab, 16–17
Customize Grammar Settings dialog box, 55–56
Cut (Ctrl+X) key combination, 35

D

data
  clearing from worksheet cells, 311
  database, 446
  enter/edit in Excel, 712–716
  finding, 332–333
  finding and replacing data, 333–334
  sharing between applications, 659–676
data documents, importing, 159–163
data form, database, 432–433
Data Series shortcut menu, 578–579
data series, editing in charts, 577–579
data source, mail merge, 152–154
data tables, 469–472
  one-input, 469
  two-input, 469
data types, Excel, 713
Data➪Filter command, 440
Data➪Filter➪AutoFilter command, 441
Data➪Form command, 433–434
Data➪Pivot Table command, 473–474
Data➪Series in Columns command, 577
Data➪Series in Rows command, 577
Data➪Sort command, 437
Data➪Table command, 470–471
Database command, 160
Database dialog box, 161
Database toolbar, Insert Database button, 160
databases, 429–448
  adding new records, 433
  attributes, 446
  creating, 431–432
  criteria searches, 434–436
  data, 446
  data form, 432–433
  deleting records, 433–434

(continued)

databases *(continued)*
  design steps, 446–447
  designing, 445–447
  editing records, 433
  Excel limitations, 444
  field naming conventions, 432
  fields, 430
  improvements over previous Excel
    versions, 432
  key field, 437
  mail merging, 445
  normalization process, 444
  overview, 429–431
  ranges, 432
  records, 430, 432–436
  search wildcards, 435
  sorting with AutoFormat command, 436–440
  undoing sorts, 440
Datasheet window
  changing data series, 577–579
  editing charts, 576–582
  editing data, 575–576
  entering data, 575–576
  inserting charts into presentations, 574–576
date-based series, 316–318
Date/Time format, 714–715
dates
  entering in Excel, 714–715
  worksheet entries, 305–306
  worksheet formats, 355–356
Decimal tabs, 42
default presentations, 528–531
  to create presentation, 529
Define Name dialog box, 321–322
Delete Cells dialog box, 120
Delete dialog box, 320
Delete key, 34, 535
deleting, slides, 538
Deprec8.xlm v1.0, 745–746
desktop publishing
  AutoFormat command, 223–225
  columns, 221–223, 243–244
  framing objects, 237–243
  graphic images, 226–234, 244–245
  graphs, 245
  headlines, 244

inserting graphs into documents, 235–237
  margins, 243–244
  Newsletter Wizard, 245–246
  organizational tools, 243–245
  subheads, 244
  tables, 245
destination documents, 660
dictionaries
  custom, 335–336
  `Custom.dic`, 50
  main, 50
direct formatting options, 86
directories, changing Excel default working,
    513–514
discontiguous ranges, 282
Display presentations (Ctrl+F6) key
    combination, 533
displayed values, worksheet, 307
divisions, 86
document summary information, printing, 105
documents
  adding sound/video, 673
  adding to Binder, 653–655
  adjusting margins in Print Preview mode,
    100–101
  annotations, 60–62
  AutoFormat, 223–225
  automatic formatting, 223–225
  automatic hyphenation, 56–57
  automatic spell checking, 52
  AutoText entries, 57–60
  bulleting, 57
  character formatting, 67–75
  character spacing, 71–72
  checking grammar while typing, 55
  checking spelling, 50–52
  copying text, 45–46
  copying/moving text between, 45–46
  creating/working with, 25–66
  cutting/pasting Clipboard text, 35
  deleting, 266
  deleting text, 34
  deleting within binders, 656
  desktop publishing, 221–247
  embedding, 659
  embedding data, 160–163

embedding objects, 669–671
establishing links, 664–669
fields, 145–165
first-line indents, 77–80
footers, 88–90
footnotes, 91–94
formatting, 67–95
framing objects, 237–243
Grammar Checker, 53–56
hanging indents, 77–80
headers, 88–90
hyphenation, 56–57
importing, 159–163, 261–262
importing Excel worksheet data documents, 159–160
index, 173–178
inserting clip art, 36
inserting columns, 221–223
inserting empty frame, 238–239
inserting graphics images, 35–36, 230–232
inserting graphs, 235–237
justifying text, 81
keyboard navigation shortcuts, 36–37
line spacing, 43–44
linking, 659
locating objects in Print Preview mode, 100–101
locking for annotations only, 62
macros, 205–219
margins, 40
moving text, 45–46
moving/copying within binder, 656
Normal view, 38
object framing, 237–243
OLE links, 160–163
opening, 695–696
opening existing, 702
outlines, 130–142
page formatting, 83–86
page numbers, 90
paragraph borders, 82–83
paragraph formatting, 75–83
paragraph marks, 75
paragraph numbers, 57
paragraph spacing, 45
portability, 663
preventing unwanted page breaks, 263–264
previewing/printing, 97–112
printing, 101–108
printing from Binder, 657
printing part of, 104–105
readability statistics, 55
red wavy lines, 52
renaming within Binder, 656
saving, 699–703
saving in previous version formats, 266–267
scrolling, 37
searching/replacing text, 46–49
section breaks, 87
section formatting, 86–88
selecting text, 37–38
selecting/deleting text blocks, 34
special character search, 47–48
Spelling Checker, 50–52
styles, 181–196
styles versus direct formatting options, 86
summaries, 63–65
synonyms, 53
tables, 113–130
tables of contents, 165–171
tables of figures, 172–173
tabs, 40–43
templates, 25–34, 196–202
text alignment, 80–81
text search/replace, 46–49
Thesaurus, 53
typing habits, 35
vertical alignment, 87
viewing, 38–39
word wrap, 34–35
working within binder, 656–657
working with text, 34–38
wrapping text around frames, 241–242
Dot file extension, 183, 199
Double line spacing (Ctrl+2) key combination, 44
doughnut charts, 402, 573
Draw⇨Align command, 542
Draw⇨Bring Forward command, 543
Draw⇨Regroup command, 540
Draw⇨Send Backward command, 543
Draw⇨Snap to Grid command, 542

drawing freeform shapes, 545
drawing shapes, 544–545
Drawing toolbar, 368–372, 528, 544
    adding macro buttons, 382–383
    assigning macros to buttons, 454–456
    AutoShape button, 546
    Bring To Front tool, 373
    Freeform tool, 371
    Freehand tool, 371
    Send To Back tool, 373
    Text Box button, 376
    tools, 369
drawing
    arcs, 371
    circles, 371
    ellipses, 371
    filled objects, 371
    freehand, 371
    lines, 370
    rectangles, 370
    squares, 370
dynamic fields, 145
dynamic pivot tables, 472

E

Edit➪Clear command, 311, 321
Edit➪Copy command, 35, 45, 312, 541, 565, 664
Edit➪Cut command, 35, 313, 541
Edit➪Delete command, 311, 321, 432
Edit➪Delete Item command, 641
Edit➪Delete Slide command, 531
Edit➪Fill command, 314
Edit➪Fill➪Series command, 316
Edit➪Find command, 46, 332
Edit➪Go To command, 62
Edit➪Links command, 667–668
Edit➪Paste command, 35, 45, 312, 541, 565
Edit➪Paste Special command, 664–665, 669
Edit➪Replace command, 46, 48, 332
Edit➪Undo command, 306
Edit➪Undo Style command, 184
editing
    embedded objects, 671
    objects as one, 619

ellipses, drawing, 371
embedded charts, 387–391
    converting file formats, 672
embedding, 659
    with Object command, 670
    when to use, 663
embossing, presentations, 560
endnotes
    See also footnotes
    changing footnotes to, 94
Envelope Address dialog box, 156
Envelope Options dialog box, 110
    Printing Options tab, 111
Envelopes and Labels dialog box, 110, 263
envelopes, printing, 110–111, 155–157, 262–263
examples, book, 760–761
Excel
    adding graphics to worksheets, 365–383
    Amort.xlm v4.1, 744–746
    amortization schedule, 507–511
    analysis techniques, 463–479
    AutoFormat, 405–406
    AutoSum, 330–331
    break-even analysis, 495–500
    cash-flow management, 493–495
    CD-ROM, 739–746
    changing printer properties, 423–425
    chart plotting, 406–409
    charts, 385–410
    data table analysis, 469–472
    database limitations, 444
    databases, 429–448
    Deprec8.xlm v1.0, 745–746
    Drawing toolbar, 368–372
    entering information, 301–337
    exiting, 294
    Format Painter, 359–360
    formatting worksheets, 339–364
    Formula bar, 302
    goal seeking analysis, 463–466
    IRA calculator, 500–507
    linking to Word documents, 160–163
    macro language improvements, 456
    macros, 449–461
    mortgage analysis, 507–511
    opening workspace file on start up, 294

pivot table analysis, 472–478
Power Utility pak, 739–744
Print Preview mode, 418
printing features, 411–427
questions, 513–519
sending files over a network, 425–426
shortcut menus, 344
Solver, 466–469
Sound Recorder, 309
spell checking, 334–336
toolbars, 286–288
Tooltips, 287
top ten questions, 513–519
transferring data documents to Word, 159–160
using version 4.0 menu structure, 514
Visual Basic for Applications (VBA), 481–491
what-if analysis, 463–479
WordArt, 379–381
workbook tabs, 711
workbooks, 274–300
workplace applications, 493–512
worksheets added to PowerPoint, 564–566
Xlstart folder, 513
Excel basics, 705–719
  building formulas, 716
  data types, 713
  entering/editing data, 712–716
  Formatting toolbar, 708
  numbers, 714
  opening existing workbook, 710
  printing worksheets, 716–717
  saving worksheets, 717
  screen, 706
  spreadsheets, 705–706
  Standard toolbar, 707
  text entry, 715–716
  times and dates, entering, 714–715
  workbook concept, 709–710
  workbook navigation, 710–712
  workbook tabs, 711
  workbook window, 710–711
  worksheet navigation, 710–712
Excel GoTo dialog box, 712
extract range, database, 432

F

fast save, 700
Fax Wizard, 31, 251–254
Fax Wizard dialog box, 251–254
faxes, cover sheet, 251–254
field characters {} curly braces in Word, 146
field codes
  printing, 151
  switches, 149–150
  viewing, 148
Field dialog box, 146–147
Field Options dialog box, 147
field type, 146
fields
  {} curly braces, 146
  characters, 146
  creating, 150–151
  database, 430
  database key, 437
  database naming conventions, 432
  dynamic, 145
  field code switches, 149–150
  formatting, 148–150
  inserting, 146–147
  instructions, 146
  locking contents, 150
  mail merge, 152–155
  merge, 152–155
  moving between, 148
  printing field codes, 151
  TC, 165, 168–170
  unlocking contents, 150
  updating, 148
  using in Word 146–151
  viewing codes, 148
  Word, 145–165
file extensions
  .ASD, 267
  .BAK, 293
  .BMP, 228
  .DOT, 183, 199
file formats, converting embedded objects, 672
File Save As dialog box, 699–700
File Save As type list box, 699

Index ◆ F

File Save dialog box, 531
File⇨Close command, 294
File⇨Exit command, 294, 531, 671
File⇨Export⇨Timex Data Link Watch command, 645
File⇨Macro command, 210
File⇨New command, 275, 549, 695, 725
File⇨Open command, 34, 275, 295, 531, 696, 698
File⇨Pack & Go command, 603
File⇨Page Setup command, 40, 86, 413
File⇨Print command, 101, 106, 393, 411, 423, 531, 595, 643, 701, 734
File⇨Print Binder command, 657
File⇨Print Preview command, 417
File⇨Properties command, 63, 289, 533
File⇨Save All command, 700–701
File⇨Save As command, 288, 698–699
File⇨Save Binder As command, 656
File⇨Save Changes command, 671
File⇨Save command, 393, 531, 589, 717
File⇨Save Workspace command, 293–294
File⇨Send command, 426, 605
File⇨Slide Setup command, 593
File⇨Update Presentation command, 589
files
   comma-delimited, 159
   organizing, 299
   sending over network, 425–426
   workspace, 293–294
Fill Series command, 316–318
filled objects, drawing, 371
filters, graphic, 226
Find (Ctrl+F) key combination, 46
Find (Shift+Insert) key combination, 47
Find dialog box, 46–47, 332
   Special button, 47
first-line indents, 77–80
fixed costs, 495
folders, Xlstart, 513
Font command, 69
Font dialog box, 69–71, 194, 561
   Character Spacing tab, 71
   Font tab, 71
   formatting options, 70

fonts
   CD-ROM, 747–748
   changing, 73–74
   chart, 582–583
   default, 268
   Excel default, 513–514
   TrueType, 350
   worksheets, 349–351
footers, 88–90
   deleting, 89
   line spacing, 90
   margin settings, 89
   positioning, 89
   travel presentation, 614–615
Footnote and Endnote dialog box, 91
footnotes, 91–94
   changing to endnotes, 94
   deleting, 93
   editing existing, 93
   moving, 93
   moving between, 93
   options, 94
form letters, 152–155
Format 3-D View dialog box, 586–587
Format Axis dialog box, 400, 585
   Font tab, 583
Format Cells dialog box, 715–716
   Alignment tab, 346
   Border tab, 352
   Font tab, 350
   Number tab, 354
   Patterns tab, 352
   Protection tab, 362
Format Chart Area dialog box, 401
   Patterns tab, 586
   Font tab, 399
Format Data Series dialog box
   Data Labels tab, 580
   Patterns tab, 579
Format Object command, 374
Format Object dialog box
   Font tab, 377
   Patterns tab, 374–375
Format Painter, 359–360
Format⇨3-D View command, 586

Format➪Apply Design Template command, 533
Format➪AutoFormat command, 223, 339, 405, 436, 581
Format➪AutoFormat➪Options command, 224
Format➪Borders and Shading command, 127, 234
Format➪Bullet command, 558
Format➪Bullets and Numbering command, 57, 136
Format➪Cells command, 346, 352
Format➪Chart Type command, 403, 580, 586
Format➪Colors and Lines command, 545–546
Format➪Column command, 343
Format➪Column➪Hide command, 345
Format➪Column➪Unhide command, 345
Format➪Columns command, 221
Format➪Custom Background command, 612
Format➪Font command, 70, 268, 561
Format➪Paragraph command, 43, 76
Format➪Row command, 344
Format➪Selected Axis command, 585
Format➪Selected Chart Area command, 586
Format➪Slide Layout command, 539, 557
Format➪Style command, 185–187, 360
Format➪Style Gallery command, 192
Format➪Tabs command, 40–43
formats, Date/Time, 714–715
Formatting toolbar, 70, 528
   (Alt+V+T) key combination, 51
   applying styles, 183–184
   Center button, 35
   defining styles by example, 187–188
   drop-down Style list, 184
   Excel, 708–709
   number formatting buttons, 354
   Style list box, 188
   Text Shadow button, 560
   Word, 692–695
formatting
   character, 67–75
   direct formatting options, 86
   levels, 67–68
   search/replace, 49
Formula bar, 302
   Cancel button, 712
   cell data editing, 310
   creating formulas, 323–324

formulas, 301, 713
   allowed elements, 324–326
   arithmetic operators, 325
   building in Excel, 716
   comparison operators, 325
   creating by pointing, 324
   displaying, 326–327
   editing, 326–327
   recalculation options, 327–328
   worksheet, 323–328
Frame dialog box, 239–240
frames
   absolutely positioned paragraphs, 237
   existing object, 238
   inserting empty, 238–239
   moving, 240–241
   removing, 242–243
   sizing, 241
   wrapping text around, 241–242
freeform shapes, drawing, 545
Front (Ctrl+F6) key combination, 276
full save, 700
function macros (Excel), 450
Function Wizard, 331–332
Function Wizard dialog box, 331
functions, worksheets, 328–332

G

Go To (Ctrl+G) key combination, 62
Go To (F5) key, 62, 278
Go To command, 62, 712
Go To dialog box, 278
Goal Seek command, 464–466
Goal Seek dialog box, 464
Goal Seek Status dialog box, 465
goal-seeking analysis (Excel), 464–466
Grammar Checker, 53–56
   document readability statistics, 55
Grammar command, 53
Grammar dialog box, 54
grammar, checking while typing, 55
graphic filters, 226
graphic images, 244–245

(continued)

graphic images *(continued)*
  adding borders, 234
  bitmapped, 227–228
  callouts, 234
  clip art, 227–228
  cropping/scaling, 232–234
  editing, 234
  inserting into document, 230–232
  object, 227–229
  pixels, 227
  resources, 229
  scaling, 228
  supported types, 226
  understanding, 226–229
  using, 230–234
graphic objects
  assigning Excel macros to, 456–457
  borders, 374–375
  bringing to front, 373
  copying, 373
  formatting, 374
  grouping, 372
  hiding/unhiding, 376
  moving, 373
  patterns, 374–375
  resizing, 374
  selecting, 372
  sending to back, 373
  shortcut menu, 369–370
  sizing handles, 374
graphic placeholders, 376
graphics
  adding to worksheets, 365–383
  clip art, 36
  inserting into documents, 35–36
  inserting into worksheets, 366–368
  inserting into worksheets with Copy/Paste commands, 366–367
  password protection, 370
  supported types, 367–368
graphs, 245
  inserting into documents, 235–237
Gridlines command, 401

gridlines
  adding to charts, 401
  chart, 386
  hiding worksheet, 345
  printing table, 264–265
  tables, 114
  turning off while printing, 421
group objects as one, 619
Group styles menu, 610
grouping objects, 540
growth series, 316–318
gutter, 84

H

handles, shapes, 546
Handout Master screen, 602–603
handouts
  presentation, 599–602
  travel presentation, 613–614
hanging indents, 77–80
hard (nonbreaking) hyphens, 57
Header and Footer dialog box, Notes and Handouts tab, 614
Header and Footer toolbar, 88
Header dialog box, 422
header record, mail merge, 152
headers, 88–90
  deleting, 89
  line spacing, 90
  margin settings, 89
  positioning, 89
  travel presentation, 614–615
  outline, 131–137
headlines, 244
help, Answer Wizard 13
hyphenation, 56–57
Hyphenation command, 56
Hyphenation dialog box, 56
hyphens
  nonbreaking (hard), 57
  optional, 57

I

icons
   in book, 7–8
   Shortcut to Winword, 26
images, graphic, 226–234
indents
   first-line, 77–80
   handing, 77–80
   paragraphs, 77–80
Index and Tables dialog box
   Index tab, 175
   Table of Contents tab, 166–167
   Table of Figures tab, 172
index, 173–178
   building large, 177–178
   entries, 173–174
   inserting into document, 174–175
   marking entries, 173–174
   multilevel entries, 175–176
   page number ranges, 176–177
Individual Retirement Account (IRA) calculator worksheet, 500–507
information, workbook summary, 289–290
Insert Cells dialog box, 120
Insert Data dialog box, 163
Insert dialog box, 283, 302
Insert Field (Ctrl+F9) key combination, 147, 168, 173
Insert file dialog box, 538
Insert Object dialog box, 566
Insert Picture dialog box, 36, 230
Insert Sound dialog box, 567–568
Insert Table dialog box, 114–115
Insert Word Table dialog box, 566–567
Insert⇨Appointment command, 636
Insert⇨Caption command, 172
Insert⇨Cells command, 319
Insert⇨Chart⇨As New Sheet command, 388
Insert⇨Chart⇨On This Sheet command, 388
Insert⇨Clip Art command, 733
Insert⇨Contact command, 642
Insert⇨Field command, 146
Insert⇨Footnote command, 91
Insert⇨Frame command, 238
Insert⇨Function command, 331
Insert⇨Index and Tables command, 141, 166, 173
Insert⇨Legend command, 400
Insert⇨Microsoft Graph command, 576
Insert⇨Microsoft Word Table command, 566
Insert⇨Name⇨Define command, 321
Insert⇨New Slide command, 531, 537
Insert⇨Note command, 308
Insert⇨Object command, 564, 589, 664–666, 670
Insert⇨Page Break command, 420
Insert⇨Page Numbers command, 90
Insert⇨Picture command, 230, 366
Insert⇨Sound command, 567–568
Insert⇨Task command, 641
Insert⇨Titles command, 398
inserting, slides, 537–538
installation
   completing the process, 690
   Microsoft Office, 679–690
instructions, field, 146
integers, worksheet entries, 304
interoffice memo, 255–256
invoices, 257–258
IRA calculator worksheet, 500–507

J

Jasc Media Center, 749–750
justified text, 81

K

kerning, 71–72, 75
key combinations
    character formatting, 72–73
    navigating in worksheets, 711–712
    paragraph formatting, 78
key field, database, 437
keyboards
    applying styles, 184–185
    cropping graphic images, 233–234
    document navigation shortcuts, 36–37
    macro shortcut key assignments, 213
    moving frames, 240
    navigating within worksheets, 278–279
    Outlining toolbar key equivalents, 133–134
    scaling graphic images, 233
    selecting table cells, 119
    selecting text, 37–38
    selecting/deleting text blocks, 34
    sizing frames, 241
    table navigation, 117
keys
    Backspace, 34, 535
    constraint, 545
    Delete, 34, 535
    F5 (Go To), 62, 278
    F5 (Page), 37
    F7 (Spelling), 51
    F11 (Move Between Fields), 148
    navigating in worksheets, 711–712
    Return, 278
    Tab, 116–117, 278

L

labels, Avery, 157–158
landscape orientation (sideways) printing, 106
Language command, 200
Language dialog box, 201
languages, Visual Basic for Applications (VBA), 481–491
layout, 620, 722
leader tabs, 43
left-aligned tabs, 42
legends, charts, 400, 572
Letter Wizard, 31
line charts, 402, 573
Line Numbers dialog box, 87
line spacing, 43–44, 81
    default measurements, 44
linear series, 316–318
lines
    drawing, 370
    formatting, 375–376
Links command, 667
Links dialog box, 667
links, 662, 664–666
    breaking/restoring, 668–669
    changing update settings, 667
    establishing in documents, 664–669
    restoring, 668–669
    updating, 667
    when to use, 663
lists, bulleted, 557–559
Lock Field (Ctrl+F11) key combination, 150

M

Macro dialog box, 210, 215–216
Macro Options dialog box, 458
Macro Recorder (Excel), 450–453
    See also macros
    changing macro options, 458–459
    creating macros, 451–452
    running macros, 453, 457
    stopping, 452–453
Macro Recorder toolbar, 214
Macro toolbar, 207–208
macros, 205–219
    See also Macro Recorder (Excel)
    adding buttons to Drawing toolbar, 382–383
    adding to menu, 212
    adding to toolbar, 211–212
    alternatives to, 206
    assigning to graphic objects (Excel), 456–457
    creating, 209–214

creating with Macro Recorder (Excel), 451–452
defining, 205–206
examples, 216–217
key assignments, 209–210, 213
Macro Recorder toolbar, 214
Macro toolbar, 207–208
pausing a recording, 213
preparing to create, 209–210
printing key assignments, 105
recording, 210–214
relative versus absolute cell references, 459
running, 214–215
running automatically, 217–218
sharing, 760–761
storing, 208
uses for (Excel), 450
Visual Basic for Applications (VBA), 481–491
Visual Basic for Applications programming language, 206
Mail Merge Helper dialog box, 153
mail merge
  adding fields to main document, 154–155
  combining documents, 152–153
  data source, 152–154
  database, 445
  fields, 152–155
  finishing, 152
  form letters, 152–155
  header record, 152
  main document, 152–153
  merging data, 155
mailing labels, printing, 157–158
main dictionary, 50
main document, mail merge, 152–153
margins, 40, 84
Mark Index Entry dialog box, 173–174
markers, chart, 573
Master Document view, 39
Master Layout dialog box, 555
Maximum function, 330
Meeting Requests, Schedule+, 642–643
meetings, scheduling, 643
Memo Wizard, 32, 255–256
Memo Wizard dialog box, 255–256
memos, interoffice, 255–256

merge fields, 152–155
messages, Can't change part of table, 472
Microsoft ClipArt Gallery dialog box, 547
Microsoft Excel dialog box, 685
Microsoft Exchange, New Message window, 605
Microsoft Graph 5.0, 235–237
  changing chart type, 579–581
  chart types, 573
  PowerPoint charts, 573–591
Microsoft Office
  See also individual applications
  Access, 12, 160–163
  applications, 11–12
  Excel, 11, 705–719
  installation, 679–690
  overview, 11–21
  PowerPoint, 12, 523–548, 721–735
  Schedule+, 12, 625–650
  Word, 11, 691–703
Microsoft Office 95
  Add-Ins dialog box, 292
  Custom dialog box, 683
  Setup dialog box, 681
  Setup welcome screen, 680
Microsoft Organizational Chart, 589–590
Microsoft PowerPoint dialog box, 687
Microsoft Schedule+ dialog box, 688
Microsoft Word dialog box, 686
Microsoft WordArt, 379–381
Minimum function, 330
misspelled words, red wavy lines, 52
modes, Print Preview (Excel), 418
Modify Style dialog box, 190
mortgage analysis worksheet, 507–511
mouse
  cropping graphic images, 233–234
  dragging/dropping text, 46
  moving frames, 240
  navigating within worksheets, 277–279
  scaling graphic images, 233
  scrolling document windows, 37
  selecting table cells, 119
  selecting text, 37–38
  selecting/deleting text blocks, 34

(continued)

mouse *(continued)*
  sizing frames, 241
  table navigation, 116–117
  worksheet pointers, 277
move slides, 538–539
multimedia, Excel features, 310

N

Name and Organization dialog box, 680
named ranges, worksheets, 278, 280, 321–322
navigation
  in Word, 696–697
  keystrokes, 696
  workbooks/worksheets, 710–712
networks
  sending files over, 425–426
  sharing presentations, 605
New command, 26
New dialog box, 26–27
New Presentation dialog box, 528–529, 608
  General tab, 532, 722
  options, 722
New Slide dialog box, 531, 537, 621, 725
New Style dialog box, 186
Newline (Shift+Enter) key combination, 40, 76
Newline command, 40, 76
Newsletter Wizard, 32, 245–246
Next Field (Alt+F1) key combination, 148
Next Field (F11) key, 148
Next Worksheet (Ctrl+PgDn) key
      combination, 279
nonbreaking (hard) hyphens, 57
nonbreaking hyphens (Ctrl+Shift+Hyphen)
      key combination, 57
Normal style, redefining, 191
Normal view, 38
`Normal.dot` template, 25–27, 198, 200–201
Note Options dialog box, 94
notes
  adding to worksheet cells, 308–309
  presentation, 599–602
  travel presentation, 613–614
NoteWorthy Composer, 752–754
number formats, worksheets, 353–359

numbered lists, creating, 268
numbers
  entering in Excel, 714
  worksheet entries, 303–304

O

Object command, 670–671
  linking, 665–666
Object dialog box
  Create from File tab, 666
  Create New tab, 665
  unable to find objects, 671
object images, 227–229
objects
  See also graphic objects
  aligning, 542–543
  copy formatting one to another, 619
  copying, 540–541
  cropping, 541
  editing embedded, 671
  embedding in documents, 669–671
  framing, 237–243
  framing existing, 238
  group/edit as one, 619
  linking, 664–669
  locating in Print Preview mode, 100–101
  move with cut-and-copy, 541
  moving, 540–541
  selecting/grouping, 540
  stacking, 543
  working with, 540–543
Office Binder and Shortcut Bar
      dialog box, 684
Office Manager, Office Shortcut Bar, 12–19
Office Shortcut Bar, 12–19
  adding buttons, 13
  adding/removing programs, 19–20
  Answer Wizard button, 13
  closing, 19
  customizing, 14–19
  docking, 14
  Schedule+, 627
  shortcut menu, 291

sizing, 14
understanding, 12–14
versus Start menu, 13
Office Tools option, 689
OLE (Object Linking and Embedding), 160, 659–676
   adding sound/video to office documents, 673
   changing links update settings, 667
   clients, 660
   converting file formats of embedded objects, 672
   Copy/Paste, 663
   creating an example, 673–674
   defining, 659–662
   editing embedded objects, 671
   embedding, 662
   embedding objects, 669–671
   establishing links in your documents, 664–669
   linking, 662
   linking to Word documents, 160–163
   linking versus embedding, 662
   protocol, 659
   servers, 660
   sharing data, 659–676
OLE2, 573, 661
on-screen
   annotations, add/erase, 621
   slide shows, 596–599
One-and-a-half line spacing (Ctrl+5) key combination, 44
one-input data tables, 469
Open Data Source dialog box, 160–161
Open dialog box, 275, 295, 710
   Advanced button, 297–298
   Preview mode, 296
Open toolbar, buttons, 296
operators
   database comparison, 434
   worksheet formulas, 324–326
optional hyphens, 57
optional hyphens (Ctrl+Hyphen) key combination, 57
Options command, 39
Options dialog box, 535

AutoFormat tab, 224
changing view options, 39
Custom Lists tab, 315
Edit tab, 302
Grammar tab, 55
Print tab, 106–108
Save tab, 267
organization, book, 2–7
Organizational Chart Style dialog box, 589
organizational charts, 589–590, 607–610
Organizer dialog box, 191, 216
Outline view, 38, 142
   editing, 535
   editing text, 731
outlines, 130–142
   adding body text, 138–139
   body text, 131
   changing headings, 134–137
   changing structure, 132–134
   converting headings to body text, 134–135, 140–141
   creating, 137–141
   creating a table of contents, 141–142
   expanding/collapsing headings, 135, 139–140
   headings, 131–137
   moving headings, 136
   numbering, 136–137
   printing, 142
   selecting text, 132
   subtext, 131
   understanding, 130–131
Outlining toolbar, 132–133, 732

P

Pack & Go Wizard, 603–605
Pack & Go Wizard dialog box, 603–604
Page (F5) key, 37
page breaks
   controlling while printing, 420–421
   preventing unwanted, 263–264
page formatting, 83–86
   margin gutter, 84
   margins, 84
   mirror margins, 84

(continued)

page formatting *(continued)*
　paper size, 85
　printer paper source, 85
　printing orientation, 85
Page Layout view, 39, 223
page numbers, 90
Page Numbers dialog box, 90
Page Setup dialog box, 413
　Header/Footer tab options, 415
　Layout tab, 86–87
　Margins tab, 84, 414
　Page tab options, 413–414
　Paper Size tab, 85
　Paper Source tab, 85
　Sheet tab options, 415–416
Paint Shop Pro, 750–752
paper
　orientation, 85
　selecting size, 85
Paragraph Borders and Shadings dialog box, 82–83
Paragraph dialog box, 43–44, 195, 264
　Indents and Spacing tab, 44, 76
　Text Flow tab, 76–77
paragraph formatting, 75–83
　aligning, 80–81
　applying, 76–78
　borders, 82–83
　displaying paragraph marks, 75
　first-line indents, 77
　hanging indents, 77–80
　indents, 77–80
　line spacing, 81
　paragraph marks, 75
　paragraph spacing, 81
　shortcut keys, 78
　spacing, 81
paragraphs
　formatting, 75–83
　indenting, 35
　numbering, 57
　spacing, 45
　styles, 182–183
passwords
　graphics protection, 370
　worksheet protection, 363

Paste (Ctrl+V) key combination, 35
Paste command, 664
Paste Links command, 664
Paste Special command, 318–319, 664–665
　embedding objects, 669
Paste Special dialog box, 318–319, 664
patterns
　graphic objects, 374–375
　worksheets, 351–353
Personal Macro Workbook, storing macros, 459–460
Picture Borders and Shading dialog box, 100–101
Picture command, 36, 366
Picture dialog box, 233, 366–367
pictures
　See also clip art, 36
　inserting into document, 36, 230–232
pie charts, 402, 573
Pivot Table Wizard, 472–478
Pivot Table Wizard dialog box, 473–476
pivot tables, 472–478
　cross-tabulations, 472
　dynamic, 472
　formatting data, 476
　viewing, 476–478
pixels, 227
placeholders, graphic objects, 376
Pleading Wizard, 33
point sizes, changing, 73–74
pointers, worksheet, 277
polygon, 545
portability of documents, 663
ports, printer, 108
Power Utility Pak, 739–744
　installation instructions, 743
　new features, 740–743
　registration, 744
PowerPoint, 48
　add sound to presentations, 567–568
　AutoLayout feature, 553
　changing slide layout, 539–540
　chart types, 580
　charts, 573–591
　columns, 559–560
　copy/move slides, 538

default presentations, 528–531
deleting slides, 538
editing in Slide view, 536
enhancing presentations, 549–570
Excel worksheets, 564–566
inserting charts into presentations, 574–576
inserting slides, 537–538
lists, 557–559
Microsoft Organizational Chart, 589–590
moving between slides, 536–537
open new presentations, 532–533
organization chart, 607–610
printing presentations, 593–606
questions, 619–622
rearranging slides, 539
saving presentations, 533
shapes, 544–548
shortcuts, 527
Slide Master, 554–557
slides, working with, 536–540
summary information, 533–534
toolbars, 528
travel presentation, 611–615
Viewer, 602–603
Word tables, 564, 566–567
WordArt, 561
working with objects, 540–543
working with presentations, 531–534
working with text, 535–536
workplace applications, 607–617
PowerPoint basics, 721–735
  adding clip art to presentations, 733–734
  adding slides, 730
  AutoContent Wizard, 723–726
  blank presentation, 725
  creating presentations, 722–726
  editing slide's contents, 731–733
  editing text in different views, 731–733
  moving among slides, 730
  notes pages view, 728–729
  opening a presentation, 726
  printing presentations, 734
  saving/closing presentations, 726
  Slide Sorter view, 728–729
  terminology, 721–722
  using a template, 725
  Views, 727–729

PowerPoint window, 523–527
  Notes Page view, 525–526
  Outline view, 524
  shortcut menu, 527
  Slide Show view, 526
  Slide Sorter view, 525
Presentation dialog box, Presentation Designs tab, 532
presentation window, 523–527
  shortcut buttons, 527
presentations, 721
  add clip art, 733–734
  adding sound, 567–568
  as templates, 620
  audience handouts, 599–602
  AutoLayout feature, 553
  blank, 725
  build slides, 597–598
  colors, 560–561
  creating in PowerPoint, 722–726
  default, 528–531
  editing in Slide view, 536
  enhancing, 549–570
  entering summary information, 533–534
  Excel worksheets, 564–566
  fonts, 560–561
  format title/text, 619
  hiding/unhiding slides, 599
  on-screen slide shows, 596–599
  opening, 726
  opening new, 532–533
  PowerPoint Viewer, 602–603
  printing, 593–606, 734
  printing parts of, 595–596
  Reporting Progress, 530
  saving, 533
  saving/closing, 726
  sending over a network, 605
  shadowing/embossing, 560–561
  speaker's notes, 599–602
  styles, 560–561
  subscript, 561
  superscript, 561
  travel, 611–615
  view without PowerPoint, 620

(continued)

presentations *(continued)*
   Word tables, 564, 566–567
   working with, 531–534
preview slide transitions, 620
Previous Field (Shift+F11) key
      combination, 148
Print (Ctrl+P) key combination, 103, 701–702
Print (Ctrl+Shift+F12) key combination, 103
Print Binder command, 657
Print Binder dialog box, 657
Print command, 734
Print dialog box, 101–102, 412, 595, 644,
      701, 717
   options, 102–103
   Print what list box, 105
Print Preview command, 98
Print Preview mode, 98
   adjusting margins, 100–101
   borders, 101
   Excel, 418
   locating objects, 100–101
   shading documents, 101
Print Preview toolbar, 99
Printer Properties dialog box, 103
   Details tab, 109
   Device Options tab, 425
   Fonts tab, 424
   Graphics tab, 424
   Paper tab, 423
printers
   changing properties, 423–425
   changing setup, 108–109
   paper source, 85
   ports, 108
printing
   annotations, 105
   AutoText entries, 105
   Avery labels, 157–158
   background printing, 97
   charts, 393
   controlling page breaks, 420–421
   database criteria search results, 435
   database report based on specific data, 442
   document summary information, 105
   documents, 97–112
   documents from binder, 657

   envelopes, 110–111, 155–157, 262–263
   Excel basics, 411–416
   field codes, 151
   inserting headers/footers in worksheets,
      421–422
   macro key assignments, 105
   mailing labels, 157–158
   nonconsecutive worksheets, 421
   outlines, 142
   paper orientation, 85
   part of a document, 104–105
   presentation parts, 595–596
   presentations, 593–606, 734
   previewing print jobs, 417–418
   Schedule+, 643–645
   selected text, 104–105
   setting multiple worksheet print ranges, 417
   setting worksheet print range, 416–417
   sideways (landscape orientation), 106
   slides in reverse order, 620
   styles, 105
   table gridlines, 264–265
   travel presentation notes pages, 615
   troubleshooting, 104
   turning off gridlines while printing, 421
   VBA (Visual Basic for Applications)
      code, 489
   Word, 701–702
   worksheet area, 517
   worksheet titles, 420
   worksheet titles on each page, 518
   worksheets, 716–717
Prior Worksheet (Ctrl+PgUp) key
      combination, 279
programming languages, Visual Basic for
      Applications (VBA), 206, 481–491
programs
   See also applications
   adding/removing, 19–20
progressive disclosure slide, 597–598
Prompt for Properties option, 700
Properties dialog box
   Statistics tab, 64
   Summary tab, 63, 290, 534
protocols, OLE, 659

Q

Query Options dialog box
  Select Fields tab, 162
  Sort Records tab, 162
questions
  add/erase on-screen annotations in a slide show, 621
  AutoSave doesn't save all changes to document, 267–268
  bulleted list, 268
  cell formatting, 516
  cell/range shortcuts, 515–516
  change slide layout, 620
  changing default font, 268
  changing Excel default working directory, 513–514
  changing Excel standard font, 513–514
  combining cell contents, 517
  copy formatting of one object to another, 619
  create new slides without New slide dialog box, 621
  deleting documents without leaving Word, 266
  displaying multiple Excel workbooks, 514
  envelope printing, 262–263
  format title/text for entire presentation, 619
  group and edit objects as one, 619
  importing documents, 261–262
  numbered lists, 268
  PowerPoint presentation as template, 620
  preventing slash (/) or hyphen (-) date formatting, 515
  preventing unwanted page breaks, 263–264
  preview slide transitions, 620
  print slides in reverse order, 620
  printing area of worksheet, 517
  printing table gridlines, 264–265
  printing worksheet titles on each page, 518
  running previous versions of Word on the same computer, 266
  specifying default workbook on Excel start up, 513
  using Excel 4.0 menu structure, 514
  view presentations without PowerPoint, 620
  Word format converters, 266–267

R

radar charts, 403, 573
ranges
  cell, 281–283
  database, 432
  discontiguous, 282
  selection shortcuts, 516
readability statistics, documents, 55
rearranging slides, 539
Record Macro dialog box, 211
Record New Macro dialog box (Excel), 451
records
  adding new, 433
  criteria searches, 434–436
  data form, 432–433
  database, 430, 432–436
  deleting, 433–434
  editing, 433
  printing criteria search results, 435
rectangles, drawing, 370
red wavy lines, 52
relative cell references, 328
  versus absolute cell references, 459
Rename Sheet dialog box, 280
Replace (Ctrl+H) key combination, 46
Replace dialog box, 48–49, 333
reports, printing database records based on specific data, 442
restoring links, 668–669
Resume Wizard, 33
Return key, navigating within worksheets, 278
Review AutoFormat Changes dialog box, 225
Right-aligned tabs, 42
rotating shapes, 546
Row Height dialog box, 344
rows
  adjusting in tables, 126–127
  adjusting worksheet heights, 343–344
  deleting worksheet, 320–321

(continued)

rows *(continued)*
   hiding worksheet, 345
   inserting worksheet, 319–320
   tables, 116–117
Ruler (Alt+V+R) key combination, 51
Ruler command, 40
rulers
   custom tabs, 41
   default tabs, 40
   displaying, 558

S

Save As command, 717
Save As dialog box, 289, 698, 718
Save Binder As dialog box, 655
Save command, 717
Save Options dialog box, 289
Save Workspace dialog box, 293–294
saving
   and closing presentations, 726
   documents, Word, 697
   worksheets, 717
   presentations, 533
scaling, 232
scatter charts, 403
Schedule Logon dialog box, 625–626
Schedule+, 625–650
   add/delete/edit contacts, 642
   Appointment window, 633, 636–640
   changing/deleting appointments, 640
   Meeting Requests, 642–643
   printing, 643–645
   Recurring meetings, 640
   starting, 625–627
   Times Data Link Watch Wizard, 645–648
   To Do list, 641
Schedule+ toolbar, 628–629
Schedule+ window, 626
   components, 627–635
   Contacts tab, 635
   Daily tab, 629
   Monthly tab, 631–632
   Planner tab, 632–633
   To Do tab, 634
   Weekly tab, 629–630
scroll bars, 37
scroll box, 37
searches
   advanced, 297–299
   database criteria, 434–436
   document formatting, 49
   special characters, 47–48
   text, 46–49
   workbook files, 295–299
section formatting, 86–88
   section breaks, 87
   vertical alignment, 87
Section⇨Print command, 657
sections, 86
Select (Ctrl+A) key combination, 38
Select Presentation Template dialog box, 551
selecting objects, 540
Send command, 605
series, 316–318
series axis, charts, 385, 572
Series dialog box, 317
server applications, 660
servers, 660
settings, update links, 67
Shading dialog box, 380, 563
Shadow dialog box, 381
shadowing, presentations, 560
shapes, 544–548
   changing color and style, 545–546
   drawing, 544–545
   drawing freeform, 545
   handles, 546
   rotating/sizing, 546
shareware, CD-ROM, 739
Shift key, select objects, 540
shortcut buttons, 527
shortcut keys, assigning to styles, 188–189
shortcut menus, 527
shortcuts
   document navigation, 36–37
   Word start up, 26
   worksheet cell/range, 515–516
sidebars, book, 8
Single line spacing (Ctrl+1) key combination, 44

sizing handles, graphic objects, 374
sizing shapes, 546
Slide Color Scheme dialog box, 555
Slide Layout dialog box, 527, 540, 553
Slide Master, 554–557
    applying background to slides, 612–613
slide masters, 722
Slide Setup dialog box, 593–594
Slide Show command, 596
Slide Show dialog box, 596
slide shows
    add/erase on-screen annotations, 621
    build slides, 597–598
    on-screen, 596–599
    polishing, 598
Slide Transition dialog box, 615
Slide view, editing, 536, 731
slides, 721
    adding columns, 559–560
    adding in PowerPoint, 730
    applying background, 612–613
    build, 597–598
    changing layout, 539–540, 620
    copy/move, 538–539
    creating new, 621
    deleting, 538
    editing, 536
    editing contents, 731–733
    hiding, 599
    inserting, 537–538
    moving among, 730
    moving between, 536–537
    navigating, 730
    outline view, 535
    preview transitions, 620
    print in reverse order, 620
    printing set up, 593–594
    rearranging, 539
    unhiding, 599
    working with, 536–540
Solver (Excel), 466–469
    add-in, 467
    changing cells, 464
    constraints, 466
    installing to Tools menu, 467
    target cell, 466

Solver Parameters dialog box, 468
Solver Results dialog box, 469
Sort command, 129–130
Sort dialog box, 130, 437
sorting
    database, 436–440
    table information, 129–130
sound
    adding to presentations, 567–568
    adding to documents, 673
sound notes, adding to worksheet cells, 309
source documents, 660
Spacing Between Characters dialog box, 380, 563
spacing, paragraph, 81
special characters, searching for, 47–48
Special Effects dialog box, 380
Spelling (F7) key, 51
Spelling Checker
    as you type, 52
    `Custom.dic`, 50
    main dictionary, 50
    performance enhancements, 51
    red wavy lines, 52
Spelling command, 50
Spelling dialog box, 50–52, 335
spelling, checking in worksheets, 334–336
Split Table (Ctrl+Shift+Enter) key combination, 123
spreadsheets, 705–706
    versus workbooks, 273–274
squares, drawing, 370
stacking objects, 543
Standard toolbar, 528
    AutoSum button, 330
    Chart Type button, 581
    clip Art button, 733
    Excel, 707–708
    MS Organizational Chart button, 589
    Word, 692–694
    Word AutoText button, 57
    Word Print button, 97
    Word Print Preview button, 98
    Word Show/Hide button, 75
Start menu, versus Office Shortcut Bar, 13
statistics, document readability, 55

status bar (Alt+T+O) key combination, 51
Style dialog box, 186, 361
Style Gallery, 193–194
Style Gallery dialog box, 193–194
styles, 181–196
   applying, 183–185, 194–196
   applying with keyboards, 184–185
   assigning shortcut keys, 188–189
   basing on another style, 189–191
   character, 182–183
   copying, 191–192
   defining, 185–192, 194–196
   defining by example, 187–188
   deleting, 191–192
   displaying as you work, 192–193
   formatting, 186–187
   Formatting toolbar, 183–184
   keyboard shortcuts, 185
   naming conventions, 187
   Normal, 191
   paragraph, 182–183
   printing, 105
   renaming, 191–192
   Style Gallery, 193–194
   understanding, 181–183
   undoing, 184
   versus direct formatting options, 86
   worksheets, 349–351, 360–361
subheads, 244
subscript, 74
   presentations, 561
subtext, outlines, 131
Sum function, 330
summary, document, 63–65
summary information
   entering, 533–534
   printing, 105
   workbook, 289–290
superscript, 74
   presentations, 561
Switch (Alt+Tab) key combination, 13, 36
switches, field code, 149–150
synonyms, 53
system resources, multiple application effects, 13

T

Tab (Ctrl+Tab) key combination, 116
Tab key
   navigating within worksheets, 278
   table navigation, 116–117
Table AutoFormat dialog box, 124, 264–265
Table Borders and Shading command, 265
Table dialog box, 471
Table of Contents Options dialog box, 168
table of contents
   building, 165–170
   creating, 170–171
   creating from outline, 141–142
   formatting on the fly, 170
   nonstandard styles, 168
   showing/hiding TC entries, 169
   style and outline headings, 166–167
   TC entries, 165, 168–170
   TOC codes, 167
Table⇨Cell Height and Width command, 124–125
Table⇨Convert Text to Table command, 128
Table⇨Delete Cells command, 120
Table⇨Gridlines command, 114
Table⇨Insert Cells command, 120
Table⇨Insert Table command, 114, 234
Table⇨Merge Cells command, 123
Table⇨Sort command, 130
Table⇨Split Table command, 123
Table⇨Table AutoFormat command, 124, 264
tables, 113–180, 245
   add to presentations, 564, 566–567
   bordering, 127–128
   cell, 113–114
   column widths, 124–125
   columns, 116–117
   converting text to, 128–129
   creating, 114–119
   deleting cells, 120–122
   editing, 119–123
   entering text, 118
   Excel data, 469–472
   formatting, 124–128

gridlines, 114
inserting cells, 120–122
keyboard navigation, 117
merging cells, 123
mouse navigation, 116–117
row adjustments, 126–127
rows, 116–117
selecting cells, 119
selecting rows/columns, 116–117
side-by-side paragraphs, 128
sorting information, 129–130
spacing between columns, 125–126
splitting, 123
Tab key, 116–117
tabs, 116–117
understanding, 113–114
tabs, 40–43
clearing, 43
custom, 40–41
default measurement, 40
leader, 43
moving, 43
table, 116–117
types, 41
Tabs command, 40–43
Tabs dialog box, 40–43
target cell, Solver, 466
Task dialog box, 641
TC fields, 165, 168–170
templates, 25–34, 196–202, 721
activating Wizards, 28
APA Style, 758–760
applying, 199–202
AutoContent Wizard, 725
basing on existing template, 199
boilerplate text, 27
categories, 27–28
changing default, 200
creating, 199–202
.Dot file extension, 199
editing, 34
from presentations, 620
global settings, 200
invoice, 257–258
modifying existing, 199–200

`Normal.dot`, 25–27, 198, 200
opening new, 26–27
predefined, 187–198
travel presentation, 611–612
understanding, 181–183, 196–198
Weekly Time Sheet, 249–251
Wizards, 28–33
working with, 198–201
text
adding to charts, 399
aligning, 80–81
AutoText entries, 57–60
boilerplate, 27
centering, 35
centering worksheet, 347–348
character spacing, 71–72
checking grammar while typing, 55
converting to tables, 128–129
copying, 45–46
deleting, 34
dragging/dropping, 46
editing in Outline view, 535
editing in PowerPoint views, 731–733
editing worksheet, 376
entering, 34
entering in Excel, 715–716
format for presentations, 619
formatting worksheet, 377
hyphenation, 56–57
indenting, 35
inserting into document, 695
justifying, 81
justifying worksheet, 348–349
moving, 45–46
printing selected, 105
red wavy lines under, 52
rotating worksheet, 378
searching/replacing, 46–49
selecting, 37–38
selecting in outlines, 132
table cell, 118
working with, 535–536
worksheet entries, 305
wrapping around frame, 241–242
wrapping worksheet, 348

text blocks, selecting/deleting, 34
text boxes, adding to worksheets, 376–379
text editing, Word, 697
text entry, Excel, 715–716
text formatting charts, 399
Thesaurus, 53
Thesaurus (Shift+F7) key combination, 53
Thesaurus command, 53
Thesaurus dialog box, 53
time sheets, 249–251
times
    worksheet formats, 355–356
    worksheet entries, 305–306
times/dates, entering in Excel, 714–715
Timex Data Link Watch Wizard, 645–648
Titles dialog box, 398, 584
titles
    adding to charts, 398
    charts, 584
    format for presentation, 619
    printing worksheet, 420
To Do list, using, 641
Toggle Field (Shift+F9) key combination, 148
toggles, 440
toolbars, 528
    adding folders/programs to, 17–18
    adding new buttons, 15
    assigning AutoText entry to, 58–59
    Borders, 82
    changing colors, 16–17
    changing default template folder, 18–19
    Chart, 397–398
    creating new, 17–18
    customizing, 14–19
    Database, 160
    Drawing, 368–372, 528, 544
    Drawing (Excel), 454
    Excel, 286–288
    floating, 288
    Formatting, 70, 183–184, 528
    Formatting (Excel), 708
    Formatting (Word), 692
    Header and Footer, 88
    Macro, 207–208
    Macro Recorder, 214
    moving buttons, 15

Office Shortcut Bar, 12–19
Open, 296
Outlining, 132–133, 732
Print Preview, 99
removing buttons, 16
Standard, 330, 528, 581, 589
Standard (Excel), 707
Standard (Word), 57, 75, 97–98, 692
Visual Basic, 489–490
Visual Basic (Excel), 452
WordArt, 379, 562
Toolbars dialog box, 287, 528
Tools⇨Mail Merge command, 153
Tools⇨Add-Ins command, 290
Tools⇨Add-Ins command, 467
Tools⇨Animation Settings, 597
Tools⇨Assign Macro command, 383, 456
Tools⇨AutoSave command, 290
Tools⇨Build Slide Text command, 598
Tools⇨Crop⇨Picture command, 541
Tools⇨Customize command, 543, 562
Tools⇨Envelopes and Labels command, 110, 263
Tools⇨Goal Seek command, 464–466
Tools⇨Grammar command, 53
Tools⇨Hide Slide command, 599
Tools⇨Macro command, 209–210, 214, 382, 457–458
Tools⇨Options command, 52, 315, 376, 535
Tools⇨Protection command, 361–362
Tools⇨Protection⇨Protect Workbook command, 362
Tools⇨Record Macro⇨Record at Mark command, 452
Tools⇨Record Macro⇨Record New Macro command, 451, 459
Tools⇨Slide Transition command, 615
Tools⇨Solver command, 467
Tools⇨Spelling command, 50, 334
Tools⇨Thesaurus command, 53
Tooltips, help feature, 287
transitions, travel presentation, 615–616
travel presentation, 611–615
    handouts, 613–614
    headers/footers, 614–615
    notes, 613

printing notes pages, 615
slide background, 612–613
template, 611
transitions, 615–616
troubleshooting, printing problems, 104
TrueType fonts, 350
two-input data tables, 469
TypeRodent, 758
typing habits, avoiding bad, 35
typing, checking spelling, 52

U

unattached text, charts, 399
underlying values, worksheet, 307
Undo AutoFormat command, 436
Unlock Field (Ctrl+Shift+F11) key combination, 150
utilities
   Carrier Pigeon, 760–761
   CD-ROM, 749–760
   Jasc Media Center, 749–750
   NoteWorthy Composer, 752–754
   Paint Shop Pro, 750–752
   TypeRodent, 758
   WinZip95, 755–757

V

value axis, charts, 385, 572
values, 301, 713
VBA (Visual Basic for Applications) programming language, 206, 481–491
   applications code, 484–488
   comments, 485
   control statements, 486
   displaying dialog boxes, 487
   editing code, 489
   entering data, 486
   footers, 485
   headers, 485
   InputBox function, 488
   modules, 481–482

MsgBox function, 487
printing code, 489
procedure, 481
programming language, 481–491
resources, 490
selecting data, 486
similarities to Microsoft Visual Basic, 483
statements, 481
user input, 487–488
Visual Basic toolbar, 489–490
vertical alignment, 87
video, adding to documents, 673
View menu, 38
View⇨Datasheet command, 576
View⇨Header and Footer command, 88, 614
View⇨Master⇨Handout Master command, 602
View⇨Master⇨Slide Master command, 554, 612
View⇨Notes Pages command, 599, 613
View⇨Outline command, 38, 132, 535, 727
View⇨Ruler command, 100, 558–559
View⇨Slide Show command, 596
View⇨Toolbars command, 183, 207, 286, 368, 397, 546
Viewer, PowerPoint, 602–603
viewing, presentations without PowerPoint, 620
views
   Master Document, 39
   Normal, 38
   Notes Page, 525–526
   Outline, 38, 142, 524
   Page Layout, 39, 223
   PowerPoint, 727–729
   Slide Show, 526
   Slide Sorter, 525
Visual Basic for Applications (VBA) programming language, 206, 481–491
Visual Basic toolbar, 489–490
   recording macros (Excel), 452

W

wavy lines, 52
Weekly Time Sheet template, 249–251
what-if analysis, 463–479
wildcards, database criteria search, 435
Window⇨Freeze Panes command, 286
Window⇨Remove Split command, 286
Window⇨Split command, 285
Windows Help file, 737–738
WinZip95, 755–757
Wizards
    Agenda, 28–29
    Answer, 13
    AutoContent, 549–553
    Award, 29–30
    Calendar, 30
    Chart, 386–391
    Fax, 31, 251–254
    Function, 331–332
    Letter, 31
    Memo, 32, 255–256
    Newsletter, 32, 245–246
    Pack & Go, 603–605
    Pivot Table, 472–478
    Pleading, 33
    Resume, 33
    template, 28–33
Word
    creating/working with documents, 25–66
    desktop publishing, 221–247
    document views, 38
    fields, 145–165
    formatting documents, 67–95
    Grammar Checker, 53–56
    importing Excel data documents, 159–160
    index, 173–178
    macros, 205–219
    questions, 261–269
    running previous versions on the same computer, 266
    saving documents in previous version formats, 266–267
    Shortcut to Winword icon, 26
    Spelling Checker, 50–52
    start up shortcut, 26
    styles, 181–196
    tables added to PowerPoint, 564, 566–567
    tables of contents, 165–171
    tables of figures, 172–173
    templates, 196–202
    Thesaurus, 53
    top ten questions, 261–269
    workplace applications, 249–259
Word basics, 691–703
    Automatic Save option, 700
    Fast Saves, 700
    File⇨Save All command, 700–701
    Formatting toolbars, 62
    navigation, 696–697
    open existing documents, 702
    opening documents, 695–696
    printing, 701–702
    Prompt for Document Properties option, 700
    Save As dialog box, 698
    saving documents, 697
    screen, 691–692
    Standard toolbar, 692
    starting, 691
    text editing, 697
    Word window, 692
Word utilities, CD-ROM, 757–760
Word window, 692
word wrap, 34–35
WordArt, 379–381
    PowerPoint, 561
    special effects, 561–564
WordArt dialog box, 561
WordArt Format menu options, 562
WordArt toolbar, 379, 561–562
    Format list box, 381
workbook concept, 709–710
workbook screen, 706
workbook tabs, 711
workbooks, 273–300
    adding summary information, 289–290
    advanced searches, 297–299
    AutoSave, 290–293
    closing, 294
    displaying multiple, 514

file organization, 299
file searches, 295–299
finding, 295–299
opening, 710
opening existing, 275–276
opening multiple, 276
opening new, 275
protecting, 361–362
saving, 288–294
saving in other file formats, 293
saving workspace file, 293–294
sending files over a network, 425–426
specifying default on start up, 513
understanding, 273–276
versus spreadsheets, 273–274
worksheets
  ###### signs in, 303
  adding, 283–284
  adding graphics to, 365–383
  adding notes to cells, 308–309
  adding sound notes to cells, 309
  adding text boxes, 376–379
  adding to presentations, 564–566
  adjacent, 280–281
  alignments, 346–347
  AutoFormat, 339–343
  automatic cell formatting, 304
  AutoSum, 330–331
  borders, 351–353
  break-even analysis, 495–500
  building series, 316–318
  cash-flow management, 493–495
  cell format protection, 361–362
  cell formatting, 516
  cell references, 328
  cell/range shortcuts, 515–516
  centering text, 347–348
  changing printer properties, 423–425
  chart sheets, 387–391
  closing panes, 286
  colors, 351–353
  column widths, 343–344
  combining cell contents, 517
  controlling page breaks while printing, 420–421
  copying cells, 312–319
  copying formats with Format Painter, 359–360
  copying information in, 284–285
  custom dictionary, 335–336
  custom number formats, 356–359
  data editing, 310–311
  data entry, 301–307
  database, 429–448
  date entries, 305–306
  date formats, 355–356
  deleting, 283–284
  deleting cells, 320–321
  deleting columns, 320–321
  deleting rows, 320–321
  displayed values versus underlying values, 307
  displaying formulas, 326–327
  Drawing toolbar, 368–372
  embedded charts, 387–391
  finding and replacing data, 333–334
  finding data, 332–333
  floating toolbars, 288
  fonts, 349–351
  Format Painter, 359–360
  formatting, 339–364
  Formula bar, 302
  Formula bar cell data editing, 310
  formulas, 301, 323–328
  Function Wizard, 331–332
  functions, 328–332
  graphic placeholders, 376
  hiding columns, 345
  hiding gridlines, 345
  hiding rows, 345
  hiding/unhiding graphic objects, 376
  inserting cells, 319–320
  inserting columns, 319–320
  inserting graphics, 366–367
  inserting graphics with Copy/Paste command, 366–367
  inserting headers/footers while printing, 421–422
  inserting rows, 319–320
  integer entries, 304
  IRA calculator, 500–507
  justifying text, 348–349

(continued)

worksheets *(continued)*
  key combinations to navigate, 711–712
  making macros available to, 459–460
  mortgage analysis/amortization schedule, 507–511
  moving cells, 312–319
  moving information in, 284–285
  multimedia capabilities, 310
  multiple print ranges, 417
  named range, 278, 280, 321–322
  navigating between, 279–280
  navigating within, 277–279, 711–712
  number entries, 303–304
  number formats, 353–355
  parts of, 276–277
  patterns, 351–353
  pointer shapes, 277
  preventing slash (/) or hyphen (-) date formatting, 515
  previewing print jobs, 417–418
  printing, 716–717
  printing area, 517
  printing nonconsecutive sheets, 421
  printing titles, 420
  printing titles on each page, 518
  rearranging, 283–284
  renaming tabs, 280
  saving, 717
  selecting cell ranges, 281–283
  selecting multiple, 280–281
  series, 316–318
  setting print range, 416–417
  Sound Recorder, 309
  spell checking, 334–336
  splitting windows, 285–286
  style formats, 349–351
  styles, 360–361
  supported graphics files, 367–368
  text entries, 305
  time entries, 305–306
  time formats, 355–356
  turning off gridlines while printing, 421
  undoing entries, 306
  values, 301

Visual Basic for Applications (VBA), 481–491
  working with, 276–286
  wrapping text, 348
workspace file, 293–294
  opening on Excel start up, 294

X

Xlstart folder, 513
XY scatter charts, 573

DUMMIES PRESS

The fun & easy way to learn about computers and more!

12/20/94

Windows 3.1 For Dummies,™ 2nd Edition
by Andy Rathbone

ISBN: 1-56884-182-5
$16.95 USA/$22.95 Canada

MORE Windows For Dummies™
by Andy Rathbone

ISBN: 1-56884-048-9
$19.95 USA/$26.95 Canada

DOS For Dummies,® 2nd Edition
by Dan Gookin

ISBN: 1-878058-75-4
$16.95 USA/$21.95 Canada

The Internet For Dummies™ 2nd Edition
by John R. Levine & Carol Baroudi

ISBN: 1-56884-222-8
$19.99 USA/$26.99 Canada

Personal Finance For Dummies™
by Eric Tyson

ISBN: 1-56884-150-7
$16.95 USA/$21.95 Canada

PCs For Dummies,™ 2nd Edition
by Dan Gookin & Andy Rathbone

ISBN: 1-56884-078-0
$16.95 USA/$21.95 Canada

Macs For Dummies,® 2nd Edition
by David Pogue

ISBN: 1-56884-051-9
$19.95 USA/$26.95 Canada

Over 12 Million in print!

Here's a complete listing of IDG's ...For Dummies Titles

Title	Author	ISBN	Price
DATABASE			
Access 2 For Dummies™	by Scott Palmer	1-56884-090-X	$19.95 USA/$26.95 Canada
Access Programming For Dummies™	by Rob Krumm	1-56884-091-8	$19.95 USA/$26.95 Canada
Approach 3 For Windows For Dummies™	by Doug Lowe	1-56884-233-3	$19.99 USA/$26.99 Canada
dBASE For DOS For Dummies™	by Scott Palmer & Michael Stabler	1-56884-188-4	$19.95 USA/$26.95 Canada
dBASE For Windows For Dummies™	by Scott Palmer	1-56884-179-5	$19.95 USA/$26.95 Canada
dBASE 5 For Windows Programming For Dummies™	by Ted Coombs & Jason Coombs	1-56884-215-5	$19.99 USA/$26.99 Canada
FoxPro 2.6 For Windows For Dummies™	by John Kaufeld	1-56884-187-6	$19.95 USA/$26.95 Canada
Paradox 5 For Windows For Dummies™	by John Kaufeld	1-56884-185-X	$19.95 USA/$26.95 Canada
DESKTOP PUBLISHING / ILLUSTRATION / GRAPHICS			
CorelDRAW! 5 For Dummies™	by Deke McClelland	1-56884-157-4	$19.95 USA/$26.95 Canada
CorelDRAW! For Dummies™	by Deke McClelland	1-56884-042-X	$19.95 USA/$26.95 Canada
Harvard Graphics 2 For Windows For Dummies™	by Roger C. Parker	1-56884-092-6	$19.95 USA/$26.95 Canada
PageMaker 5 For Macs For Dummies™	by Galen Gruman	1-56884-178-7	$19.95 USA/$26.95 Canada
PageMaker 5 For Windows For Dummies™	by Deke McClelland & Galen Gruman	1-56884-160-4	$19.95 USA/$26.95 Canada
QuarkXPress 3.3 For Dummies™	by Galen Gruman & Barbara Assadi	1-56884-217-1	$19.99 USA/$26.99 Canada
FINANCE / PERSONAL FINANCE / TEST TAKING REFERENCE			
QuickBooks 3 For Dummies™	by Stephen L. Nelson	1-56884-227-9	$19.99 USA/$26.99 Canada
Quicken 8 For DOS For Dummies™, 2nd Edition	by Stephen L. Nelson	1-56884-210-4	$19.95 USA/$26.95 Canada
Quicken 5 For Macs For Dummies™	by Stephen L. Nelson	1-56884-211-2	$19.95 USA/$26.95 Canada
Quicken 4 For Windows For Dummies™, 2nd Edition	by Stephen L. Nelson	1-56884-209-0	$19.95 USA/$26.95 Canada
The SAT I For Dummies™	by Suzee Vlk	1-56884-213-9	$14.99 USA/$20.99 Canada
GROUPWARE / INTEGRATED			
Lotus Notes 3/3.1 For Dummies™	by Paul Freeland & Stephen Londergan	1-56884-212-0	$19.95 USA/$26.95 Canada
Microsoft Office 4 For Windows For Dummies™	by Roger C. Parker	1-56884-183-3	$19.95 USA/$26.95 Canada
Microsoft Works 3 For Windows For Dummies™	by David C. Kay	1-56884-214-7	$19.99 USA/$26.99 Canada

FOR MORE INFORMATION OR TO ORDER, PLEASE CALL ▶ 800. 762. 2974

For volume discounts & special orders please call
Tony Real, Special Sales, at 415. 655. 3048

DUMMIES PRESS

Title	Author	ISBN	Price
INTERNET / COMMUNICATIONS / NETWORKING			12/20/94
CompuServe For Dummies™	by Wallace Wang	1-56884-181-7	$19.95 USA/$26.95 Canada
Modems For Dummies™, 2nd Edition	by Tina Rathbone	1-56884-223-6	$19.99 USA/$26.99 Canada
Modems For Dummies™	by Tina Rathbone	1-56884-001-2	$19.95 USA/$26.95 Canada
MORE Internet For Dummies™	by John R. Levine & Margaret Levine Young	1-56884-164-7	$19.95 USA/$26.95 Canada
NetWare For Dummies™	by Ed Tittel & Deni Connor	1-56884-003-9	$19.95 USA/$26.95 Canada
Networking For Dummies™	by Doug Lowe	1-56884-079-9	$19.95 USA/$26.95 Canada
ProComm Plus 2 For Windows For Dummies™	by Wallace Wang	1-56884-219-8	$19.99 USA/$26.99 Canada
The Internet For Dummies™, 2nd Edition	by John R. Levine & Carol Baroudi	1-56884-222-8	$19.99 USA/$26.99 Canada
The Internet For Macs For Dummies™	by Charles Seiter	1-56884-184-1	$19.95 USA/$26.95 Canada
MACINTOSH			
Macs For Dummies®	by David Pogue	1-56884-173-6	$19.95 USA/$26.95 Canada
Macintosh System 7.5 For Dummies™	by Bob LeVitus	1-56884-197-3	$19.95 USA/$26.95 Canada
MORE Macs For Dummies™	by David Pogue	1-56884-087-X	$19.95 USA/$26.95 Canada
PageMaker 5 For Macs For Dummies™	by Galen Gruman	1-56884-178-7	$19.95 USA/$26.95 Canada
QuarkXPress 3.3 For Dummies™	by Galen Gruman & Barbara Assadi	1-56884-217-1	$19.99 USA/$26.99 Canada
Upgrading and Fixing Macs For Dummies™	by Kearney Rietmann & Frank Higgins	1-56884-189-2	$19.95 USA/$26.95 Canada
MULTIMEDIA			
Multimedia & CD-ROMs For Dummies™, Interactive Multimedia Value Pack	by Andy Rathbone	1-56884-225-2	$29.95 USA/$39.95 Canada
Multimedia & CD-ROMs For Dummies™	by Andy Rathbone	1-56884-089-6	$19.95 USA/$26.95 Canada
OPERATING SYSTEMS / DOS			
MORE DOS For Dummies™	by Dan Gookin	1-56884-046-2	$19.95 USA/$26.95 Canada
S.O.S. For DOS™	by Katherine Murray	1-56884-043-8	$12.95 USA/$16.95 Canada
OS/2 For Dummies™	by Andy Rathbone	1-878058-76-2	$19.95 USA/$26.95 Canada
UNIX			
UNIX For Dummies™	by John R. Levine & Margaret Levine Young	1-878058-58-4	$19.95 USA/$26.95 Canada
WINDOWS			
S.O.S. For Windows™	by Katherine Murray	1-56884-045-4	$12.95 USA/$16.95 Canada
MORE Windows 3.1 For Dummies™, 3rd Edition	by Andy Rathbone	1-56884-240-6	$19.99 USA/$26.99 Canada
PCs / HARDWARE			
Illustrated Computer Dictionary For Dummies™	by Dan Gookin, Wally Wang, & Chris Van Buren	1-56884-004-7	$12.95 USA/$16.95 Canada
Upgrading and Fixing PCs For Dummies™	by Andy Rathbone	1-56884-002-0	$19.95 USA/$26.95 Canada
PRESENTATION / AUTOCAD			
AutoCAD For Dummies™	by Bud Smith	1-56884-191-4	$19.95 USA/$26.95 Canada
PowerPoint 4 For Windows For Dummies™	by Doug Lowe	1-56884-161-2	$16.95 USA/$22.95 Canada
PROGRAMMING			
Borland C++ For Dummies™	by Michael Hyman	1-56884-162-0	$19.95 USA/$26.95 Canada
"Borland's New Language Product" For Dummies™	by Neil Rubenking	1-56884-200-7	$19.95 USA/$26.95 Canada
C For Dummies™	by Dan Gookin	1-878058-78-9	$19.95 USA/$26.95 Canada
C++ For Dummies™	by Stephen R. Davis	1-56884-163-9	$19.95 USA/$26.95 Canada
Mac Programming For Dummies™	by Dan Parks Sydow	1-56884-173-6	$19.95 USA/$26.95 Canada
QBasic Programming For Dummies™	by Douglas Hergert	1-56884-093-4	$19.95 USA/$26.95 Canada
Visual Basic "X" For Dummies™, 2nd Edition	by Wallace Wang	1-56884-230-9	$19.99 USA/$26.99 Canada
Visual Basic 3 For Dummies™	by Wallace Wang	1-56884-076-4	$19.95 USA/$26.95 Canada
SPREADSHEET			
1-2-3 For Dummies™	by Greg Harvey	1-878058-60-6	$16.95 USA/$21.95 Canada
1-2-3 For Windows 5 For Dummies™, 2nd Edition	by John Walkenbach	1-56884-216-3	$16.95 USA/$21.95 Canada
1-2-3 For Windows For Dummies™	by John Walkenbach	1-56884-052-7	$16.95 USA/$21.95 Canada
Excel 5 For Macs For Dummies™	by Greg Harvey	1-56884-186-8	$19.95 USA/$26.95 Canada
Excel For Dummies™, 2nd Edition	by Greg Harvey	1-56884-050-0	$16.95 USA/$21.95 Canada
MORE Excel 5 For Windows For Dummies™	by Greg Harvey	1-56884-207-4	$19.95 USA/$26.95 Canada
Quattro Pro 6 For Windows For Dummies™	by John Walkenbach	1-56884-174-4	$19.95 USA/$26.95 Canada
Quattro Pro For DOS For Dummies™	by John Walkenbach	1-56884-023-3	$16.95 USA/$21.95 Canada
UTILITIES / VCRs & CAMCORDERS			
Norton Utilities 8 For Dummies™	by Beth Slick	1-56884-166-3	$19.95 USA/$26.95 Canada
VCRs & Camcorders For Dummies™	by Andy Rathbone & Gordon McComb	1-56884-229-5	$14.99 USA/$20.99 Canada
WORD PROCESSING			
Ami Pro For Dummies™	by Jim Meade	1-56884-049-7	$19.95 USA/$26.95 Canada
MORE Word For Windows 6 For Dummies™	by Doug Lowe	1-56884-165-5	$19.95 USA/$26.95 Canada
MORE WordPerfect 6 For Windows For Dummies™	by Margaret Levine Young & David C. Kay	1-56884-206-6	$19.95 USA/$26.95 Canada
MORE WordPerfect 6 For DOS For Dummies™	by Wallace Wang, edited by Dan Gookin	1-56884-047-0	$19.95 USA/$26.95 Canada
S.O.S. For WordPerfect™	by Katherine Murray	1-56884-053-5	$12.95 USA/$16.95 Canada
Word 6 For Macs For Dummies™	by Dan Gookin	1-56884-190-6	$19.95 USA/$26.95 Canada
Word For Windows 6 For Dummies™	by Dan Gookin	1-56884-075-6	$16.95 USA/$21.95 Canada
Word For Windows For Dummies™	by Dan Gookin	1-878058-86-X	$16.95 USA/$21.95 Canada
WordPerfect 6 For Dummies™	by Dan Gookin	1-878058-77-0	$16.95 USA/$21.95 Canada
WordPerfect For Dummies™	by Dan Gookin	1-878058-52-5	$16.95 USA/$21.95 Canada
WordPerfect For Windows For Dummies™	by Margaret Levine Young & David C. Kay	1-56884-032-2	$16.95 USA/$21.95 Canada

FOR MORE INFORMATION OR TO ORDER, PLEASE CALL ▶ 800.762.2974

For volume discounts & special orders please call Tony Real, Special Sales, at 415. 655. 3048

DUMMIES QUICK REFERENCES

Fun, Fast, & Cheap!

CorelDRAW! 5 For Dummies™ Quick Reference
by Raymond E. Werner
ISBN: 1-56884-952-4
$9.99 USA/$12.99 Canada
NEW!

Windows "X" For Dummies™ Quick Reference, 3rd Edition
by Greg Harvey
ISBN: 1-56884-964-8
$9.99 USA/$12.99 Canada
NEW!

Word For Windows 6 For Dummies™ Quick Reference
by George Lynch
ISBN: 1-56884-095-0
$8.95 USA/$12.95 Canada
SUPER STAR

WordPerfect For DOS For Dummies™ Quick Reference
by Greg Harvey
ISBN: 1-56884-009-8
$8.95 USA/$11.95 Canada
SUPER STAR

Title	Author	ISBN	Price
DATABASE			
Access 2 For Dummies™ Quick Reference	by Stuart A. Stuple	1-56884-167-1	$8.95 USA/$11.95 Canada
dBASE 5 For DOS For Dummies™ Quick Reference	by Barry Sosinsky	1-56884-954-0	$9.99 USA/$12.99 Canada
dBASE 5 For Windows For Dummies™ Quick Reference	by Stuart J. Stuple	1-56884-953-2	$9.99 USA/$12.99 Canada
Paradox 5 For Windows For Dummies™ Quick Reference	by Scott Palmer	1-56884-960-5	$9.99 USA/$12.99 Canada
DESKTOP PUBLISHING / ILLUSTRATION/GRAPHICS			
Harvard Graphics 3 For Windows For Dummies™ Quick Reference	by Raymond E. Werner	1-56884-962-1	$9.99 USA/$12.99 Canada
FINANCE / PERSONAL FINANCE			
Quicken 4 For Windows For Dummies™ Quick Reference	by Stephen L. Nelson	1-56884-950-8	$9.95 USA/$12.95 Canada
GROUPWARE / INTEGRATED			
Microsoft Office 4 For Windows For Dummies™ Quick Reference	by Doug Lowe	1-56884-958-3	$9.99 USA/$12.99 Canada
Microsoft Works For Windows 3 For Dummies™ Quick Reference	by Michael Partington	1-56884-959-1	$9.99 USA/$12.99 Canada
INTERNET / COMMUNICATIONS / NETWORKING			
The Internet For Dummies™ Quick Reference	by John R. Levine	1-56884-168-X	$8.95 USA/$11.95 Canada
MACINTOSH			
Macintosh System 7.5 For Dummies™ Quick Reference	by Stuart J. Stuple	1-56884-956-7	$9.99 USA/$12.99 Canada
OPERATING SYSTEMS / DOS			
DOS For Dummies® Quick Reference	by Greg Harvey	1-56884-007-1	$8.95 USA/$11.95 Canada
UNIX			
UNIX For Dummies™ Quick Reference	by Margaret Levine Young & John R. Levine	1-56884-094-2	$8.95 USA/$11.95 Canada
WINDOWS			
Windows 3.1 For Dummies™ Quick Reference, 2nd Edition	by Greg Harvey	1-56884-951-6	$8.95 USA/$11.95 Canada
PRESENTATION / AUTOCAD			
AutoCAD For Dummies™ Quick Reference	by Ellen Finkelstein	1-56884-198-1	$9.95 USA/$12.95 Canada
SPREADSHEET			
1-2-3 For Dummies™ Quick Reference	by John Walkenbach	1-56884-027-6	$8.95 USA/$11.95 Canada
1-2-3 For Windows 5 For Dummies™ Quick Reference	by John Walkenbach	1-56884-957-5	$9.95 USA/$12.95 Canada
Excel For Windows For Dummies™ Quick Reference, 2nd Edition	by John Walkenbach	1-56884-096-9	$8.95 USA/$11.95 Canada
Quattro Pro 6 For Windows For Dummies™ Quick Reference	by Stuart A. Stuple	1-56884-172-8	$9.95 USA/$12.95 Canada
WORD PROCESSING			
Word For Windows 6 For Dummies™ Quick Reference	by George Lynch	1-56884-095-0	$8.95 USA/$11.95 Canada
WordPerfect For Windows For Dummies™ Quick Reference	by Greg Harvey	1-56884-039-X	$8.95 USA/$11.95 Canada

FOR MORE INFORMATION OR TO ORDER, PLEASE CALL ▶ 800.762.2974

For volume discounts & special orders please call Tony Real, Special Sales, at 415. 655. 3048

PC PRESS

12/20/94

Windows 3.1 SECRETS™
by Brian Livingston
ISBN: 1-878058-43-6
$39.95 USA/$52.95 Canada
Includes Software.

MORE Windows 3.1 SECRETS™
by Brian Livingston
ISBN: 1-56884-019-5
$39.95 USA/$52.95 Canada
Includes Software.

Windows GIZMOS™
by Brian Livingston
& Margie Livingston
ISBN: 1-878058-66-5
$39.95 USA/$52.95 Canada
Includes Software.

Windows 3.1 Connectivity SECRETS™
by Runnoe Connally, David Rorabaugh, & Sheldon Hall
ISBN: 1-56884-030-6
$49.95 USA/$64.95 Canada
Includes Software.

Windows 3.1 Configuration SECRETS™
by Valda Hilley
& James Blakely
ISBN: 1-56884-026-8
$49.95 USA/$64.95 Canada
Includes Software.

Internet SECRETS™
by John R. Levine
& Carol Baroudi
ISBN: 1-56884-452-2
$39.99 USA/$54.99 Canada
Includes Software.
Available: January 1995

Internet GIZMOS™ For Windows
by Joel Diamond, Howard Sobel, & Valda Hilley
ISBN: 1-56884-451-4
$39.99 USA/$54.99 Canada
Includes Software.
Available: December 1994

Network Security SECRETS™
by David Stang
& Sylvia Moon
ISBN: 1-56884-021-7
Int'l. ISBN: 1-56884-151-5
$49.95 USA/$64.95 Canada
Includes Software.

PC SECRETS™
by Caroline M. Halliday
ISBN: 1-878058-49-5
$39.95 USA/$52.95 Canada
Includes Software.

WordPerfect 6 SECRETS™
by Roger C. Parker
& David A. Holzgang
ISBN: 1-56884-040-3
$39.95 USA/$52.95 Canada
Includes Software.

DOS 6 SECRETS™
by Robert D. Ainsbury
ISBN: 1-878058-70-3
$39.95 USA/$52.95 Canada
Includes Software.

Paradox 4 Power Programming SECRETS,™ 2nd Edition
by Gregory B. Salcedo
& Martin W. Rudy
ISBN: 1-878058-54-1
$44.95 USA/$59.95 Canada
Includes Software.

Paradox For Windows "X" Power Programming SECRETS™
by Gregory B. Salcedo
& Martin W. Rudy
ISBN: 1-56884-085-3
$44.95 USA/$59.95 Canada
Includes Software.

Hard Disk SECRETS™
by John M. Goodman, Ph.D.
ISBN: 1-878058-64-9
$39.95 USA/$52.95 Canada
Includes Software.

WordPerfect 6 For Windows Tips & Techniques Revealed
by David A. Holzgang
& Roger C. Parker
ISBN: 1-56884-202-3
$39.95 USA/$52.95 Canada
Includes Software.

Excel 5 For Windows Power Programming Techniques
by John Walkenbach
ISBN: 1-56884-303-8
$39.95 USA/$52.95 Canada
Includes Software.
Available: November 1994

INFO WORLD

...SECRETS™

FOR MORE INFORMATION OR TO ORDER, PLEASE CALL ▶ 800.762.2974

For volume discounts & special orders please call Tony Real, Special Sales, at 415. 655. 3048

PC PRESS

12/20/94

"A lot easier to use than the book Excel gives you!"

Lisa Schmeckpeper, New Berlin, WI, on PC World Excel 5 For Windows Handbook

Official Hayes Modem Communications Companion
by Caroline M. Halliday

ISBN: 1-56884-072-1
$29.95 USA/$39.95 Canada
Includes software.

PC World Excel 5 For Windows Handbook, 2nd Edition
by John Walkenbach & Dave Maguiness

ISBN: 1-56884-056-X
$34.95 USA/$44.95 Canada
Includes software.

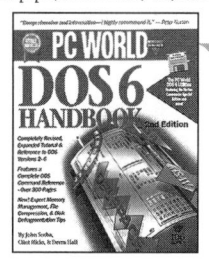

PC World DOS 6 Handbook, 2nd Edition
by John Socha, Clint Hicks, & Devra Hall

ISBN: 1-878058-79-7
$34.95 USA/$44.95 Canada
Includes software.

PC World Word For Windows 6 Handbook
by Brent Heslop & David Angell

ISBN: 1-56884-054-3
$34.95 USA/$44.95 Canada
Includes software.

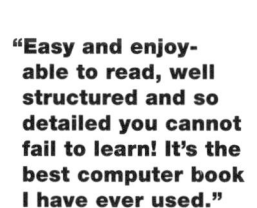

PC World Microsoft Access 2 Bible, 2nd Edition
by Cary N. Prague & Michael R. Irwin

ISBN: 1-56884-086-1
$39.95 USA/$52.95 Canada
Includes software.

"Easy and enjoyable to read, well structured and so detailed you cannot fail to learn! It's the best computer book I have ever used."

John Wildsmith, Gateshead, England, on PC World Microsoft Access 2 Bible, 2nd Edition

PC World WordPerfect 6 Handbook
by Greg Harvey

ISBN: 1-878058-80-0
$34.95 USA/$44.95 Canada
Includes software.

QuarkXPress For Windows Designer Handbook
by Barbara Assadi & Galen Gruman

ISBN: 1-878058-45-2
$29.95 USA/$39.95 Canada

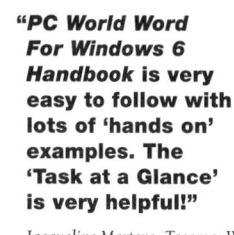

Official XTree Companion, 3rd Edition
by Beth Slick

ISBN: 1-878058-57-6
$19.95 USA/$26.95 Canada

PC World DOS 6 Command Reference and Problem Solver
by John Socha & Devra Hall

ISBN: 1-56884-055-1
$24.95 USA/$32.95 Canada

Client/Server Strategies: A Survival Guide for Corporate Reengineers
by David Vaskevitch

ISBN: 1-56884-064-0
$29.95 USA/$39.95 Canada

"PC World Word For Windows 6 Handbook is very easy to follow with lots of 'hands on' examples. The 'Task at a Glance' is very helpful!"

Jacqueline Martens, Tacoma, WA

"Thanks for publishing this book! It's the best money I've spent this year!"

Robert D. Templeton, Ft. Worth, TX, on MORE Windows 3.1 SECRETS

FOR MORE INFORMATION OR TO ORDER, PLEASE CALL ▶ 800. 762. 2974

For volume discounts & special orders please call
Tony Real, Special Sales, at 415. 655. 3048

MACWORLD BOOKS

12/20/94

"An essential guide for anyone managing Mac networks."

Reese Jones, CEO, Farallon Computing, on Macworld Networking Handbook

Demystify the Mac!

Macworld books are built like your Macintosh — Powerful, Easy, Fun, and at a Great Value!

"I sell Macs and will recommend this book to my customers. Best computer book I have ever owned."

John Schultz, McLean, VA, on Macworld Macintosh SECRETS

Macworld System 7.5 Bible, 3rd Edition
by Lon Poole
ISBN: 1-56884-098-5
$29.95 USA/$39.95 Canada

NATIONAL BESTSELLER!

Macworld Mac & Power Mac SECRETS,™ 2nd Edition
by David Pogue & Joseph Schorr
ISBN: 1-56884-175-2
$39.95 USA/$54.95 Canada
Includes 3 disks chock full of software.

Macworld Complete Mac Handbook + Interactive CD, 3rd Edition
by Jim Heid
ISBN: 1-56884-192-2
$39.95 USA/$54.95 Canada
Includes an interactive CD-ROM.

Macworld Ultimate Mac CD-ROM
by Jim Heid
ISBN: 1-56884-477-8
$19.95 USA/$26.99 Canada
CD-ROM includes version 2.0 of QuickTime, and over 65 MB of the best shareware, freeware, fonts, sounds, and more!

Macworld Networking Bible, 2nd Edition
by Dave Kosiur & Joel M. Snyder
ISBN: 1-56884-194-9
$29.95 USA/$39.95 Canada

Macworld Photoshop 3 Bible, 2nd Edition
by Deke McClelland
ISBN: 1-56884-158-2
$39.95 USA/$54.95 Canada
Includes stunning CD-ROM with add-ons, digitized photos, new filters from Kai's Power Tools, and more.

NEW!

Macworld Photoshop 2.5 Bible
by Deke McClelland
ISBN: 1-56884-022-5
$29.95 USA/$39.95 Canada

NATIONAL BESTSELLER!

Macworld FreeHand 4 Bible
by Deke McClelland
ISBN: 1-56884-170-1
$29.95 USA/$39.95 Canada

Macworld Illustrator 5.0/5.5 Bible
by Ted Alspach
ISBN: 1-56884-097-7
$39.95 USA/$54.95 Canada
Includes CD-ROM with QuickTime tutorials.

FOR MORE INFORMATION OR TO ORDER, PLEASE CALL ▶ 800. 762. 2974

For volume discounts & special orders please call Tony Real, Special Sales, at 415. 655. 3048

MACWORLD BOOKS

12/20/94

"Macworld Complete Mac Handbook Plus CD covered everything I could think of and more!"

Peter Tsakiris, New York, NY

"Thanks for the best computer book I've ever read — Photoshop 2.5 Bible. Best $30 I ever spent. I love the detailed index...Yours blows them all out of the water. This is a great book. We must enlighten the masses!"

Kevin Lisankie, Chicago, Illinois

"Macworld Guide to ClarisWorks 2 is the easiest computer book to read that I have ever found!"

Steven Hanson, Lutz, FL

Macworld QuarkXPress 3.2/3.3 Bible
by Barbara Assadi & Galen Gruman
ISBN: 1-878058-85-1
$39.95 USA/$52.95 Canada
Includes disk with QuarkXPress XTensions and scripts.

Macworld PageMaker 5 Bible
by Craig Danuloff
ISBN: 1-878058-84-3
$39.95 USA/$52.95 Canada
Includes 2 disks with Pagemaker utilities, clip art, and more.

Macworld FileMaker Pro 2.0/2.1 Bible
by Steven A. Schwartz
ISBN: 1-56884-201-5
$34.95 USA/$46.95 Canada
Includes disk with ready-to-run databases.

Macworld Word 6 Companion, 2nd Edition
by Jim Heid
ISBN: 1-56884-082-9
$24.95 USA/$34.95 Canada

Macworld Guide To Microsoft Word 5/5.1
by Jim Heid
ISBN: 1-878058-39-8
$22.95 USA/$29.95 Canada

Macworld ClarisWorks 2.0/2.1 Companion, 2nd Edition
by Steven A. Schwartz
ISBN: 1-56884-180-9
$24.95 USA/$34.95 Canada

Macworld Guide To Microsoft Works 3
by Barrie Sosinsky
ISBN: 1-878058-42-8
$22.95 USA/$29.95 Canada

Macworld Excel 5 Companion, 2nd Edition
by Chris Van Buren & David Maguiness
ISBN: 1-56884-081-0
$24.95 USA/$34.95 Canada

Macworld Guide To Microsoft Excel 4
by David Maguiness
ISBN: 1-878058-40-1
$22.95 USA/$29.95 Canada

FOR MORE INFORMATION OR TO ORDER, PLEASE CALL ▶ 800. 762. 2974

For volume discounts & special orders please call Tony Real, Special Sales, at 415. 655. 3048

ORDER FORM

12/20/94

IDG BOOKS

Order Center: **(800) 762-2974** *(8 a.m.–6 p.m., EST, weekdays)*

Quantity	ISBN	Title	Price	Total

Shipping & Handling Charges				
	Description	**First book**	**Each additional book**	**Total**
Domestic	Normal	$4.50	$1.50	$
	Two Day Air	$8.50	$2.50	$
	Overnight	$18.00	$3.00	$
International	Surface	$8.00	$8.00	$
	Airmail	$16.00	$16.00	$
	DHL Air	$17.00	$17.00	$

*For large quantities call for shipping & handling charges.
**Prices are subject to change without notice.

Ship to:
Name _____
Company _____
Address _____
City/State/Zip _____
Daytime Phone _____

Payment: ☐ Check to IDG Books (US Funds Only)
☐ VISA ☐ MasterCard ☐ American Express
Card # _____ Expires _____
Signature _____

Subtotal _____

CA residents add
applicable sales tax _____

IN, MA, and MD
residents add
5% sales tax _____

IL residents add
6.25% sales tax _____

RI residents add
7% sales tax _____

TX residents add
8.25% sales tax _____

Shipping _____

Total _____

Please send this order form to:
IDG Books Worldwide
7260 Shadeland Station, Suite 100
Indianapolis, IN 46256

*Allow up to 3 weeks for delivery.
Thank you!*

Register for only $9.95!
The Power Utility Pak 2.0a
Add-In Tools for Microsoft® Excel

"The Power Utility Pak starts where Excel leaves off, providing extra functionality and useful shortcuts." — Craig Stinson, *PC Magazine*

The Power Utility Pak...
is a useful collection of 23 Excel utilities, plus 22 new worksheet functions.

Pro-Quality Tools
The Power Utility Pak was developed by John Walkenbach, author of *Excel for Windows 95 Bible*. As a special offer, he's making the registered version available to purchasers of this book for only $9.95. The Power Utility Pak normally sells for $39.95.

Order Today
To receive your copy, just complete the coupon below and include a check or money order for $9.95 + $4.00 to cover shipping and handling.

Source Code Also Available!
You can also purchase the complete XLS source files for only $20.00. Learn how the utilities were written, and pick up useful tips and programming techniques in the process.

YES! Please send the *Power Utility Pak* to...

Name: _____

Company: _____

Address: _____

City: _____ State: _____ Zip: _____

Daytime Phone: _____

❏ Power Utility Pak registration ($9.95) + $4.00 s&h $13.95

❏ Complete Package: Registration ($9.95) & VBA source
   files ($20.00) + $4.00 s&h $33.95

Credit cards are accepted for the <u>complete package only</u>. Your card will be billed $33.95.

Credit card number: _____ Expires: _____

❏ Visa ❏ MasterCard ❏ Discover Signature: _____

Make checks or money orders (U.S. funds only) payable to *JWalk and Associates*. No telephone orders for this special offer.

JWalk and Associates Inc.
P.O. Box 12861
La Jolla, CA 92039-2861

OB

IDG BOOKS WORLDWIDE LICENSE AGREEMENT

Important — read carefully before opening the software packet. This is a legal agreement between you (either an individual or an entity) and IDG Books Worldwide, Inc. (IDG). By opening the accompanying sealed packet containing the software disc, you acknowledge that you have read and accept the following IDG License Agreement. If you do not agree and do not want to be bound by the terms of this Agreement, promptly return the book and the unopened software packet to the place you obtained them for a full refund.

1. License. This License Agreement (Agreement) permits you to use one copy of the enclosed Software program(s) on a single computer. The Software is in "use" on a computer when it is loaded into temporary memory (i.e., RAM) or installed into permanent memory (e.g., hard disk, CD-ROM, or other storage device) of that computer.

2. Copyright. The entire contents of this disc and the compilation of the Software are copyrighted and protected by both United States copyright laws and international treaty provisions. The individual programs on the disc are copyrighted by the authors of each program respectively. Each program has its own use permissions and limitations. You may only (a) make one copy of the Software for backup or archival purposes, or (b) transfer the Software to a single hard disk, provided that you keep the original for backup or archival purposes. To use each program, you must follow the individual requirements and restrictions detailed for each in Appendix E of this Book. Do not use a program if you do not want to follow its Licensing Agreement. None of the material on this disc or listed in this Book may ever be distributed, in original or modified form, for commercial purposes.

3. Other Restrictions. You may not rent or lease the Software. You may transfer the Software and user documentation on a permanent basis provided you retain no copies and the recipient agrees to the terms of this Agreement. You may not reverse engineer, decompile, or disassemble the Software except to the extent that the foregoing restriction is expressly prohibited by applicable law. If the Software is an update or has been updated, any transfer must include the most recent update and all prior versions. Each shareware program has its own use permissions and limitations. These limitations are contained in the individual license agreements that are on the software disc. The restrictions include a requirement that after using the program for a period of time specified in its text, the user must pay a registration fee or discontinue use. By opening the package which contains the software disc, you will be agreeing to abide by the licenses and restrictions for these programs. Do not open the software package unless you agree to be bound by the license agreements.

4. Limited Warranty. IDG Warrants that the Software and disc are free from defects in materials and workmanship for a period of sixty (60) days from the date of purchase of this Book. If IDG receives notification within the warranty period of defects in material or workmanship, IDG will replace the defective disc. IDG's entire liability and your exclusive remedy shall be limited to replacement of the Software, which is returned to IDG with a copy of your receipt. This Limited Warranty is void if failure of the Software has resulted from accident, abuse, or misapplication. Any replacement Software will be warranted for the remainder of the original warranty period or thirty (30) days, whichever is longer.

5. No Other Warranties. To the maximum extent permitted by applicable law, IDG and the author disclaim all other warranties, express or implied, including but not limited to implied warranties of merchantability and fitness for a particular purpose, with respect to the Software, the programs, the source code contained therein and/or the techniques described in this Book. This limited warranty gives you specific legal rights. You may have others which vary from state/jurisdiction to state/jurisdiction.

6. No Liability For Consequential Damages. To the extent permitted by applicable law, in no event shall IDG or the author be liable for any damages whatsoever (including without limitation, damages for loss of business profits, business interruption, loss of business information, or any other pecuniary loss) arising out of the use of or inability to use the Book or the Software, even if IDG has been advised of the possibility of such damages. Because some states/jurisdictions do not allow the exclusion or limitation of liability for consequential or incidental damages, the above limitation may not apply to you.

7. U.S.Government Restricted Rights. Use, duplication, or disclosure of the Software by the U.S. Government is subject to restrictions stated in paragraph (c) (1) (ii) of the Rights in Technical Data and Computer Software clause of DFARS 252.227-7013, and in subparagraphs (a) through (d) of the Commercial Computer—Restricted Rights clause at FAR 52.227-19, and in similar clauses in the NASA FAR supplement, when applicable.

CD-ROM Installation Instructions

The CD-ROM comes with a Windows Help file that gives you information about each item on the CD-ROM. Most items are templates or macro-based utilities that you must copy to an appropriate directory on your hard drive; the Windows Help file gives more information. Some items are programs that come with their own installation utilities. In these cases, the Windows Help file lets you execute those installation utilities with a mouse click.

Here's how to get to the Windows Help file on the CD-ROM:

1. Place the CD-ROM into your CD-ROM drive and close the door.
2. Double-click on the My Computer icon on the desktop. When the My Computer window opens, double-click on the CD-ROM icon it contains. The following window appears; it shows the CD-ROM's contents.

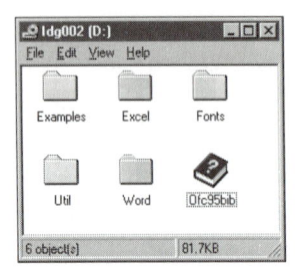

3. Double-click on the Ofc95bib icon. The Windows Help file opens, similar to the following window.

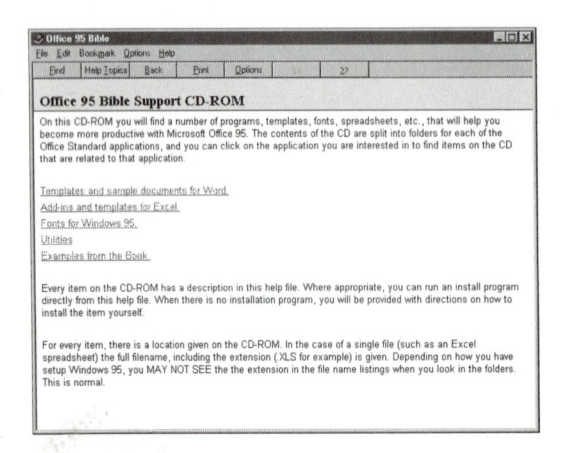

Navigate the Windows Help file to learn more about each item on the CD-ROM.

IDG BOOKS WORLDWIDE REGISTRATION CARD

RETURN THIS REGISTRATION CARD FOR FREE CATALOG

Title of this book: Microsoft Office for Windows 95 Bible, Standard Ed.

My overall rating of this book: ❑ Very good [1] ❑ Good [2] ❑ Satisfactory [3] ❑ Fair [4] ❑ Poor [5]

How I first heard about this book:
❑ Found in bookstore; name: [6] _____
❑ Book review: [7] _____
❑ Advertisement: [8] _____
❑ Catalog: [9] _____
❑ Word of mouth; heard about book from friend, co-worker, etc.: [10] _____
❑ Other: [11] _____

What I liked most about this book:
_____
_____

What I would change, add, delete, etc., in future editions of this book:
_____
_____

Other comments:
_____

Number of computer books I purchase in a year: ❑ 1 [12] ❑ 2-5 [13] ❑ 6-10 [14] ❑ More than 10 [15]

I would characterize my computer skills as: ❑ Beginner [16] ❑ Intermediate [17] ❑ Advanced [18] ❑ Professional [19]

I use ❑ DOS [20] ❑ Windows [21] ❑ OS/2 [22] ❑ Unix [23] ❑ Macintosh [24] ❑ Other: [25] _____ (please specify)

I would be interested in new books on the following subjects:
(please check all that apply, and use the spaces provided to identify specific software)

❑ Word processing: [26] _____
❑ Spreadsheets: [27] _____
❑ Data bases: [28] _____
❑ Desktop publishing: [29] _____
❑ File Utilities: [30] _____
❑ Money management: [31] _____
❑ Networking: [32] _____
❑ Programming languages: [33] _____
❑ Other: [34] _____

I use a PC at (please check all that apply): ❑ home [35] ❑ work [36] ❑ school [37] ❑ other: [38] _____

The disks I prefer to use are ❑ 5.25 [39] ❑ 3.5 [40] ❑ other: [41] _____

I have a CD ROM: ❑ yes [42] ❑ no [43]

I plan to buy or upgrade computer hardware this year: ❑ yes [44] ❑ no [45]

I plan to buy or upgrade computer software this year: ❑ yes [46] ❑ no [47]

Name: _____ **Business title:** [48] _____ **Type of Business:** [49] _____

Address (❑ home [50] ❑ work [51] /Company name: _____)

Street/Suite# _____

City [52] /**State** [53] /**Zipcode** [54]: _____ **Country** [55] _____

❑ **I liked this book!** You may quote me by name in future IDG Books Worldwide promotional materials.

My daytime phone number is _____

IDG BOOKS
THE WORLD OF COMPUTER KNOWLEDGE

❏ **YES!**
Please keep me informed about IDG's World of Computer Knowledge. Send me the latest IDG Books catalog.

BUSINESS REPLY MAIL
FIRST CLASS MAIL   PERMIT NO. 2605   FOSTER CITY, CALIFORNIA

IDG Books Worldwide
919 E Hillsdale Blvd, STE 400
Foster City, CA 94404-9691

NO POSTAGE
NECESSARY
IF MAILED
IN THE
UNITED STATES